*The Republic Pictures Checklist*

# The Republic Pictures Checklist

*Features, Serials, Cartoons, Short Subjects and Training Films of Republic Pictures Corporation, 1935–1959*

by LEN D. MARTIN

McFarland & Company, Inc., Publishers
*Jefferson, North Carolina, and London*

***Acknowledgments:*** I would like to thank the following institutions and individuals for their invaluable assistance in providing books, films, and other research materials in the compilation of this book: Rice University, University of Houston, Budget Films, Film Favorites, Bob Selig, Pat Ray, Bill Mooney, Pat Mooney, and Randy Franklin of Collector's Showcase.

A very special thanks, again, to my wife, Ann, who aided immensely in the editing of this book.

---

*The present work is a reprint of the library bound edition of* The Republic Pictures Checklist: Features, Serials, Cartoons, Short Subjects and Training Films of Republic Pictures Corporation, 1935–1959, *first published in 1998 by McFarland.*

---

LIBRARY OF CONGRESS CATALOGUING-IN-PUBLICATION DATA

Martin, Len D., 1939–
   The Republic Pictures checklist : features, serials, cartoons, short subjects and training films of Republic Pictures Corporation, 1935–1959 / by Len D. Martin.
      p.   cm.
   Includes bibliographical references and index.

   ISBN-13: 978-0-7864-2740-6
   (softcover : 50# alkaline paper) ∞

   1. Republic Pictures Corporation — Catalogs.   2. Motion pictures — United States — Catalogs.   I. Title.
   PN1999.R4M35   2006
   016.79143'75 — dc21                                                                98-12993

British Library cataloguing data are available

©1998 Len D. Martin. All rights reserved

*No part of this book may be reproduced or transmitted in any form or by any means, electronic or mechanical, including photocopying or recording, or by any information storage and retrieval system, without permission in writing from the publisher.*

*On the cover:* John Wayne in *Wake of the Red Witch* (1948); background ©2006 PhotoSpin

Manufactured in the United States of America

*McFarland & Company, Inc., Publishers*
   *Box 611, Jefferson, North Carolina 28640*
   *www.mcfarlandpub.com*

# Contents

| | |
|---|---|
| *Preface* | vii |
| *Historical Overview* | 1 |
| | |
| FEATURE FILMS (1935–1959) | 3 |
| SERIALS (1936–1955) | 237 |
| CARTOONS (1947–1949) | 275 |
| SHORT SUBJECTS (1940–1955) | 277 |
| TRAINING FILMS (1941–1945) | 283 |
| | |
| Appendix A: Films Listed by Release Date | 285 |
| Appendix B: Academy Award Nominations and Winners | 299 |
| Appendix C: Movie Series | 302 |
| Appendix D: Western Stars and Western Series | 305 |
| | |
| *Bibliography* | 313 |
| *Chapter Title Index* | 315 |
| *Name Index* | 323 |

# *Preface*

This book is not intended to be an in-depth critical or historical examination of Republic Pictures Corporation or their product. Rather it is intended as a comprehensive handbook to the output of a studio known for its serials, B westerns, and features.

In doing research for this book, it was not uncommon to find different running times and release dates for certain titles along with different releases for the same title. I have tried to furnish the reader with as accurate information as possible. I have also decided not to include re-release dates as Republic re-released their product numerous times during the life of the studio.

Periodicals consulted were *The New York Times*, *The Los Angeles Times*, and *Variety*.

Abbreviations used in this book are as follows: *DIR* (director), *PRO* (producer), *A-PRO* (associate producer), *E- PRO* (executive producer), *SUP* (supervisor) *SP* (screenplay), *B&W* (black & white), and G.B. title (Great Britain title).

Len D. Martin,
*Houston, Texas*
*September 1997*

# Historical Overview

Republic Pictures Corporation had its beginnings in 1915 when Herbert J. Yates, one time member of the executive staff of the American Tobacco Company, entered the motion picture business with Hedwig Laboratories and, in 1918, launched Republic Laboratories in New York. He then took over Eastman Kodak Company's motion picture laboratories and in turn acquired Rothacker Laboratories in Chicago in 1924, which became known as Consolidated Film Laboratories.

Laboratory connections brought Yates into association with production and motion picture financing, and in May, 1935, Yates decided to foreclose on the following companies utilizing Consolidated Film Laboratories, and merge them into one operating unit, Republic Pictures Corporation. The companies were Mascot Pictures, under Nat Levine; Monogram Pictures, under Trem Carr and W. L. Johnston; Liberty Pictures, under M. H. Hoffman; Majestic Pictures, under Phil Goldstone and Larry Darmour; and Supreme Pictures, under A. W. Hackel. Goldstone and Darmour had earlier turned over Majestic to Yates, and each went their separate ways rather than be part of the new organization.

It should be noted that friction soon developed between Yates, Carr and Johnston, leading to Monogram's withdrawing from the organization and reinstituting Monogram Pictures in 1937.

Republic's first release of 1935 was a western, *Westward Ho!*, starring John Wayne, who would stay with Republic for the next 17 years, and their second release, *Tumbling Tumbleweeds*, featured a singing cowboy, Gene Autry, who would later, with Roy Rogers, be a top star at Republic. The rest of the releases for 1935 would be a mixture of new Republic releases, together with the final releases of the combining companies, each carrying the logo of the newly formed Republic Pictures

By 1936, with Nat Levine in charge of serial production, Republic entered the serial market with their first release, *Darkest Africa*, a jungle adventure starring Clyde Beatty. Nat Levine would leave Republic after 18 months to go to M-G-M, but the serial format had been established at Republic, and for the next 19 years, Republic, also known as "The Thrill Factory," would produce serials that thrilled and excited the audiences, although their later serials utilized a majority of stock footage.

Republic was primarily a "B" picture unit, specializing in second features, and from the late '30s to the late '40s Republic knew what the public wanted and it gave it to them: B westerns, serials, dramas, series pictures, and musicals.

Occasionally, Republic would try its hand at producing and distributing an "A" feature, such as *Man of Conquest, Dark Command, The Fighting Seabees, Sands of Iwo Jima, Moonrise, Macbeth, Wake of the Red Witch, The Quiet Man,* and so on, but it was B pictures and serials that they knew how to produce and how to market.

In 1945, the stockholders of Consolidated Film Industries, Inc., voted the merger and consolidation of Consolidated Film Industries, Inc., and Republic Pictures Corporation, with Setay Company, Inc., the corporate name of which was changed to Republic Pictures Corporation.

By the 1950s Republic was beginning to die as a studio. Television, a changing public, profits, Yates' inability to adapt to the changing times, and a continuation of their B westerns and features which relied more and more on stock footage, all combined to bring about Republic's downfall.

With the advent of television, Yates used Hollywood Television Service not only to show Republic's product, but to produce series as well. Republic had the knowledge and technical expertise to make good television series, but they did not utilize it. Of the four series they made for television, *Stories of the Century, Fu Manchu, Frontier Doctor,* and *Stryker of Scotland Yard,* a British made series, only *Stories of the Century* proved good enough to win Republic an Emmy.

Although television brought in some profit for Republic, it actually hurt the studio's producing unit, because the market was now flooded with B westerns.

When the science-fiction craze of the '50s hit, Republic's releases were sparse and what films they did release were from other sources, with the exception of two feature versions of their science-fiction serials in 1958, *Satan's Satellites,* and *Missile Monsters.*

Although widescreen was introduced in 1953, Republic did not adapt to it until 1956, and the anamorphic lens purchased by Republic was a French lens built by Professor Ernst Abbe. Republic claimed authorship of the lens with the screen billing *Naturama by Republic Pictures Corporation,* but only 22 features were produced in the next three years. It should also be noted that Republic never adapted to stereophonic sound.

The final factors in the demise of Republic include to the following: Yates' sinking all the company profits into big budget pictures for his wife (Vera Ralston), which did not return a fair profit; post–World War II inflation; union demands for residuals on post–1948 features released to television; the passing of the theatrical Saturday matinee due to television; and the public demand for bigger and better films.

By 1959 Republic was dead as a studio; of the five features released that year, only one was a studio-produced feature, *Plunderers of Painted Flats*. The other releases were two feature versions of serials, and two foreign releases. On July 1, 1959, Yates relinquished control of Republic to Victor M. Carter, a California banker and real estate operator. The Carter administration decided not to get into the motion picture business and sold the Republic lot to CBS. Thus, the studio that had thrilled viewers for almost a quarter of a century was no more.

In 1960, the name was changed from Republic Pictures Corporation to Republic Corporation, and today Republic Pictures still exists as a division of Spelling Entertainment, but their releases are only present-day. With the advent of home video, many of Republic's older titles began being re-released, so we can once again be thrilled by the "Thrill Factory."

# Feature Films (1935–1959)

Following is a complete list of feature films produced or distributed by Republic Pictures Corporation. Release dates are approximate release dates. Omitted from this listing are the 1935 Mascot features, which bore the Mascot logo and were released through Republic exchanges.

**1. Above Us the Waves** (10/26/56) B&W 92 mins. (War). *DIR:* Ralph Thomas. *PRO:* William MacQuitty, Sidney Box. *SP:* Robin Estridge. Based on the book by C. E. T. Warren, James Benson. A London Independent Producers Film. A Rank Production. A Republic Presentation. *CAST:* John Mills, John Gregson, Donald Sinden, James Robertson Justice, Michael Medwin, James Kenney, O. E. Hasse, William Russell, Thomas Heathcoate, Lee Patterson, Theodore Bikel, Lyndon Brook, Harry Towb, Anthony Newley, Anthony Wager, William Franklyn, Leslie Weston, Guido Lorraine. *SYN:* A British Commander (Mills) persuades his superiors to use midget submarines to sink the giant German pocket battleship *Tirpitz* by planting underwater explosives on her hull while moored in a Norwegian fjord. *NOTES:* Released in Britain in 1955.

**2. Accused of Murder** (12/21/56) Trucolor/Naturama 74 mins. (Mystery). *DIR/PRO:* Joseph Kane. *SP:* Bob Williams, W. R. Burnett. Based on the novel *Vanity Row* by W.R. Burnett. *CAST:* David Brian, Vera Ralston, Sidney Blackmer, Virginia Grey, Warren Stevens, Lee Van Cleef, Barry Kelley, Richard Karlan, Frank Puglia, Elisa Cook, Jr., Ian MacDonald, Claire Carleton, Greta Thyssen, Hank Worden, Wally Cassell, Robert Shayne, Scott Simon, John Damler, Gil Rankin, Joseph Corey, Leon Tyler, Harry Lewis, David Bair, William (Bill) Henry, Bob Carney, Victor Sen Yung. *SYN:* A detective (Brian) sets out to prove a nightclub singer (Ralston) innocent of murdering a crooked lawyer (Blackmer).

**3. Adventures of Captain Fabian** (10/6/51) B&W 100 mins. (Adventure). *DIR/PRO:* William Marshall. *SP:* Charles Gross, Errol Flynn. Based on the novel *Fabulous Ann Madlock* by Robert T. Shannon. A Silver Films Production. A Republic Presentation. *CAST:* Errol Flynn, Micheline Presle, Vincent Price, Agnes Moorehead, Victor Francen, Jim Gerald, Helena Manson, Howard Vernon, Roger Blin, Valentine Camax, Georges Flateau, Zanie Campan, Reggie Nalder, Charles Fawcett, Aubrey Bower. *SYN:* In early New Orleans, a sea captain (Flynn) falls for an ambitious servant girl (Presle) who uses him to gain entrance into rich households. *NOTES:* Screenwriter Charles Gross was uncredited. One of Flynn's poorer efforts and done near the end of his career. This was also the second collaborative production between William Marshall and Errol Flynn; their first being an obscure 1951 film, *Hello God*, never released in the United States.

**4. Affair in Reno** (2/15/57) B&W/Naturama 75 mins. (Crime). *DIR:* R. G. Springsteen. *PRO:* Sidney Picker. *SP:* John K. Butler. Story by Gerald Drayson Adams. *CAST:* John Lund, Doris Singleton, Angela Greene, John Archer, Alan Hale, Jr., Harry Bartell, Howard McNear, Richard Deacon, Thurston Hall, Billy Vincent. *SYN:* A public relations man (Lund) is hired by a millionaire to go to Reno to prevent his daughter (Greene) from marrying an opportunistic gambler (Archer).

**5. Affairs of Cappy Ricks** (5/24/37) B&W 57 mins. (Comedy). *DIR:* Ralph Staub. *A-PRO:* Burt Kelley. *SP:* Lester Cole. Story by Peter B. Kyne. *CAST:* Walter Brennan, Mary Brian, Lyle Talbot, Frank Shields, Frank Melton, Georgia Caine, Phyllis Barry, William B. Davidson, Frank Shannon, Howard Brooks, Anthony Pawley, Sherry Hall, Don Rowan, Will Stanton. *SYN:* An old salt (Brennan) spends most of his time trying to show his two daughters (Brian, Barry) the real values in life. *NOTES:* The 2nd and final entry in the "Cappy Ricks" series. After dismal reviews, Republic decided not to continue with this series. This was a far inferior film to another "Cappy Ricks" production in 1937, *The Gogetter*, a Warner Bros.–Cosmopolitan feature.

**6. Affairs of Geraldine** (11/18/46) B&W 68 mins. (Comedy). *DIR:* George Blair. *A-PRO:* Armand Schaefer. *SP:* John K. Butler. Based on an unpublished story *Blossoms for Effie* by Lee Loeb and Arthur Strawn. *CAST:* Jane Withers, James Lydon, Raymond Walburn, Donald Meek, Charles Quigley, Grant Withers, William Haade, Michael Branden, Johnny Sands, David Holt, Tanis Chandler, Harry Cheshire, Josephine Whittell, Donia Russey, Edith M. Griffith, George Carleton. *SYN:* A young woman (Jane Withers) suddenly inherits a fortune, but her mother's dying request that her brothers (Grant Withers, Haade) find a good husband for her, causes her to leave home and head for the big city, where she becomes involved with a con-man (Walburn) and a bigamist (Quigley).

**7. Affairs of Jimmy Valentine** (3/25/42) B&W 71 mins. (Crime). *DIR:* Bernard Vorhaus. *A-PRO:* Leonard Fields. *SP:* Olive Cooper, Robert Tasker. *CAST:* Dennis O'Keefe, George E.

Stone, Gloria Dickson, Ruth Terry, Harry Shannon, Spencer Charters, Roman Bohnen, Roscoe Ates, Jed Prouty, Rand Brooks, Joe Cunningham. *SYN:* A reporter (O'Keefe) and the daughter (Terry) of a radio station owner (Shannon) set out to locate a retired criminal, Jimmy Valentine, which eventually leads them to a small town and several murders. *NOTES:* A remake of Republic's 1936 film, *The Return of Jimmy Valentine*. Re-edited for TV at 54 mins. [TV title: *Unforgotten Crime*.]

8. **African Manhunt** (1/5/55) B&W 65 mins. (Adventure). *DIR:* Seymour Friedman. *PRO:* Jerry Thomas. *SP:* Arthur Hoerl. A Trinity Production. A Republic Presentation. *CAST:* Myron Healey, Karin Booth, John Kellogg, Ross Elliott, Raphael Bennett, James Edwards, Lawrence Dobkin. *SYN:* A woman (Booth) and her two male friends (Healey, Elliott) escort a wanted criminal (Kellogg) to the coast from central Africa. *NOTES:* Extensive use of stock footage.

9. **Alias Billy the Kid** (4/17/46) B&W 56 mins. (Western). *DIR:* Thomas Carr. *A-PRO:* Bennett Cohen. *SP:* Betty Burbridge, Earle Snell. Story by Norman Sheldon. *CAST:* Sunset Carson, Peggy Stewart, Tom London, Roy Barcroft, Tex Terry, Tom Chatterton, Russ Whiteman, Pierce Lyden, Stanley Price, James Linn, Edward Cassidy, Jack Kirk, Jack Rockwell, Jack O'Shea. *SYN:* A ranger (Carson) trails an escaped outlaw (Whiteman) to his gang, becomes involved with a female outlaw leader (Stewart), and finds the culprit (Barcroft) behind the killing of a fellow ranger. *NOTES:* Nowhere in this film is the name "Billy the Kid" mentioned, referred to, or even hinted at. Sunset Carson's real name was Michael Harrison.

10. **Alias the Champ** (10/15/49) B&W 60 mins. (Crime-Sports). *DIR:* George Blair. *A-PRO:* Stephen Auer. *SP:* Albert DeMond. *CAST:* Robert Rockwell, Barbara Fuller, Audrey Long, Jim Nolan, John Harmon, Sammy Menacker, Joseph Crehan, John Hamilton, Stephen Chase, Frank Scannell, Frank Yaconelli, Emmett Vogan, John Wald, Gorgeous George (Wagner), Mike Ruby, James Lennon, Henry "Bomber" Kulkovich (Henry Kulky), Billy Varga, Bobby Manogoff, George Temple, Super Swedish Angel McDonald, Jack "Sockeye" McDonald. *SYN:* An East coast mobster (Nolan) and his henchman (Harmon) try to muscle in on the professional wrestling game by framing a wrestler (Gorgeous George) for the murder of his ring opponent (Menacker) when he won't do business with them. Eventually, a police lieutenant (Rockwell), who is also a wrestling code administrator, clears the wrestler and brings the criminals to justice.

11. **The Alibi** (3/24/43) B&W 66 mins. (Mystery). *DIR:* Brian Desmond Hurst. *PRO:* Josef Somlo. *SP:* Lesley Storm, Jacques Companeez, Justine & Carter. Based on *L'Alibi* by Marcel Archard. A British-Lion Corona Film. A Republic Presentation. *CAST:* Margaret Lockwood, Hugh Sinclair, James Mason, Raymond Lovell, Enid Stamp-Taylor, Hartley Power, Jane Carr, Rodney Ackland, Edana Romney, Elisabeth Welch, Olga Lindo, Muriel George, George Merritt, Judy Gray, Philip Leaver, Derek Blomfield, Claire Wear's Embassy Orchestra. *SYN:* A nightclub psychic (Lovell) kills a man and uses the

bar hostess (Lockwood) to obtain his alibi. *NOTES:* Released in Britain in 1942 at a running time of 82 mins. A remake of the 1939 French film, *L'Alibi,* which starred Erich Von Stroheim.

**12. All Over Town** (8/8/37) B&W 62 mins. (Comedy). *DIR:* James W. Horne. *A-PRO:* Leonard Fields. *SP:* Jack Townley, Jerome Chodorov. Story by Richard English. *CAST:* Ole Olsen, Chic Johnson, Mary Howard, Harry Stockwell, Franklin Pangborn, James Finlayson, Eddie Kane, Stanley Fields, D'Arcy Corrigan, Lew Kelly, John Sheehan, Earle Hodgins, Gertrude Astor, Blanche Payson, Otto Hoffman, Fred Kelsey, Alan Ladd. *SYN:* Olsen and Johnson try to save a theatrical boarding house from being foreclosed on by the bank.

**13. Along the Navajo Trail** (12/15/45) B&W 66 mins. (Western). *DIR:* Frank McDonald. *A-PRO:* Edward J. White. *SP:* Gerald Geraghty. Story by William Colt MacDonald. *CAST:* Roy Rogers, George "Gabby" Hayes, Dale Evans, Estelita Rodriguez, Douglas Fowley, Nestor Paiva, Sam Flint, Emmett Vogan, Roy Barcroft, David Cota, Pat Brady, Edward Cassidy, Poppy Del Vando, Rosemonde James, Tex Terry, Budd Buster, Eddie Kane, Frank O'Connor, Bert Moorhouse, Frank Stephens, Marin Sais, Marlene Ames, Hank Bell, Kit Guard, George Morrell, Bob Nolan and the Sons of the Pioneers, "Trigger." *SYN:* Roy, with the aid of a band of gypsies, helps break up a cattle syndicate pressuring local ranchers. *NOTES:* Re-edited for TV at 54 mins.

**14. Along the Oregon Trail** (8/30/47) Trucolor 64 mins. (Western). *DIR:* R. G. Springsteen. *A-PRO:* Melville Tucker. *SP:* Earle Snell. *CAST:* Monte Hale, Adrian Booth (Lorna Gray), Max Terhune, Clayton Moore, Roy Barcroft, LeRoy Mason, Will Wright, Wade Crosby, Tom London, Forrest Taylor, Kermit Maynard, Frank Ellis, Foy Willing and the Riders of the Purple Sage. *SYN:* A trail guide (Hale) leads a group exploring the Oregon Trail into uncharted territory, uncovering a greedy land baron (Moore), who is manipulating local Indians in order to scare off the pioneers.

**15. Angel and the Badman** (2/15/47) B&W 100 mins. (Western). *DIR/SP:* James Edward Grant. *PRO:* John Wayne. Story by James Edward Grant. *CAST:* John Wayne, Gail Russell, Harry Carey, Sr., Bruce Cabot, Irene Rich, Lee Dixon, Stephen Grant, Tom Powers, Paul Hurst, Olin Howlin, John Halloran, Joan Barton, Craig Woods, Marshall Reed, Hank Worden, Jack Kirk. *SYN:* An outlaw (Wayne) is nursed back to health by a Quaker family when he collapses on their doorstep and falls in love with the daughter (Russell). Realizing that his outlaw days are numbered, he begins to change his ways, even though he is obsessed with killing the murderer (Cabot) of his foster-father. *NOTES:* This was the first film produced by and starring John Wayne. Released in a "Computer-colorized" version in the 1980s by the new Republic Studios. Working title was *The Angel and the Outlaw.*

**16. An Angel Comes to Brooklyn** (11/27/45) B&W 70 mins. (Musical-Comedy). *DIR:* Leslie Goodwins. *A-PRO:* Leonard Sillman. *E-PRO:* Armand Schaefer. *SP:* Stanley Paley, June Carroll. Story by June Carroll and Lee Wainer. *CAST:* Kaye Dowd, Robert Duke, David Street, Barbara Perry,

Charles Kemper, Marguerite D'Alvarez, Robert Scheerer, Alice Tyrrell, June Carroll, Rodney Bell, Rodney Betzi Beaton, Jay Presson, Joe Cappo, Sheree North, Billi Haywood, Cliff Allen, C. Montague Shaw, Eula Morgan, Harry Rose, Frank Scannell, Mike Ricigliano, Jack McClendon, Jimmy Conlin, Ralph Dunn. *SYN:* A guardian angel (Kemper) comes down to earth to help a bunch of kids put on a show.

17. **Angel in Exile** (9/3/48) B&W 90 mins. (Drama). *DIR:* Allan Dwan, Philip Ford. *E-PRO:* Herbert J. Yates. *SP:* Charles Lawson. *CAST:* John Carroll, Adele Mara, Thomas Gomez, Barton MacLane, Alfonso Bedoya, Grant Withers, Paul Fix, Art Smith, Tom Powers, Ian Wolfe, Howland Chamberlin, Elsa Zepeda, Mary Currier. *SYN:* An ex-con (Carroll) uses a Mexican mine as a cover in his plan to filter out gold hidden away from a past robbery, but has a change of heart when the local villagers look at his success with the mine as a message from God.

18. **Angel on the Amazon** (11/1/48) B&W 86 mins. (Adventure). *DIR/PRO:* John H. Auer. *SP:* Lawrence Kimble. Story by Earl Felton. *CAST:* George Brent, Vera Ralston, Brian Aherne, Constance Bennett, Fortunio Bonanova, Alfonso Bedoya, Gus Schilling, Richard Crane, Walter Reed, Ross Elliott, Konstantin Shayne, Charles LaTorre, Elizabeth Dunne, Alberto Morin, Dick Jones, Alfredo de Sa, Tony Martinez, Jerry Groves, John Trebach,

Manuel Paris. *SYN:* An explorer (Brent) and his party crash-land in the jungle and are rescued by a mysterious woman (Ralston) who lives in the jungle. [British title: *Drums Along the Amazon.*]

**19. Angels with Broken Wings** (6/27/41) B&W 72 mins. (Musical-Comedy). *DIR:* Bernard Vorhaus. *A-PRO:* Albert J. Cohen. *SP:* George Carleton Brown, Bradford Ropes. Story by George Carleton Brown. *CAST:* Binnie Barnes, Gilbert Roland, Mary Lee, Billy Gilbert, Jane Frazee, Edward Norris, Katherine Alexander, Leo Gorcey, Lois Ranson, Leni Lynn, Marilyn Hare, Sidney Blackmer, Tom Kennedy. *SYN:* A group of kids try to arrange a marriage between a couple (Blackmer, Alexander).

**20. The Apache Kid** (9/12/41) B&W 56 mins. (Western). *DIR/A-PRO:* George Sherman. *SP:* Eliot Gibbons, Richard Murphy. *CAST:* Don ("Red") Barry, Lynn Merrick, LeRoy Mason, Robert Fiske, John Elliott, Forbes Murray, Monte Montague, Al St. John, Fred "Snowflake" Toones, Charles King, Frank Brownlee, John Cason, Cactus Mack, Kenne Duncan, Hal Price, Buddy Roosevelt, Buck Moulton, Tommy Coats. *SYN:* A cowboy (Barry) leads a wagon train to Oregon unaware that he is helping his crooked uncle (Fiske) who has a government contract to build a road.

**21. Apache Rose** (2/15/47) Trucolor 75 mins. (Western). *DIR:* William Whitney. *A-PRO:* Edward J. White. *SP:* Gerald Geraghty. *CAST:* Roy Rogers, Dale Evans, Olin Howlin, George Meeker, John Laurenz, Russ Vincent, Minerva Urecal, LeRoy Mason, Donna DeMario (Donna Martell), Terry Frost, Conchita Lemus, Tex Terry, Bob Nolan and the Sons of the Pioneers, "Trigger." *SYN:* An oil wildcatter (Rogers) tries to obtain the rights to an old Spanish land grant, while gamblers, headquartered on a ship offshore, conspire to get the land first. *NOTES:* Roy Rogers' first color western. Re-edited for TV at 54 mins.

**22. The Arizona Cowboy** (4/1/50) B&W 67 mins. (Western). *DIR:* R. G. Springsteen. *A-PRO:* Franklin Adreon. *SP:* Bradford Ropes. *CAST:* Rex Allen, Teala Loring, Gordon Jones, Minerva Urecal, James Cardwell, Roy Barcroft, Stanley Andrews, Harry Cheshire, Edmund Cobb, Joseph Crehan, Steve Darrell, Douglas Evans, John Elliott, Chris-Pin Martin, Frank Reicher, George Lloyd, Lane Bradford, "Koko." *SYN:* After World War II, a cowboy (Allen) returns home and sets out to prove his father (Elliott) innocent of a land swindle. *NOTES:* Rex Allen's first Republic western and he became known by the film's title. Running times are listed at 57 mins. and 67 mins. The 67 min. time listed above is the actual running time of this feature.

**23. The Arizona Gunfighter** (9/24/37) B&W 58 mins. (Western). *DIR:* Sam Newfield. *PRO:* A. W. Hackel. *SP:* George Plympton. Story by Harry Olmstead. *CAST:* Bob Steele, Jean Carmen, Ted Adams, Ernie Adams, Lew Meehan, Steve Clark, John Merton, Karl Hackett, Al C. Henderson, Frank Ball, Sherry Tansey, Jack Kirk, Hal Price, Budd Buster, Horace B. Carpenter, Tex Palmer, Archie Ricks, Allen Greer, Roy Bucko, Oscar Gahan, Silver Tip Baker. *SYN:* A cowboy (Steele) sets out to find the men (Hackett, Merton) who murdered his father; when he finds them he kills them but is shot himself and is nursed back to health by an outlaw leader (Ted Adams) who wants to reform.

24. **The Arizona Kid** (9/29/39) B&W 61 mins. (Western). *DIR/PRO:* Joseph Kane. *SP:* Luci Ward, Gerald Geraghty. Story by Luci Ward. *CAST:* Roy Rogers, George "Gabby" Hayes, Sally March, Stuart Hamblen, Dorothy Sebastian, Earl Dwire, David Kerwin, Peter Fargo, Fred Burns, Edward Cassidy, Jack Ingram, Ted Mapes, Frank McCarroll, Ben Corbett, Georgia Simmons, Robert Middlemass, Herman Hack, Tom Smith, "Trigger." *SYN:* During the Civil War, a Union captain (Rogers) must hunt down and bring to justice his friend (Kerwin) who is a member of a band of guerrillas. *NOTES:* Re-edited for TV at 54 mins.

25. **Arizona Manhunt** (9/15/51) B&W 60 mins. (Western). *DIR:* Fred C. Brannon. *A-PRO:* Rudy Ralston. *SP:* William Lively. *CAST:* Michael Chapin, Eilene Janssen, James Bell, Lucille Barkley, Roy Barcroft, Hazel Shaw, John Baer, Harry Harvey, Stuart Randall, Ted Cooper. *SYN:* The Rough-Ridin' Kids (Chapin, Janssen) aid a sheriff (Bell) in tracking down an outlaw gang. *NOTES:* The 3rd entry in the "Rough-Ridin' Kids" series.

**Arizona Terror** *see* **Arizona Terrors**

26. **Arizona Terrors** (1/6/42) B&W 56 mins. (Western). *DIR/A-PRO:* George Sherman. *SP:* Doris Schroeder, Taylor Caven. *CAST:* Don ("Red") Barry, Lynn Merrick, Al St. John, Reed Hadley, John Maxwell, Frank Brownlee, Rex Lease, Lee Shumway, Tom London, John Merton, Fred "Snowflake" Toones, Curley Dresden, Herman Hack, Bud Osborne, Jack Kirk, Kermit Maynard. *SYN:* A cowboy (Barry) tries to save a group of landowners from being kicked off their property by a tyrant (Hadley), who claims the land is his through a Spanish land grant. [Alternate title: *Arizona Terror.*]

27. **Arkansas Judge** (1/28/41) B&W 72 mins. (Western-Drama). *DIR:* Frank McDonald. *A-PRO:* Armand Schaefer. *SP:* Dorrell and Stuart McGowan. Adapted by Ian Hunter, Ring Lardner, Jr., Gertrude Purcell. Based on *False Witness* by Irving Stone. *CAST:* Leon Weaver, Frank Weaver, June Weaver, Roy Rogers, Spring Byington, Pauline Moore, Frank M. Thomas, Veda Ann Borg, Eily Malyon, Loretta Weaver, Minerva Urecal, Beatrice Maude, Harrison Greene, Barry Macollum, George Rosener, Monte Blue, Frank Darien, Russell Hicks, Edwin Stanley. *SYN:* The Weaver Brothers (Leon, Frank) and Elviry (June Weaver) help to prove a scrubwoman (Byington) innocent of theft charges. *NOTES:* The 6th entry in the "Weaver Brothers and Elviry" series. [British title: *False Witness.*]

**Army Capers** (G.B. title) *see* **The WAC from Walla Walla**

28. **Army Girl** (7/15/38) B&W 90 mins. (Drama). *DIR:* George Nicholls, Jr., B. Reeves Eason. *A-PRO:* Sol C. Siegel. *SP:* Barry Trivers, Samuel Ornitz. Story by Charles L. Clifford. *CAST:* Madge Evans, Preston Foster, James Gleason, H. B. Warner, Ruth Donnelly, Neil Hamilton, Heather Angel, Billy Gilbert, Ralph Morgan, Barbara Pepper, Ralph Byrd, Guinn "Big Boy" Williams, Robert Warwick, Allen Vincent, Pepito, Paul Stanton, Dewey Robinson, *SYN:* Saga of the growing pains the U.S. Army

experienced when going from horses to tanks. The daughter (Evans) of an Army post commander (Warner), falls for tank specialist (Foster) who sets out to prove that tanks can do more than cavalry. *NOTES:* Academy Award nominee — Best Cinematography, Best Score, and Best Sound. [British title: *The Last of the Cavalry.*]

**29. Arson Gang Busters** (3/28/38) B&W 64 mins. (Crime). *DIR:* Joseph Kane. *A-PRO:* Herman Schlom. *SP:* Alex Gottlieb, Norman Burnstine. *CAST:* Robert Livingston, Rosalind Keith, Jackie Moran, Warren Hymer, Jack LaRue, Clay Clement, Selmer Jackson, Emory Parnell, Walter Sande, Jack Rice, Lloyd Whitlock, Dick Wessel. *SYN:* A firefighter (Livingston) goes undercover as an arsonist to investigate a group of shady insurance underwriters who have been burning down buildings to cash in insurance policies. Working title was *Fire Over the Waterfront.* [Alternate title: *Arson Racket Squad.*] [British title: *Fire Fighters.*]

**Arson Racket Squad** *see* **Arson Gang Busters**

**30. At Dawn We Die** (3/20/43) B&W 85 mins. (War-Spy). *DIR:* George King. *PRO:* George King, John Stafford. *SP:* Anatole de Grunwald, Katherine Strueby. Based on *Jean Baptiste* by Dorothy Hope. A British-Lion Production. A Republic Presentation. *CAST:* John Clements, Godfrey Tearle, Hugh Sinclair, Greta Gynt, Judy Kelly, Yvonne Arnaud, Karel Stepanek, Bransby Williams, F. R. Wendhausen, Allan Jeayes, Gabrielle Brune, David Keir, Brefni O'Roarke, Gibb McLaughlin. *SYN:* A British agent (Clements) becomes involved with freedom fighters in occupied France. *NOTES:* Released in Britain in 1942. [Original British title: *Tomorrow We Live.*]

**31. Atlantic City** (9/15/44) B&W 86 mins. (Musical). *DIR:* Ray McCarey. *A-PRO:* Albert J. Cohen. *SP:* Doris Gilbert, Frank Gill, Jr., George Carleton Brown. Story by Arthur Caesar. *CAST:* Constance Moore, Brad Taylor, Charley Grapewin, Jerry Colonna, Robert B. Castaine, Adele Mara, Pierre Watkin, Harry Tyler, Stanley Andrews, Donald Kerr, Charles Williams, Daisy Lee Mothershed, Jack Kenney, Al Shean, Gus Van, Charles Marsh, Paul Whiteman and His Orchestra, Louis Armstrong and His Orchestra, Buck and Bubbles, Dorothy Dandridge, Belle Baker, Joe Frisco. *SYN:* An ambitious entrepreneur (Taylor) builds an entertainment empire on the Atlantic City Boardwalk, but alienates his wife (Moore) and friends in doing so, but, when the amusement pier he's constructed burns down, he learns that friends matter more than money. [Rerelease title: *Atlantic City Honeymoon.*]

**Atlantic City Honeymoon** *see* **Atlantic City**

**32. The Atomic Kid** (12/8/54) B&W 86 mins. (Comedy). *DIR:* Leslie H. Martinson. *PRO:* Maurice Duke. *SP:* Benedict Freedman, John Fenton Murray. Story by Blake Edwards. *CAST:* Mickey Rooney, Robert Strauss, Elaine Davis, Bill Goodwin, Whit Bissell, Joey Forman, Hal March, Peter Leeds, Fay Roope, Stanley Adams, Robert Emmett Keane, Bill Welsh, Charles Conrad, Milton Frome, Don Haggerty, Dan Riss, Ray Walker, Peter Brocco, Robert Nichols, Paul Dubov, Frank Richards, Tommy Walker, Sig Frohlich. *SYN:* A prospector (Rooney) looking for uranium is caught in the center of an atomic blast and survives because of a peanut butter sandwich (!) he was eating at the time. This gives him the power to do all sorts of comical things like winning at Las Vegas slot machines without touching them.

33. **The Avengers** (6/26/50) B&W 92 mins. (Adventure). *DIR/A-PRO:* John H. Auer. *SP:* Lawrence Kimble, Aeneas MacKenzie. Based on *Don Careless* by Rex Beach. *CAST:* John Carroll, Adele Mara, Mona Maris, Roberto Airaldi, Jorge Villoldo, Vincent Padula, Vivian Bay, Cecile Lezard, Juan Olaguivel, Fernando Lamas, Andre LeBlanc. *SYN:* In South America, a mysterious adventurer (Carroll), known as "Don Careless," falls in love with the governor's daughter (Mara), and prevents the overthrow of her father (Villoldo). *NOTES:* The film debut of Fernando Lamas.

34. **Back in the Saddle** (3/14/41) B&W 73 mins. (Western). *DIR:* Lew Landers. *A-PRO:* Harry Grey. *SP:* Richard Murphy, Jesse Lasky, Jr. *CAST:* Gene Autry, Smiley Burnette, Mary Lee, Edward Norris, Jacqueline Wells (Julie Bishop), Addison Richards, Arthur Loft, Edmund Elton, Joe McGuinn, Edmund Cobb, Robert Barron, Reed Howes, Stanley Blystone, Curley Dresden, Fred "Snowflake" Toones, Frank Ellis, Jack O'Shea, Victor Cox, Herman Hack, Bob Burns, Ralph Bucko, Jack Montgomery, Frankie Marvin, John Indrisano, Art Dillard, Bob Woodward, Bill Nestell, Bob Card, Roy Bucko, Jess Cavan, Jack C. Smith, "Champion." *SYN:* When pollution from a copper mine starts poisoning the ranchers' cattle, Gene sets out to bring peace between the local ranchers and the owners of the copper mine. *NOTES:* Re-edited for TV at 54 mins.

35. **Bad Man of Deadwood** (9/5/41) B&W 61 mins. (Western). *DIR/A-PRO:* Joseph Kane. *SP:* James R. Webb. *CAST:* Roy Rogers, George "Gabby" Hayes, Carol Adams, Henry Brandon, Herbert Rawlinson, Sally Payne, Hal Taliaferro, Jay Novello, Horace Murphy, Monte Blue, Ralf Harolde, Jack Kirk, Yakima Canutt, Curley Dresden, Fred Burns, Lynton Brent, Lloyd Ingraham, George Lloyd, Robert Frazer, Archie Twitchell, Karl Hackett, Harry Harvey, Eddie Acuff, Tom London, Jack Rockwell, Ernie Adams, Jack O'Shea, George Morrell, Wally West, Bob Woodward, Pascale Perry, Horace B. Carpenter, Harrison Greene, "Trigger." *SYN:* Roy joins a traveling medicine show and together they help a town regain control of its destiny by kicking out a group of crooked businessmen. *NOTES:* Re-edited for TV at 54 mins.

36. **Bal Tabarin** (6/1/52) B&W 84 mins. (Drama-Musical). *DIR:* Philip Ford. *A-PRO:* Herman Millakowsky. *SP:* Houston Branch. *CAST:* Muriel Lawrence, William Ching, Claire Carleton, Steve Brodie, Steven Geray, Carl Milletaire, Jan Rubini, Tom Powers, Gregory Gay, Adrienne d'Ambricourt, Herbert Deans. *SYN:* A singer (Lawrence) hides out in a Paris nightclub from the crooks who murdered her boss.

37. **Bandit King of Texas** (8/29/49) B&W 60 mins. (Western). *DIR:* Fred C. Brannon. *A-PRO:* Gordon Kay. *SP:* Olive Cooper. *CAST:* Allan ("Rocky") Lane, Eddy Waller, Helene Stanley, Jim Nolan, Harry Lauter, Robert Bice, John Hamilton, Lane Bradford, George

Lloyd, Steve Clark, I. Stanford Jolley, Danni Nolan, Richard Emory, "Black Jack." *SYN:* A government investigator (Lane) sets out to stop land swindlers who sell bogus land to settlers and then murder them for their money.

**38. Bandits of Dark Canyon** (12/15/47) B&W 59 mins. (Western). *DIR:* Philip Ford. *A-PRO:* Gordon Kay. *SP:* Bob Williams. *CAST:* Allan ("Rocky") Lane, Bob Steele, Eddy Waller, Roy Barcroft, John Hamilton, Linda Johnson, Gregory Marshall, Francis Ford, Eddie Acuff, LeRoy Mason, Norman Willis, "Black Jack." *SYN:* A Texas Ranger (Lane) helps an escaped convict (Steele) clear his name on a phony murder charge.

**39. Bandits of the Badlands** (9/14/45) B&W 55 mins. (Western). *DIR:* Thomas Carr. *A-PRO:* Bennett Cohen. *SP:* Doris Schroeder. *CAST:* Sunset Carson, Peggy Stewart, Monte Hale, Forrest Taylor, Si Jenks, John Merton, Wade Crosby, Jack Ingram, Alan Ward, Fred Graham, Post Park, Foxy O'Callahan, Bert LeBaron, Bob Reeves. *SYN:* An ex-Ranger (Carson) seeks the killer of his brother.

**40. Bandits of the West** (8/8/53) B&W 54 mins. (Western). *DIR:* Harry Keller. *A-PRO:* Rudy Ralston. *SP:* Gerald Geraghty. *CAST:* Allan ("Rocky") Lane, Eddy Waller, Cathy Downs, Roy Barcroft, Trevor Bardette, Ray Montgomery, Byron Foulger, Harry Harvey, Robert Bice, "Black Jack." *SYN:* A U. S.

Mashal (Lane) is sent to prevent sabotage on the installation of the first natural gas system.

**41. Bar-Z Bad Men** (4/22/37) B&W 57 mins. (Western). *DIR:* Sam Newfield. *PRO:* A. W. Hackel. *SP:* George Plympton. Story by James P. Olson. *CAST:* Johnny Mack Brown, Lois January, Ernie Adams, Jack Rockwell, Tom London, Dick Curtis, Milburn Morante, Horace Murphy, Tex Palmer, Budd Buster, Frank Ball, George Morrell, Horace B. Carpenter, Art Dillard, Oscar Gahan. *SYN:* A rancher (Brown), accused of cattle rustling, sets out to find the real rustlers and clear his name.

**42. Barnyard Follies** (12/6/40) B&W 68 mins. (Musical). *DIR:* Frank McDonald. *A-PRO:* Armand Schaefer. *SP:* Dorrell McGowan, Stuart McGowan. Story by Robert T. Shannon. *CAST:* Mary Lee, Rufe Davis, June Storey, Jed Prouty, Victor Kilian, Joan Woodbury, Carl "Alfalfa" Switzer, Robert E. Homans, Dorothy Harrison, Harry Cheshire, Mary Jane De Zurik, Carolyn De Zurik, James J. Jeffries, The Kidoodlers, Ralph Bowman (John Archer), Isabel Randolph. *SYN:* A girl (Lee) and her friends try to save their 4-H club by putting on a show with a group of stranded performers.

**Battleshock** *see* **A Woman's Devotion**

**43. Beginning of the End** (6/28/57) B&W 73 mins. (Science-Fiction). *DIR/PRO:* Bert I. Gordon. *SP:* Fred Freiberger, Lester Gorn. An AB-PT Production. A Republic Presentation. *CAST:* Peggie Castle, Peter Graves, Morris Ankrum, Richard Benedict, James Seay, Thomas Browne Henry, Than Wyenn, John Close, Don C. Harvey, Larry J. Blake, Steve Warren, Frank Connor, Don Eltner, Frank Chase, Pierre Watkin, Frank Wilcox. *SYN:* Giant grasshoppers, which have eaten fruits and vegetables grown with radioactive material, threaten to destroy Chicago. *NOTES:* Double billed in some areas with *The Unearthly*.

**44. Behind City Lights** (9/10/45) B&W 68 mins. (Drama). *DIR:* John English. *A-PRO:* Joseph Bercholz. *SP:* Richard Weil. Adapted by Gertrude Walker. Original story by Vicki Baum. *CAST:* Lynne Roberts, Peter Cookson, Jerome Cowan, Esther Dale, William Terry, Victor Kilian, Moroni Olsen, William Forrest, Emmett Vogan, Joseph J. Greene, Frank Scannell, Tom London, George Carleton, Bud Geary. *SYN:* A country girl (Roberts) walks out on her wedding and heads to the city, where after some misadventures with crooks and the law, she returns home to her fiance (Cookson).

**45. Behind the News** (12/20/40) B&W 75 mins. (Drama). *DIR:* Joseph Santley. *A-PRO:* Robert North. *SP:* Isabel Dawn, Boyce DeGaw. Story by Dore Schary, Allen Rivkin. *CAST:* Lloyd Nolan, Doris Davenport, Frank Albertson, Robert Armstrong, Paul Harvey, Charles Halton, Eddie Conrad, Harry Tyler, Dick Elliott, Archie Twitchell, Veda Ann Borg, Eddie Fetherston, Milton Parsons. *SYN:* A journalism school scholarship winner (Albertson) joins a newspaper and befriends a boozy former news reporter (Nolan) and together the two of them go on to upset a crime scheme. *NOTES:* Remade by Republic in 1955 as *Headline Hunters*. Academy Award Nominee — Best Sound.

**46. Belle LeGrand** (1/27/51) B&W 90 mins. (Western). *DIR:* Allan Dwan. *PRO:* Herbert J. Yates. *SP:* D. D. Beauchamp. Story by Peter B. Kyne. *CAST:* Vera Ralston, John Carroll, Muriel Lawrence, William Ching, Hope Emerson, Grant Withers, Stephen Chase, John Qualen, Henry (Harry) Morgan, Charles Cane, Thurston Hall, Marietta Canty, Glenn Vernon, Sam Flint, Edward Cassidy, Isabel Randolph, Don Beddoe, John Holland, Frank Wilcox, Paul Maxey, Pierre Watkin, John Hart, Edward Keane, Russell Hicks, Rodney Bell, John Close, John Vosper, John Hamilton, Howard Mitchell, Perry Ivins, Jimmy Ogg, Maude Eburne, Carl "Alfalfa" Switzer, Eddie Dunn, Chester Clute, Queenie Smith, Hal Price, William Schallert, Gino Corrado, Ruth Robinson, Fred Hoose, Dick Elliott, Andrew Tombes, Art Baker, James Arness, James Kirkwood, Emory Parnell, Peter Brocco, Don C. Harvey, Jerry Miley, Joseph Granby, Sam Sebby, Thomas Browne Henry. *SYN:* In Virginia City, a lady gambler (Ralston) joins forces with a silver miner (Carroll) to help him keep his mine from an unscrupulous banker (Chase), but he has eyes for her sister (Lawrence). *NOTES:* The film debut of Muriel Lawrence.

**47. Belle of Old Mexico** (3/1/50) Trucolor 70 mins. (Musical-Drama). *DIR:* R. G. Springsteen. *A-PRO:* Edward J. White. *SP:* Bradford Ropes, Francis Swann. *CAST:* Estelita Rodriguez, Robert Rockwell, Dorothy Patrick, Thurston Hall, Florence Bates, Dave Willock, Gordon Jones, Fritz Feld, Anne O'Neal, Nacho Galindo, Joe Venuti, Edward Gargan, Carlos Molina and His Orchestra. *SYN:* A college president (Rockwell) goes south of the border to adopt the kid sister of a pal from World War II, but it turns out that she is a full grown lady (Rodriguez).

**48. Bells of Capistrano** (9/15/42) B&W 78 mins. (Western). *DIR:* William Morgan. *A-PRO:* Harry Grey. *SP:* Lawrence Kimble. *CAST:* Gene Autry, Smiley Burnette, Virginia Grey, Lucien Littlefield, Morgan Conway, Claire DuBrey, Charles Cane, Joe Strauch, Jr., Marla Shelton, Tristram Coffin, Jay Novello, Alan Bridge, Terrisita Osta, Eddie Acuff, Jack O'Shea, Julian Rivero, William Forrest, Bill Telaak, Ken Christy, Dick Wessel, Eddie Jauregui, Guy Usher, Ralph Peters, Joe McGuinn, Howard Hickman, William Kellogg (Bruce Kellogg), Carla Ramos, Fernando Ramos, Peggy Satterlee, Ray Jones, Frankie Marvin, "Champion." *SYN:* Gene helps a young woman (Grey) who owns a rodeo show and is facing some unscrupulous competition from a rival rodeo show. *NOTES:* Gene's last feature before entering service during World War II. Re-edited for TV at 54 mins.

**49. Bells of Coronado** (1/8/50) Trucolor 67 mins. (Western). *DIR:* William Witney. *A-PRO:* Edward J. White. *SP:* Sloan Nibley. *CAST:* Roy Rogers, Dale Evans, Pat Brady, Grant Withers, Leo Cleary, Clifton Young, Robert Bice, Stuart Randall, John Hamilton, Edmund Cobb, Eddie Lee, Rex Lease, Lane Bradford, Foy Willing and the Riders of the Purple Sage, "Trigger." *SYN:* An insurance investigator (Rogers), sent to find missing uranium ore, learns that a local businessman (Withers) has been selling it to foreign spies who plan to send it to their homeland, and he and his men set out to stop the spies before they can ship the uranium out. *NOTES:* Re-edited for TV at 54 mins.

# Bells of San Angelo

**50. Bells of Rosarita** (6/19/45) B&W 68 mins. (Western). *DIR:* Frank McDonald. *A-PRO:* Edward J. White. *SP:* Jack Townley. *CAST:* Roy Rogers, George "Gabby" Hayes, Dale Evans, Adele Mara, Grant Withers, Janet Martin, Addison Richards, Roy Barcroft, Syd Saylor, Edward Cassidy, Kenne Duncan, Rex Lease, Earle Hodgins, Robert Wilke, Ted Adams, Wally West, Bob Nolan and the Sons of the Pioneers, Robert Mitchell Boy Choir, Poodles Hanneford, Helen Talbot, Charles Sullivan, Hank Bell, Forbes Murray, Eddie Kane, Tom London, Marin Sais, Rosemonde James, Marian Kerrigan, Sam Ash, Craig Lawrence, Barbara Elliott, Mary McCarty, Tom Plank, George Barton, George "Shug" Fisher, Duke Taylor, Cactus Mack, Frank McDonald, Edward J. White, Paul Power, Billy Cartledge, Roger Creed, Frank McCarroll, Carl Leviness, Jesse Graves, Jack Richardson, Gil Perkins, Buster Brodie, Billy Cummings, Larry Williams, Irving Fulton, "Trigger." *GUEST STARS:* Bill Elliott, "Thunder," Allan ("Rocky") Lane, "Feather," Don ("Red") Barry, "Cyclone," Robert Livingston, "Shamrock," Sunset Carson, "Silver." *SYN:* Roy and "Gabby" call in other cowboy actors to help a girl (Evans) keep her circus when it is being taken over by her late father's partner (Withers). *NOTES:* Republic's first western to use other cowboy stars as guests. Director McDonald and associate-producer White appear in cameos. Re-edited for TV at 54 mins.

**51. Bells of San Angelo** (4/15/47) Trucolor 71 mins. (Western). *DIR:* William Witney. *A-PRO:* Edward J. White. *SP:* Sloan Nibley. Story by Paul

Gangelin. CAST: Roy Rogers, Dale Evans, Andy Devine, John McGuire, Olaf Hytten, David Sharpe, Fritz Leiber, Hank Patterson, Fred "Snowflake" Toones, Eddie Acuff, Dale Van Sickel, Ralph Bucko, Bob Nolan and the Sons of the Pioneers, "Trigger." SYN: A border patrolman (Rogers) and a writer (Evans) of western lore go after a gang smuggling silver across the Mexican border. NOTES: The first Roy Rogers film in which Andy Devine appeared. Re-edited for TV at 54 mins.

**52. Beneath Western Skies** (3/3/44) B&W 56 mins. (Western). DIR: Spencer G. Bennet. A-PRO: Louis Gray. SP: Albert DeMond, Bob Williams. Story by Albert DeMond. CAST: Robert Livingston, Smiley Burnette, Effie Laird, Frank Jaquet, Tom London, Charles Miller, Joe Strauch, Jr., LeRoy Mason, Kenne Duncan, Charles Dorety, Jack Kirk, Jack Ingram, John James, Budd Buster, Robert Wilke, Tom Steele, Herman Hack, Carl Sepulveda, Roy Bucko, Robert Kortman, Forrest Taylor, Marshall Reed, Bud Geary. SYN: John Paul Revere (Livingston) suffers amnesia and winds up as a pawn for an outlaw gang until he regains his memory and then he rounds them up. NOTES: The 4th and final entry in the "John Paul Revere" series.

**53. Beware of Ladies** (1/12/37) B&W 62 mins. (Drama). DIR: Irving Pichel. PRO: Nat Levine. SP: L. C. Dublin. CAST: Donald Cook, Judith Allen, George Meeker, Goodee Montgomery, Russell Hopton, William Newell, Dwight Frye, Thomas E. Jackson, Josephine Whittell, William Crowell, Robert Strange, Robert Emmett Keane, Eric Wilton, Phil Dunham. SYN: A newspaper reporter (Allen) falls for a hopeful district attorney (Cook) and brings about his downfall when a compromising photo is obtained by her estranged husband (Meeker).

**Beyond the Border** *see* **Mexicana**

**54. Beyond the Last Frontier** (9/18/43) B&W 57 mins. (Western). DIR: Howard Bretherton. A-PRO: Louis Gray. SP: John K. Butler, Morton Grant. CAST: Eddie Dew, Smiley Burnette, Harry Woods, Robert Mitchum, Kermit Maynard, Lorraine Miller, Ernie Adams, Curley Dresden, Henry Wills, Tom Steele, Frank O'Connor, Art Dillard, Al Taylor, Cactus Mack, Jack Rockwell, Jack Kirk, Charles Miller, Richard Cramer, Wheaton Chambers. SYN: A Texas Ranger (Dew) goes undercover and joins a gang of outlaws to put an end to their illegal gun running trade. NOTES: The 1st entry in the "John Paul Revere" series.

**55. The Big Bonanza** (12/30/44) B&W 68 mins. (Western). DIR: George Archainbaud. A-PRO: Edward J. White. SP: Dorrell McGowan, Stuart McGowan, Paul Gangelin. Story by Robert Presnell, Leonard Praskins. CAST: Richard Arlen, Robert Livingston, Jane Frazee, George "Gabby" Hayes, Lynne Roberts, Bobby Driscoll, J. M. Kerrigan, Russell Simpson, Frank Reicher, Cordell Hickman, Hayward Soo Hoo, Roy Barcroft, Fred Kohler, Jr., Monte Hale, Charles King, Jack Rockwell, Henry Wills, Fred Graham, Dan White, Robert Wilke, Tom Steele. SYN: A Union officer (Arlen), accused of cowardice, returns home and learns that it was his friend (Livingston) who framed him. NOTES: The film debut of Monte Hale.

**The Big Gamble** *see* **The Inside Story**

**56. The Big Show** (11/16/36) B&W 59 mins. (Western-Comedy). *DIR:* Mack V. Wright. *PRO:* Nat Levine. *SP:* Dorrell McGowan, Stuart McGowan. Story by Stuart and Dorrell McGowan. *CAST:* Gene Autry, Smiley Burnette, Kay Hughes, Sally Payne, William Newell, Max Terhune, Charles Judels, Rex King, Harry Worth, Mary Russell, Christine Maple, Jerry Larkin, Jack O'Shea, Wedgewood Norrell, Antrim Short, June Johnson, Grace Durkin, Slim Whitaker, George Chesebro, Edward Hearn, Cliff Lyons, Tracy Layne, Jack Rockwell, Frankie Marvin, Cornelius Keefe, Martin Stevenson, Horace B. Carpenter, Helen Servis, Frances Morris, Richard Beach, Jeanne Lafayette, Art Mix, I. Stanford Jolley, Vic Lacardo, Sally Rand, The SMU 50, The Jones Boys, The Beverly Hill Billies, The Light Crust Doughboys, Bob Nolan and the Sons of the Pioneers [Leonard Slye (Roy Rogers), Tim Spencer, Hugh Farr, Karl Farr], "Champion." *SYN:* A western star (Autry) skips out on an appearance at the Texas Centennial in Dallas and his screen double (Autry) takes over for him, which confuses each's fiancee, (Hughes, Payne) as well as gangsters who are looking for the star. *NOTES:* Gene Autry plays a dual role in this film. The screen debut of Max Terhune. Filmed at the Texas Centennial Exposition. [Re-release title: *Home in Oklahoma.*]

**57. The Big Show-Off** (1/22/45) B&W 60 mins. (Drama). *DIR:* Howard Bretherton. *PRO:* Sydney M. Williams. *SP:* Laslo Vadnay, Richard Weil. *CAST:* Arthur Lake, Dale Evans, Lionel Stander, George Meeker, Paul Hurst, Marjorie Manners, Sammy Stein, Louis (Duke) Adlon, Dan Tobey, Emmett Lynn, Douglas Wood, Anson Weeks and His Orchestra. *SYN:* A pianist (Lake) pretends to be a famous wrestler in order to impress a girl (Evans).

**58. Bill and Coo** (3/28/48) Trucolor 61 mins. (Children's). *DIR:* Dean Riesner. *PRO:* Ken Murray. *SP:* Royal Foster, Dean Riesner. Based on an idea from Ken Murray's "Blackouts." A Ken Murray Production. A Republic Presentation. *CAST: VOICES OF:* Ken Murray, George Burton, Elizabeth Walters. *SYN:* The tale of a bird sanctuary, Chirpendale, whose inhabitants are threatened by a menace, Jimmy the Crow. *NOTES:* Film has no human actors.

**59. Bill Cracks Down** (3/22/37) B&W 61 mins. (Comedy). *DIR:* William Nigh. *A-PRO:* William Berke. *SP:* Dorrell McGowan, Stuart McGowan. Story by Owen Francis, Morgan B. Cox. *CAST:* Grant Withers, Beatrice Roberts, Ranny Weeks, Judith Allen, William Newell, Pierre Watkin, Julia Thayer, Roger Williams, Georgia Caine, Greta Meyer, Edgar Norton, Harry Depp, Eugene King, Landers Stevans, Eddie Anderson. *SYN:* A father (Watkin) leaves his playboy son (Weeks) the family business, a steel mill, in the hopes he gains some experience working under the superintendent (Withers), or he will lose his inheritance. [British title: *Men of Steel.*]

**60. Billy the Kid Returns** (9/4/38) B&W 58 mins. (Western). *DIR:* Joseph Kane. *A-PRO:* Charles E. Ford. *SP:* Jack Natteford. *CAST:* Roy Rogers, Smiley Burnette, Mary Hart (Lynn Roberts), Morgan Wallace, Fred Kohler, Sr., Wade Boteler, Edwin Stanley, Horace Murphy, Joseph Crehan, Robert Emmett Keane,

Dorothy Vaughan, Frank O'Connor, Al Taylor, George Letz (George Montgomery), Chris-Pin Martin, Jim Corey, Lloyd Ingraham, Bob McKenzie, Oscar Gahan, Jack Kirk, Art Dillard, Fred Burns, Betty Roadman, Rudy Sooter, Betty Jane Haney, Patsy Lee Parsons, Ray Nichols, Ralph Dunn, Bob Card. *SYN:* Billy the Kid (Rogers) becomes a lawman and brings justice to Lincoln county. *NOTES:* Re-edited for TV at 54 mins.

The Black Devils of Kali (G.B. title) see Mystery of the Black Jungle

61. Black Hills Ambush (5/20/52) B&W 54 mins. (Western). *DIR/A-PRO:* Harry Keller. *SP:* Ronald Davidson, M. Coates Webster. *CAST:* Allan ("Rocky") Lane, Eddy Waller, Leslye Banning, Roy Barcroft, Michael Hall, John Vosper, Edward Cassidy, John Cason, Wesley Hudman, Michael Barton, "Black Jack." *SYN:* A marshal (Lane) is called in by an old pal (Waller) to help him stop a gang of outlaws who are ruining his shipping business.

62. The Black Hills Express (8/15/43) B&W 56 mins. (Western). *DIR:* John English. *A-PRO:* Edward J. White. *SP:* Norman S. Hall. Story by Fred Myton. *CAST:* Don ("Red") Barry, Ariel Heath, Wally Vernon, George J. Lewis, William Halligan, Hooper Atchley, Charles Miller, Pierce Lyden, Jack Rockwell, Robert Kortman, Al Taylor, LeRoy Mason, Milton Kibbee, Wheaton Chambers, Marshall Reed, Curley Dresden, Ray Jones, Frank Ellis, Carl Sepulveda. *SYN:* A cowboy (Barry) sets out to clear himself from a string of stagecoach robberies and find the real culprits.

63. Blackmail (7/24/47) B&W 67 mins. (Crime). *DIR:* Lesley Selander. *A-PRO:* William J. O'Sullivan. *SP:* Royal K. Cole, Albert DeMond. Story by Robert Leslie Bellen. *CAST:* William Marshall, Adele Mara, Ricardo Cortez, Grant Withers, Stephanie Bachelor, Richard Fraser, Roy Barcroft, George J. Lewis, Gregory Gay, Tristram Coffin, Eva Novak, Bud Wolfe. *SYN:* A detective (Marshall) is hired by a gambler-playboy (Cortez) to protect him from a blackmailer (Fraser).

64. The Blocked Trail (3/12/43) B&W 58 mins. (Western). *DIR:* Elmer Clifton. *A-PRO:* Louis Gray. *SP:* John K. Butler, Jacquin Frank. Based on characters created by William Colt MacDonald. *CAST:* Bob Steele, Tom Tyler, Jimmie Dodd, Helen Deverall, George J. Lewis, Walter Sodering, Charles Miller, Kermit Maynard, Pierce Lyden, Carl Mathews, Hal Price, Budd Buster, Earle Hodgins, Bud Osborne, Al Taylor, Art Dillard, Bud Geary. *SYN:* The Three Mesquiteers (Livingston, Tyler, Dodd) are suspected of murder and set out to clear their names. *NOTES:* The 49th entry in the "Three Mesquiteers" series.

65. The Blonde Bandit (1/11/50) B&W 60 mins. (Drama). *DIR:* Harry Keller. *A-PRO:* Sidney Picker. *SP:* John K. Butler. *CAST:* Dorothy Patrick, Gerald Mohr, Robert Rockwell, Larry J. Blake, Charles Cane, Richard Irving, Argentina Brunetti, Alex Frazer, Nana Bryant, David Clarke, Jody Gilbert, Monte Blue, Eve Whitney, Norman Rudd, Bob Scott, Robert Wilke, Philip Van Zandt, Ted Jacques, Walter Clinton, Eva Novak, Keith Richards, Lester Dorr, Roy Gordon. *SYN:* A woman (Patrick) is talked into taking part in a

robbery by a criminal bookie (Mohr), and when he is captured, she refuses to get evidence against him because she loves him, and promises to wait for him while he does his time.

**66. Blue Montana Skies** (5/4/39) B&W 56 mins (Western). *DIR:* B. Reeves Eason. *A-PRO:* Harry Grey. *SP:* Gerald Geraghty. *CAST:* Gene Autry, Smiley Burnette, June Storey, Harry Woods, Tully Marshall, Alan Bridge, Glenn Strange, Dorothy Granger, Edmund Cobb, Robert Winkler, Jack Ingram, Augie Gomez, John Beach, Elmo Lincoln, Allan Cavan, Jay Wilsey (Buffalo Bill, Jr.), Buck Moulton, Ray Henderson, Wally West, Ted Mapes, Curley Dresden, Frankie Marvin, Walt Shrum and His Colorado Hillbillies, "Champion." *SYN:* A federal investigator (Autry) sets out to capture a band of fur smugglers near the Canadian border. *NOTES:* Elmo Lincoln was the first screen *Tarzan* in 1918. Re-edited for TV at 54 mins.

**67. The Bold Caballero** (2/3/36) Magnacolor 69 mins. (Western). *DIR:* Wells Root. *PRO:* Nat Levine. *SP:* Wells Root from his original screenplay *The Return of Zorro*, and the character created by Johnson McCulley. *CAST:* Robert Livingston, Heather Angel, Sig Rumann, Ian Wolfe, Robert Warwick, Emily Fitzroy, Charles Stevens, Walter Long, Ferdinand Munier, King Martin (Chris-Pin Martin), Carlos de Valdez, John Merton, Jack Kirk, Slim Whitaker, Vinegar Roan, George Plues, Henry Morris, Chief Thunder Cloud, Pascale Perry, Jack Roberts, William Emile, Gurdial Singh, Steve Clark, Herman Hack, Rube Dalroy, Bill Wolfe, Si Jenks, Harrison Greene, Jimmy Aubrey, Jack Rockwell, Artie Ortego, Dick Botiller, Wally West, Eddie Phillips, Sherry Tansey, Henry Hall, Ben Corbett, Bud McClure. *SYN:* In old Spanish California, Zorro (Livingston), framed for the murder of the Governor (Warwick) by the Commandante (Rumann), who is oppressing the Spanish colonists, must prove his innocence and free the colonists. *NOTES:* This was one of Republic's first efforts in color filmmaking (Magnacolor), and the first feature in the "Zorro" series. Only B&W prints are available. [British title: *The Bold Cavalier.*]

**The Bold Cavalier** (G.B. title) *see* **The Bold Caballero**

**68. The Bold Frontiersman** (4/15/48) B&W 60 mins. (Western). *DIR:* Philip Ford. *A-PRO:* Gordon Kay. *SP:* Bob Williams. *CAST:* Allan ("Rocky") Lane, Eddy Waller, Roy Barcroft, John Alvin, Francis McDonald, Fred Graham, Edward Cassidy, Edmund Cobb, Harold Goodwin, Jack Kirk, Ken Terrell, Marshall Reed, Al Murphy, "Black Jack." *SYN:* A government investigator (Lane) is sent to recover the gold from an outlaw gang that drought-parched ranchers have raised to build a dam.

**69. Boothill Brigade** (8/2/37) B&W 56 mins. (Western). *DIR:* Sam Newfield. *PRO:* A. W. Hackel. *SP:* George Plympton. Story by Harry Olmstead. *CAST:* Johnny Mack Brown, Claire Rochelle, Dick Curtis, Horace Murphy, Frank LaRue, Edward Cassidy, Bobby Nelson, Frank Ball, Steve Clark, Frank Ellis, Lew Meehan, Tex Palmer, Sherry Tansey, Jim Corey. *SYN:* A ranch foreman (Brown) sets out to stop an unscrupulous land baron (Cassidy) from stealing his employer's (LaRue) ranch. *NOTES:* Johnny Mack Brown's final film for Republic and A. W. Hackel before moving over to Universal Pictures.

**70. Boots and Saddles** (10/11/37) B&W 59 mins. (Western). *DIR:* Joseph Kane. *A-PRO:* Sol C. Siegel. *SP:* Jack Natteford, Oliver Drake. Story by Jack Natteford. *CAST:* Gene Autry, Smiley Burnette, Judith Allen, Ra Hould (Ronald Sinclair), Guy Usher, Gordon (Bill) Elliott, John Ward, Frankie Marvin, Chris-Pin Martin, Stanley Blystone, Bud Osborne, Merrill McCormick, Max Terhune, Jerry Frank, Bob Reeves, Nelson McDowell, Al Taylor, "Champion." *SYN:* A ranch foreman (Autry) helps a teenage English boy (Hould) to keep his ranch, and sets out to stop a rival horse dealer (Elliott) from stealing his Army contract.

**71. The Border Legion** (12/5/40) B&W 58 mins. (Western). *DIR/PRO:* Joseph Kane. *SP:* Olive Cooper, Louis Stevens. Additional treatment by George Carleton Brown. Based on the book by Zane Grey. *CAST:* Roy Rogers, George "Gabby" Hayes, Carol Hughes, Joe Sawyer, Maude Eburne, Jay Novello, Hal Taliaferro, Dick Wessel, Paul Porcasi, Robert Emmett Keane, Ted Mapes, Fred Burns, Post Park, Art Dillard, Chick Hannon, Chuck Baldra, Jack Kirk, Eddie Acuff, Monte Montague, Pascale Perry, Bob Card, Edward Peil, Sr., Ed Brady, Lew Kelly, Victor Cox, Curley Dresden, George Kesterson (Art Mix), Cactus Mack, Bob Woodward, Jack Montgomery, "Trigger." *SYN:* A wanted fugitive (Rogers), framed for a crime he did not commit, joins an outlaw gang to bring them to justice and clear his name. *NOTES:* Re-edited for TV at 54 mins. Previously filmed as a silent in 1924 with Antonio Moreno, in 1930 with Richard Arlen, and in 1934 as *The Last Roundup* with Randolph Scott. [TV title: *West of the Badlands.*]

**72. Border Phantom** (6/7/37) B&W 58 mins. (Western). *DIR:* S. Roy Luby. *PRO:* A. W. Hackel. *SP:* Fred Myton. Story by Fred Myton. *CAST:* Bob Steele, Harley Wood, Don Barclay, Karl Hackett, Horace Murphy, Miki Morita, Perry Murdock, Hans Joby, Frank Ball, Budd Buster, Clyde McClary, Horace B. Carpenter. *SYN:* A cowboy (Steele) and his sidekick (Barclay) set out to stop the smuggling of Chinese brides into the U.S. from Mexico.

**73. Border Saddlemates** (4/15/52) B&W 67 mins. (Western). *DIR:* William Witney. *A-PRO:* Edward J. White. *SP:* Albert DeMond. *CAST:* Rex Allen, Mary Ellen Kay, Slim Pickens, Roy Barcroft, Forrest Taylor, Jimmy Moss, Zon Murray, Keith McConnell, Mark Hanna, Bud Osborne, Billy Dix, Pat O'Malley, Joe Yrigoyen, Post Park, James Magill, The Republic Rhythm Riders, "Koko." *SYN:* A government agent (Allen), posing as a veterinarian, sets out to stop a gang smuggling counterfeit U.S. currency from Canada into Montana.

**74. Bordertown Gunfighters** (10/1/43) B&W 55 mins. (Western). *DIR:* Howard Bretherton. *A-PRO:* Edward J. White. *SP:* Norman S. Hall. *CAST:* Bill Elliott, George "Gabby" Hayes, Anne Jeffreys, Ian Keith, Harry Woods, Roy Barcroft, Bud Geary, Carl Sepulveda, Edward Earle, Karl Hackett, Charles King, Edward Keane, Frank McCarroll, Wheaton Chambers, Ken Terrell, Bill Wolfe, Rose Plummer, Al Haskell, Foxy O'Callahan, Neal Hart, Frosty Royce,

Ralph Bucko, Marshall Reed, Jim Massey, "Sonny." *SYN:* Bill and "Gabby" set out to put an end to an illegal lottery scheme in Texas being operated by an unscrupulous gambler (Keith).

**75. Bordertown Trail** (8/11/44) B&W 55 mins. (Western) *DIR:* Lesley Selander. *A-PRO:* Louis Gray. *SP:* Bob Williams, Jesse Duffy. *CAST:* Sunset Carson, Smiley Burnette, Ellen Lowe, Weldon Heyburn, Addison Richards, Francis McDonald, Jack Luden, Rex Lease, John James, Jack Kirk, Henry Wills, Cliff Parkinson, Neal Hart, Chick Hannon, Jack O'Shea, Robert Wilke, Ted Wells, Fusty Cecil, Earl Dobbins, Roy Darmour. *SYN:* A U. S. border patrolman (Carson) sets out to stop a gang of smugglers.

**76. Born to be Wild** (2/16/38) B&W 66 mins. (Drama-Adventure). *DIR:* Joseph Kane. *A-PRO:* Harold Shumate. *SP:* Nathaniel West. Story by Nathaniel West. *CAST:* Ralph Byrd, Doris Weston, Ward Bond, Robert Emmett Keane, Bentley Hewlett, Charles Williams, Davison Clark, Byron Foulger, George Anderson, Edwin Stanley, Ben Hendricks, Jr., Stelita, Lew Kelly, Harrison Greene, George Magrill, Herbert Heywood, Anna Demetrio, Stooge. *SYN:* Two truckers (Byrd, Bond) set out to deliver a shipment of dynamite to a distant town where it will be used to blow up a dam. *NOTES:* This film was scripted by famed writer Nathanael West (*Miss Lonelyhearts, The Day of the Locust*). West and his wife, Eileen McKenney (whose early life was the basis for the feature *My Sister Eileen*, 1942, 1955), were killed in an automobile accident in 1940.

**77. Born to Gamble** (10/4/35) B&W 66 mins. (Drama). *DIR:* Phil Rosen. *PRO:* M. H. Hoffman. *SP:* E. Morton Hough. Based on *The Greek Poropulos* by Edgar Wallace. A Liberty/Republic Picture. *CAST:* Onslow Stevens, H. B. Warner, Maxine Doyle, Eric Linden, Lois Wilson, William Janney, Ben Alexander, Lucien Prival. *SYN:* A brother (Stevens) sets out to avenge the murder of his three older brothers (Linden, Janney, Alexander) who had an inherited weakness for gambling. *NOTES:* Onslow Stevens plays a dual role in this film. Working title was *I'll Bet You.*

**Bourbon St. Shadows** *see* **Invisible Avenger**

**78. Bowery Boy** (12/30/40) B&W 71 mins. (Drama). *DIR:* William Morgan. *A-PRO:* Armand Schaefer. *SP:* Robert Chapin, Harry Kronman, Eugene Solow. Story by Samuel Fuller, Sidney Sutherland. *CAST:* Dennis O'Keefe, Louise Campbell, James Lydon, Helen Vinson, Roger Pryor, Paul Hurst, Edward Gargan, Selmer Jackson, John Kelly, Howard Hickman, Frederick Burton, Jack Carr. *SYN:* A crusading doctor (O'Keefe) and his nurse (Campbell) help clear up a tainted food epidemic while a juvenile delinquent (Lydon) gets involved with a mobster (Pryor) and his gang.

**79. Brazil** (11/30/44) B&W 91 mins. (Musical-Comedy). *DIR:* Joseph Santley. *A-PRO:* Robert North. *SP:* Frank Gill, Jr., Laura Kerr. Story by Richard English. *CAST:* Tito Guizar, Virginia Bruce, Edward Everett Horton, Robert Livingston, Fortunio Bonanova, Richard Lane, Frank Puglia, Aurora Miranda, Alfredo de Sa, Henry DaSilva,

Rico de Montez, Leon Lenoir, Veloz and Yolanda, GUEST STAR: Roy Rogers. SYN: A South American songwriter (Guizar), having had initial success with the tune "Brazil," struggles to come up with a follow-up hit for the national Brazilian song contest, while trying to tame an American authoress (Bruce). NOTES: Aurora Miranda was the sister of Carmen Miranda. Academy Award Nominee — Best Score, Best Song, and Best Sound.

**80. Brimstone** (8/15/49) Trucolor 90 mins. (Western). *DIR/A-PRO:* Joseph Kane. *SP:* Thames Williamson. Story by Norman S. Hall. *CAST:* Rod Cameron, Adrian Booth, Walter Brennan, Forrest Tucker, Jack Holt, Jim Davis, James Brown, Guinn "Big Boy" Williams, Jack Lambert, Will Wright, David Williams, Harry Cheshire, Hal Taliaferro, Herbert Rawlinson, Stanley Andrews, Charlita, Jack Perrin, George Chesebro, Charles Cane, Hank Bell, Emmett Lynn, Jack O'Shea. *SYN:* A U.S. Marshal (Cameron) is sent to a territory to put an end to the cattle rustling that is going on there, and learns that his friend (Tucker), who is the sheriff, and a local rancher (Brennan) are the ones doing the cattle rustling.

**81. Buckaroo Sheriff of Texas** (5/1/51) B&W 60 mins. (Western). *DIR:* Philip Ford. *A-PRO:* Rudy Ralston. *SP:* Arthur E. Orloff. *CAST:* Michael Chapin, Eilene Janssen, James Bell, Hugh O'Brian, Steve Pendleton, Tristram Coffin, William Haade, Alice Kelley, Selmer Jackson, Edward Cassidy, George Taylor, Steve Dunhill, Billy Dix, Eddie Dunn, *SYN:* The Rough Ridin' Kids (Chapin, Janssen) set out to stop a crooked land baron (Coffin) from stealing land from the local ranchers.

*NOTES:* The 1st entry in the "Rough-Ridin' Kids" series.

**82. Bulldog Drummond at Bay** (7/31/37) B&W 63 mins. (Mystery). *DIR:* Norman Lee. *PRO:* Walter C. Mycroft. *SP:* James Parrish, Patrick Kirwin. Based on the book by H. C. "Sapper" McNeile. An Associated British Picture/Wardour Film. A Republic Presentation. *CAST:* John Lodge, Wilfrid Hyde-White, Dorothy Mackaill, Victor Jory, Claud Allister, Hugh Miller, Leslie Perrins, Richard Bird, Brian Buchel, Jim Gerald, Maire O'Neill, William Dewhurst, Frank Cochrane, Annie Esmond. *SYN:* Bulldog Drummond (Lodge) is out to stop foreign agents who are after the secret plans of a remote-controlled British warplane. *NOTES:* Released in Britain in March, 1937 at a running time of 78 mins.

**83. Bulldog Edition** (9/20/36) B&W 57 mins. (Drama). *DIR:* Charles Lamont. *PRO:* Nat Levine. *A-PRO:* Sol C. Siegel. *SP:* Karen DeWolf, Richard English. Story by Richard English. Based on *Back in Circulation* by Danny Ahearn. *CAST:* Ray Walker, Evalyn Knapp, Regis Toomey, Cy Kendall, William Newell, Oscar Apfel, Betty Compson, Robert Warwick, Ivan Miller, Matty Fain, George Lloyd, Frank Puglia, Ruth Gillette, Edward J. LeSaint, Lynn Roberts. *SYN:* A feud develops between two newspapers searching for the ultimate in circulation figures. [British title: *Lady Reporter.*]

**84. Bullfighter and the Lady** (5/15/51) B&W 87 mins. (Drama). *DIR:* Budd Boetticher. *PRO:* John Wayne. *SP:* James Edward Grant. Story by Budd Boetticher and Ray Nazarro. *CAST:* Robert Stack, Joy Page, Gilbert Roland,

Virginia Grey, John Hubbard, Katy Jurado, Antonio Gomez, Ismael Perez, Rodolfo Acosta, Ruben Padilla, Dario Ramirez. *SYN:* An American (Stack) falls in love with a lovely senorita, (Page), and, to impress her, convinces a renowned matador (Roland) to make him his protege. He becomes over confident and causes the matador's death, incurring the hatred of the locals and the girl. He redeems himself by reentering the ring and decimating a bull in the matador's honor. *NOTES:* Academy Award nominee for Best Motion Picture Story. Boetticher, a former college football player and boxer who traveled to Mexico in the 1930's and began a lifelong passion for bullfighting as a matador, served as the technical advisor for Rouben Mamoulian's *Blood and Sand* in 1941 and went on to direct another bullfighting film, *The Magnificent Matador*, in 1955, a 20th Century–Fox release. Following great success as a director of westerns he spent seven years, beginning in 1960, working on a documentary about the famous matador Carlos Arruza. While filming this documentary, *Arruza*, most of his crew, along with bullfighter Carlos Arruza, were killed in an automobile crash. The documentary was finally released by Avco-Embassy Pictures in 1972.

**85. Burning Gold** (5/22/36) B&W 58 mins. (Drama). *DIR:* Sam Newfield. *PRO:* Nat Levine. *SP:* Earle Snell. Story by Stuart Anthony. *CAST:* William Boyd, Judith Allen, Lloyd Ingraham, Fern Emmett, Frank Mayo, Bud Flanagan (Dennis O'Keefe). *SYN:* An oil driller (Boyd) strikes it rich, marries a local gal (Allen), then loses everything when his well catches fire.

**86. Calendar Girl** (1/31/47) B&W 88 mins. (Musical). *DIR/A-PRO:* Allan Dwan. *SP:* Mary Loos, Richard Sale, Lee Loeb. Story by Lee Loeb. *CAST:* Jane Frazee, William Marshall, Gail Patrick, Kenny Baker, Victor McLaglen, Irene Rich, James Ellison, Janet Martin, Franklin Pangborn, Gus Schilling, Charles Arnt, Lou Nova, Emory Parnell. *SYN:* An artist (Ellison) causes romance problems for a young couple (Marshall, Frazee) when he selects the girl as his next calendar model. *NOTES:* The final film of Kenny Baker—he retired after this film.

**87. California Firebrand** (4/1/48) Trucolor 63 mins. (Western). *DIR:* Philip Ford. *A-PRO:* Melville Tucker. *SP:* J. Benton Cheney, John K. Butler. *CAST:* Monte Hale, Adrian Booth, Paul Hurst, Alice Tyrrell, Tristram Coffin, LeRoy Mason, Douglas Evans, Sarah Edwards, Daniel M. Sheridan, Duke York, Lanny Rees, Glenn Strange, Foy Willing and the Riders of the Purple Sage. *SYN:* A drifter (Hale) pretends to be a dangerous gunfighter as he defends a gold mining town against a group of outlaws. *NOTES:* LeRoy Mason died 10/13/47 during filming of this feature. Tristram Coffin plays a dual role in this film.

**88. California Gold Rush** (2/4/46) B&W 51 mins. (Western). *DIR:* R. G. Springsteen. *A-PRO:* Sidney Picker. *SP:* Bob Williams. Based on the comic strip created by Fred Harman. *CAST:* Bill Elliott, Bobby (Robert) Blake, Alice Fleming, Peggy Stewart, Kenne Duncan, Russell Simpson, Dick Curtis, Joel Friedkin, Monte Hale, Tom London, Wen Wright, Dickie Dillon, Jack Kirk, Mary Arden, Budd Buster, Bud Osborne, Neal Hart, Frank Ellis, Jim

Mitchell, Herman Hack, Freddie Chapman, Jess Cavan, Pascale Perry, Silver Harr, Ben Johnson, "Thunder." *SYN:* Red Ryder (Elliott) is sent for by the Duchess (Fleming) to stop a gang of outlaws that are trying to drive a stagecoach line out of business. *NOTES:* Ben Johnson was a stunt double for Bill Elliott. The 13th entry in the "Red Ryder" feature series.

**89. California Joe** (12/29/43) B&W 55 mins. (Western). *DIR:* Spencer G. Bennet. *A-PRO:* Edward J. White. *SP:* Norman S. Hall. *CAST:* Don ("Red") Barry, Wally Vernon, Helen Talbot, Twinkle Watts, Brian O'Hara, Terry Frost, Edward Earle, LeRoy Mason, Charles King, Pierce Lyden, Edmund Cobb, Karl Hackett, Robert Kortman, Edward Keane, Tom London, Jack O'Shea, Robert Wilke, Ernest Hilliard, Larry Steers, Foxy O'Callahan, Bob Burns, Lee Morgan, Jack Kirk. *SYN:* During the Civil War, a Union cavalry lieutenant (Barry) is sent to stop a group of Confederate sympathizers who want to make California a separate empire.

**California Outpost** *see* **Old Los Angeles**

**90. California Passage** (12/15/50) B&W 90 mins. (Western). *DIR/A-PRO:* Joseph Kane. *SP:* James Edward Grant. *CAST:* Forrest Tucker, Adele Mara, Estelita Rodriguez, Jim Davis, Peter Miles, Charles Kemper, Bill Wiliams, Rhys Williams, Paul Fix, Francis McDonald, Eddy Waller, Charles Stevens, Iron Eyes Cody, Alan Bridge, Ruth Brennan, Marshall Reed, Hal Taliaferro, Rory Mallinson, I. Stanford Jolley, Frank Richards. *SYN:* A saloon owner (Tucker), framed by his partner (Davis) for stealing gold shipments, flees the authorities. When his girl (Mara) is kidnapped by the partner, he returns to rescue her and exact justice.

**91. Call of the Canyon** (8/17/42) B&W 71 mins. (Western). *DIR:* Joseph Santley. *A-PRO:* Harry Grey. *SP:* Olive Cooper. Story by Maurice Rapf, Olive Cooper. *CAST:* Gene Autry, Smiley Burnette, Pat Brady, Bob Nolan and the Sons of the Pioneers, Ruth Terry, Thurston Hall, Joe Strauch, Jr., Cliff Nazarro, Dorothea Kent, Edmund MacDonald, Marc Lawrence, John Harmon, John Holland, Eddy Waller, Budd Buster, Frank Jaquet, Lorin Raker, John Duncan, Broderick O'Farrell, Raphael Bennett, Carey Harrison, Anthony Marsh, Fred Santley, Frank Ward, Freddie Walburn, Earle Hodgins, Red Knight, Al Taylor, Jimmy Lucas, Edna Johnson, Frankie Marvin, Charles Flynn, Bob Burns, Charles Williams, Joy Barton, "Champion." *SYN:* Gene gets mixed up with a crooked meatpacker and a radio sales lady and singer (Terry) who wants to rent his ranch to do her broadcast. *NOTES:* Re-edited for TV at 54 mins.

**The Call of the Ring** (G.B. title) *see* **The Duke Comes Back**

**92. Call of the Rockies** (7/14/44) B&W 58 mins. (Western). *DIR:* Lesley Selander. *A-PRO:* Louis Gray. *SP:* Bob Williams. *CAST:* Sunset Carson, Smiley Burnette, Ellen Hall, Frank Jaquet, Harry Woods, Kirk Alyn, Charles Williams, Jack Kirk, Tom London, Robert Kortman, Edmund Cobb, Jack O'Shea, Rex Lease, Frank McCarroll, Herman Hack, Bill Nestell, Robert Wilke, Kit Guard, Carl Sepulveda, Horace B. Carpenter, Roy Bucko, Nolan

Leary, Brandon Beach, Harry Wilson, Franklyn Farnum. *SYN:* Two freight haulers (Carson, Burnette) lose their cargo to outlaws, and then go after the outlaw ringleaders. *NOTES:* Sunset Carson's first starring film.

**93. Call of the South Seas** (4/7/44) B&W 55 mins. (Adventure). *DIR:* John English. *A-PRO:* Walter H. Goetz. *SP:* Albert DeMond. *CAST:* Janet Martin, Allan ("Rocky") Lane, William (Bill) Henry, Roy Barcroft, Wally Vernon, Adele Mara, Duncan Renaldo, Frank Jaquet, Anna Demetrio, Richard Alexander. *SYN:* When a gang of crooks, on the run from the FBI, invade a Pacific island and start harassing the locals, a federal agent (Lane) goes undercover as a beachcomber and infiltrates the gang to stop them.

**94. Call of the Yukon** (4/18/38) B&W 70 mins. (Western-Adventure). *DIR:* B. Reeves Eason, John T. Coyle. *A-PRO:* Armand Schaefer. *SP:* Gertrude Orr, William Bartlett. Based on *Swift Lightning* by James Oliver Curwood. *CAST:* Richard Arlen, Beverly Roberts, Lyle Talbot, Ray Mala, Garry Owen, Ivan Miller, James Lono, Emory Parnell, Billy Dooley, Al St. John, Anthony Hughes, Nina Campana, "Buck," the Wonder Dog. *SYN:* A lady reporter (Roberts) and a trapper (Arlen) battle snowslides, ice storms, falling trees, rain, and starvation in the Arctic while trying to reach civilization.

**95. Call the Mesquiteers** (3/7/38) B&W 55 mins. (Western). *DIR:* John English. *A-PRO:* William Berke. *SP:* Luci Ward. Story by Bernard McConville. Based on characters created by William Colt MacDonald. *CAST:* Robert Livingston, Ray ("Crash") Corrigan, Max Terhune, Lynn Roberts, Earle Hodgins, Sammy McKim, Eddy Waller, Maston Williams, Eddie Hart, Pat Gleason, Roger Williams, Warren Jackson, Hal Price, Frank Ellis, Curley Dresden, Jack Ingram, Ralph Peters, Ethan Laidlaw, Tom Steele, Al Taylor, "Flash." *SYN:* The Three Mesquiteers (Livingston, Corrigan, Terhune) are accused of robbery and must clear their names. *NOTES:* The 13th entry in the "Three Mesquiteers" series. [British and re-release title: *Outlaws of the West.*]

**96. Calling All Marines** (9/20/39) B&W 67 mins. (Spy). *DIR:* John H. Auer. *A-PRO:* Armand Schaefer. *SP:* Earl Felton. Story by Harrison Carter. *CAST:* Don ("Red") Barry, Helen Mack, Warren Hymer, Robert Kent, Cy Kendall, Leon Ames, Selmer Jackson, Janet McLeay, Walter McGrail, George Chandler, Jay Novello, James Flavin. *SYN:* A mobster (Barry) is recruited by an international spy ring to infiltrate the U.S. Marine Corps to steal plans for a new aerial torpedo being developed by engineers. Stealing another man's papers to enlist, he is eventually exposed and then jailed; released, he goes to the spy ring who wants to kill him to keep him from talking. He escapes from them, through the help of his friend (Hymer), and, having a change of heart, aids the Marines in rounding up the spies.

**97. Calling Wild Bill Elliott** (4/30/43) B&W 55 mins. (Western). *DIR:* Spencer G. Bennet. *A-PRO:* Harry Grey. *SP:* Anthony Coldeway. Story by Luci Ward. *CAST:* Bill Elliott, George "Gabby" Hayes, Anne Jeffreys, Herbert Heyes, Dee "Buzzy" Henry, Fred Kohler, Jr., Roy Barcroft, Charles King, Frank Hagney, Bud Geary, Lynton

Brent, Frank McCarroll, Eve March, Burr Caruth, Forbes Murray, Ted Mapes, Cliff Parkinson, Herman Hack, Yakima Canutt, "Sonny." *SYN:* Bill and "Gabby" help put an end to a crooked governor (Heyes) and his gang of militia who have been seizing the local ranches. *NOTES:* Bill Elliott's first Republic feature and possibly the first sound feature to incorporate the name of the star into the title.

**98. Campus Honeymoon** (2/1/48) B&W 61 mins. (Musical Comedy). *DIR:* Richard Sale. *A-PRO:* Fanchon. *SP:* Richard Sale, Jerry Gruskin. Story by Thomas R. St. George. *CAST:* Lyn Wilde, Lee Wilde, Adele Mara, Richard Crane, Hal Hackett, Wilson Wood, Stephanie Bachelor, Teddy Infuhr, Edwin Maxwell, Boyd Irwin, Kay Morley, Charles Smith, Edward Gargan, Maxine Semon, William H. Simon, Jr. *SYN:* Two returning war vets (Crane, Hackett) cannot obtain veteran housing because they are unmarried, so they fake a wedding with two sisters (Lyn and Lee Wilde) so they can obtain the houses.

**99. Canyon City** (11/24/43) B&W 56 mins. (Western). *DIR:* Spencer G. Bennet. *A-PRO:* Edward J. White. *SP:* Robert Yost. *CAST:* Don ("Red") Barry, Wally Vernon, Helen Talbot, Twinkle Watts, Morgan Conway, Emmett Vogan, Stanley Andrews, Roy Barcroft, LeRoy Mason, Pierce Lyden, Forbes Murray, Edward Peil, Sr., Eddie Gribbon, Tom London, Jack Kirk, Kenne Duncan, Bud Geary, Bud Osborne, Hank Worden. *SYN:* A cowboy (Barry) and his sidekick (Vernon) are out to prove that a big city promoter (Conway) is out to rob the ranchers of their land.

**100. Cappy Ricks Returns** (9/10/35) B&W 67 mins. (Drama). *DIR:* Mack V. Wright. *PRO:* Trem Carr. *SP:* George Waggner. Based on the novel by Peter B. Kyne. *CAST:* Robert McWade, Ray Walker, Florine McKinney, Lucien Littlefield, Bradley Page, Lois Wilson, Oscar Apfel, Kenneth Harlan. *SYN:* Cappy Ricks (McWade) comes out of retirement to battle a roofing materials lobby which is pushing legislation to outlaw the use of shingles on roofs, because such a law would ruin his lumber company. *NOTES:* The 1st entry in the "Cappy Ricks" series.

**101. Captain Tugboat Annie** (11/17/45) B&W 70 mins. (Drama). *DIR:* Phil Rosen. *A-PRO:* James S. Burkett. *SP:* George E. Callahan. Based on characters created by Norman Reilly Raine. *CAST:* Jane Darwell, Edgar Kennedy, Charles Gordon, Mantan Moreland, Pamela Blake, Hardie Albright, H. B. Warner, Saundra Berkova, Jack Norton, Barton Yarborough, Fritz Feld, Anthony Warde, Joseph Crehan, Pierre Watkin, Cyril Delevanti, Guy Wilkerson, Robert Elliott, Kernan Cripps, Harold Lang, Marion McGuire, Betty Sinclair, Edward Earle, Victor Potel, Sam Flint, Ralph Linn, Eddy Chandler, Harry Depp. *SYN:* Two rival tugboat operators (Darwell, Kennedy), out to win a big shipping contract, put aside their differences to combat a deadly waterfront fire. *NOTES:* The final film of Robert Elliott — he retired after this film.

**102. Captive of Billy the Kid** (1/22/52) B&W 54 mins. (Western). *DIR:* Fred C. Brannon. *A-PRO:* Harry Keller. *SP:* M. Coates Webster, Richard Wormser. *CAST:* Allan ("Rocky") Lane, Penny Edwards, Grant Withers, Clem Bevans,

Roy Barcroft, Clayton Moore, Mauritz Hugo, Gary Goodwin, Frank McCarroll, Richard Emory, Steve Clark, "Black Jack." *SYN:* A sheriff (Lane) goes under cover to trap the outlaws who are after the treasure of Billy the Kid.

**Cargo of Brides** *see* **A Perilous Journey**

103. **Carolina Cannonball** (1/28/55) B&W 74 mins. (Western-Comedy). *DIR:* Charles Lamont. *A-PRO:* Sidney Picker. *SP:* Barry Shipman. Story by Frank Gill, Jr. *CAST:* Judy Canova, Andy Clyde, Ross Elliott, Sig Rumann, Leon Askin, Jack Kruschen, Frank Wilcox, Roy Barcroft. *SYN:* A girl (Canova), her grandfather (Clyde), and a special agent (Elliott) set out to stop foreign agents (Rumann, Askin, Kruschen) who are trying to steal America's first atomic powered guided missile that crashed in a ghost town, and the girl and her grandfather are using it as a boiler on their steam-driven trolley.

104. **Carolina Moon** (7/15/40) B&W 65 mins. (Western) *DIR:* Frank McDonald. *A-PRO:* William Berke. *SP:* Winston Miller. Story by Connie Lee. *CAST:* Gene Autry, Smiley Burnette, June Storey, Mary Lee, Eddy Waller, Hardie Albright, Frank Dale, Terry Nibert, Robert Fiske, Etta McDaniel, Paul White, Fred Ritter, Ralph Sanford, Jack Kirk, Jimmy Lewis and his Texas Cowboys, "Champion." *SYN:* Gene and Frog (Burnette) are after a con man (Albright) who has bilked the owners out of their land. *NOTES:* Re-edited for TV at 54 mins.

105. **Carson City Cyclone** (3/3/43) B&W 55 mins. (Western). *DIR:* Howard Bretherton. *A-PRO:* Edward J. White. *SP:* Norman S. Hall. *CAST:* Don ("Red") Barry, Lynn Merrick, Noah Beery, Sr., Bryant Washburn, Emmett Lynn, Roy Barcroft, Stuart Hamblen, Bud Osborne, Jack Kirk, Bud Geary, Curley Dresden, Tom London, Frank Ellis, Horace B. Carpenter, Edward Cassidy, Reed Howes, Jack O'Shea, Tom Steele, Frank McCarroll, Roy Brent, Pascale Perry. *SYN:* A young lawyer (Barry) sets out to prove himself innocent of a murder charge.

106. **The Carson City Kid** (7/1/40) B&W 57 mins. (Western). *DIR/PRO:* Joseph Kane. *SP:* Robert Yost, Gerald Geraghty. Based on *Diamond Carlisle* by Joseph Kane. *CAST:* Roy Rogers, George "Gabby" Hayes, Bob Steele, Noah Beery, Jr., Pauline Moore, Francis McDonald, Hal Taliaferro, Arthur Loft, George Rosener, Chester Gan, Hank Bell, Ted Mapes, Jack Ingram, Jack Kirk, Jack Rockwell, Tom Smith, Art Dillard, Hal Price, Yakima Canutt, Kit Guard, Curley Dresden, Oscar Gahan, Chick Hannon, Al Taylor, "Trigger." *SYN:* A gunslinger, the Carson City Kid (Rogers), searches out a gambling hall owner (Steele) who killed his younger brother. *NOTES:* Re-edited for TV at 54 mins.

107. **Carson City Raiders** (5/13/48) B&W 60 mins. (Western). *DIR:* Yakima Canutt. *A-PRO:* Gordon Kay. *SP:* Earle Snell. *CAST:* Allan ("Rocky") Lane, Eddy Waller, Frank Reicher, Beverly Jons, Hal Landon, Steve Darrell, Harold Goodwin, Dale Van Sickel, Tom Chatterton, Edmund Cobb, Holly Bane, Robert Wilke, Herman Hack, "Black Jack." *SYN:* An express company agent (Lane) goes to Carson City to put an end to a gang of outlaws who are trying to grab control of a freight-wagon company.

The Carter Case (G.B. and Alternate title) *see* **Mr. District Attorney in the Carter Case**

**108. Casanova in Burlesque** (2/19/44) B&W 72 mins. (Musical-Comedy). *DIR:* Leslie Goodwins. *A-PRO:* Albert J. Cohen. *SP:* Frank Gill, Jr. Story by John Wales. *CAST:* Joe E. Brown, June Havoc, Dale Evans, Marjorie Gateson, Lucien Littlefield, Ian Keith, Roger Imhof, Harry Tyler, Patricia Knox, Sugar Geise, Jerome Franks, Jr., Marga Dean. *SYN:* A professor of Shakespeare (Brown) spends his summers as a burlesque comedian and, when he is blackmailed into putting one of the strippers (Havoc) in the lead of his upcoming production of "The Taming of the Shrew," the rest of the cast walks out and he is forced to call on his burlesque associates to be in the show.

**The Castaway** *see* **The Cheaters**

**109. The Catman of Paris** (4/20/46) B&W 65 mins. (Mystery). *DIR:* Lesley Selander. *A-PRO:* Marek M. Libkov. *SP:* Sherman L. Lowe. *CAST:* Carl Esmond, Lenore Aubert, Adele Mara, Douglass Dumbrille, Gerald Mohr, Fritz Feld, Francis Pierlot, Georges Renavent, Francis McDonald, Maurice Cass, Alphonse Martell, Paul Marion, John Dehner, Anthony Caruso, Carl Neubert, Elaine Lange, Tanis Chandler, George Davis, Albert Petit, Jean deBriac, Gino Corrado, Louis Mercier, Eugene Borden, Steve Darrell, Armand Roland, Claire DuBrey, Hector V. Sarno, Robert Wilke. *SYN:* An amnesia victim (Esmond) is suspected of murder until two crime experts (Mohr, Feld) find clues leading to the real killer. *NOTES:* Robert Wilke plays the role of the Catman. Double billed in some areas with *Valley of the Zombies*.

**110. Cavalry** (10/5/36) B&W 63 mins. (Western). *DIR:* Robert North Bradbury. *PRO:* A. W. Hackel. *SP:* George Plympton. Story by Robert North Bradbury. *CAST:* Bob Steele, William Welch, Karl Hackett, Frances Grant, Earl Ross, Hal Price, Edward Cassidy, Perry Murdock, Martin Turner, Pinky Barnes, Budd Buster, William Desmond, Earl Dwire, Horace B. Carpenter. *SYN:* After the Civil War, a cavalry officer (Steele) is sent West to stop a group from forming a separate state.

**111. Champ for a Day** (8/15/53) B&W 90 mins. (Crime). *DIR/A-PRO:* William A. Seiter. *SP:* Irving Shulman. Based on *The Disappearance of Dolan* by William Fay. *CAST:* Alex Nicol, Audrey Totter, Charles Winninger, Hope Emerson, Joseph Wiseman, Barry Kelley, Henry (Harry) Morgan, Jesse White, Horace MacMahon, Grant Withers, Eddy Waller, Dick Wessel, Hal Baylor. *SYN:* A boxer (Nicol) and his girl (Totter) set out to find who murdered his manager.

**Change of Heart** *see* **Hit Parade of 1943**

**112. Chatterbox** (4/27/43) B&W 77 mins. (Comedy). *DIR:* Joseph Santley. *A-PRO:* Albert J. Cohen. *SP:* George Carleton Brown, Frank Gill, Jr. *CAST:* Joe E. Brown, Judy Canova, John Hubbard, Rosemary Lane, Chester Clute, Emmett Vogan, Gus Schilling, Anne Jeffreys, George Byron, Art Whitney, Frank Melton, Gary Bruce, Matty Kemp, Ray Parsons, Mary Armstrong, The Mills Brothers, Roy Barcroft, Earle Hodgins, Nora Lane, Joe Phillips, Edward Earle, Herbert Heyes, Sam Flint, Gordon DeMain, Spade Cooley,

Marie Windsor, Ruth Robinson, Robert Conway, Pierce Lyden, Billy Bletcher, Ben Taggart, Dickie Dilton. SYN: A radio cowboy (Brown) is signed for a film and, when he falls off his horse and is rescued by a girl (Canova), the publicity surrounding the event makes him appear the fool until a dangerous stunt makes him the hero.

**113. The Cheaters** (7/15/45) B&W 87 mins. (Comedy). DIR/PRO: Joseph Kane. SP: Frances Hyland. Story by Frances Hyland and Albert Ray. CAST: Joseph Schildkraut, Billie Burke, Eugene Pallette, Ona Munson, Raymond Walburn, Ann Gillis, Ruth Terry, Robert Livingston, David Holt, Robert Greig, Norma Varden, Byron Foulger, St. Luke's Choristers. SYN: At Christmas time, a family takes in a down-and-out actor (Schildkraut) and they learn that their rich uncle died and left his entire fortune to an actress (Munson) he never met. They go searching for her for their share of the inheritance. They locate her, take her in as part of the family, and through the intercession of the actor, she agrees to share the inheritance with them. [Re-release title: *The Castaway*.]

**114. The Cherokee Flash** (12/13/45) B&W 55 mins. (Western). DIR: Thomas Carr. A-PRO: Bennett Cohen. SP: Betty Burbridge. CAST: Sunset Carson, Linda Stirling, Tom London, Roy Barcroft, John Merton, Bud Geary, Frank Jaquet, Fred Graham, Joe McGuinn, Pierce Lyden, James Linn, Bud Osborne, Edmund Cobb, Herman Hack, Bill Wolfe, Hank Bell, Chick Hannon, Roy Bucko, Ralph Bucko, George Sowards, George Chesebro, Tommy Coats, Cactus Mack, Duke Green. SYN: An aging gunslinger (Barcroft) goes to his foster son (Carson) for help when members of his old gang try to stop him from retiring. NOTES: Roy Barcroft in his first sympathetic role.

**115. Cheyenne Wildcat** (9/30/44) B&W 56 mins. (Western). DIR: Lesley Selander. A-PRO: Louis Gray. SP: Randall Faye. Based on the comic strip created by Fred Harman. CAST: Bill Elliott, Bobby (Robert) Blake, Alice Fleming, Peggy Stewart, Francis McDonald, Roy Barcroft, Tom London, Tom Chatterton, Kenne Duncan, Bud Geary, Jack Kirk, Sam Burton, Bud Osborne, Robert Wilke, Rex Lease, Tom Steele, Charles Morton, Forrest Taylor, Franklyn Farnum, Wee Willie Keeler, Universal Jack, Tom Smith, Rudy Bowman, Horace B. Carpenter, Frank Ellis, Steve Clark, Bob Burns, Jack O'Shea, Dickie Dillon, "Thunder." SYN: Red Ryder (Elliott) helps an ex-convict (McDonald) prove that he did not kill his old bank partner (Chatterton). NOTES: The 4th entry in the "Red Ryder" feature series.

**116. The Chicago Kid** (6/29/45) B&W 68 mins. (Crime). DIR: Frank McDonald. A-PRO: Edward J. White. SP: Jack Townley. Additional dialogue by Albert Beich. Story by Karl Brown. CAST: Don ("Red") Barry, Otto Kruger, Tom Powers, Lynne Roberts, Henry Daniell, Chick Chandler, Joseph Crehan, Jay Novello, Paul Harvey, Addison Richards, Kenne Duncan. SYN: A young man (Barry) turns to a life of crime when his father dies in prison and he seeks vengeance on the man (Kruger) whose testimony sent his father to prison.

**The Chinese Orange Mystery** see **The Mandarin Mystery**

**117. Circus Girl** (3/1/37) B&W 64 mins. (Romance). *DIR:* John H. Auer. *PRO:* Nat Levine. *E-PRO:* Herman Schlom. *A-PRO:* Charles A. Browne. *SP:* Adele Buffington, Bradford Ropes. Adapted by Adele Buffington. Based on a *Cosmopolitan Magazine* story by Frank R. Adams. *CAST:* Robert Livingston, June Travis, Donald Cook, Betty Compson, Charlie Murray, Sr., Lucille Osborne, Donald Kerr, Emma Dunn, John Wray, John Holland, Kathryn Sheldon, Lynn Roberts, The Escalante Family. *SYN:* A circus aerialist (Cook), injured in a fall, tries to kill his partners (Livingston, Travis) who he blames for his injuries. *NOTES:* Trapeze sequences are performed by the Escalante family, a famous circus act of the day. Footage of the aerial action and costumes were used in several features and serials.

**118. Circus Girl** (4/20/56) Trucolor 88 mins. (Drama). *DIR:* Veit Harlan. *PRO:* Eberhard Meichsner. *SP:* Peter Francke, Maria Osten-Sacken. A Republic Presentation. *CAST:* Kristina Soederbaum, Willy Birgel, Adrian Hoven, Rene Deltgen, Rolf Von Nauckhoff, Hermann Schomberg, Paul Busch, Jr., Gilbert Houcke, Karl Martell, Herbert Hubner, Sujata Jayawardena, Theodor Loos, Rolf Wanka, Otto Gebuhr. *SYN:* Unknown. *NOTES:* Filmed in Germany.

**Citadel of Crime** (G.B. title) *see* **462. A Man Betrayed**

**119. Citadel of Crime** (7/24/41) B&W 58 mins. (Crime). *DIR/A-PRO:* George Sherman. *SP:* Don Ryan. *CAST:* Robert Armstrong, Frank Albertson, Linda Hayes, Russell Simpson, Skeets Gallagher, William Haade, Jay Novello, Paul Fix, Bob McKenzie, Wade Crosby, William Benedict. *SYN:* A federal agent (Albertson) goes after moonshiners when they recruit a local man (Armstrong) to supply them with illegal liquor. Working title was *Ten Nights in a Barroom.* [British and re-release title: *Outside the Law.*]

**120. City of Shadows** (6/2/55) B&W 70 mins. (Crime). *DIR:* William Witney. *A-PRO:* William J. O'Sullivan. *E-PRO:* Herbert J. Yates. *SP:* Houston Branch. *CAST:* Victor McLaglen, John Baer, Kathleen Crowley, Anthony Caruso, June Vincent, Richard Reeves, Paul Maxey, Frank Ferguson, Richard Travis, Kay E. Kuter, Nicolas Coster, Gloria Pall, Fern Hall. *SYN:* A gangster (McLaglen) is able to circumvent the law through the help of a lawyer (Baer) he took under his wing and sent to law school, but when the lawyer falls in love, he decides to go straight and turns in his boss.

**121. City That Never Sleeps** (6/12/53) B&W 90 mins. (Crime). *DIR/A-PRO:* John H. Auer. *SP:* Steve Fisher. *CAST:* Gig Young, Mala Powers, William Talman, Edward Arnold, Marie Windsor, Paula Raymond, Otto Hulett, Wally Cassell, Ron Hagerthy, James Andelin, Tom Poston, Bunny Kacher, Philip L. Boddy, Thomas Jones, Leonard Diebold, Emmett Vogan, Tom Irish, Walter Woolf King, Helen Gibson, Gil Herman, Clark Howat, Chill Wills, Tom Steele, Dale Van Sickel. *SYN:* Done in semidocumentary style and taking place in one night, a Chicago cop (Young) must choose between leaving the police force, leaving his wife (Raymond) for a stripper (Powers), and taking a bribe from a crooked lawyer (Arnold) to arrest the lawyer's right-hand man (Talman). *NOTES:* Chill Wills is also the narrator of this film. This film was shot on location in Chicago.

**Cloak Without Dagger** (G.B. title) *see* **Operation Conspiracy**

122. **Code of Scotland Yard** (10/24/48) B&W 92 mins. (Drama). *DIR/PRO:* George King. *SP:* Katherine Strueby. Based on a play by Edward Percy. A British-Lion-Pennant Pictures Production. A Republic Presentation. *CAST:* Oscar Homolka, Derek Farr, Muriel Pavlow, Kenneth Griffith, Manning Whiley, Kathleen Harrison, Garry Marsh, Jan Van Loewen, Irene Handl, Johnnie Schofield, Diana Dors. *SYN:* When a bookkeeper (Griffith) discovers that his employer (Homolka) is an escaped convict from Devil's Island, the bookkeeper tries to blackmail him. Fearing that exposure would ruin the career of his concert violinist daughter (Pavlow), he and his partner (Whiley) kill the clerk. When his partner is killed in an auto accident and he comes under suspicion by Scotland Yard, he saves his daughter from scandal by committing suicide. *NOTES:* Released in Britain in 1946. [Original British title: *The Shop at Sly Corner*.]

123. **Code of the Outlaw** (1/30/42) B&W 57 mins. (Western). *DIR:* John English. *A-PRO:* Louis Gray. *SP:* Barry Shipman. Based on characters created by William Colt MacDonald. *CAST:* Bob Steele, Tom Tyler, Rufe Davis, Weldon Heyburn, Melinda Leighton, Donald Curtis, John Ince, Kenne Duncan, Phil Dunham, Max Walzman, Chuck Morrison, Carleton Young, Al Taylor, Robert Frazer, Forrest Taylor, Richard Alexander, Jack Ingram, Wally West, Edward Peil, Sr., Bud Osborne, Hank Worden, Cactus Mack, Jack Kirk. *SYN:* The Three Mesquiteers (Steele, Tyler, and Davis) go after mine payroll bandits. *NOTES:* The 42nd entry in the "Three Mesquiteers" series.

124. **Code of the Prairie** (10/6/44) B&W 56 mins. (Western). *DIR:* Spencer G. Bennet. *A-PRO:* Louis Gray. *SP:* Albert DeMond, Anthony Coldeway. Story by Albert DeMond. *CAST:* Sunset Carson, Smiley Burnette, Peggy Stewart, Weldon Heyburn, Tom Chatterton, Roy Barcroft, Bud Geary, Tom London, Jack Kirk, Tom Steele, Robert Wilke, Frank Ellis, Rex Lease, Henry Wills, Ken Terrell, Charles King, Nolan Leary, Hank Bell, Karl Hackett, Jack O'Shea, Horace B. Carpenter. *SYN:* A cowboy (Carson) and sidekick (Burnette) rid a town of outlaws.

125. **Code of the Silver Sage** (3/25/50) B&W 60 mins. (Western). *DIR:* Fred C. Brannon. *A-PRO:* Gordon Kay. *SP:* Arthur E. Orloff. *CAST:* Allan ("Rocky") Lane, Eddy Waller, Roy Barcroft, Kay Christopher, Lane Bradford, William Ruhl, Richard Emory, Kenne Duncan, Rex Lease, Hank Patterson, John K. Butler, Forrest Taylor, "Black Jack." *SYN:* An undercover agent (Lane) is sent West to stop a madman (Barcroft) from becoming dictator of Arizona.

126. **Colorado** (9/15/40) B&W 57 mins. (Western). *DIR/PRO:* Joseph Kane. *SP:* Louis Stevens, Harrison Jacobs. *CAST:* Roy Rogers, George "Gabby" Hayes, Pauline Moore, Milburn Stone, Maude Eburne, Hal Taliaferro, Vester Pegg, Fred Burns, Lloyd Ingraham, Jay Novello, Chuck Baldra, Tex Palmer, Joseph Crehan, Edward

Cassidy, George Rosener, Robert Fiske, Arthur Loft, "Trigger." *SYN:* During the Civil War, a Union lieutenant (Rogers) is sent to Denver to look into Indian problems. *NOTES:* Re-edited for TV at 54 mins.

**127. The Colorado Kid** (12/6/37) B&W 56 mins. (Western). *DIR:* Sam Newfield. *PRO:* A. W. Hackel. *SP:* Charles Francis Royal. Story by Harry Olmstead. *CAST:* Bob Steele, Marion Weldon, Karl Hackett, Ernie Adams, Ted Adams, Frank LaRue, Horace Murphy, Kenne Duncan, Frank Ball, John Merton, Horace B. Carpenter, Wally West, Budd Buster. *SYN:* A cowboy (Steele), unjustly accused of murder, escapes from jail to find the real killer.

**128. Colorado Pioneers** (11/14/45) B&W 57 mins. (Western). *DIR:* R. G. Springsteen. *A-PRO:* Sidney Picker. *SP:* Earle Snell. Story by Peter Whitehead. Based on the comic strip created by Fred Harman. *CAST:* Bill Elliott, Bobby (Robert) Blake, Alice Fleming, Roy Barcroft, Bud Geary, Billy Cummings, Freddie Chapman, Frank Jaquet, Tom London, Monte Hale, Buckwheat Thomas, George Chesebro, Emmett Vogan, Tom Chatterton, Edward Cassidy, Fred Graham, Cliff Parkinson, Horace B. Carpenter, Bill Wolfe, Jess Cavan, Howard Mitchell, Jack Rockwell, George Morrell, Jack Kirk, Gary Armstrong, Robert Anderson, Roger Williams, Richard Lydon, Robert Goldschmidt, Romey Foley, "Thunder." *SYN:* While in Chicago selling cattle, Red Ryder (Elliott) has a bunch of tough kids put in his custody and sends them back to his ranch for straightening out. When he gets back to the ranch with the kids, he has to find out who has been trying to force the Duchess (Fleming) to sell her land. *NOTES:* The 11th entry in the "Red Ryder" feature series.

**129. Colorado Sundown** (2/8/52) B&W 67 mins. (Western). *DIR:* William Witney. *A-PRO:* Edward J. White. *SP:* Eric Taylor, William Lively. Story by Eric Taylor. *CAST:* Rex Allen, Mary Ellen Kay, Slim Pickens, June Vincent, Fred Graham, John Daheim (John Day), Louise Beavers, Chester Clute, Clarence Straight, Bud Osborne, Harry Harvey, Hal Price, Rex Lease, Tex Terry, The Republic Rhythm Riders, "Koko." *SYN:* A cowboy (Allen) travels to the Colorado Territory where a friend (Pickens) is supposed to inherit a large timber ranch, but when he arrives, he finds that the ownership of the land is being contested by a brother (Graham) and sister (Vincent), and another heir (Kay).

**130. Colorado Sunset** (7/31/39) B&W 61 mins. (Western). *DIR:* George Sherman. *A-PRO:* William Berke. *SP:* Betty Burbridge, Stanley Roberts. Story by Luci Ward, Jack Natteford. *CAST:* Gene Autry, Smiley Burnette, June Storey, Barbara Pepper, Larry "Buster" Crabbe, Robert Barrat, Patsy Montana, Purnell Pratt, William Farnum, Kermit Maynard, Jack Ingram, Elmo Lincoln, Frankie Marvin, Ethan Laidlaw, Fred Burns, Jack Kirk, Budd Buster, Edward Cassidy, Slim Whitaker, Murdock MacQuarrie, Ralph Peters, Herman Hack, Chuck Baldra, Francis Ford, The CBS-KMBC Texas Rangers, "Champion." *SYN:* Gene and his friends end up with a dairy farm instead of a cattle ranch and find themselves in the midst of a war between the local dairy ranchers and a "protective" association. *NOTES:* Re-edited for TV at 54 mins.

**131. Come Next Spring** (3/9/56) Trucolor 98 mins. (Drama). *DIR:* R. G. Springsteen. *PRO:* Herbert J. Yates. *SP:* Montgomery Pittman. *CAST:* Ann Sheridan, Steve Cochran, Walter Brennan, Sherry Jackson, Richard Eyer, Edgar Buchanan, Sonny Tufts, Harry Shannon, Rad Fulton, Mae Clarke, Roscoe Ates, Wade Ruby, James Best. *SYN:* A drifter (Cochran) returns to his wife (Sheridan) and daughter (Jackson) and their Arkansas farm and tries for a second chance with his family.

**132. Come On, Cowboys!** (5/24/37) B&W 59 mins. (Western). *DIR:* Joseph Kane. *A-PRO:* Sol C. Siegel. *SP:* Betty Burbridge. *CAST:* Robert Livingston, Ray ("Crash") Corrigan, Max Terhune, Maxine Doyle, Willie Fung, Edward Peil, Sr., Horace Murphy, Ann Bennett, Edward Cassidy, Roger Williams, Fern Emmett, Yakima Canutt, George Burton, Merrill McCormick, Loren Riebe, Victor Allen, Al Taylor, George Plues, Milburn Morante, Carleton Young, George Morrell, Ernie Adams, Jim Corey, Jack Kirk. *SYN:* The Three Mesquiteers (Livingston, Corrigan, Terhune) help unmask a counterfeit ring that uses a carnival for a front. *NOTES:* The 7th entry in the "Three Mesquiteers" series. Re-edited for TV at 54 mins.

**133. Come On, Leathernecks** (8/8/38) B&W 65 mins. (Drama). *DIR:* James Cruze. *A-PRO:* Herman Schlom. *SP:* Sidney Salkow, Dorrell McGowan, Stuart McGowan. Story by Sidney Salkow. *CAST:* Richard Cromwell, Marsha Hunt, Leon Ames, Edward Brophy, Bruce MacFarlane, Robert Warwick, Howard Hickman, James Bush, Walter Miller, Anthony Warde, Ralph Dunn, Harry Strang, Alan Ladd. *SYN:* After graduating from Annapolis, a man (Cromwell) must choose between joining the Marines or a professional football team. *NOTES:* Alan Ladd has an uncredited bit role as a club waiter. Director James Cruze's final film.

**134. Come On, Rangers** (11/25/38) B&W 57 mins. (Western). *DIR:* Joseph Kane. *A-PRO:* Charles E. Ford. *SP:* Gerald Geraghty, Jack Natteford. *CAST:* Roy Rogers, Mary Hart, Raymond Hatton, J. Farrell MacDonald, Purnell Pratt, Harry Woods, Bruce MacFarlane, Lane Chandler, Lee Powell, Chester Gunnels, Frank McCarroll, Chick Hannon, Jack Kirk, Al Taylor, Horace B. Carpenter, Robert Wilke, Al Ferguson, Allan Cavan, Ben Corbett, Burr Caruth. *SYN:* A group of Texas Rangers are brought back into action by one of their fellow rangers (Rogers) to battle corrupt politicians. *NOTES:* Re-edited for TV at 54 mins.

**135. Comin' Round the Mountain** (3/31/36) B&W 55 mins. (Western). *DIR:* Mack V. Wright. *PRO:* Nat Levine. *SP:* Oliver Drake, Dorrell McGowan. Story by Oliver Drake. *CAST:* Gene Autry, Ann Rutherford, Smiley Burnette, LeRoy Mason, Raymond Brown, Ken Cooper, Tracy Layne, Bob McKenzie, John Ince, Frank Lackteen, Laurita Puente, Jim Corey, Al Taylor, Steve Clark, Frank Ellis, Hank Bell, Dick Botiller, Frankie Marvin, "Champion." *SYN:* A Pony Express rider (Gene) helps a girl (Rutherford) to save her ranch by helping her win a contract to sell horses to the Pony Express.

**Concerto** (G.B. title) *see* **I've Always Loved You**

**136. The Congress Dances** (1/11/57) Trucolor/Cinemascope 90 mins. (Musical). *DIR:* Unknown. *PRO:* Unknown. *SP:* Kurt Nachmann. Based on the 1932 UFA film screenplay of the same name by Norbert Falk, Robert Liebmann. A Cosmos-Neusser-West German Film. A Republic Presentation. *CAST:* Johanna Matz, Rudolf Prack, Hannelore Bollmann, Marte Harell, Jester Naefe, Hans Moser, Josef Meinrad, Gunther Philipp, Karl Schonbock, Oskar Sima, Paul Westermeier. *SYN:* Lackluster remake of the 1932 musical. Prack plays the double role of a Czar (Prack) and his unhappy double who romances and negotiates in 1814 during the Congress of Vienna. *NOTES:* Rudolf Prack plays a dual role in this film. A remake of the 1932 German film of the same title.

**137. Conquest of Cheyenne** (7/29/46) B&W 55 mins. (Western). *DIR:* R. G. Springsteen. *A-PRO:* Sidney Picker. *SP:* Earle Snell. Story by Bert Horswell, Joseph F. Poland. Based on the comic strip created by Fred Harman. *CAST:* Bill Elliott, Bobby (Robert) Blake, Alice Fleming, Peggy Stewart, Jay Kirby, Emmett Lynn, Milton Kibbee, Tom London, Kenne Duncan, George Sherwood, Frank McCarroll, Jack Kirk, Tom Chatterton, Ted Mapes, Jack Rockwell, "Thunder." *SYN:* When oil is discovered on Cheyenne Jackson's (Stewart) ranch, Red Ryder (Elliott) sets out to stop the town banker (Kibbee) from buying up the local ranches in the area. *NOTES:* The 16th entry in the "Red Ryder" feature series and Elliott's and Fleming's last "Red Ryder" film. Blake would continue on in seven more with Allan ("Rocky") Lane.

**138. Corpus Christi Bandits** (4/20/45) B&W 55 mins. (Western). *DIR:* Wallace A. Grissell. *A-PRO:* Stephen Auer. *SP:* Norman S. Hall. *CAST:* Allan ("Rocky") Lane, Helen Talbot, Twinkle Watts, Tom London, Francis McDonald, Jack Kirk, Roy Barcroft, Kenne Duncan, Robert Wilke, Ruth Lee, Edward Cassidy, Emmett Vogan, Dickie Dillon, Freddie Chapman, Shelby Bacon, Neal Hart, Horace B. Carpenter, Hal Price, Frank Ellis, Frank McCarroll, Henry Wills, Cliff Parkinson, Carl Faulkner, Eva Novak, George Bell. *SYN:* A World War II pilot (Lane) learns how his grandfather (Lane) became a bandit and then redeemed himself. *NOTES:* Allan Lane plays a dual role in this film.

**139. Country Fair** (5/5/41) B&W 74 mins. (Comedy). *DIR:* Frank McDonald. *A-PRO:* Armand Schaefer. *SP:* Dorrell McGowan, Stuart McGowan. Story by Jack Townley. *CAST:* Eddie Foy, Jr., June Clyde, Guinn "Big Boy" Williams, William Demarest, Harold Huber, Ferris Taylor, Maurice Cass, Harold Peary, Whitey Ford, Lulu Belle and Scotty (Myrtle and Scott Wiseman), The Vass Family, The Simp-Phonies. *SYN:* A fast-talking campaign manager (Foy) tries to talk a girl (Clyde) into marrying him should his candidate for governor (Demarest) win. She immediately sets about helping the opponent (Peary).

**140. Country Gentlemen** (10/24/36) B&W 66 mins. (Comedy). *DIR:* Ralph Staub. *PRO:* Nat Levine. *SP:* Joseph Hoffman, Gertrude Orr. Story by Milton Raison, Jack Harvey, Jo Graham. Additional dialogue by John P. Medbury. *CAST:* Ole Olsen, Chic Johnson, Joyce Compton, Lila Lee, Pierre Watkin, Donald Kirke, Ray ("Crash") Corrigan, Sammy McKim, Wade Boteler, Ivan Miller, Olin Howland, Frank Sheridan, Harry Harvey, Joe Cunningham, "Prince," the Great Dane. *SYN:* Two con men (Olsen, Johnson) have their scheme backfire when they sell phony oil well shares at a veterans home and the well comes in.

**141. The Covered Trailer** (11/10/39) B&W 63 mins. (Comedy). *DIR/A-PRO:* Gus Meins. *SP:* Jack Townley. Story by Jack Townley, M. Coates Webster. *CAST:* James Gleason, Lucille Gleason, Russell Gleason, Harry Davenport, Mary Beth Hughes, Tommy Ryan, Maurice Murphy, Maude Eburne, Spencer Charters, Tom Kennedy, Hobart Cavanaugh, Pierre Watkin, Frank Dae, Richard Tucker, Willie Best, Walter Fenner. *SYN:* The Higgins family (The Gleasons, Davenport, Hughes, Ryan) give up their planned cruise when an expected check fails to arrive, and, rather than let their neighbors know, the family members go on a fishing trip instead. When the cruise ship they were suppose to be on sinks, the neighbors think they have drowned. *NOTES:* The 4th entry in the "Higgins Family" series.

**142. Covered Wagon Days** (4/22/40) B&W 56 mins. (Western). *DIR/A-PRO:* George Sherman. *A-PRO:* Harry Grey. *SP:* Earle Snell. Based on characters created by William Colt MacDonald. *CAST:* Robert Livingston, Raymond Hatton, Duncan Renaldo, Kay Griffith, George Douglas, Ruth Robinson, Paul Marion, John Merton, Tom Chatterton, Guy D'Ennery, Tom London,, Reed Howes, Richard Alexander, Art Mix, Jack Montgomery, Edward Hearn, Frank McCarroll, Jack Kirk, Al Taylor, Lee Shumway, Barry Hays, Elias Gomboa, Herman Hack, Ken Terrell, Tex Palmer. *SYN:* The Three Mesquiteers (Livingston, Hatton, Renaldo) get mixed up with murder and silver smugglers. *NOTES:* The 29th entry in the "Three Mesquiteers" series. Re-edited for TV at 54 mins.

**143. Covered Wagon Raid** (6/30/50) B&W 60 mins. (Western). *DIR:* R. G. Springsteen. *A-PRO:* Gordon Kay. *SP:* M. Coates Webster. *CAST:* Allan ("Rocky") Lane, Eddy Waller, Alex Gerry, Lyn Thomas, Byron Barr, Dick Curtis, Pierce Lyden, Sherry Jackson, Rex Lease, Lester Dorr, Lee Roberts, Edmund Cobb, Wee Willie Keeler, Marshall Reed. *SYN:* An insurance investigator (Lane) is sent West to find out why pioneers trying to settle a rich valley are continuously being robbed and murdered.

**144. Cowboy and the Senorita** (5/13/44) B&W 78 mins. (Western). *DIR:* Joseph Kane. *A-PRO:* Harry Grey. *SP:* Gordan Kahn. Story by Bradford Ropes. *CAST:* Roy Rogers, Mary Lee, Dale Evans, John Hubbard, Guinn "Big Boy" Williams, Fuzzy Knight, Dorothy Christy, Lucien Littlefield, Hal Taliaferro, Jack Kirk, Jack O'Shea, Jane Beebe, Ben Rochelle, Rex Lease, Lynton Brent, Julian Rivero, Robert Wilke, Wally West, Spanky McFarland, Kirk Alyn, Bob Nolan and the Sons of the Pioneers, Cappella and Patricia, Tito and Corinne Valdes, "Trigger." *SYN:* Roy comes to the aid of a young girl (Lee) who has been left a gold mine that will be turned over to her on her 16th birthday, and routs the crook (Hubbard) who is trying to steal the mining rights from her. *NOTES:* The first teaming of Roy Rogers and Dale Evans, who would go on to make 29 films together for Republic, finally marrying in 1947. Re-edited for TV at 54 mins.

**145. Cowboy Serenade** (1/22/42) B&W 66 mins. (Western). *DIR:* William Morgan. *A-PRO:* Harry Grey. *SP:* Olive Cooper. *CAST:* Gene Autry, Smiley Burnette, Fay McKenzie, Cecil Cunningham, Rand Brooks, Addison Richards, Tristram Coffin, Lloyd "Slim" Andrews, Melinda Leighton, John Berkes, Forrest Taylor, Hank Worden, Si Jenks, Ethan Laidlaw, Hal Price, Otto Ham, Lorin Raker, Bud Wolfe, Forbes Murray, Bud Geary, Frankie Marvin, Tom London, Ken Terrell, Ralph Kirby, Ken Cooper, Rick Anderson, "Champion." *SYN:* Gene goes after professional gamblers when they get control of a cattle herd. *NOTES:* Re-edited for TV at 54 mins. [British title: *Serenade of the West.*]

**146. Cowboys from Texas** (11/29/39) B&W 57 mins. (Western). *DIR:* George Sherman. *A-PRO:* Harry Grey. *SP:* Oliver Drake. Based on characters created by William Colt MacDonald. *CAST:* Robert Livingston, Raymond Hatton, Duncan Renaldo, Carole Landis, Charles Middleton, Ivan Miller, Betty Compson, Ethan Laidlaw, Yakima Canutt, Walter Wills, Edward Cassidy, Forbes Murray, Bud Osborne, Charles King, Horace Murphy, Harry Strang, Jack Kirk, David Sharpe, Lew Meehan, Jack O'Shea. *SYN:* The Three Mesquiteers (Livingston, Hatton, Renaldo) are out to stop a feud between cattlemen and homesteaders. *NOTES:* The 26th entry in the "Three Mesquiteers" series.

**147. Crazylegs** (2/15/54) B&W 87 mins. (Biography). *DIR:* Francis D. Lyon. *PRO/SP:* Hall Bartlett. *CAST:* Elroy "Crazylegs" Hirsch, Lloyd Nolan, Joan Vohs, James Millican, Bob Waterfield, Bob Kelley, James Brown, John Brown, Norman Field, Louise Lorimer, Joseph Crehan, Joel Marston, Bill Brundige, Win Hirsch, Melvyn Arnold. *SYN:* The film biography of pro football Hall of Famer and one-time University of Wisconsin athletic director, Elroy "Crazylegs" Hirsch, who plays himself. *NOTES:* Academy Award Nominee for Best Film Editing. Date given is general release date. Narrated by Lloyd Nolan. [Alternate title: *Crazylegs, All-American.*]

**Crazylegs, All-American** see **Crazylegs**

**148. The Crime of Dr. Crespi** (9/24/35) B&W 64 mins. (Horror). *DIR/PRO:* John H. Auer. *SP:* Lewis Graham, Edwin Olmstead. Story by John H. Auer. Adapted from *The Premature Burial* by Edgar Allan Poe. A Liberty/Republic Picture. *CAST:* Erich Von Stroheim, Dwight Frye, Paul Guilfoyle, Harriet Russell, John Bohn, Geraldine Kay, Jeanne Kelly (Jean Brooks), Patsy Berlin, Joe Verdi, Dean Raymond. *SYN:* A doctor (Von Stroheim) injects his rival (Bohn) with a drug that induces suspended animation so he can bury him and then watch his reaction upon finding himself in a coffin.

**149. Crime of the Century** (2/28/46) B&W 57 mins. (Crime). *DIR:* Philip Ford. *A-PRO:* Walter H. Goetz. *SP:* O'Leta Rhinehart, William Hagens, Gertrude Walker. Story by O'Leta Rhinehart, William Hagens. *CAST:* Stephanie Bachelor, Michael Browne, Martin Kosleck, Betty Shaw, Paul Stanton, Mary Currier, Ray Walker, Tom London. *SYN:* A reporter (Browne) gets involved in murder and kidnapping when he sets out to find a missing industrialist.

**150. The Crooked Circle** (11/11/57) B&W/Naturama 72 mins. (Crime-

Sports). *DIR:* Joseph Kane. *A-PRO:* Rudy Ralston. *SP:* Jack Townley. *CAST:* John Smith, Fay Spain, Steve Brodie, Don Kelly, Robert Armstrong, John Doucette, Philip Van Zandt, Richard Karlan, Bob Swan, Don Haggerty, Peter Mamakos. *SYN:* The younger brother (Smith) of an ex-fighter, (Kelly) decides to leave home and enter the ring in New York. He falls in with gangsters who force him to throw fights. When he decides to fight honestly, the gangsters try to kill him, but a sportswriter, (Brodie) learns what has happened and leads the police to save him.

**151. The Crooked Road** (5/10/40) B&W 69 mins. (Drama). *DIR:* Phil Rosen. *A-PRO:* Robert North. *SP:* Garnett Weston, Joseph Krumgold. Story by Edward E. Paramore, Jr., Richard Blake. *CAST:* Edmund Lowe, Irene Hervey, Henry Wilcoxon, Paul Fix, Arthur Loft, Claire Carleton, Charles Lane. *SYN:* An escaped prisoner (Lowe), because of his past, gets blackmailed and framed for murder. Eventually he is found innocent but, when it is learned that he is an escaped prisoner, he is returned to prison.

**152. Cross Channel** (9/29/55) B&W 61 mins. (Crime). *DIR:* R. G. Springsteen. *PRO:* William N. Boyle. *SP:* Rex Rienits. *CAST:* Wayne Morris, Yvonne Furneaux, Arnold Marle, Patrick Allen, Carl Jaffe, Peter Sinclair, Charles Laurence, Michael Golden, June Ashley, Jack Lambert, Jacques Cey. *SYN:* A charter boat captain (Morris) is framed for murder by a gang of jewel smugglers and must prove himself innocent of the charges against him. *NOTES:* This British actioner is one of four directed in England in 1955 by R. G. "Bud" Springsteen. Released in Britain in July, 1955.

**Cruising Casanovas** (G.B. title) *see* **Gobs and Gals**

**153. Cuban Fireball** (3/5/51) B&W 78 mins. (Musical). *DIR:* William Beaudine. *A-PRO:* Sidney Picker. *SP:* Charles E. Roberts, Jack Townley. Story by Charles E. Roberts. *CAST:* Estelita Rodriguez, Warren Douglas, Mimi Aguglia, Leon Belasco, Donald MacBride, Rosa Turich, John Litel, Tim Ryan, Russ Vincent, Edward Gargan, Victoria Horne, Jack Kruschen, Pedro de Cordoba, Olan Soule, Tony Barr, Luther Crockett. *SYN:* A young woman (Rodriguez), on her way to Los Angeles to collect an inheritance, disguises herself as an old woman to throw off the men who are following her for her inheritance.

**154. The Cyclone Kid** (5/31/42) B&W 55 mins. (Western). *DIR/A-PRO:* George Sherman. *SP:* Richard Murphy. *CAST:* Don ("Red") Barry, John James, Lynn Merrick, Alex Callam, Joel Friedkin, Lloyd "Slim" Andrews, Rex Lease, Joe McGuinn, Monte Montague, Frank LaRue, Edmund Cobb, Budd Buster, Hal Price, Jack Rockwell, Al Taylor, Jack O'Shea, Curley Dresden, Bob Woodward, Joe Cody, Rose Plummer. *SYN:* An outlaw (Barry) is convinced by his brother (James) to reform.

**155. Dakota** (12/25/45) B&W 82 mins. (Western). *DIR/A-PRO:* Joseph Kane. *SP:* Lawrence Hazard. Adapted by Howard Estabrook. Story by Carl Foreman. *CAST:* John Wayne, Vera Hruba Ralston, Walter Brennan, Ward Bond, Mike Mazurki, Ona Munson, Olive Blakeney, Hugo Haas, Nicodemus Stewart, Paul Fix, Grant Withers, Robert Livingston, Olin Howlin, Pierre Watkin, Robert Barrat, Jonathan Hale,

Bobby (Robert) Blake, Paul Hurst, Eddy Waller, Sarah Padden, Jack LaRue, George Cleveland, Selmer Jackson, Claire DuBrey, Roy Barcroft, Yakima Canutt, Larry Thompson, Jack Roper, Fred Graham, Cliff Lyons, Al Murphy, Houseley Stevenson, William Haade, Dick Wessel, Rex Lease, Betty Shaw, Martha Carroll, Adrian Booth, Linda Stirling, Cay Forester, Eugene Borden, Hector V. Sarno, Michael Visaroff, Victor Varconi, Paul E. Burns, Art Miles, Dorothy Christy, Virginia Wave, Peter Cusanelli, Russ Kaplan. *SYN:* A young couple (Wayne, Ralston), eager to settle in the Dakota territory, come across a gang of crooks who are buying up land from unsuspecting farmers because a railroad is to be built on their land.

**156. Dakota Incident** (7/23/56) Trucolor 88 mins. (Western). *DIR:* Lewis R. Foster. *A-PRO:* Michael Baird. *SP:* Frederic Louis Fox. *CAST:* Linda Darnell, Dale Robertson, John Lund, Ward Bond, Regis Toomey, Skip Homeier, Irving Bacon, John Doucette, Whit Bissell, William Fawcett, Malcolm Atterbury, Diane Du Bois, Charles Horvath, Eva Novak, Boyd "Red" Morgan, Fred Coby, Rankin Mansfield. *SYN:* A group of strangers (Robertson, Darnell, Lund, Bond, Toomey, Bissell) are thrown together in a struggle for survival when they are attacked by Indians.

**157. The Dakota Kid** (7/1/51) B&W 60 mins. (Western). *DIR:* Philip Ford. *A-PRO:* Rudy Ralston. *SP:* William Lively. *CAST:* Michael Chapin, Eilene Janssen, James Bell, Danny Morton, Margaret Field, Robert Shayne, Roy Barcroft, Mauritz Hugo, House Peters, Jr., Lee Bennett, Mike Ragan. *SYN:* The Rough Ridin' Kids (Chapin, Janssen) help a sheriff (Bell) when an outlaw (Morton) poses as his nephew. *NOTES:* The 2nd entry in the "Rough-Ridin' Kids" series.

**158. Dancing Feet** (1/20/36) B&W 69 mins. (Musical). *DIR:* Joseph Santley. *A-PRO:* Colbert Clark. *SP:* Jerome Chodorov, Olive Cooper, Wellyn Totman. Story by David Silverstein, Rob Eden. *CAST:* Ben Lyon, Joan Marsh, Eddie Nugent, Isabel Jewell, James Burke, Purnell Pratt, Vince Barnett, Nick Condos, Herbert Rawlinson, Lillian Harmer, Herbert Corthell, James Burtis, Harry C. Bradley, Cy Kendall, Lynton Brent, Wilson Benge, Fern Emmett, Gladys Gale, Grace Hale, J. C. Edwards and Band. *SYN:* A rich society girl (Marsh) becomes a dancer to show her grandfather (Pratt) that she can make a living on her own.

**Danger Rides the Range** (G.B. title) *see* **Three Texas Steers**

**159. Dangerous Holiday** (6/7/37) B&W 58 mins. (Drama). *DIR/SP:* Nicholas Barrows. *A-PRO:* William Berke. Story by Karen DeWolf, Barry Shipman. *CAST:* Ra Hould (Ronald Sinclair), Hedda Hopper, Guinn "Big Boy" Williams, Jack LaRue, Jed Prouty, Lynn Roberts, William Bakewell, Fern Emmett, Virginia Sale, Franklin Pangborn, Grady Sutton, William Newell, Thomas E. Jackson, Olaf Hytten, Jack Mulhall, Harvey Clark, Wade Boteler, Carleton Young, Michael Jeffrey. *SYN:* A violin prodigy (Hould) runs away from home because he cannot be like other kids his age and have fun.

**Dangerous Moonlight** (G.B. title) *see* **Suicide Squadron**

**160. Daniel Boone, Trail Blazer** (10/5/56) Trucolor 76 mins. (Western-Adventure). *DIR:* Albert C. Gannaway, Ismael Rodriguez. *PRO:* Albert C. Gannaway. *SP:* Tom Hubbard, Jack Patrick. An Albert C. Gannaway Production. A Republic Presentation. *CAST:* Bruce Bennett, Lon Chaney, Jr., Faron Young, Kem Dibbs, Damian O'Flynn, Jacqueline Evans, Nancy Rodman, Freddy Fernandez, Carol Kelly, Eduardo Noriega, Fred Kohler, Jr., Gordon Mills, Claude Brook, Lee Morgan, Joe Ainley. *SYN:* Daniel Boone (Bennett) and his band of settlers travel from Yadkin Valley, North Carolina, to Kentucky and convince a Shawnee chief (Chaney, Jr.) that the settlers want nothing but peace. *NOTES:* Filmed in Mexico.

**161. Daredevils of the Clouds** (8/10/48) B&W 60 mins. (Drama). *DIR:* George Blair. *A-PRO:* Stephen Auer. *SP:* Norman S. Hall. Story by Ronald Davidson. *CAST:* Robert Livingston, Mae Clarke, James Cardwell, Grant Withers, Edward Gargan, Ray Teal, Jimmie Dodd, Pierre Watkin, Jayne Hazard, Robert Wilke, Frank Melton, Russell Arms, Hugh Prosser, Charles Sullivan. *SYN:* The owner (Livingston) of a small airline company fights to keep his company from being taken over by a larger airline.

**162. Dark Command** (4/15/40) B&W 94 mins. (Western). *DIR:* Raoul Walsh. *A-PRO:* Sol C. Siegel. *SP:* Grover Jones, Lionel Houser, F. Hugh Herbert. Adapted by Jan Fortune. Based on *Dark Command: A Kansas Iliad* by W. R. Burnett. *CAST:* John Wayne, Claire Trevor, Walter Pidgeon, Roy Rogers, George "Gabby" Hayes, Porter Hall, Marjorie Main, Raymond Walburn, Joe Sawyer, Helen MacKellar, J. Farrell MacDonald, Trevor Bardette, Alan Bridge, Ferris Taylor, Ernie Adams, Harry Cording, Edward Hearn, Edmund Cobb, Glenn Strange, Mildred Gover, Tom London, Richard Alexander, Yakima Canutt, Hal Taliaferro, Jack Rockwell, Harry Woods, Dick Rich, John Merton, Frank Hagney, John Dilson, Clinton Rosemond, Budd Buster, Howard Hickman, Al Taylor, Jack Low, Edward Earle, Joe McGuinn, Harry Strang, Tex Cooper, Jack Montgomery, Cliff Lyons, Hank Bell, Al Haskell, Tom Smith, Bob Woodward. *SYN:* In 1859 Kansas, because of the slave state/free state issue, a school teacher (Pidgeon) becomes a guerrilla leader, and it is up to the sheriff (Wayne) to track him down after he burns down the town. *NOTES:* This film, with a budget of three-quarters of a million dollars, was the most expensive and successful film of Republic's early years, and was based on the exploits of Quantrill's Raiders. Released in a "Computer-colorized" version in the 1980s by the new Republic studios. Academy Award Nominee—Best Art Direction, Best Score.

**163. Darkest Africa** (5/21/36) B&W 73 mins. (Jungle-Adventure). *SYN:* Feature version of the 15-chapter serial. *See* **957. Darkest Africa**.

**164. Daughter of the Jungle** (2/8/49) B&W 69 mins. (Adventure). *DIR:* George Blair. *A-PRO:* Franklin Adreon. *SP:* William Lively. Story by Sol Shor. *CAST:* Lois Hall, James Cardwell, William Wright, Sheldon Leonard, Jim Nolan, Frank Lackteen, George Carleton, Francis McDonald, Jim Bannon, Charles Soldani, Alex Montoya, Al Kikume, Leo C. Richmond, George Piltz. *SYN:* A jungle girl (Hall) leads a group of survivors from a plane crash back to civilization. NOTES: 1949 was the year for jungle pictures, and Republic tried to cash in on the craze with this film.

**165. A Day to Remember** (3/29/55) B&W 92 mins. (Drama). DIR: Ralph Thomas. PRO: Betty E. Box. SP: Robin Estridge. Based on *The Hand and the Flower* by Jerrard Tickell. A Group Films Production. A Republic Presentation. CAST: Stanley Holloway, Donald Sinden, Joan Rice, Odile Versois, James Hayter, Harry Fowler, Edward Chapman, Peter Jones, Bill Owen, Meredith Edwards, George Couloris, Vernon Gray, Thora Hird, Theodore Bikel, Brenda DeBanzie, Lilly Kahn, Arthur Hill, Patricia Raine, Marianne Stone, Harold Lang, Germaine Delbat, Robert Le Beal, Georgette Anys, Marcel Poncin, Jacques Cey, Jacqueline Robert, Richard Molinas. SYN: The story of the road trip of the British "Hand and Flowers" dart team to an area of France where many of the players had served in the war. NOTES: Released in Britain in 1953.

**166. Days of Buffalo Bill** (2/8/46) B&W 56 mins. (Western). DIR: Thomas Carr. A-PRO: Bennett Cohen. SP: William Lively, Doris Schroeder. CAST: Sunset Carson, Peggy Stewart, Tom London, James Craven, Rex Lease, Edmund Cobb, Eddie Parker, Michael Sloane, Jay Kirby, George Chesebro, Edward Cassidy, Frank O'Connor, Jess Cavan, Pascale Perry, Kit Guard, Tex Cooper, Tommy Coats, Roy Bucko. SYN: A cowboy (Carson) is framed for murder and sets out to prove his innocence. NOTES: Nowhere in this film is Buffalo Bill Cody seen or mentioned.

**167. Days of Jesse James** (12/20/39) B&W 63 mins. (Western). DIR/PRO: Joseph Kane. SP: Earle Snell. Story by Jack Natteford. CAST: Roy Rogers, George "Gabby" Hayes, Don ("Red") Barry, Pauline Moore, Harry Woods, Arthur Loft, Wade Boteler, Ethel Wales, Scotty Beckett, Harry Worth, Glenn Strange, Olin Howland, Monte Blue, Jack Rockwell, Fred Burns, Bud Osborne, Jack Ingram, Carl Sepulveda, Forrest Dillon, Hansel Warner, Lynton Brent, Pascale Perry, Eddie Acuff, Horace B. Carpenter, "Trigger." SYN: A railroad detective (Rogers) sets out to prove that Jesse James (Barry) and his gang did not rob the Northfield bank, but were framed by a sheriff (Woods) and crooked banker (Loft). NOTES: Re-edited for TV at 54 mins. Don "Red" Barry also played Jesse James again in the 1954 United Artists film, *Jesse James' Women*, his only directed film.

**168. Days of Old Cheyenne** (5/15/43) B&W 56 mins. (Western). DIR: Elmer Clifton. A-PRO: Edward J. White. SP: Norman S. Hall. CAST: Don ("Red") Barry, Lynn Merrick, William Haade, Emmett Lynn, Herbert Rawlinson, Charles Miller, William Ruhl, Harry McKim, Robert Kortman, Nolan Leary, Kenne Duncan, Eddie Parker, Bob Reeves, Art Dillard. SYN: A drifter (Barry) is used as a pawn by a crooked politician (Haade) until he turns the tables on him.

**169. Dead Man's Gulch** (2/12/43) B&W 56 mins. (Western). DIR: John English. A-PRO: Edward J. White. SP: Norman S. Hall, Bob Williams. Story by Norman S. Hall. CAST: Don ("Red") Barry, Lynn Merrick, Clancy Cooper, Emmett Lynn, Bud McTaggart, Jack Rockwell, John Vosper, Pierce Lyden, Lee Shumway, Rex Lease, Al Taylor,

Robert Frazer, Robert Fiske, Charles Sullivan, Frank Brownlee. *SYN:* Interesting Barry oater directed at a breakneck pace by serial veteran English. A former Pony Express rider (Barry) finds out he is being used by a bunch of crooks to maintain a freight line monopoly.

**170. Death Valley Gunfighter** (3/29/49) B&W 60 mins. (Western). *DIR:* R. G. Springsteen. *A-PRO:* Gordon Kay. *SP:* Bob Williams. *CAST:* Allan ("Rocky") Lane, Eddy Waller, Jim Nolan, Gail Davis, William (Bill) Henry, Harry Harvey, Mauritz Hugo, George Chesebro, Forrest Taylor, George Lloyd, Lane Bradford. *SYN:* A peace officer (Lane) helps the owner (Waller) of a mercury mine defeat the outlaws who are after it.

**171. Death Valley Manhunt** (11/24/43) B&W 55 mins. (Western). *DIR:* John English. *A-PRO:* Edward J. White. *SP:* Norman S. Hall, Anthony Coldeway. Story by Fred Myton, Edward J. White. *CAST:* Bill Elliott, George "Gabby" Hayes, Anne Jeffreys, Weldon Heyburn, Herbert Heyes, Davison Clark, Pierce Lyden, Charlie Murray, Jr., Jack Kirk, Eddie Phillips, Bud Geary, Al Taylor, Marshall Reed, Edward Keane, Curley Dresden, "Sonny." *SYN:* Bill and "Gabby" set out to stop the manager (Heyburn) of an oil company from cheating independent oil drillers out of their wells.

**172. Death Valley Outlaws** (9/26/41) B&W 56 mins. (Western). *DIR/A-PRO:* George Sherman. *SP:* Don Ryan, Jack Lait, Jr. Story by Don Ryan. *CAST:* Don ("Red") Barry, Lynn Merrick, Milburn Stone, Bob McKenzie, Karl Hackett, Rex Lease, Jack Kirk, Michael Owen, Fred "Snowflake" Toones, Robert Kortman, Curley Dresden, John Cason, Griff Barnette, Lee Shumway, Wally West, Harry Strang, Reed Howes, George J. Lewis, Tex Palmer, Sam Lufkin. *SYN:* A cowboy (Barry) goes after the outlaws that killed his best friend and learns that his long lost brother (Owen) is a member of the gang.

**173. Deerslayer** (11/22/43) B&W 67 mins. (Western-Adventure). *DIR:* Lew Landers. *PRO/SP:* P. S. Harrison, E. B. Derr. Based on the novel by James Fenimore Cooper. Adapted by John W. Krafft. A Cardinal Picture Production. A Republic Presentation. *CAST:* Bruce Kellogg, Jean Parker, Larry Parks, Warren Ashe, Wanda McKay, Yvonne DeCarlo, Addison Richards, Johnny Michaels, Philip Van Zandt, Trevor Bardette, Robert Warwick, Chief Many Treaties, Clancy Cooper, Princess Whynemah, William Edmunds. *SYN:* Natty Bumpo (Kellogg), also known as Deerslayer, aids a settler (Parker) and her companions who are caught in the midst of an Indian war when an Indian princess (DeCarlo) is kidnapped by the Hurons. *NOTES:* This film was a financial disaster at the box office, and because of this, Republic no longer accepted action films from other sources until the 1950s. Remade in 1957 by 20th Century–Fox, and in 1978 as a TV movie.

**174. The Denver Kid** (10/1/48) B&W 60 mins. (Western). *DIR:* Philip Ford. *A-PRO:* Gordon Kay. *SP:* Bob Williams. *CAST:* Allan ("Rocky") Lane, Eddy Waller, William (Bill) Henry, Douglas Fowley, Rory Mallinson, George Lloyd, George Meeker, Emmett Vogan, Hank Patterson, Bruce Edwards, Peggy Wynne,

Tom Steele, Carole Gallagher, Marshall Reed, "Black Jack." SYN: A border patrolman (Lane) goes after a vicious killer.

**175. Desert Bandit** (5/24/41) B&W 56 mins. (Western). DIR/A-PRO: George Sherman. SP: Bennett Cohen, Eliot Gibbons. Story by Bennett Cohen. CAST: Don ("Red") Barry, Lynn Merrick, William Haade, James Gillette, Dick Wessel, Tom Chatterton, Tom Ewell, Robert Strange, Charles Moore, Ernie Stanton, Curley Dresden, Jim Corey, Merrill McCormick, Charles King, Jack Montgomery, Jack O'Shea, Pascale Perry. SYN: A Texas Ranger (Barry) goes after gun smugglers along the Mexican border.

**176. Desert of Lost Men** (11/19/51) B&W 54 mins. (Western). DIR/A-PRO: Harry Keller. SP: M. Coates Webster. CAST: Allan ("Rocky") Lane, Irving Bacon, Mary Ellen Kay, Roy Barcroft, Ross Elliott, Cliff Clark, Boyd "Red" Morgan, Leo Cleary, Kenneth MacDonald, Steve Pendleton, Herman Hack, "Black Jack." SYN: A federal marshal (Lane) goes under cover and works his way into a gang of thieves so that he can bring them to justice.

**177. Desert Patrol** (6/6/38) B&W 56 mins. (Western). DIR: Sam Newfield. PRO: A. W. Hackel. SP: Fred Myton. CAST: Bob Steele, Rex Lease, Marion Weldon, Ted Adams, Forrest Taylor, Budd Buster, Steve Clark, Jack Ingram, Julian Madison, Tex Palmer. SYN: A Texas Ranger (Steele) tracks down and brings to justice a gang of smugglers who have murdered a fellow ranger.

**178. Desperadoes of Dodge City** (9/15/48) B&W 60 mins. (Western). DIR: Philip Ford. A-PRO: Gordon Kay. SP: Bob Williams. CAST: Allan ("Rocky") Lane, Eddy Waller, Mildred Coles, Roy Barcroft, Tristram Coffin, William Phipps, James Craven, John Hamilton, Edward Cassidy, House Peters, Jr., Dale Van Sickel, Peggy Wynne, Ted Mapes, Robert Wilke, "Black Jack." SYN: A cowboy (Lane) sets out to protect a wagon train of homesteaders from a band of outlaws.

**179. Desperadoes' Outpost** (10/8/52) B&W 54 mins. (Western). DIR: Philip Ford. A-PRO: Rudy Ralston. SP: Arthur E. Orloff, Albert DeMond. CAST: Allan ("Rocky") Lane, Eddy Waller, Roy Barcroft, Myron Healey, Lyle Talbot, Claudia Barrett, Lane Bradford, Lee Roberts, Edward Cassidy, Charles Evans, Zon Murray, Slim Duncan, "Black Jack." SYN: A federal agent (Lane) is sent to investigate the destruction of a stagecoach line.

**180. A Desperate Adventure** (8/6/38) B&W 67 mins. (Comedy-Romance). DIR/A-PRO: John H. Auer. SP: Barry Trivers. Story by Hans Kraly, M. Coates Webster. CAST: Ramon Novarro, Marian Marsh, Margaret Tallichet, Eric Blore, Andrew Tombes, Tom Rutherford, Maurice Cass, Erno Verebes, Michael Kent, Cliff Nazarro, Rolfe Sedan, Gloria Rich, Lois Collier. SYN: A French painter (Novarro) finds romance in Paris with his dream girl (Marsh) while searching for a missing painting. [British title: *It Happened in Paris*.]

**181. Destination Big House** (6/1/50) B&W 60 mins. (Crime). DIR: George Blair. A-PRO: William Lackey. SP: Eric Taylor. Story by Mortimer Braus. CAST: Dorothy Patrick, Robert Rockwell, James Lydon, Robert Armstrong, Larry J. Blake, John Harmon, Claire DuBrey, Richard Benedict, Mickey Knox, Danny Morton, Mack Williams, Olan Soule, Peter Prouse, Norman Field. SYN: A school teacher (Patrick), vacationing in the woods, gets involved with a gangster (Rockwell) and stolen money.

**182. The Devil Pays Off** (11/10/41) B&W 70 mins. (Drama). DIR: John H. Auer. A-PRO: Albert J. Cohen. SP: Lawrence Kimble, Malcolm Stuart Boylan. Story by George Worthing Yates, Julian Zimet. CAST: J. Edward Bromberg, Osa Massen, William Wright, Margaret Tallichet, Abner Biberman, Martin Kosleck, Charles D. Brown, Ivan Miller, Roland Varno. SYN: A cashiered Navy man (Bromberg) redeems his honor by exposing a plot to sell ships to an enemy government. NOTES: Academy Award Nominee— Best Sound.

**Diary of a Bride** (G.B. title) see **I, Jane Doe**

**183. Dick Tracy** (12/27/37) B&W 73 mins. (Adventure). SYN: Feature version of the 15 chapter serial. See **960. Dick Tracy**.

**184. The Divided Heart** (8/11/55) B&W 89 mins. (Drama). DIR: Charles Crichton. PRO: Michael Truman. SP: Jack Whittingham, Richard Hughes. An Ealing Film. A Republic Presentation. CAST: Cornell Borchers, Yvonne Mitchell, Armin Dahlen, Alexander Knox, Geoffrey Keen, Liam Redmond, Eddie Byrne, Theodore Bikel, Ferdy Mayne, Andre Mikhelson, Pamela Stirling, Martin Stephens, Michel Ray, Martin Keller, Krystyna Rumistrzewicz, Mark Guebhard, Gilgi Hauser, Maria Leontovitsch, Marianne Walla, Dorit Welles, Hans Kuhn, John Schlesinger, Philo Hauser, Guy Deghy, Carl Duering, Dora Lavrencic, Richard Molinas, John Welsh, Nicholas Stuart, Hans Elwenspoek, Frederick Schrecker, Alec McCowen, Orest Orloff, Ilona Ference, Randal Kinkead, Arthur Cortez. SYN: A 10-year-old war orphan (Ray) is caught in the midst of a court battle when his real mother (Mitchell), who was found alive after the war, tries to take him from his foster parents (Dahlen, Borchers). NOTES: Based on a true story from *Life* magazine. Released in Britain in 1954.

**185. Doctor at Sea** (2/23/56) Technicolor/VistaVision 93 mins. (Comedy). DIR: Ralph Thomas. PRO: Betty E. Box. SP: Richard Gordon, Nicholas Phipps, Jack Davies. Based on the book by Richard Gordon. A Rank Film Production. A Republic Presentation. CAST: Dirk Bogarde, Brigitte Bardot, Brenda DeBanzie, James Robertson Justice, Maurice Denham, Michael Medwin, Hubert Gregg, James Kenney, Raymond Huntley, Geoffrey Keen, George Coulouris, Noel Purcell, Jill Adams, Joan Sims, Thomas Heathcoate, Toke Townley, Cyril Chamberlain, Paul Carpenter, Frederick Piper, Abe Barker, Michael Shepley, Eugene Deckers, Stuart Saunders, Harold Kasket, Martin Benson, Mary Laura Wood, Joan Hickson, Ekali Sokou, Felix Felton. SYN: Dr. Simon Sparrow (Bogarde) is a medical officer on a ship carrying only two women (De Banzie, Bardot), who pursue the captain (Justice) and Sparrow, which leads to several misadventures. NOTES: Released in Britain in 1955.

**186. Doctor in the House** (2/2/55) Eastmancolor 92 mins. (Comedy). DIR:

Ralph Thomas. *PRO:* Betty E. Box. *SP:* Richard Gordon, Nicholas Phipps, Ronald Wilkinson. Based on the book by Richard Gordon. A Rank Film Production. A Republic Presentation. *CAST:* Dirk Bogarde, Muriel Pavlow, Kenneth More, Donald Sinden, Kay Kendall, James Robertson Justice, Donald Houston, Suzanne Cloutier, Geoffrey Keen, George Coulouris, Jean Taylor-Smith, Harry Locke, Ann Gudrun, Joan Sims, Maureen Pryor, Shirley Eaton, Geoffrey Sumner, Nicholas Phipps, Amy Veness, Richard Wattis, Lisa Gastoni, Shirley Burniston, Joan Hickson, George Benson, Martin Boddey, Cyril Chamberlain, Ernest Clark, Mark Dignam, Felix Felton, Wyndham Goldie, Douglas Ives, Eliot Makeham, Anthony Marlowe, Brian Oulton, Mona Washbourne. *SYN:* Four medical students (Bogarde, More, Sinden, Houston) get into a series of scrapes as they study to become doctors. *NOTES:* The original "Doctor" comedy that spawned a series of films and a popular television sitcom. Released in Britain in 1954.

**187. Doctors Don't Tell** (8/20/41) B&W 65 mins. (Drama). *DIR:* Jacques Tourneur. *A-PRO:* Albert J. Cohen. *SP:* Theodore Reeves, Isabel Dawn. Story by Theodore Reeves. *CAST:* John Beal, Florence Rice, Edward Norris, Ward Bond, Douglas Fowley, Grady Sutton, Bill Shirley, Joseph Crehan, Paul Porcasi, Russell Hicks, Howard Hickman. *SYN:* Two interns (Beal, Norris) fall in love with a woman (Rice) When she learns that one of them (Norris) has dealings with criminals, she chooses the other. *NOTES:* The title was taken from a *Liberty* magazine serial.

**188. Don Juan's Night of Love** (5/26/55) B&W 71 mins. (Comedy). *DIR:* Mario Soldati. *PRO:* Niccolo Theodoli. *SP:* Mario Soldati, Vittorio Nino Novarese, Giorgio Lassani, Augusto S. Frassineti. A Republic Presentation. *CAST:* Raf Vallone, Silvana Pampanini, Michele Phillippe, Jacques Castelot, Giulio Donnini, Roland Armontel, Gualtiero Tumiati. *SYN:* Unknown.

**189. Don't Fence Me In** (10/20/45) B&W 71 mins. (Western). *DIR:* John English. *A-PRO:* Donald H. Brown. *SP:* Dorrell McGowan, Stuart McGowan. Additional dialogue by John K. Butler. *CAST:* Roy Rogers, George "Gabby" Hayes, Dale Evans, Robert Livingston, Moroni Olsen, Marc Lawrence, Lucille Gleason, Andrew Tombes, Paul Harvey, Tom London, Douglas Fowley, Stephen Barclay, Edgar Dearing, Helen Talbot, Michael Branden, Ray Teal, Eddie Fetherston, John Ince, Lee Phelps, Kenner G. Kemp, Charles Teske, Arleen Claire, Phil Dennis, Sherry Hall, James Linn, Diane Quilland, Brick Sullivan, Frank Fanning, Sam Ash, Bob Nolan and the Sons of the Pioneers, "Trigger." *SYN:* A magazine writer (Evans) heads west to do an article about a supposedly long-dead outlaw (Hayes) and causes problems when she uncovers the fact that he is still alive. *NOTES:* Re-edited for TV at 54 mins.

**190. Doomed at Sundown** (7/7/37) B&W 54 mins. (Western). *DIR:* Sam Newfield. *PRO:* A. W. Hackel. *SP:* George Plympton. Story by Fred Myton. *CAST:* Bob Steele, Lorraine Hayes (Laraine Day), Warner Richmond, Harold Daniels, David Sharpe, Horace B. Carpenter, Earl Dwire, Sherry Tansey, Budd Buster, Jack C. Smith, Jack Kirk, Horace Murphy, Charles King, Lew Meehan, Jack Ingram. *SYN:*

A sheriff's son (Steele) joins an outlaw gang to capture his father's killers. NOTES: Film debut of Laraine Day, though she was billed as Lorraine Hayes.

**Double Identity** *see* **Hurricane Smith**

**191. Double Jeopardy** (6/23/55) B&W 70 mins. (Crime). *DIR:* R. G. Springsteen. *A-PRO:* Rudy Ralston. *SP:* Don Martin. *CAST:* Rod Cameron, Gale Robbins, Allison Hayes, Jack Kelly. *SYN:* A real estate agent (Cameron) is accused of murder and sets out to prove his innocence.

**192. Down Dakota Way** (9/9/49) Trucolor 67 mins. (Western) *DIR:* William Witney. *A-PRO:* Edward J. White. *SP:* John K. Butler, Sloan Nibley. *CAST:* Roy Rogers, Dale Evans, Pat Brady, Monte Montana, Elisabeth Risdon, Byron Barr, James Cardwell, Roy Barcroft, Emmett Vogan, Foy Willing and the Riders of the Purple Sage, "Trigger." *SYN:* When a veterinarian is murdered because he found a herd of cattle had hoof-and-mouth disease, Roy goes after the rancher that killed him.

**193. Down in "Arkansaw"** (10/8/38) B&W 65 mins. (Comedy). *DIR:* Nick Grinde. *A-PRO:* Armand Schafer. *SP:* Dorrell McGowan, Stuart McGowan. *CAST:* Leon Weaver, June Weaver, Frank Weaver, Ralph Byrd, June Storey, Pinky Tomlin, Berton Churchill, Guinn "Big Boy" Williams, Walter Miller, Gertrude Green, Selmer Jackson, Arthur Loft, John Dilson, Alan Bridge, Karl Hackett, Ivan Miller. *SYN:* A government man (Byrd), with the help of the Weaver Brothers (Leon Weaver, Frank Weaver) and Elviry (June Weaver), wins the approval of selling a town on the plan of building a dam. NOTES: The 1st entry in the "Weaver Brothers and Elviry" series.

**194. Down Laredo Way** (8/5/53) B&W 54 mins. (Western). *DIR:* William Witney. *A-PRO:* Rudy Ralston. *SP:* Gerald Geraghty. *CAST:* Rex Allen, Slim Pickens, Dona Drake, Marjorie Lord, Roy Barcroft, Judy Nugent, Percy Helton, Clayton Moore, Zon Murray, "Koko." *SYN:* A rodeo star (Allen) and his partner (Pickens) go after a diamond smuggling ring.

**195. Down Mexico Way** (10/15/41) B&W 77 mins. (Western). *DIR:* Joseph Santley. *A-PRO:* Harry Grey. *SP:* Olive Cooper, Albert Duffy. Story by Dorrell McGowan, Stuart McGowan. *CAST:* Gene Autry, Smiley Burnette, Fay McKenzie, Harold Huber, Sidney Blackmer, Joe Sawyer, Andrew Tombes, Murray Alper, Arthur Loft, Duncan Renaldo, Paul Fix, Julian Rivero, Ruth Robinson, Thornton Edwards, Eddie Dean, Esther Estrella, Sam Appel, Helen MacKellar, Elias Gamboa, Rico de Montez, Charles Rivero, Paquita del Rey, Jose Manero, Carmela Cansino, Reed Howes, Hank Bell, Fred Burns, Al Haskell, Jack O'Shea, Frankie Marvin, The Herrara Sisters, "Champion." *SYN:* When a group of swindlers fleece the people of Sage City, Gene and Frog (Burnette) chase them to Mexico and prevent them from swindling a Mexican rancher.

**196. Down to the Sea** (5/30/36) B&W 69 mins. (Drama). *DIR:* Lewis D. Collins. *PRO:* Nat Levine. *SP:* Wellyn Totman, Robert Lee Johnson. Story by Eustace Adams, Wellyn Totman, William A. Ulman, Jr. *CAST:* Russell

Hardie, Ben Lyon, Ann Rutherford, Irving Pichel, Fritz Leiber, Vince Barnett, Maurice Murphy, Nigel de Brulier, Paul Porcasi, Victor Potel, Karl Hackett, Francisco Maran, Frank Yaconelli, Mike Tellegen, John Picorri. *SYN:* Two Greek brothers, (Hardie, Lyon), who are sponge divers in Florida, both love the same girl (Rutherford), whose father (Pichel) runs most of the sponge trade. [Alternate title: *Down Under the Sea.*]

**Down Under the Sea** *see* **Down to the Sea**

**197. Driftwood** (9/15/47) B&W 88 mins. (Drama). *DIR:* Allan Dwan. *SP:* Mary Loos, Richard Sale. *CAST:* Ruth Warrick, Walter Brennan, Dean Jagger, Charlotte Greenwood, Natalie Wood, Jerome Cowan, H. B. Warner, Margaret Hamilton, Hobart Cavanaugh, Francis Ford, Alan Napier, Howland Chamberlin, James Bell, Teddy Infuhr, James Kirkwood, Ray Teal, Zeke Holland. *SYN:* An orphan (Wood), adopted by a pharmacist (Brennan), becomes involved in the lives of most of the people in a far West town that is ravaged by an epidemic.

**Drums Along the Amazon** (G.B. title) *see* **Angel on the Amazon**

**198. Drums of Fu Manchu** (11/27/43) B&W 68 mins. (Adventure). *SYN:* Feature version of the 15 chapter serial. *NOTES:* Working titles for the feature version were *Fu Manchu*, and *Fu Manchu Strikes*. See **965. Drums of Fu Manchu.**

**199. Duel at Apache Wells** (1/25/57) B&W/Naturama 70 mins. (Western).

*DIR/A-PRO:* Joseph Kane. *SP:* Bob Williams. *CAST:* Anna Maria Alberghetti, Ben Cooper, Jim Davis, Harry Shannon, Francis McDonald, Bob Steele, Frank Puglia, Argentina Brunetti, Ian MacDonald, John Dierkes, Ric Roman, Dick Elliott. *SYN:* A young man (Cooper) returns home to his Arizona ranch after a four-year absence to find his father murdered and to face the crook (Davis) who has taken over his ranch.

**200. The Duke Comes Back** (11/29/37) B&W 62 mins. (Drama-Sports). *DIR:* Irving Pichel. *A-PRO:* Herman Schlom. *SP:* Adele Buffington, Edmond Seward. Based on *The Duke Comes Back* by Lucian Cary. *CAST:* Allan ("Rocky") Lane, Heather Angel, Genevieve Tobin, Frederick Burton, Joseph Crehan, Ben Welden, John Russell, Selmer Jackson, Art Lasky, George Lynn, Victor Adams, George Cooper, Byron Foulger, Fred "Snowflake" Toones, Clyde Dilson. *SYN:* An ex-prizefighter (Lane) returns to the ring to help his father-in-law (Burton) who has money problems. *NOTES:* The film debut of John Russell. Remade by Republic in 1949 as *Duke of Chicago*. [British title: *The Call of the Ring*.]

**201. Duke of Chicago** (3/15/49) B&W 59 mins. (Crime-Sports). *DIR:* George Blair. *A-PRO:* Stephen Auer. *SP:* Albert DeMond. Based on *The Duke Comes Back* by Lucian Cary. *CAST:* Tom Brown, Audrey Long, Grant Withers, Paul Harvey, Skeets Gallagher, Lois Hall, Matt McHugh, Joseph Crehan, Harvey Parry, George Beban, Jr., Keith Richards, DeForest Kelley, Frankie Van, Dan Tobey, Dale Van Sickel. *SYN:* A retired prizefighter (Brown) gets involved with gangsters when he is forced out of retirement to make enough money to save his father-in-law's (Harvey) publishing firm. *NOTES:* A remake of the 1937 film, *The Duke Comes Back*.

**202. Durango Valley Raiders** (8/22/38) B&W 55 mins. (Western). *DIR:* Sam Newfield. *PRO:* A. W. Hackel. *SP:* George Plympton. Story by Harry Olmstead. *CAST:* Bob Steele, Louise Stanley, Karl Hackett, Ted Adams, Forrest Taylor, Steve Clark, Horace Murphy, Jack Ingram, Ernie Adams, Julian Madison, Budd Buster, Frank Ball. *SYN:* A cowboy (Steele) goes undercover as a masked bandit to get the goods on a group of outlaws terrorizing the local ranchers. *NOTES:* Bob Steele's last film for producer A. W. Hackel.

**203. Earl Carroll Sketchbook** (8/22/46) B&W 90 mins. (Musical). *DIR:* Albert S. Rogell. *A-PRO:* Robert North. *SP:* Frank Gill, Jr., Parke Levy. Story by Frank Gill, Jr. *CAST:* Constance Moore, William Marshall, Bill Goodwin, Johnny Coy, Vera Vague, Edward Everett Horton, Hillary Brooke, Dorothy Babb, Robert E. Homans. *SYN:* A singer (Moore) and her songwriter boyfriend (Marshall) turn to writing radio jingles. [British title: *Hats Off to Rhythm*.]

**204. Earl Carroll Vanities** (4/5/45) B&W 95 mins. (Musical). *DIR:* Joseph Santley. *A-PRO:* Albert J. Cohen. *SP:* Frank Gill, Jr. Story by Cortland Fitzsimmons. *CAST:* Dennis O'Keefe, Constance Moore, Eve Arden, Otto Kruger, Alan Mowbray, Stephanie Bachelor, Pinky Lee, Leon Belasco, Beverly Lloyd, Edward Gargan, Mary Forbes, Tom Dugan, Chester Clute, Jim Alexander, Tom London, Robert Greig, Wilton Graff, Tommy Ivo, Parkyakarkus, Lillane and Mario, Woody Herman and

His Orchestra. SYN: Broadway producer Earl Carroll (Kruger) searches for a star for his new show, and discovers a visiting European princess (Moore) who is in America trying to get a loan to bail her country out of debt. NOTES: Academy Award Nominee — Best Song.

**205. Earl of Puddlestone** (8/31/40) B&W 67 mins. (Comedy). *DIR/A-PRO:* Gus Meins. *SP:* Val Burton, Ewart Adamson. *CAST:* James Gleason, Lucille Gleason, Russell Gleason, Harry Davenport, Lois Ranson, Tommy Ryan, Eric Blore, Betty Blythe, Forrester Harvey, William Halligan, Mary Ainslee, William Brady, Ben Carter, James C. Morton, Aubrey Mather, Mary Kenyon, Raymond Burr. *SYN:* The Higgins family (The Gleasons, Ransom, Ryan, Davenport) invent imaginary titled relatives to impress their wealthy neighbors.

*NOTES:* Raymond Burr's first film. He has an uncredited bit part as a chauffeur. There were no Director and Associate Producer screen credits due to the untimely death of Gus Meins. The 7th entry in the "Higgins Family" series and the final one to star the Gleasons, Davenport and Ryan. [British title: *Jolly Old Higgins.*]

**206. Eighteen and Anxious** (11/15/57) B&W 93 mins. (Drama). *DIR:* Joe Parker. *PRO:* Edmond Chevie. *SP:* Dale Eunson, Katherine Eunson. An AB-PT Production. A Republic Presentation. *CAST:* Mary Webster, William Campbell, Martha Scott, Jackie Loughery, Jim Backus, Ron Hagerthy, Jackie Coogan, Damian O'Flynn, Katherine Barrett, Charlotte Wynters, Yvonne Craig, Joyce Andre, Slick Slavin, Benny Rubin. *SYN:* A young girl (Webster) is secretly married to a young man who is killed while drag racing and has his baby. Unable to prove she was married and, refusing to care for the baby, she runs off to Las Vegas with a jazz trumpeter (Campbell), who cares nothing for her, and eventually marries a disk jockey (Hagerthy). NOTES: Later re-released as part of an adults-only birth-of-a-baby exploitation film. [Alternate title: *No Greater Sin.*]

**207. The El Paso Kid** (5/22/46) B&W 54 mins. (Western). *DIR:* Thomas Carr. *A-PRO:* Bennett Cohen. *SP:* Norman Sheldon. *CAST:* Sunset Carson, Marie Harmon, Hank Patterson, Edmund Cobb, Robert Filmer, Wheaton Chambers, John Carpenter, Tex Terry, Zon Murray, Robert Wilke, Edward Cassidy, Post Park, Charles Sullivan. *SYN:* An outlaw (Carson) decides to break away from his gang and go on his own, but is mistaken for a hero when he stops a stagecoach robbery by his old gang because he wanted to rob it, and is made sheriff of a town and redeems himself.

**208. El Paso Stampede** (9/8/53) B&W 54 mins. (Western). *DIR:* Harry Keller. *A-PRO:* Rudy Ralston. *SP:* Arthur E. Orloff. *CAST:* Allan ("Rocky") Lane, Eddy Waller, Phyllis Coates, Stephen Chase, Roy Barcroft, Edward Clark, Tom Monroe, Stanley Andrews, William Tannen, John Hamilton, "Black Jack." *SYN:* A government agent (Lane) teams up with grain merchant (Waller) to stop rustlers who are stealing cattle intended to feed U.S. troops fighting the Spanish in Cuba. *NOTES:* Allan "Rocky" Lane's last western for Republic. The picture of unseen rustler "Jose Delgado" is Grant Withers.

**El Rancho Grande** *see* **Rancho Grande**

**End of the Rainbow** (G.B. title) *see* **Northwest Outpost**

**209. End of the Road** (11/10/44) B&W 61 mins. (Crime). *DIR/A-PRO:* George Blair. *SP:* Denison Clift, Gertrude Walker. Additional dialogue by Albert Beich. Based on a *New Yorker* magazine article by Alva Johnston. *CAST:* Edward Norris, John Abbott, June Storey, Jonathan Hale, Pierre Watkin, Ted Hecht, Kenne Duncan, Eddy Fields, Ferris Taylor, Emmett Vogan, Charles Williams, Edward Van Sloan. *SYN:* A mystery writer (Norris), who believes in the innocence of a man convicted of murder, sets out to find the real killer.

**The Enemy Within** (G.B. title) *see* **The Red Menace**

**210. Escape By Night** (9/1/37) B&W 67 mins. (Drama). *DIR:* Hamilton MacFadden. *A-PRO/SP:* Harold Shumate. *CAST:* William Hall, Anne Nagel, Dean Jagger, Steffi Duna, Ward Bond, Murray Alper, Charles Waldron, George Meeker, Anthony Warde, Ralph Sanford, Arthur Aylesworth, Wallis Clark, John Dilson, "Bill," the Dog. *SYN:* A bunch of gangsters hide out from the law at an isolated farm whose only occupants are a blind man (Waldron) and his Seeing Eye dog.

**211. The Eternal Sea** (5/5/55) B&W 103 mins. (War-Biography). *DIR/A-PRO:* John H. Auer. *SP:* Allen Rivkin. Story by William Wister Haines. *CAST:* Sterling Hayden, Alexis Smith, Dean Jagger, Ben Cooper, Virginia Grey, Hayden Rorke, Douglas Kennedy, Louis Jean Heydt, Richard Crane, Morris Ankrum, Frank Ferguson, John Maxwell. *SYN:* The story of Rear Admiral

John M. Hoskins (Hayden), who continued to command a carrier and fought to stay on active duty when carrier-borne jet aircraft came along, even though he lost a leg in a Japanese attack on his carrier, the *Princeton*.

**Eventful Journey** (G.B. title) *see* **Hitch Hike Lady**

212. **Exiled to Shanghai** (12/20/37) B&W 65 mins. (Drama). *DIR:* Nick Grinde. *A-PRO:* Armand Schaefer. *SP:* Wellyn Totman. Story by Wellyn Totman. *CAST:* Wallace Ford, June Travis, Dean Jagger, William Bakewell, Arthur Lake, Jonathan Hale, William Harrigan, Sarah Padden, Syd Saylor, Charles Trowbridge, Johnny Arthur, Maurice Cass, Minerva Urecal, Sally Payne. *SYN:* A couple of newsreel men (Ford, Jagger) invents a transmission system that revolutionizes the news business. *NOTES:* In this film no one is exiled and Shanghai is never mentioned.

213. **Exposed** (9/8/47) B&W 59 mins. (Crime). *DIR:* George Blair. *A-PRO:* William J. O'Sullivan. *SP:* Royal K. Cole, Charles Moran. Story by Charles Moran. *CAST:* Adele Mara, Robert Scott, Adrian Booth, Robert Armstrong, William Haade, Bob Steele, Harry Shannon, Charles Evans, Joyce Compton, Russell Hicks, Paul E. Burns, Colin Campbell, Edward Gargan, Mary Gordon, Patricia Knox. *SYN:* A female private eye (Mara), hired by a man (Hicks) to investigate his stepson (Scott), turns up dead and, with the help of his assistant (Haade), sets out to find his killer.

214. **Eyes of Texas** (7/15/48) Trucolor 70 mins. (Western) *DIR:* William Witney. *A-PRO:* Edward J. White. *SP:* Sloan Nibley. *CAST:* Roy Rogers, Lynne Roberts, Andy Devine, Nana Bryant, Roy Barcroft, Danny Morton, Francis Ford, Pascale Perry, Stanley Blystone, Bob Reeves, Bob Nolan and the Sons of the Pioneers, "Trigger," "Bullet." *SYN:* A U.S. Marshal (Rogers) goes after land grabbers whose leader is a lady lawyer (Bryant). *NOTES:* Lynne Roberts last Republic film. Re-edited for TV at 54 mins.

215. **The Fabulous Senorita** (4/1/52) B&W 80 mins. (Comedy). *DIR:* R. G. Springsteen. *SP:* Charles E. Roberts, Jack Townley. Story by Jack Townley, Charles R. Marion. *CAST:* Estelita Rodriguez, Robert Clarke, Nestor Paiva, Marvin Kaplan, Rita Moreno, Leon Belasco, Tito Renaldo, Tom Powers, Emory Parnell, Olin Howlin, Vito Scotti, Martin Garralaga, Nita Del Rey. *SYN:* A Cuban businessman's daughter (Rodriguez) who is pledged to marry a wealthy banker's son (Renaldo), instead falls in love with a college professor (Clarke).

216. **The Fabulous Suzanne** (12/15/46) B&W 71 mins. (Comedy). *DIR/A-PRO:* Steve Sekely. *SP:* Tedwell Chapman, Randall Faye. Story by Tedwell Chapman, William Bowers. *CAST:* Barbara Britton, Rudy Vallee, Otto Kruger, Richard Denning, William (Bill) Henry, Veda Ann Borg, Irene Agay, Grady Sutton, Frank Darien, Harry Tyler, Eddy Fields, Alvin Hammer. *SYN:* A waitress (Britton), who has the uncanny ability to pick a winning horse from a racing form, decides to head to New York and try her hand in the stock market.

217. **The Fabulous Texan** (11/9/47) B&W 95 mins. (Western). *DIR:* Edward Ludwig. *PRO:* Edmund Grainger. *SP:*

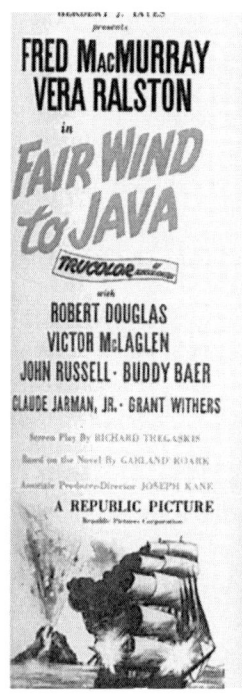

Lawrence Hazard, Horace McCoy. Story by Hal Long. *CAST:* Bill Elliott, John Carroll, Catherine McLeod, Albert Dekker, Andy Devine, Patricia Knight, Ruth Donnelly, Johnny Sands, Harry Davenport, Robert Barrat, Douglass Dumbrille, Reed Hadley, Roy Barcroft, Russell Simpson, James Brown, Jim Davis, George Beban, Jr., John Miles, Robert Coleman, Tommy Kelly, Frank Ferguson, Glenn Strange, Selmer Jackson, Harry Cheshire, John Hamilton, Harry Woods, Karl Hackett, Edward Cassidy, Pierre Watkin, Tristram Coffin, Stanley Andrews, Olin Howlin, Kenneth MacDonald, Edythe Elliott, Crane Whitley, Jack Ingram, Ted Mapes, Pierce Lyden, Al Ferguson, Ethan Laidlaw, Franklyn Farnum, Ray Teal. *SYN:* Two Confederate officers (Elliott, Carroll) return to Texas after the Civil War and find the state ruled by the State Police under the rule of a corrupt official (Dekker). Each vow in his own way to rid the state of corrupt rule. One (Carroll) becomes an outlaw when his father (Davenport) is murdered and the other (Elliott) becomes a U. S. Marshal.

218. **Faces in the Fog** (11/30/44) B&W 71 mins. (Drama). *DIR:* John English. *A-PRO:* Herman Millakowsky. *SP:* Jack Townley. *CAST:* Jane Withers, Paul Kelly, Lee Patrick, John Litel, Eric Sinclair, Dorothy Peterson, Gertrude Michael, H. B. Warner, Richard Byron, Roger Clark, Adele Mara, Bobby Stebbins, Charles Trowbridge, Helen Talbot, Joel McGinnis, Tom London, Emmett Vogan. *SYN:* A boy (Sinclair) marries his girlfriend (Withers) and assumes the blame for a hit-and-run accident that she had.

219. **Fair Wind to Java** (4/28/53) Trucolor 92 mins. (Adventure). *DIR/*

*A-PRO:* Joseph Kane. *SP:* Richard Tregaskis. Based on the book by Garland Roark. *CAST:* Fred MacMurray, Vera Ralston, Robert Douglas, Victor McLaglen, John Russell, Buddy Baer, Claude Jarman, Jr., Grant Withers, Howard Petrie, Paul Fix, William Murphy, Sujata, Philip Ahn, Stephen Bekassy, Keye Luke, John Halloran, Howard Chuman, Maiola Kalili, Al Kikume, Blackie Whiteford, Chuck Hayward, Richard Reeves, Virginia Brissac. *SYN:* A trader (MacMurray) in the Dutch East Indies locates a fortune in diamonds and has to fight a pirate band to try keep them.

**220. False Faces** (5/28/43) B&W 56 mins. (Mystery). *DIR/A-PRO:* George Sherman. *SP:* Curt Siodmak. *CAST:* Stanley Ridges, William (Bill) Henry, Rex Williams, Veda Ann Borg, Janet Shaw, Joseph Crehan, Chester Clute, John Maxwell, Dick Wessel, Billy Nelson, Nicodemus Stewart, Etta McDaniel. *SYN:* A district attorney (Ridges) sets out to prove his son (Williams) innocent of a nightclub singer's murder.

**False Witness** (G.B. title) *see* **Arkansas Judge**

**221. The Far Frontier** (12/29/48) Trucolor 67 mins. (Western). *DIR:* William Witney. *A-PRO:* Edward J. White. *SP:* Sloan Nibley. *CAST:* Roy Rogers, Gail Davis, Andy Devine, Francis Ford, Roy Barcroft, Clayton Moore, Robert Strange, Holly Bane, Lane Bradford, John Bagni, Clarence Straight, Edmund Cobb, Tom London, Anthony Caruso, Foy Willing and the Riders of the Purple Sage, "Trigger." *SYN:* Roy helps the Border Patrol to round up smugglers (Bradford, Barcroft) who are smuggling wanted criminals back into the U.S. from Mexico, and also helps prove a border patrolman (Moore) innocent of murder. *NOTES:* Andy Devine's last appearance in a Roy Rogers western. Re-edited for TV at 54 mins.

**Farmyard Follies** (G.B. title) *see* **Hoosier Holiday**

**222. The Fatal Witness** (9/15/45) B&W 59 mins. (Mystery). *DIR:* Lesley Selander. *A-PRO:* Rudolph E. Abel. *SP:* Jerry Sackheim, Cleve F. Adams. Story by Rupert Croft-Cooke. *CAST:* Evelyn Ankers, Richard Fraser, George Leigh, Barbara Everest, Barry Bernard, Frederic Worlock, Virginia Farmer, Colin Campbell, Crauford Kent, Peggy Jackson. *SYN:* A man is slain, and a Scotland Yard inspector (Fraser), who falls in love with the victim's niece (Ankers), nabs the killer.

**223. Federal Agent** (4/14/36) B&W 60 mins. (Spy). *DIR:* Sam Newfield. *SP:* Barry Baringer. *CAST:* William Boyd, Charles A. Browne, Irene Ware, George Cooper, Lentia Lace, Don Alvarado. *SYN:* A federal agent (Boyd) goes after foreign spies who are after a new chemical explosive.

**224. Federal Agent at Large** (3/12/50) B&W 60 mins. (Crime). *DIR:* George Blair. *A-PRO:* Stephen Auer. *SP:* Albert DeMond. *CAST:* Dorothy Patrick, Robert Rockwell, Kent Taylor, Estelita Rodriguez, Thurston Hall, Frank Puglia, Roy Barcroft, Denver Pyle, Jonathan Hale, Robert Kent, Kenneth MacDonald, Sonia Darrin, Frank McFarland, John McGuire. *SYN:* A treasury agent (Taylor) goes undercover as a mobster to infiltrate a gold-smuggling ring in Mexico and learns that a woman (Patrick) is the leader of the gang and they are using an archaeologist's (Rockwell) digs to smuggle the gold out of Mexico.

**225. Federal Man-Hunt** (2/2/39) B&W 64 mins. (Prison). *DIR:* Nick Grinde. *A-PRO:* Armand Schaefer. *SP:* Maxwell Shane. Story by Samuel Fuller, William Lively. *CAST:* Robert Livingston, June Travis, John Gallaudet, Ben Welden, Horace MacMahon, Charles Halton, Gene Morgan, Matt McHugh, Sibyl Harris, Jerry Tucker, Margaret Mann, Frank Conklin. *SYN:* When a hardened criminal (Gallaudet) pretends to marry his girl (Travis) in the Alcatraz prison chapel and uses the event to cover his prison break, a Federal investigator (Livingston) is called in to track him and bring him to justice. [British title: *Flight from Justice*.]

**226. The Feud Maker** (4/18/38) B&W 55 mins. (Western). *DIR:* Sam Newfield. *PRO:* A. W. Hackel. *SP:* George Plympton. Story by Harry Olmstead. *CAST:* Bob Steele, Marion Weldon, Karl Hackett, Frank Ball, Budd Buster, Lew Meehan, Roger Williams, Forrest Taylor, Jack C. Smith, Steve Clark, Lloyd Ingraham, Sherry Tansey, Wally West, Tex Palmer. *SYN:* A cowboy (Steele) sets out to stop the feud between the farmers and cattlemen.

**227. The Fighting Chance** (12/15/55) B&W 70 mins. (Drama). *DIR:* William Witney. *PRO:* Herbert J. Yates. *SP:* Houston Branch. Story by Robert Blees. *CAST:* Rod Cameron, Julie London, Ben Cooper, Taylor Holmes, Howard Wendell, Mel Welles, Bob Steele, Paul Birch, Carl Milletaire, Rodolfo Hoyos, John Damler, Sam Scar. *SYN:* A woman (London) causes problems between a horse trainer (Cameron) and a jockey (Cooper).

**228. Fighting Coast Guard** (6/1/51) B&W 86 mins. (War). *DIR/A-PRO:* Joseph Kane. *SP:* Kenneth Gamet. Story by Charles Marquis Warren. *CAST:* Brian Donlevy, Forrest Tucker, Ella Raines, John Russell, Richard Jaeckel, William Murphy, Martin Milner, Steve Brodie, Hugh O'Brian, Tom Powers, Jack Pennick, Olin Howlin, Damian O'Flynn, Morris Ankrum, James Flavin, Roy Roberts, Sandra Spence, Eric Pedersen, Bob Nolan and the Sons of the Pioneers. *SYN:* A group of shipyard workers, spurred on by the attack on Pearl Harbor, join the Coast Guard and see action in major battles in the South Pacific. *NOTES:* Actual wartime footage is used for the beachhead landings.

**229. The Fighting Devil Dogs** (1/29/43) B&W 69 mins. (Spy). *SYN:* Feature version of the 12 chapter serial. *See* **968. The Fighting Devil Dogs**.

**230. The Fighting Kentuckian** (10/5/49) B&W 100 mins. (Adventure). *DIR/SP:* George Waggner. *PRO:* John Wayne. A John Wayne Production. *CAST:* John Wayne, Vera Ralston, Philip Dorn, Oliver Hardy, Marie Windsor, John Howard, Hugo Haas, Grant Withers, Odette Myrtil, Paul Fix, Mae Marsh, Jack Pennick, Mickey Simpson, Fred Graham, Mabelle Koenig, Shy Waggner, Crystal White, Hank Worden, Charles Cane, Cliff Lyons, Chuck Roberson, Major Sam Harris, Roy Acuff and His Smoky Mountain Boys. *SYN:* In Mobile, Alabama, a Kentucky rifleman (Wayne), returning from the battle of New Orleans, falls in love with the daughter (Ralston) of a French general (Haas) and helps them to defeat land

JOHN
WAYNE
in
THE FIGHTING
KENTUCKIAN
co-starring
VERA PHILIP OLIVER
RALSTON • DORN • HARDY
featuring
MARIE WINDSOR • JOHN HOWARD
HUGO HAAS • GRANT WITHERS • ODETTE MYRTIL • PAUL FIX
Written and Directed by GEORGE WAGGNER
A JOHN WAYNE PRODUCTION
A REPUBLIC PICTURE

grabbers who are after their land. NOTES: One of Oliver Hardy's few roles without his partner, Stan Laurel. Released in a "Computer-colorized" version in the 1980s by the new Republic studios. Working title was *A Strange Caravan*.

**231. The Fighting Seabees** (3/10/44) B&W 100 mins. (War). *DIR:* Edward Ludwig. *A-PRO:* Albert J. Cohen. *SP:* Borden Chase, Aeneas MacKenzie. Story by Borden Chase. *CAST:* John Wayne, Susan Hayward, Dennis O'Keefe, William Frawley, Leonid Kinskey, J. M. Kerrigan, Grant Withers, Paul Fix, Ben Welden, William Forrest, Addison Richards, Jay Norris, Duncan Renaldo. *SYN:* During World War II on a remote Pacific island, a construction crew, working for the Navy and having no military training, is slaughtered when Japanese invade the island. The head (Wayne) of the construction company and a Navy commander (O'Keefe) journey to Washington, where it is agreed to establish a new Navy unit, the Seabees, where the men recruited will be trained and sent to another island. *NOTES:* Released in a "Computer-colorized" version in the 1990s by the new Republic studios. Academy Award nominee — Best Score.

**232. Fighting Thoroughbreds** (1/6/39) B&W 65 mins. (Sports). *DIR:* Sidney Salkow. *A-PRO:* Armand Schaefer. *SP:* Wellyn Totman, Franklin Coen. Story by Clarence E. Marks, Robert Wyler. *CAST:* Ralph Byrd, Mary Carlisle, Robert Allen, George "Gabby" Hayes, Marvin Stephens, Charles Wilson, Kenne Duncan, Victor Kilian, Eddie Brian. *SYN:* When a Kentucky

Derby winner sires a colt that becomes the possession of a fallen aristocrat (Hayes) and his granddaughter (Carlisle), the owner (Wilson) of the Derby winner does his best to bring about their ruination.

**233. The Fighting Wildcats** (12/27/57) B&W 75 mins. (Crime). *DIR:* Arthur Crabtree. *PRO:* Kay Luckwell, Bill Luckwell, Derek Winn. *SP:* Norman Hudis. Story by Lance Z. Hargreaves, Norman Hudis. An Astral Film Production. A Republic Presentation. *CAST:* Keefe Brasselle, Kay Callard, Karel Stepanek, Maya Koumani, Bruce Seton, Harry Fowler, Ursula Howells, Richard Shaw, Sheldon Lawrence, Alex Gallier. *SYN:* An American mercenary (Brasselle) is hired to kill a visiting Arab dignitary. *NOTES:* Released in Britain in March, 1957. [Original British title: *West of Suez.*]

**Fire Fighters** (G.B. title) *see* **Arson Gang Busters**

**234. Firebrands of Arizona** (12/1/44) B&W 55 mins. (Western). *DIR:* Lesley Selander. *A-PRO:* Louis Gray. *SP:* Randall Faye. *CAST:* Sunset Carson, Smiley Burnette, Peggy Stewart, Earle Hodgins, Roy Barcroft, Rex Lease, Tom London, Jack Kirk, Bud Geary, Robert Wilke, LeRoy Mason, Charles Morton, Fred "Snowflake" Toones, Pierce Lyden, Budd Buster, Bob Burns, Jack O'Shea, Hank Bell, Frank Ellis, Frank McCarroll, Jess Cavan, Bob Woodward, Dickie Dillon, Roy Butler, Phil Dunham, Grace Cunard, Maxine Doyle, Pascale Perry, Horace B. Carpenter, Bill Nestell, Tom Smith, Victor Cox, William Desmond, Tom Steele. *SYN:* Confusion reigns in the West as Sunset's hypochondriacal sidekick, Frog Millhouse (Burnette), is mistaken for a notorious robber, Beefsteak Discoe (Burnette). *NOTES:* Smiley Burnette plays a dual role in this film, and this was the last film to star Sunset Carson and Smiley Burnette and was also Smiley Burnette's last film for Republic.

**235. The Flame** (11/24/47) B&W 96 mins. (Crime). *DIR/A-PRO:* John H. Auer. *SP:* Lawrence Kimble. Story by Robert T. Shannon. *CAST:* John Carroll, Vera Ralston, Robert Paige, Broderick Crawford, Henry Travers, Blanche Yurka, Constance Dowling, Hattie McDaniel, Victor Sen Yung, Harry Cheshire, John Miljan, Garry Owen, Eddie Dunn, Vince Barnett, Hal K. Dawson, Jeff Corey, Ashley Cowan, Cyril Ring, Howard Mitchell, Martha Holliday, John Albright, John Trebach. *SYN:* A brother (Carroll) plots with his girlfriend (Ralston) to get his sick brother's (Paige) fortune.

**236. Flame of Barbary Coast** (5/28/45) B&W 91 mins. (Western). *DIR/A-PRO:* Joseph Kane. *SP:* Borden Chase. Story by Prescott Chaplin. *CAST:* John Wayne, Ann Dvorak, Joseph Schildkraut, William Frawley, Virginia Grey, Russell Hicks, Jack Norton, Paul Fix, Manart Kippen, Eve Lynne, Marc Lawrence, Butterfly McQueen, Rex Lease, Hank Bell, Al Murphy, Adele Mara, Emmett Vogan, Hugh Prosser, Eddie Parker, Jack O'Shea, Frank Jaquet, Eddie Acuff, Stuart Hamblen, Frank Hagney, Tom London, Charles Sullivan, Bud Geary, Bill Wolfe. *SYN:* When a Montana cattleman (Wayne) loses his money to a card cheat (Schildkraut) in San Francisco, he goes back to Montana, learns cards from an ace gambler, and returns to San Francisco to open his own gambling saloon only to lose it in the 1906 earthquake. *NOTES:* Released in a "Computer-colorized" version in the 1980s by the new Republic studios. Academy Award Nominee — Best Sound, Best Score. [Alternate title: *Flame of the Barbary Coast.*]

**Flame of Sacramento** *see* **In Old Sacramento**

**Flame of the Barbary Coast** *see* **Flame of Barbary Coast**

237. **Flame of the Islands** (1/6/56) Trucolor 90 mins. (Crime). *DIR/PRO:* Edward Ludwig. *SP:* Bruce Manning. Story by Adele Comandini. *CAST:* Howard Duff, Yvonne DeCarlo, Zachary Scott, Kurt Kasznar, Barbara O'Neil, James Arness, Frieda Inescort, Lester Matthews, Donald Curtis, Nick Stewart, John Pickard, Leslie Denison, Peter Adams. *SYN:* A woman (De Carlo) starts a gambling club in the Bahamas, acts as the club's hostess and singer, and gets involved with gangsters wanting control of her establishment.

238. **Flame of Youth** (9/22/49) B&W 60 mins. (Crime). *DIR:* R. G. Springsteen. *A-PRO:* Lou Brock. *SP:* Robert Libott, Frank Burt, Bradford Ropes. Story by Albert DeMond. *CAST:* Barbara Fuller, Ray McDonald, Danni Nolan, Tony Barrett, Carol Brannan, Anita Carrell, Michael Carr, Don Beddoe, Denver Pyle, Willard Waterman, Arthur Walsh, Kathryn Lang, Maurice Doner, Stephen Chase, Charles Flynn, Audrey Farr. *SYN:* A group of high-school students turn to crime to make money by stealing automobile accessories.

239. **Flaming Fury** (7/28/49) B&W 59 mins. (Crime). *DIR:* George Blair. *A-PRO:* Sidney Picker. *SP:* John K. Butler. *CAST:* Roy Roberts, George Cooper, David Wolfe, Billy Wayne, Peter Brocco, Ransom Sherman, Paul Marion, Celia Lovsky, Cliff Clark, Jimmie Dodd, G. Pat Collins, Bob Purcell. *SYN:* A rookie (Cooper) with the Los Angeles Fire Department's arson squad goes undercover to track down a gang of crooks who are setting fires to hide their crimes.

240. **Flight at Midnight** (8/28/39) B&W 66 mins. (Drama). *DIR:* Sidney Salkow. *A-PRO:* Armand Schaefer. *SP:* Eliot Gibbons. Story by Daniel Moore, Hugh King. *CAST:* Phil Regan, Jean Parker, Roscoe Turner, Robert Armstrong, Noah Beery, Jr., Harlan Briggs, Helen Lynd, Barbara Pepper, Harry Hayden, Raymond Bailey. *SYN:* A pilot (Regan), is shunned when, due to his carelessness, his airplane mechanic pal (Beery, Jr.) is killed. He redeems himself when he saves his girl's (Parker) life. *NOTES:* Roscoe Turner, who plays himself in this film, was a crack speed pilot in the 1930s who went on to become a distinguished aviation expert.

**Flight from Justice** (G.B. title) *see* **Federal Man-Hunt**

241. **Flight Nurse** (3/1/54) B&W 90 mins. (War). *DIR:* Allan Dwan. *PRO:* Herbert J. Yates. *SP:* Alan LeMay. *CAST:* Joan Leslie, Forrest Tucker, Arthur Franz, Jeff Donnell, Ben Cooper, James Holden, Kristine Miller, Maria Palmer, Richard Simmons, James Brown, Hal Baylor. *SYN:* An Air Force nurse (Leslie) must choose between two men (Tucker, Franz) while serving on the front lines during the Korean War.

242. **The Flying Squadron** (??/??/52) B&W 60 mins. *DIR:* Luigi Capuano.

PRO: Unknown. SP: Unknown. A Republic Presentation. CAST: Massimo Serato, Dina Sassoli, Guido Selano, Andrea Checchi, Mario Ferrari, Maria G. Francia, Giovanni Grasso, Umberto Spadaro. SYN: Unknown. NOTES: Filmed in Italy. The author has done extensive research and has found no other information about this film. It is one of those obscure foreign films that came and went.

**243. Flying Tigers** (10/8/42) B&W 102 mins. (War) DIR: David Miller. A-PRO: Edmund Grainger. SP: Kenneth Gamet. Story by Barry Trivers, Kenneth Gamet. CAST: John Wayne, John Carroll, Anna Lee, Paul Kelly, Gordon Jones, Mae Clarke, Addison Richards, Edmund MacDonald, Bill Shirley, Tom Neal, Bud McTaggart, David Bruce, Chester Gan, Jimmie Dodd, Gregg Barton, John James, Charles Lane, Tom Seidel, Richard Loo, Richard Crane, Willie Fung. SYN: The leader (Wayne) of the All American Volunteer Group in China, known as the "Flying Tigers," has to deal with a hot-shot pilot (Carroll) who threatens the whole air group because of his reckless antics. NOTES: John Wayne's first appearance in a war film. Released in a "Computer-colorized" version in the 1980s by the new Republic studios. Academy Award Nominee — Best Sound, Best Score, and Best Special Effects.

**244. Follow Your Heart** (8/11/36) B&W 82 mins. (Opera). DIR: Aubrey Scott. PRO: Nat Levine. SP: Nathanael West, Lester Cole, Samuel Ornitz, Olive Cooper. Based on an idea by Dana Burnett. CAST: Marion Talley, Michael Bartlett, Nigel Bruce, Luis Alberni, Henrietta Crosman, Vivienne Osborne, Walter Catlett, Eunice Healy, John Eldredge, Clarence Muse, Ben Blue, Mickey Rentschler, Si Jenks, Margaret Irving, Josephine Whittell, The Hall Johnson Choir. SYN: A young vocalist (Talley) is unsure about whether she should follow in the footsteps of her operatic mother, until an opera company becomes stranded in town and she is given the chance to sing. NOTES: The only film appearance of opera star Marion Talley. Screenwriter Olive Cooper was uncredited.

**245. Forbidden Heaven** (10/26/36) B&W 67 mins. (Political). DIR: Reginald Barker. PRO: Trem Carr. SP: Sada Cowan, Jefferson Parker. Story by Christine Jope-Slade. CAST: Charles Farrell, Charlotte Henry, Beryl Mercer, Fred Walton, Phyllis Barry, Eric Wilton, Barry Winton, Eric Snowden. SYN: A British worker (Farrell) rescues a homeless girl (Henry), falls in love, and ends up marrying her.

**246. Forced Landing** (11/26/35) B&W 61 mins. (Mystery). DIR: Melville Brown. PRO: M. H. Hoffman. SP: W. Scott Darling. Story by William Boehnel, M. Helprin. CAST: Esther Ralston, Onslow Stevens, Sidney Blackmer, Toby Wing, Eddie Nugent, Barbara Pepper, Willard Robertson, Bradley Page, Kane Richmond, Ralf Harolde, Arthur Aylesworth, Julia Griffith, Barbara Bedford, Lionel Belmore, George Cleveland. SYN: A transcontinental flight to New York, with a group of kidnappers on board, is forced down during a storm. NOTES: William Boehnel was a newspaperman and film critic at the time of this film.

**247. Forged Passport** (4/24/39) B&W 60 mins. (Crime). DIR/A-PRO: John H. Auer. SP: Franklin Coen, Lee

Strong
BRAVE MEN FLYING IN THE FACE
DEATH THAT WE MAY Live
JOHN WAYNE
JOHN CARROLL · ANNA LEE
FLYING TIGERS
A
Republic Picture

Loeb. Story by James R. Webb, Lee Loeb. *CAST:* Paul Kelly, June Lang, Lyle Talbot, Billy Gilbert, Cliff Nazarro, Maurice Murphy, Christian Rub, John Hamilton, Dewey Robinson, Bruce MacFarlane, Ivan Miller, Frank Puglia. *SYN:* A U.S. border patrol agent (Kelly), stationed in Tijuana, loses his job after a friend is gunned down due to his investigation, and when he discovers that the bullet was meant for him, he embarks on a mission of vengeance to find the killer.

**248. Forgotten Girls** (3/15/40) B&W 68 mins. (Mystery). *DIR:* Phil Rosen. *A-PRO:* Robert North. *SP:* Joseph Moncure March, George Beck, F. Hugh Herbert. Story by Frank McDonald. *CAST:* Louise Platt, Donald Woods, Wynne Gibson, Robert Armstrong, Eduardo Ciannelli, Jack LaRue, Barbara Pepper, Charles D. Brown, Sarah Padden, Ann Baldwin. *SYN:* A woman (Platt) is framed for murder by her stepmother (Gibson), and with the help of a reporter (Woods), gets out of prison and proves her innocence.

**249. Fort Dodge Stampede** (8/24/51) B&W 60 mins. (Western). *DIR/A-PRO:* Harry Keller. *SP:* Richard Wormser. *CAST:* Allan ("Rocky") Lane, Chubby Johnson, Mary Ellen Kay, Roy Barcroft, Trevor Bardette, Bruce Edwards, Wesley Hudman, William Forrest, Chuck Roberson, Rory Mallinson, Jack Ingram, Kermit Maynard, Wally West, "Black Jack." *SYN:* A deputy sheriff (Lane) and a gang of outlaws goes after stolen money buried in the deserted town of Fort Dodge.

**250. Frankie and Johnnie** (6/25/36) B&W 66 mins. (Drama). *DIR:* Chester Erskine, John H. Auer. *PRO:* William Saal. *SP:* Moss Hart, Lou Goldberg. Story by Jack Kirkland. *CAST:* Helen Morgan, Chester Morris, Florence Reed, Walter Kingsford, William Harrigan, John Larkin, Cora Witherspoon, Lilyan Tashman. *SYN:* The story of Frankie (Morgan), a singer in a casino, Johnnie (Morris), a gambler, and Nellie Bly (Tashman), the girl Frankie falls for after he and Johnnie are married. *NOTES:* One of the first films to be based on a song. This film, originally filmed by RKO in 1934, was shelved because RKO thought it was so bad that it would not make any money (they were right), and also because of censorship problems with the Hays code. It was finally released by Republic in 1936. Lilyan Tashman died before the picture was released, two years after it was made, and was unbilled in the screen credits on the picture's release.

**251. The French Key** (5/18/46) B&W 67 mins. (Mystery). *DIR/A-PRO:* Walter Colmes. *SP:* Frank Gruber. *CAST:* Albert Dekker, Mike Mazurki, Evelyn Ankers, John Eldredge, Frank Fenton, Selmer Jackson, Byron Foulger, Joe De Rita, Marjorie Manners, David Gorcey, Michael Branden, Sammy Stein, Alan Ward, Walter Soderling, Emmett Vogan. *SYN:* Two men (Dekker, Mazurki) find a dead man in their room clutching a gold coin and to avoid being blamed for the murder, they set out to track down the real killer.

**252. Friendly Neighbors** (11/7/40) B&W 67 mins. (Drama). *DIR:* Nick Grinde. *A-PRO:* Armand Schaefer. *SP:* Dorrell McGowan, Stuart McGowan. *CAST:* Leon Weaver, Frank Weaver, June Weaver, Lois Ranson, Spencer Charters, Cliff Edwards, John Hartley, Loretta Weaver, Al Shean, Thurston

Hall, Margaret Seddon, Clarence Wilson, J. Farrell MacDonald, Al St. John. SYN: The Weavers (Leon, Frank, June) are forced to leave their land because of drought and end up settling in a small town that needs their help. NOTES: The 5th entry in the "Weaver Brothers and Elviry" series.

**253. Frisco Tornado** (10/1/50) B&W 60 mins. (Western). DIR: R. G. Springsteen. A-PRO: Gordon Kay. SP: M. Coates Webster. CAST: Allan ("Rocky") Lane, Eddy Waller, Martha Hyer, Stephen Chase, Ross Ford, Mauritz Hugo, Lane Bradford, Hal Price, Rex Lease, George Chesebro, Edmund Cobb, Bud Geary, Ted Adams, "Black Jack." SYN: A U.S. Marshal (Lane) sets out to break up a protection racket run by insurance salesmen who provide protection coverage against a gang of outlaws ravaging a small cattle town.

**254. Frisco Waterfront** (12/3/35) B&W 66 mins. (Political). DIR: Arthur Lubin. PRO: Trem Carr. SP: Norman Houston. CAST: Ben Lyon, Helen Twelvetrees, Rod La Rocque, Russell Hopton, James Burke, Henry Kolker, Purnell Pratt, Barbara Pepper, Lee Shumway. SYN: The story of a man's (Lyon) rise to power, from unemployed World War I vet to powerful dockworker, to lawyer to politician, as told through flashbacks. [Alternate title: *When We Look Back*]

**Frontier Horizon** see **524. New Frontier**

**255. Frontier Investigator** (5/2/49) B&W 60 mins. (Western). DIR: Fred C. Brannon. A-PRO: Gordon Kay. SP: Bob Williams. CAST: Allan ("Rocky") Lane, Gail Davis, Eddy Waller, Roy Barcroft, Robert Emmett Keane, Clayton Moore, Francis Ford, Claire Whitney, Harry Lauter, Tom London, George Lloyd, Marshall Reed, "Black Jack." SYN: A cowboy (Lane) searches for the killer of his brother, and gets mixed up in a stagecoach war.

**256. Frontier Pony Express** (4/12/39) B&W 58 mins. (Western). DIR/A-PRO: Joseph Kane. SP: Norman S. Hall. CAST: Roy Rogers, Mary Hart, Raymond Hatton, Edward Keane, Noble Johnson, Monte Blue, Donald Dillaway, William Royle, Ethel Wales, George Letz, Charles King, Bud Osborne, Fred Burns, Jack Kirk, Bob McKenzie, Ernie Adams, Hank Bell, Jack O'Shea, House Peters, Jr., Art Dillard, Chris-Pin Martin, "Trigger." SYN: A Pony Express rider (Rogers), operating between California and the frontier territory, becomes involved in a plot by a Confederate spy (Dillaway) and southern politician (Keane) to get California to enter the Civil War on the rebel side. NOTES: Re-edited for TV at 54 mins.

**257. Frontier Vengeance** (10/10/40) B&W 57 mins. (Western). DIR: Nate Watt. A-PRO: George Sherman, Edward J. White. SP: Bennett Cohen, Barry Shipman. Story by Bennett Cohen. CAST: Don ("Red") Barry, Betty Moran, George Offerman, Jr., Ivan Miller, Obed Pickard, Cindy Walker, Kenneth MacDonald, Griff Barnette, Yakima Canutt, Jack Lawrence, Matty Roubert, Fred "Snowflake" Toones, Jack Rockwell. SYN: A cowboy (Barry) becomes involved with rival stagecoach lines, and helps a woman (Moran) win a stage line contract.

**258. Fugitive from Sonora** (7/1/43) B&W 57 mins. (Western). DIR: Howard Bretherton. *A-PRO:* Edward J. White. *SP:* Norman S. Hall. *CAST:* Don ("Red") Barry, Wally Vernon, Lynn Merrick, Harry Cording, Ethan Laidlaw, Pierce Lyden, Gary Bruce, Kenne Duncan, Tommy Coats, Frank McCarroll, Karl Hackett, Charles Sullivan, Augie Gomez, Kansas Moehring, Jamesson Shade. *SYN:* A former outlaw (Barry) gets mixed up in a range war. *NOTES:* Wally Vernon's first role as Barry's sidekick.

**259. Fugitive Lady** (7/15/51) B&W 78 mins. (Mystery). *DIR:* Sidney Salkow. *PRO:* Mike J. Frankovich. *SP:* John O'Dea. Based on the novel by Doris Miles Disney. A Venus Production. A Republic Presentation. *CAST:* Janis Paige, Binnie Barnes, Massimo Serato, Eduardo Ciannelli, Antonio Centa, Alba Arnova, Dino Galvani, Rosina Galli, John Fostini, Luciana Danieli, Michael Tor, Alex Serbaroli, Joop Van Hulzen, Giulio Marchetti. *SYN:* When a man (Ciannelli) falls to his death from a cliff, an insurance agent (Centa) suspects foul play and investigates to find out if it was the wife (Paige) or stepsister (Barnes) that killed him.

**260. The Gallant Legion** (5/24/48) B&W 88 mins. (Western). *DIR/A-PRO:* Joseph Kane. *SP:* Gerald Drayson Adams. Story by John K. Butler, Gerald Geraghty. *CAST:* Bill Elliott, Adrian Booth, Joseph Schildkraut, Bruce Cabot, Andy Devine, Jack Holt, Grant Withers, Adele Mara, James Brown, Hal Landon, Tex Terry, Lester Sharpe, Hal Taliaferro, Russell Hicks, Herbert Rawlinson, Marshall Reed, Steve Drake, Harry Woods, Roy Barcroft, Bud Osborne, Hank Bell, Jack Ingram, George Chesebro, Rex Lease, Noble Johnson, Emmett Vogan, John Hamilton, Trevor Bardette, Gene Stutenroth, Ferris Taylor, Iron Eyes Cody, Kermit Maynard, Jack Kirk, Merrill McCormick, Augie Gomez, Cactus Mack, Fred Kohler, Jr., Glenn Strange, Joseph Crehan, Peter Perkins, Jack Perrin. *SYN:* A Texas Ranger (Elliott) and a journalist (Booth) set out to stop a corrupt official (Schildkraut) and his chief henchman (Cabot) from breaking up the Texas Rangers and splitting Texas into two sections.

**261. The Gambling Terror** (2/15/37) B&W 53 mins. (Western). *DIR:* Sam Newfield. *PRO:* A. W. Hackel. *SP:* George Plympton, Fred Myton. *CAST:* Johnny Mack Brown, Iris Meredith, Charles King, Ted Adams, Earl Dwire, Dick Curtis, Horace Murphy, Bobby Nelson, Frank Ellis, Frank Ball, Sherry Tansey, Steve Clark, George Morrell, Art Dillard, Tex Palmer, Jack Montgomery, Budd Buster, Lloyd Ingraham, Ray Henderson, Emma Tansey, Buck Morgan, Clyde McClary, Herman Hack, Oscar Gahan, Roy Bucko. *SYN:* A cowboy (Brown) pretends to be a gambler in order to stop a crook (Dwire) who demands protection money from ranchers.

**The Gang Made Good** (G.B. title) *see* **Tuxedo Junction**

**262. Gangs of Chicago** (5/19/40) B&W 66 mins. (Crime). *DIR:* Arthur Lubin. *A-PRO:* Robert North. *SP:* Karl Brown. *CAST:* Lloyd Nolan, Barton MacLane, Lola Lane, Ray Middleton, Astrid Allwyn, Leona Roberts, Horace MacMahon, Howard Hickman, Charles Halton, Addison Richards, John Harmon, Dwight Frye, Alan Ladd. *SYN:* A criminal lawyer (Nolan), who as a lad witnessed his thief father gunned down by cops, becomes a lawyer for the local mob boss (MacLane). His former friend (Middleton), working undercover for the FBI, sets out to get the goods on the mob and persuade his friend to go on the right side of the law. NOTES: The film debut of Ray Middleton.

**263. Gangs of New York** (5/23/38) B&W 67 mins. (Crime). *DIR:* James Cruze. *A-PRO:* Armand Schaefer. *SP:* Wellyn Totman, Samuel Fuller, Charles Francis Royal. Additional dialogue by Jack Townley. Story by Samuel Fuller. Suggested by *Gangs of New York* by Herbert Asbury. *CAST:* Charles Bickford, Ann Dvorak, Alan Baxter, Wynne Gibson, Harold Huber, Willard Robertson, Maxie Rosenbloom, Charles Trowbridge, John Wray, Jonathan Hale, Fred Kohler, Sr., Howard Phillips, Robert Gleckler, Elliott Sullivan, Maurice Cass. *SYN:* A cop (Bickford) takes the place of a top gangster (Bickford), who is in prison and runs his gang from there, and has the gang keep records in order to collect enough evidence to put all of the gang in prison. *NOTES:* Charles Bickford plays a dual role in this film.

**264. Gangs of Sonora** (7/10/41) B&W 56 mins. (Western). *DIR:* John English. *A-PRO:* Louis Gray. *SP:* Albert DeMond, Doris Schroeder. Based on characters created by William Colt MacDonald. *CAST:* Robert Livingston, Bob Steele, Rufe Davis, June Johnson, Bud McTaggart, Helen MacKellar, Robert Frazer, William Farnum, Budd Buster, Hal Price, Bud Osborne, Wally West, Bud Geary, Jack Kirk, Al Taylor, Griff Barnette, Curley Dresden, Jack Lawrence, Hank Patterson. *SYN:* The Three Mesquiteers (Livingston, Steele, Davis) go after a crooked town boss (Frazer) who is trying to prevent Wyoming from becoming a state, and aid a woman (MacKellar) in taking over a newspaper after the editor was killed. *NOTES:* The 38th entry in the "Three Mesquiteers" series and Robert Livingston's last appearance as a "Mesquiteer."

**Gangs of the City** *see* **Public Enemies**

**265. Gangs of the Waterfront** (7/3/45) B&W 55 mins. (Crime). *DIR/A-PRO:* George Blair. *E-PRO:* Armand Schaefer. *SP:* Albert Beich. Story by Samuel Fuller. *CAST:* Robert Armstrong, Stephanie Bachelor, Martin Kosleck, Marian Martin, William Forrest, Wilton Graff, Eddie Hall, Jack O'Shea, Davison Clark, Dick Elliott, Blake Edwards. *SYN:* A taxidermist (Armstrong) goes after the mobster that killed his brother.

**266. Gaucho Serenade** (5/10/40) B&W 66 mins. (Western). *DIR:* Frank McDonald. *A-PRO:* William Berke. *SP:* Betty Burbridge, Bradford Ropes. *CAST:* Gene Autry, Smiley Burnette, June Storey, Duncan Renaldo, Mary Lee, Clifford Severn, Jr., Lester Matthews, Smith Ballew, Joseph Crehan, William Ruhl, Wade Boteler, Ted Adams, Wendell Niles, Fred Burns, Julian Rivero, George Lloyd, Edward Cassidy, Joe Dominguez, Olaf Hytten, Fred "Snowflake" Toones, Gene Morgan, Jack Kirk, Harry Strang, Hank Worden, Kernan Cripps, Jim Corey, Tom London, Walter Miller, Frankie Marvin, Ralph Bucko, Al Taylor, Jean Procter, The Velascos (Fred and Mary), Jose Eslava Orchestra, "Champion." *SYN:* Gene works with cattle ranchers to fight a corrupt meat packing company and also helps a young man (Severn, Jr.) run his ranch. [Re-release title: *Keep Rollin'.*]

**267. Gauchos of Eldorado** (10/24/41) B&W 56 mins. (Western). *DIR:* Les Orlebeck. *A-PRO:* Louis Gray. *SP:* Earle Snell. Based on characters created by William Colt MacDonald. *CAST:* Bob Steele, Tom Tyler, Rufe Davis, Lois Collier, Duncan Renaldo, Rosina Galli, Norman Willis, William Ruhl, Tony Roux, Raphael Bennett, Yakima Canutt, Edmund Cobb, Eddie Dean, Terry Frost, John Merrill Holmes, John Merton, Virginia Farmer, Si Jenks, Ted Mapes, Bob Woodward, Ray Jones, Horace B. Carpenter. *SYN:* The Three Mesquiteers (Tyler, Steele, Davis) go after a dishonest banker (Willis) who is cheating the townspeople. *NOTES:* The 40th entry in the "Three Mesquiteers" series.

**268. Gay Blades** (1/25/46) B&W 67 mins. (Comedy). *DIR/A-PRO:* George Blair. *SP:* Albert Beich. Adapted by Marcel Klauber. Based on a magazine story by Jack Goodman, Albert Rice. *CAST:* Allan ("Rocky") Lane, Jean Rogers, Edward Ashley, Frank Albertson, Ann Gillis, Robert Armstrong, Paul Harvey, Ray Walker, Jonathan Hale, Russell Hicks, Emmett Vogan, Edward Gargan, Ned Young. *SYN:* A Hollywood talent scout (Rogers) goes to New York and tries to persuade a hockey player (Lane) to star in a movie titled "The Behemoth."

**269. The Gay Ranchero** (1/10/48) Trucolor 72 mins. (Western). *DIR:* William Witney. *A-PRO:* Edward J. White. *SP:* Sloan Nibley. *CAST:* Roy Rogers, Tito Guizar, Jane Frazee, Andy Devine, Estelita Rodriguez, George Meeker, LeRoy Mason, Dennis Moore, Keith Richards, Betty Gagnon, Robert Rose, Ken Terrell, Bob Nolan and the Sons of the Pioneers, "Trigger." *SYN:* A sheriff (Rogers) and a bullfighter (Guizar) are after gold hijackers who use modern airplanes for their hijacking, and who try to gain control of an airport. *NOTES:* This was a posthumous screen appearance for LeRoy Mason. He had died the previous year while filming *California Firebrand*. Re-edited for TV at 54 mins.

**270. The Gay Vagabond** (5/12/41) B&W 66 mins. (Comedy). *DIR:* William Morgan. *A-PRO:* Robert North. *SP:* Ewart Adamson, Taylor Caven. *CAST:* Roscoe Karns, Ruth Donnelly, Ernest Truex, Margaret Hamilton, Abner Biberman, Bernadene Hayes, Lynn Merrick, Rod Bacon, Gloria Franklin, Carol Adams, Byron Foulger, Paul "Tiny" Newlan. *SYN:* A twin (Karns), who is a skirt-chasing adventurer, visits his meek, reclusive brother (Karns) and causes mix-ups for both. *NOTES:* Roscoe Karns plays a dual role in this film.

**271. A Gentle Gangster** (5/10/43) B&W 57 mins. (Comedy-Drama). *DIR:* Phil Rosen. *PRO:* A. W. Hackel. *SP:* Jefferson Parker, Al Martin. *CAST:* Barton MacLane, Molly Lamont, Dick Wessel, Joyce Compton, Jack LaRue, Cy Kendall, Rosella Towne, Ray Teal, Crane Whitley, Elliott Sullivan, Anthony Warde. *SYN:* A gangster (LaRue) from the past threatens to disrupt the life of a fellow gangster (MacLane) and his pals who have given up the life of crime and settled down with their girlfriends in a small town.

**272. The Gentleman from Louisiana** (8/15/36) B&W 67 mins. (Crime). *DIR:* Irving Pichel. *PRO:* Nat Levine. *SP:* Gordon Rigby, Joseph Fields. Story by Jerome Chodorov, Bert Granet.

CAST: Eddie Quillan, Charles "Chic" Sale, Charlotte Henry, Marjorie Gateson, John Miljan, Pierre Watkin, Charles Wilson, Ruth Gillette, Holmes Herbert, Matt McHugh, John Kelly, Arthur Wanzer, Snub Pollard, Kenneth Lawton, Lowden Adams, Gertrude W. Hoffman, Harrison Greene. SYN: A jockey (Quillan) gets railroaded by some crooks, only to emerge victorious on the track and regain respect.

273. **Geraldine** (4/1/54) B&W 90 mins. (Musical). DIR: R. G. Springsteen. A-PRO: Sidney Picker. SP: Peter Milne, Frank Gill, Jr. Story by Peter Milne, Doris Gilbert. CAST: John Carroll, Mala Powers, Jim Backus, Stan Freberg, Kristine Miller, Leon Belasco, Ludwig Stossel, Earl Lee, Alan Reed, Nana Bryant, Carolyn Jones. SYN: A top recording star (Freberg) wants to record a tune of a music instructor (Carroll).

274. **The Ghost Goes Wild** (3/8/47) B&W 66 mins. (Comedy-Mystery). DIR: George Blair. A-PRO: Armand Schaefer. SP: Randall Faye. Story by Randall Faye, Taylor Caven. CAST: James Ellison, Anne Gwynne, Ruth Donnelly, Stephanie Bachelor, Grant Withers, Lloyd Corrigan, Emil Rameau, Jonathan Hale, Charles Halton, Edward Everett Horton, Edward Gargan, Gene Garrick, Michael Hughes, William Austin. SYN: An artist (Ellison), masquerading as a spiritualist to escape a court date, inadvertently conjures up a real ghost and gets more than he bargained for.

275. **Ghost of Zorro** (6/30/59) B&W 69 mins. (Western). SYN: Feature version of the 12 chapter serial. See **970. Ghost of Zorro.**

276. **Ghost Town Gold** (10/26/36) B&W 55 mins. (Western). DIR: Joseph Kane. PRO: Nat Levine. SP: John Rathmell, Oliver Drake. Story by Bernard McConville. Based on characters created by William Colt MacDonald. CAST: Robert Livingston, Ray ("Crash") Corrigan, Max Terhune, Kay Hughes, LeRoy Mason, Burr Caruth, Robert Kortman, Milburn Morante, Frank Hagney, Don Roberts, F. Herrick Herrick, Robert C. Thomas, Yakima Canutt, Horace Murphy, Earle Hodgins, Edward Peil, Sr., Harry Harvey, Hank Worden, Bud Osborne, Bob Burns, Wally West, I. Stanford Jolley. SYN: The Three Mesquiteers (Livingston, Corrigan, Terhune) go after stolen bank money hidden in a ghost town. NOTES: The first appearance of Max Terhune as a Mesquiteer. The 2nd entry in the "Three Mesquiteers" series.

277. **Ghost Valley Raiders** (3/26/40) B&W 57 mins. (Western). DIR/A-PRO: George Sherman. SP: Bennett Cohen. Story by Connie Lee. CAST: Don ("Red") Barry, Lona Andre, LeRoy Mason, Tom London, Jack Ingram, Horace Murphy, Ralph Peters, Curley Dresden, Yakima Canutt, John Beach, Bud Osborne, Al Taylor, Jack Montgomery, Fred Burns. SYN: A cowboy (Barry) goes undercover as a bandit to capture the gang terrorizing stagecoach riders. NOTES: Don "Red" Barry's first series western.

278. **G.I. War Brides** (8/12/46) B&W 69 mins. (Comedy). DIR: George Blair. A-PRO: Armand Schaefer. SP: John K. Butler. CAST: Anna Lee, James Ellison, Harry Davenport, William (Bill) Henry, Stephanie Bachelor, Doris Lloyd, Robert Armstrong, Joe Sawyer, Mary McLeod, Carol Savage, Patricia Walker, Helen Gerald, Patrick O'Moore,

Maxine Jennings, Russell Hicks, Francis Pierlot, Pierre Watkin, Eugene Lay, Lois Austin, Virginia Carroll. SYN: A woman (Bachelor) pretends to be an English war bride so she can get through immigration and find her boyfriend. [British title: *War Brides*.]

**279. The Girl from Alaska** (4/16/42) B&W 75 mins. (Western). *DIR:* Nick Grinde. *A-PRO:* Armand Schaefer. *SP:* Edward T. Lowe, Robert Ormand Case. Based on *The Golden Portage* by Robert Ormond Case. *CAST:* Ray Middleton, Jean Parker, Jerome Cowan, Robert Barrat, Ray Mala, Francis McDonald, Raymond Hatton, Milton Parsons, Nestor Paiva. *SYN:* A prospector (Middleton), who believes he has killed an officer of the law, saves the gold claim of a woman (Parker) from a felon (Cowan) and learns that he is not a murderer. *NOTES:* Re-edited for TV at 54 mins.

**280. Girl from God's Country** (7/30/40) B&W 75 mins. (Drama). *DIR:* Sidney Salkow. *A-PRO:* Armand Schaefer. *SP:* Elizabeth Meehan, Robert Lee Johnson, Malcolm Stuart Boylan. Based on *Island Doctor* by Ray Millholland. *CAST:* Chester Morris, Jane Wyatt, Charles Bickford, Ray Mala, Kate Lawson, John Bleifer, Mamo Clark, Ferike Boros, Don Zelaya, Clem Bevans, Edward Gargan, Spencer Charters, Thomas E. Jackson, Victor Potel, Si Jenks, Gene Morgan, "Ace," the Wonder Dog. *SYN:* A doctor (Morris), wanted for the mercy killing of his father, flees to the frozen North and ends up saving the life of the policeman (Bickford) who is after him. *NOTES:* Re-edited for TV at 54 mins.

**281. Girl from Havana** (9/11/40) B&W 69 mins. (Drama). *DIR:* Lew Landers. *A-PRO:* Robert North. *SP:* Karl Brown, Malcolm Stuart Boylan. *CAST:* Dennis O'Keefe, Claire Carleton, Victor Jory, Steffi Duna, Gordon Jones, Bradley Page, Addison Richards, Abner Biberman, William Edmunds, Richard Cramer, Trevor Bardette, Jay Novello, Frank Lackteen. *SYN:* Two friends (O'Keefe, Jory) venture into the oil drilling business and their site is threatened by rebel uprisings, and their friendship by a woman (Carleton).

**282. The Girl from Mandalay** (4/14/36) B&W 68 mins. (Drama). *DIR:* Howard Bretherton. *PRO:* Nat Levine. *A-PRO:* Victor Zobel. *SP:* Wellyn Totman, Endre Bohem. Based on *Tiger Valley* by Reginald Campbell. *CAST:* Conrad Nagel, Kay Linaker, Donald Cook, Esther Ralston, Harry Stubbs, Reginald Barlow, George Regas, David Clyde, Jack Santos, Joe Bautista, John Bouer, Daisy Belmore, Harry Allen. *SYN:* A lonely Britisher in Mandalay (Nagel) marries a local nightclub entertainer (Linaker) after his fiancee leaves him.

**The Girl from Mexico** (G.B. title) *see* **Mexacali Rose**

**283. Girl in the Woods** (6/1/58) B&W 71 mins. (Drama) *DIR:* Tom Gries. *PRO:* Harry L. Mandell. *SP:* Oliver Crawford, Marcel Klauber. Based on *Blood on the Branches* by Oliver Crawford. An AB-PT Picture. A Republic Presentation. *CAST:* Forrest Tucker, Margaret Hayes, Barton MacLane, Diana Francis, Murvyn Vye, Paul Langton, Joyce Compton, Kim Charney, Mickey Finn, Bartlett Robinson, Harry Raybould, George Lynn, Joey Ray. *SYN:* A lumberjack (Tucker), caught in the middle of rivalry between two logging companies, has to prove his innocence when he is accused of murder. *NOTES:* Forrest Tucker's last film for Republic.

**284. The Girl Who Dared** (8/5/44) B&W 56 mins. (Mystery-Thriller). *DIR:* Howard Bretherton. *A-PRO:* Rudolph E. Abel. *SP:* John K. Butler. Based on the novel *Blood on Her Shoe* by Medora Field. *CAST:* Lorna Gray, Peter Cookson, Grant Withers, Veda Ann Borg, John Hamilton, Willie Best, Vivien Oakland, Roy Barcroft, Kirk Alyn, Tom London. *SYN:* Murder strikes a group voyaging to a remote island off the coast of Georgia, and a woman (Gray) plays detective to find the killer.

**285. Girls of the Big House** (11/2/45) B&W 68 mins. (Prison). *DIR:* George Archainbaud. *A-PRO:* Rudolph E. Abel. *E-PRO:* Armand Schaefer. *SP:* Houston Branch. *CAST:* Lynn Roberts, Virginia Christine, Marian Martin, Adele Mara, Richard Powers (Tom Keene), Geraldine Wall, Tala Birell, Norma Varden, Stephen Barclay, Mary Newton, Erskine Sanford, Sarah Edwards, Ida Moore, William Forrest, Verna Felton. *SYN:* A woman (Roberts), framed and sent to prison for theft, must learn to adjust to prison rules and standards. While in prison, she is attacked by one of the inmates (Christine), who is eventually found dead, and is implicated in her death. Her attorney–boy friend (Powers) investigates, finds she is innocent of both charges, and secures her release.

**286. Git Along Little Dogies** (3/27/37) B&W 60 mins. (Western). *DIR/PRO:* Joseph Kane. *A-PRO:* Armand Schaefer. *SP:* Dorrell McGowan, Stuart McGowan. *CAST:* Gene Autry, Smiley Burnette, Judith Allen, Weldon Heyburn, William Farnum, Willie Fung, Carleton Young, G. Raymond Nye, Frankie Marvin, George Morrell, Horace B. Carpenter, Rose Plummer, Earl Dwire, Lynton Brent, Jack Kirk, Al Taylor, Frank Ellis, Jack C. Smith, Murdock MacQuarrie, Oscar Gahan, Monte Montague, Sam McDaniel, Eddie Parker, Bob Burns, Will and Gladys Ahern, Maple City Four, The Cabin Kids, "Champion." *SYN:* Gene settles a conflict between cattle ranchers and oil drillers over range land, stops a crooked oilman (Heyburn) from delaying in bringing in the well, and wins the love of a banker's daughter (Allen). *NOTES:* Re released 10/15/44. [British title: *Serenade of the West.*]

**287. Glamorous Night** (12/15/37) B&W 65 mins. (Drama). *DIR:* Brian Desmond Hurst. *PRO:* Walter C. Mycroft. *SP:* Dudley Leslie, Hugh Brooke, William Freshman. Based on the play by Ivor Novello. An Associated British Production. A Republic Presentation. *CAST:* Mary Ellis, Otto Kruger, Victor Jory, Barry Mackay, Trefor Jones, Maire O'Neill, Antony Holles, Charles Carson, Felix Aylmer, Finlay Currie, Jeanne Carpenter. *SYN:* A king (Kruger) who becomes infatuated with a gypsy girl (Ellis) thinks about abdicating, and his prime minister (Jory) tries to use this development to put himself on the throne. *NOTES:* Released in Britain in April, 1937 at a running time of 81 mins.

**288. The Glass Alibi** (4/27/46) B&W 68 mins. (Thriller). *DIR/PRO:* W. Lee Wilder. *SP:* Mindret Lord. A W. W. Production. A Republic Presentation. *CAST:* Paul Kelly, Douglas Fowley, Anne Gwynne, Maris Wrixon, Jack Conrad, Selmer Jackson, Cyril Thornton, Cy

Kendall, Walter Soderling, Victor Potel, George Chandler, Phyllis Adair, Ted Stanhope, Dick Scott, Eula Guy, Forrest Taylor. *SYN:* A reporter (Fowley) marries a wealthy Santa Monica socialite (Wrixon) knowing that she has a heart ailment and only has six months to live, but when she does not die, he and his girlfriend (Gwynne) plot her murder, as a "perfect" crime. *NOTES:* W. Lee Wilder is the brother of director Billy Wilder.

**289. Go-Get-'Em Haines** (10/22/36) B&W 63 mins. (Western). *DIR:* Sam Newfield. *A-PRO:* George A. Hirliman. *SP:* George W. Sayre. *CAST:* William Boyd, Sheila Terry, Eleanor Hunt, LeRoy Mason, Lloyd Ingraham, Clarence Geldert, Louis Natheaux, Lee Shumway, Jimmy Aubrey. *SYN:* A federal agent (Boyd) goes after a gang of crooks.

**290. Gobs and Gals** (5/1/52) B&W 86 mins. (Comedy). *DIR:* R. G. Springsteen. *A-PRO:* Sidney Picker. *SP:* Arthur T. Horman. *CAST:* George Bernard, Bert Bernard, Robert Hutton, Cathy Downs, Gordon Jones, Florence Marly, Leon Belasco, Emory Parnell, Leonid Kinskey, Tommy Rettig, Minerva Urecal, Donald MacBride, Henry Kulky. *SYN:* Two bored sailors (The Bernards) on a South Seas island get their chief officer (Hutton) in a mess of trouble when they send romantic letters to various feminine pen pals and enclose his picture with every letter. [British title: *Cruising Casanovas.*]

**291. Gold Mine in the Sky** (7/5/38) B&W 60 mins. (Western). *DIR:* Joseph Kane. *A-PRO:* Charles E. Ford. *SP:* Jack Natteford, Betty Burbridge. Story by Betty Burbridge. *CAST:* Gene Autry, Smiley Burnette, Carol Hughes, Craig Reynolds, Cupid Ainsworth, LeRoy Mason, Frankie Marvin, Robert E. Homans, Eddie Cherkose, Ben Corbett, Milburn Morante, Jim Corey, George Guhl, Fred "Snowflake" Toones, George Letz, Charles King, Lew Kelly, Joe Whitehead, Matty Roubert, Anita Bolster, Earl Dwire, Maude Prickett, Al Taylor, Art Dillard, Herman Hack, George Plues, The Stafford Sisters, J. L. Frank's Golden West Cowboys, "Champion." *SYN:* Gene is a singing ranch foreman who becomes executor of the owner's will and it's his job to see that the late owner's daughter (Hughes), doesn't sell the ranch or marry unless he has final approval of her intended. *NOTES:* Re-released 1/15/46. Re-edited for TV at 54 mins.

**292. The Golden Stallion** (11/15/49) Trucolor 67 mins. (Western). *DIR:* William Witney. *A-PRO:* Edward J. White. *SP:* Sloan Nibley. *CAST:* Roy Rogers, Dale Evans, Estelita Rodriguez, Pat Brady, Douglas Evans, Frank Fenton, Greg McClure, Dale Van Sickel, Clarence Straight, Jack Sparks, Karl Hackett, Chester Conklin, Foy Willing and the Riders of the Purple Sage, "Trigger." *SYN:* A horse trader (Rogers) captures a wild herd of horses that diamond smugglers have been using to smuggle diamonds across the border.

**The Golden Trail** (G.B. title) *see* **Riders of the Whistling Skull**

**293. Goodnight Sweetheart** (6/17/44) B&W 67 mins. (Drama). *DIR:* Joseph Santley. *A-PRO:* Edward J. White. *SP:* Isabel Dawn, Jack Townley. Story by Frank Fenton, Joseph Hoffman. *CAST:* Robert Livingston, Ruth Terry, Henry Hull, Grant Withers,

Thurston Hall, Lloyd Corrigan, Maude Eburne, Olin Howlin, Lucien Littlefield, Ellen Lowe, Chester Conklin, Emmett Lynn, William Benedict. *SYN:* A big-city reporter (Livingston) moves to a small town to take over a newspaper he owns half interest in, and stirs up trouble during a mayoral election.

**294. Grand Canyon Trail** (11/5/48) Trucolor 67 mins. (Western). *DIR:* William Witney. *A-PRO:* Edward J. White. *SP:* Gerald Geraghty. *CAST:* Roy Rogers, Jane Frazee, Andy Devine, Robert Livingston, Roy Barcroft, Charles Coleman, Emmett Lynn, Ken Terrell, James Finlayson, Tommy Coats, Zon Murray, Foy Willing and the Riders of the Purple Sage, "Trigger." *SYN:* A mining engineer (Livingston) tries to swindle an owner (Lynn) out of his old silver mine because he suspects that the mine is rich in silver. When he is found dead, Roy is accused of the killing and has to prove his innocence. *NOTES:* The first appearance of the Riders of the Purple Sage, who replaced the Sons of the Pioneers. Re-edited for TV at 54 mins.

**295. Grand Ole Opry** (6/25/40) B&W 68 mins. (Musical-Comedy). *DIR:* Frank McDonald. *A-PRO:* Armand Schaefer. *SP:* Dorrell McGowan, Stuart McGowan. *CAST:* Leon Weaver, Frank Weaver, June Weaver, Lois Ranson, Allan ("Rocky") Lane, Henry Kolker, John Hartley, Loretta Weaver, Purnell Pratt, Claire Carleton, Ferris Taylor, George Dewey Hay, Roy Acuff and His Smoky Mountain Boys. *SYN:* The Weavers (Leon, Frank June) outwit a group of corrupt city politicians and manage to get Leon elected as the governor of the state. *NOTES:* The 4th entry in the "Weaver Brothers and Elviry" series.

**296. Grandpa Goes to Town** (4/19/40) B&W 66 mins. (Comedy). *DIR/A-PRO:* Gus Meins. *SP:* Jack Townley. *CAST:* James Gleason, Lucille Gleason, Russell Gleason, Harry Davenport, Lois Ranson, Maxie Rosenbloom, Tommy Ryan, Ledda Godoy, Noah Beery, Sr., Douglas Meins, Garry Owen, Ray Turner, Lee "Lasses" White, Walter Miller, Emmett Lynn, Joe Caits, Cliff Nazarro, Arturo Godoy. *SYN:* The Higgins family (The Gleasons, Ryan, Ranson, Davenport) buy a hotel in a ghost town and it becomes a thriving business when Sidney (Russell Gleason) believes that a scene of a gold strike being filmed nearby is real and spreads the news about the strike. *NOTES:* Walter Miller, one of the best known romantic leads of the silents, died before this film's release. He played the director of a film within the film. The 6th entry in the "Higgins Family" series.

**297. The Great Flamarion** (3/30/45) B&W 78 mins. (Drama). *DIR:* Anthony Mann. *PRO:* W. Lee Wilder. *SP:* Anne Wigton, Heinz Herald, Richard Weil. Story by Anne Wigton. Based on the character "Big Shot" created by Vicki Baum in *Collier's* magazine. A W. W. Production. A Republic Presentation. *CAST:* Erich Von Stroheim, Mary Beth Hughes, Dan Duryea, Stephen Barclay, Lester Allen, Esther Howard, Michael Mark, Joseph Granby, John Hamilton, Tony Ferrell, Velasco and Lopez. *SYN:* Told in flashback, a performer (Von Stroheim), who makes his living as a vaudeville marksman, plots to kill his assistant's (Hughes) husband (Duryea) when he thinks she is in love with him.

**298. Great Stagecoach Robbery** (2/15/45) B&W 56 mins. (Western). *DIR:* Lesley Selander. *A-PRO:* Louis

Gray. *SP:* Randall Faye. Based on the comic strip created by Fred Harman. *CAST:* Bill Elliott, Bobby (Robert) Blake, Alice Fleming, Francis McDonald, Don Costello, Sylvia Arslan, Bud Geary, Leon Tyler, Freddie Chapman, Henry Wills, Hank Bell, Robert Wilke, John James, Tom London, Dickie Dillon, Bobby Dillon, Raymond ZeBrack, Patsy May, Chris Wren, Horace B. Carpenter, Grace Cunard, Frederick Howard, "Thunder." *SYN:* Red Ryder (Elliott) tries to prevent a young man (James) from entering into a life of crime because of his outlaw father (McDonald). *NOTES:* The 7th entry in the "Red Ryder" feature series.

**299. The Great Train Robbery** (2/28/41) B&W 62 mins. (Drama-Crime). *DIR/A-PRO:* Joseph Kane. *SP:* Olive Cooper, Garnett Weston, Robert T. Shannon. *CAST:* Bob Steele, Claire Carleton, Milburn Stone, Helen MacKellar, Si Jenks, Monte Blue, Hal Taliaferro, George Guhl, Jay Novello, Yakima Canutt, Dick Wessel, Lew Kelly, Guy Usher, Jack Ingram, Philip Trent. *SYN:* A railroad detective (Steele) is sent to guard a shipment of gold and to try and stop his brother (Stone) from stealing it. *NOTES:* Remade in 1949 as *The Last Bandit*. Re-edited for TV at 54 mins.

**300. The Green Buddha** (7/9/55) B&W 62 mins. (Crime). *DIR:* John Lemont. *PRO:* William N. Boyle. *SP:* Paul Erickson. A Republic Presentation. *CAST:* Wayne Morris, Mary Germaine, Walter Rilla, Mary Merrall, Arnold Marle, Lloyd Lamble, Kenneth Griffith, Leslie Linder, George Woodbridge, Percy Herbert, Marcia Ashton, Victor Platt, Wolf Frees, Frank Atkinson, Bartlett Mullins, Dan Lester. *SYN:* An American charter pilot (Morris) finds himself mixed up with international thieves who have stolen a costly antique jade figure from an exhibit. *NOTES:* Released in Britain in 1954.

**301. Grissly's Millions** (1/16/45) B&W 71 mins. (Mystery). *DIR:* John English. *A-PRO:* Walter H. Goetz. *SP:* Muriel Roy Bolton. *CAST:* Paul Kelly, Virginia Grey, Don Douglas, Elisabeth Risdon, Robert Barrat, Clem Bevans, Eily Malyon, Adele Mara, Francis Pierlot, Addison Richards, Paul Fix, Byron Foulger, Joan Blair, Grady Sutton, Frank Jaquet, Will Wright, Louis Mason, Tom London. *SYN:* When an aged millionaire (Barrat) dies and leaves all of his wealth to his favorite granddaughter (Grey), the rest of the relatives plot to do away with her. *NOTES:* Re-edited for TV at 54 mins. Working title was *The Crowded Coffin*.

**302. Gun Lords of Stirrup Basin** (5/18/37) B&W 57 mins. (Western). *DIR:* Sam Newfield. *PRO:* A. W. Hackel. *SP:* George Plympton, Fred Myton. Story by Harry Olmstead. *CAST:* Bob Steele, Louise Stanley, Karl Hackett, Ernie Adams, Frank LaRue, Frank Ball, Steve Clark, Lew Meehan, Frank Ellis, Jim Corey, Budd Buster, Lloyd Ingraham, Jack Kirk, Horace Murphy, Milburn Morante, Bobby Nelson, Tex Palmer, Emma Tansey, Horace B. Carpenter, Herman Hack, Sherry Tansey, Chuck Baldra, Jack Evans, Rose Plummer. *SYN:* The son (Steele) of a cattleman and the daughter (Stanley) of a homesteader thwart the plans of a lawyer (Hackett) when he tries to turn cattlemen against homesteaders. [TV title: *Gunlords of Stirrup Basin*.]

**303. The Gun Ranger** (2/9/37) B&W 56 mins. (Western). *DIR:* Robert North

Bradbury. *PRO:* A. W. Hackel. *SP:* George Plympton. Story by Homer King Gordon. *CAST:* Bob Steele, Eleanor Stewart, John Merton, Ernie Adams, Earl Dwire, Budd Buster, Frank Ball, Horace Murphy, Lew Meehan, Hal Taliaferro, Horace B. Carpenter, Jack Kirk, George Morrell, Tex Palmer, Oscar Gahan, Archie Ricks, Clyde McClary. *SYN:* A lawman (Steele) goes after the murderer of a girl's (Stewart) father.

**304. Gunfire at Indian Gap** (12/13/57) B&W/Naturama 70 mins. (Western). *DIR:* Joseph Kane. *A-PRO:* Rudy Ralston. *SP:* Barry Shipman. *CAST:* Vera Ralston, Anthony George, George Macready, Barry Kelley, John Doucette, George Keymas, Chubby Johnson, Glenn Strange, Dan White, Steve Warren, Chuck Hicks, Sarah Selby. *SYN:* At a relay station, outlaws wait for a stagecoach carrying a shipment of gold.

**Gunlords of Stirrup Basin** *see* **Gun Lords of Stirrup Basin**

**305. Gunmen of Abilene** (2/6/50) B&W 60 mins. (Western). *DIR:* Fred C. Brannon. *A-PRO:* Gordon Kay. *SP:* M. Coates Webster. *CAST:* Allan ("Rocky") Lane, Eddy Waller, Roy Barcroft, Donna Hamilton, Peter Brocco, Selmer Jackson, Duncan Richardson, Arthur Walsh, Don C. Harvey, Donald Dillaway, George Chesebro, Steve Clark, Tom Steele, "Black Jack." *SYN:* A U.S. Marshal (Lane) goes undercover to stop outlaws from stealing a gold shipment.

**306. Guns and Guitars** (6/22/36) B&W 58 mins. (Western). *DIR:* Joseph Kane. *PRO:* Nat Levine. *SP:* Dorrell McGowan, Stuart McGowan. *CAST:* Gene Autry, Dorothy Dix, Smiley Burnette, Tom London, Charles King, J. P. McGowan, Earle Hodgins, Frankie Marvin, Eugene Jackson, Jack Rockwell, Ken Cooper, Tracy Layne, Wes Warner, Jim Corey, Frank Stravenger, Harrison Greene, Pascale Perry, Bob Burns, Jack Don, Jack Kirk, Audry Davis, Al Taylor, George Morrell, Sherry Tansey, Jack Evans, George Plues, Art Davis, Denver Dixon, "Champion." *SYN:* Framed for the murder of a local sheriff, Gene finds the guilty party and gets himself elected sheriff. *NOTES:* Re-edited for TV at 54 mins.

**307. Guns in the Dark** (5/13/37) B&W 56 mins. (Western). *DIR:* Sam Newfield. *PRO:* A. W. Hackel. *SP:* Charles Francis Royal. Story by E. B. Mann. *CAST:* Johnny Mack Brown, Claire Rochelle, Dick Curtis, Julian Madison, Ted Adams, Sherry Tansey, Slim Whitaker, Lew Meehan, Tex Palmer, Francis Walker, Frank Ellis, Budd Buster, Oscar Gahan, Merrill McCormick, Richard Cramer, Steve Clark, Syd Saylor, Jack C. Smith, Roger Williams, Jim Corey, Chick Hannon. *SYN:* A gunslinger (Brown) hangs up his guns when he mistakenly believes that he killed his best friend in a barroom brawl.

**308. Gunsmoke Ranch** (5/5/37) B&W 56 mins. (Western). *DIR:* Joseph Kane. *A-PRO:* Sol C. Siegel. *SP:* Oliver Drake. *CAST:* Robert Livingston, Ray ("Crash") Corrigan, Max Terhune, Kenneth Harlan, Julia Thayer, Sammy McKim, Burr Caruth, Allen Connor, Yakima Canutt, Horace B. Carpenter, Jane Keckley, Bob Walker, Jack Ingram, Loren Riebe, Jack Kirk, Vinegar Roan, Wes Warner, Jack Padjan, Fred "Snowflake" Toones, John Merton, Bob McKenzie, Edward Peil, Sr., Fred Burns, Oscar and Elmer (Ed Platt, Lou Foulton). *SYN:* The Three Mesquiteers (Livingston, Corrigan, Terhune) set out to stop a land thief who is trying to take advantage of refugees during a flood. *NOTES:* Re-edited for TV at 54 mins. The 6th entry in the "Three Mesquiteers" series.

**309. A Guy Could Change** (1/27/46) B&W 65 mins. (Drama).*DIR/A-PRO:* William K. Howard. *SP:* Al Martin. Story by F. Hugh Herbert. *CAST:* Allan ("Rocky") Lane, Jane Frazee, Twinkle Watts, Bobby (Robert) Blake, Wallace Ford, Adele Mara, Mary Treen, Joseph Crehan, Eddie Quillan, Gerald Mohr, George Chandler, William Haade, Betty Shaw. *SYN:* A man (Lane) is forced to bring up his daughter (Watts) alone, but his job keeps him busy, and he ignores her until he meets a woman (Frazee) who shames him into taking care of his daughter. *NOTES:* The final film of director William K. Howard—he retired after this film.

**310. Hands Across the Border** (1/5/44) B&W 73 mins. (Western). *DIR:* Joseph Kane. *A-PRO:* Harry Grey. *SP:* Bradford Ropes, J. Benton Cheney. *CAST:* Roy Rogers, Ruth Terry, Guinn "Big Boy" Williams, Onslow Stevens, Mary Treen, Joseph Crehan, Duncan Renaldo, Frederick Burton, LeRoy Mason, Larry Steers, Julian Rivero, Janet Martin, Betty Marion, Roy Barcroft, Kenne Duncan, Jack Kirk, Jack O'Shea, Curley Dresden, Bob Reeves, The Wiere Brothers, Bob Nolan and the Sons of the Pioneers, "Trigger." *SYN:* Roy helps a woman (Terry) and her father (Crehan) keep their contract to supply the government with horses by entering a race to win a government contract for them. *NOTES:* Re-edited for TV at 54 mins.

**311. Happy-Go-Lucky** (12/5/36) B&W 69 mins. (Musical-Drama). *DIR:* Aubrey Scotto. *PRO:* Nat Levine. *SP:* Raymond L. Schrock, Olive Cooper. Story by Eric Taylor, Wellyn Totman, Endre Bohem. *CAST:* Phil Regan, Evelyn Venable, Jed Prouty, William Newell, Jonathan Hale, Harlan Briggs, Stanley Andrews, Claude King, Carleton Young, Karl Hackett, Guy Kingsford, Howard Hickman, Willie Fung. *SYN:* A woman (Venable) searches for her missing husband (Regan) in Shanghai, and finds him in a nightclub as a tap-dancer suffering from amnesia.

**312. Harbor of Missing Men** (3/26/50) B&W 60 mins. (Crime). *DIR:* R. G. Springsteen. *A-PRO:* Sidney Picker. *SP:* John K. Butler. *CAST:* Richard Denning, Barbara Fuller, Steven Geray, Aline Towne, Percy Helton, George Zucco, Paul Marion, Ray Teal, Robert Osterloh, Fernanda Eliscu, Gregory Gay, Jimmie Kelly, Barbara Stanley, Neyle Morrow, Charles LaTorre. *SYN:* A fishing boat owner (Denning), who augments his income by using his boat for smuggling, becomes a hunted man when he is robbed of the money he was to deliver to his boss (Zucco).

**Harvest Days** (G.B. title) *see* **509. Mountain Rhythm**

**313. The Harvester** (4/18/36) B&W 72 mins. (Drama). *DIR:* Joseph Santley. *PRO:* Nat Levine. *SP:* Gertrude Orr, Homer Croy, Robert Lee Johnson, Elizabeth Meehan. Based on the book by Gene Stratton-Porter. *CAST:* Alice Brady, Russell Hardie, Ann Rutherford, Frank Craven, Cora Sue Collins, Emma Dunn, Eddie Nugent, Joyce Compton, Roy Atwell, Spencer Charters, Russell Simpson, Phyllis Fraser, Fern Emmett,

Burr Caruth, Lucille Ward, Harry Bowen, Grace Hayle. *SYN:* An Indiana farm mother (Brady) tries to marry her daughter (Compton) off to a farmer (Hardie).

**Hats Off to Rhythm** (G.B. title) *see* **Earl Caroll Sketchbook**

314. **Havana Rose** (9/15/51) B&W 77 mins. (Musical-Comedy). *DIR:* William Beaudine. *A-PRO:* Sidney Picker. *SP:* Charles E. Roberts, Jack Townley. *CAST:* Estelita Rodriguez, Bill Williams, Hugh Herbert, Florence Bates, Fortunio Bonanova, Leon Belasco, Nacho Galindo, Martin Garralaga, Rosa Turich, Tom Kennedy, Manuel Paris, Bob Easton, Felix and His Martiniques. *SYN:* An ambassador's daughter (Rodriguez) constantly messes up her father's attempts to secure a loan for his country.

315. **Headin' for God's Country** (8/26/43) B&W 78 mins. (War-Drama). *DIR:* William Morgan. *A-PRO:* Armand Schaefer. *SP:* Elizabeth Meehan, Houston Branch. Story by Houston Branch. *CAST:* William Lundigan, Virginia Dale, Harry Davenport, Harry Shannon, Addison Richards, J. Frank Hamilton, Eddie Acuff, Wade Crosby, Skelton Knaggs, John Bleifer, Charles Lung, Ernie Adams, Eddie Lee, James B. Leong, Anna Q. Nilsson, Eddy Waller. *SYN:* A stranger (Lundigan), in an isolated town in Alaska, is shunned by the townspeople and jailed for vagrancy. To get even, he plants a story in the newspaper that the U.S. is at war and the locals get ready for an attack. The story turns out to be true with the bombing of Pearl Harbor, and a local spy (Shannon) has signaled the Japanese to attack the town, and the townspeople, ready for an attack, defeat them. *NOTES:* "God's country" is the tag name for Alaska.

316. **Headline Hunters** (9/15/55) B&W 70 mins. (Drama). *DIR:* William Witney. *A-PRO:* William J. O'Sullivan. *SP:* Frederic Louis Fox, John K. Butler. *CAST:* Rod Cameron, Julie Bishop, Ben Cooper, Raymond Greenleaf, Chubby Johnson, John Warburton, Nacho Galindo, Virginia Carroll, Howard Wright, Stuart Randall, Edward Colmans, Joe Besser. *SYN:* A cub reporter (Cooper) joins a big city paper to be near his idol (Cameron), who has now taken to drink and doesn't care about his job. Eager to take assignments, he gets into trouble when he becomes involved with a crime ring and gets framed for murder. He joins forces with the older reporter to break up the crime ring. *NOTES:* A remake of Republic's 1940 film, *Behind the News*.

317. **Heart of the Golden West** (11/16/42) B&W 65 mins. (Western). *DIR/A-PRO:* Joseph Kane. *SP:* Earl Felton. *CAST:* Roy Rogers, Smiley Burnette, George "Gabby" Hayes, Ruth Terry, Walter Catlett, Paul Harvey, Edmund MacDonald, Leigh Whipper, William Haade, Hal Taliaferro, Cactus Mack, Hank Bell, Fred Burns, Carl Mathews, Horace B. Carpenter, Frank McCarroll, Art Dillard, Bob Nolan and the Sons of the Pioneers, The Hall Johnson Choir, "Trigger." *SYN:* When a trucking company charges too much to haul cattle, Roy convinces the ranchers to ship their cattle by steamboat. *NOTES:* Re-edited for TV at 54 mins.

318. **Heart of the Rio Grande** (3/11/42) B&W 70 mins. (Western). *DIR:* William Morgan. *A-PRO:* Harry Grey.

SP: Lillie Hayward, Winston Miller. Story by Newlin B. Wildes. CAST: Gene Autry, Smiley Burnette, Fay McKenzie, Edith Fellows, Pierre Watkin, Joe Strauch, Jr., William Haade, Sarah Padden, Jean Porter, Milton Kibbee, Edmund Cobb, Budd Buster, Frank Mills, Howard Mitchell, Allan Wood, Nora Lane, Mady Lawrence, Buck Woods, Harry Depp, George Porter, Frankie Marvin, Jeannie Hebers, Katherine Frye, Jane Graham, Patsy Fay Northrup, Jan Lester, Gloria Gardner, Gladys Gardner, Jimmy Wakely Trio (Jimmy Wakely, Johnny Bond, Dick Rinehart), "Champion." SYN: Gene helps a spoiled girl (McKenzie) turn her ranch into a dude ranch. NOTES: Re-edited for TV at 54 mins.

**319. Heart of the Rockies** (9/6/37) B&W 56 mins. (Western). DIR: Joseph Kane. A-PRO: Sol C. Siegel. SP: Jack Natteford, Oliver Drake. Story by Bernard McConville. Based on characters created by William Colt MacDonald. CAST: Robert Livingston, Ray ("Crash") Corrigan, Max Terhune, Lynn Roberts, Sammy McKim, J. P. McGowan, Yakima Canutt, Hal Taliaferro, George Simmons, Maston Williams, Guy Wilkerson, Ranny Weeks, George Pearce, Nelson McDowell, Herman's Mountaineers. SYN: The Three Mesquiteers (Livingston, Corrigan, Terhune) learn that a mountain family is behind the cattle rustling and illegal game trapping that has been going on and they set out to bring them to justice. NOTES: The 9th entry in the "Three Mesquiteers" series and the first film of the series to be directed by Joseph Kane.

**320. Heart of the Rockies** (3/30/51) B&W 67 mins. (Western). DIR: William Witney. A-PRO: Edward J. White. SP: Eric Taylor. CAST: Roy Rogers, Penny Edwards, Gordon Jones, Ralph Morgan, Fred Graham, Mira McKinney, Dee "Buzzy" Henry, William Gould, Pepe Hern, Rand Brooks, Foy Willing and the Riders of the Purple Sage, "Trigger," "Bullet." SYN: A rancher (Morgan) tries to stop Roy from putting a highway across his land because he fears that the authorities are going to discover the unscrupulous manner in which he acquired his property.

**321. Heart of Virginia** (4/25/48) B&W 60 mins. (Sports). DIR: R. G. Springsteen. A-PRO: Sidney Picker. SP: Jerry Sackheim, John K. Butler. CAST: Janet Martin, Robert Lowery, Frankie Darro, Paul Hurst, Sam McDaniel, Tom Chatterton, Bennie Bartlett, Glenn Vernon, Edmund Cobb. SYN: A jockey (Darro) fears the racetrack because he feels responsible for the death of a fellow rider during a race.

**322. Hearts in Bondage** (5/26/36) B&W 72 mins. (War-Drama). DIR: Lew Ayres. PRO: Nat Levine. SP: Bernard Schubert, Olive Cooper, Karl Brown. Story by Wallace MacDonald. CAST: James Dunn, Mae Clarke, David Manners, Charlotte Henry, Henry B. Walthall, Fritz Leiber, George Irving, Irving Pichel, J. M. Kerrigan, Frank McGlynn, Sr., Ben Alexander, Oscar Apfel, Clay Clement, Edward Gargan, Russell Hicks, George "Gabby" Hayes, Douglas Wood, Bodil Rosing, Erville Alderson, John Hyams, Etta McDaniel, Warner Richmond, Lloyd Ingraham, Lane Chandler, Hooper Atchley, Smiley Burnette, Eugene Jackson, Earl Aby, Henry Roquemore, Frankie Marvin, Arthur Wanzer, Helen Seamon, Cecil Watson, Maurice Brierre, Clinton Rosemond,

Pat Flaherty. SYN: The Civil War battle between the ships Monitor and Merrimac serves as the backdrop for the romance between a naval hero (Dunn) and his sweetheart (Clarke). NOTES: This was the only film solely directed by Lew Ayres.

323. **Heldorado** (12/15/46) B&W 70 mins. (Western). DIR: William Witney. A-PRO: Edward J. White. SP: Gerald Geraghty, Julian Zimet. CAST: Roy Rogers, George "Gabby" Hayes, Dale Evans, Paul Harvey, Barry Mitchell (Brad Dexter), John Bagni, John Phillips, James Taggart, Rex Lease, Steve Darrell, Doye O'Dell, LeRoy Mason, Charles Williams, Eddie Acuff, Clayton Moore, Virginia Carroll, Keith Richards, Victor Potel, Eddie Kane, George Chandler, Emmett Vogan, George "Shug" Fisher, Joaquin Bascon, Jack Sparks, Walter Lawrence, Phil Arnold, Sam Ash, Frank Henry, Tex Terry, Bob Nolan and the Sons of the Pioneers, "Trigger." SYN: During Las Vegas' Helldorado parade and rodeo, a ranger (Rogers) works with the sheriff to break up a gang of racketeers trying to pass money on which taxes have not been paid. NOTES: Re-edited for TV at 54 mins. [Alternate title: *Helldorado*.]

324. **Hell Canyon Outlaws** (10/6/57) B&W 72 mins. (Western). DIR: Paul Landres. PRO: Thomas F. Woods. SP: Allan Kaufman, Max Glandbard. A Zukor Production. A Republic Presentation. CAST: Dale Robertson, Brian Keith, Rossana Rory, Dick Kallman, Don Megowan, Mike Lane, Buddy Baer, Charles Fredericks, Alexander Lockwood, James Nusser, James Maloney, William Pullen, George Ross, George Pembroke, Vincent Padula, Tom Hubbard. SYN: A sheriff (Robertson) seeks vengeance against the outlaws who have been instrumental in seeing him lose his job and taken over the town. [British title: *The Tall Trouble*.]

325. **Hell Ship Mutiny** (12/6/57) B&W 66 mins. (Adventure). DIR: Lee Sholem, Elmo Williams. E-PRO: Jon Hall. A-PRO: George Bilson. SP: DeVallon Scott, Wells Root. A Lovina Production. A Republic Presentation. CAST: Jon Hall, John Carradine, Peter Lorre, Roberta Haynes, Mike Mazurki, Charles Mauu, Stanley Adams, Danny Richards, Jr., Felix Locher, Peter Coe, Michael Barrett, Salvador Bagues, "Salty" the Chimp. SYN: A sea captain (Hall) helps a South Sea island princess (Haynes) rid her domain of two smugglers (Carradine, Mazurki) who have been forcing the natives to dive for pearls against their will. NOTES: Executive producer Hall cast his father, Felix Locher, as the island chief Parea, thus allowing him to make his film debut at age 75.

**Helldorado** *see* **Heldorado**

326. **Hellfire** (6/26/49) Trucolor 90 mins. (Western). DIR: R. G. Springsteen. A-PRO: William J. O'Sullivan. E-PRO/SP: Dorrell McGowan, Stuart McGowan. An Elliott-McGowan Production. CAST: Bill Elliott, Marie Windsor, Forrest Tucker, Jim Davis, H. B. Warner, Paul Fix, Grant Withers, Emory Parnell, Esther Howard, Jody Gilbert, Louis R. Faust, Harry Woods, Denver Pyle, Trevor Bardette, Dewey Robinson, Harry Tyler, Roy Barcroft, Hank Worden, Kenneth MacDonald, Paula Hill, Eva Novak, Richard Alexander, Edward Keane, Elizabeth Marshall, Keenan Elliott, Olin Howlin, Stanley Price. SYN: A gambler (Elliott), who

turns to preaching when a minister (Warner) saves his life, promises to build him a church without using violence, and tries to convince an outlaw (Windsor) to give herself up so he can collect the $5,000 reward on her to build the church.

**327. Hell's Crossroads** (3/8/57) Trucolor/Naturama 73 mins. (Western). *DIR:* Franklin Adreon. *PRO:* Rudy Ralston. *A-PRO:* Michael Baird. *SP:* John K. Butler, Barry Shipman. Story by John K. Butler. *CAST:* Stephen McNally, Peggie Castle, Robert Vaughn, Barton MacLane, Harry Shannon, Henry Brandon, Douglas Kennedy, Grant Withers, Myron Healey, Frank Wilcox, Jean Howell, Morris Ankrum. *SYN:* A woman (Castle) convinces the governor to pardon her lover (McNally) and brother (Vaughn), who are members of the James gang, if Jesse James is brought in dead or alive, and it is her brother, Bob Ford, who kills Jesse. *NOTES:* After several minor films, this was the first starring big-screen role for TV star Vaughn.

**328. Hell's Half Acre** (6/1/54) B&W 90 mins. (Mystery). *DIR/A-PRO:* John H. Auer. *SP:* Steve Fisher. *CAST:* Wendell Corey, Evelyn Keyes, Elsa Lanchester, Marie Windsor, Nancy Gates, Leonard Strong, Jesse White, Keye Luke, Philip Ahn, Robert Shield, Clair Widenaar, Robert Costa. *SYN:* In Hawaii, a gangster (Corey) gives his life so that his wife (Keyes), who believed he died at Pearl Harbor, will be free to remarry and his son will still believe his dad died at Pearl Harbor, a hero.

**329. Hell's Outpost** (12/15/54) B&W 90 mins. (Western-Drama). *DIR/A-*

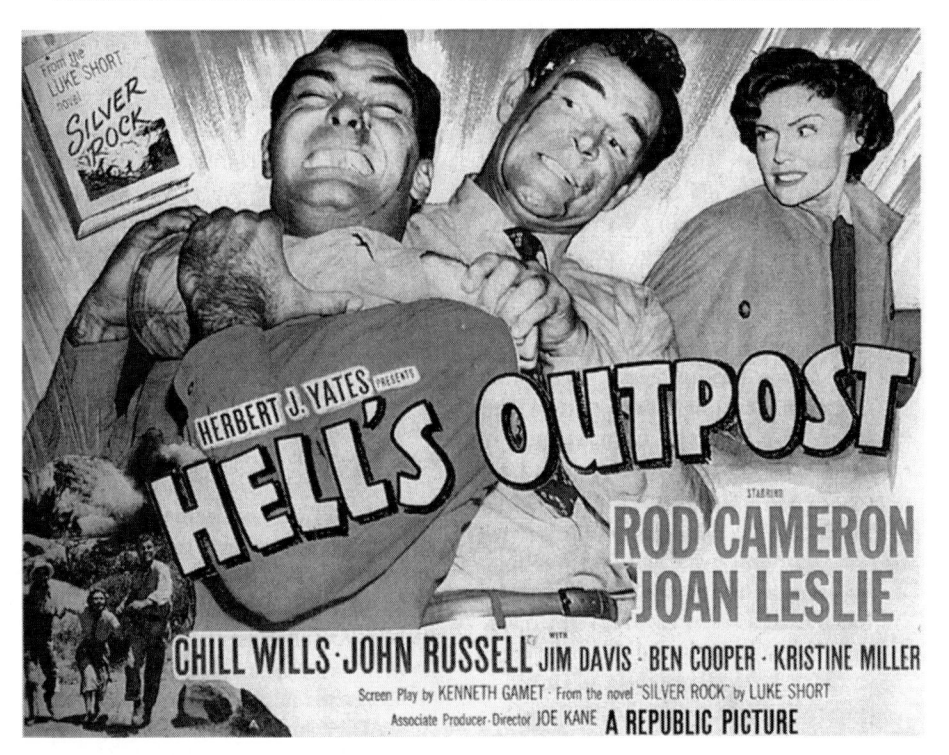

*PRO:* Joseph Kane. *SP:* Kenneth Gamet. Based on *Silver Rock* by Luke Short. *CAST:* Rod Cameron, Joan Leslie, John Russell, Chill Wills, Jim Davis, Kristine Miller, Ben Cooper, Taylor Holmes, Barton MacLane, Ruth Lee, Arthur Q. Bryan, Oliver Blake, Harry Woods, Dee "Buzzy" Henry, John Dierkes, Sue England, Almira Sessions, Elizabeth Slifer, Don Kennedy, Paul Stader, George Dockstader, Don Brodie, Alan Bridge, Edward Clark, Gil Harman, James Lilburn, Ruth Brennan. *SYN:* A Korean War vet (Cameron), works himself into part-ownership of a mine, tries to rebuild it, but is opposed by a crooked banker (Russell) who wants the mine for himself.

**330. Here Comes Elmer** (11/15/43) B&W 74 mins. (Musical-Comedy) *DIR:* Joseph Santley. *A-PRO:* Armand Schaefer. *SP:* Jack Townley, Stanley Davis. *CAST:* Al Pearce, Dale Evans, Frank Albertson, Gloria Stuart, Wally Vernon, Nick Cochrane, Will Wright, Thurston Hall, Ben Welden, Chester Clute, Luis Alberni, Tom Kennedy, Artie Auerbach, William Comstock, Pinky Tomlin, Wendell Niles, Arlene Harris, The Sportsmen, The King Cole Trio, Jan Garber and His Orchestra. *SYN:* When a radio star (Pearce) removes a singer (Harris) from his show, her father (Wright) quits sponsoring them and they have to find a new sponsor. *NOTES:* Al Pearce plays a dual role in this film. [British title: *Hitch Hike to Happiness.*]

**The Hero of Pine Ridge** (G.B. title) *see* **Yodelin' Kid from Pine Ridge**

**331. Heroes of the Hills** (7/29/38) B&W 55 mins. (Western). *DIR:* George Sherman. *A-PRO:* William Berke. *SP:*

Betty Burbridge, Stanley Roberts. Story by Jack Natteford, Stanley Roberts. Based on characters created by William Colt MacDonald. CAST: Robert Livingston, Ray ("Crash") Corrigan, Max Terhune, Priscilla Lawson, LeRoy Mason, James Eagles, Roy Barcroft, Barry Hayes, Carleton Young, Forrest Taylor, John P. Wade, Maston Williams, John Beach, Jerry Frank, Roger Williams, Kit Guard, Jack Kirk, Curley Dresden. SYN: The Three Mesquiteers (Livingston, Corrigan, Terhune) decide to turn their ranch into a prison farm because of their belief in prison reform, but are opposed by a contractor (Barcroft) who thinks a prison should be built instead. NOTES: This was Priscilla Lawson's only Republic feature. She is best remembered as Princess Aura in Universal's *Flash Gordon* serial. The 16th entry in the "Three Mesquiteers" series.

**332. Heroes of the Saddle** (1/12/40) B&W 59 mins. (Western). DIR: William Witney. A-PRO: Harry Grey. SP: Jack Natteford. Based on characters created by William Colt MacDonald. CAST: Robert Livingston, Raymond Hatton, Duncan Renaldo, Patsy Lee Parsons, Loretta Weaver, Byron Foulger, William Royle, Vince Barnett, Jack Roper, Reed Howes, Ethel May Halls, Al Taylor, Patsy Carmichael, Kermit Maynard, Tom Hanlon, Tex Terry, Douglas Deems, Darwood Kaye, Matt McHugh, Harrison Greene, Chief John Big Tree. SYN: The Three Mesquiteers (Livingston, Renaldo, Hatton) try to adopt the orphaned daughter (Parsons) of an old friend, but are met by miles of red tape, and they find that the orphanage is being used by a corrupt political machine. NOTES: The 27th entry in the "Three Mesquiteers" series.

**333. Hi, Neighbor!** (7/27/42) B&W 72 mins. (Comedy). DIR: Charles Lamont. A-PRO: Armand Schaefer. SP: Dorrell McGowan, Stuart McGowan. CAST: Jean Parker, John Archer, Janet Beecher, Marilyn Hare, Bill Shirley, Pauline Drake, Fred Sherman, Vera Vague, Don Wilson, Harry Cheshire, Roy Acuff and His Smoky Mountain Boys, Lillian Randolph, Lulu Belle and Scotty. SYN: The students of a small college, threatened with bankruptcy, decide to put on a show using country western stars of the time to save the college.

**334. Hi-Yo-Silver** (4/10/40) B&W 69 mins. (Western). CAST: Raymond Hatton, Dick Jones. SYN: Feature version of the 15 chapter serial, *The Lone Ranger*. NOTES: Republic added Raymond Hatton's narration to piece together the reels by telling the story to young Dick Jones. These two were not in the original serial. See **987. The Lone Ranger**.

**335. Hidden Guns** (1/30/56) B&W 66 mins. (Western). DIR: Albert C. Gannaway. PRO: Albert C. Gannaway, C. J. Ver Halen, Jr. SP: Albert C. Gannaway, Sam Roeca. An Albert C. Gannaway Production. A Republic Presentation. CAST: Bruce Bennett, Richard Arlen, John Carradine, Faron Young, Lloyd Corrigan, Angie Dickinson, Damian O'Flynn, Irving Bacon, Tom Hubbard, Ron Kennedy, Bill Ward, Raymond L. Morgan, Edmund Cobb, Ben Welden, Guinn "Big Boy" Williams, Gordon Terry, Michael Darrin, Bill Coontz. SYN: A sheriff (Arlen) and his son (Young) set out to reform a community run by a gambler (Bennett) and his henchmen, but when the father is gunned down by the hired killers, it is left up to the son to clean the town. *NOTES:* Erich Von Stroheim, Jr., the son of the great director, served as assistant director. An unusual aspect of this film is the use of a choral group to comment on and develop the action.

**336. Hidden Homicide** (2/25/59) B&W 70 mins. (Mystery). *DIR:* Tony Young. *PRO:* Derek Winn. *SP:* Tony Young, Bill Luckwell. Based on *Murder at Shinglestrand* by Paul Capon. A Rank/Bill & Michael Luckwell Production. A Republic Presentation. *CAST:* Griffith Jones, James Kenney, Patricia Laffan, Bruce Seton, Maya Koumani, Robert Raglan, Richard Shaw, Charles Farrell, Peter Carver, Danny Green, John Moore, David Chivers, Norman Wynne, Frank Hawkins, Jan Wilson, Joe Wadham, John Watson. *SYN:* A lady hitchhiker (Laffan) helps a novelist (Jones) search for the murderer of his uncle. *NOTES:* Released in Britain in January, 1959.

**337. Hidden Valley Outlaws** (4/2/44) B&W 56 mins. (Western). *DIR:* Howard Bretherton. *A-PRO:* Louis Gray. *SP:* John K. Butler, Bob Williams. Story by John K. Butler. *CAST:* Bill Elliott, George "Gabby" Hayes, Anne Jeffreys, Roy Barcroft, Kenne Duncan, John James, Charles Miller, Fred "Snowflake" Toones, Budd Buster, Tom London, LeRoy Mason, Earle Hodgins, Yakima Canutt, Jack Kirk, Tom Steele, Bud Geary, Frank McCarroll, Edward Cassidy, Robert Wilke, Charles Morton, Cactus Mack, Forbes Murray, Frank O'Connor, "Sonny." *SYN:* Bill and "Gabby" set out to stop an unscrupulous land grabber and former outlaw (Barcroft) and his chief henchman, "The Whistler" (Mason), from swindling the local ranchers out of their land. *NOTES:* The last of Bill Elliott's westerns in which he played himself.

**338. Hideout** (3/8/49) B&W 61 mins. (Crime). *DIR:* Philip Ford. *A-PRO:* Sidney Picker. *SP:* John K. Butler. Based on the *Saturday Evening Post* story "Fourteen Hours from Chi" by William Porter. *CAST:* Adrian Booth, Lloyd Bridges, Ray Collins, Sheila Ryan, Alan Carney, Jeff Corey, Fletcher Chandler, Don Beddoe, Charles Halton, Emory Parnell, Nana Bryant, Paul E. Burns, Douglas Evans, "Smoki" Whitfield. *SYN:* When a diamond cutter (Halton) is found murdered, a city attorney (Bridges) sets out to solve the crime and learns that the town's leading citizen is a con man (Collins) who doublecrossed his partners (Corey, Carney) and settled in town.

**339. The Higgins Family** (3/29/38) B&W 65 mins. (Comedy). *DIR:* Gus Meins. *A-PRO:* Sol C. Siegel. *SP:* Paul Gerard Smith, Jack Townley. Story by Richard English. *CAST:* James Gleason, Lucille Gleason, Russell Gleason, Lynn Roberts, Harry Davenport, William Bakewell, Paul Harvey, Wallis Clark, Sally Payne, Richard Tucker, Doreen McKay, Gay Seabrook, Richard Cramer, Franklin Parker. *SYN:* A bored husband, Joe Higgins, (James Gleason), involved in advertising, has to put up with wife's, Lil Higgins, (Lucille Gleason) radio aspirations which puts a strain on their marriage. *NOTES:* Republic wanted to create a "family" series of pictures like MGM's "Hardy Family" series and Fox's "Jones Family" series. The "Higgins Family" series was to be Republic's answer and this was their 1st entry in the series.

**High and Happy** *see* **Hit Parade of 1947**

340. **Hills of Oklahoma** (6/1/50) B&W 67 mins. (Western). *DIR:* R. G. Springsteen. *A-PRO:* Franklin Adreon. *SP:* Olive Cooper, Victor Arthur. Story by Olive Cooper. *CAST:* Rex Allen, Elisabeth Fraser, Elisabeth Risdon, Robert Karnes, Fuzzy Knight, Roscoe Ates, Robert Emmett Keane, Trevor Bardette, Lee Phelps, Edmund Cobb, Rex Lease, Ted Adams, Lane Bradford, Michael Carr, Johnny Downs, "Koko." *SYN:* The leader of a cattlemen's association (Allen) has to deal with rustlers as he drives his cattle to market. *NOTES:* A reworking of Republic's 1942 feature, *Call of the Canyon*.

341. **The Hit Parade** (4/26/37) B&W 77 mins. (Musical). *DIR:* Gus Meins. *PRO:* Nat Levine. *A-PRO:* Colbert Clark. *SP:* Bradford Ropes, Samuel Ornitz. Story by Bradford Ropes. *CAST:* Frances Langford, Phil Regan, Louise Henry, Pert Kelton, Edward Brophy, Max Terhune, Inez Courtney, Monroe Owsley, Pierre Watkin, Stanley Fields, Johnny Arthur, J. Farrell MacDonald, William Demarest, George Givot, Sammy White, Paul Garner, Sam Wolfe, Richard Hakins, Yvonne Manoff, Mildred Winston, Barbara Johnston, Ed Thorgersen, Carl Hoff and Band, Duke Ellington and His Orchestra, Eddie Duchin Orchestra, Molasses and January, Pick and Pat, Al Pearce and His Gang, Oscar and Elmer (Ed Platt, Lou Fulton), The Voice of Experience. *SYN:* An agent (Regan) is determined to promote a new singing sensation (Langford) to spite a rich society girl (Henry), because she became a success and abandoned him, only to find out that his new singing sensation is being pursued by a parole officer. *NOTES:* Sequels followed in 1940, 1943, 1947, and 1950. The "Hit Parade" series was Republic's answer to Paramount's "Big Broadcast" series. [Alternate title: *I'll Reach for a Star*.]

342. **Hit Parade of 1941** (10/15/40) B&W 83 mins. (Musical). *DIR:* John H. Auer. *A-PRO:* Sol C. Siegel. *SP:* Bradford Ropes, F. Hugh Herbert, Maurice Leo. Additional sequences by Sid Kuller, Ray Golden. *CAST:* Kenny Baker, Frances Langford, Hugh Herbert, Mary Boland, Ann Miller, Patsy Kelly, Phil Silvers, Sterling Holloway, Donald MacBride, Barnett Parker, Franklin Pangborn, Six Hits and a Miss, Borrah Minevitch and His Harmonica Rascals. *SYN:* A radio station owner (Baker), seeking sponsors, agrees to use the no-talent daughter (Miller) of a department store owner (Boland) when she agrees to be a sponsor. The daughter cannot carry a tune and this necessitates using a songstress (Langford) to overdub her voice, and soon complications follow. *NOTES:* The film debut of Phil Silvers. Academy Award Nominee — Best Score, Best Song. [Re-release title: *Romance and Rhythm*.]

343. **Hit Parade of 1943** (3/26/43) B&W 90 mins. (Musical). *DIR:* Albert S. Rogell. *A-PRO:* Albert J. Cohen. *SP:* Frank Gill, Jr. Additional dialogue by Frances Hyland. *CAST:* John Carroll, Susan Hayward, Gail Patrick, Eve Arden, Melville Cooper, Walter Catlett, Mary Treen, Tom Kennedy, Astrid Allwyn, Tim Ryan, Jack Williams, The Harlem Sandman, Dorothy Dandridge, Pops and Louie, The Music Maids, 3 Cheers, Chinita, Golden Gate Quartet, Freddy Martin and His Orchestra, Count Basie and His Orchestra, Ray McKinley and Orchestra. *SYN:* A washed-up songwriter (Carroll), steals a tune written by another songwriter

(Hayward). She confronts him with the theft and, when he begs her to ghost-write for him, she agrees, hoping to expose his deceit when he becomes famous. NOTES: The final film of Astrid Allwyn — she retired after this film. AAN — Best Score, Beat Song. [Re-release title: *Change of Heart*.]

**344. Hit Parade of 1947** (3/22/47) B&W 90 mins. (Musical). *DIR/A-PRO:* Frank McDonald. *SP:* Mary Loos. Story by Parke Levy. *CAST:* Eddie Albert, Constance Moore, Joan Edwards, Gil Lamb, Bill Goodwin, William Frawley, Richard Lane, Frank Fenton, Ralph Sanford, Frank Scannell, Knox Manning, Del Sharbutt, Albert Ruiz, Harland Tucker, Chester Clute, Woody Herman and His Orchestra, *GUEST STARS:* Bob Nolan and the Sons of the Pioneers, Roy Rogers, and "Trigger." *SYN:* A songwriter (Albert) and a trio of other performers (Moore, Edwards, and Lamb) form a musical nightclub act calling themselves "The Tune Toppers" but, when they are signed to a Hollywood contract, they learn that it was only one of them (Moore) that Hollywood wanted, and the other members go their separate ways. *NOTES:* The film debut of Joan Edwards. The final film of Constance Moore — she retired after this film. [TV title: *High and Happy*]

**345. Hit Parade of 1951** (10/15/50) B&W 85 mins. (Musical). *DIR/A-PRO:* John H. Auer. *SP:* Elizabeth Reinhardt, Aubrey Wiseberg, Lawrence Kimble. Story by Aubrey Wiseberg. *CAST:* John Carroll, Marie McDonald, Estelita Rodriguez, Frank Fontaine, Grant Withers, Mikhail Rasumny, Paul Cavanagh, Edward Gargan, Gus Schilling, Rose Rosett, Wade Crosby, Duke York, Al Murphy, Steve Flagg (Michael St. Angel), Firehouse Five Plus Two, Bobby Ramos Band. *SYN:* A consistant losing gambler (Carroll) meets his exact double (Carroll), a singer, and switches places with him bringing chaos and confusion. *NOTES:* John Carroll plays a dual role in this film. This was the last entry in Republic's five-picture "Hit Parade" series, and the first since 1947.

**346. Hit the Saddle** (3/3/37) B&W 61 mins. (Western). *DIR:* Mack V. Wright. *PRO:* Nat Levine. *SP:* Oliver Drake. Story by Oliver Drake, Maurice Geraghty. Based on characters created by William Colt MacDonald. *CAST:* Robert Livingston, Ray ("Crash") Corrigan, Max Terhune, Rita Cansino (Rita Hayworth), J. P. McGowan, Edward Cassidy, Sammy McKim, Yakima Canutt, Harry Tenbrook, Robert Smith, Ed Bowland, George Plues, Jack Kirk, Russ Powell, Bob Burns, Allan Cavan, George Morrell, Wally West, Budd Buster, Kernan Cripps, "Volcano," the Stallion Horse. *SYN:* The Three Mesquiteers (Livingston, Corrigan, Terhune) go after a gang of outlaws rustling wild horses in a federally protected area, and Stony (Livingston) falls for a saloon singer (Cansino). *NOTES:* Nineteen-year-old Rita Hayworth, billed as Rita Cansino, makes an early screen appearance as a saloon songstress. At the end of the film, she announces that she is going to Hollywood to become a movie star (and she did!). Re-edited for TV at 54 mins. The 5th entry in the "Three Mesquiteers" series.

**347. Hitch Hike Lady** (1/3/36) B&W 77 mins. (Drama). *DIR:* Aubrey Scotto. *PRO:* Nat Levine. *SP:* Gordon Rigby, Lester Cole. Story by Wallace MacDonald. *CAST:* Alison Skipworth, Mae

Clarke, Arthur Treacher, James Ellison, Warren Hymer, Beryl Mercer, J. Farrell MacDonald, Lionel Belmore, Otis Harlan, Charles Wilson, Wilbur Mack, Clay Clement, George "Gabby" Hayes, Dell Henderson, Harold Waldridge, Christian Rub. *SYN:* An elderly English housekeeper (Skipworth) saves her hard-earned money to go to the U.S. to visit her son, whom she believes to be doing well, but is actually a prisoner in San Quentin. [British title: *Eventful Journey.*]

**Hitch Hike to Happiness** (G.B. title) *see* **Here Comes Elmer**

**348. Hitchhike to Happiness** (7/16/45) B&W 71 mins. (Musical). *DIR:* Joseph Santley. *A-PRO:* Donald H. Brown. *SP:* Jack Townley. Story by Manuel Seff, Jerry Horwin. *CAST:* Al Pearce, Dale Evans, Brad Taylor, William Frawley, Jerome Cowan, William Trenk, Arlene Harris, Joyce Compton, Maude Eburne, Irving Bacon, Lynn Romer, Jeanne Romer. *SYN:* A would-be playwright (Pearce), who takes a job as a waiter in a small New York City restaurant frequented by show biz folk in hopes of getting his big break, gets to show his play to a Hungarian producer (Trenk) which turns out to be a hit. *NOTES:* Academy Award Nominee — Best Score.

**Hitting the Headlines** (G.B. title) *see* **Yokel Boy**

**349. Hollywood Stadium Mystery** (2/21/38) B&W 66 mins. (Mystery). *DIR:* David Howard. *A-PRO:* Armand Schaefer. *SP:* Stuart Palmer, Dorrell McGowan, Stuart McGowan. Story by Stuart Palmer. *CAST:* Neil Hamilton, Evelyn Venable, Jimmy Wallington, Barbara Pepper, Lucien Littlefield, Lynn Roberts, Charles Williams, James Spottswood, Reed Hadley, Robert E. Homans, William Haade, Pat Flaherty, Dan Tobey, Smiley Burnette, Al Bayne. *SYN:* A fighter is mysteriously killed before his big match with the champ and the D.A. (Hamilton) is assigned to investigate the case. [Alternate title: *The Stadium Murders.*]

**Home in Oklahoma** *see* **The Big Show**

**350. Home in Oklahoma** (11/8/46) B&W 72 mins. (Western). *DIR:* William Witney. *A-PRO:* Edward J. White. *SP:* Gerald Geraghty. *CAST:* Roy Rogers, George "Gabby" Hayes, Dale Evans, Carol Hughes, George Meeker, Lanny Rees, Ruby Dandridge, George Lloyd, Arthur Space, Frank Reicher, George Carleton, John Walsh, Bob Nolan and the Sons of the Pioneers, "Trigger." *SYN:* An editor of a small-town newspaper (Rogers) and city reporter (Evans) search for the killer of a local rancher. *NOTES:* Re-edited for TV at 54 mins.

**351. Home in Wyomin'** (4/29/42) B&W 67 mins. (Western). *DIR:* William Morgan. *A-PRO:* Harry Grey. *SP:* Robert Tasker, M. Coates Webster. Story by Stuart Palmer. *CAST:* Gene Autry, Smiley Burnette, Fay McKenzie, Olin Howlin, Chick Chandler, Joe Strauch, Jr., Forrest Taylor, James Seay, George Douglas, Charles Lane, Hal Price, Bud Geary, Ken Cooper, Jean Porter, James H. McNamara, Kermit Maynard, Roy Butler, William Benedict, Cyril Ring, Spade Cooley, Ted Mapes, Jack Kirk, William Kellogg (Bruce Kellogg), Betty Farrington, Rex Lease, Tom Hanlon, Lee Shumway,

"Champion." *SYN:* Gene goes back to Wyoming to help a friend who is having financial problems with his rodeo. *NOTES:* Re-edited for TV at 54 mins.

**352. Home on the Prairie** (2/3/39) B&W 58 mins. (Western). *DIR:* Jack Townley. *A-PRO:* Harry Grey. *SP:* Charles Arthur Powell, Paul Franklin. *CAST:* Gene Autry, Smiley Burnette, June Storey, George Cleveland, Jack Mulhall, Walter Miller, Gordon Hart, Hal Price, Earle Hodgins, Ethan Laidlaw, John Beach, Jack Ingram, Bob Woodward, Olin Francis, Fred Burns, Dorothy Vernon, Chuck Baldra, Art Dillard, Burr Caruth, Sherven Brothers' Rodeoliers, "Champion." *SYN:* A border inspector (Autry), whose job is to make sure no diseased animals enter the U.S., goes after two unscrupulous cattlemen (Miller, Hart) who try to bring in their infected cattle and put the blame for the infection on an innocent rancher (Storey). *NOTES:* Re-edited for TV at 54 mins. [Alternate title: *Ridin' the Range.*]

**353. Home on the Range** (4/18/46) Magnacolor 55 mins. (Western). *DIR:* R. G. Springsteen. *A-PRO:* Louis Gray. *SP:* Betty Burbridge. Story by Betty Burbridge, Bernard McConville. *CAST:* Monte Hale, Adrian Booth, Tom Chatterton, Bobby (Robert) Blake, LeRoy Mason, Roy Barcroft, Kenne Duncan, Budd Buster, Jack Kirk, John Hamilton, Bob Nolan and the Sons of the Pioneers. *SYN:* A rancher (Hale) wants to set up a preservation area to protect the wild creatures, but runs into opposition from the local ranchers before he is successful. *NOTES:* Monte Hale's first series western.

**354. Homesteaders of Paradise Valley** (4/1/47) B&W 59 mins. (Western). *DIR:* R. G. Springsteen. *A-PRO:* Sidney Picker. *SP:* Earle Snell. Based on the comic strip created by Fred Harman. *CAST:* Allan ("Rocky") Lane, Bobby (Robert) Blake, Martha Wentworth, Ann E. Todd, Gene Stutenroth (Roth), John James, Mauritz Hugo, Emmett Vogan, Milton Kibbee, Tom London, Edythe Elliott, George Chesebro, Edward Cassidy, Jack Kirk, Herman Hack. *SYN:* Red Ryder (Lane) and Little Beaver (Blake) lend a hand to a group of homesteaders who are constructing a dam in Paradise Valley. *NOTES:* Re-edited for TV at 54 mins. The 20th entry in the "Red Ryder" feature series.

**355. Homicide for Three** (12/8/48) B&W 60 mins. (Thriller). *DIR:* George Blair. *A-PRO:* Stephen Auer. *SP:* Bradbury Foote, Albert DeMond. Based on *Puzzle for Puppets* by Patrick Quentin. *CAST:* Audrey Long, Warren Douglas, Grant Withers, Lloyd Corrigan, Stephanie Bachelor, George Lynn, Tala Birell, Benny Baker, Joseph Crehan, Sid Tomack, Dick Elliott, Eddie Dunn, John Newland, Billy Curtis, Patsy Moran. *SYN:* A newlywed couple (Douglas, Long) gets mixed up with gangsters when they stay in an apartment that was formerly shared by three show girls who sent them to jail and they are now out seeking revenge. [British title: *An Interrupted Honeymoon.*]

**356. Honeychile** (10/20/51) Trucolor 90 mins. (Western-Musical-Comedy). *DIR:* R. G. Springsteen. *A-PRO:* Sidney Picker. *SP:* Jack Townley, Charles E. Roberts. Additional dialogue by Barry Trivers. *CAST:* Judy Canova, Eddie Foy, Jr., Alan Hale, Jr., Walter Catlett, Claire Carleton, Karolyn Grimes, Brad Morrow, Roy Barcroft, Leonid Kinskey, Gus Schilling, Irving Bacon, Fuzzy Knight,

Roscoe Ates, Ida Moore, Sarah Edwards, Emory Parnell, Dick Elliott, Dick Wessel, William Fawcett, Robin Winans, Stanley Blystone, Donia Bussey, John Crawford, Cecil Elliott, Cecil Weston. *SYN:* A hillbilly songwriter (Canova) writes a song called "Honeychile" and a pair of publishers (Foy, Jr., Catlett) want the rights to the song, but she won't sell until her boyfriend (Hale, Jr.) gets in trouble after some crooks fix a chuckwagon race.

**357. Hoodlum Empire** (4/15/52) B&W 98 mins. (Crime). *DIR/A-PRO:* Joseph Kane. *E-PRO:* Herbert J. Yates. *SP:* Bruce Manning, Bob Considine. *CAST:* Brian Donlevy, Claire Trevor, Forrest Tucker, Vera Ralston, Luther Adler, John Russell, Gene Lockhart, Grant Withers, Taylor Holmes, Roy Barcroft, William Murphy, Richard Jaeckel, Don Beddoe, Roy Roberts, Richard Benedict, Phillip Pine, Damian O'Flynn, Pat Flaherty, Ric Roman, Douglas Kennedy, Don Haggerty, Francis Pierlot, Sarah Spencer, Thomas Browne Henry, Jack Pennick, Dick Wessel, Paul Livermore, Fred Kohler, Jr., Tony Dante, Tom Monroe, Leah Waggner, Betty Ball, William Schallert, John Phillips, Joe Bailey, Lee Shumway, Charles Trowbridge, Elizabeth Flournoy, John Halloran, John Pickard, Gil Herman, Mervin Williams, Mikel Conrad, Richard Reeves, Matty Fain, Stanley Waxman, Sydney Mason, Whit Bissell, Sid Tomack, Edward Foster, Dick Paxton, Sam Scar, George Volk, Don Michael Drysdale, Walter (Andy) Brennan, Jr. *SYN:* A crusading Senator (Donlevy) sets out to destroy a gangster's (Adler) criminal empire with the help of a reformed mobster (Russell) who has gone straight. *NOTES:* Republic had originally planned this film as the life of gangster Frank Costello, with George Raft in the title role, but Raft rejected the part and the film was rewritten.

**358. Hoosier Holiday** (9/15/43) B&W 72 mins. (Musical). *DIR:* Frank McDonald. *A-PRO:* Armand Schaefer. *SP:* Dorrell McGowan, Stuart McGowan. Based on an idea by Edward James. *CAST:* George Dewey Hay, Dale Evans, Isabel Randolph, George Byron, Emma Dunn, Thurston Hall, Nicodemus Stewart, Ferris Taylor, Georgia Davis, George "Shug" Fisher, Lillian Randolph, "Sleepy" Williams and His Three Shades of Rhythm, The Hoosier Hot Shots, The Music Maids. *SYN:* The Baker Boys (Hoosier Hotshots), a local singing group adored by the community, decide to enlist in the Air Corps but find that they are opposed by the head of the local draft board (Hall) who refuses their enlistment because he thinks they are buffoons. [British title: *Farmyard Follies.*]

**359. House by the River** (3/25/50) B&W 88 mins. (Crime). *DIR:* Fritz Lang. *PRO:* Howard Welsch. *A-PRO:* Robert Peters. *SP:* Mel Dinelli. Based on *Floodtide* by Sir Alan P. Herbert. A Fidelity Picture Production. A Republic Presentation. *CAST:* Louis Hayward, Lee Bowman, Jane Wyatt, Dorothy Patrick, Ann Shoemaker, Jody Gilbert, Peter Brocco, Howland Chamberlin, Margaret Seddon, Sarah Padden, Kathleen Freeman, Will Wright, Leslie Kimmell, Effie Laird. *SYN:* A writer (Hayward), who lives with his wife (Wyatt) in a decaying mansion on the banks of a river, accidentally kills his housemaid while attempting to seduce her and puts the blame on his crippled brother (Bowman).

**360. The House of a Thousand Candles** (4/3/36) B&W 68 mins. (Spy). *DIR:* Arthur Lubin. *PRO:* Nat Levine. *SP:* H. W. Hanemann, Endre Bohem. Based on the book by Meredith Nicholson. *CAST:* Phillips Holmes, Mae Clarke, Irving Pichel, Rosita Moreno, Fred Walton, Hedwig Reicher, Lawrence Grant, Fredrik Vogeding, Michael Fitzmaurice, Rafael Storm, Mischa Auer, Paul Ellis, Keith Daniels, Olaf Hytten, Charles de Ravenne, Lal Chand Mehra, Charles Martin, Max Wagner, Count Stefanelli. *SYN:* International spies are out to stop a British courier (Holmes) and his girl (Clarke) from taking a secret coded message from London to Geneva.

**361. Hurricane Smith** (7/20/41) B&W 69 mins. (Western). *DIR:* Bernard Vorhaus. *A-PRO:* Robert North. *SP:* Robert Presnell. Story by Charles G. Booth. *CAST:* Ray Middleton, Jane Wyatt, Harry Davenport, J. Edward Bromberg, Henry Brandon, Carter Johnson, Charles Trowbridge, Frank Darien, Howard Hickman, Emmett Vogan. *SYN:* A cowboy (Middleton), falsely accused of theft, escapes from jail, catches up with the real crooks, and gets the money away from them, but instead of returning the money and clearing his name, he gets married and uses the money to start a new life, only to have one of the original crooks (Bromberg) show up to blackmail him. *NOTES:* Republic's only attempt to make Ray Middleton a top western star, which was not a success due to a mediocre script. [TV title: *Double Identity*.]

**The Hypnotist** (G.B. title) *see* **Scotland Yard Dragnet**

**362. I Cover the Underworld** (5/19/55) B&W 70 mins. (Crime). *DIR:* R. G. Springsteen. *PRO:* Herbert J. Yates. *SP:* John K. Butler. *CAST:* Sean McClory, Joanne Jordan, Ray Middleton, Jaclynne Greene, Lee Van Cleef, James Griffith, Hugh Sanders, Roy Roberts, Peter Mamakos, Robert Crosson, Frank Gerstle, Willis Bouchey, Philip Van Zandt. *SYN:* A divinity student (McClory) offers his services to the city police chief (Middleton) to pose as his jailed gangster brother (McClory) in order to break up his brother's gang and bring them to justice. *NOTES:* Sean McClory plays a dual role in this film. Ray Middleton's last film for Republic.

**363. I Dream of Jeanie** (6/15/52) Trucolor 90 mins. (Musical-Biography). *DIR:* Allan Dwan. *PRO:* Herbert J. Yates. *SP:* Alan LeMay. *CAST:* Ray Middleton, Bill Shirley, Muriel Lawrence, Eileen Christy, Lynn Bari, Richard Simmons, Robert Neil, Andrew Tombes, James Dobson, Percy Helton, Glenn Turnbull, Louise Beavers, James Kirkwood, Switzer, Carl "Alfalfa" Switzer, Freddie Moultrie, Rex Allen (Narrator/Mr. Tambo). *SYN:* A bookkeeper (Shirley), turns composer and writes the songs that will make him famous. *NOTES:* This was the third, and worst, screen biography of composer Stephen Foster; the other two biographies being Mascot's *Harmony Lane* (1935), and Fox's *Swanee River* (1939). Republic's last studio produced musical.

**364. I, Jane Doe** (5/25/48) B&W 85 mins. (Drama). *DIR/A-PRO:* John H. Auer. *SP:* Lawrence Kimble, Decla Dunning. *CAST:* Ruth Hussey, John Carroll, Vera Ralston, Gene Lockhart, John Howard, Benay Venuta, Adele Mara, Roger Dann, James Bell, Leon Belasco, John Litel, Eric Feldary, Francis Pierlot, Marta Mitrovich, John Albright, Louis

Mercier, Gene Gary, Henry Rowland, Walden Boyle, E. L. Davenport, Roy Darmour, Ed Rees, Howard Mitchell, Nolan Leary, Eva Novak, Martha Holliday, Myron Healey, Charles Flynn, Harry Strang, Chuck Hamilton, Stanley Blystone, Jack Clifford, Sonia Darrin, Frank Reicher, Boyd Irwin, Willy Wickerhauser, Frederic Brunn, Cliff Clark, Jeff Corey, Frances Robinson, Dave Anderson, Sammy McKim, Bobby Stone, Ray Hirsch, James Dale, Jerry Lynn Myers. *SYN:* A French girl (Ralston), on trial for murder, has come to the U.S. to find her husband (Carroll), and accidentally kills him when she finds out he has remarried and he wants to have her deported. [British title: *Diary of a Bride*.]

**365. I Stand Accused** (10/28/38) B&W 63 mins. (Crime). *DIR/A-PRO:* John H. Auer. *SP:* Gordan Kahn, Alex Gottlieb. *CAST:* Robert Cummings, Helen Mack, Lyle Talbot, Thomas Beck, Gordon Jones, Robert Paige, Leona Roberts, Robert Middlemass, Thomas E. Jackson, John Hamilton, Howard Hickman, Harry Stubbs, Robert Strange. *SYN:* A lawyer (Cummings) becomes a mouthpiece for the mob and, when he has enough of them, goes to his former partner (Talbot), who is now the District Attorney, and gives him enough evidence to put them away.

**366. I Was a Convict** (3/6/39) B&W 62 mins. (Drama-Comedy). *DIR:* Aubrey Scotto. *A-PRO:* Herman Schlom. *SP:* Ben Markson, Robert D. Andrews. Story by Robert D. Andrews. *CAST:* Barton MacLane, Beverly Roberts, Clarence Kolb, Janet Beecher, Horace MacMahon, Ben Welden, Leon Ames,

Clara Blandick, Russell Hicks, John Harmon, Chester Clute. *SYN:* A millionaire businessman (Kolb), released from jail after serving time for income tax fraud, makes two of his cellmates, Ace (MacLane) and Missouri (MacMahon), executives in his company. Ace plans to steal what he can from the company, but has a change of heart when he falls in love with the businessman's daughter (Roberts). [Alternate title: *I Was in Prison*.]

**I Was in Prison** *see* **I Was a Convict**

367. **Ice-Capades** (8/20/41) B&W 88 mins. (Musical-Drama). *DIR:* Joseph Santley. *A-PRO:* Robert North. *SP:* Jack Townley, Robert Harari, Olive Cooper, Melville Shavelson, Milt Josefsberg. Story by Isabel Dawn, Boyce DeGaw. *CAST:* James Ellison, Jerry Colonna, Dorothy Lewis, Barbara Jo Allen (Vera Vague), Alan Mowbray, Phil Silvers, Gus Schilling, Tim Ryan, Harry Clark, Renie Riano, Carol Adams, Lois Dworshak, Megan Taylor, Vera Hruba, Red McCarthy, Phil Taylor, Belita, Jackson and Lynam, The Benoits, Dench and Stewart. *SYN:* A newsreel cameraman (Ellison) misses his assignment to cover some Lake Placid ice skaters, but instead, fakes it in New York's Central Park with an unknown skater (Lewis). *NOTES:* The film debuts of Belita and Vera Hruba (Ralston). Academy Award Nominee — Best Score. [Alternate title: *Music in the Moonlight*.]

368. **Ice-Capades Revue** (12/24/42) B&W 79 mins. (Musical). *DIR:* Bernard Vorhaus. *A-PRO:* Robert North. *SP:* Bradford Rogers, Gertrude Purcell. Story by Robert T. Shannon, Mauri Grashin. *CAST:* Richard Denning, Ellen Drew, Jerry Colonna, Barbara Jo Allen (Vera Vague), Harold Huber, Marilyn Hare, Bill Shirley, Pierre Watkin, Si Jenks, Sam Bernard, George Byron, Charles Williams, William Newell, Edward Keane, Roy Butler, Harrison Greene, Broderick O'Farrell, Cyril Ring, Jimmy Conlin, Mary McCarty, Betty Farrington, Elmer Jerome, Hal Price, Lee Shumway, Stanley Blystone, George Sherwood, Dave Willock, Edwin Stanley, Frank Jaquet, Beatrice Maude, Kathryn Sheldon, Emil Van Horn, Jack Norton, Irene Shirley, Frank Brownlee, Donna Atwood, Lois Dworshak, Vera Hruba, Megan Taylor, Joe Jackson, Jr., Robin Lee, Rod McCarthy, Phil Taylor, Eric Waite, Jackson and Lynam, The Benoits, Dench and Stewart. *SYN:* A New England country girl (Drew) inherits a bankrupt ice show and has to fight an unscrupulous rival producer (Watkin) to stage it. [British and Re-release title: *Rhythm Hits the Ice*.]

369. **Idaho** (3/10/43) B&W 70 mins. (Western). *DIR/A-PRO:* Joseph Kane. *SP:* Roy Chanslor, Olive Cooper. *CAST:* Roy Rogers, Smiley Burnette, Virginia Grey, Harry Shannon, Ona Munson, Dick Purcell, Onslow Stevens, Arthur Hohl, Hal Taliaferro, Rex Lease, Tom London, Jack Ingram, James Bush, Bob Nolan and the Sons of the Pioneers, The Robert Mitchell Boy Choir, "Trigger." *SYN:* Roy helps a judge (Shannon), an ex-convict, clear his name when he is framed for bank robbery, and ends up putting the saloon owner (Munson) and her gang behind bars. *NOTES:* Re-edited for TV at 54 mins.

370. **Identity Unknown** (4/2/45) B&W 71 mins. (Drama). *DIR:* Walter Colmes. *A-PRO:* Howard Bretherton, Walter Colmes. *SP:* Richard Weil. Based on *Johnny March* by Robert Newman. A

Republic Presentation. *CAST:* Richard Arlen, Cheryl Walker, Roger Pryor, Bobby Driscoll, Lola Lane, Ian Keith, John Forrest, Sarah Padden, Forrest Taylor, Frank Marlowe, Harry Tyler, Nelson Leigh, Charles Williams, Charles Jordan, Dick Scott, Marjorie Manners, Eddie Baker. *SYN:* A soldier (Arlen) returns home from World War II suffering from amnesia, and uses the name "Johnny March" as he searches for his real identity.

**I'll Reach for a Star** *see* **The Hit Parade**

**371. In Old Amarillo** (5/15/51) B&W 67 mins. (Western). *DIR:* William Witney. *A-PRO:* Edward J. White. *SP:* Sloan Nibley. *CAST:* Roy Rogers, Estelita Rodriguez, Penny Edwards, Pinky Lee, Roy Barcroft, Pierre Watkin, Kenneth Howell, Elisabeth Risdon, William Holmes, Kermit Maynard, Alan Bridge, The Roy Rogers Riders, "Trigger," "Bullet." *SYN:* Roy sets out to stop a crook (Barcroft) who wants to buy cattle cheaply off of drought ridden ranchers.

**372. In Old Caliente** (6/19/39) B&W 57 mins. (Western). *DIR/A-PRO:* Joseph Kane. *SP:* Norman Houston, Gerald Geraghty. *CAST:* Roy Rogers, Mary Hart, George "Gabby" Hayes, Jack LaRue, Katherine DeMille, Frank Puglia, Harry Woods, Paul Marion, Ethel Wales, Merrill McCormick, Fred Burns, Blackie Whiteford, Tom Smith, Ted Mapes, Al Taylor, Jim Corey, Bill Nestell, "Trigger." *SYN:* Roy sets out to find the thief that robbed his employer and has put the blame on immigrants in the area. *NOTES:* Re-edited for TV at 54 mins.

**373. In Old California** (6/11/42) B&W 88 mins. (Western). *DIR:* William McGann. *A-PRO:* Robert North. *SP:* Gertrude Purcell, Frances Hyland. Story by J. Robert Bren, Gladys Atwater. *CAST:* John Wayne, Binnie Barnes, Albert Dekker, Helen Parrish, Patsy Kelly, Edgar Kennedy, Dick Purcell, Harry Shannon, Charles Halton, Emmett Lynn, Bob McKenzie, Milton Kibbee, Paul Sutton, Anne O'Neal, Minerva Urecal, Robert E. Homans, Hooper Atchley, Pearl Early, Ruth Robinson, Frank Jaquet, Jack O'Shea, Jack Kirk, Lynne Carver, James C. Morton, Horace B. Carpenter, Olin Howlin, Chester Conklin, Ralph Peters, Forrest Taylor, Richard Alexander, Donald Curtis, George Lloyd, Stanley Blystone, Slim Whitaker, Frank Ellis, Frank Hagney, Bud Osborne, Ed Brady, Wade Crosby, Guy Usher, Martin Garralaga, Rex Lease, Karl Hackett, Art Mix, Merrill McCormick, Frank McGlynn, Sr., Bob Woodward, Harry McKim. *SYN:* Set in California after the Gold Rush, a pharmacist (Wayne) has a run-in with the town boss (Dekker) when he tries to take his girl (Barnes), and ends up almost being lynched when he is accused of a poisoning that he did not commit.

**374. In Old Cheyenne** (3/28/41) B&W 58 mins. (Western). *DIR/A-PRO:* Joseph Kane. *SP:* Olive Cooper. Story by John W. Krafft. *CAST:* Roy Rogers, George "Gabby" Hayes, Joan Woodbury, J. Farrell MacDonald, Sally Payne, George Rosener, William Haade, Hal Taliaferro, Jack Kirk, Bob Woodward, Jim Corey, Cactus Mack, George Lloyd, William Benedict, Jack O'Shea, Edward Peil, Sr., Merrill McCormick, Ted Mapes, Fred Burns, Ben Corbett, Nick Thompson, Frank Ellis, "Trigger." *SYN:* Roy is sent West by his newspaper to cover a story about a range war between cattlemen and an outlaw leader (Rosener). NOTES: Re-edited for TV at 54 mins.

**In Old Los Angeles** see **Old Los Angeles**

**375. In Old Missouri** (4/17/40) B&W 67 mins. (Drama). DIR: Frank McDonald. A-PRO: Armand Schaefer. SP: Dorrell McGowan, Stuart McGowan. CAST: Leon Weaver, Frank Weaver, June Weaver, June Storey, Marjorie Gateson, Thurston Hall, Alan Ladd, Loretta Weaver, Andrew Tombes, Mildred Shay, Willis Claire, Leonard Carey, Earle S. Dewey, Forbes Murray, The Hall Johnson Choir. SYN: The Weavers (Leon, Frank, June) are sharecroppers who discover that their millionaire boss (Hall) is in worse shape than they are. NOTES: The 3rd entry in the "Weaver Brothers and Elviry" series.

**376. In Old Monterey** (8/14/39) B&W 73 mins. (Western). DIR: Joseph Kane. A-PRO: Armand Schaefer. SP: Dorrell McGowan, Stuart McGowan, Gerald Geraghty. Story by George Sherman, Gerald Geraghty. CAST: Gene Autry, Smiley Burnette, June Storey, George "Gabby" Hayes, Stuart Hamblen, Billy Lee, Jonathan Hale, Robert Warwick, William Hall, Eddie Conrad, Curley Dresden, Victor Cox, Ken Carson, Robert Wilke, Hal Price, Tom Steele, Jack O'Shea, Rex Lease, Edward Earle, James Mason, Fred Burns, Dan White, Frank Ellis, Jim Corey, Curley Bradley, Shorty Carlson, Jack Ross, I. Stanford Jolley, The Hoosier Hot Shots, Sarie and Sallie, The Ranch Boys, "Champion." SYN: Gene is sent to buy up lands for use in bombing maneuvers, and has to deal with unscrupulous ranchers who are trying to make an illegal profit off of the government. NOTES: Joseph Kane's last directed Gene Autry film. Re-edited for TV at 54 mins.

**377. In Old Oklahoma** (12/6/43) B&W 102 mins. (Western-Drama). DIR: Albert S. Rogell. A-PRO: Robert North. SP: Ethel Hill, Eleanore Griffin. Adapted by Thomson Burtis from his story *War of the Wildcats*. CAST: John Wayne, Martha Scott, Albert Dekker, George "Gabby" Hayes, Marjorie Rambeau, Dale Evans, Grant Withers, Sidney Blackmer, Paul Fix, Cecil Cunningham, Irving Bacon, Byron Foulger, Anne O'Neal, Richard Graham, Robert Warwick, Stanley Andrews, Will Wright, Harry Shannon, Emmett Vogan, Charles Arnt, Edward Gargan, Harry Woods, Tom London, Dick Rich, Slim Whitaker, LeRoy Mason, Lane Chandler, Arthur Loft, Bud Geary, Fred Graham, Kenne Duncan, Hooper Atchley, George Chandler, Wade Crosby, Curley Dresden, Roy Barcroft, Jack Kirk, Yakima Canutt, Shirley Rickert, Oril Taller, Linda Scott, Juanita Colteaux, Bob Reeves, Jess Cavan, Charles Agnew, Pat Hogan, Bonnie Jean Harley, Pearl Early, Linda Brent, Rhonda Fleming. SYN: A cowboy (Wayne) comes to the aid of an Indian tribe when a crooked oilman (Dekker) wants to drill on their land and keep the profits for himself. NOTES: The film debut of Rhonda Fleming. Academy Award Nominee — Best Score, Best Sound. Initial release title was *War of the Wildcats*. It was changed to *In Old Oklahoma* a few weeks after release and the re-release title was then changed back to *War of the Wildcats*. [British and Re-release title: *War of the Wildcats*.]

**378. In Old Sacramento** (5/31/46) B&W 89 mins. (Western). DIR/A-PRO:

Joseph Kane. SP: Frances Hyland. Adapted by Frank Gruber. Story by Jerome Odlum. Based on *Diamond Carlisle* by Joseph Kane. CAST: Bill Elliott, Constance Moore, Hank Daniels, Ruth Donnelly, Eugene Pallette, Lionel Stander, Jack LaRue, Grant Withers, Bobby (Robert) Blake, Charles Judels, Paul Hurst, Victoria Horne, Dick Wessel, Hal Taliaferro, Jack O'Shea, H. T. Tsiang, Marshall Reed, Wade Crosby, Eddy Waller, William Haade, Boyd Irwin, Lucien Littlefield, Ethel Wales, Elaine Lange, William B. Davidson, Ellen Corby, Fred Burns. SYN: A gentleman gambler and stagecoach robber, Johnny Barrett, known as "Spanish Jack" (Elliott), falls for a singing star (Moore). She protects him from the sheriff and local vigilantes, but, when a young prospector (Daniels) falls for her, he decides to give her up and is killed while committing another robbery. NOTES: This film marked the beginning of Bill Elliott's "A" pictures for Republic. This was the third film based on Kane's story. The previous versions were *Diamond Carlisle*, filmed in 1924 with George Chesebro, and *The Carson City Kid*, filmed in 1940 with Roy Rogers. [Re-release title: *Flame of Sacramento*.]

379. **In Old Vienna** (??/??/55) B&W 72 mins. (Drama-Musical). DIR: Unknown. PRO: Unknown. SP: Unknown. A Republic Presentation. CAST: Robert Killick, Heinz Roettinger, Mostyn Bell, Martin Berliner, Emil Feldmar, Fred Grundei, Georg Hartmann, Henriette Hiess, Kurt Jaggberg, Peter Larsen, Hanni Loser, Paul Roberts, Herbert Stepanek, Marianne Schonauer, Dagmar Thomas. SYN: The struggles of composers Schubert, Strauss, and Beethoven in the city of Vienna. NOTES: Filmed in Austria.

**In Rosie's Room** (G.B. title) *see* **Rosie the Riveter**

380. **The Inner Circle** (8/7/46) B&W 57 mins. (Mystery). DIR: Philip Ford. A-PRO: William J. O'Sullivan. SP: Dorrell McGowan, Stuart McGowan. Based on a radio script by Leonard St. Clair, Lawrence Edmund Taylor. CAST: Adele Mara, Warren Douglas, William Frawley, Ricardo Cortez, Virginia Christine, Ken Niles, Will Wright, Dorothy Adams, Martha Montgomery, Edward Gargan, Fred Graham, Eddie Parker, Robert Wilke. SYN: A private detective (Douglas) is framed for the murder of a news commentator and scandal reporter, and with the assistance of his secretary (Mara), sets out to find the guilty party.

381. **The Inside Story** (3/14/48) B&W 87 mins. (Comedy). DIR/A-PRO: Allan Dwan. SP: Mary Loos, Richard Sale. Story by Ernest Lehman, Geza Herczeg. CAST: Marsha Hunt, William Lundigan, Charles Winninger, Gail Patrick, Florence Bates, Gene Lockhart, Hobart Cavanaugh, Allen Jenkins, Roscoe Karns, Robert Shayne, Will Wright, William Haade, Frank Ferguson, Tom Fadden. SYN: Told in flashback, in a small Vermont town in 1933, a New York hotel guest puts $1000 in the hotel safe and the money is taken illegally from the safe to pay off a debt; the money circulates all over town until it is returned to its original spot in the nick of time. NOTES: This was Gail Patrick's final film as an actress. She would become a television producer using her married name, Gail Patrick Davis, her most notable series being *Perry Mason*. [Re-release title: *The Big Gamble*.]

**Inside the Underworld** *see* **Storm Over Lisbon**

**382. Insurance Investigator** (3/23/51) B&W 60 mins. (Crime). *DIR:* George Blair. *A-PRO:* William Lackey. *SP:* Gertrude Walker. Story by Gertrude Walker, Beth Brown. *CAST:* Richard Denning, Audrey Long, John Eldredge, Hillary Brooke, Reed Hadley, Jonathan Hale, Roy Barcroft, Wilson Wood, William Tannen, Phillip Pine, Crane Whitley, Ruth Lee, Patricia Knox, M'Liss McClure, Maurice Samuels. *SYN:* When an insurance investigator (Denning) investigates the death of a real estate operator, it leads to the discovery of an "accidental" death racket to cash in on insurance policies.

**383. International Counterfeiters** (2/14/58) B&W 70 mins. (Crime). *DIR:* Franz Cap. *PRO:* Arthur Brauner. *SP:* Paul H. Rameau. Based on an idea by Arthur Brauner. A CCC Production. A Republic Presentation. *CAST:* Gordon Howard, Irina Garden, Kurt Meisel, Hans Nielsen, Paul Bildt, Barbara Ruetting. *SYN:* Unknown.

**An Interrupted Honeymoon** (G.B. title) see **Homicide for Three**

**384. Invisible Avenger** (12/2/58) B&W 60 mins. (Mystery). *DIR:* James Wong Howe, John Sledge, Ben Parker. *PRO:* Eric Sayers, Emanuel Denby. *SP:* George Bellak, Betty Jeffries. *CAST:* Richard Derr, Mark Daniels, Helen Westcott, Jeanne Neher, Dan Mullin, Lee Edwards, Jack Doner, Steve Dano, Leo Bruno, Sam Page. *SYN:* While investigating the murder of a New Orleans jazzman, Lamont Cranston, "The Shadow" (Derr) finds that the mystery will lead him to an exiled Latin American dictator. *NOTES:* In 1962 this film was re-released as *Bourbon St. Shadows* with additional footage tacked on, under the direction of Parker. The film's original director Howe was a noted cinematographer in the 1940s and 1950s. [TV and Re-release title: *Bourbon St. Shadows*]

**385. Invisible Enemy** (4/4/38) B&W 66 mins. (Crime). *DIR:* John H. Auer. *SP:* Albert J. Cohen, Alex Gottlieb, Norman Burnstine. Story by Albert J. Cohen, Robert T. Shannon. *CAST:* Alan Marshal, Tala Birell, Mady Correll, C. Henry Gordon, Herbert Mundin, Gerald Oliver Smith, Ivan Simpson, Elsa Buchanan, Dwight Frye, Leonard Willey, Ian MacLaren, Egon Brecher. *SYN:* A special agent (Marshal) is out to stop a master criminal (Gordon) from destroying international oil companies. *NOTES:* Released before World War II, this film anticipates the importance of oil to the war effort.

**386. The Invisible Informer** (8/19/46) B&W 57 mins. (Mystery). *DIR:* Philip Ford. *A-PRO:* William J. O'Sullivan. *SP:* Sherman L. Lowe. Story by Gerald Drayson Adams. *CAST:* Linda Stirling, William (Bill) Henry, Adele Mara, Gerald Mohr, Peggy Stewart, Donia Bussey, Claire DuBrey, Tristram Coffin, Tom London, Charles Lane, Cy Kendall, Francis McDonald. *SYN:* A pair of private detectives (Stirling, Henry) set out to track down a missing necklace, and run into a trail of bodies which have either been strangled or torn apart by police dogs.

**387. Iron Mountain Trail** (5/8/53) B&W 54 mins. (Western). *DIR:* William Witney. *A-PRO:* Edward J. White. *SP:* Gerald Geraghty. Story by William Lively. *CAST:* Rex Allen, Slim Pickens, Grant Withers, Nan Leslie, Roy Barcroft, Forrest Taylor, Alan Bridge, John Hamilton, George Lloyd, "Koko." *SYN:* A postal inspector (Allen) is sent to California to find out why mail delivery is taking so long by clipper ship, and a land-sea race is set up to see which method delivers the mail most efficiently.

**388. It Could Happen to You** (5/28/37) B&W 71 mins. (Drama). *DIR:* Phil Rosen. *A-PRO:* Leonard Fields. *SP:* Samuel Ornitz, Nathanael West. Story by Nathanael West. *CAST:* Alan Baxter, Andrea Leeds, Owen Davis, Jr., Astrid Allwyn, Walter Kingsford, Al Shean, Christian Rub, Elsa Janssen, Edward Colebrook, Stanley King, Nina Campana, Frank Yaconelli, John Hamilton, Paul Stanton. *SYN:* A brother (Davis, Jr.) defends his half-brother (Baxter) of a murder charge, and gets him acquitted but, feeling remorse about his crime, he pronounces himself guilty and serves as his own executioner.

**389. I've Always Loved You** (12/2/46) Technicolor 117 mins. (Musical). *DIR/PRO:* Frank Borgaze. *SP:* Borden Chase. Based on *Concerto* by Borden Chase. *CAST:* Philip Dorn, Catherine McLeod, William Carter, Maria Ouspenskaya, Felix Bressart, Fritz Feld, Elizabeth Patterson, Vanessa Brown, Lewis Howard, Adele Mara, Gloria Donovan, Stephanie Bachelor, Cora Witherspoon, Arthur Rubenstein. *SYN:* An orchestra conductor (Dorn) engages in a professional rivalry with a young female pupil (McLeod), and ruins her career by playing the orchestra too loudly during her concert at Carnegie Hall. *NOTES:* Republic's first and only Technicolor feature production. Arthur Rubenstein ghosted for Philip Dorn on the soundtrack. Working title was *Concerto*. [British title: *Concerto*.]

**It Happened in Paris** (G.B. title) see **A Desperate Adventure**

390. **Jaguar** (1/20/56) B&W 66 mins. (Mystery-Adventure). DIR: George Blair. PRO: Mickey Rooney, Maurice Duke. SP: John Fenton Murray, Benedict Freedman. CAST: Sabu, Chiquita, Barton MacLane, Jonathan Hale, Touch Connors (Mike Connors), Jay Novello, Fortunio Bonanova, Nacho Galindo, Rodd Redwing, Pepe Hern, Raymond Rosas. SYN: In Africa, a young boy (Sabu) fears he may be reverting back to his savage nature when he is suspected of murder while on an oil expedition.

**Jamboree** (G.B. title) see **Rookies on Parade**

391. **Jamboree** (5/5/44) B&W 71 mins. (Musical). DIR: Joseph Santley. A-PRO: Armand Schaefer. SP: Jack Townley. Story by Jack Townley, Taylor Caven. CAST: Ruth Terry, George Byron, Paul Harvey, Edwin Stanley, Don Wilson, Isabel Randolph, Rufe Davis, Shirley Mitchell, George "Shug" Fisher, Feddie Fisher and His Schnickelfritz Band, The Music Maids, Ernest Tubb and His Texas Troubadors. SYN: A struggling country band (Freddie Fisher and his Schnickelfritz Band) is abandoned at a farm by their manager (Byron) when they can't land a job, but once he learns that a rich radio sponsor (Harvey) is willing to sponsor a band and another band (Ernest Tubbs and His Texas Troubadors) is in contention, he goes back to the farm to get them and they land the job.

392. **Jealousy** (7/23/45) B&W 71 mins. (Mystery). DIR/PRO: Gustav Machaty. SP: Arnold Phillips, Gustav Machaty. Based on a story by Dalton Trumbo. CAST: John Loder, Jane Randolph, Karen Morley, Nils Asther, Hugo Haas, Holmes Herbert, Michael Mark, Mauritz Hugo, Peggy Leon, Mary Arden, Noble "Kid" Chissell. SYN: When a famous refugee novelist (Asther) is found murdered, his wife (Randolph) is suspected of the crime and a surgeon (Loder), whom she loves, must prove her innocence.

393. **Jeepers Creepers** (10/27/39) B&W 69 mins. (Drama). DIR: Frank McDonald. A-PRO: Armand Schaefer. SP: Dorrell McGowan, Stuart McGowan. CAST: Leon Weaver, Frank Weaver, June Weaver, Roy Rogers, Maris Wrixon, Billy Lee, Lucien Littlefield, Thurston Hall, Loretta Weaver, Johnny Arthur. SYN: When coal is discovered on the Weavers' (Leon, Frank, June) farm, a rich industrialist (Hall) proceeds to cheat them out of their land. NOTES: The 2nd entry in the "Weaver Brothers and Elviry" series. [British title: *Money Isn't Everything*.]

394. **Jesse James at Bay** (10/17/41) B&W 56 mins. (Western). DIR/A-PRO: Joseph Kane. SP: James R. Webb. Story by Harrison Jacobs. CAST: Roy Rogers, George "Gabby" Hayes, Sally Payne, Pierre Watkin, Ivan Miller, Hal Taliaferro, Gale Storm, Roy Barcroft, Jack Kirk, William Benedict, Jack O'Shea, Rex Lease, Edward Peil, Sr., Jack Rockwell, Kit Guard, Curley Dresden, Hank Bell, Bill Wolfe, Lloyd Ingraham, Karl Hackett, Budd Buster, Fred Burns, Ray Jones, Fern Emmett, Bob Woodward, Chuck Morrison, Chester Conklin, Charles Moore, Theodore Lorch, Pascale Perry, Al Taylor, Luke Cosgrove, Rick Anderson, Bob Reeves, George

Kesterson (Art Mix), Ken Card, Paul Sells, "Trigger." *SYN:* When Jesse James (Rogers) comes back to Missouri to find that a crooked banker (Barcroft) is cheating the homesteaders out of their land, he starts robbing trains to give the money to the homesteaders to save their land. *NOTES:* Roy Rogers plays a dual role in this film. Re-edited for TV at 54 mins.

**395. Jesse James, Jr.** (3/25/42) B&W 56 mins. (Western). *DIR/A-PRO:* George Sherman. *SP:* Richard Murphy, Doris Schroeder, Taylor Caven. Story by Richard Murphy. *CAST:* Don ("Red") Barry, Lynn Merrick, Al St. John, Douglas Walton, Karl Hackett, Lee Shumway, Stanley Blystone, Jack Kirk, Robert Kortman, George Chesebro, Frank Brownlee, Forbes Murray, Jim Corey, Kermit Maynard, Ken Cooper, Tommy Coats. *SYN:* A cowboy (Barry) tries to stop outlaws who are out to wreck a telegraph. [TV title: *Sundown Fury*]

**396. Jim Hanvey, Detective** (4/5/37) B&W 71 mins. (Mystery). *DIR:* Phil Rosen. *A-PRO:* Albert E. Levoy. *SP:* Joseph Krumgold, Olive Cooper. Based on a magazine story by Octavus Roy Cohen. *CAST:* Guy Kibbee, Tom Brown, Lucie Kaye, Catharine Doucet, Edward Brophy, Edward Gargan, Helen Jerome Eddy, Theodore Von Eltz, Kenneth Thomson, Howard Hickman, Oscar Apfel, Charles Williams, Wade Boteler, Robert Emmett Keane, Harry Tyler, Frank Darien, Robert E. Homans. *SYN:* An ace detective (Kibbee) is called in by an insurance company to investigate the theft of an emerald.

**397. Joan of Ozark** (8/1/42) B&W 80 mins. (Musical-Comedy-Spy). *DIR:* Joseph Santley. *A-PRO:* Harriet Parsons. *SP:* Monte Brice, Bradford Ropes. Story by Eve Greene, Robert Harari. Additional dialogue by Jack Townley. *CAST:* Judy Canova, Joe E. Brown, Eddie Foy, Jr., Jerome Cowan, Wolfgang Zilzer, Alexander Granach, Anne Jeffreys, Otto Reichow, Hans Von Twardowski, William Dean, Paul Fung, Donald Curtis, George Eldredge, Olin Howlin, Ralph Peters, Chester Clute, Emmett Lynn, Kam Tong, Cyril Ring, Eric Alden, Ralph McCullough, Lloyd Whitlock, Horace B. Carpenter, Bobby Stone, Bud Jamison, Tyler Gibson, William Sundholm, William Worth, Robert Cherry, Bill Nestell, William Vaughn (William von Brincken), Harry Hayden, Gladys Gale, Charles Miller, Laura Treadwell, Nora Lane, Bob Stevenson, Peppy and Peanuts, Jason Robards, Sr., Ernest Hilliard, Richard Keene, Bert Moorhouse, Fred Santley, Pat Gleason, Charles Williams, Joan Tours, Sally Cairns, Eleanor Bayley, Billy Lane, Jane Allen, Ruby Morie, Kay Gordon, Aileen Morris, Jean O'Connell, June Earl, Patsy Bedell, Pearl Tolson, Jeanette Dixon, Helen Seamon, Barbara Clark, Mary Jo Ellis, Midgie Dare, Audren Brier, Maxine Ardell. *SYN:* A girl (Canova) shoots a pigeon one day while quail hunting in the Ozarks, and it turns out that it is a Nazi carrier pigeon which she turns over to the FBI. She is declared a hero incurring the wrath of the Nazi spy head (Cowan), who runs a New York nightclub as a front. He sends a theatrical agent (Brown), who pretends to be a government agent, to bring her to New York on the pretext of singing at the nightclub so they can do away with her. [British title: *Queen of Spies*]

**398. Johnny Doughboy** (12/31/42) B&W 64 mins. (Musical). *DIR/A-PRO:* John H. Auer. *SP:* Lawrence Kimble. Story by Frederick Kohner. *CAST:* Jane Withers, Henry Wilcoxon, Patrick Brook, William Demarest, Ruth Donnelly, Etta McDaniel, Jolene Westbrook, Bobby Breen, Baby Sandy, Carl "Alfalfa" Switzer, Spanky McFarland, Butch and Buddy, Cora Sue Collins, Robert Coogan, Grace Costello, Karl Kiffe, The Falkner Orchestra. *SYN:* A girl (Withers), disappointed with romance with a middle-aged playwright (Wilcoxon), finally comes upon happiness when she joins the "Junior Victory Caravan," a young people's version of the "Hollywood Caravan," touring army camps to give the fighting men a boost of morale. *NOTES:* Jane Withers plays a dual role in this film. The final film of Bobby Breen and Baby Sandy — he retired after this film and she retired also — at age 4. Academy Award Nominee — Best Score.

**399. Johnny Guitar** (8/23/54) Trucolor 110 mins. (Western). *DIR:* Nicholas Ray. *PRO:* Herbert J. Yates. *SP:* Philip Yordan. Based on the novel by Roy Chanslor. *CAST:* Joan Crawford, Sterling Hayden, Mercedes McCambridge, Scott Brady, Ward Bond, Ben Cooper, Ernest Borgnine, John Carradine, Royal Dano, Frank Ferguson, Paul Fix, Rhys Williams, Ian MacDonald, Will Wright, John Maxwell, Robert Osterloh, Trevor Bardette, Sumner Williams, Sheb Wooley, Denver Pyle, Clem Harvey, Frank Marlowe. *SYN:* A ruthless saloon owner (Crawford) and her guitar-playing, ex-lover, gunman (Hayden), must defend themselves from a town boss (Bond), and a female rancher (McCambridge).

**400. Join the Marines** (1/25/37) B&W 70 mins. (Drama). *DIR:* Ralph

Staub. PRO: Nat Levine. SP: Joseph Krumgold, Olive Cooper. Story by Karl Brown. CAST: Paul Kelly, June Travis, Purnell Pratt, Reginald Denny, Warren Hymer, Irving Pichel, Sterling Holloway, Ray ("Crash") Corrigan, John Holland, Carleton Young, John Sheehan, Arthur Hoyt, Richard Beach, Howard Hickman, Val Duran, Landers Stevens. SYN: A New York City cop (Kelly), wrongly accused of drunkenness and kicked off the force, redeems himself when he joins the Marines and swiftly rises through the ranks, winning both a commission and his girl (Travis).

**Jolly Old Higgins** (G.B. title) *see* **Earl of Puddlestone**

**401. Journey to Freedom** (6/21/57) B&W 60 mins. (Spy). DIR: Robert C. Dertano. PRO: Stephen C. Apostolof. SP: Herbert F. Niccolls. Story by Herbert F. Niccolls, Stephen C. Apostolof. A Stephen C. Apostolof Production. A Republic Presentation. CAST: Jacques Scott, Genevieve Aumont, George Graham, Morgan Lane, Jean Ann Lewis, Peter Besbas, Don McArt, Dan O'Dowd, Barry O'Hara, Fred Kohler, Jr., Tor Johnson, Don Marlowe, Miles Shepard. SYN: An activist (Scott) for the "Voice of Freedom," is chased from Bulgaria to the U.S. by Soviet agents and, when he is injured in a car accident, a nurse (Aumont) helps him regain his health, falls in love with him, and joins him in his escape from the Soviet agents.

**402. Jubilee Trail** (5/15/54) Trucolor 103 mins. (Western). DIR/A-PRO: Joseph Kane. PRO: Herbert J. Yates. SP: Bruce Manning. Based on the novel by Gwen Bristow. CAST: Vera Ralston, Joan Leslie, Forrest Tucker, John Russell, Ray Middleton, Pat O'Brien, Buddy Baer, Jim Davis, Barton MacLane, Richard Webb, James Millican, Nina Varela, Martin Garralaga, Charles Stevens, Jack Elam, Nacho Galindo, Don Beddoe, John Holland, William Haade, Alan Bridge, Marshall Reed, Emmett Lynn, Charles Sullivan, Emil Sitka, Ralph Brooks, John Halloran, Sayre Dearing, Stephen Chase, Dan White, Walter (Andy) Brennan, Jr., Eugene Borden, Morris Buchanan, Rodolfo Hoyos, Rico Alaniz, Bud Wolfe, Paul Stader, Maurice Jara, Rosa Turich, Manuel Lopez, Frances Dominguez, Perry Lopez, Claire Carleton, Victor Sen Yung, Grant Withers, Frank Puglia, Glenn Strange, Joe Dominguez, Felipe Turich, Tex Terry, Rocky Shahan, Chuck Hayward, Pilar Del Rey, Jack O'Shea, Tina Menard, Dee "Buzzy" Henry, Don Haggerty, Ted Smile, Raymond Johnson, Manuel Paris, James Lilburn, Bob Burrows, Gloria Varela, Linda Danceil, Pepe Hern, Alma Beltran, Anna Navarro, Edward Colmans, George Navarro, John Mooney, Peter Ortiz, Richard Dodge. SYN: A dance hall singer (Ralston) helps an Eastern woman (Leslie) cope with frontier life in California after her husband (Russell) is killed.

**Judy Goes to Town** (G.B. title) *see* **Puddin' Head**

**403. Jungle Stampede** (7/29/50) B&W 60 mins. (Documentary-Travelogue). DIR: George Breakston. A-PRO: George Breakston, Yorke Coplen. CAST: George Breakston, Yorke Coplen, Stan Lawrence-Brown, Miguel Roginsky, Herman Schopp. Narrated by Ronald Davidson. SYN: A pictorial account of the African expedition led by Breakston and Coplan.

A GIRL DELINQUENT ...A JET PROPELLED GANG... OUT FOR FAST KICKS!

# JUVENILE JUNGLE
### in NATURAMA

STARRING
**COREY ALLEN · REBECCA WELLES
RICHARD BAKALYAN
ANNE WHITFIELD · JOE DI REDA**
with JOE CONLEY · WALTER COY · TAGGART CASEY

Produced by SIDNEY PICKER · Directed by WILLIAM WITNEY · Written by ARTHUR T. HORMAN
REPUBLIC PICTURES Presents A CORONADO Production

**404. Juvenile Jungle** (4/24/58) B&W/ Naturama 69 mins. (Crime). *DIR:* William Witney. *PRO:* Sidney Picker. *SP:* Arthur T. Horman. A Coronado Production. A Republic Presentation. *CAST:* Corey Allen, Rebecca Welles, Richard Bakalyan, Anne Whitfield, Joe DiReda, Walter Coy, Taggart Casey, Hugh Lawrence, Leon Tyler, Harvey Grant, Louise Arthur. *SYN:* A teen (Allen) kidnaps the daughter (Whitfield) of a wealthy merchant for a big ransom, but has a change of heart when he falls in love with her. *NOTES:* Double-billed in some areas with *Young and Wild*.

**405. Kansas Cyclone** (6/24/41) B&W 58 mins. (Western). *DIR/A-PRO:* George Sherman. *SP:* Oliver Drake, Doris Schroeder. Story by Louis Sarecky. *CAST:* Don ("Red") Barry, Lynn Merrick, William Haade, Milton Kibbee, Harry Worth, Dorothy Sebastian, Jack Kirk, Forrest Taylor, Charles Moore, Eddie Dean, Reed Howes, Guy Usher, Edward Peil, Sr., Yakima Canutt, Cactus Mack, Bob Woodward, Tex Terry, George J. Lewis, Augie Gomez, Buddy Roosevelt, William Kellogg (Bruce Kellogg). *SYN:* A U.S. Marshal (Barry) goes undercover as a geologist to break up a gang that has been robbing Wells Fargo stagecoaches. *NOTES:* Re-edited for TV at 54 mins.

**406. The Kansas Terrors** (10/6/39) B&W 57 mins. (Western). *DIR:* George Sherman. *A-PRO:* Harry Grey. *SP:* Jack Natteford, Betty Burbridge. Story by Luci Ward. Based on characters created by William Colt MacDonald. *CAST:* Robert Livingston, Raymond Hatton, Duncan Renaldo, Jacqueline Wells (Julie Bishop), Howard Hickman, George Douglas, Frank Lackteen, Myra Marsh, Yakima Canutt, Ruth Robinson, Richard Alexander, Merrill McCormick, Artie Ortego, Curley Dresden, Al Haskell, Henry Wills, Dick Botiller, Joe Dominguez. *SYN:* Mesquiteers Stony (Livingston) and Rusty (Hatton) deliver horses to a remote Caribbean island and end up helping the rebel leader, Rico (Renaldo), overthrow the island's unjust leader. In the end Rico ends up joining Stony and Rusty as they once again become the "Three Mesquiteers." *NOTES:* The oddest part of this film comes when Livingston, who had earlier filmed *The Lone Ranger Rides Again* (1939), seems to reprise the part with costume and white horse. The first film to star Duncan Renaldo as a Mesquiteer. Re-edited for TV at 54 mins. The 25th entry in the "Three Mesquiteers" series.

**Keep Rollin'** *see* **Gaucho Serenade**

**The Kid Colossus** (G.B. title) *see* **Roogie's Bump**

**407. The Kid from Cleveland** (9/5/49) B&W 89 mins. (Sports). *DIR:* Herbert Kline. *A-PRO:* Walter Colmes. *SP:* John Bright. Story by Herbert Kline, John Bright. *CAST:* George Brent, Lynn Bari, Russ Tamblyn, Tommy Cook, Louis Jean Heydt, Ann Doran, K. Elmo Lowe, John Beradino, Bill Veeck, Lou Boudreau, Tris Speaker, Hank Greenberg, Bob Feller, Gene Bearden, LeRoy "Satchel" Paige, Bob Lemon, Steve Gromek, Joe Gordon, Mickey Vernon, Ken Keltner, Ray Boone, Dale Mitchell, Larry Doby, Bob Kennedy, Jim Hegan, Franklin Lewis, Gordon Cobbledock, Ed MacAuley, Bill Summers, Bill Grieve. *SYN:* A sports announcer (Brent) takes a juvenile delinquent (Tamblyn), abandoned by his stepfather, under his wing and introduces him to the Cleveland Indians, who do their best to straighten the kid out. NOTES: Actual footage of the 1948 World Series is included in this film.

**408. King of the Cowboys** (4/9/43) B&W 67 mins. (Western). *DIR:* Joseph Kane. *A-PRO:* Harry Grey. *SP:* Olive Cooper, J. Benton Cheney. Story by Hal Long. *CAST:* Roy Rogers, Smiley Burnette, Peggy Moran, Gerald Mohr, Dorothea Kent, Lloyd Corrigan, James Bush, Russell Hicks, Irving Bacon, Stuart Hamblen, Emmett Vogan, Eddie Dean, Forrest Taylor, Dick Wessel, Jack Kirk, Edward Earle, Yakima Canutt, Charles King, Jack O'Shea, Norman Willis, Rex Lease, Bud Geary, Lynton Brent, William Gould, Harry Burns, Earle Hodgins, Dick Rich, Herbert Heyes, Raphael Bennett, John Dilson, Edward Peil, Sr., Charles Sullivan, Ralph Peters, Jack Ingram, Jack Ray, Kate Lawson, Elmer Jerome, Fred Johnson, Richard Alexander, Harrison Greene, Edward Cassidy, Hugh Sothern, Herbert Rawlinson, Eddie Dew, Reed Howes, Roy Bucko, Bob Nolan and the Sons of the Pioneers, "Trigger." *SYN:* A special agent (Rogers), appointed by the governor (Hicks) to discover who has been sabotaging military warehouses, learns that the saboteurs are working out of a traveling tent show, and joins it as a rodeo performer to ferret them out. *NOTES:* The final film of Peggy Moran—she retired after this film. Re-edited for TV at 54 mins.

**409. King of the Gamblers** (5/10/48) B&W 60 mins. (Sports-Crime). *DIR:* George Blair. *A-PRO:* Stephen Auer. *SP:* Albert DeMond, Bradbury Foote. *CAST:* Janet Martin, William Wright, Thurston Hall, Stephanie Bachelor, George Meeker, Wally Vernon, William (Bill) Henry, James Cardwell, Jonathan Hale, Selmer Jackson, Howard J. Negley, John Holland, George Anderson, Ralph Dunn, John Albright. *SYN:* A football player (Wright), framed for the murder of another football player who threatened to expose a game-fixing operation, sets out to prove his innocence and find the murderer of his fellow player.

**410. King of the Newsboys** (3/18/38) B&W 65 mins. (Drama). *DIR/A-PRO:* Bernard Vorhaus. *SP:* Louis Weitzenkorn, Peggy Thompson. Story by Samuel Ornitz, Horace McCoy. *CAST:* Lew Ayres, Helen Mack, Alison Skipworth, Victor Varconi, Sheila Bromley, Alice White, Horace MacMahon, William Benedict, Victor Ray Cooke, Jack Pennick, Mary Kornman, Gloria Rich, Oscar O'Shea, Marjorie Main, Anthony Warde, Ralph Dunn, Byron Foulger, Emmett Vogan, Ferris Taylor, Ethan Laidlaw, Dale Van Sickel, Howard Hickman, John Baird, Inez Palange, Allan Cavan, Alphonse Martell, Horace B. Carpenter, Ben Taggart, Paul Stanton, Joe Cunningham, Harry Semels, Frances Morris, Jack Chefe, Harry Wilson, Charles Sullivan, Robert Livingston. *SYN:* A man (Ayres) becomes big in the newspaper trucking business and tries to get his girl (Mack) back from a mobster (Varconi).

**411. King of the Pecos** (3/9/36) B&W 54 mins. (Western). *DIR:* Joseph Kane. *S-PRO:* Paul Malvern. *SP:* Bernard McConville, Dorrell McGowan, Stuart McGowan. Story by Bernard McConville. *CAST:* John Wayne, Muriel Evans, Cy Kendall, Jack Clifford, J. Frank Glendon, Herbert Heywood, Arthur Aylesworth, John

Beck, Mary MacLaren, Bradley Metcalfe, Yakima Canutt, Edward Hearn, Earl Dwire, Tex Palmer, Jack Kirk, Horace B. Carpenter, Tracy Layne, Tex Phelps, Bud Pope. *SYN:* A law student (Wayne) returns home to avenge the murder of his parents by the local cattle baron (Kendall), which he first attempts to do legally, but his efforts are thwarted and he resorts to taking the law into his own hands.

**412. Ladies in Distress** (6/13/38) B&W 66 mins. (Drama). *DIR:* Gus Meins. *A-PRO:* Harry Grey. *SP:* Dorrell McGowan, Stuart McGowan. Story by Dore Schary. *CAST:* Alison Skipworth, Polly Moran, Robert Livingston, Virginia Grey, Max Terhune, Berton Churchill, Leonard Penn, Horace MacMahon, Allen Vincent, Eddie Acuff, Charles Anthony Hughes, Jack Carr, Walter Sande, Billy Wayne. *SYN:* The lady mayor (Skipworth) of a town, a former schoolteacher, decides to make it a better place in which to live, and she enlists the aid of an ex-pupil (Livingston), to help her get the job done.

**The Lady and the Doctor** (G.B. title) *see* **The Lady and the Monster**

**413. The Lady and the Monster** (4/17/44) B&W 86 mins. (Science-Fiction-Horror). *DIR/A-PRO:* George Sherman. *SP:* Dane Lussier, Frederick Kohner. Based on the novel *Donovan's Brain* by Curt Siodmak. *CAST:* Vera Hruba Ralston, Erich Von Stroheim, Richard Arlen, Mary Nash, Sidney Blackmer, Helen Vinson, Charles Cane, William (Bill) Henry, Juanita Quigley, Josephine Dillon, Tom London, Jack Kirk, Sam Flint, Edward Keane, Lane Chandler, Wallis Clark, Harry Hayden, Antonio Triana, Lola Montes, Maxine Doyle, William Benedict, Herbert Clifton, Harry Depp, Lee Phelps, Janet Martin, Frank Graham (Narrator). *SYN:* A scientist (Von Stroheim) and his assistant (Arlen) develop a machine to keep alive the brain of a dead financier, which eventually takes over the mind of the assistant, forcing him into killing the financier's enemies. *NOTES:* The final film of Helen Vinson—she retired after this film. Production titles were *Monster and the Lady* and *The Monster*. This was the first film based on Curt Siodmak's novel. It would be filmed again in 1953 as *Donovan's Brain*, which adhered closer to the book, and again in 1965 as *The Brain* (aka *Vengeance*). [British title: *The Lady and the Doctor*.] [Re-release title: *The Tiger Man*.]

**414. Lady, Behave!** (12/22/37) B&W 70 mins. (Comedy). *DIR:* Lloyd Corrigan. *A-PRO:* Albert E. Levoy. *SP:* Joseph Krumgold, Olive Cooper. Story by Joseph Krumgold. *CAST:* Sally Eilers, Neil Hamilton, Joseph Schildkraut, Grant Mitchell, Patricia Farr, Marcia Mae Jones, George Ernest, Warren Hymer, Robert Greig, Charles Richman, Spencer Charters, Mary Gordon. *SYN:* A woman (Eilers) pretends to be her sister (Farr) to get her out of a marriage as she is already married.

**415. Lady for a Night** (1/5/42) B&W 87 mins. (Drama-Western). *DIR:* Leigh Jason. *A-PRO:* Albert J. Cohen. *SP:* Isabel Dawn, Boyce DeGaw. Story by Garrett Fort. *CAST:* John Wayne, Joan Blondell, Ray Middleton, Blanche Yurka, Edith Barrett, Leonid Kinskey, Philip Merivale, Hattie Noel, Dorothy Burgess, Patricia Knox, Montagu Love, Lew Payton, Guy Usher, Margaret Armstrong, Ivan Miller, Carmel Myers, Betty Hill, Marilyn Hare, Corinne

Valdez, Pierre Watkin, Jack George, Gertrude Astor, Minerva Urecal, Dudley Dickerson, Paul White, Dolores Gray, Dewey Robinson, The Hall Johnson Choir. SYN: A riverboat queen (Blondell), who runs her casino with her gambler partner (Wayne), marries a society gambler (Middleton) in order to be accepted into society, but then finds herself shunned by his family and charged with his murder. She is eventually found innocent and returns to her previous life on the riverboat with her partner. NOTES: John Wayne plays a secondary role in this film; it is Joan Blondell's film.

**416. Lady from Louisiana** (4/22/41) B&W 82 mins. (Drama). DIR/A-PRO: Bernard Vorhaus. SP: Vera Caspary, Michael Hogan, Guy Endore. Story by Edward James, Francis Faragoh. CAST: John Wayne, Ona Munson, Ray Middleton, Henry Stephenson, Helen Westley, Jack Pennick, Dorothy Dandridge, Shimen Ruskin, Jacqueline Dalya, Paul Scardon, Major James H. MacNamara, James C. Morton, Maurice Costello. SYN: In New Orleans, a crusading lawyer (Wayne) fights the leader (Stephenson) of a local lottery racket, not knowing that it is the assistant (Middleton) who is skimming profits; he also meets and falls in love with a woman (Munson), not knowing that she is the lottery leader's daughter. NOTES: Maurice Costello, a matinee idol in the silent film days, plays a small part in this, his final film before retirement. Working title was *Lady from New Orleans*.

**417. A Lady Possessed** (1/26/52) B&W 87 mins. (Thriller). DIR: William Spier, Roy Kellino. PRO: James Mason. SP: James Mason, Pamela Kellino. Based on *Del Palma* by Pamela Kellino. A Portland Production. A Republic Presentation. CAST: James Mason, June Havoc, Stephen Dunne, Fay Compton, Pamela Kellino, Steven Geray, Diana Graves, Odette Myrtil, Eileen Erskine, John Monaghan, Enid Mosier, Judy Osborne, Constance Cavendish, Alma Lawton, Anna Grevier, Tonyna Micky Dolly, Hazel Franklyn. SYN: A woman (Havoc) imagines she is the dead wife of the owner (Mason) of a country estate.

**Lady Reporter** (G.B. title) *see* **Bulldog Edition**

**418. The Lady Wants Mink** (3/30/53) Trucolor 92 mins. (Comedy). DIR/A-PRO: William A. Seiter. SP: Dane Lussier, Richard Arlen Simmons. Story by Leonard Neubauer, Lou Schor. CAST: Dennis O'Keefe, Ruth Hussey, Eve Arden, William Demarest, Gene Lockhart, Hope Emerson, Hillary Brooke, Tommy Rettig, Earl Robie, Mary Field, Isabel Randolph, Thomas Browne Henry, Brad Johnson, Mara Corday, Robert Shayne, Jean Fenwick, Jean Vachon, Vici Raaf, Mary Alan Hokanson, Angela Greene, Barbara Billingsley, Arthur Walsh, Howard J. Negley, Max Wagner, Rodney Bell, Joseph Mell, Sydney Mason, Frank Gerstle, Wayne Treadway, Bobby Diamond, Dennis Ross, Gail Bonney, Wade Crosby, Slim Duncan, Michael Barton. SYN: A husband (O'Keefe) cannot afford to buy his wife (Hussey) a mink coat, so she buys minks and tries to grow one, resulting in the family being displaced from their home and having to live in the country, to which they become accustomed.

**419. Lake Placid Serenade** (12/23/44) B&W 85 mins. (Musical). DIR:

Steve Sekley. *A-PRO:* Harry Grey. *SP:* Dick Irving Hyland, Doris Gilbert. Story by Frederick Kohner. *CAST:* Vera Hruba Ralston, Robert Livingston, Eugene Pallette, Barbara Jo Allen (Vera Vague), Walter Catlett, William Frawley, Ruth Terry, Stephanie Bachelor, Lloyd Corrigan, John Litel, Ludwig Stossel, Andrew Tombes, Marietta Canty, Twinkle Watts, Janina Frostova, Felix Sadovsky, Janet Martin, Mike Macy, Sewell Shurtz, Janna de Loos, Demetrius Alexis, Erno Kiraly, Hans Herbert, Ferdinand Munier, Nora Lane, John Dehner, Frank Mayo, Pat Gleason, Dick Scott, Ernie Adams, Charles Williams, Ruth Warren, Bert Moorhouse, Eric Alden, Stuart Hall, Craig Lawrence, Geoffrey Ingham, John Hamilton, Stanley Andrews, Virginia Carroll, Eddie Kane, Chester Clute, McGowan and Mack, Ray Noble and His Orchestra, Harry Owens and His Royal Hawaiians, The Merry Meisters, *GUEST STAR*: Roy Rogers. *SYN:* A skater (Ralston), representing her country at a Lake Placid carnival, is unable to return home due to the outbreak of war, and while being taken care of by her paternal uncle (Pallette), falls in love with his junior partner (Livingston). *NOTES:* The film debut of Janna de Loos.

**420. The Laramie Trail** (4/3/44) B&W 55 mins. (Western). *DIR:* John English. *PRO:* Louis Gray. *SP:* J. Benton Cheney. Based on *Mystery at Spanish Hacienda* by Jackson Gregory. *CAST:* Robert Livingston, Smiley Burnette, Linda Brent, Emmett Lynn, John James, George J. Lewis, Leander de Cordova,

Slim Whitaker, Bud Osborne, Bud Geary, Roy Barcroft, Kenne Duncan, Marshall Reed, Martin Garralaga. *SYN:* A Virginian, Johnny Rapidan (Livingston), heads out West and arrives at a Spanish hacienda where he meets a young man (James) falsely accused of murder, and sets out to prove him innocent and bring in the real killer. *NOTES:* The 1st and only entry in Republic's proposed "Johnny Rapidan" series.

**421. Larceny on the Air** (1/11/37) B&W 67 mins. (Crime). *DIR:* Irving Pichel. *PRO:* Nat Levine. *A-PRO:* Sol C. Siegel. *SP:* Richard English, Endre Bohem. Story by Richard English. *CAST:* Robert Livingston, Grace Bradley, Willard Robertson, Pierre Watkin, Granville Bates, William Newell, Byron Foulger, Wilbur Mack, Matty Fain, Smiley Burnette, Josephine Whittell, Charles Timblin, William Griffith, DeWolf Hopper (William Hopper), Frank DuFrane, Florence Gill. *SYN:* A doctor (Livingston) sets out to stop the corrupt selling of quack cures by delivering talks over the radio, and continuing his work through an investigation that gets him mixed up with the mob.

**422. The Last Bandit** (2/25/49) Trucolor 78 mins. (Western). *DIR/A-PRO:* Joseph Kane. *SP:* Thames Williamson. Story by Luci Ward, Jack Natteford. *CAST:* Bill Elliott, Adrian Booth, Forrest Tucker, Andy Devine, Jack Holt, Minna Gombell, Grant Withers, Virginia Brissac, Louis R. Faust, Stanley Andrews, Martin Garralaga, Joseph Crehan, Charles Middleton, Rex Lease, Emmett Lynn, Gene Roth, George Chesebro, Hank Bell, Jack O'Shea, Tex Terry, Steve Clark, George Eldredge, Chick Hannon. *SYN:* A security guard (Elliott) on a train tries to stop his brother (Tucker) from robbing the gold shipment he is guarding. *NOTES:* The final film of Charles Middleton — he died 4/22/49. A remake of Republic's 1941, *The Great Train Robbery.*

**423. The Last Command** (8/3/55) Trucolor 110 mins. (Biography-Western). *DIR/A-PRO:* Frank Lloyd. *PRO:* Herbert J. Yates. *SP:* Warren Duff. Story by Sy Bartlett. *CAST:* Sterling Hayden, Anna Maria Alberghetti, Richard Carlson, Arthur Hunnicutt, Ernest Borgnine, J. Carrol Naish, Ben Cooper, John Russell, Virginia Grey, Jim Davis, Eduard Franz, Otto Kruger, Russell Simpson, Roy Roberts, Slim Pickens, Hugh Sanders, Kermit Maynard, Harry Woods, Morris Ankrum. *SYN:* Jim Bowie (Hayden), developer of the knife which bears his name, is a Mexican citizen living in early 19th century Texas. When Texans begin agitating for secession from Mexico, Bowie tries to recommend a course of moderation, since he used to be friends with Santa Anna (Naish). Finally, when the repressive reactions to the unrest bring tensions to the breaking point, Bowie joins Crockett (Hunnicutt), Travis (Carlson), and the rest of the Texans in the Alamo as they hold off the Mexicans for 13 days before the walls are breached and everyone within is killed. *NOTES:* John Wayne had wanted to do a project about the Alamo for a long time, but negotiations with Republic fell through because, either Republic head Herbert J. Yates backed off from the high-projected cost of the project, or Wayne rejected the film when Yates refused to fund it unless his costar was Vera Hruba Ralston, Yates' wife; he had already worked with her on several other films and would not do it again. Either way,

Wayne left Republic in 1952, never to return. Wayne's version of the story, *The Alamo*, would not be released until 1960, but Yates, seemingly to spite his departing star, pushed this version into production.

**424. The Last Crooked Mile** (8/9/46) B&W 67 mins. (Crime). *DIR:* Philip Ford. *A-PRO:* Rudolph E. Abel. *SP:* Jerry Sackheim. Based on the radio play by Robert L. Richards. *CAST:* Don ("Red") Barry, Ann Savage, Adele Mara, Tom Powers, Sheldon Leonard, Nestor Paiva, Harry Shannon, Ben Welden, John Miljan, Charles D. Brown, John Dehner, Anthony Caruso, George Chandler, Earle Hodgins. *SYN:* A private detective (Barry), hired by an insurance investigator (Powers) to recover money taken in a bank robbery, learns that the thieves died in an auto accident, the money was nowhere to be found, and the car is now part of a carnival exhibit.

**425. Last Frontier Uprising** (2/1/47) Trucolor 67 mins. (Western). *DIR:* Lesley Selander. *A-PRO:* Louis Gray. *SP:* Harvey Gates. Story by Jerome Odlum. *CAST:* Monte Hale, Adrian Booth, James Taggert, Roy Barcroft, Tom London, Philip Van Zandt, Edmund Cobb, John Ince, Frank O'Connor, Bob Blair, Doye O'Dell, Foy Willing and the Riders of the Purple Sage. *SYN:* A government agent (Hale), sent to Texas to buy horses, finds himself up against a gang of horse thieves, which he brings to justice.

**426. The Last Musketeer** (3/1/52) B&W 67 mins. (Western). *DIR:* William Witney. *A-PRO:* Edward J. White. *SP:* Arthur E. Orloff. *CAST:* Rex Allen, Mary Ellen Kay, Slim Pickens, James Anderson, Boyd "Red" Morgan, Monte Montague, Michael Hall, Alan Bridge, Stan Jones, The Republic Rhythm Riders, "Koko." *SYN:* A cowboy (Allen) sets out to stop a ruthless businessman (Anderson) from taking over all the land in a district from the cattle ranchers so he can build a dam and become wealthy selling electric power.

**The Last of the Cavalry** (G.B. title) *see* **Army Girl**

**427. Last Stagecoach West** (7/15/57) B&W/Naturama 67 mins. (Western). *DIR:* Joseph Kane. *PRO:* Rudy Ralston. *SP:* Barry Shipman. A Ventura Production. A Republic Presentation. *CAST:* Jim Davis, Mary Castle, Victor Jory, Lee Van Cleef, Grant Withers, Roy Barcroft, John Alderson, Glenn Strange, Francis McDonald, Willis Bouchey, Lewis Martin, Tristram Coffin, Kelo Henderson, Percy Helton, Henry Wills. *SYN:* A mail stagecoach, operated by a father (Jory) and daughter (Castle), is competing with the new railroad mail service, and a railway detective (Davis) is sent to stop the saboteurs from bringing the rail system to a halt and find out who is behind the sabotage.

**428. Laughing Anne** (7/1/54) Technicolor 90 mins. (Adventure). *DIR/PRO:* Herbert Wilcox. *SP:* Pamela Bower. Based on *Between the Tides* by Joseph Conrad. An Imperadio Production. A Republic Presentation. *CAST:* Wendell Corey, Margaret Lockwood, Forrest Tucker, Ronald Shiner, Robert Harris, Jacques Brunius, Daphne Anderson, Helen Shingler, Danny Green, Harold Lang, Edgar Norfolk, Sean Lynch, Gerard Lohan, Andy Ho, Maurice Bush, David Crowley, Jack Cooper, Rudolph Offenbach, Christopher Rhodes,

John Serret, Michael Oldham, Bernard Robel, Joe Powell, Julian Sherrier, Nandi. *SYN:* In 1890, a singer (Lockwood), prone to laughing fits, and her former boxer husband (Tucker), try to steal the cargo of a sea captain (Corey) and end up losing their lives. *NOTES:* Released in Britain in 1953.

**429. Laughing Irish Eyes** (3/4/36) B&W 70 mins. (Sports-Musical). *DIR:* Joseph Santley. *A-PRO:* Colbert Clark. *SP:* Olive Cooper, Ben Ryan, Stanley Rauh. Story by Sidney Sutherland, Wallace Sullivan. *CAST:* Phil Regan, Walter C. Kelly, Evalyn Knapp, Ray Walker, Mary Gordon, Warren Hymer, Betty Compson, J. M. Kerrigan, Herman Bing, Raymond Hatton, Clarence Muse, Russell Hicks, Maurice Black, John Indrisano, John Sheehan, Robert E. Homans. *SYN:* An American fight promoter (Kelly) travels to Ireland to find a boxer and returns with an Irish tenor (Regan) who wins the middleweight title, as well as the heart of the promoter's daughter (Knapp).

**430. Law of the Golden West** (5/9/49) B&W 60 mins. (Western). *DIR:* Philip Ford. *A-PRO:* Melville Tucker. *SP:* Norman S. Hall. *CAST:* Monte Hale, Paul Hurst, Gail Davis, Roy Barcroft, John Holland, Scott Elliott, Lane Bradford, Harold Goodwin, John Hamilton. *SYN:* A young Buffalo Bill Cody (Hale) sets out to find who murdered his father, which took place during a train robbery, with only a hotel room key as a clue. *NOTES:* This film uses stock footage from Republic's 1940 *Dark Command*.

**431. The Lawless Eighties** (5/31/57) B&W/Naturama 70 Mins. (Western). *DIR/A-PRO:* Joseph Kane. *PRO:* Rudy Ralston. *SP:* Kenneth Gamet. Based on *Brother Van* by Alson Jesse Smith. A Ventura Production. A Republic Presentation. *CAST:* Larry "Buster" Crabbe, John Smith, Marilyn Saris, Ted de Corsia, Anthony Caruso, John Doucette, Frank Ferguson, Sheila Bromley, Walter Reed, Dee "Buzzy" Henry, Will J. White, Bob Swan. *SYN:* A circuit rider (Crabbe) who comes upon some outlaws abusing a group of Indians, goes to inform the authorities, but is shot and wounded; left to die, he is found by a gunfighter (Smith), who nurses him back to health, and together they go after the outlaws.

**432. Lawless Land** (4/6/37) B&W 55 mins. (Western). *DIR:* Albert Ray. *PRO:* A. W. Hackel. *SP:* Andrew Bennison. *CAST:* Johnny Mack Brown, Louise Stanley, Ted Adams, Julian Rivero, Horace Murphy, Frank Ball, Edward Cassidy, Ana Camargo, Roger Williams, Frances Kellogg, Chiquita Hernandez Orchestra. *SYN:* A Texas Ranger (Brown) is sent to a western town to invesigate several murders.

**433. The Lawless Nineties** (2/15/36) B&W 55 mins. (Western). *DIR:* Joseph Kane. *S-PRO:* Paul Malvern. *SP:* Joseph F. Poland. Story by Joseph F. Poland, Scott Pembroke. *CAST:* John Wayne, Ann Rutherford, Harry Woods, George "Gabby" Hayes, Alan Bridge, Lane Chandler, Fred "Snowflake" Toones, Etta McDaniel, Tom Brower, Cliff Lyons, Jack Rockwell, Al Taylor, Charles King, George Chesebro, Tom London, Sam Flint, Henry Hall, Earl Seaman, Tracy Layne, Philo McCullough, Chuck Baldra, Lloyd Ingraham, Monte Blue, Lew Meehan, Horace B. Carpenter, Sherry Tansey, Curley Dresden, Tex Palmer, Jack Kirk, Edward Hearn, Steve

Clark, Jimmy Harrison. *SYN:* A federal agent (Wayne), dispatched from Washington to Wyoming to make sure that an honest election is held in the voting for statehood, has to deal with raiders terrorizing the area.

**434. Lawless Range** (11/4/35) B&W 54 mins. (Western). *DIR:* Robert North Bradbury. *PRO:* Paul Malvern. *S-PRO:* Trem Carr. *SP:* Lindsley Parsons. A Republic-Lone Star Production. *CAST:* John Wayne, Sheila Mannors (Sheila Bromley), Earl Dwire, Frank McGlynn, Jr., Jack Curtis, Yakima Canutt, Wally Howe, Glenn Strange, Jack Kirk, Chuck Baldra, Charles Sargent, Fred Burns, Slim Whitaker, Julia Griffin, Charles Brinley, Robert Kortman, Sam Flint, Tex Palmer, Henry Hall, Pascale Perry, Herman Hack, Ray Henderson, Sherry Tansey, Francis Walker, Fred Parker, Frank Ellis. *SYN:* A government agent (Wayne) is out to stop a banker (McGlynn, Jr.) from making a valley a ghost town to get his hands on a secret gold mine. *NOTES:* This film was shot as a Monogram film; it was released as a Republic film.

**435. A Lawman Is Born** (6/21/37) B&W 58 mins. (Western). *DIR:* Sam Newfield. *PRO:* A. W. Hackel. *SP:* George Plympton. Story by Harry Olmstead. *CAST:* Johnny Mack Brown, Iris Meredith, Warner Richmond, Mary MacLaren, Dick Curtis, Earle Hodgins, Charles King, Frank LaRue, Al St. John, Steve Clark, Jack C. Smith, Sherry Tansey, Wally West, Budd Buster, Lew Meehan, Tex Palmer, Oscar Gahan. *SYN:* A young man (Brown) becomes sheriff and goes after a gang of land-grabbing cattle rustlers.

**436. Lay That Rifle Down** (7/7/55) B&W 71 mins. (Comedy). *DIR:* Charles Lamont. *A-PRO:* Sidney Picker. *SP:* Barry Shipman. *CAST:* Judy Canova, Robert Lowery, Jil Jarmyn, Jacqueline de Wit, Richard Deacon, Robert Burton, James Bell, Leon Tyler, Tweeny Canova, Pierre Watkin, Marjorie Bennett, William Fawcett, Paul E. Burns, Edmund Cobb, Donald MacDonald, Mimi Gibson, Rudy Lee. *SYN:* A woman (Canova), working as a domestic in a small hotel run by her aunt (de Wit) and who dreams of becoming charming and wealthy, enrolls in a correspondence charm course which is run by swindlers who descend on her aunt and try to cheat her out of her money. *NOTES:* Judy Canova's last film for Republic.

**437. Leadville Gunslinger** (3/22/52) B&W 54 mins. (Western). *DIR/A-PRO:* Harry Keller. *SP:* M. Coates Webster. *CAST:* Allan ("Rocky") Lane, Eddy Waller, Grant Withers, Elaine Riley, Roy Barcroft, Richard Crane, I. Stanford Jolley, Kenneth MacDonald, Mickey Simpson, Ed Hinton, Art Dillard, Wesley Hudman, "Black Jack." *SYN:* A U.S. Marshal (Lane) masquerades as a member of an outlaw gang to find out why they are trying to drive his friend (Waller) off his ranch.

**438. The Leathernecks Have Landed** (2/17/36) B&W 67 mins. (Adventure). *DIR:* Howard Bretherton. *PRO:* Ken Goldsmith. *SP:* Seton I. Miller. Story by Wellyn Totman, James Gruen. *CAST:* Lew Ayres, Isabel Jewell, James Ellison, James Burke, J. Carrol Naish, Clay Clement, Maynard Holmes, Ward Bond, Paul Porcasi, Christian Rub, Joe Sawyer, Henry Mowbray, John Webb Dillon, Claude King, Louis Vincenot, Lal Chand Mehra, Frank Tang, Ray Benard, Beal Wong, Robert Strange,

Victor Wong, C. Montague Shaw. *SYN:* A Marine (Ayres), stationed in China and cashiered out of the service when his friend is killed in a barroom brawl, joins up with a pair of gunrunners (Burke, Jewell), but has a change of heart and redeems himself when he captures the gang. [British title: *The Marines Have Landed.*]

**439. The Leavenworth Case** (1/6/36) B&W 66 mins. (Mystery). *DIR:* Lewis D. Collins. *SP:* Albert Demond, Sidney Sutherland. Based on the novel *The Leavenworth Case: A Lawyer's Story* by Anna Katherine Green. *CAST:* Donald Cook, Jean Rouverol, Norman Foster, Erin O'Brien-Moore, Maude Eburne, Warren Hymer, Frank Sheridan, Gavin Gordon, Clay Clement, Ian Wolfe, Peggy Stratford, Archie Robbins, Lucille Ward, Belle Mitchell, Marie Rice, Carl Stockdale, Dagmar Oakland, Bess Stafford. *SYN:* When a woman (Rouverol) is suspected of the murder of her father (Sheridan), it is up to a detective (Clement) to prove her innocence. *NOTES:* Due to careless direction, the murderer is apparent at the moment of the crime, which spoils the rest of the movie. The novel upon which the film is based was written in the 1878, and is considered to be the granddaddy of many mystery stories to follow. Filmed first as a silent in 1923.

**440. "Lightnin'" Crandall** (3/24/37) B&W 60 mins. (Western). *DIR:* Sam Newfield. *PRO:* A. W. Hackel. *SP:* Charles Francis Royal. Story by E. B. Mann. *CAST:* Bob Steele, Lois January, Charles King, Frank LaRue, Ernie Adams, Earl Dwire, Dave O'Brien, Lew Meehan, Horace Murphy, Lloyd Ingraham, Richard Cramer, Jack C. Smith, Sherry Tansey, Tex Palmer, Ed Carey, Art Felix. *SYN:* A gunman (Steele) heads to Arizona and finds himself in the middle of a range war.

**441. Lightnin' in the Forest** (3/26/48) B&W 58 mins. (Crime). *DIR:* George Blair. *A-PRO:* Sidney Picker. *SP:* John K. Butler. Story by J. Benton Cheney. *CAST:* Lynn Roberts, Don ("Red") Barry, Warren Douglas, Adrian Booth, Lucien Littlefield, Claire DuBrey, Roy Barcroft, Paul Harvey, Al Eben, Jerry Jerome, George Chandler, Eddie Dunn, Dale Van Sickel, Bud Wolfe, Hank Worden. *SYN:* An Eastern girl (Roberts) takes a trip to the North Woods and meets a vacationing psychiatrist (Douglas) for a series of adventures.

**442. Lights of Old Santa Fe** (11/6/44) B&W 76 mins. (Western). *DIR:* Frank McDonald. *A-PRO:* Harry Grey. *SP:* Gordon Kahn, Bob Williams. *CAST:* Roy Rogers, George "Gabby" Hayes, Dale Evans, Lloyd Corrigan, Richard Powers (Tom Keene), Claire DuBrey, Arthur Loft, Roy Barcroft, Lucien Littlefield, Sam Flint, Jack Kirk, Bob Nolan and the Sons of the Pioneers, "Trigger." *SYN:* Roy is out to stop a rival rodeo owner (Powers) who wants to buy out his friends' (Hayes, Evans) rodeo. *NOTES:* Re-edited for TV at 54 mins.

**443. Lisbon** (8/17/56) Trucolor/Naturama 90 mins. (Drama). *DIR/PRO:* Ray Milland. *SP:* John Tucker Battle. Story by Martin Rackin. *CAST:* Ray Milland, Maureen O'Hara, Claude Rains, Yvonne Furneaux, Francis Lederer, Percy Marmont, Jay Novello, Edward Chapman, Harold Jamieson, Humberto Madeira. *SYN:* An American smuggler (Milland) is hired to rescue a rich man behind the Iron Curtain by the man's wife (O'Hara), who wants him dead for his money, and the killer (Rains) she has hired to do the job.

**444. London Blackout Murders** (1/15/43) B&W 58 mins. (Thriller-War-Spy). *DIR/A-PRO:* George Sherman. *SP:* Curt Siodmak. *CAST:* John Abbott, Mary McLeod, Lloyd Corrigan, Lester Matthews, Anita Bolster, Louis Borell, Billy Bevan, Lumsden Hare, Frederic Worlock, Carl Harbord, Keith Hitchcock, Tom Stevenson. *SYN:* During the World War II bombing raids on London and subsequent blackouts, a psychotic surgeon (Abbott) murders those he believes to be enemies of England with a deadly hypodermic needle. [British title: *Secret Motive.*]

**445. Lone Star Raiders** (12/23/40) B&W 57 mins. (Western). *DIR:* George Sherman. *A-PRO:* Louis Gray. *SP:* Joseph Moncure March, Barry Shipman. Story by Charles Francis Royal. Based on characters created by William Colt MacDonald. *CAST:* Robert Livingston, Bob Steele, Rufe Davis, June Johnson, George Douglas, Sarah Padden, John Elliott, John Merton, Rex Lease, Bud Osborne, Jack Kirk, Tom London, Hal Price. *SYN:* The Three Mesquiteers (Livingston, Steele, Davis) come to the aid of an old woman (Padden), who inherits a horse ranch, and prevent outlaws from stealing her horses, which she has contracted to sell to the Army. *NOTES:* Re-edited for TV at 54 mins. The 34th entry in the "Three Mesquiteers" series.

**446. Lone Texas Ranger** (5/20/45) B&W 56 mins. (Western). *DIR:* Spencer G. Bennet. *A-PRO:* Louis Gray. *SP:* Bob Williams. Based on the comic strip created by Fred Harman. *CAST:* Bill Elliott, Bobby (Robert) Blake, Alice Fleming, Roy Barcroft, Helen Talbot, Jack McClendon, Rex Lease, Tom Chatterton, Jack Kirk, Nelson McDowell, Larry Olsen, Dale Van Sickel, Frank O'Connor, Robert Wilke, Bud Geary, Budd Buster, Hal Price, Horace B. Carpenter, Nolan Leary, Tom Steele, Earl Dobbins, Bill Stevens, Howard Frederick, *VOICE OF:* Leroy Mason. *SYN:* Red Ryder (Elliott) kills a sheriff (Chatterton) in a holdup and has to convince his son (McClendon) that his dad was crooked and had been using his position to cover up a number of crimes. *NOTES:* Re-edited for TV at 54 mins. The 8th entry in the "Red Ryder" feature series.

**447. Lonely Heart Bandits** (8/29/50) B&W 60 mins. (Crime). *DIR:* George Blair. *A-PRO:* Stephen Auer. *SP:* Gene Lewis. *CAST:* Dorothy Patrick, John Eldredge, Barbara Fuller, Robert Rockwell, Ann Doran, Richard Travis, Dorothy Granger, Eric Sinclair, Kathleen Freeman, Frank Kreig, Harry Cheshire, William Schallert, Howard J. Negley, John Crawford, Eddie Dunn, Sammy McKim, Leonard Penn. *SYN:* A gangster (Eldredge) and his wife (Patrick), who figure there's money to be made in the lonely hearts business, swindle lovelorn victims out of their money and then murder them. *NOTES:* This film was inspired by the Lonely Heart Murders that took place in the late 1940s. [Alternate title: *Lonely Hearts Bandits.*]

**Lonely Hearts Bandits** *see* **Lonely Heart Bandits**

**448. The Lonely Trail** (5/25/36) B&W 58 mins. (Western). *DIR:* Joseph Kane. *S-PRO:* Paul Malvern. *PRO:* Nat

Levine. *SP:* Bernard McConville, Jack Natteford. Story by Bernard McConville. *CAST:* John Wayne, Ann Rutherford, Cy Kendall, Robert Kortman, Fred "Snowflake" Toones, Etta McDaniel, Sam Flint, Dennis Meadows (Dennis Moore), Jim Toney, Yakima Canutt, Lloyd Ingraham, Bob Burns, James Marcus, Rodney Hildebrand, Eugene Jackson, Floyd Shackelford, Jack Kirk, Jack Ingram, Bud Pope, Tex Phelps, Tracy Layne, Clyde Kenny, Horace B. Carpenter, Oscar Gahan, Francis Walker, Clifton Young. *SYN:* Returning to his home in Texas after serving with the Union army, a rancher (Wayne) is hired by the governor (Flint) to clean up the state of corrupt carpetbaggers and their leader (Kendall). *NOTES:* Remade in 1941 as *West of Cimarron*.

**Lost** (G.B. title) *see* **Tears for Simon**

**449. Lost Planet Airmen** (7/25/51) B&W 65 mins. (Action). *SYN:* Feature version of the 12 chapter serial, *King of the Rocketmen*. *NOTES:* Working titles for the feature version were *The Lost Planet* and *Lost Planetmen*. See **984. King of the Rocket Men.**

**450. Love, Honor and Goodbye** (9/15/45) B&W 87 mins. (Comedy). *DIR:* Albert S. Rogell. *A-PRO:* Harry Grey. *SP:* Lee Loeb, Arthur Phillips, Dick Irving Hyland. Story by Art Arthur, Albert S. Rogell. *CAST:* Virginia Bruce, Edward Ashley, Victor McLaglen, Nils Asther, Helen Broderick, Veda Ann Borg, Jacqueline Moore, Robert Greig, Victoria Horne, Ralph Dunn, Therese Lyon. *SYN:* A woman (Bruce) suspects her husband (Ashley) of cheating on her, so she adopts a disguise to try and catch him in the act.

**451. Macbeth** (10/1/48) B&W 106 mins. A Mercury Production. A Republic Presentation. *DIR/PRO/SP:* Orson Welles. *E-PRO:* Charles K. Feldman. Dialogue director: William Alland. Adapted from the play by William Shakespeare. *CAST:* Orson Welles, Jeanette Nolan, Dan O'Herlihy, Roddy McDowall, Edgar Barrier, Alan Napier, Erskine Sanford, John Dierkes, Keene Curtis, Peggy Webber, Lionel Braham, Archie Heugly, Christopher Welles, Morgan Farley, Lurene Tuttle, Brainerd Duffield, William Alland, George "Shorty" Chirello, Gus Schilling, Robert Alan, Jerry Farber, Charles Lederer. *SYN:* Shakespeare's story of a lord (Welles) who falls prey to his own vanity under the prodding of his wife (Nolan) and decides to murder in order to secure his kingdom. *NOTES:* The film debuts of Jeanette Nolan and John Dierkes. This film was later edited down to 89 minutes and re-released in December, 1950.

**452. Madonna of the Desert** (2/23/48) B&W 60 mins. (Drama). *DIR:* George Blair. *A-PRO:* Stephen Auer. *SP:* Albert De Mond. Story by Frank Wisbar. *CAST:* Lynn Roberts, Don ("Red") Barry, Don Castle, Sheldon Leonard, Paul Hurst, Roy Barcroft, Paul E. Burns, Betty Blythe, Grazia Narciso, Martin Garralaga, Frank Yaconelli, Maria Genardi, Renee Donatt, Vernon Cansino. *SYN:* Two crooks (Roberts, Barry) set out to steal a statue of the Madonna, which is said to have miraculous powers, from a rancher (Castle), and with the help of the statue he thwarts their plans.

**453. The Madonna's Secret** (2/16/46) B&W 79 mins. (Mystery). *DIR:* William Thiele. *A-PRO:* Stephen Auer. *SP:* Bradbury Foote, William Thiele. Story by Bradbury Foote, William

Thiele. *CAST:* Francis Lederer, Gail Patrick, Ann Rutherford, Edward Ashley, Linda Stirling, John Litel, Leona Roberts, Michael Hawks, Clifford Brooke, Pierre Watkin, Will Wright, Geraldine Wall, John Hamilton. *SYN:* When a young model (Stirling) is found murdered, her sister (Rutherford), sets out to find her killer, believing it to be the painter (Lederer) that painted her portrait. *NOTES:* Director William Thiele's final U.S. film.

**454. Magic Fire** (3/29/56) Trucolor 94 mins. (Biography). *DIR/PRO:* William Dieterle. *SP:* Beritita Harding, E. A. Dupont, David Chantler. Based on the novel by Bertita Harding. A Republic Presentation. *CAST:* Yvonne DeCarlo, Carlos Thompson, Rita Gam, Valentina Cortese, Alan Badel, Peter Cushing, Frederick Valk, Gerhard Riedmann, Erik Schumann, Robert Freytag, Heinz Klingenberg, Charles Regnier, Fritz Rasp, Kurt Grosskurth, Hans Quest, Jan Hendriks. *SYN:* A biography of German composer Richard Wagner (Badel), concentrating on his love life, with only excerpts of his greatest works. *NOTES:* Filmed on location in Germany.

**455. The Magnificent Rogue** (2/15/47) B&W 74 mins. (Drama-Comedy). *DIR:* Albert S. Rogell. *A-PRO:* William J. O'Sullivan. *SP:* Dane Lussier. Adapted by Sherman L. Lowe. Story by Gerald Drayson Adams, Richard Sokolove. *CAST:* Lynn Roberts, Warren Douglas, Gerald Mohr, Stephanie Bachelor, Adele Mara, Grady Sutton, Donia Bussey, Ruth Lee, Charles Coleman, Dorothy Christy. *SYN:* A woman (Roberts) takes over her husband's (Douglas) shady business dealings when he is sent off to World War II, and when he returns, he has a hard time trying to get her to relinquish the business.

**456. The Main Street Kid** (1/1/48) B&W 64 mins. (Drama-Comedy). *DIR:* R. G. Springsteen. *A-PRO:* Sidney Picker. *SP:* Jerry Sackheim. Additional dialogue by John K. Butler. Based on a radio play by Caryl Coleman. *CAST:* Al Pearce, Janet Martin, Alan Mowbray, Adele Mara, Arlene Harris, Emil Rameau, Byron Barr, Douglas Evans, Roy Barcroft, Phil Arnold, Sarah Edwards, Earle Hodgins, Dick Elliott. *SYN:* A man (Pearce) uses his mind reading powers to expose a gang of crooks.

**457. Main Street Lawyer** (11/3/39) B&W 72 mins. (Drama). *DIR:* Dudley Murphy. *A-PRO:* Robert North. *SP:* Joseph KrumGold, Devery Freeman. Story by Harry Hamilton. *CAST:* Edward Ellis, Anita Louise, Margaret Hamilton, Harold Huber, Clem Bevans, Robert Baldwin, Henry Kolker, Beverly Roberts, Willard Robertson, Richard Lane, Ferris Taylor, Wallis Clark. *SYN:* A country lawyer (Ellis) defends his daughter (Louise) when she is accused of murder. *NOTES:* Working title was *Abraham Lincoln Boggs*. Remade in 1956 as *When Gangland Strikes*. [British title: *Small Town Lawyer*.]

**458. Make Haste to Live** (8/1/54) B&W 90 mins. (Drama). *DIR/A-PRO:* William A. Seiter. *SP:* Warren Duff. Based on a novel by Mildred Gordon. *CAST:* Dorothy McGuire, Stephen McNally, Mary Murphy, Edgar Buchanan, John Howard, Ron Hagerthy, Pepe Hern, Eddy Waller, Carolyn Jones. *SYN:* Released after eighteen years in prison, a man (McNally) seeks revenge against his wife (McGuire) who let him go there for her murder, which never happened.

**459. Mama Runs Wild** (12/22/37) B&W 67 mins. (Comedy). *DIR/A-PRO:* Ralph Staub. *SP:* Gordan Kahn, Paul Gerard Smith, Frank Rowan. Hal Yates. Story by Gordan Kahn. *CAST:* Mary Boland, Ernest Truex, William (Bill) Henry, Lynn Roberts, Max Terhune, Joseph Crehan, Dorothy Page, Dewey Robinson, Julius Tannen, Sammy McKim, John Sheehan, James C. Morton. *SYN:* When a woman (Boland) runs for mayor and promises to close the town bar, her husband (Truex) becomes the opposing candidate.

**460. A Man Alone** (10/17/55) Trucolor 96 mins. (Western). *DIR:* Ray Milland. *PRO:* Herbert J. Yates. *SP:* John Tucker Battle. Story by Mort Briskin. *CAST:* Ray Milland, Mary Murphy, Ward Bond, Raymond Burr, Arthur Space, Lee Van Cleef, Alan Hale, Jr., Douglas Spencer, Thomas Browne Henry, Grandon Rhodes, Martin Garralaga, Kim Spalding, Howard J. Negley, Julian Rivero, Lee Roberts, Minerva Urecal, Thorpe Whiteman, Dick Rich, Frank Hagney. *SYN:* A gunfighter (Milland) hides out in the house of a sick sheriff (Bond) and his daughter (Murphy) when a lynch mob wants to hang him for two murders he did not commit. *NOTES:* The directorial debut of Ray Milland.

**461. A Man Betrayed** (1/8/37) B&W 58 mins. (Crime). *DIR:* John H. Auer. *A-PRO:* William Berke. *SP:* Dorrell McGowan, Stuart McGowan. *CAST:* Eddie Nugent, Kay Hughes, Lloyd Hughes, John Wray, Edwin Maxwell, Theodore Von Eltz, Thomas E. Jackson, William Newell, Smiley Burnette, Christine Maple, John Hamilton, Ralf Harolde, Grace Durkin, Carleton Young, Mary Bovard, Sam Ash, Pat Gleason. *SYN:* A man (Nugent) is framed for a crime and must prove his innocence. Working title was *Missing Men*.

**462. A Man Betrayed** (3/7/41) B&W 83 mins. (Drama). *DIR:* John H. Auer. *A-PRO:* Armand Schaefer. *SP:* Isabel Dawn. Adapted by Tom Kilpatrick. Story by Jack Moffitt. *CAST:* John Wayne, Frances Dee, Edward Ellis, Wallace Ford, Ward Bond, Harold Huber, Alexander Granach, Barnett Parker, Edwin Stanley, Tim Ryan, Harry Hayden, Russell Hicks, Pierre Watkin, Ferris Taylor, Joseph Crehan, Robert E. Homans, Tristram Coffin, Dick Elliott, Joe Devlin, Minerva Urecal. *SYN:* A small-town lawyer (Wayne) arrives in the big city to prove that the death of a basketball player was actually a murder, not suicide, and falls in love with the daughter (Dee) of a corrupt politician (Ellis). *NOTES:* Working title was *Citadel of Crime*. [British title: *Citadel of Crime*.] [Re-release and TV title: *Wheel of Fortune*.]

**463. Man from Cheyenne** (1/16/42) B&W 60 mins. (Western). *DIR/A-PRO:* Joseph Kane. *SP:* Winston Miller. *CAST:* Roy Rogers, George "Gabby" Hayes, Sally Payne, Lynne Carver, William Haade, James Seay, Gale Storm, Jack Ingram, Jack Kirk, Fred Burns, Jack Rockwell, Al Taylor, Chick Hannon, Art Dillard, Frank Brownlee, Pat Brady, Bob Nolan and the Sons of the Pioneers, "Trigger." *SYN:* A government agent (Rogers) is sent to Wyoming to track down modern cattle rustlers. *NOTES:* Re-edited for TV at 54 mins.

**464. Man from Frisco** (7/1/44) B&W 91 mins. (Drama). *DIR:* Robert J. Florey. *A-PRO:* Albert J. Cohen. *SP:* Ethel Hill, Arnold Manoff. Story and Adaptation by George Worthing Yates, George Carleton Brown. CAST: Michael O'Shea, Anne Shirley, Gene Lockhart, Dan Duryea, Ray Walker, Robert Warwick, Forbes Murray, Ann Shoemaker, Tommy Bond, Charles Wilson, Edward Peil, Sr., Bill Nestell, Roy Barcroft, Russell Simpson, Erville Alderson, Olin Howlin, Stanley Andrews, Martin Garralaga, Ira Buck Woods, Stephanie Bachelor, Charles Sullivan, William Haade, Sid Gould, Tom London, George Cleveland, Nolan Leary, Hal Price, Jack Low, Harry Tenbrook, Richard Alexander, Sam Bernard, Lee Shumway, George Lloyd, Judy Cook, Eddy Waller, Tom Chatterton, Minerva Urecal, Jack Gardner, Rex Lease, Roy Darmour, Effie Laird, Virginia Carroll, Marjorie "Babe" Kane, Patricia Knox, Gino Corrado, Frank Moran, Norman Nesbitt, Chester Conklin, Rosina Galli, Monte Montana, Frank Marlowe, Ben Taggart, Sam Flint, Grace Lenard, Weldon Heyburn, Jimmy Conlin, Harrison Greene, John Hamilton, Bud Geary, Kenne Duncan, Jack Kirk, Larry Williams, Maxine Doyle, John Sheehan, George Neise (Narrator). SYN: An engineer (O'Shea) in a shipyard convinces the owners to use his new, revolutionary building technique, which makes for better, cheaper ships.

**465. Man from Music Mountain** (8/15/38) B&W 58 mins. (Western). DIR: Joseph Kane. A-PRO: Charles E. Ford. SP: Betty Burbridge, Luci Ward. Story by Bernard McConville. CAST: Gene Autry, Smiley Burnette, Carol Hughes, Sally Payne, Ivan Miller, Edward Cassidy, Lew Kelly, Howard Chase, Al Terry, Frankie Marvin, Earl Dwire, Lloyd Ingraham, Lillian Drew,

Al Taylor, Joe Yrigoyen, Dick Elliott, Hal Price, Cactus Mack, Gordon Hart, Rudy Sooter, Harry Harvey, Meredith McCormack, Chris Allen, Lee Shumway, Bill Wolfe, Horace B. Carpenter, Tex Phelps, Murdock MacQuarrie, Polly Jenkins and Her Plowboys, "Champion." *SYN:* When drought-plagued farmers sell their land to a gang of crooks and move to a ghost town through the promise of power lines from Boulder Dam, Gene sets out to help them make a success of the town. *NOTES:* Re-edited for TV at 54 mins.

**466. Man from Music Mountain** (10/30/43) B&W 71 mins. (Western). *DIR:* Joseph Kane. *A-PRO:* Harry Grey. *SP:* Bradford Ropes, J. Benton Cheney. *CAST:* Roy Rogers, Ruth Terry, Paul Kelly, Ann Gillis, George Cleveland, Pat Brady, Renie Riano, Paul Harvey, Hank Bell, Jay Novello, Hal Taliaferro, I. Stanford Jolley, Jack O'Shea, Tom Smith, Charles Morton, Roy Barcroft, Slim Whitaker, Fred Burns, Bob Burns, Jane Isbell, Robert Kortman, Timmy Miller, Isabel Lamal, Roy Butler, Bob Nolan and the Sons of the Pioneers, "Trigger." *SYN:* A man (Rogers) returns to his hometown to make a radio appearance, gets mixed up in a feud between the cattlemen and sheepherders, and takes on the role of deputy sheriff to solve the dispute. *NOTES:* Re-edited for TV at 54 mins. [TV title: *Texas Legionnaires*]

**467. The Man from Oklahoma** (8/1/45) B&W 68 mins. (Western). *DIR:* Frank McDonald. *A-PRO:* Louis Gray. *SP:* John K. Butler. *CAST:* Roy Rogers, George "Gabby" Hayes, Dale Evans, Roger Pryor, Arthur Loft, Maude Eburne, Sam Flint, Si Jenks, June Bryde (June Gittleson), Elaine Lange, Charles Soldani, Edmund Cobb, George Sherwood, Eddie Kane, George Chandler, Wally West, Tex Terry, Robert Wilke, Bobbie Priest, Dorothy Bailer, Rosemonde James, Melva Anstead, Beverly Reedy, Geraldine Farnum, Tom London, Horace B. Carpenter, Cactus Mack, Bob Nolan and the Sons of the Pioneers, "Trigger." *SYN:* Roy sets out to solve a feud between rival ranchers. *NOTES:* Re-edited for TV at 54 mins.

**468. The Man from Rainbow Valley** (6/15/46) Trucolor 56 mins. (Western). *DIR:* R. G. Springsteen. *A-PRO:* Louis Gray. *SP:* Betty Burbridge. *CAST:* Monte Hale, Adrian Booth, Jo Ann Marlowe, Ferris Taylor, Emmett Lynn, Tom London, Bud Geary, Kenne Duncan, Doye O'Dell, Bert Roach, The Sagebrush Serenaders (Enright Busse, John Scott, Frank Wilder). *SYN:* A cowboy (Hale) is on the hunt for a stolen stallion which is supposed to be used in a promotional stunt publicizing a cartoon strip. *NOTES:* Hale's second western is photographed in Trucolor, which is an offshoot of Magnacolor, and Republic would use this process for all of their color films.

**469. The Man from the Rio Grande** (10/18/43) B&W 57 mins. (Western). *DIR:* Howard Bretherton. *A-PRO:* Edward J. White. *SP:* Norman S. Hall. *CAST:* Don ("Red") Barry, Wally Vernon, Twinkle Watts, Harry Cording, Nancy Gay, Kirk Alyn, Paul Scardon, Roy Barcroft, Kenne Duncan, Jack Kirk, Kansas Moehring, LeRoy Mason, Earle Hodgins, Ken Terrell, Robert E. Homans, Tom London, Bud Geary, Jack O'Shea. *SYN:* A cowboy (Barry) and his pal (Vernon) set out to make sure a little girl (Watts), who is an ice-skater, is not cheated out of her inheritance.

Man from Tangier (G.B. title) *see* Thunder Over Tangier

**470. The Man from Thunder River** (6/11/43) B&W 57 mins. (Western). *DIR:* John English. *A-PRO:* Harry Grey. *SP:* J. Benton Cheney. *CAST:* Bill Elliott, George "Gabby" Hayes, Anne Jeffreys, Ian Keith, John James, Georgia Cooper, Jack Ingram, Eddie Lee, Charles King, Bud Geary, Jack Rockwell, Edward Cassidy, Roy Brent, Al Taylor, Alan Bridge, Edmund Cobb, Robert Barron, Jack O'Shea, Curley Dresden, Frank McCarroll, "Sonny." *SYN:* Bill and "Gabby" clear their friend (James) of a murder charge and stop the outlaw gang that is stealing gold from their friend's mine.

**471. The Man in the Road** (4/12/57) B&W 83 mins. (Thriller-Spy). *DIR:* Lance Comfort. *PRO:* Charles A. Leeds. *SP:* Guy Morgan. Based on the novel *He Was Found in the Road* by Antony Armstrong. A Gibraltar Production. A Republic Presentation. *CAST:* Derek Farr, Ella Raines, Donald Wolfit, Lisa Daniely, Karel Stepanek, Cyril Cusack, Olive Sloane, Bruce Beeby, Russell Napier, Frederick Piper, John Welsh, Alfred Maron. *SYN:* A man (Farr), suffering from amnesia, wakes up in a nursing home and is told that he is an accountant bound for Russia, but in reality, he finds out that he is a scientist that enemy agents want in Russia. With the help of an American woman (Raines) at the nursing home, he escapes and turns the spies over to the police. *NOTES:* The final film of Ella Raines. Released in Britain in 1956.

**472. The Man Is Armed** (10/19/56) B&W 70 mins. (Crime). *DIR:* Franklin

Adreon. *A-PRO:* Edward J. White. *SP:* Richard Landau, Robert C. Dennis. Story by Don Martin. *CAST:* Dane Clark, William Talman, May Wynn, Robert Horton, Barton MacLane, Fredd Wayne, Richard Benedict, Richard Reeves, Harry Lewis, Bob Jordan, Larry J. Blake, Darlene Fields, John Mitchum. *SYN:* A man (Clark) unknowingly helps a gang pull off a big heist, and the gang discovers that the man is more trouble than he is worth and, as a result, things do not go as planned.

**Man Mad** (G.B. title) *see* **No Place to Land**

**473. Man of Conquest** (5/15/39) B&W 105 mins. (Western-Biography). *DIR:* George Nicholls, Jr. *A-PRO:* Sol C. Siegel. *SP:* Wells Root, Edward E. Paramore, Jr. Adaptation by Jan Fortune. Story by Wells Root, Harold Shumate. *CAST:* Richard Dix, Gail Patrick, Edward Ellis, Joan Fontaine, Victor Jory, Robert Barrat, George "Gabby" Hayes, Ralph Morgan, Robert Armstrong, C. Henry Gordon, Janet Beecher, Pedro de Cordoba, Max Terhune, George Letz, Guy Wilkerson, Hal Taliaferro, Ethan Laidlaw, Ferris Taylor, Kathleen Lockhart, Leon Ames, Charles Stevens, Lane Chandler, Sarah Padden, Tex Cooper, William Benedict, Edmund Cobb. *SYN:* The story of Sam Houston (Dix), beginning in Tennessee with Andrew Jackson (Ellis), who teaches him the clever way of politics, his twice governorship of the state, his first marriage to Eliza Allen (Fontaine) which ended in divorce, his travels to Arkansas, where he is adopted by the Cherokees, his second marriage to Margaret Lea (Patrick), his involvement with the Texans' fight for freedom against Mexico, and the battle of San Jacinto where he defeats Santa Anna (Gordon), and finally, becoming governor of Texas and bringing Texas into the Union as a State. *NOTES:* In the brief scenes of the battle of the Alamo, Robert Armstrong played Jim Bowie, Robert Barrat played Davy Crockett, and Victor Jory played William Travis. Academy Award Nominee — Best Interior Decoration, Best Sound, and Best Original Score.

**Man of the Frontier** *see* **632. Red River Valley**

**474. Man or Gun** (5/30/58) B&W/Naturama 79 mins. (Western). *DIR:* Albert C. Gannaway. *PRO:* Vance Skarstedt. *SP:* Vance Skarstedt, James C. Cassity. An Albert C. Gannaway Production. A Republic Presentation. *CAST:* Macdonald Carey, Audrey Totter, James Craig, James Gleason, Warren Stevens, Harry Shannon, Jil Jarmyn, Robert Burton, Ken Lynch, Karl Davis, Julian Burton, Carl York, Harry Keekas, Mel Gaines, Ron McNeil, Lawrence Grant. *SYN:* A drifter (Carey) frees a town from the tyrannical grip of a power-hungry family.

**475. The Man Who Died Twice** (6/6/58) B&W/Naturama 70 mins. (Drama-Crime). *DIR:* Joseph Kane. *PRO:* Rudy Ralston. *SP:* Richard C. Sarafian. *CAST:* Rod Cameron, Vera Ralston, Mike Mazurki, Gerald Milton, Richard Karlan, Louis Jean Heydt, Don Megowan, John Maxwell, Robert Anderson, Paul Picerni, Don Haggerty, Luana Anders, Jesslyn Fax. *SYN:* A man (Cameron) searches for the killer of his brother (Megowan), who was involved in a narcotics racket, and suspects his wife (Ralston), a nightclub singer, who suffered a nervous breakdown shortly after her husband and two undercover narcotic agents were killed. *NOTES:* Vera Ralston's final screen appearance and Joseph Kane's last directed feature for Republic.

**476. The Mandarin Mystery** (12/23/36) B&W 63 mins. (Mystery-Comedy). *DIR:* Ralph Staub. *PRO:* Nat Levine. *A-PRO:* Victor Zobel. *SP:* John Francis Larkin, Rex Taylor, Gertrude Orr, Cortland Fitzsimmons. Based on *The Chinese Orange Mystery* by Ellery Queen (Manfred B. Lee, Frederic Dannay). *CAST:* Eddie Quillan, Charlotte Henry, Rita LaRoy, Wade Boteler, Franklin Pangborn, George Irving, Kay Hughes, William Newell, George Walcott, Edwin Stanley, Anthony Merrill, Richard Beach, Edgar Allen, Monte Vandergrift, Bert Roach, Grace Durkin, Mary Russell, June Johnson, Mary Bovard. *SYN:* Ellery Queen (Quillan) sets out to recover a valuable Chinese Mandarin stamp and gets involved with a stamp collector (Irving) and murder. *NOTES:* This was the last of the "Ellery Queen" films produced by Republic. Another series of "Ellery Queen" films were produced by Columbia Pictures between 1940 and 1942; four starring Ralph Bellamy and three starring William Gargan. [Alternate title: *The Chinese Orange Mystery*.]

**477. Manhattan Merry-Go-Round** (11/13/37) B&W 82 mins. (Musical). *DIR:* Charles F. Riesner. *A-PRO/SP:* Harry Sauber. Musical Sequences supervised by Harry Grey. Based on the musical revue *Manhattan Merry-Go-Round* by Frank Hummert. *CAST:* Phil Regan, Leo Carrillo, Ann Dvorak, Tamara Geva, James Gleason, Henry Armetta, Luis Alberni, Smiley Burnette, Selmer Jackson, Eddie Kane, Moroni Olsen, Nellie V. Nichols, Gennaro Curci, Sam Finn, Al Herman, Bob Perry, Jack Adair, Thelma Wunder, Joe DiMaggio, Max Terhune, Gene Autry, The Lathrops, Rosalean and Seville, Ted Lewis and His Band, Cab Calloway and His Cotton Club Orchestra, Jack Jenny and His Orchestra, Louis Prima and His Band, Kay Thompson and Her Ensemble. *SYN:* A gangster (Carrillo) wants to take over a sound recording company by using strong-arm methods in coercing disagreeable performers. *NOTES:* Academy Award Nominee—Best Art Direction. [Alternate title: *Manhattan Music Box*] [British title: *Manhattan Music Box*]

**Manhattan Music Box** (G.B. and Alternate title) *see* **Manhattan Merry-Go-Round**

**478. The Mantrap** (4/13/43) B&W 57 mins. (Mystery). *DIR/A-PRO:* George Sherman. *SP:* Curt Siodmak. *CAST:* Henry Stephenson, Lloyd Corrigan, Joseph Allen, Jr., Dorothy Lovett, Edmund MacDonald, Alice Fleming, Tom Stevenson, Frederic Worlock, Jane Weeks. *SYN:* A retired Scotland Yard man (Stephenson), who writes books on criminology, is called to aid in a case as a tribute to his 70th birthday, and he solves the case using his old fashioned methods.

**The Marines Have Landed** (G.B. title) *see* **The Leathernecks have Landed**

**479. Marshal of Amarillo** (7/25/48) B&W 60 mins. (Western). *DIR:* Philip Ford. *A-PRO:* Gordon Kay. *SP:* Bob Williams. *CAST:* Allan ("Rocky") Lane, Eddy Waller, Mildred Cole, Clayton Moore, Roy Barcroft, Trevor Bardette, Minerva Urecal, Denver Pyle, Charles

Williams, Tom Chatterton, Peter Perkins, Tom London, Lynn Castile, "Black Jack." *SYN:* A U.S. Marshal (Lane) and his sidekick (Waller) investigate a murder at a stage line halfway house and try to stop a gang of outlaws from wrecking the stage line.

**480. Marshal of Cedar Rock** (2/1/53) B&W 54 mins. (Western). *DIR:* Harry Keller. *A-PRO:* Rudy Ralston. *SP:* Albert DeMond. Story by M. Coates Webster. *CAST:* Allan ("Rocky") Lane, Eddy Waller, Phyllis Coates, Roy Barcroft, William (Bill) Henry, Robert Shayne, John Crawford, John Hamilton, Kenneth MacDonald, Herb Lytton, "Black Jack." *SYN:* A U.S. Marshal (Lane) sets out to prove the innocence of a man (Henry) falsely accused of robbery, and to find out who is cheating the ranchers out of their land.

**481. Marshal of Cripple Creek** (8/15/47) B&W 58 mins. (Western). *DIR:* R. G. Springsteen. *A-PRO:* Sidney Picker. *SP:* Earle Snell. Based on the comic strip created by Fred Harman. *CAST:* Allan ("Rocky") Lane, Bobby (Robert) Blake, Martha Wentworth, Trevor Bardette, Tom London, Roy Barcroft, Gene Stutenroth (Gene Roth), William Self, Helen Wallace. *SYN:* Red Ryder (Lane) and Little Beaver (Blake), together with a reformed outlaw (Bardette), set out to find who is hijacking gold shipments out of a Colorado mining town. *NOTES:* Re-edited for TV at 54 mins. This was the 23rd and final feature in the "Red Ryder" feature series for Republic. Eagle-Lion studios would produce 4 more "Red Ryder" Cinecolor features in 1949; *Ride, Ryder, Ride, Roll Thunder Roll, The Fighting Redhead,* and *Cowboy and the Prizefighter,* and all would star Jim Bannon (Red Ryder), Little Brown Jug (Little Beaver) and Marin Sais (Duchess), and were directed by Lewis D. Collins.

**482. Marshal of Laredo** (10/7/45) B&W 56 mins. (Western). *DIR:* R. G. Springsteen. *A-PRO:* Sidney Picker. *SP:* Bob Williams. Based on the comic strip created by Fred Harman. *CAST:* Bill Elliott, Bobby (Robert) Blake, Alice Fleming, Peggy Stewart, Roy Barcroft, Tom London, George Carleton, Wheaton Chambers, Tom Chatterton, George Chesebro, Don Costello, Bud Geary, Robert Grady, Sarah Padden, Jack O'Shea, Lane Bradford, Ken Terrell, Dorothy Granger, Dick Scott, Jack Kirk, Mary Arden. *SYN:* When a lawyer (Grady) becomes involved with outlaws and then decides to reform, the outlaws frame him for murder and Red Ryder (Elliott) and Little Beaver (Blake) must prove his innocence and bring the real outlaws to justice. *NOTES:* Re-edited for TV at 54 mins. The 10th entry in the "Red Ryder" feature series.

**483. Marshal of Reno** (7/2/44) B&W 54 mins. (Western). *DIR:* Wallace A. Grissell. *A-PRO:* Louis Gray. *SP:* Anthony Coldeway. Story by Anthony Coldeway, Taylor Caven. Based on the comic strip created by Fred Harman. *CAST:* Bill Elliott, Bobby (Robert) Blake, Alice Fleming, George "Gabby" Hayes, Herbert Rawlinson, Tom London, Jay Kirby, Charles King, Jack Kirk, Kenne Duncan, LeRoy Mason, Robert Wilke, Fred Burns, Tom Steele, Edmund Cobb, Fred Graham, Blake Edwards, Hal Price, Bud Geary, Jack O'Shea, Al Taylor, Marshall Reed, Tom Chatterton, Carl Sepulveda, Ken Terrell, Horace B. Carpenter, Charles Sullivan, George Chesebro, Augie Gomez, Pascale Perry, Jim Corey, *VOICE OF:*

Roy Barcroft. *SYN:* Red Ryder (Elliott) helps the town of Blue Springs to become the county seat by putting an end to the crime wave from Rockland, which wants to be county seat also. *NOTES:* The 2nd entry in the "Red Ryder" feature series. Donald "Red" Barry had played "Red Ryder" in the 1940 serial, *Adventure of Red Ryder.* The last feature to have George "Gabby" Hayes as co-sidekick along with Blake.

**484. The Maverick Queen** (5/3/56) Trucolor/Naturama 92 mins. (Western). *DIR/A-PRO:* Joseph Kane. *PRO:* Herbert J. Yates. *SP:* Kenneth Gamet, DeVallon Scott. Based on the novel by Zane Grey, completed by Romer Grey. *CAST:* Barbara Stanwyck, Barry Sullivan, Scott Brady, Mary Murphy, Wallace Ford, Howard Petrie, Jim Davis, Emile Meyer, Walter Sande, George Keymas, John Doucette, Taylor Holmes, Pierre Watkin, Karen Scott, Carol Brewster, William Loftos, Jack Harden, Herb Jones, Bob Swan, Tristram Coffin, Jack O'Shea. *SYN:* A Pinkerton detective (Sullivan), pretending to be an outlaw to break up the Wild Bunch Gang, falls for a woman (Stanwyck), owner of a hotel/saloon called "The Maverick Queen," not knowing that her partners are Butch Cassidy (Brady) and the Sundance Kid (Petrie), leaders of the Wild Bunch Gang. *NOTES:* This story, adapted from an unfinished story by Zane Grey, was completed by his son Romer and published in 1950. This film was photographed on location in Colorado, and was Republic's first film shot in "Naturama," the studio's own widescreen process, and billed on screen as "Naturama by Republic Pictures Corporation."

**485. Meet the Boy Friend** (7/12/37) B&W 63 mins. (Romance-Comedy). *DIR:* Ralph Staub. *A-PRO:* Colbert Clark. *SP:* Bradford Ropes. Story by Jack Raymond, Robert Arthur. *CAST:* David Carlyle (Robert Paige), Carol Hughes, Warren Hymer, Pert Kelton, Andrew Tombes, Gwili Andre, Smiley Burnette, Syd Saylor, Leonid Kinskey, Selmer Jackson, Cy Kendall, Robert Middlemass, Mary Gordon, Oscar and Elmer, The Beverly Hill Billies. *SYN:* A woman (Hughes) sets out to rescue the country's top crooner (Carlyle), known as "America's Boy Friend," from a marriage to a shady actress (Andre).

**486. Meet the Missus** (11/29/40) B&W 64 mins. (Comedy). *DIR:* Malcolm St. Clair. *A-PRO:* Robert North. *SP:* Val Burton, Ewart Adamson, Taylor Caven. *CAST:* Roscoe Karns, Ruth Donnelly, Spencer Charters, George Ernest, Lois Ranson, Polly Moran, Astrid Allwyn, Alan Ladd, Harry Woods, Dorothy Ann Seese, Harry Tyler. *SYN:* The Higgins family (Karns, Donnelly, Charters, Ernest) run into money and marriage problems when Sidney (Ernest) loses five thousand dollars worth of bonds, and Joe Higgins (Karns) decides to marry off grandpa Higgins (Charters) to a rich widow (Moran). *NOTES:* The 8th entry in the "Higgins Family" series.

**487. Melody and Moonlight** (10/11/40) B&W 72 mins. (Musical). *DIR:* Joseph Santley. *A-PRO:* Robert North. *SP:* Bradford Ropes. Story by David Silverstein. *CAST:* Johnny Downs, Barbara Jo Allen, Jerry Colonna, Mary Lee, Frank Jenks, Claire Carleton, Jonathan Hale, Marten Lamont, Jane Frazee, The Kidoodlers. *SYN:* A bellhop (Downs), with high hopes of being a tap dancer with a debutante (Frazee), runs into problems with her millionaire father

(Hale) who doesn't care for the idea, but eventually comes around and sponsors the radio show that they appear on.

**Melody Girl** (G.B. title) *see* **Sing Dance, Plenty Hot**

**488. Melody Ranch** (11/15/40) B&W 83 mins. (Western-Musical). *DIR:* Joseph Santley. *A-PRO:* Sol C. Siegel. *SP:* John C. Moffitt, F. Hugh Herbert. Special comedy sequences by Sid Culler, Ray Golden. *CAST:* Gene Autry, Jimmy Durante, Ann Miller, Barton MacLane, Barbara Jo Allen, George "Gabby" Hayes, Jerome Cowan, Mary Lee, Joe Sawyer, Horace MacMahon, Clarence Wilson, William Benedict, Ruth Gifford, Maxine Ardell, Veda Ann Borg, George Chandler, Jack Ingram, Lloyd Ingraham, John Merton, Horace Murphy, Tom London, Edmund Cobb, Slim Whitaker, Curley Dresden, Dick Elliott, Billy Bletcher, Art Mix, George Chesebro, Tiny Jones, Herman Hack, Jack Kirk, Merrill McCormick, Wally West, Frankie Marvin, Carl Cotner, Tex Cooper, Chick Hannon, Tom Smith, Jim Corey, Ralph Bucko, Jane Keckley, Frank Hagney, Jack Montgomery, Priscilla Bonner, Joe Yrigoyen, Bob Wills and His Texas Playboys, "Champion." *SYN:* Gene pays a visit to his hometown, is made honorary sheriff for the Frontier Days Celebration, and rids the town of three brothers (MacLane, Sawyer, McMahon) and their gang who are running the town. *NOTES:* Re-edited for TV at 54 mins.

**489. Melody Trail** (9/24/35) B&W 60 mins. (Western-Musical). *DIR:* Joseph Kane. *PRO:* Nat Levine. *SP:* Sherman L. Lowe. Story by Sherman L. Lowe, Betty Burbridge. *CAST:* Gene Autry, Smiley Burnette, Ann Rutherford, Wade Boteler, Alan Bridge, Willy Costello, Marie Quillan, Fern Emmett, Gertrude Messinger, Tracy Layne, George DeNormand, Marion Downing, Ione Reed, Jane Barnes, Abe Lefton, Tex Cooper, Herman Hack, Chick Hannon, Tom Smith, "Buck," the Wonder Dog, "Champion." *SYN:* When Gene and Frog (Burnette) lose their rodeo winnings to a gypsy thief, they end up working at a ranch house and also help stop a gang of rustlers. *NOTES:* Re-edited for TV at 54 mins.

**Men of Steel** (G.B. title) *see* **Bill Cracks Down**

**490. Mercy Island** (10/10/41) B&W 72 mins. (Adventure). *DIR:* William Morgan. *A-PRO:* Armand Schaefer. *SP:* Malcolm Stuart Boylan. Based on the novel by Theodore Pratt. *CAST:* Ray Middleton, Gloria Dickson, Otto Kruger, Don Douglas, Forrester Harvey, Terry Kilburn. *SYN:* Set in the Florida Keys, a group of travelers become shipwrecked on a remote island inhabited by a recluse (Kruger) who is a wanted man. *NOTES:* Academy Award Nominee — Best Score.

**491. Mexacali Rose** (3/29/39) B&W 60 mins. (Western). *DIR:* George Sherman. *A-PRO:* Harry Grey. *SP:* Gerald Geraghty. Story by Luci Ward, Connie Lee. *CAST:* Gene Autry, Smiley Burnette, Noah Beery, Sr., Luana Walters, William Farnum, William Royle, LeRoy Mason, Wally Albright, Kathy Frey, Roy Barcroft, Dick Botiller, Vic Demourelle, John Beach, Henry Otho, Joe Dominguez, Al Haskell, Merrill McCormick, Fred "Snowflake" Toones, Sherry Hall, Al Taylor, Josef Swickard, Tom London, Jack Ingram, Eddie Parker, Suzanne Kaaren, "Champion."

SYN: Gene and Frog (Burnette), together with a Mexican bandit (Beery, Sr.), help to protect a mission for poor Mexican children from oil swindlers. [British title: *The Girl from Mexico*.]

**492. Mexicana** (11/15/45) B&W 83 mins. (Musical). *DIR/A-PRO:* Alfred Santell. *SP:* Frank Gill, Jr. *CAST:* Tito Guizar, Constance Moore, Leo Carrillo, Estelita Rodriguez, Howard Freeman, Steven Geray, Jean Stevens, St. Luke's Choristers, Peter Meremblum, Junior Orchestra. *SYN:* A singing idol (Guizar), who gets tired of his fans ripping the shirt off his back every time he appears in public, persuades a visiting soprano (Moore) to pose as his wife so that the fans will go easier on his wardrobe. *NOTES:* The film debut of Estelita Rodriguez. [Alternate title: *Beyond the Border*.]

**493. Michael O'Halloran** (5/15/37) B&W 68 mins. (Drama). *DIR:* Karl Brown. *A-PRO:* Herman Schlom. *SP:* Adele Buffington. Based on *Michael O'Halloran* by Gene Stratton-Porter. *CAST:* Wynne Gibson, Warren Hull, Jackie Moran, Charlene Wyatt, Sidney Blackmer, Hope Manning, G. P. Huntley, Jr., Robert Greig, Helen Howell, Vera Gordon, Pierre Watkin, Dorothy Vaughan, Bodil Rosing, Guy Usher. *SYN:* A 10-year-old newsboy (Moran), who is eternally devoted to his disabled sister (Wyatt), are orphaned and a woman (Gibson), who is going through a divorce, takes in the kids and ends up falling for them and when her husband (Blackmer) sees this touching trio, he decides to cancel the divorce proceedings. *NOTES:* The author has found this film listed in several publications — under the above title and also under the working title. Remade in 1948 by Windsor Pictures for Monogram Studios under the same title. Working title was *Any Man's Wife*.

**494. Mickey, the Kid** (7/3/39) B&W 68 mins. (Drama). *DIR:* Arthur Lubin. *A-PRO:* Herman Schlom. *SP:* Doris Malloy, Gordan Kahn. Story by Alice Altschuler. *CAST:* Bruce Cabot, Ralph Byrd, ZaSu Pitts, Tommy Ryan, Jessie Ralph, June Storey, J. Farrell MacDonald, John Qualen, Robert Elliott, Scotty Beckett, James Flavin, Archie Twitchell. *SYN:* A criminal (Cabot) raises his young son (Ryan) in the slums, and when he kills a bank teller in a robbery, he and his son go on the run together. They hijack a school bus, and when it is wrecked in a snowdrift, the father, who goes for help, is shot. The son saves the kids by building a fire and becoming a hero.

**Midnight Melody** *see* **Murder in the Music Hall**

**495. Million Dollar Pursuit** (5/30/51) B&W 59 mins. (Crime). *DIR:* R. G. Springsteen. *A-PRO:* Stephen Auer. *E-PRO:* Herbert J. Yates. *SP:* Albert DeMond, Bradbury Foote. Story by Albert DeMond. *CAST:* Penny Edwards, Grant Withers, Norman Budd, Steve Flagg (Michael St. Angel), Rhys Williams, Mikel Conrad, Paul Hurst, Denver Pyle, Ted Pavelec, John DeSimone, Don Beddoe, Edward Cassidy, Edward Clark, John Hamilton, George Brand, Jack Shea. *SYN:* A small-time hoodlum (Budd) decides to rob a department store and make himself known as a mastermind of robbery, but his big mouth ruins those plans, and another mob takes over and gives him a lesser role in the heist.

**496. Missile Monsters** (3/28/58) B&W 75 mins. (Action). *SYN:* Feature version of the 12 chapter serial, *Flying Disc Man from Mars. See* **969. Flying Disc Man from Mars.**

**497. Missing Women** (2/23/51) B&W 60 mins. (Crime). *DIR:* Philip Ford. *A-PRO:* Stephen Auer. *SP:* John K. Butler. *CAST:* Penny Edwards, James Millican, John Gallaudet, John Alvin, Fritz Feld, James Brown, Robert Shayne, Marlo Dwyer, William Forrest, John Hedloe, Mary Alan Hokanson, Patricia Joiner. *SYN:* A newlywed (Edwards), whose husband (Hedloe) is killed by a gang of car thieves, plans her revenge by getting into prison and learning about the car-theft racket so she can get to the murderers of her husband.

**498. A Missouri Outlaw** (11/25/41) B&W 58 mins. (Western). *DIR/A-PRO:* George Sherman. *SP:* Doris Schroeder, Jack Lait, Jr. *CAST:* Don ("Red") Barry, Lynn Merrick, Noah Beery, Sr., Paul Fix, Al St. John, Frank LaRue, Kenne Duncan, John Merton, Carleton Young, Frank Brownlee, Fred "Snowflake" Toones, Karl Hackett, Lee Shumway, Raphael Bennett, Bob McKenzie, Kermit Maynard, Frank McCarroll, Curley Dresden, Herman Hack. *SYN:* A cowboy (Barry) goes after the men that killed his father (Beery, Sr.).

**499. The Missourians** (11/25/50) B&W 60 mins. (Western). *DIR:* George Blair. *A-PRO:* Melville Tucker. *SP:* Arthur E. Orloff. *CAST:* Monte Hale, Paul Hurst, Roy Barcroft, Lyn Thomas, Howard J. Negley, Robert Neil, Lane Bradford, John Hamilton, Sarah Padden, Charles Williams, Perry Ivins. *SYN:* When a Polish refugee (Neil) attempts to buy a ranch and the other ranchers try to stop him, a sheriff (Hale) comes to his defense to put an end to the prejudice.

**500. Mr. District Attorney** (3/26/41) B&W 69 mins. (Crime). *DIR:* William Morgan. *A-PRO:* Leonard Fields. *SP:* Karl Brown, Malcolm Stuart Boylan. Based on the radio program *Mr. District Attorney* by Phillips H. Lord. *CAST:* Dennis O'Keefe, Florence Rice, Peter Lorre, Stanley Ridges, Minor Watson, Charles Arnt, Joan Blair, Charles Halton, Alan Edwards, George Watts, Sarah Edwards, Helen Brown, Ben Welden. *SYN:* A novice District Attorney (O'Keefe), fresh out of law school, botches up his first case and, assisted by a newspaper reporter (Rice), is assigned by his boss, District Attorney Hinton (Ridges), to track down a former politician (Lorre) who had vanished four years earlier with a large payoff. *NOTES:* Two sequels followed, *Mr. District Attorney in the Carter Case* (1941) and *Secrets of the Underground* (1943). Dennis O'Keefe also starred in a 1947 version by Columbia Pictures, also titled *Mr. District Attorney*, and it too was based on the radio show.

**501. Mr. District Attorney in the Carter Case** (12/18/41) B&W 67 mins. (Drama). *DIR:* Bernard Vorhaus. *A-PRO:* Leonard Fields. *SP:* Sidney Sheldon, Ben Roberts. Based on the radio program *Mr. District Attorney* by Phillips H. Lord. *CAST:* James Ellison, Virginia Gilmore, Franklin Pangborn, Paul Harvey, Lynne Carver, Spencer Charters, Douglas Fowley, John Eldredge, Eddie Acuff, John Sheehan, Bradley Page. *SYN:* An assistant District Attorney (Ellison), together with his reporter girlfriend (Gilmore) track down clues in the murder of a publisher of a fashion magazine. NOTES: This film was preceded by *Mr. District Attorney* (1941) and was followed by *Secrets of the Underground* (1943). Sidney Sheldon's debut as a screenwriter before he became a successful novelist in the 1970s. [Alternate title: *The Carter Case.*] [British title: *The Carter Case.*]

**502. Mojave Firebrand** (3/19/44) B&W 55 mins. (Western). *DIR:* Spencer G. Bennet. *A-PRO:* Edward J. White. *SP:* Norman S. Hall. *CAST:* Bill Elliott, George "Gabby" Hayes, Anne Jeffreys, LeRoy Mason, Jack Ingram, Harry McKim, Karl Hackett, Forrest Taylor, Hal Price, Marshall Reed, Kenne Duncan, Bud Geary, Jack Kirk, Fred Graham, Tom London, Frank Ellis, Tom Steele, Bob Burns, Jess Cavan, Art Dillard, Bud Osborne, Larry Steers, "Sonny." *SYN:* Bill arrives in the town of Epitaph and helps his friend "Gabby" and the townspeople regain their town from an unscrupulous businessman (Mason) and his gang.

**Money Isn't Everything** (G.B. title) see **Jeepers Creepers**

**503. Money to Burn** (12/31/39) B&W 69 mins. (Comedy). *DIR/A-PRO:* Gus Meins. *SP:* Jack Townley. Story by Jack Townley, Taylor Caven. *CAST:* James Gleason, Lucille Gleason, Russell Gleason, Harry Davenport, Lois Ranson, Tommy Ryan, Thurston Hall, Winifred Harris, Douglas Meins, Lucien Littlefield, Herbert Rawlinson, Jack Rice, Andrew Tombes, Gladys Blake, Jean Fenwick. *SYN:* Lil Higgins (Lucille Gleason) buys up all the dog biscuits in town to enter a contest that offers a $50,000 prize, but what she doesn't know is that Joe Higgins (James Gleason) works for the agency that is handling the contest holder's account, which thus disqualifies her entry. *NOTES:* The 5th entry in the "Higgins Family" series.

**504. Moonlight Masquerade** (6/10/42) B&W 67 mins. (Musical-Drama). *DIR/A-PRO:* John H. Auer. *SP:* Lawrence Kimble. Story by John H. Auer. *CAST:* Dennis O'Keefe, Jane Frazee, Betty Kean, Eddie Foy, Jr., Erno Verebes, Franklin Pangborn, Paul Harvey, Jed Prouty, Tommye Adams (Abigail Adams), The Three Chocolateers. *SYN:* Complications ensue when two oil company co-owners (Harvey, Prouty) agree to leave controlling interest in their company to their respective son and daughter, (O'Keefe, Frazee), if the two marry by the time she turns 21, but the problem is that they have never met and have preconceived notions of what the other must be like.

**505. Moonrise** (10/1/48) B&W 90 mins. (Drama). *DIR:* Frank Borzage. *PRO/SP:* Charles F. Haas. Based on the novel by Theodore Strauss. A Marshall Grant Production. A Republic Presentation. *CAST:* Dane Clark, Gail Russell, Ethel Barrymore, Allyn Joslyn, Rex Ingram, Henry (Harry) Morgan, David Street, Selena Royle, Harry Carey, Jr., Irving Bacon, Lloyd Bridges, Houseley Stevenson, Phil Brown, Harry Cheshire, Lila Leeds, Virginia Mullen, Oliver Blake, Tom Fadden, Charles Lane, Clem Bevans, Helen Wallace, Michael Branden (Archie Twitchell), Bill Borzage, James L. Kelly, Ed Rees, Casey MacGregor, John Harmon, Monte Lowell, Jimmy Hawkins, Gary Armstrong, Dee "Buzzy" Henry, Jimmy Crane, Harry Lauter, Bob Hoffman, Joel McGinnis, Tim Hawkins, Doreen McCann, Candy

Toxton, Steven Peck, Johnny Calkins, Tommy Ivo, Michael Dill, Linda Lombard, Stelita Ravel, Renee Donatt, George Backus, Monte Montague. *SYN:* The son (Clark) of a murderer, who was hanged for his crimes, is haunted by his father's past and tormented by his peers in a small southern town where his only friend is a young girl (Russell) who is in love with him. When he is attacked by another youth (Carey, Jr.), he kills him in self-defense, and feeling guilty of murder, flees to the swamps where he stays with a former schoolteacher (Barrymore), who convinces him that he is not a product of "bad blood" and that he should turn himself in to the law. *NOTES:* Academy Award Nominee—Best Sound.

**Morning Call** (G.B. title) *see* **Strange Case of Dr. Manning**

**506. Moscow Strikes Back** (10/1/42) B&W 55 mins. (Documentary-War). *DIR:* None. *PRO:* Central Newsreel Studios of Moscow. American produced version by Nicholas Napoli. English commentary written by Albert Maltz, Elliott Paul. An Artkino Picture. A Republic Presentation. *CAST:* Narrated by Edward G. Robinson. *SYN:* A documentary of the Russian winter counteroffensive of 1941. *NOTES:* Although this documentary was produced by Artinko Pictures, the releasing rights were given to Republic Pictures. Reviewed as an Artkino release 8/12/42.

**507. Mountain Moonlight** (7/12/41) B&W 68 mins. (Comedy). *DIR:* Nick Grinde. *A-PRO:* Armand Schaefer. *SP:* John W. Krafft, Mauri Grashin, Dorrell McGowan, Stuart McGowan. *CAST:* Leon Weaver, June Weaver, Frank Weaver, Betty Rhodes, John Archer, Loretta Weaver, George Ernest, Andrew Tombes, George Chandler, Harry Hayden, Roscoe Ates, Leonard Carey, George Meeker, Edwin Stanley, Kane Richmond, Frank Sully, Johnny Arthur. *SYN:* The Weavers (Frank, Leon, June) head to Washington when they discover that their ancestors loaned the government some cash back in 1790, and they stand to gain some sizeable returns, with interest. *NOTES:* The 7th entry in the "Weaver Brothers and Elviry" series. Working title was *Thunder Over the Ozarks*. [British title: *Moving in Society*.]

**508. Mountain Rhythm** (6/29/39) B&W 61 mins. (Western). *DIR:* B. Reeves Eason. *A-PRO:* Harry Grey. *SP:* Gerald Geraghty. Story by Connie Lee. *CAST:* Gene Autry, Smiley Burnette, June Storey, Maude Eburne, Ferris Taylor, Walter Fenner, Jack Pennick, Hooper Atchley, Bernard Suss, Edward Cassidy, Jack Ingram, Tom London, Roger Williams, Frankie Marvin, "Champion." *SYN:* When the owner of a resort hotel schemes to buy the ranchers' grazing land at a low profit for his own use, Gene helps the ranchers to purchase their grazing land by rounding up and selling their cattle.

**509. Mountain Rhythm** (1/8/43) B&W 70 mins. (Comedy). *DIR:* Frank McDonald. *A-PRO:* Armand Schaefer. *SP:* Dorrell McGowan, Stuart McGowan. Story by Ray Harris. *CAST:* Leon Weaver, Frank Weaver, June Weaver, Lynn Merrick, Frank M. Thomas, Sally Payne, Dick Jones, Joseph Allen, Jr., Billy Roy, Earle S. Dewey, Sam Flint, Ben Erway. *SYN:* The Weavers (Leon Frank, June) try to start a farm as their contribution to the war effort, but run into problems from a nearby school run by snobs for snobby children. NOTES: The 11th and final entry in the "Weaver Brothers and Elviry" series. [British title: *Harvest Days*]

**Moving in Society** (G.B. title) *see* **Mountain Moonlight**

**510. Murder in the Music Hall** (4/10/46) B&W 84 mins. (Mystery). DIR: John English. A-PRO: Herman Millakowsky. SP: Frances Hyland, Laszlo Gorog. Story by Arnold Phillips, Maria Matray. CAST: Vera Hruba Ralston, William Marshall, Helen Walker, Nancy Kelly, William Gargan, Ann Rutherford, Julie Bishop, Jerome Cowan, Edward Norris, Paul Hurst, Frank Orth, Jack LaRue, James Craven, Fay McKenzie, Tom London, Joe Yule, Mary Field, Anne Nagel, Ilka Gruning, Inez Palange, William Austin, Spec O'Donnell, Billy Vernon, Nolan Leary, LeRoy Mason, Brooks Benedict, Lee Phelps, Virginia Carroll, Lillian Bronson, Wheaton Chambers, John Wald, James Farley, Red McCarthy, Patti Phillippi, John Jolliffe, Henry Lie, Conden and Bohland. SYN: When a producer-blackmailer (Norris), who lives next door to a music hall is killed, a music hall ice skating star (Ralston) and orchestra leader (Marshall) set out to solve the murder. NOTES: Vera Ralston's final appearance in films as an ice-skater. [Re-release title: *Midnight Melody*]

**Music in the Moonlight** *see* **Ice-Capades**

**511. My Best Gal** (3/28/44) B&W 67 mins. (Musical). DIR: Anthony Mann. A-PRO: Harry Grey. SP: Olive Cooper, Earl Felton. Story by Richard Brooks. CAST: Jane Withers, James Lydon, Frank Craven, Fortunio Bonanova, George Cleveland, Franklin Pangborn, Mary Newton, Jack Boyle. SYN: A drugstore assistant (Withers), who comes from a show business family, but wants no part of show business, tries to find a backer for a musical written by a budding composer (Lydon).

**512. My Buddy** (10/12/44) B&W 69 mins. (Crime). DIR: Steve Sekely. A-PRO: Edward J. White. SP: Arnold Manoff. Story by Prescott Chaplin. CAST: Don ("Red") Barry, Ruth Terry, Lynn Roberts, Alexander Granach, Emma Dunn, John Litel, George E. Stone, Jonathan Hale, Ray Walker, Joe Devlin, Matt McHugh, Jack Ingram, George Humbert, Gayne Whitman, Edward Earle, Emmett Vogan, Jimmy Zaner, Jack Baxley, Connie Leon, Milton Kibbee, Almeda Fowler, Sam Bernard, Constance Purdy, Blake Edwards, Sven Hugo Borg, George Lloyd, Lee Shumway, Marshall Reed, Roy Darmour, Lynton Brent, Harry Strang, Jack Gardner, Russ Whiteman, Boots Brown, Robert Middlemass, Nolan Leary, Ralph Linn, Frank Marlowe, Charles Sullivan, Larry Steers, Jack Rockwell, Charles Sherlock, Noble "Kid" Chissell, John Bagni, Jay Norris, Arthur Loft, Jack Mulhall, Larry Burke, The Poison Gardner Trio. SYN: A priest (Litel) delivers testimony before the Washington Post-War Planning Committee and talks about his friend (Barry) and the man's experiences after returning home from World War I, a story we see in flashback. Returning from the war, and unable to get a job, he is forced to put off his marriage to his girl (Roberts), and gets involved in bootlegging and ends up going to prison where he forms a gang. Released from prison, a gang war erupts and he ends up killing his former boss (Granach) and is then himself killed in a rooftop shootout. The film ends with the priest once more before the committee, explaining how a note was left to the priest, begging to tell the veteran's story so this might never happen to another. *NOTES:* This plot was similar to the 1939 Warner Bros. film, *The Roaring Twenties.* It was also a plea not to let this happen to our returning vets from World War II, as it did to those returning from World War I.

**513. My Pal Trigger** (7/10/46) B&W 79 mins. (Western). *DIR:* Frank McDonald. *A-PRO:* Armand Schaefer. *SP:* Jack Townley, John K. Butler. Story by Paul Gangelin. *CAST:* Roy Rogers, George "Gabby" Hayes, Dale Evans, Jack Holt, LeRoy Mason, Roy Barcroft, Sam Flint, Kenne Duncan, Ralph Sanford, Francis McDonald, Harlan Briggs, William Haade, Alan Bridge, Paul E. Burns, Frank Reicher, Fred Graham, Ted Mapes, Bob Nolan and the Sons of the Pioneers, "Trigger." *SYN:* Roy plans to mate a prize mare with a stallion belonging to a rancher friend (Hayes). Another rancher (Holt) tries to steal the stallion, but it escapes and mates with Roy's mare, and when he catches up to the stallion, he shoots it. He puts the blame on Roy who escapes from authorities, taking his mare with him. The mare's colt is born and grows up to be the famed horse, Trigger. *NOTES:* This film was Roy's personal favorite. "Trigger" originally named "Golden Cloud" was purchased by Roy in 1938 for $2,500 and was ridden by Roy in his first starring role in *Under Western Stars* (1938). When studio boss, Herbert J. Yates, threatened to take "Trigger" away, Roy told him sorry but he'd already bought the horse for $2,500. Remade in 1951 as *Rodeo King and the Senorita*. Re-edited for TV at 54 mins

**514. My Wife's Relatives** (5/20/39) B&W 65 mins. (Comedy). *DIR:* Gus Meins. *A-PRO:* Sol C. Siegel. *SP:* Jack Townley. Story by Dorrell McGowan, Stuart McGowan. *CAST:* James Gleason, Lucille Gleason, Russell Gleason, Harry Davenport, Mary Hart, Purnell Pratt, Maude Eburne, Marjorie Gateson, Tommy Ryan, Henry Arthur, Sally Payne, Edward Keane. *SYN:* Joe Higgins (James Gleason) opens his own candy factory to impress his daughter's (Hart) boyfriend (Arthur) and parents (Pratt, Gatteson), who also own a candy factory, but trouble erupts when Lil (Lucille Gleason) loses her diamond ring, then offers a reward for its recovery, and the misquoted ad states that it's in one of the candy bars. *NOTES:* The 2nd entry in the "Higgins Family" series.

**515. The Mysterious Miss X** (1/10/39) B&W 62 mins. (Mystery-Comedy). *DIR:* Gus Meins. *A-PRO:* Herman Schlom. *SP:* Olive Cooper. Story by George Worthing Yates. *CAST:* Michael Whalen, Mary Hart, Mabel Todd, Chick Chandler, Frank M. Thomas, Regis Toomey, Don Douglas, Wade Boteler, Dorothy Tree, Eddie Acuff, Pierre Watkin, Harlan Briggs. *SYN:* Two vaudevillians from England (Whalen, Chandler), stranded in America, are mistaken for Scotland Yard detectives and before they know it, are helping police solve a hotel murder.

**516. The Mysterious Mr. Valentine** (9/3/46) B&W 56 mins. Crime). *DIR:* Philip Ford. *A-PRO:* Donald H. Brown. *SP:* Milton Raison. *CAST:* William

(Bill) Henry, Linda Stirling, Virginia Christine, Thomas E. Jackson, Barbara Woodell, Kenne Duncan, Virginia Brissac, Lyle Latell, Ernie Adams, Tristram Coffin, Arthur Space, Robert Bice. SYN: When a young woman's (Stirling) car has a blowout, it unexpectedly sets off a mystery that leads to blackmail and murder.

**517. Mystery Broadcast** (11/23/43) B&W 63 mins. (Mystery). DIR/A-PRO: George Sherman. SP: Dane Lussier, Gertrude Walker. CAST: Frank Albertson, Ruth Terry, Nils Asther, Wynne Gibson, Paul Harvey, Mary Treen, Addison Richards, Joseph Crehan, Alice Fleming, Francis Pierlot, Ken Carpenter, Emmett Vogan. SYN: When her popular mystery show has ratings trouble, a radio writer (Terry) becomes intrigued with an unsolved murder case and when she airs it, it brings about several murders associated with the case, and she almost gets herself killed.

**518. Mystery of the Black Jungle** (10/20/55) B&W 72 mins. (Jungle Adventure). DIR: Ralph Murphy. PRO: Giorgio Venturini. SP: Ralph Murphy, Gian Paolo Callegari. Based on the novel *Misterio Nero Bosco* by Emilio Salgari. A Cosmopolitan Production. A Republic Presentation. CAST: Giorgio Venturini, Ralph Murphy, Gian Paolo Callegari, Emilio Salgari, Lex Barker, Jane Maxwell, Luigi Tosi, Paul Muller, Jack Rex, Pamela Palma. SYN: An adventurer (Barker) and his comrades travel to India, where they meet up with a tribe of idol worshippers. [British title: *The Black Devils of Kali*.]

**519. Navajo Trail Raiders** (10/15/49) B&W 60 mins. (Western). DIR: R. G. Springsteen. A-PRO: Gordon Kay. SP: M. Coates Webster. CAST: Allan ("Rocky") Lane, Eddy Waller, Robert Emmett Keane, Barbara Bestar, Hal Landon, Dick Curtis, Dennis Moore, Ted Adams, Forrest Taylor, Marshall Reed, Steve Clark, Chick Hannon, "Black Jack." SYN: A government investigator (Lane) goes after outlaws who are raiding supply trains to a western town.

**520. Navy Blues** (4/19/37) B&W 68 mins. (Spy). DIR: Ralph Staub. A-PRO: Burt Kelly. SP: Gordon Kahn, Eric Taylor. Story by Gordon Kahn, Eric Taylor. CAST: Dick Purcell, Mary Brian, Warren Hymer, Joe Sawyer, Edward Woods, Horace MacMahon, Chester Clute, Lucille Gleason, Ruth Fallows, Alonzo Price, Mel Ruick, Carleton Young. SYN: A sailor (Purcell), pretending to be a naval intelligence officer to impress a girl (Brian), gets both of them involved with a group of spies plotting to assassinate a visiting diplomat.

**521. Navy Born** (6/2/36) B&W 68 mins. (Drama). DIR: Nate Watt. PRO: Nat Levine. SP: Marcus Goodrich, Albert DeMond, Olive Cooper, Claire Church. Story by Mildred Cram. CAST: William Gargan, Claire Dodd, Douglas Fowley, George Irving, Dorothy Tree, William Newell, Addison Randall (Jack Randall), Claudia Coleman, Douglas Wood, Paul Fix, Hooper Atchley, M. Lou Wastal, Larry Steers, Myra Marsh, Charles Marsh, George Guhl, Harry Strang, Elsa Newell, Gladys Gale, Lloyd Whitlock, Billie Van Every, Hal Price, Don Brodie, Lucille Ward. SYN: When a boy (Van Every) is orphaned when his parents die in an automobile accident, a naval officer (Gargan), who had promised the child's father that if anything happened he would care for him, meets opposition from the boy's aunt (Dodd).

**522. Nevada City** (6/20/41) B&W 58 mins. (Western). *DIR/A-PRO:* Joseph Kane. *SP:* James R. Webb. *CAST:* Roy Rogers, George "Gabby" Hayes, Sally Payne, Fred Kohler, Jr., George Cleveland, Billy Lee, Joseph Crehan, Pierre Watkin, Jack Ingram, Art Mix, Syd Saylor, Hank Bell, Yakima Canutt, Rex Lease, Henry Wills, Bob Woodward, Jack Kirk, Fred Burns, Chuck Baldra, Jack C. Smith, "Trigger." *SYN:* Two stagecoach drivers (Rogers, Hayes) try to settle a feud between their boss (Crehan) and the owner of the railroad (Cleveland), which was instigated by a business man (Watkin) wanting to control all freight business. *NOTES:* Re-edited for TV at 54 mins.

**523. The New Frontier** (10/5/35) B&W 59 mins. (Western). *DIR:* Carl Pierson. *PRO:* Paul Malvern. *S-PRO:* Trem Carr. *SP:* Robert Emmett. A Republic-Lone Star Production. *CAST:* John Wayne, Muriel Evans, Murdock MacQuarrie, Allan Cavan, Mary MacLaren, Warner Richmond, Alan Bridge, Glenn Strange, Sam Flint, Earl Dwire, Frank Ball, Hooper Atchley, Jack Kirk, Chuck Baldra, Tex Phelps, Herman Hack, Pat Harmon, Art Dillard, Sherry Tansey. *SYN:* The leader (Wayne) of a pioneer caravan arrives in a small town and learns that his father, the sheriff, has been murdered by a saloon owner (Richmond). He enlists the aid of a former outlaw gang that he befriended to bring the killer of his father to justice.

**524. New Frontier** (8/10/39) B&W 57 mins. (Western). *DIR:* George Sherman. *A-PRO:* William Berke. *SP:* Betty Burbridge, Luci Ward. Based on characters created by William Colt MacDonald. *CAST:* John Wayne, Raymond Hatton, Ray ("Crash") Corrigan, Phylis Isley (Jennifer Jones), Eddy Waller, Sammy McKim, LeRoy Mason, Harrison Greene, Reginald Barlow, Burr Caruth, Dave O'Brien, Hal Price, Jack Ingram, Bud Osborne, Slim Whitaker, Bob Burns, Bob Reeves, Frank Ellis, Walt LaRue, Jody Gilbert, Oscar Gahan, Charles Murphy, Herman Hack, Wilbur Mack, Curley Dresden, Cactus Mack, George Chesebro, Bill Wolfe, George Plues. *SYN:* The Three Mesquiteers (Wayne, Corrigan, Hatton) save a group of settlers from a land-grabbing construction company which wants to build a dam where the ranchers have settled. *NOTES:* The screen debut of Jennifer Jones, who originally was billed as Phyllis Isley. The 24th entry in the "Three Mesquiteers" series and John Wayne and Ray Corrigan's last appearances as "Mesquiteers." [TV title: *Frontier Horizon.*]

**525. The Night Hawk** (10/1/38) B&W 63 mins. (Crime). *DIR:* Sidney Salkow. *A-PRO:* Herman Schlom. *SP:* Earl Felton. *CAST:* Robert Livingston, June Travis, Robert Armstrong, Ben Welden, Lucien Littlefield, Joseph Downing, Roland Got, Cy Kendall, Paul Fix, Billy Burrud, Charles Wilson, Dwight Frye, Paul McVey, Robert E. Homans. *SYN:* A newspaper reporter (Livingston), who declares war on the mob after hoods have killed his best friend, a customs agent, teams up with a mob hit man (Armstrong) who is out to get revenge on other gangsters who stole an iron lung which was meant for his dying kid brother (Burrad).

**526. The Night Riders** (4/12/39) B&W 58 mins. (Western). *DIR:* George

Sherman. A-PRO: William Berke. SP: Betty Burbridge, Stanley Roberts. Based on characters created by William Colt MacDonald. CAST: John Wayne, Ray ("Crash") Corrigan, Max Terhune, Doreen McKay, Ruth Rogers, George Douglas, Tom Tyler, Kermit Maynard, Sammy McKim, Walter Wills, Ethan Laidlaw, Edward Peil, Sr., Tom London, Jack Ingram, Bill Nestell, Cactus Mack, Lee Shumway, Hal Price, Hank Worden, Roger Williams, Olin Francis, Francis Walker, Hugh Prosser, Jack Kirk, Yakima Canutt, Glenn Strange, David Sharpe, Bud Osborne, Georgia Summers, Eva McKenzie, Tommy Coats, Tex Palmer, Horace Murphy, Frank O'Connor, Allan Cavan, Bob Card, Art Dillard. SYN: The Three Mesquiteers (Wayne, Corrigan, Terhune) are forced to don masks and capes to become 'night riders' in order to expose a gambler (Douglas), posing as a Spanish nobleman, who has snatched ranch land and evicted the landowners. NOTES: The 21st entry in the "Three Mesquiteers" series. Working title was *Lone Star Bullets*.

**527. Night Riders of Montana** (2/28/51) B&W 60 mins. (Western). DIR: Fred C. Brannon. A-PRO: Gordon Kay. SP: M. Coates Webster. CAST: Allan ("Rocky") Lane, Chubby Johnson, Roy Barcroft, Claudia Barrett, Arthur Space, Myron Healey, Mort Thompson, Marshall Bradford, Lester Dorr, Ted Adams, George Chesebro, Don C. Harvey, Zon Murray, Bud Osborne, John Hamilton, "Black Jack." SYN: A ranger (Lane), called in to stop rustlers from terrorizing ranchers, suspects that a woman (Barrett) may be the leader since her ranch has been left alone.

**528. Night Time in Nevada** (9/5/48) Trucolor 67 mins. (Western). *DIR:* William Witney. *A-PRO:* Edward J. White. *SP:* Sloan Nibley. *CAST:* Roy Rogers, Adele Mara, Andy Devine, Grant Withers, Marie Harmond (Marie Harmon), Joseph Crehan, George Carleton, Holly Bane, Steve Darrell, Hank Patterson, Rex Lease, Bob Reeves, Forrest Taylor, Jim Nolan, Bob Nolan and the Sons of the Pioneers, "Trigger." *SYN:* When a man (Withers) murders his partner (Nolan) over a mine claim and the dead man's daughter (Mara) shows up for her share of the claim, he sets out to rustle cattle belonging to Roy to pay off her share of the claim. Roy then sets out to get his cattle back and prove that the man murdered his partner and the mine is rightfully hers. *NOTES:* The Sons of the Pioneers final film with Roy Rogers. Re-edited for TV at 54 mins.

**529. Night Train to Memphis** (7/12/46) B&W 66 mins. (Drama). *DIR:* Lesley Selander. *A-PRO/SP:* Dorrell McGowan, Stuart McGowan. *CAST:* Roy Acuff and His Smoky Mountain Boys, Allan ("Rocky") Lane, Adele Mara, Irving Bacon, Joseph Crehan, Emma Dunn, Roy Barcroft, Kenne Duncan, LeRoy Mason, Nicodemus Stewart, Nina Mae McKinney, Francis McDonald. *SYN:* A Tennessee mountain man (Acuff) tries to convince his brother (Lane) and the townfolks that the railroad that is being built through the area will benefit them in the long run.

**No Greater Sin** *see* **Eighteen and Anxious**

**530. No Man's Woman** (10/27/55) B&W 70 mins. (Mystery). *DIR:* Franklin Adreon. *A-PRO:* Rudy Ralston. *SP:* John K. Butler. Story by Don Martin. *CAST:* Marie Windsor, John Archer, Patric Knowles, Nancy Gates, Jil Jarmyn, Richard Crane, Fern Hall, Louis Jean Heydt, John Gallaudet, Douglas Wood, Percy Helton, Morris Ankrum. *SYN:* A police inspector (Archer) investigates five suspects in the murder of a woman who showed no mercy in her business dealings.

**531. No Place to Land** (10/3/58) B&W/Naturama 78 mins. (Drama). *DIR/PRO:* Albert C. Gannaway. *SP:* Vance Skarstedt. An Albert C. Gannaway Production. A Republic Presentation. *CAST:* John Ireland, Mari Blanchard, Gail Russell, Jackie Coogan, Robert Middleton, Douglas Henderson, Bill Ward, Robert E. Griffin, John Carpenter, Bill Coontz, Whitey Hughes, William Peter Blatty, James Macklin, Patric Dennis Leigh, Burt Topper. *SYN:* A cropduster (Ireland) decides he is not the marrying kind and rejects his girl (Blanchard) for his job. [British title: *Man Mad.*]

**532. Nobody's Darling** (8/27/43) B&W 71 mins. (Musical). *DIR:* Anthony Mann. *A-PRO:* Harry Grey. *SP:* Olive Cooper. Story by F. Hugh Herbert. *CAST:* Louis Calhern, Gladys George, Jackie Moran, Mary Lee, Lee Patrick, Bennie Bartlett, Marcia Mae Jones, Roberta Smith, Lloyd Corrigan, Jonathan Hale, Sylvia Field, Billy Dawson, Beverly Boyd. *SYN:* A young girl (Lee), upset by her parent's (Calhern, George) separation, sets out to make a name for herself. *NOTES:* Mary Lee was billed as "America's Little Sister."

**533. North of the Great Divide** (11/15/50) Trucolor 67 mins. (Western). *DIR:* William Witney. *A-PRO:* Edward J. White. *SP:* Eric Taylor. *CAST:* Roy Rogers, Penny Edwards, Gordon Jones, Roy Barcroft, Jack Lambert, Douglas Evans, Keith Richards, Iron Eyes Cody, Noble Johnson, Holly Bane, Foy Willing and the Riders of the Purple Sage, "Trigger," "Bullet." *SYN:* An Indian agent (Rogers) sets out to protect the Indian salmon fishing rights from a crook (Barcroft) who has dammed up the river and overfishes the salmon before they can travel upstream to where the Indians are camped and as a result, are starving. *NOTES:* Re-edited for TV at 54 mins. Some TV prints are in black and white. [Alternate title: *West of the Great Divide.*]

**534. Northwest Outpost** (6/25/47) B&W 91 mins. (Western-Musical). *DIR/A-PRO:* Allan Dwan. *E-PRO:* Herbert J. Yates. *SP:* Elizabeth Meehan, Richard Sale. Story by Angela Stuart. Adapted by Laird Doyle. Music score by Rudolph Friml. *CAST:* Nelson Eddy, Ilona Massey, Joseph Schildkraut, Hugo Haas, Elsa Lanchester, Lenore Ulric, Peter Whitney, Tamara Shayne, Erno Verebes, George Sorel, Rick Vallin, Henry Brandon, Michael Visaroff, Muni Seroff, Gene Gary Sentries, Max Willenz, Nina Hansen, Eugene Sigaloff, Michael Mark, Richard Alexander, George Paris, Ray Teal, Zoya Karabanova, Inna Gest, John Bleifer, Molio Sheron, Gregory Golubeff, Peter Seal, Nicco Romoff, John Peters, Jay Silverheels, Constantine Romanoff, Peter Gurs, Marvin Press, Abe Dinovitch, Nick Kobliansky, Countess Rosanska, Dina Smirnova, Antonina Barnett, Lola De Tolly, Myra Sokolskaya, George Blagoi, Sam Savitsky, Igor Dolgoruki, Nestor Eristoff, The American G.I. Chorus. *SYN:* Set in 19th-century California at a Russian fort, a woman (Massey) who has traveled from the mother country in search of her husband (Schildkraut), learns he is a political prisoner, and she tries to persuade an American (Eddy) in the employ of the settlement's Russian governor (Haas) to help her husband escape. *NOTES:* Republic's only attempt at producing an operetta. This was Nelson Eddy's final film. He retired from films and entered into nightclub entertainment. [British title: *End of the Rainbow.*]

**535. The Notorious Mr. Monks** (2/28/58) B&W/Naturama 70 mins. (Drama). *DIR:* Joseph Kane. *PRO:* Rudy Ralston. *SP:* Richard C. Sarafian. Story by Peter Paul Fix. A Ventura Production. A Republic Presentation. *CAST:* Vera Ralston, Don Kelly, Paul Fix, Leo Gordon, Luana Anders, Tom Brown, Lyle Talbot, Emory Parnell, Fuzzy Knight, Grandon Rhodes. *SYN:* A young man (Kelly) is picked up hitchhiking by a drunken driver (Fix) and taken to the man's home, where he meets the man's wife (Ralston), which leads to murder.

**536. O, My Darling Clementine** (12/31/43) B&W 70 mins. (Musical). *DIR:* Frank McDonald. *A-PRO:* Armand Schaefer. *SP:* Dorrell McGowan, Stuart McGowan. *CAST:* Harry Cheshire, Isabel Randolph, Frank Albertson, Lorna Gray (Adrian Booth), Irene Ryan, Eddie Parks, Loie Bridge, Patricia Knox, Tom Kennedy, Edwin Stanley, Emmett Vogan, Roy Acuff and His Smoky Mountain Boys, The Tennessee Ramblers, The Radio Rogues. *SYN:* A group of hillbilly road musicians become stranded in a high-class Dixie town, and their manager (Albertson) decides to put on a show to win over the townfolks. [Alternate title: *Oh, My Darling Clementine.*]

**Oh, My Darling Clementine** *see* **O, My Darling Clementine**

537. **Oh, Susanna!** (8/19/36) B&W 59 mins. (Western). *DIR:* Joseph Kane. *PRO:* Nat Levine. *S-PRO:* Armand Schaefer. *SP:* Oliver Drake. *CAST:* Gene Autry, Smiley Burnette, Frances Grant, Earle Hodgins, Donald Kirke, Boothe Howard, Clara Kimball Young, Frankie Marvin, Edward Peil, Sr., Carl Stockdale, Gerald Roscoe, Roger Gray, Fred Burns, Walter James, Fred "Snowflake" Toones, Earl Dwire, Bruce Mitchell, Jack Kirk, George Morrell, Pascale Perry, Tommy Coats, Bill McCall, Horace B. Carpenter, Silver Tip Baker, The Light Crust Doughboys, "Champion." *SYN:* Gene is tossed from a speeding train after thieves rob him while he's on his way to Mineral Springs. Two drifters (Burnette, Hodgins) find him, patch him up, and join him on the road to Mineral Springs, where Gene finds the thieves who robbed him.

538. **Oh! Susanna** (3/3/51) Trucolor 90 mins. (Western). *DIR/A-PRO:* Joseph Kane. *SP:* Charles Marquis Warren. *CAST:* Rod Cameron, Adrian Booth, Forrest Tucker, Chill Wills, William Ching, Jim Davis, Wally Cassell, James Lydon, Douglas Kennedy, William Haade, John Compton, James Flavin, Charles Stevens, Alan Bridge, Marion Randolph, Marshall Reed, John Pickard, Ruth Brennan, Louise Kane. *SYN:* At a remote frontier outpost, an Army officer (Cameron), who is at odds with his commanding officer (Tucker), tries to prevent an Indian uprising by overseeing Black Hills gold miners to assure that Indian treaties are not broken. *NOTES:* Louise Kane is the daughter of Joseph Kane.

539. **Oklahoma Annie** (3/24/52) Trucolor 90 mins. (Western-Musical). *DIR:* R. G. Springsteen. *A-PRO:* Sidney Picker. *SP:* Jack Townley. Story by Jack Townley, Charles E. Roberts. *CAST:* Judy Canova, John Russell, Grant Withers, Roy Barcroft, Emmett Lynn, Frank Ferguson, Minerva Urecal, Houseley Stevenson, Almira Sessions, Allen Jenkins, Maxine Gates, Emory Parnell, Denver Pyle, House Peters, Jr., Andrew Tombes, Fuzzy Knight, Si Jenks, Marian Martin, Herb Vigran, Hal Price, Fred Hoose, Lee Phelps, Bobby Taylor, William Fawcett, Bob Reeves. *SYN:* A country girl shopkeeper (Canova), who is in love with the town's new sheriff, (Russell), captures a bank robber, is given a job as his deputy, and together, they rid the town of crooked politicians. *NOTES:* The final film of Marian Martin.

540. **Oklahoma Badlands** (2/22/48) B&W 59 mins. (Western). *DIR:* Yakima Canutt. *A-PRO:* Gordon Kay. *SP:* Bob Williams. *CAST:* Allan ("Rocky") Lane, Eddy Waller, Mildred Coles, Roy Barcroft, Gene Stutenroth (Gene Roth), Earle Hodgins, Dale Van Sickel, Jay Kirby, Claire Whitney, Terry Frost, Hank Patterson, House Peters, Jr., Jack Kirk, Bob Woodward, "Black Jack." *SYN:* A cowboy (Lane) sets out to stop a gang of landgrabbers who are trying to run a rancher (Coles) off her land.

541. **Oklahoma Renegades** (8/29/40) B&W 57 mins. (Western). *DIR:*

Nate Watt. *A-PRO:* Harry Grey. *SP:* Earle Snell, Doris Schroeder. Story by Charles Condon. Based on characters created by William Colt MacDonald. *CAST:* Robert Livingston, Raymond Hatton, Duncan Renaldo, Lee "Lasses" White, Florine McKinney, Al Herman, William Ruhl, Eddie Dean, James Seay, Harold Daniels, Jack Lescoulie, Frosty Royce, Yakima Canutt, Hank Bell, Harry Strang, Art Dillard, Ken Terrell, Al Taylor, Pascale Perry, Tom Smith. *SYN:* The Three Mesquiteers (Livingston, Hatton, Renaldo) help veterans of the Spanish-American war who are being cheated out of their homesteads. *NOTES:* The 31st entry in the "Three Mesquiteers" series and Duncan Renaldo and Raymond Hatton's last appearance as "Mesquiteers."

**542. The Old Barn Dance** (1/29/38) B&W 60 mins. (Western). *DIR:* Joseph Kane. *A-PRO:* Sol C. Siegel. *SP:* Bernard McConville, Charles Francis Royal. *CAST:* Gene Autry, Smiley Burnette, Helen Valkis, Sammy McKim, Ivan Miller, Earl Dwire, Hooper Atchley, Raphael Bennett, Carleton Young, Frankie Marvin, Earle Hodgins, Gloria Rich, Denver Dixon, Chuck Baldra, Jack Kenney, Bill Nestell, Dick Weston (Roy Rogers), Walt Shrum and His Colorado Hillbillies, The Stafford Sisters, The Maple City Four, "Champion." *SYN:* Gene and his pals, put out of the horse selling business because of a tractor company, are forced to work as singers on the radio sponsored by the same tractor company that drove them out of business. When they learn that the company's tractors have been nothing but trouble for the ranchers, they go after the crooks. *NOTES:* Re-edited for TV at 54 mins.

**543. The Old Corral** (12/21/36) B&W 56 mins. (Western). *DIR:* Joseph Kane. *PRO:* Nat Levine. *S-PRO:* Armand Schaefer. *SP:* Joseph F. Poland, Sherman L. Lowe. Story by Bernard McConville. *CAST:* Gene Autry, Smiley Burnette, Hope Manning, Cornelius Keefe, Lon Chaney, Jr., John Bradford, Milburn Morante, Abe Lefton, Merrill McCormick, Charles Sullivan, Buddy Roosevelt, Lynton Brent, Frankie Marvin, Jack Ingram, Oscar and Elmer, Bob Nolan and the Sons of the Pioneers (Leonard Slye [Roy Rogers], Tim Spencer, Hugh Farr, Karl Farr), "Champion." *SYN:* Gene is the singing sheriff of a small sagebrush town and has to deal with singing bandits (Sons of the Pioneers), a young singer (Manning) who left her club in Chicago after witnessing a murder, and Chicago gangsters. [British title: *Texas Serenade.*]

**544. The Old Frontier** (7/29/50) B&W 60 mins. (Western). *DIR:* Philip Ford. *A-PRO:* Melville Tucker. *SP:* Bob Williams. *CAST:* Monte Hale, Paul Hurst, Claudia Barrett, William (Bill) Henry, Tristram Coffin, William Haade, Victor Kilian, Lane Bradford, Denver Pyle, Almira Sessions, Tom London. *SYN:* The sheriff (Hale) of a town goes after a gang of bank robbers and learns that the town's leading attorney (Coffin) is their leader.

**545. The Old Homestead** (8/17/42) B&W 68 mins. (Drama). *DIR:* Frank McDonald. *A-PRO:* Armand Schaefer. *SP:* Dorrell McGowan, Stuart McGowan. *CAST:* Leon Weaver, Frank Weaver, June Weaver, Dick Purcell, Jed Prouty, Anne Jeffreys, Maris Wrixon, Robert Conway, Linda Brent. *SYN:* When a small town is hit by a crime wave, the mayor (June Weaver) pretends to be crooked and hires a mobster (Purcell) to eliminate the opposition, but her plan backfires when a crooked politician (Prouty) aligns with the mob. Eventually, things work out, and the crooks are brought to justice. *NOTES:* The 10th entry in the "Weaver Brothers and Elviry" series.

**546. Old Los Angeles** (4/25/48) B&W 88 mins. (Western). *DIR/A-PRO:* Joseph Kane. *SP:* Gerald Drayson Adams, Clements Riley. Story by Clements Riley. *CAST:* Bill Elliott, John Carroll, Catherine McLeod, Joseph Schildkraut, Andy Devine, Estelita Rodriguez, Virginia Brissac, Grant Withers, Tito Renaldo, Roy Barcroft, Henry Brandon, Julian Rivero, Earle Hodgins, Augie Gomez, House Peters, Jr. *SYN:* A Missouri cowboy (Elliott) travels to Los Angeles to prospect for gold with his brother (Brandon), but when he finds that he has been murdered by outlaws, he vows to bring the gang to justice. [Alternate title: *In Old Los Angeles.*] [Re-release title: *California Outpost.*]

**547. Old Oklahoma Plains** (7/25/52) B&W 60 mins. (Western). *DIR:* William Witney. *A-PRO:* Edward J. White. *SP:* Milton Raison. Story by Albert DeMond. *CAST:* Rex Allen, Slim Pickens, Elaine Edwards, Roy Barcroft, John Crawford, Joel Marston, Russell Hicks, Fred Graham, Stephen Chase, Cactus Mack, Chick Hannon, The Republic Rhythm Riders, "Koko." *SYN:* In 1926, a former cavalry officer (Allen) helps the Army clear cattle from an area of range so that they can conduct tank maneuvers, but the ranchers do not like the idea because they fear the Army will no longer buy their horses if tanks replace the cavalry. *NOTES:* Uses extensive stock footage from Republic's 1938 *Army Girl.*

**548. Old Overland Trail** (2/25/53) B&W 60 mins. (Western). *DIR:* William Witney. *A-PRO:* Edward J. White. *SP:* Milton Raison. *CAST:* Rex Allen, Slim Pickens, Roy Barcroft, Virginia Hall, Gil Herman, Wade Crosby, Leonard Nimoy, Zon Murray, Harry Harvey, The Republic Rhythm Riders, "Koko." *SYN:* An agent (Allen) for the Bureau of Indian Affairs is assigned to prevent an Indian war on immigrants that is being instigated by a railroad contractor (Barcroft) who wants the Indians to drive the immigrants from their land into his cheap labor camps.

**549. On the Old Spanish Trail** (10/15/47) Trucolor 75 mins. (Western). *DIR:* William Witney. *A-PRO:* Edward J. White. *SP:* Sloan Nibley. Story by Gerald Geraghty. *CAST:* Roy Rogers, Tito Guizar, Jane Frazee, Andy Devine, Estelita Rodriguez, Charles McGraw, Fred Graham, Steve Darrell, Marshall Reed, Wheaton Chambers, Edward Cassidy, Jack O'Shea, Bob Nolan and the Sons of the Pioneers, "Trigger." *SYN:* Roy teams up with a "Robin Hood" type bandit (Guizar) from Mexico to help a faltering musical troupe (Sons of the Pioneers) and to stop a masked outlaw known as "The Gypsy." *NOTES:* Re-edited for TV at 54 mins.

**550. One Exciting Week** (6/8/46) B&W 69 mins. (Comedy). *DIR:* William Beaudine. *A-PRO:* Donald H. Brown. *SP:* Jack Townley, John K. Butler. Story by Dennis Murray. *CAST:* Al Pearce, Pinky Lee, Jerome Cowan, Shemp Howard, Arlene Harris, Mary Treen, Lorraine Krueger, Maury Dexter, Will Wright, Arthur Loft, Chester Clute, The Teen-Agers. *SYN:* A Merchant Marine hero (Pearce), on his way home to join in a celebration, sustains a blow in a fight with a gang of crooks which causes him to lose his memory, and they convince him that he is their gang leader and he is to assume the identity of the hero (himself) in order to receive the cash award the town plans to give him.

**One for All** (G.B. title) *see* **The President's Mystery**

**551. One Man's Law** (6/29/40) B&W 57 mins. (Western). *DIR/A-PRO:* George Sherman. *SP:* Bennett Cohen, Jack Natteford. *CAST:* Don ("Red") Barry, Janet Waldo, George Cleveland, Dub Taylor, Carleton Young, Edmund Cobb, Dick Elliott, James H. McNamara, Robert Frazer, Rex Lease, Edward Peil, Sr., Fred "Snowflake" Toones, Bud Osborne, Horace B. Carpenter, Jack Kirk, Cactus Mack, Jim Corey, Curley Dresden, Roy Brent, William Kellogg (Bruce Kellogg), Barry Hays, Guy Usher, Matty Roubert, Jack Ingram, Charles King, Stanley Price. *SYN:* A cowboy (Barry) is persuaded to become sheriff after his pal (Taylor) brags about his reputation, and he unites the citizens of the town to ward off a gang of outlaws sent by a nearby town that is in competition for a railroad franchise. *NOTES:* Re-edited for TV at 54 mins.

**552. $1,000 a Minute** (10/22/35) B&W 70 mins. (Comedy). *DIR:* Aubrey Scotto. *PRO:* Nat Levine. *SP:* Joseph Fields, Jack Natteford, Claire Church. Story by Everett Freeman. *CAST:* Roger Pryor, Leila Hyams, Edgar Kennedy, Edward Brophy, Purnell Pratt, Morgan Wallace, Sterling Holloway, Herman Bing, Franklin Pangborn, William Austin, Arthur Hoyt, George "Gabby" Hayes, Russell Hicks, Claude King, Spencer Charters, Lee Phelps, Ian Wolfe, James Burtis, Harry C. Bradley, Rolfe Sedan, Fern Emmett. *SYN:* A news reporter (Pryor) has been picked, on a bet, to spend $720,000 in 12 hours, but since he just covered a bank robbery, he is the number 1 suspect of the police, and he has to spend the money and keep one step in front of the police. *NOTES:* Academy Award Nominee — Best Sound.

**553. Operation Conspiracy** (9/27/57) B&W 69 mins. (Spy). *DIR:* Joseph Sterling. *PRO/SP:* A. R. Rawlinson. A Balblair Production. A Republic Presentation. *CAST:* Philip Friend, Mary MacKenzie, Leslie Dwyer, Allan Cuthbertson, John G. Heller, Chin Yu, Bill Nagy, Patrick Jordan, Patricia Haines, Stuart Mitchell, Ivor Dean, Marianne Stone, Maria Mercedes, Frank Thornton, Gerry Levey, Boris Ranevsky. *SYN:* In World War II, a woman's (MacKenzie) interference is the cause of an intelligence officer (Friend) failing to capture a spy. Years later, she is now a reporter and he is still in intelligence, and together they capture the spy (Heller) who is now a dress designer. *NOTES:* Released in Britain in 1955. [British title: *Cloak Without Dagger.*]

**554. The Oregon Trail** (1/15/36) B&W 59 mins. (Western). *DIR:* Scott Pembroke. *PRO:* Nat Levine. *S-PRO:* Paul Malvern. *SP:* Jack Natteford, Robert Emmett, Lindsley Parsons. Story by Robert Emmett, Lindsley Parsons. *CAST:* John Wayne, Ann Rutherford, Joe Girard, Yakima Canutt, Frank Rice, E. H. Calvert, Ben Hendricks, Jr., Harry Harvey, Fern Emmett, Jack Rutherford, Marian Farrell, Roland Ray, Edward J. LeSaint, Gino Corrado, Octavio Giraud. *SYN:* An army captain (Wayne) goes in search of his father when he disappears while leading a supply train to California.

**555. Oregon Trail** (7/14/45) B&W 55 mins. (Western). *DIR:* Thomas Carr. *A-PRO:* Bennett Cohen. *SP:* Betty Burbridge. Story by Frank Gruber. *CAST:* Sunset Carson, Peggy Stewart, Frank Jaquet, Si Jenks, Mary Carr, Lee Shumway, Bud Geary, Kenne Duncan, Steve Winston, Tex Terry, Tom London, Earle Hodgins, Monte Hale, Rex Lease, John Merton, Cactus Mack, Bud Osborne, Henry Wills, Horace B. Carpenter, Tommy Coats, George Magrill, Sheila Stewart, Jamesson Shade. *SYN:* A cowboy (Carson) joins a wagon train heading west to find the murderer of his father and to stop a power hungry empire builder (Duncan). *NOTES:* Scene with Monte Hale and Rex Lease was edited out of release print. Silent film star Mary Carr was the mother of director Thomas Carr.

**556. Oregon Trail Scouts** (5/5/47) B&W 58 mins. (Western). *DIR:* R. G. Springsteen. *A-PRO:* Sidney Picker. *SP:* Earle Snell. Based on the comic strip created by Fred Harman. *CAST:* Allan ("Rocky") Lane, Bobby (Robert) Blake, Martha Wentworth, Roy Barcroft, Emmett Lynn, Edmund Cobb, Earle Hodgins, Edward Cassidy, Frank Lackteen, Billy Cummings, Jack Kirk, Jack O'Shea, Chief Yowlachie. *SYN:* Red Ryder (Lane), desiring trapping rights on Indian land, comes to their aid when he learns a gang of crooks have kidnapped Little Beaver (Blake), grandson of the chief. Red thwarts the crooks' attempts to take over the Indian land and rescues Little Beaver, who decides to stay with Red. *NOTES:* The 21st entry in the "Red Ryder" feature series.

**557. Orphans of the Street** (12/5/38) B&W 64 mins. (Mystery). *DIR:* John H. Auer. *A-PRO:* Herman Schlom. *SP:* Eric Taylor, Jack Townley, Olive Cooper. Story by Earl Felton. *CAST:* Tommy Ryan, Robert Livingston, Ralph Morgan, Harry Davenport, James Burke, Sidney Blackmer, Victor Kilian, Hobart Cavanaugh, Herbert Rawlinson, Robert Gleckler, Ian Wolfe, Reed Hadley, Don Douglas, Paul Everton, "Ace," the Wonder Dog. *SYN:* A young boy (Ryan), after learning that his dead father's inheritance can no longer cover the costs of military school, is sent to a state home. He runs away, taking with him a trusty police dog (Ace), and gets mixed up in a dog show and a murder.

**558. O.S.S. 117 Is Not Dead** (2/13/59) B&W/Dyaliscope 82 mins. (Spy-Crime). *DIR:* Jean Sacha. *A-PRO:* Leon Canel. *SP:* Jacques Berland, Jean Levitte. Story by Jean De Bruce. A Republic Presentation. *CAST:* Magali Noel, Ivan Desney, Yves Vincent, Danik Patisson, Beatrice Arnac, Marie Dea, Georges Lannes, Andre Le Gall, Jacqueline Pierreux, Gamil Ratib, Andre Valmy, Joelle Bernard, Lorraine Bruce, Colette Castel, Anne-Marie Mersen, Charles Millot, Karl Martell, Maurice Sarfati, Louis Massis, Jo Davray. *SYN:* Unknown. *NOTES:* Filmed in France. Based on the spy books by Jean De Bruce, whose central character is Hubert Bonisseur de la Bruce, alias "O.S.S. 117." This series of films did well in Europe, but failed to find an American audience because the leading role of "O.S.S. 117" was played by a different actor in every film. The earliest the author can find any "O.S.S. 117" features released is in the 1960s; if this film had another title, or was re-released in the 1960s, it is unknown.

**559. Out California Way** (12/5/46) Trucolor 67 mins. (Western). *DIR*: Lesley Selander. *A-PRO*: Harry Grey. *SP*: Betty Burbridge. Story by Barry Shipman. *CAST*: Monte Hale, Adrian Booth, Bobby (Robert) Blake, John Dehner, Nolan Leary, Fred Graham, Tom London, Jimmy Starr, Edward Keane, Robert Wilke, Brooks Benedict, St. Luke's Choristers, Foy Willing and the Riders of the Purple Sage, *GUEST STARS*: Roy Rogers, Dale Evans, Allan ("Rocky") Lane, Don ("Red") Barry, "Trigger." *SYN*: A cowboy (Hale) comes to Hollywood to be a western star but finds he is in competition with a fading cowboy star (Dehner).

**560. Out of the Storm** (9/11/48) B&W 61 mins. (Crime). *DIR*: R. G. Springsteen. *A-PRO*: Sidney Picker. *SP*: John K. Butler. Story by Gordon Rigby. *CAST*: James Lydon, Lois Collier, Marc Lawrence, Richard Travis, Robert Emmett Keane, Helen Wallace, Harry Hayden, Roy Barcroft, Charles Lane, Iris Adrian, Byron Foulger, Claire DuBrey, "Smoki" Whitfield, Charles Sullivan, Rex Lease, Edgar Dearing. *SYN*: A clerk (Lydon) at a shipping plant, steals a large sum of money when his plant is robbed, but after struggling with his conscience, he returns the money and confesses his crime to an insurance investigator (Travis).

**561. The Outcast** (8/15/54) Trucolor 90 mins. (Western). *DIR*: William Witney. *A-PRO*: William J. O'Sullivan. *SP*: John K. Butler, Richard Wormser. Based on the *Esquire* magazine story by Todhunter Ballard. *CAST*: John Derek, Joan Evans, Jim Davis, Catherine McLeod, Ben Cooper, Taylor Holmes, Nana Bryant, Slim Pickens, Frank Ferguson, James Millican, Bob Steele, Nacho Galindo, Harry Carey, Jr., Bill Walker, Dee "Buzzy" Henry, Nicolas Coster, Hank Worden. *SYN*: When a young man (Derek) heads West to claim his late father's ranch, he finds that his uncle (Davis) has claimed the ranch, through a phony will, as his, he vows to get back what rightfully belongs to him and goes looking for the valid will and promises a showdown with his uncle.

**562. Outcasts of the City** (1/10/58) B&W 61 mins. (Romance-Drama). *DIR/PRO*: Boris L. Petroff. *SP*: Stephen Longstreet. A Boris L. Petroff Production. A Republic Presentation. *CAST*: Osa Massen, Robert Hutton, Maria Palmer, Nestor Paiva, John Hamilton, George Neise, Leon Tyler, Larry J. Blake, Norbert Schiller, Michael Dale, George Sanders, John Close, John Clark, John Harding, James Wilson. *SYN*: In post World War II Germany, an American officer (Hutton) falls in love with a German girl (Massen) and has to prove his innocence when her former lover (Neise) returns, threatens him and the girl, and is later found murdered.

**563. Outcasts of the Trail** (6/8/49) B&W 60 mins. (Western). *DIR*: Philip Ford. *A-PRO*: Melville Tucker. *SP*: Olive Cooper. *CAST*: Monte Hale, Paul Hurst, Jeff Donnell, Roy Barcroft, John Gallaudet, Milton Parsons, Tommy Ivo, Minerva Urecal, Ted Mapes, George Lloyd, Steve Darrell, Tom Steele, Hank Bell, Hank Patterson. *SYN*: The daughter (Donnell) and son (Ivo) of a convicted stagecoach robber (Gallaudet), who has gone straight and returned the money, are shunned by the community and when she gets herself mixed up in a robbery, it is up to Pat Garrett (Hale) to clear her and her family's name, and bring the real crooks to justice.

**564. Outlaws of Cherokee Trail** (9/10/41) B&W 56 mins. (Western). *DIR:* Les Orlebeck. *A-PRO:* Louis Gray. *SP:* Albert DeMond. Based on characters created by William Colt MacDonald. *CAST:* Bob Steele, Tom Tyler, Rufe Davis, Lois Collier, Tom Chatterton, Rex Lease, Joel Friedkin, Roy Barcroft, Philip Trent, Peggy Lynn, Bud Osborne, Chief Yowlachie, John James, Lee Shumway, Karl Hackett, Chuck Morrison, Billy Burtis, Griff Barnette, Bud Geary, Al Taylor, Henry Wills, Sarah Padden, Iron Eyes Cody, Cactus Mack. *SYN:* The Three Mesquiteers (Steele, Tyler, Davis) find themselves in Indian territory pitted against an outlaw gang and when the daughter (Collier) of a ranger captain is kidnapped, they set out to rescue her. *NOTES:* The 39th entry in the "Three Mesquiteers" series. [Alternate title: *Outlaws of the Cherokee Trail.*]

**565. Outlaws of Pine Ridge** (10/27/42) B&W 56 mins. (Western). *DIR:* William Witney. *A-PRO:* Edward J. White. *SP:* Norman S. Hall. *CAST:* Don ("Red") Barry, Lynn Merrick, Noah Beery, Sr., Donald Kirke, Emmett Lynn, Francis Ford, Clayton Moore, Stanley Price, George J. Lewis, Forrest Taylor, Wheaton Chambers, Roy Brent, Ken Terrell, Al Taylor, Tex Terry, Jack O'Shea, Cactus Mack, Tom Steele, Horace B. Carpenter, Duke Green, Duke Taylor, Jess Cavan. *SYN:* A cowboy (Barry) stops an outlaw gang in Pine Ridge from disrupting a local election and keeping a man (Beery, Sr.) from getting elected to governor.

**566. Outlaws of Santa Fe** (4/4/44) B&W 56 mins. (Western). *DIR:* Howard Bretherton. *A-PRO:* Edward J. White. *SP:* Norman S. Hall. *CAST:* Don ("Red") Barry, Helen Talbot, Wally Vernon, Twinkle Watts, Charles Morton, Herbert Heyes, Bud Geary, LeRoy Mason, Kenne Duncan, Nolan Leary, Walter Soderling, Edmund Cobb, Frank McCarroll, Robert Kortman, Ernie Adams, Emmett Lynn, Jack Kirk, Pierce Lyden, Forrest Taylor, Bob Burns, Jack O'Shea, Fred Graham. *SYN:* A former outlaw (Barry), who learns that his father was a lawman and not an outlaw, sets out to find the man who killed him. *NOTES:* Don "Red" Barry's last series western.

**567. Outlaws of Sonora** (4/14/38) B&W 55 mins. (Western). *DIR:* George Sherman. *A-PRO:* William Berke. *SP:* Betty Burbridge, Edmond Kelso. Story by Betty Burbridge. Based on characters created by William Colt MacDonald. *CAST:* Robert Livingston, Ray ("Crash") Corrigan, Max Terhune, Jack Mulhall, Otis Harlan, Jean Joyce, Stelita Peluffo, Tom London, Gloria Rich, Edwin Mordant, Ralph Peters, George Chesebro, Frank LaRue, Jack Ingram, Merrill McCormick, Curley Dresden, Jim Corey, George Cleveland, Earl Dwire, Jack Kirk, Fred Burns, Blackjack Ward, Jack O'Shea, Art Dillard. *SYN:* When an outlaw (Livingston), who resembles Stony (Livingston), pretends to be transporting a cache of money from a cattlemen's association to a nearby town, but is actually robbing them, the Three Mesquiteers (Livingston, Corrigan, Terhune) go after him to bring him to justice and clear Stony's name. *NOTES:* Robert Livingston plays a dual role in this film. The 14th entry in the "Three Mesquiteers" series.

**Outlaws of the Cherokee Trail** *see* **Outlaws of Cherokee Trail**

**Outlaws of the West** (G.B. and Re-release title) *see* **Call the Mesquiteers**

**568. Outside of Paradise** (2/7/38) B&W 68 mins. (Musical). *DIR:* John H. Auer. *A-PRO/SP:* Harry Sauber. *CAST:* Phil Regan, Penny Singleton, Bert Gordon, Leonid Kinskey, Ruth Coleman, Mary Forbes, Lionel Pape, Ralph Remley, Renie Riano, Linda Hayes, Joe E. Marks, David Kerman, Billy Young, Cliff Nazarro, Harry Allen. *SYN:* An Irish singer/bandleader (Regan) inherits a half-interest in an Irish castle and wants to turn it into a nightclub but meets opposition from the co-owner (Singleton).

**Outside the Law** (G.B. and Re-release title) *see* **119. Citadel of Crime**

**569. Overland Mail Robbery** (11/20/43) B&W 56 mins. (Western). *DIR:* John English. *A-PRO:* Louis Gray. *SP:* Bob Williams, Robert Yost. Story by Robert Yost. *CAST:* Bill Elliott, George "Gabby" Hayes, Anne Jeffreys, Alice Fleming, Weldon Heyburn, Kirk Alyn, Roy Barcroft, Nancy Gay, Peter Michael, Bud Geary, Tom London, Jack Kirk, Kenne Duncan, Jack Rockwell, Frank McCarroll, Jack O'Shea, LeRoy Mason, Hank Bell, Cactus Mack, Ray Jones, Tom Steele, Frank Ellis, Maxine Doyle, Diane Henry, "Sonny." *SYN:* Bill and "Gabby" help an easterner (Alyn) take over the family stagecoach line after his father and brother are murdered, and also help him fight off the gang of sibling outlaws, headed by their crooked and tough mother (Fleming), responsible for their deaths. *NOTES:* Alice Fleming, who plays the heavy in this film, would later play "Duchess" in the *Red Ryder* series with Bill Elliott.

**570. Overland Stage Raiders** (9/20/38) B&W 55 mins. (Western). *DIR:* George Sherman. *A-PRO:* William Berke. *SP:* Luci Ward. Story by Bernard McConville, Edmond Kelso. Based on characters created by William Colt MacDonald. *CAST:* John Wayne, Ray ("Crash") Corrigan, Max Terhune, Louise Brooks, Anthony Marsh, Gordon Hart, Roy James, Olin Francis, Fern Emmett, Henry Otho, George Sherwood, Ralph Bowman (John Archer), Archie Hall (Arch Hall, Sr.), Frank LaRue, Yakima Canutt, Slim Whitaker, Milton Kibbee, Jack Kirk, Bud Osborne, Dirk Thane, Edwin Gaffney, Bud McClure, John Beach, Curley Dresden, Tommy Coats, George Plues, Fred Burns, George Morrell, Bill Wolfe. *SYN:* The Three Mesquiteers (Wayne, Corrigan, Terhune) buy an airplane and a stake in an airport in order to fly out gold from a remote mining camp after previous shipments by motor coach have been hijacked. *NOTES:* Silent screen star Louise Brooks' last film. The 18th entry in the "Three Mesquiteers" series.

**571. The Painted Stallion** (2/11/38) B&W 67 mins. (Western). *SYN:* Feature version of the 12-chapter serial. *See* **993. The Painted Stallion.**

**Pale Arrow** (G.B. title) *see* **Pawnee**

**572. Pals of the Golden West** (11/15/51) B&W 68 mins. (Western). *DIR:* William Witney. *A-PRO:* Edward J. White. *SP:* Robert DeMond, Eric Taylor. Story by Sloan Nibley. *CAST:* Roy Rogers, Dale Evans, Estelita Rodriguez, Pinky Lee, Anthony Caruso, Roy Barcroft, Edwardo Jimenez, Ken Terrell, Emmett Vogan, Maurice Jara, The Roy Rogers Riders, "Trigger," "Bullet."

SYN: A U.S. border patrolman (Rogers) sets out to stop diseased cattle, which are infected with hoof-and-mouth disease, from being smuggled into the U.S. NOTES: Roy Rogers' last film for Republic.

**573. Pals of the Pecos** (4/8/41) B&W 56 mins. (Western). *DIR:* Les Orlebeck. *A-PRO:* Louis Gray. *SP:* Oliver Drake, Herbert Delmas. Story by Oliver Drake. Based on characters created by William Colt MacDonald. *CAST:* Robert Livingston, Bob Steele, Rufe Davis, Robert Winkler, June Johnson, Pat O'Malley, Dennis Moore, Roy Barcroft, John Holland, Tom London, Robert Frazer, George Chesebro, Chuck Morrison, Bud Osborne, Jack Kirk, Forrest Taylor, Frank Ellis, Eddie Dean. *SYN:* The Three Mesquiteers (Livingston, Steele, Davis) set out to stop a stagecoach line from being shut down. *NOTES:* One of the few Mesquiteers films that does not occur in the modern West. The 36th entry in the "Three Mesquiteers" series.

**574. Pals of the Saddle** (8/28/38) B&W 55 mins. (Western). *DIR:* George Sherman. *A-PRO:* William Berke. *SP:* Betty Burbridge, Stanley Roberts. Based on characters created by William Colt MacDonald. *CAST:* John Wayne, Ray ("Crash") Corrigan, Max Terhune, Doreen McKay, Joe Forte, George Douglas, Frank Milan, Ted Adams, Harry Depp, Dave Weber, Don Orlando, Charles Knight, Jack Kirk, Monte Montague, Olin Francis, Curley Dresden, Art Dillard, Tex Palmer. *SYN:* The Three Mesquiteers (Wayne, Corrigan, Terhune) and an undercover government agent (McKay) set out to stop enemy agents trying to smuggle a deadly chemical, Monium, from which poisonous gas can be made, into Mexico to sell to foreign powers. *NOTES:* John Wayne's debut as a Mesquiteer. The first "B" western to utilize a spy theme during the pre-World War II period. The 17th entry in the "Three Mesquiteers" series.

**575. Panama Sal** (10/18/57) B&W/Naturama 70 mins. (Drama). *DIR:* William Witney. *PRO:* Edward J. White. *SP:* Arnold Belgard. A Vineland Production. A Republic Presentation. *CAST:* Elena Verdugo, Edward Kemmer, Carlos Rivas, Harry Jackson, Joe Flynn, Christine White, Albert Carrier, Jose Gonzalez-Gonzalez, Billie Bird. *SYN:* A playboy (Kemmer) meets a native girl (Verdugo) in a Panamanian waterfront and tries to transform her into a Beverly Hills socialite, but when the new setting proves to be too much, she runs away, and realizing he loves her, goes after her.

**576. Paradise Express** (2/22/37) B&W 60 mins. (Drama). *DIR:* Joseph Kane. *PRO:* Nat Levine. *SP:* Jack Natteford, Betty Burbridge. Story by Allan Elston, Paul Perez. *CAST:* Grant Withers, Dorothy Appleby, Arthur Hoyt, Maude Eburne, Harry Davenport, Donald Kirke, Arthur Loft, Lew Kelly, Anthony Pawley, Fern Emmett, John Holland, Bob McClung, Bruce Mitchell, Guy Wilkerson, George Cleveland, Ralph McCullough. *SYN:* A man (Withers) helps two old-timers (Cleveland, Davenport), who are nearly forced to close down their railroad stations by a trucking company, by winning a railroad race to the town of Paradise.

**577. Pardon My Stripes** (1/26/42) B&W 64 mins. (Comedy). *DIR:* John H. Auer. *A-PRO:* Albert J. Cohen. *SP:* Lawrence Kimble, Stuart Palmer. Story by Mauri Grashin, Robert T. Shannon. *CAST:* William (Bill) Henry, Sheila Ryan, Edgar Kennedy, Harold Huber, Paul Hurst, Cliff Nazarro, Tom Kennedy, Edwin Stanley, Dorothy Granger, George McKay, Maxine Leslie. *SYN:* A college football player (Henry), who runs the wrong way for a touchdown, scores big when a gangster, who won a bundle on the game, gives him a job and assigns him to take a large sum of money from California to Chicago. He misses his plane when he meets a female reporter (Ryan), hires his own plane, and then accidentally drops the money into a prison courtyard. He then gets himself sent to prison so he can retrieve the money.

**578. Paroled—to Die** (1/11/38) B&W 55 mins. (Western). *DIR:* Sam Newfield. *PRO:* A. W. Hackel. *SP:* George Plympton. Story by Harry Olmstead. *CAST:* Bob Steele, Kathleen Eliot, Karl Hackett, Horace Murphy, Steve Clark, Budd Buster, Sherry Tansey, Frank Ball, Jack C. Smith, Horace B. Carpenter. *SYN:* A rancher (Steele), framed by the town boss (Hackett) for robbery and murder, eventually clears his name and brings the boss and his men to justice.

**579. Passkey to Danger** (5/11/46) B&W 58 mins. (Comedy-Mystery). *DIR:* Lesley Selander. *PRO:* Marek M. Libkov. *A-PRO:* William J. O'Sullivan. *SP:* O'Leta Rhinehart, William Hagens. *CAST:* Kane Richmond, Stephanie Bachelor, Adele Mara, Gregory Gay, Gerald Mohr, John Eldredge, George J. Lewis, Fred Graham, Tom London, Donia Bussey, Charles Williams, Charles Wilson. *SYN:* An advertising executive

(Richmond) turns detective when he discovers a team of embezzling brothers who are also in trouble with the mob. The brothers, whose last name is Spring, believe the ad man is trying to blackmail them when an ad campaign called "The Three Springs" comes out.

580. Pawnee (9/7/57) Trucolor 80 mins. (Western). *DIR:* George Waggner. *PRO:* Jack J. Gross, Philip N. Krasne. *SP:* George Waggner, Louis Vittes, Endre Bohem. *CAST:* George Montgomery, Bill Williams, Lola Albright, Francis McDonald, Robert E. Griffin, Dabbs Greer, Kathleen Freeman, Charlotte Austin, Ralph Moody, Anne Barton, Raymond Hatton, Charles Horvath, Robert Nash. *SYN:* The adopted son of a Pawnee chief (Montgomery), determined to learn more about his own people, becomes a scout on a wagon train following the Oregon Trail, and when the wagon train is attacked by his own tribe, he rejects his adopted tribe to stay with his own race. [British title: *Pale Arrow*.]

581. A Perilous Journey (4/5/53) B&W 90 mins. (Western). *DIR:* R. G. Springsteen. *A-PRO:* William J. O'Sullivan. *SP:* Richard Wormser. Based on *The Golden Tide* by Vingie Roe. *CAST:* Vera Ralston, David Brian, Scott Brady, Charles Winninger, Hope Emerson, Eileen Christy, Leif Erickson, Veda Ann Borg, Ian MacDonald, Virginia Grey, Dorothy Ford, Ben Cooper, Kathleen Freeman, Barbara Hayden, Paul Fierro, Angela Greene, John Dierkes, Fred Graham, Trevor Bardette, Richard Reeves, Bob Carney, Charles Evans, Philip Van Zandt, Byron Foulger, Denver Pyle, Harry Tyler, Emil Sitka, Jack O'Shea, Brandon Beach, Frank Hagney, Stanley Blystone, Richard Alexander, Charles Cane, Gloria Clark, Alden Aldrich. *SYN:* In 1850, a woman (Ralston), in search of her gambler-husband who left her years ago, joins a group of 48 other women, who are mail-order brides, as they hire a ship and sail to California via Panama. [Alternate title: *Cargo of Brides*]

582. Petticoat Politics (1/31/41) B&W 67 mins. (Comedy). *DIR:* Erle C. Kenton. *A-PRO:* Robert North. *SP:* Ewart Adamson, Taylor Caven. *CAST:* Roscoe Karns, Ruth Donnelly, Spencer Charters, George Ernest, Lois Ranson, Polly Moran, Paul Hurst, Pierre Watkin, Alan Ladd, Harry Woods, Claire Carleton, Jeff Corey, Charles Moore, George Meader, Emmett Vogan, "Pom Pom." *SYN:* Joe Higgins (Karns) decides to retire from the candy factory and spend the rest of his days quietly duck hunting, but Lil Higgins (Donnelly), who has heard from the insurance man that retired people cannot just relax or they will die, pushes Joe into running for mayor on the Women's Reform ticket. *NOTES:* The 9th and final entry in the "Higgins Family" series.

583. The Phantom Cowboy (2/14/41) B&W 56 mins. (Western). *DIR/A-PRO:* George Sherman. *SP:* Doris Schroeder. *CAST:* Don ("Red") Barry, Virginia Carroll, Milburn Stone, Neyle Marx, Rex Lease, Nick Thompson, Bud Osborne, Ernest Wilson, Burr Caruth, Frank Ellis, Art Dillard, Jack O'Shea, Chuck Baldra, Hank Bell, Leander de Cordova, Jim Corey, Matty Roubert, Hank Patterson. *SYN:* When the real "El Lobo" (Marx) is killed by a pair of outlaws (Stone, Lease), a cowboy (Barry) assumes his identity in order to keep homesteaders from being driven off their land.

**584. Phantom of the Plains** (9/7/45) B&W 56 mins. (Western). *DIR:* Lesley Selander. *A-PRO:* R. G. Springsteen. *SP:* Earle Snell, Charles Kenyon. Based on the comic strip created by Fred Harman. *CAST:* Bill Elliott, Bobby (Robert) Blake, Alice Fleming, Ian Keith, William Haade, Virginia Christine, Bud Geary, Henry Hall, Fred Graham, Jack Kirk, Jack Rockwell, Tom London, Earle Hodgins, Rose Plummer. *SYN:* Red Ryder (Elliott) and Little Beaver (Blake) must convince the Duchess (Fleming) that her soon-to-be husband (Keith) is not an Englishman, but a wife murderer. *NOTES:* Re-edited for TV at 54 mins. The 9th entry in the "Red Ryder" feature series.[Alternate title: *Texas Manhunt*]

**585. The Phantom Plainsman** (6/16/42) B&W 57 mins. (Western). *DIR:* John English. *A-PRO:* Louis Gray. *SP:* Robert Yost, Barry Shipman. Story by Robert Yost. Based on characters created by William Colt MacDonald. *CAST:* Bob Steele, Tom Tyler, Rufe Davis, Robert O. Davis (Rudolph Anders), Lois Collier, Charles Miller, Alex Callam, Monte Montague, Henry Rowland, Richard Crane, Jack Kirk, Vince Barnett, Lloyd Ingraham, Al Taylor, Bud Geary, Herman Hack, Edward Cassidy. *SYN:* The Three Mesquiteers (Steele, Tyler, Davis), working on the horse ranch of their pacifist boss (Miller) who refuses to sell his steeds to any army, learn that Nazis, traveling incognito, have been purchasing his horses to send to Germany. The Mesquiteers foil the plans of the Nazis and their boss sells his horses to the U.S. Army. *NOTES:* The 45th entry in the "Three Mesquiteers" series and Rufe Davis' last appearance as a "Mesquiteer."

**586. The Phantom Speaks** (5/10/45) B&W 69 mins. (Crime-Fantasy). *DIR:* John English. *A-PRO:* Donald H. Brown. *E-PRO:* Armand Schaefer. *SP:* John K. Butler. *CAST:* Richard Arlen, Stanley Ridges, Lynn Roberts, Tom Powers, Charlotte Wynters, Jonathan Hale, Pierre Watkin, Marian Martin, Garry Owen, Ralf Harolde, Doreen McCann, Joseph Granby, Frank Fanning, Eddie Parker, Charles Sullivan, Robert E. Homans, Tom Chatterton, Edward Cassidy, Edmund Cobb, Nolan Leary, Jack Perrin, Bob Alden, Jack Ingram, Robert Malcolm, Walter Shumway, *VOICE OF:* Roy Barcroft. *SYN:* An executed killer (Powers) takes over the mind of a mild-mannered scientist (Ridges) and has him commit his heinous crimes of revenge. *NOTES:* Plot is similar to Universal's 1940 release *Black Friday*, which also featured Stanley Ridges in a similar role. Double-billed in some areas with *The Vampire's Ghost*.

**587. The Phantom Stallion** (2/10/54) B&W 54 mins. (Western). *DIR:* Harry Keller. *A-PRO:* Rudy Ralston. *SP:* Gerald Geraghty. *CAST:* Rex Allen, Slim Pickens, Carla Balenda, Harry Shannon, Don Haggerty, Peter Price, Rosa Turich, Zon Murray, "Koko." *SYN:* A cowboy (Allen) comes to the aid of a rancher (Shannon) who is having his best horses disappear, and which appears to be the work of a wild horse herd.

**588. The Pilgrim Lady** (1/22/47) B&W 67 mins. (Comedy-Romance). *DIR:* Lesley Selander. *A-PRO:* William J. O'Sullivan. *SP:* Dane Lussier. *CAST:* Lynn Roberts, Warren Douglas, Alan Mowbray, Veda Ann Borg, Clarence Kolb, Helen Freeman, Doris Merrick,

Russell Hicks, Ray Walker, Charles Coleman, Carlyle Blackwell, Jr., Harry Cheshire, Dorothy Christy, Paul E. Burns, Tom Dugan, Jack Rice, William Haade, William Benedict. *SYN:* A refined college teacher (Freeman), who writes a spicy novel under a pseudonym and has it published, drafts her niece (Roberts) to stand in as the author of the book rather than having to reveal her true identity.

**589. Pioneer Marshal** (11/24/49) B&W 60 mins. (Western). *DIR:* Philip Ford. *A-PRO:* Melville Tucker. *SP:* Bob Williams. *CAST:* Monte Hale, Paul Hurst, Nan Leslie, Roy Barcroft, Damian O'Flynn, Myron Healey, Ray Walker, John Hamilton, Clarence Straight, Robert B. Williams, Marshall Reed. *SYN:* A lawman (Hale) pretends to be an outlaw as he pursues an embezzler (Healey) to a town that is a haven for outlaws.

**590. Pioneers of the West** (3/12/40) B&W 56 mins. (Western). *DIR:* Les Orlebeck. *A-PRO:* Harry Grey. *SP:* Jack Natteford, Karen DeWolf, Gerald Geraghty. Based on characters created by William Colt MacDonald. *CAST:* Robert Livingston, Raymond Hatton, Duncan Renaldo, Noah Beery, Sr., Beatrice Roberts, George Cleveland, Lane Chandler, Hal Taliaferro, Yakima Canutt, John Dilson, Joe McGuinn, Earl Askam, George Chesebro, Jack Kirk, Herman Hack, Bob Burns, Tex Terry, Chuck Baldra, Hansel Warner, Art Dillard, Ray Jones, Artie Ortego. *SYN:* The Three Mesquiteers (Livingston, Hatton, Renaldo) come to the rescue of a group of settlers who are being driven off their land because of high taxes. *NOTES:* Re-edited for TV at 54 mins. The 28th entry in the "Three Mesquiteers" series.

**591. Pistol Packin' Mama** (12/15/43) B&W 64 mins. (Musical-Crime). *DIR:* Frank Woodruff. *A-PRO:* Edward J. White. *SP:* Edward Dein, Fred Schiller. Story by Arthur Caesar, Edward Dein. *CAST:* Ruth Terry, Robert Livingston, Wally Vernon, Jack LaRue, Kirk Alyn, Eddie Parker, Helen Talbot, Lydia Bilbrook, George Lessey, Joseph Kirk, The King Cole Trio. *SYN:* The owner of a Nevada gambling den (Terry) assumes a new identity as she goes after a New York club owner (Livingston), who cheated her. Getting a job in his club as a singer, not only does she con him into playing cards for his club and wins, but also outshoots a gangster (LaRue) and his mob. *NOTES:* Ruth Terry plays a dual role in this film. The title song was popularized by Al Dexter who does not appear in this film.

**592. The Pittsburgh Kid** (8/29/41) B&W 76 mins. (Sports). *DIR:* Jack Townley. *A-PRO:* Armand Schaefer. *SP:* Houston Branch, Earl Felton. Based on *Kid Tinsel* by Octavus Roy Cohen. *CAST:* Billy Conn, Jean Parker, Dick Purcell, Alan Baxter, Veda Ann Borg, Jonathan Hale, Ernest Whitman, John Kelly, Etta McDaniel, Dick Elliott, John Harmon, Robert Barron, Arthur Donovan, Henry Armstrong, Freddie Steele, Jack Roper, Sam Balter, Dan Tobey. *SYN:* A boxer (Conn), whose manager dies, is enticed to sign with an unscrupulous manager (Hale), but signs instead with his old manager's daughter (Parker) and goes on to be champ. *NOTES:* Billy Conn was a real-life boxer who played himself in this film. He was knocked out by Joe Louis, "The Brown Bomber," in 1941 and again in 1946.

**593. Plainsman and the Lady** (11/11/46) B&W 87 mins. (Western). *DIR/*

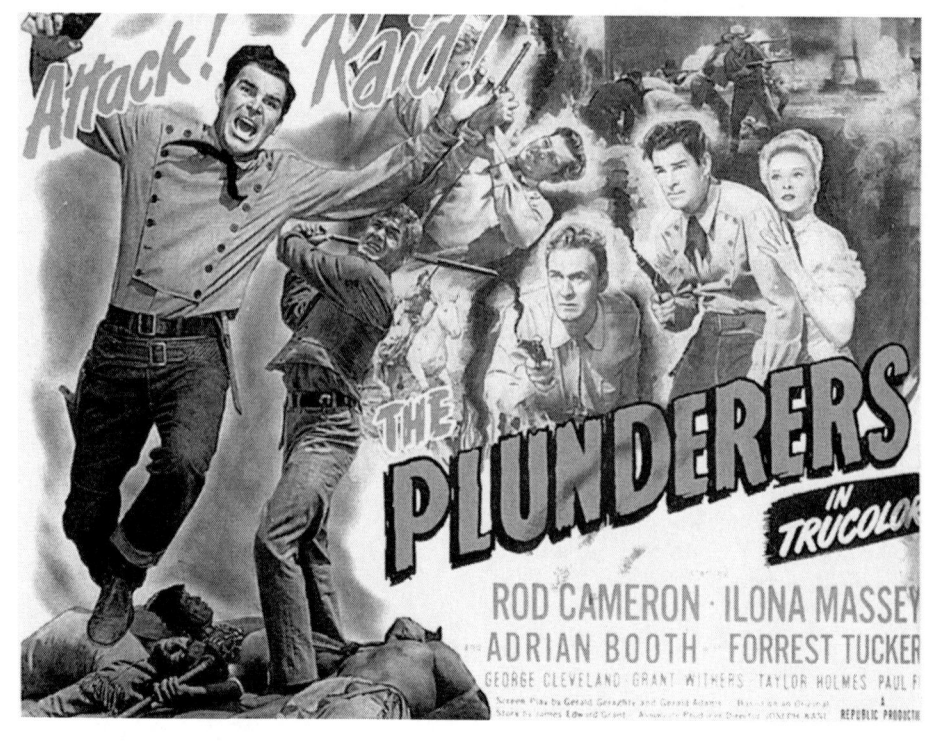

A-PRO: Joseph Kane. SP: Richard Wormser. Story by Michael Uris, Ralph Spence. CAST: Bill Elliott, Vera Ralston, Gail Patrick, Joseph Schildkraut, Don ("Red") Barry, Andy Clyde, Raymond Walburn, Reinhold Schunzel, Paul Hurst, Russell Hicks, William B. Davidson, Charles Judels, Eva Puig, Jack Lambert, Stuart Hamblen, Noble Johnson, Hal Taliaferro, Byron Foulger, Pierre Watkin, Eddy Waller, Charles Morton, Martin Garralaga, Guy Beach, Joseph Crehan, Grady Sutton, Eddie Parks, Norman Willis, Tex Terry, Chuck Roberson, Rex Lease, Henry Wills, Daniel Day Tolman, David Williams, Hank Bell, Roy Barcroft, Jack O'Shea, Carl Sepulveda, Iron Eyes Cody, Lola and Fernando. SYN: In St. Joseph, Missouri, the owner (Schunzel) of the Pony Express hires a cowboy (Elliott) to protect his line from a rival stagecoach owner (Schildkraut) who wants to destroy the Pony Express.

**594. The Plunderers** (12/1/48) Trucolor 87 mins. (Western). DIR/A-PRO: Joseph Kane. SP: Gerald Geraghty, Gerald Drayson Adams. Story by James Edward Grant. CAST: Rod Cameron, Ilona Massey, Adrian Booth, Forrest Tucker, George Cleveland, Grant Withers, Taylor Holmes, Paul Fix, Francis Ford, James Flavin, Russell Hicks, Maude Eburne, Mary Ruth Wade, Louis R. Faust, Hank Bell, Rex Lease, John Hart, Bud Osborne, Clayton Moore, Roy Barcroft. SYN: A lawman (Cameron) pretends to be a wanted man in order to infiltrate a gang and bring in a notorious outlaw (Tucker) and, as he is bringing him in, they have to join forces to fight off an Indian uprising. NOTES: Joseph Kane's first directed color film.

**595. Plunderers of Painted Flats** (1/23/59) B&W/Naturama 77 mins. (Western). *DIR/PRO:* Albert C. Gannaway. *SP:* Phillip Shuken, John Greene. An Albert C. Gannaway Production. *CAST:* Corinne Calvet, John Carroll, Skip Homeier, George Macready, Edmund Lowe, Bea Benaderet, Madge Kennedy, Joe Besser, Allan Lurie, Candy Candido, Rick Allen, Herb Vigran, Bob Kline, Burt Topper, Bill Foster, Lee Redman, Roy Gordon, Wade Lane, David Waldor, John Kidd. *SYN:* When a young man (Homeier), whose father is killed by the town boss (Macready), gets help from an aging gunfighter (Lowe) who is in turn, gunned down by a hired gun (Carroll), rallies the other ranchers to go after the town boss and clean up the town. *NOTES:* Republic's last studio produced film and the last original released film. Four more films would be released in 1959, a foreign film, a British film, and two serial feature versions. Republic would close their doors and sell off their remaining assets to the highest bidder, with the lot itself going to CBS.

**596. Poison Pen** (6/30/41) B&W 66 mins. (Drama). *DIR:* Paul L. Stein. *PRO:* Walter C. Mycroft. *SP:* Doreen Montgomery, William Freshman, N. C. Hunter, Esther McCracken. Based on the play by Richard Llewellyn. An Associated British Production. A Republic Presentation. *CAST:* Flora Robson, Robert Newton, Ann Todd, Geoffrey Toone, Reginald Tate, Belle Chrystal, Edward Chapman, Edward Rigby, Athole Stewart, Mary Hinton, Cyril Chamberlain, Catherine Lacey, Wally Patch, Ella Retford, Jean Clyde, Wilfrid Hyde-White, Marjorie Rhodes, Beatrice Varley, Peter Murray Hill, Empsie Bowman, Laurence Kitchin, Kenneth Connor, Megs Jenkins, Esma Cannon, Eileen Beldon, Merle Tottenham, Charles Mortimer, Roddy Hughes, Roddy McDowall. *SYN:* A number of poison pen letters are mailed to villagers in a small English community, making wild and scandalous accusations, which result in a murder and suicide. *NOTES:* Released in Britain in 1939 at a running time of 79 mins.

**597. Port of 40 Thieves** (8/13/44) B&W 58 mins. (Crime). *DIR:* John English. *A-PRO:* Walter H. Goetz. *SP:* Dane Lussier. *CAST:* Stephanie Bachelor, Richard Powers (Tom Keene), Lynn Roberts, Olive Blakeney, Russell Hicks, George Meeker, Mary Field, Ellen Lowe, Patricia Knox, John Hamilton, Harry Depp. *SYN:* A woman (Bachelor) murders her rich husband for the inheritance so she can marry her playboy lover (Meeker), but then she kills him for fear he might talk, which then leads to two more murders.

**598. Portia on Trial** (11/8/37) B&W 85 mins (Drama). *DIR:* George Nicholls, Jr. *PRO:* Albert E. Levoy. *SP:* Samuel Ornitz, Edward E. Paramore. Story by Faith Baldwin. *CAST:* Walter Abel, Frieda Inescort, Neil Hamilton, Heather Angel, Ruth Donnelly, Barbara Pepper, Clarence Kolb, Anthony Marsh, Paul Stanton, George Cooper, John Kelly, Hobart Bosworth, Ian MacLaren, Chick Chandler, Bob Murphy, Inez Palange, Leo Gorcey, Huntley Gordon, Marion Ballou, Hooper Atchley, Nat Carr, Lucie Kaye. *SYN:* A lawyer (Inescort) is forced to give up her son after her marriage is annulled, and as the son grows up, the secret behind his mother's existence begins to unfold. *NOTES:* Academy Award Nominee — Best Score. [British title: *The Trial of Portia Merriman*.]

**599. Post Office Investigator** (9/1/49) B&W 60 mins. (Crime). *DIR:* George Blair. *A-PRO:* Sidney Picker. *SP:* John K. Butler. *CAST:* Audrey Long, Warren Douglas, Jeff Donnell, Marcel Journet, Danny Morton, Richard Benedict, Jimmie Dodd, Thomas Browne Henry, Cliff Clark, Vera Marshe, Peter Brocco, Patricia Knox, Holmes Herbert, Jason Robards, Sr., Emmett Vogan. *SYN:* A female criminal (Long), specializing in rare stamps, harasses a mail carrier (Douglas) into handing over a letter she knows contains some rare stamps. Realizing he has been duped, he then helps postal investigators to recover the stolen property.

**600. Powder River Rustlers** (11/25/49) B&W 60 mins. (Western). *DIR:* Philip Ford. *A-PRO:* Gordon Kay. *SP:* Richard Wormser. *CAST:* Allan ("Rocky") Lane, Eddy Waller, Gerry Ganzer, Roy Barcroft, Francis McDonald, Cliff Clark, Douglas Evans, Bruce Edwards, Clarence Straight, Ted Jacques, Tom Monroe, Stanley Blystone, Eddie Parker, Herman Hack, "Black Jack." *SYN:* A government agent (Lane) sets out to prevent crooks from stealing the bond money the town has raised to build a needed bridge.

**601. Prairie Moon** (10/7/38) B&W 58 mins. (Western). *DIR:* Ralph Staub. *A-PRO:* Harry Grey. *SP:* Betty Burbridge, Stanley Roberts. *CAST:* Gene Autry, Smiley Burnette, Shirley Deane, Tommy Ryan, Walter Tetley, David Gorcey, Stanley Andrews, William Pawley, Warner Richmond, Raphael Bennett, Tom London, Bud Osborne, Jack Rockwell, Peter Potter, Merrill McCormick, Hal Price, Lew Meehan, Jack Kirk, Fred Burns, Al Taylor, Dan White, Chuck Baldra, Frankie Marvin, Art Baker, Buster Slaven, Mira McKinney, "Champion." *SYN:* Three tough kids (Ryan, Tetley, Gorcey) from the streets of Chicago, sent west after their father died and left them a ranch, bring their city ways to the ranch, and it is up to Gene to straighten out the kids. *NOTES:* Re-edited for TV at 54 mins. Walter Tetley was the radio actor best remembered as *The Great Gildersleeve's* nephew, LeRoy.

**602. Prairie Pioneers** (2/16/41) B&W 57 mins. (Western). *DIR:* Les Orlebeck. *A-PRO:* Louis Gray. *SP:* Barry Shipman. Story by Karl Brown. Based on characters created by William Colt MacDonald. *CAST:* Robert Livingston, Bob Steele, Rufe Davis, Esther Estrella, Robert Kellard, Guy D'Ennery, Davison Clark, Jack Ingram, Kenneth MacDonald, Lee Shumway, Mary MacLaren, Yakima Canutt, Jack Kirk, Wheaton Chambers, Frank Ellis, Cactus Mack, Curley Dresden, Frank McCarroll, Ray Henderson, Tom Smith, Bob Burns, Chuck Baldra, Dan White, Pascale Perry, Jim Corey. *SYN:* The Three Mesquiteers (Livingston, Steele, Davis) lead a wagon train out west and help prevent a family from being run off their ranch. *NOTES:* The 35th entry in the "Three Mesquiteers" series.

**603. The President's Mystery** (9/28/36) B&W 80 mins. (Drama-Mystery). *DIR:* Phil Rosen. *PRO:* Nat Levine. *SP:* Lester Cole, Nathanael West. Story by Rupert Hughes, Samuel Hopkins Adams, Anthony Abbott, Rita Weiman, S. S. Van Dine, John Erskine. Based on the *Liberty Magazine* story suggested by President Franklin D. Roosevelt. *CAST:* Henry Wilcoxon, Betty Furness, Sidney Blackmer, Evelyn Brent, Barnett Parker, Mel Ruick, Wade Boteler, John Wray,

Guy Usher, Robert E. Homans, Si Jenks, Arthur Aylesworth. *SYN:* A lawyer (Wilcoxon) forsakes his wife (Brent) and drops out of society after getting fed up with his environment and way of life and marries another woman (Furness). He keeps a low profile until he learns that his first wife has been arrested for his murder. [British title: *One for All.*]

**604. The Pretender** (8/16/47) B&W 69 mins. (Crime). *DIR/PRO:* W. Lee Wilder. *SP:* Don Martin. Additional dialogue by Doris Miller. A W. W. Production. A Republic Presentation. *CAST:* Albert Dekker, Catherine Craig, Charles Drake, Alan Carney, Linda Stirling, Tom Kennedy, Selmer Jackson, Charles Middleton, Ernie Adams, Ben Welden, John Bagni, Stanley Ross, Forrest Taylor, Greta Clement, Peggy Wynne, Eula Guy, Cay Forester, Peter Michael, Michael Mark, Dorothy Scott. *SYN:* An investment broker (Dekker), who has been embezzling from one of his clients (Craig), plots to kill her fiance so he can marry her and cover up his embezzlement. Hiring a killer, he tells him that the fiance's picture will appear in the newspaper, but when she changes her mind, and marries him, the picture of the newlyweds is printed instead, causing the killer to think that the broker is his intended target. *NOTES:* Linda Stirling's final film — she retired after this film. Ernie Adams' final feature film — he died 11/26/47.

**605. Pride of Maryland** (1/20/51) B&W 60 mins. (Sports). *DIR:* Philip Ford. *A-PRO:* William Lackey. *SP:* John K. Butler. *CAST:* Stanley Clements, Peggy Stewart, Frankie Darro, Joe Sawyer, Robert Barrat, Harry Shannon, Duncan Richardson, Stanley Logan, Joseph Crehan, Emmett Vogan, Clyde Cook, Donald Kerr, Guy Bellis. *SYN:* A young jockey (Clements), with a new style of riding that brings him acclaim, is barred from the track when he starts betting on himself.

**606. Pride of the Navy** (1/23/39) B&W 63 mins. (Drama). *DIR:* Charles Lamont. *A-PRO:* Herman Schlom. *SP:* Ben Markson, Saul Elkins. Story by James R. Webb, Joseph Hoffman. *CAST:* James Dunn, Rochelle Hudson, Gordon Oliver, Horace MacMahon, Gordon Jones, Charlotte Wynters, Joseph Crehan, Suzanne Kaaren, Charles Trowbridge. *SYN:* A man (Dunn), who is kicked out of Annapolis because of his rowdiness, becomes a speedboat designer and attracts the Navy's attention because they want him to build a small torpedo boat.

**607. Pride of the Plains** (1/5/44) B&W 56 mins. (Western). *DIR:* Wallace Fox. *A-PRO:* Louis Gray. *SP:* John K. Butler, Bob Williams. Story by Oliver Drake. *CAST:* Robert Livingston, Smiley Burnette, Nancy Gay, Stephen Barclay, Kenneth MacDonald, Charles Miller, Kenne Duncan, Jack Kirk, Bud Geary, Yakima Canutt, Budd Buster, Bud Osborne. *SYN:* John Paul Revere (Livingston) and his sidekick (Burnette) go after a gang of crooks who are trying to repeal a law which prevents them from slaughtering horses for profit. *NOTES:* Re-edited for TV at 54 mins. The 3rd entry in the "John Paul Revere" series.

**608. Prince of the Plains** (4/8/49) B&W 60 mins. (Western). *DIR:* Philip Ford. *A-PRO:* Melville Tucker. *SP:* Louise Rousseau, Albert DeMond. *CAST:* Monte Hale, Paul Hurst, Shirley

Davis, Roy Barcroft, Rory Mallinson, Harry Lauter, Lane Bradford, George Carleton, Edmund Cobb, Holly Bane. *SYN:* Bat Masterson (Hale), investigating the death of his father, uncovers a plot to take over a town and drive the ranchers off their land.

**609. Prison Nurse** (3/1/38) B&W 65 mins. (Drama-Prison). *DIR:* James Cruze. *A-PRO:* Herman Schlom. *SP:* Earl Felton, Sidney Salkow. Story by Adele Buffington. Based on the novel by Dr. Louis Berg. *CAST:* Henry Wilcoxon, Marian Marsh, Bernadene Hayes, Ben Welden, Ray Mayer, John Arledge, Addison Richards, Frank Reicher, Minerva Urecal, Selmer Jackson, Fred Kohler, Jr., Norman Willis. *SYN:* A doctor (Wilcoxon), in prison for a mercy killing, assists another doctor (Reicher), and his nurses (Marsh, Hayes, Urecal) at an outbreak of typhoid in the prison. Later, when the doctor is up for parole, he is kidnapped by three escaping inmates (Welden, Mayer, Arledge) who are killed when he wrecks the ambulance they escaped in. Thinking he is part of the gang, he is arrested and tried for murder, but a nurse (Marsh) finds a diary of one of the convicts, and the doctor is freed.

**610. Prisoners in Petticoats** (9/18/50) B&W 60 mins. (Crime). *DIR:* Philip Ford. *A-PRO:* Lou Brock. *SP:* Bradbury Foote. Story by Raymond L. Schrock, George E. Callahan. *CAST:* Valentine Perkins, Robert Rockwell, Danni Nolan, Anthony Caruso, Tony Barrett, David Wolfe, Alex Gerry, Michael Carr, Queenie Smith, Bert Conway, Rudy Rama, Marlo Dwyer, Russ Conway, Marta Mitrovich. *SYN:* A club pianist (Perkins) inadvertently gets pulled into underworld dealings when a gangster (Barrett) double-crosses her boss (Caruso) by stashing stolen money with her. Picked up by the police, she goes to prison rather than reveal her true identity, the daughter of a respected professor (Gerry). She escapes with another inmate (Nolan), who is the gangster's girlfriend, and, while the police are watching her, retrieves the money, and the gang is captured.

**611. Public Cowboy No. 1** (8/23/37) B&W 59 mins. (Western). *DIR:* Joseph Kane. *A-PRO:* Sol C. Siegel. *SP:* Oliver Drake. Story by Bernard McConville. *CAST:* Gene Autry, Smiley Burnette, Ann Rutherford, William Farnum, James C. Morton, Frank LaRue, Maston Williams, Arthur Loft, Frankie Marvin, House Peters, Jr., Milburn Morante, King Mojave, Hal Price, Jack Ingram, Raphael Bennett, George Plues, Frank Ellis, James Mason, Douglas Evans, Bob Burns, "Champion." *SYN:* Gene and Frog (Burnette) are called in by the sheriff (Farnum) to stop a group of modern cattle rustlers who are using airplanes, refrigerated trucks, and shortwave radios to rustle cattle. *NOTES:* Re-edited for TV at 54 mins.

**612. Public Enemies** (10/30/41) B&W 66 mins. (Crime). *DIR:* Albert S. Rogell. *A-PRO:* Robert North. *SP:* Edward T. Lowe, Lawrence Kimble. Story by Michael Burke. *CAST:* Phillip Terry, Wendy Barrie, Edgar Kennedy, William Frawley, Marc Lawrence, Nana Bryant, Willie Fung, Paul Fix, Russell Hicks, Tim Ryan, Duke York, Ken Lundy, Peter Leeds, Cyril Ring, Eddie Fetherston, Francis Sayles, Guy Usher, Lee Phelps, Charles McAvoy, Rod Bacon, Pat Gleason, Dick Paxton, Chuck Morrison, Jack Kennedy, Harry Holman, Frank Richards, Sammy Stein,

Francis Pierlot, Jerry Jerome, Wally Albright, Sam Bernard, Sammy McKim, Robert Winkler, Douglas Deems, Larry Harris, Eddy Waller, James C. Morton, Dick Rush, Arthur Housman. *SYN:* A reporter's (Terry) enthusiasm causes him to print a false story about a society deb (Barrie) and consequently lose his job, but when he gets involved with a gangster smuggling operation in order to win back his job, she is kidnapped by the gang and he rescues her, gets back his job and ultimately marries her. *NOTES:* Arthur Housman's final film — he died in 1942. [Alternate title: *Gangs of the City.*]

**613. Puddin' Head** (6/25/41) B&W 80 mins. (Musical-Comedy). *DIR:* Joseph Santley. *A-PRO:* Albert J. Cohen. *SP:* Jack Townley, Milt Gross. Additional dialogue by Howard Snyder, Hugh Wedlock, Jr. Story by Jack Townley. *CAST:* Judy Canova, Francis Lederer, Raymond Walburn, Slim Summerville, Astrid Allwyn, Eddie Foy, Jr., Alma Kruger, Hugh O'Connell, Chick Chandler, Paul Harvey, Nora Lane, Gerald Oliver Smith, Wendell Niles, Vince Barnett, The Sportsmen. *SYN:* A girl (Canova) and her uncle (Summerville) live on a farm located on New York City's Fifth Avenue (!), and a pair of city slickers (Walburn, Foy, Jr.) try to get them to sell out. [British title: *Judy Goes to Town.*]

**The Purple Riders** (G.B. title) *see* **The Purple Vigilantes**

**614. The Purple V** (3/12/43) B&W 58 mins. (War). *DIR/A-PRO:* George Sherman. *SP:* Bertram Millhauser, Curt Siodmak. Adapted by Bertram Millhauser. Story by Robert R. Mill. *CAST:* John Archer, Mary McLeod, Fritz Kortner, Rex Williams, Kurt Katch, Walter Sande, Peter Lawford, Kurt Kreuger, Eva Hyde, Irene Seidner, William Vaughn (William von Bricken). *SYN:* When an American R.A.F. flyer (Archer) crash-lands in Germany, while on a mission, and obtains secrets about the North African campaign from a dying German officer (Vaughn), he seeks out his old German schoolteacher (Kortner), his daughter (McLeod), and son (Williams), who are anti–Nazis, to help him escape and get back home.

**615. The Purple Vigilantes** (1/24/38) B&W 58 mins. (Western). *DIR:* George Sherman. *A-PRO:* Sol C. Siegel. *SP:* Betty Burbridge, Oliver Drake. Based on characters created by William Colt MacDonald. *CAST:* Robert Livingston, Ray ("Crash") Corrigan, Max Terhune, Joan Barclay, Earl Dwire, Earle Hodgins, Francis Sayles, George Chesebro, Robert Fiske, Jack Perrin, Ernie Adams, William Gould, Harry Strang, Edward Cassidy, Frank O'Connor, Allan Cavan, Edward Peil, Sr., Jason Robards, Sr., Frank Ellis, Jack Kirk, Dot Farley, Lee Shumway, Billy Bletcher, Merrill McCormick, Bob Burns, Bill Patton, Wally West, Herman Hack, Jim Corey, Tom Smith, Curley Dresden. *SYN:* The Three Mesquiteers (Livingston, Corrigan, Terhune) go after a gang of outlaws, wearing purple hoods and purporting to be vigilantes who are terrorizing the citizens of a town. *NOTES:* Re-edited for TV at 54 mins. The 12th entry in the "Three Mesquiteers" series. [British title: *The Purple Riders.*]

**Queen of Spies** (G.B. title) *see* **Joan of Ozark**

**616. The Quiet Man** (9/14/52) Technicolor 129 mins. (Romance-Comedy).

*DIR:* John Ford. *PRO:* John Ford, Merian C. Cooper. *SP:* Frank S. Nugent. From the story *Green Rushes* by Maurice Walsh. An Argosy Production. *CAST:* John Wayne, Maureen O'Hara, Barry Fitzgerald, Ward Bond, Victor McLaglen, Mildred Natwick, Francis Ford, Eileen Crowe, May Craig, Arthur Shields, Charles FitzSimons, James Lilburn, Sean McClory, Jack MacGowran, Ken Curtis, Mae Marsh, Joseph O'Dea, Eric Gorman, Kevin Lawless, Paddy O'Donnell, Webb Overlander, Harry Tenbrook, Major Sam Harris, Harry Tyler, Patrick Wayne, Michael Wayne, Melinda Wayne, Antonia Wayne, David Hughes, Jack Roper, Douglas Evans, Al Murphy, Don Hatswell, Tiny Jones, Hank Worden, Pat O'Malley, Bob Perry, Frank Baker. *SYN:* In the 1920s, an American boxer (Wayne), who retired from the ring after he accidentally killed a man in a match, returns to his ancestral home of Ireland to forget his past and settle down. There he meets the woman (O'Hara) he wishes to marry, but first, he must overcome the objections of her rough and tumble brother (McLaglen), whom he has already alienated in buying his property that the brother wanted, and must fight him for his acceptance. *NOTES:* Uncredited was: co-producer Michael Killanin; additional dialogue writer Richard Llewellyn; second-unit directors John Wayne and Patrick Ford; and assistant director Andrew V. McLaglen. Although partly filmed on Republic's sound-stages, Herbert J. Yates' only contribution to this film was to try to have the title changed from *The Quiet Man* to *The Prizefighter and the Colleen*. This was John Wayne's last film for Republic — see Notes under 423. When Republic released a film from another source, the title card would read "A

Republic Presentation." However, with the John Ford films, they read "A Republic Production." Ford had pitched this story to studios all around Hollywood for many years before finally convincing Republic Pictures to finance the movie, but the agreement came with a price — John Ford had to direct two other movies for Republic first ... the acclaimed *Rio Grande* and the comparatively unsuccessful *The Sun Shines Bright*. Academy Award Winner: Best Director, Best Cinematography. Academy Award Nominee: Best Picture, Best Supporting Actor, Best Screenplay, Best Art Direction, Best Sound.

**617. Racing Luck** (11/19/35) B&W 59 mins. (Sports-Mystery). *DIR:* Sam Newfield. *A-PRO:* George A. Hirliman. *SP:* Jack O'Donnell, George W. Sayre. *CAST:* William Boyd, Barbara Worth, George Ernest, Esther Muir, Ernest Hilliard, Onest Conley, Ben Hall, Henry Roquemore, Dick Curtis, Ted Caskey. *SYN:* A trainer (Boyd), whose prize horse takes first place in a big race, is disqualified when drugs are discovered in its system, and although innocent, is suspended from racing for a year, allowing him time to discover the identity of the real culprit.

**618. Rags to Riches** (7/31/41) B&W 57 mins. (Crime). *DIR/A-PRO:* Joseph Kane. *SP:* James R. Webb. *CAST:* Alan Baxter, Mary Carlisle, Jerome Cowan, Michael Morris, Ralf Harolde, Paul Porcasi, Suzanne Kaaren, Eddie Acuff, Rosina Galli, Charles Trowbridge, Daisy Lee Mothershed, Joan Blair, Francis Sayles. *SYN:* A cab driver (Baxter), accused of a crime he did not commit, is later released, gets a job as a trucker, and becomes involved in a fur smuggling ring.

**619. Raiders of Old California** (11/1/57) B&W 72 mins. (Western). *DIR/PRO:* Albert C. Gannaway. *SP:* Sam Roeca, Tom Hubbard. An Albert C. Gannaway Production. A Republic Presentation. *CAST:* Jim Davis, Arleen Whelan, Faron Young, Marty Robbins, Lee Van Cleef, Louis Jean Heydt, Harry Lauter, Douglas Fowley, Lawrence Dobkin, Bill Coontz, Don Diamond, Rick Vallin, Tom Hubbard. *SYN:* At the end of the Mexican War in the Mexican part of California, an ex-cavalry officer (Davis) and his men try to set up their own empire by pressuring the Mexicans into signing over their property, until a settler (Young) stands up for the Mexicans.

**620. Raiders of Sunset Pass** (12/30/43) B&W 57 mins. (Western). *DIR:* John English. *A-PRO:* Louis Gray. *SP:* John K. Butler. *CAST:* Eddie Dew, Smiley Burnette, Jennifer Holt, Roy Barcroft, Mozelle Cravens, Nancy Worth, Kenne Duncan, Jack Kirk, Jack Rockwell, Hank Bell, Budd Buster, Jack Ingram, Frank McCarroll, Fred Burns, Al Taylor, Charles Miller, LeRoy Mason, Maxine Doyle. *SYN:* During World War II, a rancher (Miller) has a shortage of ranch hands, rendering him unable to battle rustlers and satisfy a government contract. With the help of his daughter (Holt) and a cowboy (Dew), the local women are organized into a group called the Women's Army of the Plains, and they join forces to bring in the cattle and repel the rustlers. *NOTES:* Republic's 2nd entry in the "John Paul Revere" series and Dew's last appearance as John Paul Revere.

**621. Raiders of the Range** (3/18/42) B&W 55 mins. (Western). *DIR:* John English. *A-PRO:* Louis Gray. *SP:* Barry

Shipman. Story by Albert DeMond. Based on characters created by William Colt MacDonald. *CAST*: Bob Steele, Tom Tyler, Rufe Davis, Lois Collier, Frank Jaquet, Tom Chatterton, Charles Miller, Dennis Moore, Fred Kohler, Jr., Max Walzman, Hal Price, Charley Phillips, Bud Geary, Jack Ingram, Al Taylor, Chuck Morrison, Joel Friedkin, Bob Woodward, Tom Steele, Monte Montague, Ken Terrell, Richard Alexander, Cactus Mack, John Cason. *SYN*: The Three Mesquiteers (Steele, Tyler, Davis) come to the aid of an oil driller (Chatterton) whose operation is being sabotaged by a gang of crooks. *NOTES*: The 43rd entry in the "Three Mesquiteers" series.

**622. Rainbow Over Texas** (5/9/46) B&W 65 mins. (Western). *DIR*: Frank McDonald. *A-PRO*: Edward J. White. *SP*: Gerald Geraghty. Story by Max Brand. *CAST*: Roy Rogers, George "Gabby" Hayes, Dale Evans, Sheldon Leonard, Robert Emmett Keane, Gerald Oliver Smith, Minerva Urecal, George J. Lewis, Kenne Duncan, Pierce Lyden, Dick Elliott, Jo Ann Dean, Bud Osborne, George Chesebro, Bob Nolan and the Sons of the Pioneers, "Trigger." *SYN*: Roy goes back to his home town on a promotional tour with the Sons of the Pioneers, gets involved with a town-sponsored Pony Express race, and cleans the town of local crooks. *NOTES*: Re-edited for TV at 54 mins.

**623. Rancho Grande** (3/22/40) B&W 68 mins. (Western). *DIR*: Frank McDonald. *A-PRO*: William Berke. *SP*: Bradford Ropes, Betty Burbridge, Peter Milne. Story by Peter Milne, Connie Lee. *CAST*: Gene Autry, Smiley Burnette, June Storey, Mary Lee, Dick Hogan, Ellen Lowe, Ferris Taylor, Joseph DeStefani, Roscoe Ates, Rex Lease, Ann Baldwin, Roy Barcroft, Edna Lawrence, Jack Ingram, Bud Osborne, Slim Whitaker, Chuck Baldra, Frankie Marvin, Horace B. Carpenter, Nora Lou Martin and the Pals of the Golden West, The Brewer Kids, The Boys Choir of Saint Joseph's School, "Champion." *SYN*: Gene has to deal with an East Coast heiress (Storey) as she takes over the ranch she has inherited from her grandfather, and also a gang of crooks that threaten to ruin the new irrigation system vital to the ranch's survival. *NOTES*: Director Frank McDonald's first Gene Autry film. [TV title: *El Rancho Grande*.]

**624. Range Defenders** (6/30/37) B&W 54 mins. (Western). *DIR*: Mack V. Wright. *A-PRO*: Sol C. Siegel. *SP*: Joseph F. Poland. Based on characters created by William Colt MacDonald. *CAST*: Robert Livingston, Ray ("Crash") Corrigan, Max Terhune, Eleanor Stewart, Harry Woods, Earle Hodgins, Thomas Carr, Yakima Canutt, John Merton, Harrison Greene, Horace B. Carpenter, Frank Ellis, Fred "Snowflake" Toones, Jack O'Shea, Ernie Adams, Jack Rockwell, Merrill McCormick, Curley Dresden, Jack Kirk, George Morrell, Donald Kirke, C. L. Sherwood, Milburn Morante, Al Taylor, Clyde McClary, Jack Evans, Bob Reeves, Art Dillard, Fred Parker. *SYN*: The Three Mesquiteers (Livingston, Corrigan, Terhune) get involved in a range war when a cattleman (Woods) decides to drive all the sheepmen off the range. *NOTES*: The 8th entry in the "Three Mesquiteers" series.

**625. The Ranger and the Lady** (7/30/40) B&W 59 mins. (Western). *DIR/A-PRO*: Joseph Kane. *SP*: Stuart

Anthony, Gerald Geraghty. Story by Bernard McConville. *CAST:* Roy Rogers, George "Gabby" Hayes, Jacqueline Wells (Julie Bishop), Harry Woods, Henry Brandon, Noble Johnson, Si Jenks, Ted Mapes, Yakima Canutt, Chuck Baldra, Herman Hack, Chick Hannon, Art Dillard, LeRoy Mason, Tom London, Davison Clark, Bud McClure, Al Taylor, Victor Cox, Bill Nestell, Fred Burns, Lloyd Ingraham, Henry Wills, "Trigger." *SYN:* While Sam Houston is in Washington trying to get Texas admitted into the Union, his assistant (Brandon) has imposed a tax on the Santa Fe trail, and a Texas Ranger (Rogers) comes to the aid of a woman (Wells) wagon train owner who is ordered to pay the tax. *NOTES:* Re-edited for TV at 54 mins.

**626. Ranger of Cherokee Strip** (11/4/49) B&W 60 mins. (Western). *DIR:* Philip Ford. *A-PRO:* Melville Tucker. *SP:* Bob Williams. Story by Earle Snell. *CAST:* Monte Hale, Paul Hurst, Alice Talton, Roy Barcroft, George Meeker, Douglas Kennedy, Frank Fenton, Monte Blue, Neyle Morrow, Lane Bradford. *SYN:* A ranger (Hale) sets out to prove that a Cherokee Indian (Kennedy), who broke out of jail to talk to his chief (Blue) about leasing the Indian lands, was framed for the chief's murder, and helps to get the Indian lands back.

**627. The Red Menace** (8/1/49) B&W 87 mins. (Drama-Spy). *DIR:* R. G. Springsteen. *E-PRO:* Herbert J. Yates. *SP:* Albert DeMond, Gerald Geraghty. Story by Albert DeMond. *CAST:* Robert Rockwell, Hanne Axman, Shepard Menken, Barbara Fuller, Betty Lou Gerson, James Harrington, Lester Luther, William J. Lally, William Martel, Duke Williams, Kay Reihl, Royal Raymond, Gregg Martell, Jimmy Hawkins, Mary DeGolyer, Leo Cleary, Napoleon Simpson, Robert Purcell, Norman Budd, Lloyd G. Davies (Narrator). *SYN:* A disillusioned veteran (Rockwell) joins the Communist party, finds out it is all hogwash, and flees across country with another ex-member (Axman) to escape their retaliation. *NOTES:* This film tries to show how communists take advantage of innocent Americans by offering them sex and money to lure them into the communist grasp, and how they are ready to betray their own members if it justifies the cause. [Alternate title: *Underground Spy.*] [British title: *The Enemy Within.*]

**628. The Red Pony** (3/28/49) Technicolor 89 mins. (Drama). *DIR/PRO:* Lewis Milestone. *SP:* John Steinbeck. Based on *The Gift, The Leader of the People,* and *The Promise* by John Steinbeck. A Charles K. Feldman Production. *CAST:* Myrna Loy, Robert Mitchum, Louis Calhern, Shepperd Strudwick, Peter Miles, Margaret Hamilton, Patty King, Jackie Jackson, Beau Bridges, Nino Tempo, Tommy Sheridan, Wee Willie Davis, George Tyne, Poodles Hanneford, Grace Hanneford, Eddie Borden, Max Wagner, Alvin Hammer, Dolores Castle, William Quinlan, Little Brown Jug (Don Kay Reynolds). *SYN:* A young boy (Miles) becomes embittered at his parents (Strudwick, Loy) and ranch hand (Mitchum) when his pony, whom he has raised and trained, dies. The father, who has never been close to his son, tries to console him. The ranch hand has a mare that's about to foal, and when the colt is born, he gives it to the boy, who again loves everyone. *NOTES:* Aaron Copland wrote the stirring score, one of very few he did for films. Re-released in 1957, and remade as a TV movie in 1973 with Henry Fonda and Maureen O'Hara. The character of *Billy Buck*, as played by Robert Mitchum, was deleted from the TV version.

**629. Red River Range** (12/22/38) B&W 56 mins. (Western). *DIR:* George Sherman. *A-PRO:* William Berke. *SP:* Luci Ward, Stanley Roberts, Betty Burbridge. Story by Luci Ward. Based on characters created by William Colt MacDonald. *CAST:* John Wayne, Ray ("Crash") Corrigan, Max Terhune, Polly Moran, Lorna Gray, Kirby Grant, Sammy McKim, William Royle, Perry Ivins, Stanley Blystone, Lenore Bushman, Burr Caruth, Roger Williams, Earl Askam, Olin Francis, Edward Cassidy, Fred "Snowflake" Toones, Bob McKenzie, Jack Montgomery, Al Taylor, Theodore Lorch. *SYN:* The Three Mesquiteers (Wayne, Corrigan, Terhune) are enlisted to stop cattle thieves who use a portable slaughterhouse and refrigerated vans to dispose of their spoils. *NOTES:* It was after this film that John Wayne made *Stagecoach* for John Ford. Since Wayne was contracted to do eight films in the series, Republic held back release of the final four until *Stagecoach* had gone into general release. Wayne would never forgive Republic for releasing the final four films after his big starring role. The 20th entry in the "Three Mesquiteers" series.

**630. Red River Renegades** (7/23/46) B&W 55 mins. (Western). *DIR:* Thomas Carr. *A-PRO:* Bennett Cohen. *SP:* Norman S. Hall. *CAST:* Sunset Carson, Peggy Stewart, Bruce Langley, Tom London, LeRoy Mason, Kenne Duncan, Ted Adams, Edmund Cobb, Jack Rockwell, Tex Terry. *SYN:* Two postal inspectors (Carson, London), assisted by a female Pinkerton agent (Stewart), go undercover to solve a rash of stagecoach robberies and disappearances.

**631. Red River Shore** (12/15/53) B&W 54 mins. (Western). *DIR:* Harry Keller. *A-PRO:* Rudy Ralston. *SP:* Arthur E. Orloff, Gerald Geraghty. *CAST:* Rex Allen, Slim Pickens, Lyn Thomas, William Phipps, Douglas Fowley, Trevor Bardette, William Haade, Emmett Vogan, John Cason, Rayford Barnes, Jack Perrin, "Koko." *SYN:* A cowboy (Allen) tries to keep the citizens of a town, who have put their money together to pursue an oil interest, and have already endured mishaps, from being swindled and also, to keep the death of a crooked businessman (Bardette) from his son (Phipps).

**632. Red River Valley** (3/2/36) B&W 56 mins. (Western). *DIR/PRO:* B. Reeves Eason. *SP:* Dorrell McGowan, Stuart McGowan. *CAST:* Gene Autry, Smiley Burnette, Frances Grant, Boothe Howard, Jack Kennedy, Sam Flint, George Chesebro, Charles King, Eugene Jackson, Edward Hearn, Frank LaRue, Ken Cooper, Frankie Marvin, Cap Anderson, Monty Cass, John Wilson, Lloyd Ingraham, Hank Bell, Earl Dwire, George Morrell, "Champion." *SYN:* Gene and Frog (Burnette) pose as ditch-riders to uncover the people responsible for causing numerous mishaps at the construction site of an irrigation project. *NOTES:* Re-edited for TV at 54 mins. Remade by Republic in 1941. [TV title: *Man of the Frontier.*]

**633. Red River Valley** (12/12/41) B&W 62 mins. (Western). *DIR/A-PRO:* Joseph Kane. *SP:* Malcolm Stuart Boylan. *CAST:* Roy Rogers, George "Gabby" Hayes, Sally Payne, Trevor Bardette, Gale Storm, Robert E. Homans, Hal Taliaferro, Lynton Brent, Pat Brady, Edward Peil, Sr., Dick Wessel, Jack Rockwell, Ted Mapes, Chuck Baldra, Bob Burns, Jack Kirk, Hank Bell, Bob Nolan and the Sons of the Pioneers, "Trigger." *SYN:* When ranchers are threatened by a severe water shortage and they obtain money to build a new reservoir, Roy sets out to stop a gambler (Bardette) who has conned the ranchers out of their money. *NOTES:* Re-edited for TV at 54 mins. A loose remake of the Republic 1936 feature of the same name.

**634. The Red Rope** (7/19/37) B&W 60 mins. (Western). *DIR:* S. Roy Luby. *PRO:* A. W. Hackel. *SP:* George Plympton. Story by Johnston McCulley. *CAST:* Bob Steele, Lois January, Forrest Taylor, Charles King, Bobby Nelson, Edward Cassidy, Lew Meehan, Frank Ball, Jack Rockwell, Karl Hackett, Horace Murphy, Richard Cramer, Horace B. Carpenter, Oscar Gahan, Ray Henderson, Wally West, Sherry Tansey, Tex Palmer, Emma Tansey, Willie Fung, Fred Parker, Lionel Belmore. *SYN:* A cowboy (Steele) goes after a gang of outlaws, whose signature is a bullet and a red-stained rope, that are terrorizing the local ranchers.

**635. Redwood Forest Trail** (9/18/50) B&W 67 mins. (Western). *DIR:* Philip Ford. *A-PRO:* Franklin Adreon. *SP:* Bradford Ropes. *CAST:* Rex Allen, Jeff Donnell, Carl "Alfalfa" Switzer, Jane Darwell, Marten Lamont, Pierre Watkin, Jimmy Ogg, Dick Jones, John Cason, Jim Frasher, Bobby Larson, Robert W. Wood, Jack Larson, Ted Fries, Joseph Granby, Robert E. Burns, "Koko." *SYN:* A cowboy (Allen) sets out to prove that the murder of a landowner was committed by men wanting valuable timberland, and not by the local underprivileged city boys at a camp. *NOTES:* In this film, Smokey the Bear makes a few points about careless forest fires and the need to preserve the woods.

**The Refugee** *see* **Three Faces West**

**636. Remember Pearl Harbor!** (5/18/42) B&W 75 mins. (War-Spy). *DIR:* Joseph Santley. *A-PRO:* Albert J. Cohen. *SP:* Malcolm Stuart Boylan, Isabel Dawn. *CAST:* Don ("Red") Barry, Alan Curtis, Fay McKenzie, Sig Rumann, Ian Keith, Rhys Williams, Maynard Holmes, Diana Del Rio, Robert Emmett Keane, Sammy Stein, Paul Fung, James B. Leong. *SYN:* On the eve of Pearl Harbor, a soldier (Barry) in the Philippines gets mixed up with a group of agents working for the Japanese. When he hears the news of the attack on Pearl Harbor, he changes his ways and exposes the espionage ring, and gives his life for his country by crashing his plane into a Japanese troopship. *NOTES:* This was the first film about the attack on Pearl Harbor.

**637. Rendezvous with Annie** (7/22/46) B&W 89 mins. (Comedy). *DIR/A-PRO:* Allan Dwan. *SP:* Richard Sale, Mary Loos. *CAST:* Eddie Albert, Faye Marlowe, Gail Patrick, Philip Reed, C. Aubrey Smith, Raymond Walburn, William Frawley, Wallace Ford, Will Wright, Lucien Littlefield, Edwin Rand, James Millican, Mary Field, Richard Sale, Bob Foy. *SYN:* A lonely soldier (Albert), stationed in Britain during World War II, goes AWOL and travels to New York City to visit his wife, and when she becomes pregnant, he must prove he's the father without admitting he went AWOL.

**638. Renegades of Sonora** (11/24/48) B&W 60 mins. (Western). *DIR:* R. G. Springsteen. *A-PRO:* Gordon Kay. *SP:* M. Coates Webster. *CAST:* Allan ("Rocky") Lane, Eddy Waller, William (Bill) Henry, Douglas Fowley, Roy Barcroft, Frank Fenton, Mauritz Hugo, George J. Lewis, Holly Bane, Dale Van Sickel, Marshall Reed, House Peters, Jr., Art Dillard, "Black Jack." *SYN:* On a trip to Wyoming to purchase a ranch, a cowboy (Lane) stops in a town and finds himself accused of murder and must prove his innocence.

**639. The Return of Jimmy Valentine** (2/1/36) B&W 67 mins. (Crime). *DIR:* Lewis D. Collins. *A-PRO:* Victor Zobel. *SP:* Jack Natteford, Olive Cooper. Story by W. Scott Darling, Wallace Sullivan, Paul Armstrong, Jr. *CAST:* Roger Pryor, Charlotte Henry, Robert Warwick, James Burtis, Edgar Kennedy, J. Carrol Naish, Lois Wilson, Wade Boteler, Gayne Whitman, Dewey Robinson, Hooper Atchley, William P. Carleton, Frank Melton, Jeanie Roberts, George Lloyd, George Chesebro, Charles Wilson, Franklin Parker, Harry Bowen, Lane Chandler, Jack Mack, Gertrude Messinger, Lucille Ward. *SYN:* A newspaper, in an effort to boost circulation and combat the rising popularity of radio, offers a reward to anyone who can find the aging safecracker, Jimmy Valentine (Warwick); their ace reporter (Pryor), who wants the reward himself, sets out to find the thief with the help of Valentine's daughter (Henry). *NOTES:* An updating of the "Jimmy Valentine" stories filmed in 1920 and 1928. Robert Warwick, who played the safecracker in the 1920 film, returns to play the character in retirement. Remade by Republic in 1942 as *Affairs of Jimmy Valentine*.

**Rhythm Hits the Ice** (G.B. and Re-release title) *see* **Ice-Capades Revue**

**640. Rhythm in the Clouds** (6/21/37) B&W 64 mins. (Musical-Comedy). *DIR:* John H. Auer. *A-PRO:* Albert E. Levoy. *SP:* Olive Cooper. Adapted by Nathanael West. Story by George Mence, Ray Bond. *CAST:* Patricia Ellis, Warren Hull, William Newell, Richard Carle, Zeffie Tilbury, Charles Judels, David Carlyle, Joyce Compton, Suzanne Kaaren, Esther Howard, Eddie Parker, James C. Morton, Rolfe Sedan. *SYN:* An impoverished songwriter (Ellis) fakes a letter that gains her admittance to the apartment of a wealthy songwriter, who is out of town, and uses his name to gain attention to herself.

**641. Rhythm of the Saddle** (11/5/38) B&W 58 mins. (Western). *DIR:* George Sherman. *A-PRO:* Harry Grey. *SP:* Paul Franklin. *CAST:* Gene Autry, Smiley Burnette, Pert Kelton, Peggy Moran, LeRoy Mason, Arthur Loft, Ethan Laidlaw, Walter De Palma, Archie Hall (Arch Hall, Sr.), Eddie Hart, Eddie Acuff, Tom London, William Norton Bailey, Roger Williams, Curley Dresden, Rudy Sooter, Douglas Wright, Kelsey Sheldon, Lola Monte, Alan Gregg, Jack Kirk, Emmett Vogan, Horace B. Carpenter, Frankie Marvin, Karl Hackett, James Mason, "Champion." *SYN:* Gene is the foreman on the ranch of a wealthy rodeo-owner (Moran), who is in danger of losing her rodeo contract. Gene comes to her rescue and overcomes a number of obstacles, including a burning barn, fixed rodeo events, and a murder charge. NOTES: Re-edited for TV at 54 mins.

**Rhythm on the Ranch** (G.B. title) *see* **Rootin' Tootin' Rhythm**

**642. Ride, Ranger, Ride** (9/30/36) B&W 63 mins. (Western). *DIR:* Joseph Kane. *PRO:* Nat Levine. *SP:* Dorrell McGowan, Stuart McGowan. Story by Bernard McConville, Karen DeWolf. *CAST:* Gene Autry, Smiley Burnette, Kay Hughes, Monte Blue, George J. Lewis, Max Terhune, Robert E. Homans, Lloyd Whitlock, Chief Thunder Cloud, Frankie Marvin, Iron Eyes Cody, Sonny Chorre, Bud Pope, Nelson McDowell, Arthur Singley, Greg Star Whitespear, Robert C. Thomas, Shooting Star, The Tennessee Ramblers, "Champion." *SYN:* Gene is an undercover Texas Ranger assigned to scout for the Army and is out to stop a group of Commanches from raiding a wagon train loaded with ammunition and supplies. *NOTES:* The screen debut of Max Terhune.

**643. Ride, Tenderfoot, Ride** (9/6/40) B&W 65 mins. (Western). *DIR:* Frank McDonald. *A-PRO:* William Berke. *SP;* Winston Miller. Story by Betty Burbridge, Connie Lee. *CAST:* Gene Autry, Smiley Burnette, June Storey, Mary Lee, Warren Hull, Forbes Murray, Joe McGuinn, Joe Frisco, Isabel Randolph, Herbert Clifton, Mildred Shay, Si Jenks, Cindy Walker, Patty Saks, Jack Kirk, Slim Whitaker, Fred Burns, Robert E. Burns, Fred "Snowflake" Toones, Chuck Morrison, Frank O'Connor, Curley Dresden, Frankie Marvin, Cactus Mack, The Pacemakers, "Champion." *SYN:* Gene becomes the heir to a meat-packing plant and the owner (Storey) of a rival plant wants to put him out of business. *NOTES:* Re-edited for TV at 54 mins.

**644. Ride the Man Down** (1/1/53) Trucolor 90 mins. (Western). *DIR/A-PRO:* Joseph Kane. *SP:* Mary C. McCall, Jr. From the *Saturday Evening Post* story by Luke Short. *CAST:* Brian Donlevy, Rod Cameron, Ella Raines, Forrest Tucker, Barbara Britton, Chill Wills, J. Carrol Naish, Jim Davis, Taylor Holmes, James Bell, Paul Fix, Al Caudebec, Roydon Clark, Roy Barcroft, Douglas Kennedy, Chris-Pin Martin, Jack LaRue, Claire Carleton. *SYN:* When the owner of a large ranch passes away, neighboring ranchers want to take the land and divide it, but the foreman (Cameron) must fight to maintain the land.

**Riders for Justice** *see* **908. Westward Ho**

**645. Riders of the Black Hills** (6/15/38) B&W 55 mins. (Western). *DIR:* George Sherman. *A-PRO:* William Berke. *SP:* Betty Burbridge. Story by Betty Burbridge, Bernard McConville. Based on characters created by William Colt MacDonald. *CAST:* Robert Livingston, Ray ("Crash") Corrigan, Max Terhune, Ann Evers, Roscoe Ates, Maude Eburne, Frank Melton, Johnny Lang Fitzgerald, Jack Ingram, Edward Earle, John P. Wade, Monte Montague, Ben Hall, Frank O'Connor, Tom London, Fred "Snowflake" Toones, Bud Osborne, Milburn Morante, Jack O'Shea, Art Dillard. *SYN:* The Three Mesquiteers (Livingston, Corrigan, Terhune) set out to rescue a valuable racehorse and bring the crooks to justice.

NOTES: Re-edited for TV at 54 mins. The 15th entry in the "Three Mesquiteers" series.

**646. Riders of the Rio Grande** (5/21/43) B&W 55 mins. (Western). DIR: Howard Bretherton. A-PRO: Louis Gray. SP: Albert DeMond. Based on characters created by William Colt MacDonald. CAST: Bob Steele, Tom Tyler, Jimmie Dodd, Lorraine Miller, Edward Van Sloan, Rick Vallin, Harry Worth, Roy Barcroft, Charles King, Jack Ingram, John James, Jack O'Shea, Henry Hall, Bud Osborne. SYN: The Three Mesquiteers (Steele, Tyler, Dodd) are mistaken for hired gunmen when a banker (Van Sloan), ashamed when his son (Vallin) robs a bank, hires three killers to kill him to make up for the misdeed. NOTES: The 51st and final entry in the "Three Mesquiteers" series.

**647. Riders of the Whistling Skull** (1/4/37) B&W 58 mins. (Western). DIR: Mack V. Wright. PRO: Nat Levine. SP: Oliver Drake, John Rathmell. Story by Bernard McConville, Oliver Drake. Based on the novels *Riders of the Whistling Skull* and *The Singing Scorpion* by William Colt MacDonald. CAST: Robert Livingston, Ray ("Crash") Corrigan, Max Terhune, Mary Russell, Roger Williams, Fern Emmett, C. Montague Shaw, Yakima Canutt, John Ward, George Godfrey, Earl Ross, Frank Ellis, Chief Thunder Cloud, John Van Pelt, Edward Peil, Sr., Jack Kirk, Iron Eyes Cody, Tracy Layne, Eddie Boland, Ken Cooper, Tom Steele, Wally West. SYN: The Three Mesquiteers (Livingston, Corrigan, Terhune) are hired by an archeologist's daughter (Russell) to guide an archeological expedition to an ancient Indian city in the Southwest and rescue her father who is being held captive by a gang of outlaws. NOTES: The 4th entry in the "Three Mesquiteers" series and considered one of the best. The plot of this film was reworked into the 1948 Monogram "Charlie Chan" film, *The Feathered Serpent*. [British title: *The Golden Trail*.]

**648. Ridin' Down the Canyon** (12/30/42) B&W 55 mins. (Western). DIR: Joseph Kane. A-PRO: Harry Grey. SP: Albert DeMond. Story by Bob Williams, Norman Houston. CAST: Roy Rogers, George "Gabby" Hayes, Dee "Buzzy" Henry, Linda Hayes, Addison Richards, Lorna Gray, Olin Howlin, James Seay, Hal Taliaferro, Forrest Taylor, Roy Barcroft, Art Mix, Art Dillard, Tom London, Jack Kirk, Major Sam Harris, Bob Nolan and the Sons of the Pioneers (Pat Brady, Hugh Farr, Karl Farr, Tim Spencer, Lloyd Perryman), "Trigger." SYN: Roy sets out to capture outlaws who have rustled horses that were destined for the war effort.

**649. Ridin' on a Rainbow** (1/24/41) B&W 79 mins. (Western). DIR: Lew Landers. A-PRO: Harry Grey. SP: Bradford Ropes, Doris Malloy. Story by Bradford Ropes. CAST: Gene Autry, Smiley Burnette, Mary Lee, Carol Adams, Ferris Taylor, Georgia Caine, Byron Foulger, Ralf Harolde, Jimmy Conlin, Guy Usher, Anthony Warde, Forrest Taylor, Burr Caruth, Edward Cassidy, Ben Hall, Tom London, William V. Mong, "Champion." SYN: When a local bank is robbed, Gene's investigation takes him to a showboat where a singer's (Lee) father (Foulger) may be involved. NOTES: Academy Award Nominee — Best Song.

**650. Ridin' the Lone Trail** (11/1/37) B&W 56 mins. (Western). DIR: Sam

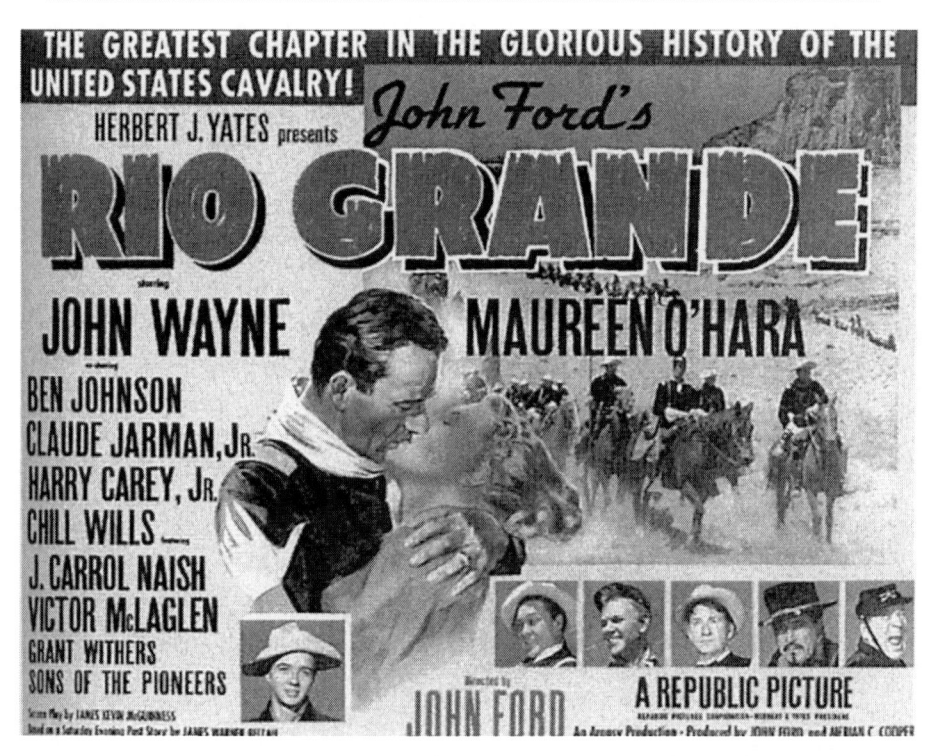

Newfield. PRO: A. W. Hackel. SP: Charles Francis Royal. Story by E. B. Mann. CAST: Bob Steele, Claire Rochelle, Charles King, Ernie Adams, Lew Meehan, Julian Rivero, Steve Clark, Hal Price, Frank Ball, Jack Kirk, Horace Murphy, Jack Evans, Bob Roper. SYN: A Texan (Steele) aids a sheriff (Clark) in rounding up a gang of road agents.

**Ridin' the Range** see **Home on the Prairie**

651. Rio Grande (11/15/50) B&W 105 mins. (Western). DIR: John Ford. PRO: John Ford, Merian C. Cooper. SP: James Kevin McGuinness. Based on *Mission With No Record* by James Warner Bellah. An Argosy Production. CAST: John Wayne, Maureen O'Hara, Ben Johnson, Claude Jarman, Jr., Harry Carey, Jr., Chill Wills, J. Carrol Naish, Victor McLaglen, Grant Withers, Peter Ortiz, Steve Pendleton, Karolyn Grimes, Alberto Morin, Stan Jones, Fred Kennedy, Chuck Roberson, Jack Pennick, Cliff Lyons, Patrick Wayne, The Sons of the Pioneers (Ken Curtis, Hugh Farr, Karl Farr, Lloyd Perryman, George "Shug" Fisher, Tommy Doss). SYN: A middle-aged commanding officer (Wayne) of a remote cavalry outpost near the Mexican border, not only has to deal with raiding Apaches, but his only son (Jarman, Jr.) who has dropped out of West Point and enlisted in his regiment, and his estranged wife (O'Hara) who has arrived at the post to look after her son and, if possible, buy back his enlistment. NOTES: This was the third in Ford's trilogy about the U. S. Cavalry troopers of the Old West. The earlier entries are *Fort Apache* (1948) and *She Wore a Yellow Ribbon* (1949), both

released by RKO. In the chronology of these three films, *Rio Grande* is the true sequel to *Fort Apache*, showing Wayne as a middle-aged commanding officer of a remote cavalry outpost. John Ford had not intended to make this film, but wanted to appease Republic Studios which asked for it, believing it would be more commercial than *The Quiet Man*, Ford's next film and one Republic had doubts about. *Rio Grande* proved to be an excellent western, and it marked the first appearance of Wayne and O'Hara together. The film debut of Patrick Wayne. John Wayne wears a small goatee in this film and this would be the only film where he wore anything approximating a beard. Working title was *Rio Bravo*.

**652. Rio Grande Raiders** (9/9/46) B&W 56 mins. (Western). *DIR:* Thomas Carr. *A-PRO:* Bennett Cohen. *SP:* Norton S. Parker. Story by Norman S. Hall. *CAST:* Sunset Carson, Linda Stirling, Bob Steele, Tom London, Tristram Coffin, Edmund Cobb, Jack O'Shea, Tex Terry, Kenne Duncan, Al Taylor, Fred Burns, Roy Bucko, Blackie Whiteford. *SYN:* A cowboy (Carson) learns that his kid brother (Steele), who has been released from prison to the custody of a crooked stagecoach operator (Coffin), has turned back to a life of crime and sets out in the hope that he will be able to turn his brother's life around. *NOTES:* Sunset Carson's last film for Republic. After this film, Carson disappeared from the screen for two years until he returned in a vastly inferior series of B-westerns for Astor Pictures.

**653. Road to Alcatraz** (7/10/45) B&W 60 mins. (Mystery). *DIR:* Nick Grinde. *A-PRO:* Sidney Picker. *PRO:* Armand Schaefer. *SP:* Dwight V. Babcock, Jerry Sackheim. Based on *Murder Stole My Missing Hours* by Francis K. Allen. *CAST:* Robert Lowery, June Storey, Grant Withers, Clarence Kolb, Charles Gordon, William Forrest, Iris Adrian, Lillian Bronson, Harry Depp, Kenne Duncan. *SYN:* A young lawyer (Lowery) sets out to prove his innocence when he is suspected of murdering his law partner. *NOTES:* Director Nick Grinde's final feature film as a director.

**654. The Road to Denver** (6/15/55) Trucolor 90 mins. (Western). *DIR/A-PRO:* Joseph Kane. *E-PRO:* Herbert J. Yates. *SP:* Horace McCoy, Allen Rivkin. Based on the *Saturday Evening Post* story "Man from Texas" by Bill Gullick. *CAST:* John Payne, Mona Freeman, Lee J. Cobb, Skip Homeier, Andy Clyde, Lee Van Cleef, Karl Davis, Glenn Strange, Dee "Buzzy" Henry, Dan White, Robert Burton, Ann Carroll, Tex Terry, Ray Middleton, Hank Worden, Fred Graham, William Haade. *SYN:* A man (Payne), tired of bailing his brother (Homeier) out of trouble, heads for Colorado and opens a stagecoach line, but it isn't long before his brother shows up working for the leader (Cobb) of an outlaw gang. *NOTES:* Although the story is set in Colorado, the location shooting for this film was done in Utah.

**655. Roarin' Lead** (12/9/36) B&W 54 mins. (Western). *DIR:* Mack V. Wright, Sam Newfield. *PRO:* Nat Levine. *SP:* Oliver Drake, Jack Natteford. Based on characters created by William Colt MacDonald. *CAST:* Robert Livingston, Ray ("Crash") Corrigan, Max Terhune, Christine Maple, Hooper Atchley, Yakima Canutt, George Chesebro, Tommy Bupp, Mary Russell, Tamara Lynn Kauffman, Beverly Luff, Theodore Frye, Katherine Frye, Jane Keckley, Harry Tenbrook, Pascale Perry, George Plues, Grace Kern, Newt Kirby, The Meglin Kiddies. *SYN:* The Three Mesquiteers (Livingston, Corrigan, Terhune) continue their fight against injustice when they are named trustees of an estate that funds an orphanage, as well as supports a cattlemen's association. When they discover mishandling of the association's monies, they put a lid on the wrongdoings. *NOTES:* The 3rd entry in the "Three Mesquiteers" series.

**656. Robin Hood of Texas** (7/15/47) B&W 71 mins. (Western). *DIR:* Lesley Selander. *A-PRO:* Sidney Picker. *SP:* John K. Butler, Earle Snell. *CAST:* Gene Autry, Lynn Roberts, Sterling Holloway, Adele Mara, James Cardwell, John Kellogg, Ray Walker, Michael Branden, Paul Bryar, James Flavin, Dorothy Vaughan, Stanley Andrews, Alan Bridge, Hank Patterson, Edmund Cobb, Lester Dorr, William Norton Bailey, Irene Mack, Opal Taylor, Eva Novak, Norma Brown, Frankie Marvin, Billy Wilkerson, Duke Green, Ken Terrell, Joe Yrigoyen, The Cass County Boys, "Champion, Jr." *SYN:* Gene aids the sheriff in searching out and capturing a gang of bank robbers. *NOTES:* This was Gene's final film for Republic studios.

**657. Robin Hood of the Pecos** (1/14/41) B&W 59 mins. (Western). *DIR/A-PRO:* Joseph Kane. *SP:* Olive Cooper. Story by Hal Long. *CAST:* Roy Rogers, George "Gabby" Hayes, Marjorie Reynolds, Cy Kendall, Leigh Whipper, Sally Payne, Eddie Acuff, Robert

Strange, William Haade, Jay Novello, Roscoe Ates, Jim Corey, Chick Hannon, Ted Mapes, Al Taylor, Frank McCarroll, Bob Burns, Chuck Baldra, George Kesterson, "Trigger." *SYN:* Following the Civil War, a group of Texans, led by a night rider (Rogers), band together to protect their state from unscrupulous northerners. *NOTES:* Re-edited for TV at 54 mins.

**658. Robinson Crusoe of Clipper Island** (1/15/37) B&W 71 mins. (Adventure). *SYN:* Feature version of the 14-chapter serial. *See* **1000. Robinson Crusoe of Clipper Island.**

**659. Rock Island Trail** (5/18/50) Trucolor 90 mins. (Western). *DIR:* Joseph Kane. *A-PRO:* Paul Malvern. *SP:* James Edward Grant. Based on *A Yankee Dared* by Frank J. Nevins. *CAST:* Forrest Tucker, Adele Mara, Adrian Booth, Bruce Cabot, Chill Wills, Barbara Fuller, Grant Withers, Jeff Corey, Roy Barcroft, Pierre Watkin, Valentine Perkins, Jimmy Hunt, Olin Howlin, Sam Flint, John Holland, Kate Lawson, Dick Elliott, Emory Parnell, Billy Wilkerson, Jack Pennick, Dick Curtis, William Haade, Richard Alexander. *SYN:* A railroad engineer (Tucker) runs into opposition from a stagecoach owner (Cabot) as he tries to extend his railway line further west from Illinois. [British title: *Transcontinent Express.*]

**660. Rocky Mountain Rangers** (5/24/40) B&W 58 mins. (Western). *DIR/A-PRO:* George Sherman. *S-PRO:* Harry Grey. *SP:* Barry Shipman, Earle Snell. Story by J. Benton Cheney. Based on characters created by William Colt MacDonald. *CAST:* Robert Livingston, Raymond Hatton, Duncan Renaldo, Rosella Towne, Sammy McKim, LeRoy Mason, Pat O'Malley, Dennis Moore, John St. Polis, Robert Blair, Burr Caruth, Jack Kirk, Hank Bell, Bud Osborne, Frank Ellis, Silver Tip Baker, Fred Burns, Buck Morgan, Curley Dresden, Pascale Perry, Herman Hack. *SYN:* The Three Mesquiteers (Livingston, Hatton, Renaldo) are Texas Rangers out to stop an outlaw gang by infiltrating the gang as outlaws. *NOTES:* Robert Livingston plays a dual role in this film. Re-edited for TV at 54 mins. The 30th entry in the "Three Mesquiteers" series.

**661. Rodeo King and the Senorita** (7/15/51) B&W 67 mins. (Western). *DIR:* Philip Ford. *A-PRO:* Melville Tucker. *SP:* John K. Butler. *CAST:* Rex Allen, Mary Ellen Kay, Buddy Ebsen, Roy Barcroft, Tristram Coffin, Bonnie DeSimone, Don Beddoe, Jonathan Hale, Harry Harvey, Rory Mallinson, Joe Forte, Buff Brady, "Koko." *SYN:* A rodeo rider (Allen) and his horse (Koko) set out to help a woman (DeSimone) run a Wild West Show after she inherits it from her murdered father (Brady). He also discovers that a crooked business partner (Coffin) is trying to bankrupt her show. *NOTES:* A remake of Republic's 1946, *My Pal Trigger.*

**662. Roll on Texas Moon** (9/12/46) B&W 68 mins. (Western). *DIR:* William Witney. *A-PRO:* Edward J. White. *SP:* Paul Gangelin, Mauri Grashin. Story by Jean Murray. *CAST:* Roy Rogers, George "Gabby" Hayes, Dale Evans, Dennis Hoey, Elisabeth Risdon, Francis McDonald, Edward Keane, Kenne Duncan, Tom London, Harry Strang, Edward Cassidy, Lee Shumway, Steve Darrell, Pierce Lyden, Bob Nolan and the Sons of the Pioneers, "Trigger." *SYN:* Roy is hired as a troubleshooter to prevent a range war between the sheepmen and cattlemen. *NOTES:* Re-edited for TV at 54 mins. The first Roy Rogers picture to be directed by William Witney. He changed the format of the Rogers films from costumers and musical extravaganzas to rapidly paced action films.

**Romance and Rhythm** *see* **Hit Parade of 1941**

663. **Romance on the Range** (5/18/42) B&W 63 mins. (Western). *DIR/A-PRO:* Joseph Kane. *SP:* J. Benton Cheney. *CAST:* Roy Rogers, George "Gabby" Hayes, Sally Payne, Linda Hayes, Edward Pawley, Harry Woods, Hal Taliaferro, Glenn Strange, Roy Barcroft, Jack Kirk, Pat Brady, Jack O'Shea, Dick Wessel, Richard Alexander, Chester Conklin, Selmer Jackson, Jack Montgomery, Henry Wills, Monte Montague, Frank Brownlee, George Kesterson (Art Mix), Bob Nolan and the Sons of the Pioneers, "Trigger." *SYN:* Roy sets out to capture a gang of fur thieves who are stealing furs through a trading post owned by a woman (Hayes). *NOTES:* Re-edited for TV at 54 mins.

664. **Romance on the Run** (5/11/38) B&W 68 mins. (Mystery-Comedy). *DIR:* Gus Meins. *A-PRO:* Herman Schlom. *SP:* Jack Townley. Story by Eric Taylor. *CAST:* Donald Woods, Patricia Ellis, Grace Bradley, Edward Brophy, William Demarest, Craig Reynolds, Andrew Tombes, Bert Roach, Leon Weaver, Edwin Maxwell, Granville Bates, Jean Joyce, Georgia Simmons. *SYN:* A private eye (Woods) is hired by an insurance company to locate some stolen jewels, and with his assistant (Ellis), chases the crooks from the city to the back roads of the South.

665. **Roogie's Bump** (8/25/54) B&W 71 mins. (Sports-Fantasy). *DIR:* Harold Young. *PRO:* John Bash, Elizabeth Dickenson. *SP:* Jack Hanley, Dan Totheroh. Story by Frank Warren, Joyce Selznick. *CAST:* Robert Marriot, Ruth Warrick, Olive Blakeney, Robert F. Simon, William Harrigan, David Winters, Michael Mann, Archie Robbins, Louise Troy, Guy Rennie, Ted Lawrence, Mike Keene, Roy Campanella, Billy Loes, Carl Erskine, Russ Meyer, The Brooklyn Dodgers, "Robbie," the dog. *SYN:* A new kid on the block (Marriot) is ostracized by the neighborhood kids who won't let him play baseball with them but, when the ghost of a onetime Brooklyn Dodger great (Harrigan), who was once in love with his grandmother, gives him a magical bump endowing him with a major-league arm, he lands a position with the Brooklyn Dodgers. [British title: *The Kid Colossus.*]

666. **Rookies on Parade** (4/17/41) B&W 69 mins. (Musical). *DIR:* Joseph Santley. *A-PRO:* Albert J. Cohen. *SP:* Karl Brown, Jack Townley, Milt Gross. Story by Sammy Cahn, Saul Chaplin. *CAST:* Bob Crosby, Ruth Terry, Gertrude Niesen, Eddie Foy, Jr., Marie Wilson, Cliff Nazarro, William Demarest, Sidney Blackmer, Horace MacMahon, William Wright, Jim Alexander, Louis DaPron, Bill Shirley. *SYN:* A pair of songwriters (Crosby, Foy, Jr.) are drafted into the Army and are assigned the task of putting on a show for their fellow soldiers. [British title: *Jamboree.*]

667. **Rootin' Tootin' Rhythm** (5/12/37) B&W 60 mins. (Western). *DIR:* Mack V. Wright. *A-PRO:* Armand Schaefer. *SP:* Jack Natteford. Story by Johnston McCulley. *CAST:* Gene Autry,

Smiley Burnette, Armida, Monte Blue, Hal Taliaferro, Ann Pendleton, Max Hoffman, Jr., Charles King, Frankie Marvin, Nina Campana, Charles Mayer, Karl Hackett, Jack Rutherford, Henry Hall, Curley Dresden, Art Davis, Milburn Morante, George Morrell, Pascale Perry, Al Clauser and His Oklahoma Outlaws, "Champion." *SYN:* Gene and Frog (Burnett) assume the identities of bandits to stop a gang of cattle rustlers. *NOTES:* Re-edited for TV at 54 mins. [British title: *Rhythm on the Ranch*.]

**668. Rose of the Yukon** (1/5/49) B&W 69 mins. (Adventure). *DIR:* George Blair. *A-PRO:* Stephen Auer. *SP:* Norman S. Hall. *CAST:* Steve Brodie, Myrna Dell, William Wright, Emory Parnell, Jonathan Hale, Benny Baker, Gene Gary, Dick Elliott, Francis McDonald, Wade Crosby, Lotus Long, Eugene Sigaloff. *SYN:* A U.S. Army major (Brodie) is sent to Alaska to investigate the mysterious resurfacing of a supposedly dead Army captain (Wright) wanted for murder.

**669. Rosie, the Riveter** (4/9/44) B&W 75 mins. (War-Comedy). *DIR:* Joseph Santley. *A-PRO:* Armand Schaefer. *SP:* Jack Townley, Aleen Leslie. Based on the Saturday Evening Post story *Room for Two* by Dorothy Curnor Handley. *CAST:* Jane Frazee, Frank Albertson, Vera Vague (Barbara Jo Allen), Frank Jenks, Maude Eburne, Lloyd Corrigan, Frank Fenton, Carl "Alfalfa" Switzer, Louise Erickson, Ellen Lowe, Arthur Loft, Tom Kennedy. *SYN:* A wartime comedy which has four female factory workers (Frazee, Vague, Erickson, Lowe) sharing a room in a boarding house with four male counterparts (Albertson, Fenton, Jenks, Loft) because of the housing shortage. [British title: *In Rosie's Room*.]

**670. Rough Riders of Cheyenne** (11/1/45) B&W 56 mins. (Western). *DIR:* Thomas Carr. *A-PRO:* Bennett Cohen. *SP:* Elizabeth Beecher. *CAST:* Sunset Carson, Peggy Stewart, Mira McKinney, Monte Hale, Wade Crosby, Kenne Duncan, Michael Sloane, Tom London, Eddy Waller, Jack O'Shea, Robert Wilke, Tex Terry, Jack Rockwell, Jack Luden, Rex Lease, Hank Bell, Henry Wills, Cactus Mack, Artie Ortego, Carl Mathews. *SYN:* Sunset sets out to finally put an end to the feud between his family and a neighboring family.

**671. Rough Riders of Durango** (1/30/51) B&W 60 mins. (Western). *DIR:* Fred C. Brannon. *A-PRO:* Gordon Kay. *SP:* M. Coates Webster. *CAST:* Allan ("Rocky") Lane, Walter Baldwin, Aline Towne, Steve Darrell, Ross Ford, Denver Pyle, Stuart Randall, Hal Price, Tom London, Russ Whiteman, Dale Van Sickel, Bob Burns, "Black Jack." *SYN:* A special courier (Lane) is sent to stop an outlaw gang from stealing wheat shipments and loan money from ranchers so they can bankrupt them and buy their land cheap.

**672. Rough Riders' Round-Up** (3/13/39) B&W 58 mins. (Western). *DIR/A-PRO:* Joseph Kane. *SP:* Jack Natteford. *CAST:* Roy Rogers, Mary Hart, Raymond Hatton, Eddie Acuff, William Pawley, Dorothy Sebastian, George Meeker, Jack Rockwell, Guy Usher, George Chesebro, Glenn Strange, Duncan Renaldo, Jack Kirk, Hank Bell, Dorothy Christy, Fred Kelsey, Eddy Waller, John Merton, George Letz, Al Haskell, Frank Ellis, Augie Gomez,

Frank McCarroll, Dan White, "Trigger." SYN: After the Spanish-American War, Roy and Rusty (Hatton) are border patrolmen who team up once again with the Rough Riders to capture a gang of gold bandits. NOTES: Re-edited for TV at 54 mins.

**673. Round-Up Time in Texas** (4/22/37) B&W 58 mins. (Western). DIR: Joseph Kane. PRO: Nat Levine. SP: Oliver Drake. CAST: Gene Autry, Smiley Burnette, Maxine Doyle, LeRoy Mason, Earle Hodgins, Dick Wessel, Buddy Williams, Elmer Fain, Cornie Anderson, Frankie Marvin, Ken Cooper, Al Ferguson, Slim Whitaker, Albert Knight, Carleton Young, Jack C. Smith, Jim Corey, Jack Kirk, George Morrell, The Cabin Kids, "Champion." SYN: Gene and Frog (Burnette) deliver a herd of horses to Gene's diamond prospector brother in South Africa and round up a gang of bandits intent on stealing the diamonds. NOTES: Re-edited for TV at 54 mins.

**674. Rovin' Tumbleweeds** (11/16/39) B&W 64 mins. (Western-Political). DIR: George Sherman. A-PRO: William Berke. SP: Betty Burbridge, Dorrell McGowan, Stuart McGowan. CAST: Gene Autry, Smiley Burnette, Mary Carlisle, Douglass Dumbrille, William Farnum, Lee "Lasses" White, Ralph Peters, Gordon Hart, Victor Potel, Jack Ingram, Sammy McKim, Reginald Barlow, Eddie Kane, Guy Usher, Horace Murphy, David Sharpe, Jack Kirk, Rose Plummer, Bob Burns, Art Mix, Horace B. Carpenter, Fred "Snowflake" Toones, Frank Ellis, Fred Burns, Edward Cassidy, Forrest Taylor, Tom Chatterton, Crauford Kent, Maurice Costello, Charles K. French, Lee Shumway, Bud Osborne, Harry Semels, Chuck Morrison, Nora Lou Martin and the Pals of the Golden West, "Champion." SYN: Gene is elected to Congress to expose a politician who is holding up a flood control bill so he can buy up large quantities of land and then sell them for a big profit after the bill is passed. [Alternate title: *Washington Cowboy.*]

**675. Rustlers of Devil's Canyon** (7/1/47) B&W 58 mins. (Western). DIR: R. G. Springsteen. A-PRO: Sidney Picker. SP: Earle Snell. Based on the comic strip created by Fred Harman. CAST: Allan ("Rocky") Lane, Bobby (Robert) Blake, Martha Wentworth, Peggy Stewart, Arthur Space, Emmett Lynn, Roy Barcroft, Tom London, Harry Carr, Pierce Lyden, Forrest Taylor, Bob Burns, Yakima Canutt. SYN: Red Ryder (Lane), after fighting in the Spanish-American War, returns home to his ranch to find that a range war is going on between homesteaders and ranchers that has been arranged by rustlers. NOTES: Re-edited for TV at 54 mins. The 22nd entry in the "Red Ryder" feature series.

**676. Rustlers on Horseback** (10/23/50) B&W 60 mins. (Western). DIR: Fred C. Brannon. A-PRO: Gordon Kay. SP: Richard Wormser. CAST: Allan ("Rocky") Lane, Eddy Waller, Roy Barcroft, Claudia Barrett, John Eldredge, George Nader, Forrest Taylor, John Cason, Stuart Randall, Douglas Evans, Tom Monroe, "Black Jack." SYN: A U.S. Marshal (Lane) and his sidekick (Waller) infiltrate a gang of outlaws to stop them from stealing ranches and then selling them to an unknowing party.

**677. Sabotage** (10/13/39) B&W 69 mins. (Spy). DIR: Harold Young. A-

*PRO:* Herman Schlom. *SP:* Lionel Houser, Alice Altschuler. *CAST:* Arleen Whelan, Gordon Oliver, Charley Grapewin, Lucien Littlefield, Paul Guilfoyle, J. M. Kerrigan, Dorothy Peterson, Don Douglas, Joe Sawyer, Maude Eburne, Horace MacMahon, John Russell, Wade Boteler, Frank Darien. *SYN:* A father (Grapewin), with the help of his fellow World War I veterans, sets out to round up the spies who are responsible for his son's (Oliver) false imprisonment. *NOTES:* The names of the spies hint they are of German origin although the plot does not say so. Working title was *Headline News*. [British title: *Spies at Work*.]

**678. Saddle Pals** (6/6/47) B&W 72 mins. (Western). *DIR:* Lesley Selander. *A-PRO:* Sidney Picker. *SP:* Bob Williams, Jerry Sackheim. Story by Dorrell McGowan, Stuart McGowan. *CAST:* Gene Autry, Lynn Roberts, Sterling Holloway, Irving Bacon, Damian O'Flynn, Charles Arnt, Jean Van, Tom London, Charles Williams, Francis McDonald, George Chandler, Edward Gargan, Carl Sepulveda, Paul E. Burns, Joel Friedkin, LeRoy Mason, Larry Steers, Edward Keane, Maurice Cass, Nolan Leary, Minerva Urecal, John S. Roberts, James Carlisle, Sam Ash, Frank O'Connor, Neal Hart, Frank Henry, Edward Peil, Sr., Bob Burns, Joe Yrigoyen, John Day, The Cass County Boys, "Champion Jr." *SYN:* Gene helps a landowner (Holloway) that is being driven off his land. *NOTES:* Re-edited for TV at 54 mins.

**679. Saddlemates** (5/16/41) B&W 56 mins. (Western). *DIR:* Les Orlebeck. *A-PRO:* Louis Gray. *SP:* Albert DeMond, Herbert Dalmas. Story by Bernard McConville, Karen DeWolf. Based on characters created by William Colt MacDonald. *CAST:* Robert Livingston, Bob Steele, Rufe Davis, Gale Storm, Forbes Murray, Cornelius Keefe, Peter George Lynn, Marin Sais, Martin Faust, Glenn Strange, Ellen Lowe, Iron Eyes Cody, Chief Yowlachie, Chief Many Treaties, Henry Wills, Bill Hazlett, Jack Kirk, Major Bill Keefer. *SYN:* The Three Mesquiteers (Livingston, Steele, Davis) become Army scouts to help hunt down a renegade Indian chief (Lynn), who is also masquerading as an Army interpreter. *NOTES:* The 37th entry in the "Three Mesquiteers" series.

**680. Saga of Death Valley** (11/17/39) B&W 58 mins. (Western). *DIR/A-PRO:* Joseph Kane. *SP:* Karen DeWolf, Stuart Anthony. *CAST:* Roy Rogers, George "Gabby" Hayes, Don ("Red") Barry, Doris Day, Frank M. Thomas, Hal Taliaferro, Jack Ingram, Tommy Baker, Buz Buckley, Lew Kelly, Fern Emmett, Horace Murphy, Lane Chandler, Fred Burns, Peter Frago, Ed Brady, Bob Thomas, Matty Roubert, Pascale Perry, Cactus Mack, Art Dillard, Horace B. Carpenter, Hooper Atchley, Frankie Marvin, Jess Cavan, Jimmy Wakely and His Rough Riders (Jimmy Wakely, Johnny Bond, Dick Rinehart), "Trigger." *SYN:* When a group of outlaws cut off the water supply to local ranchers, a man (Rogers) sets out to stop them and learns that his long lost brother (Barry), who was kidnapped as a youth, is a member of the gang. *NOTES:* The Doris Day that appears in this film is *not* the well-known actress/vocalist. Re-edited for TV at 54 mins.

**681. Sagebrush Troubador** (11/19/35) B&W 57 mins. (Western). *DIR:* Joseph Kane. *PRO:* Nat Levine. *S-PRO:* Armand Schaefer. *SP:* Oliver Drake, Joseph F. Poland. Story by Oliver Drake.

CAST: Gene Autry, Smiley Burnette, Barbara Pepper, J. Frank Glendon, Hooper Atchley, Fred Kelsey, Julian Rivero, Dennis Meadows, Tom London, Wes Warner, Frankie Marvin, Bud Pope, Tommy Gene Fairey, Art Davis, "Champion." *SYN:* Gene and Frog (Burnette) set out to find the murderer of a half-blind old rancher. *NOTES:* Re-edited for TV at 54 mins.

**682. Sailors on Leave** (9/30/41) B&W 71 ins. (Comedy). *DIR:* Albert S. Rogell. *A-PRO:* Albert J. Cohen. SP; Art Arthur, Malcolm Stuart Boylan. Story by Herbert Dalmas. *CAST:* William Lundigan, Shirley Ross, Chick Chandler, Ruth Donnelly, Mae Clarke, Cliff Nazarro, Tom Kennedy, Mary Ainslee, Bill Shirley, Garry Owen, William Haade, Jane Kean. *SYN:* A woman-hating sailor (Lundigan) is hopelessly in debt to his shipmates on board a battleship and to get even with him, they arrange a fake marriage between him and a cafe singer (Ross) which turns out to be genuine.

**683. The Saint Meets the Tiger** (7/29/43) B&W 70 mins. (Mystery). *DIR:* Paul L. Stein. *PRO:* William Sistrom. *SP:* Leslie Arliss, James Seymour, Wolfgang Wilhelm. Based on *Meet the Tiger* by Leslie Charteris. An RKO-British Production. A Republic Presentation. *CAST:* Hugh Sinclair, Jean Gillie, Gordon McLeod, Clifford Evans, Wylie Watson, Dennis Arundell, Charles Victor, Louise Hampton, John Salew, Arthur Hambling, Amy Veness, Claude Bailey, Noel Dainton, Eric Clavering, Ben Williams, Tony Quinn, John Slater, Alf Goddard. *SYN:* When a man is murdered on his doorstep, Simon Templar, "The Saint" (Sinclair), sets out to find the killer and gets involved with gold smugglers. *NOTES:* Distribution of this film went to Republic when RKO, who tried to revive "The Saint" with this film, knew they had made a mistake. Released in Britain in 1941 at a running time of 79 mins.

**684. Salt Lake Raiders** (5/1/50) B&W 60 mins. (Western). *DIR:* Fred C. Brannon. *A-PRO:* Gordon Kay. *SP:* M. Coates Webster. *CAST:* Allan ("Rocky") Lane, Eddy Waller, Roy Barcroft, Martha Hyer, Byron Foulger, Myron Healey, Clifton Young, Stanley Andrews, Rory Mallinson, Kenneth MacDonald, George Chesebro, "Black Jack." *SYN:* A cowboy (Healey), falsely accused of murder, escapes from prison trailed by a U.S. Marshal (Lane) and his deputy (Waller), but before he can prove his innocence, they are captured by outlaws who believe he has hidden a cache of gold and they force the trio to search for the gold, but because none of them actually knows where it's hidden, they cannot find it.

**685. San Antone** (2/15/53) B&W 90 mins. (Western). *DIR/A-PRO:* Joseph Kane. *SP:* Steve Fisher. Based on *The Golden Herd* by Curt Carroll. *CAST:* Rod Cameron, Arleen Whelan, Forrest Tucker, Katy Jurado, Rodolfo Acosta, Roy Roberts, Bob Steele, Harry Carey, Jr., James Lilburn, Walter (Andy) Brennan, Jr., Richard Hale, Martin Garralaga, Argentina Brunetti, Douglas Kennedy, Paul Fierro, George Cleveland, Francis McDonald, William Haade, James Craven, Marshall Reed. *SYN:* During the Civil War, a Texas rancher (Cameron), who won't choose sides, reluctantly agrees to lead a cattle drive through enemy territory, after an ex-Confederate officer (Tucker) becomes an outlaw and murders the rancher's father.

**686. San Antone Ambush** (10/1/49) B&W 60 mins. (Western). *DIR:* Philip Ford. *A-PRO:* Melville Tucker. *SP:* Norman S. Hall. *CAST:* Monte Hale, Bette Daniels, Paul Hurst, Roy Barcroft, James Cardwell, Trevor Bardette, Lane Bradford, Tommy Coats, Tom London, Edmund Cobb, Carl Sepulveda. *SYN:* An Army officer (Hale) is framed, along with an innocent rancher (Cardwell), for robbing stagecoaches of Army payrolls. They escape, capture the outlaw gang, and clear their names.

**687. The San Antonio Kid** (8/16/44) B&W 59 mins. (Western). *DIR:* Howard Bretherton. *A-PRO:* Stephen Auer. *SP:* Norman S. Hall. Based on the comic strip created by Fred Harman. *CAST:* Bill Elliott, Bobby (Robert) Blake, Alice Fleming, Linda Stirling, Tom London, Earle Hodgins, Glenn Strange, Duncan Renaldo, LeRoy Mason, Jack Kirk, Robert Wilke, Cliff Parkinson, Jack O'Shea, Tex Terry, Bob Woodward, Herman Hack, Henry Wills, Tom Steele, Joe Garcia, Billy Vincent, Bud Geary, Pascale Perry. *SYN:* The San Antonio Kid (Renaldo) is hired by Ace Hanlon (Strange) to kill Red Ryder (Elliott) when he learns that Hanlon and an oil field employee (Mason) are trying to drive the ranchers off their land for the oil rights. *NOTES:* Re-edited for TV at 54 mins. The 3rd entry in the "Red Ryder" feature series.

**688. San Fernando Valley** (9/15/44) B&W 74 mins. (Western). *DIR:* John English. *A-PRO:* Edward J. White. *SP:* Dorrell McGowan, Stuart McGowan. *CAST:* Roy Rogers, Dale Evans, Jean Porter, Andrew Tombes, Charles Smith, Edward Gargan, Dot Farley, LeRoy Mason, Pierce Lyden, Maxine Doyle, Helen Talbot, Pat Starling, Cay Forester, Marguerite Blount, Mary Kenyon, Hank Bell, Kenne Duncan, Edward Cassidy, Vernon and Draper, The Morell Trio, Bob Nolan and the Sons of the Pioneers, "Trigger." *SYN:* Roy rides into the San Fernando Valley to clean out a gang of outlaws that are terrorizing the area. *NOTES:* Roy Rogers receives his first on-screen kiss from Jean Porter in a dream sequence. Re-edited for TV at 54 mins.

**689. Sands of Iwo Jima** (3/1/50) B&W 110 mins. (War). *DIR:* Allan Dwan. *A-PRO:* Edmund Grainger. *SP:* Harry Brown, James Edward Grant. Story by Harry Brown. *CAST:* John Wayne, John Agar, Adele Mara, Forrest Tucker, Wally Cassell, James Brown, Richard Webb, Arthur Franz, Julie Bishop, James Holden, Peter Coe, Richard Jaeckel, William Murphy, George Tyne, Hal Fieberling, John McGuire, Martin Milner, Leonard Gumley, William Self, Dick Wessel, I. Stanford Jolley, David Clarke, Gil Herman, Dick Jones, Don Haggerty, Bruce Edwards, Dorothy Ford, John Whitney, Col. D. M. Shoup, Lt. Col. H. P. Crowe, Capt. Harold G. Schrier, Pfc. Rene A. Gagnon, Pfc. Ira H. Hayes, PM-3/C John H. Bradley. *SYN:* In 1943, a Marine Corps sergeant (Wayne) inherits a new group of recruits that he must turn into crack Marines within a few weeks; he drills them hard and marches them hard, not caring whether he makes any friends, but one recruit, the son (Agar) of a military hero who is one of his old friends, rebuffs him and wants out of the corps. Later, on Iwo Jima, when the sergeant dies, his death is shocking — a single bullet from an enemy sniper cuts him down without a farewell speech or a heroic act to go with it, and from his pocket the recruit takes an unfinished

A GREAT HUMAN STORY
...MAKES A MIGHTY
MOTION PICTURE
THE MARINES' GREATEST HOUR
SANDS OF
IWO JIMA
starring
JOHN WAYNE
JOHN AGAR · ADELE MARA · FORREST TUCKER
WALLY CASSELL · JAMES BROWN · RICHARD WEBB · ARTHUR FRANZ
JULIE BISHOP · JAMES HOLDEN · PETER COE · RICHARD JAECKEL
A REPUBLIC PICTURE

letter he had been writing to his son, which he slowly reads aloud. The sergeant has written his boy that he was a failure in many things, except being a good Marine. The recruit vows to finish their mission and orders the men — harshly, as the sergeant would — into battle. NOTES: The release date given above is the general release date. The film was premiered in San Francisco December 14, 1949 to qualify for the 1949 Academy Awards. This was John Wayne's first Oscar-nominated role. Three of the men "playing" members of the Marine squad, Hayes, Gagnon, and Bradley, are the real-life Marines who raised the flag at Iwo Jima and were caught in the historic photograph from which the monument in Washington, D.C., was created. Released in a "Computer-colorized" version in the 1980s by the new Republic studios. Academy Award Nominee — Best Actor, Best Original Screenplay, Best Editing, Best Sound.

**690. Santa Fe Passage** (5/12/55) Trucolor 90 mins. (Western). *DIR:* William Witney. *A-PRO:* Sidney Picker. *SP:* Lillie Hayward. Based on the story in *Esquire* magazine by Clay Fisher. *CAST:* John Payne, Faith Domergue, Rod Cameron, Slim Pickens, Irene Tedrow, George Keymas, Leo Gordon, Anthony Caruso. *SYN:* Accused of betraying a wagon train to Apaches, a guide (Payne) is shunned by his employers, but is given another chance by a man (Cameron) and woman (Domergue) to guide a large cargo of guns and other munitions through hostile Apache territory. The guide, who hates Indians, finds himself falling in love with the woman, who is a half-breed, and he must deal with his prejudices as well as an Indian attack.

*NOTES:* William Witney's last directed western for Republic.

**691. Santa Fe Saddlemates** (6/2/45) B&W 56 mins. (Western). *DIR/A-PRO:* Thomas Carr. *SP:* Bennett Cohen. *CAST:* Sunset Carson, Linda Stirling, Olin Howlin, Roy Barcroft, Rex Lease, Bud Geary, Kenne Duncan, George Chesebro, Robert Wilke, Forbes Murray, Henry Wills, Frank Jaquet, John Carpenter, Edmund Cobb, Nolan Leary, Fred Graham, George Magrill, Jack O'Shea, Carol Henry, Billy Vincent, Horace B. Carpenter, Bill McCall, Rose Plummer, Bob Reeves, Bill Wolfe, Kansas Moehring, Bill Nestell. *SYN:* A U.S. Marshal (Carson) works undercover as an outlaw to locate a diamond smuggling ring believed to be headquartered at a ranch on the Mexican border.

**692. Santa Fe Scouts** (4/16/43) B&W 55 mins. (Western). *DIR:* Howard Bretherton. *A-PRO:* Louis Gray. *SP:* Morton Grant, Betty Burbridge. Based on characters created by William Colt MacDonald. *CAST:* Bob Steele, Tom Tyler, Jimmie Dodd, Lois Collier, John James, Elizabeth Valentine, Tom Chatterton, Tom London, Budd Buster, Jack Ingram, Kermit Maynard, Rex Lease, Edward Cassidy, Yakima Canutt, Jack Kirk, Curley Dresden, Reed Howes, Bud Geary, Carl Sepulveda, Al Taylor, Kenne Duncan. *SYN:* The Three Mesquiteers (Steele, Tyler, Dodd) save a rancher framed for murder and stop outlaw squatters from unfairly taking over ranch land and watering their cattle with the rancher's water. *NOTES:* The 50th entry in the "Three Mesquiteers" series.

**693. Santa Fe Stampede** (11/18/38) B&W 56 mins. (Western). *DIR:* George

Sherman. *A-PRO:* William Berke. *SP:* Luci Ward, Betty Burbridge. Story by Luci Ward. Based on characters created by William Colt MacDonald. *CAST:* John Wayne, Ray ("Crash") Corrigan, Max Terhune, William Farnum, June Martel, LeRoy Mason, Martin Spellman, Genee Hall, Ferris Taylor, Tom London, Walter Wills, John F. Cassidy, Dick Rush, George Chesebro, Bud Osborne, Yakima Canutt, Richard Alexander, Nelson McDowell, Curley Dresden, Duke Lee, Bill Wolfe, Charles King, Ralph Peters, Horace B. Carpenter, Jerry Frank, Cliff Parkinson, Bob Woodward, Blackjack Ward, Robert Milasch, Jim Corey, Russ Powell, George Morrell, Bud McClure, Charles Murphy, Griff Barnette, John Elliott, Marin Sais, Frank O'Connor. *SYN:* An old prospector (Farnum) invites the Three Mesquiteers (Wayne, Corrigan, Terhune) to share a claim with him, and upon arriving the trio discovers him murdered, and a crooked politician (Mason), who also wants a piece of the gold claim, frames Stoney (Wayne) for the murder and it is up to the other Mesquiteers to set him free and bring the politician to justice. *NOTES:* This film is very unusual in that it contains a scene of two kids getting killed in a runaway buckboard, something which was unheard of at the time in B-Westerns. The 19th entry in the "Three Mesquiteers" series.

**694. Santa Fe Uprising** (11/15/46) B&W 55 mins. (Western). *DIR:* R. G. Springsteen. *A-PRO:* Sidney Picker. *SP:* Earle Snell. Based on the comic strip created by Fred Harman. *CAST:* Allan ("Rocky") Lane, Bobby (Robert) Blake, Martha Wentworth, Barton MacLane, Jack LaRue, Tom London, Dick Curtis, Forrest Taylor, Emmett Lynn, Hank Patterson, Edmund Cobb, Pat Michaels, Kenne Duncan, Edythe Elliott, Frank Ellis, Art Dillard, Lee Reynolds, Forest Burns. *SYN:* Red Ryder (Lane) sets out to rescue Little Beaver (Blake) after he has been kidnapped by outlaws who are trying to stop the Duchess (Wentworth) from taking over a toll road she has inherited. *NOTES:* The 17th entry in the "Red Ryder" feature series and the first to star Allan ("Rocky") Lane as "Red Ryder" and Martha Wentworth as "Duchess."

**695. Satan's Satellites** (3/28/58) B&W 75 mins. (Science Fiction). *SYN:* Feature version of the 12 chapter serial, *Zombies of the Stratosphere*. See **1009. Zombies of the Stratosphere.**

**696. Savage Frontier** (5/15/53) B&W 54 mins. (Western). *DIR:* Harry Keller. *A-PRO:* Rudy Ralston. *SP:* Dwight V. Babcock, Gerald Geraghty. *CAST:* Allan ("Rocky") Lane, Eddy Waller, Bob Steele, Dorothy Patrick, Roy Barcroft, Richard Avonde, William Phipps, Jimmy Hawkins, Lane Bradford, John Cason, Kenneth MacDonald, William (Bill) Henry, Gerry Flash, Art Dillard, "Black Jack." *SYN:* A U.S. Marshal (Lane) who is tracking down two killers, comes across an ex-con and a young robber who he sets straight on the side of law and order.

**697. The Savage Horde** (5/22/50) B&W 90 mins. (Western). *DIR/A-PRO:* Joseph Kane. *SP:* Kenneth Gamet. Story by Thames Williamson, Gerald Geraghty. *CAST:* Bill Elliott, Adrian Booth, Grant Withers, Barbara Fuller, Noah Beery, Jr., Jim Davis, Douglass Dumbrille, Will Wright, Roy Barcroft, Earle Hodgins, Stuart Hamblen, Hal Taliaferro, Bob Steele, Lloyd Ingraham,

Marshall Reed, Crane Whitley, Charles Stevens, James Flavin, Edward Cassidy, Kermit Maynard, George Chesebro, Jack O'Shea, Monte Montague, Bud Osborne, Reed Howes. *SYN:* A gunfighter (Elliott), fleeing the law because of his self-defense killing of an Army officer, risks capture to aid a group of ranchers against a cattle baron (Withers) who is trying to increase his empire by taking over the smaller ranches.

**698. Scandal Incorporated** (10/12/56) B&W 79 mins. (Crime). *DIR:* Edward Mann. *PRO/SP:* Milton Mann. *CAST:* Robert Hutton, Paul Richards, Claire Kelly, Patricia Wright, Robert Knapp, Havis Davenport, Reid Hammond, Nestor Paiva, Gordon Wynn, Guy Prescott, Donald Kirke, Marjorie Stapp, Enid Baine, Mauritz Hugo, Joe Breen, Allen O'Locklin, George Cisar, Tracey Morgan, Mimi Simpson. *SYN:* A Hollywood star (Hutton), who had a run in with the reporter of a scandal magazine, is suspected of his murder when he turns up dead, and it is up to an attorney (Richards) to prove him innocent.

**699. Scatterbrain** (7/20/40) B&W 74 mins. (Musical-Comedy). *DIR/A-PRO:* Gus Meins. *SP:* Jack Townley, Val Burton, Olive Cooper. Additional dialogue by Paul Conlan. Adapted by Joseph Moncure March. *CAST:* Judy Canova, Alan Mowbray, Ruth Donnelly, Eddie Foy, Jr., Joseph Cawthorn, Wallace Ford, Isabel Jewell, Luis Alberni, Emmett Lynn, Jimmy Starr, Cal Shrum and His Gang, Matty Malneck and His Orchestra. *SYN:* An Ozark mountain girl (Canova) mistakenly gets "discovered" by a Hollywood film producer (Cawthorn) and is sent to Hollywood where she becomes a star. *NOTES:* Judy Canova's first film for Republic. Screenwriter Olive Cooper and adaptor Joseph Moncure March were uncredited.

**700. Scotland Yard Dragnet** (2/7/58) B&W 74 mins. (Crime). *DIR/SP:* Montgomery Tully. *PRO:* Alec C. Snowden. Based on a play by Falkland Cary. A Merton Park Production. A Republic Presentation. *CAST:* Roland Culver, Patricia Roc, Paul Carpenter, William Hartnell, Kay Callard, Ellen Pollock, Gordon Needham, Martin Wyldeck, Oliver Johnston, Mary Jones, John Serret, Helene Gilmer, Patricia Wellum, Edgar Driver, Robert Sansom, Douglas Hayes, Calvin Stewart, Gordon Harris, Jill Nicholls, Jessica Cairns, Hilda Barry, Tim Fitzgerald, Tom Tann, Dennis McCarthy, Richard Stewart. *SYN:* A psychiatrist (Culver), who uses hypnotism to treat his patients, tries to hypnotize one of his patients, a test pilot (Carpenter) that suffers blackouts, into killing his wife. *NOTES:* Released in Britain in 1957 at a running time of 88 mins. [Original British title: *The Hypnotist.*]

**701. Scotland Yard Investigator** (9/30/45) B&W 68 mins. (Crime). *DIR/A-PRO:* George Blair. *PRO:* Armand Schaefer. *SP:* Randall Faye. *CAST:* C. Aubrey Smith, Erich Von Stroheim, Stephanie Bachelor, Forrester Harvey, Doris Lloyd, Eva Moore, Richard Fraser, Victor Varconi, Frederic Worlock, George Metaxa, Emil Rameau, Colin Campbell. *SYN:* A museum curator (Smith), a Scotland Yard inspector (Fraser), and an obsessed art collector (Von Stroheim) set out to track down the original painting of the *Mona Lisa,* supposedly in the possession of an antique dealer (Harvey).

**702. A Scream in the Dark** (10/15/43) B&W 53 mins. (Mystery). *DIR/*

*A-PRO:* George Sherman. *SP:* Gerald Schnitzer, Anthony Coldeway. Based on *The Morgue Is Always Open* by Jerome Odlum. *CAST:* Robert Lowery, Marie McDonald, Edward Brophy, Wally Vernon, Hobart Cavanaugh, Jack LaRue, Elizabeth Russell, Frank Fenton, William Haade, Linda Brent, Arthur Loft, Kitty McHugh. *SYN:* When a spiked umbrella is used to kill several people, a reporter (Lowery) sets out to find the killer, which may be a woman.

**703. The Sea Hornet** (11/6/51) B&W 84 mins. (Adventure). *DIR/A-PRO:* Joseph Kane. *SP:* Gerald Drayson Adams. *CAST:* Rod Cameron, Adele Mara, Adrian Booth, Chill Wills, Jim Davis, Richard Jaeckel, Ellen Corby, James Brown, Grant Withers, William Ching, William Haade, Hal Taliaferro, Emil Sitka, Byron Foulger, Monte Blue, Jack Pennick. *SYN:* A diver (Cameron) leads a search for a sunken ship full of gold, on which his pal (Brown) was killed when the ship went under. When he gets there he finds the ship has been emptied of the gold by another diver (Davis), who has hidden the treasure in his hotel, and he sets out to get the treasure and bring the murderer to justice.

**704. Sea of Lost Ships** (2/1/54) B&W 85 mins. (Adventure). *DIR/A-PRO:* Joseph Kane. *SP:* Steve Fisher. Story by Norman Reilly Raine. *CAST:* John Derek, Wanda Hendrix, Walter Brennan, Richard Jaeckel, Tom Tully, Barton MacLane, Erin O'Brien-Moore, Ben Cooper, Darryl Hickman, Roy Roberts, Tom Powers, Richard Hale, James Brown, Douglas Kennedy, Steve Brodie,

John Hudson. *SYN:* A father (Brennan) rears his own son (Jaeckel) as well as an orphan (Derek). When they both enter the Coast Guard Academy, the orphan is expelled because of fighting, and he vows to work his way back and become a hero to his girl (Hendrix), step-father, and step-brother. *NOTES:* Some sources also list release date as 10/22/53.

**705. Sea Racketeers** (8/20/37) B&W 64 mins. (Drama-Crime). *DIR:* Hamilton MacFadden. *A-PRO:* Armand Schaefer. *SP:* Dorrell McGowan, Stuart McGowan. *CAST:* Weldon Heyburn, Jeanne Madden, Warren Hymer, Dorothy McNulty, J. Carrol Naish, Joyce Compton, Charles Trowbridge, Syd Saylor, Lane Chandler, Benny Burt, Ralph Sanford, Don Rowan, Bryant Washburn. *SYN:* A Coast Guardsman (Heyburn) saves a woman (Madden) from a gang of fur smugglers that terrorizes a floating nightclub.

**Secret Motive** (G.B. title) *see* **London Blackout Murders**

**706. Secret Service Investigator** (5/31/48) B&W 60 mins. (Crime). *DIR:* R. G. Springsteen. *A-PRO:* Sidney Picker. *SP:* John K. Butler. *CAST:* Lynn Roberts, Lloyd Bridges, George Zucco, June Storey, Trevor Bardette, John Kellogg, Jack Overman, Roy Barcroft, Douglas Evans, Milton Parsons, James Flavin, Tommy Ivo, Sam McDaniel, William Benedict, Minerva Urecal. *SYN:* An unemployed World War II veteran (Bridges) is conned by a counterfeiter (Zucco) and his gang, posing as Secret Service agents, into participating in their schemes. Eventually he finds out who they are and calls real Treasury agents in to round them up.

**707. Secret Venture** (11/10/55) B&W 68 mins. (Spy). *DIR:* R. G. Springsteen. *PRO:* William N. Boyle. *SP:* Paul Erickson, Kenneth R. Hayles. *CAST:* Kent Taylor, Jane Hylton, Kathleen Byron, Karel Stepanek, Frederick Valk, Maurice Kaufmann, Martin Boddey, Arthur Lane, Michael Balfour, John Boxer, Hugo Schuster, John Warren, Fred Griffiths, Terence Brook, Patrick Dowling, Arthur Bentley, Michael Ripper, Vivienne Martin, Alexander Field. *SYN:* An American (Taylor) in England gets mixed up with an espionage ring when he gains possession of a briefcase containing a secret formula, and instead of working with Scotland Yard, he decides to round up the spies by himself. *NOTES:* Released in Britain in February, 1955.

**708. Secrets of Monte Carlo** (6/20/51) B&W 60 mins. (Crime). *DIR:* George Blair. *A-PRO:* William Lackey. *SP:* John K. Butler. *CAST:* Warren Douglas, Lois Hall, June Vincent, Stephen Bekassy, Robin Hughes, Otto Waldis, Charles LaTorre, Philip Ahn, Isabel Randolph, Charles Lung, Sue Casey, Georges Renavent, Bruce Lester, George Davis, Howard Chuman. *SYN:* An American businessman (Douglas), visiting Monte Carlo, finds himself embroiled in the theft of valuable jewels belonging to a rajah (Lung) and being pursued by a British insurance investigator (Hughes).

**709. Secrets of Scotland Yard** (7/26/44) B&W 68 mins. (Spy). *DIR/A-PRO:* George Blair. *SP:* Clift Denison. Based on *Room 40, O. B.* by Denison Clift. *CAST:* Edgar Barrier, Stephanie Bachelor, C. Aubrey Smith, Lionel Atwill, Henry Stephenson, John Abbott, Walter Kingsford, Martin Kosleck, Forrester Harvey, Frederic Worlock, Matthew Boulton, Bobby Cooper, William Edmunds, Louis Arco, Frederick Giermann, Sven Hugo Borg, Leslie Vincent, Arthur Stanning, Keith Hitchcock, Leonard Carey, Mary Gordon, Jordan Shelley, Jack George, Edward Biby, Arthur Mulliner, Major Sam Harris, Eric Wilton, Carey Harrison, Larry Steers, Bill Nind, Carl Ekberg, Antonio Filauri, Dick Ryan, Frank Brand, Nigel Horton, Richard Woodruff, Kenne Duncan. *SYN:* Germans have placed a spy in Scotland Yard in the room where secret messages are decoded. When a twin (Barrier), who works in this room for Scotland Yard, is killed by Nazi agents after deciphering an important Nazi message, the other twin (Barrier) takes his place to continue the task of decoding secret messages that will bring down the Nazi agents operating in England. *NOTES:* The directorial debut of George Blair. Edgar Barrier plays a brief dual role in this film.

**710. Secrets of the Underground** (12/18/42) B&W 70 mins. (Spy). *DIR:* William Morgan. *A-PRO:* Leonard Fields. *SP:* Robert Tasker, Geoffrey Homes (Daniel Mainwaring). Story by Geoffrey Homes. Based on the radio program *Mr. District Attorney* by Phillips H. Lord. *CAST:* John Hubbard, Virginia Grey, Lloyd Corrigan, Robin Raymond, Miles Mander, Olin Howlin, Ben Welden, Marla Shelton, Neil Hamilton, Ken Christy, Dick Rich, Pierre Watkin, Eula Morgan, George Sherwood, Herb Vigran, Nora Lane, Charles Williams, Bobby Stone, Francis Sayles, Roy Gordon, Connie Evans, George Chandler, Eddie Kane, Joey Ray, Max Wagner, Pauline Drake, Eddy Chandler, Ben Taggart. *SYN:* An assistant District Attorney (Hubbard) and his reporter girlfriend (Grey) uncover a group of Nazis using a fancy gown shop as a front for counterfeiting bogus war savings stamps. *NOTES:* This was the last of three films featuring popular radio character P. Cadwallader Jones. It was preceded by *Mr. District Attorney* and *Mr. District Attorney in the Carter Case*, both 1941.

**Serenade of the West** (G.B. title) *see* **Cowboy Serenade**

**Serenade of the West** (G.B. title) *see* **Git Along Little Dogies**

**711. Shadows of Tombstone** (9/28/53) B&W 54 mins. (Western). *DIR:* William Witney. *A-PRO:* Rudy Ralston. *SP:* Gerald Geraghty. *CAST:* Rex Allen, Slim Pickens, Jeanne Cooper, Roy Barcroft, Emory Parnell, Ric Roman, Richard Avonde, Julian Rivero, Rex Lease, "Koko." *SYN:* Two cowboys (Allen, Pickens) ride into a town and, with the help of a woman reporter (Cooper), oust a crooked sheriff (Parnell) and clean up the town.

**712. Shadows on the Sage** (9/24/42) B&W 58 mins. (Western). *DIR:* Les Orlebeck. *A-PRO:* Louis Gray. *SP:* J. Benton Cheney. Based on characters created by William Colt MacDonald. *CAST:* Bob Steele, Tom Tyler, Jimmie Dodd, Cheryl Walker, Harry Holman, Bryant Washburn, Griff Barnette, Freddie Mercer, Tom London, Yakima Canutt, Rex Lease, Curley Dresden, Eddie Dew, Horace B. Carpenter, Frank Brownlee, John Cason, Pascale Perry. *SYN:* The Three Mesquiteers (Steele, Tyler, Dodd) go after a gang of outlaws who have been stealing from miners and killing the sheriffs of a small town. *NOTES:* Bob Steele plays a dual role in this film. The 46th entry in the "Three Mesquiteers" series.

**713. The Shanghai Story** (9/1/54) B&W 90 mins. (Spy). *DIR:* Frank Lloyd. *E-PRO:* Herbert J. Yates. *SP:* Seton I. Miller, Steve Fisher. Story by Lester Yard. *CAST:* Ruth Roman, Edmond O'Brien, Richard Jaeckel, Barry Kelley, Whit Bissell, Basil Ruysdael, Marvin Miller, Yvette Dugay, Paul Picerni, Isabel Randolph, Philip Ahn, Frances Rafferty, Frank Ferguson, James Griffith, John Alvin, Frank Puglia, Victor Sen Yung, Janine Ferreau, Richard Loo. *SYN:* In Shanghai, shortly after the Communist takeover of China, a police chief (Miller) suspects a doctor (O'Brien), a sailor (Jaeckel), and several other people of being a spy, when, in reality, it is his lover (Roman) who is an undercover spy for the U.S.

**714. Shantytown** (4/20/43) B&W 65 mins. (Drama). *DIR:* Joseph Santley. *A-PRO:* Harry Grey. *SP:* Olive Cooper. Based on the play *The Goslings* by Henry Moritz. *CAST:* Mary Lee, John Archer, Marjorie Lord, Harry Davenport, Billy Gilbert, Anne Revere, J. Frank Hamilton, Frank Jenks, Cliff Nazarro, Carl "Alfalfa" Switzer, Robert E. Homans, Noel Madison, Matty Malneck and His Orchestra. *SYN:* A tomboy (Lee), who becomes infatuated with the local garage mechanic (Archer), goes onto an amateur-hour show in an effort to reunite him with his wife (Lord).

**715. She Married a Cop** (7/12/39) B&W 66 mins. (Comedy). *DIR:* Sidney Salkow. *A-PRO:* Sol C. Siegel. *SP:* Olive Cooper. *CAST:* Phil Regan, Jean Parker, Jerome Cowan, Dorothea Kent, Benny Baker, Barnett Parker, Horace MacMahon, Oscar O'Shea, Mary Gordon, Muriel Campbell, Peggy Ryan, Richard Keene. *SYN:* Two film producers (Cowan, Parker) trick an Irish singing cop (Regan) into believing he has landed the romantic lead in a film when, in reality, he is to be the singing voice for a cartoon pig. *NOTES:* Leon Schlesinger provided the brief animated sequence. Academy Award Nominee — Best Score.

**716. The She Wolf** (11/15/54) Eastman Color 95 mins. (Drama). *DIR:* Alberto Lattuado. *PRO:* Ponto De Laurentiis. *SP:* Alberto Lattuado, Luigi Malerba, Alberto Moravia, Antonio Pietrangeli. Story by Giavani Verga. A Republic presentation. *CAST:* Kerima, Ettore Manni, May Britt, Mario Passante, Maresa Gallo, Bianca Doria. *SYN:* Unknown. [Original Italian title: *La Lupa*].

**717. The Sheik Steps Out** (9/6/37) B&W 68 mins. (Musical). *DIR:* Irving Pichel. *A-PRO:* Herman Schlom. *SP:* Adele Buffington, Gordon Kahn. Story by Adele Buffington. *CAST:* Ramon Novarro, Lola Lane, Gene Lockhart, Kathleen Burke, Stanley Fields, Billy Bevan, Charlotte Treadway, Robert Coote, Leonid Kinskey, Georges Renavent, Jamiel Hasson, C. Montague Shaw, George Sorel. *SYN:* When a spoiled rich American (Lane), whose father (Lockhart) made his millions selling corkscrews, wagers her English fiance (Coote) that she can find a horse faster than any in his stable and goes off to Arabia to purchase one, she mistakes a sheik (Navarro) for a baggage porter and travel guide who decides to teach her a lesson about manners and culture.

**718. Shepherd of the Ozarks** (3/26/42) B&W 70 mins. (Comedy). *DIR:* Frank McDonald. *A-PRO:* Armand

Schaefer. *SP:* Dorrell McGowan, Stuart McGowan. *CAST:* Leon Weaver, Frank Weaver, June Weaver, Marilyn Hare, Frank Albertson, Thurston Hall, Johnny Arthur, William Haade, Wade Crosby, Joe Devlin, Fred Sherman, Guy Usher. *SYN:* When the Weavers (Leon, Frank, June) return to the Ozarks from the city, they see a mock battle occurring and they think it's the real thing, so they quickly come to the aid of what they take to be the Americans. *NOTES:* The 9th entry in the "Weaver Brothers and Elviry" series. [British title: *Susanna*].

719. **Sheriff of Cimarron** (2/28/45) B&W 56 mins. (Western). *DIR:* Yakima Canutt. *A-PRO:* Bennett Cohen. *PRO:* Thomas Carr. *SP:* Bennett Cohen. *CAST:* Sunset Carson, Linda Stirling, Jack Kirk, Jack Ingram, Riley Hill, Olin Howlin, Robert Wilke, Edward Cassidy, George Chesebro, Dickie Dillon, Tom London, Jack O'Shea, Sylvia Arslan, Henry Wills, Hal Price, Carol Henry, Horace B. Carpenter, Herman Hack, Dee Cooper, Tommy Coats, Post Park. *SYN:* A cowboy (Carson), recently released from prison, rides into a town, foils a robbery and is made sheriff. When he learns that his brother (Hill) is the leader of the local gang of outlaws and was responsible for framing him, he sets out to capture him and his gang and clear his name. *NOTES:* The directorial debut of Yakima Canutt. Sunset Carson's first solo film without a sidekick.

720. **Sheriff of Las Vegas** (12/31/44) B&W 55 mins. (Western). *DIR:* Lesley Selander. *A-PRO:* Stephen Auer. *SP:* Norman S. Hall. Based on the comic strip created by Fred Harman. *CAST:* Bill Elliott, Bobby (Robert) Blake, Alice Fleming, Peggy Stewart, Selmer Jackson, William Haade, Jay Kirby, John Hamilton, Kenne Duncan, Bud Geary, Jack Kirk, Dickie Dillon, Frank McCarroll, Freddie Chapman, Robert Wilke. *SYN:* Red Ryder (Elliott) and Little Beaver (Blake) set out to find the real killers of a local judge after the murdered man's son (Kirby) is framed for the crime. *NOTES:* The 6th entry in the "Red Ryder" feature series.

721. **Sheriff of Redwood Valley** (3/29/46) B&W 54 mins. (Western). *DIR:* R. G. Springsteen. *A-PRO:* Sidney Picker. *SP:* Earle Snell. Based on the comic strip created by Fred Harman. *CAST:* Bill Elliott, Bobby (Robert) Blake, Alice Fleming, Bob Steele, Peggy Stewart, Arthur Loft, James Craven, Tom London, Kenne Duncan, Bud Geary, John Wayne Wright, Tom Chatterton, Budd Buster, Frank McCarroll, Frank Linn, Jack Kirk, Tex Cooper. *SYN:* Red Ryder (Elliott) and Little Beaver (Blake) set out to prove the innocence of the Reno Kid (Steele) and bring the real culprit to justice. *NOTES:* The 14th entry in the "Red Ryder" feature series.

722. **Sheriff of Sundown** (11/7/44) B&W 56 mins. (Western). *DIR:* Lesley Selander. *A-PRO:* Stephen Auer. *SP:* Norman S. Hall. *CAST:* Allan ("Rocky") Lane, Linda Stirling, Max Terhune, Twinkle Watts, Duncan Renaldo, Roy Barcroft, Herbert Rawlinson, Bud Geary, Jack Kirk, Tom London, Robert Wilke, Kenne Duncan, Rex Lease, Nolan Leary, Jack O'Shea, Herman Hack, Carl Sepulveda, Cactus Mack, Horace B. Carpenter, Neal Hart, Chick Hannon, Duke Green, Foxy O'Callahan. *SYN:* When a town boss (Barcroft) and his men try to take over the town

with force, a cattleman (Lane) and his sidekicks (Terhune, Renaldo) take up their defense and manage to bring law and order to the town of Sundown.

**723. Sheriff of Tombstone** (5/7/41) B&W 56 mins. (Western). *DIR/A-PRO:* Joseph Kane. *SP:* Olive Cooper. Story by James R. Webb. *CAST:* Roy Rogers, George "Gabby" Hayes, Elyse Knox, Addison Richards, Sally Payne, Harry Woods, Zeffie Tilbury, Hal Taliaferro, Jay Novello, Jack Ingram, George Rosenor, Jack Kirk, Frank Ellis, Art Dillard, Herman Hack, Vester Pegg, Al Haskell, Ray Jones, Jess Cavan, Roy Barcroft, Jack Rockwell, Chuck Baldra, Fred Burns, Oscar Gahan, Al Taylor, Jim Corey, Bob Reeves, "Trigger." *SYN:* Roy and "Gabby," arriving in Tombstone, are mistaken for gunfighters the mayor (Richards) has sent for, and Roy, going along with the impersonation, becomes sheriff and discovers a plot by the crooked mayor to gain control of the town. *NOTES:* Re-edited for TV at 54 mins. The final film of Vester Pegg.

**724. Sheriff of Wichita** (1/22/49) B&W 60 mins. (Western). *DIR:* R. G. Springsteen. *A-PRO:* Gordon Kay. *SP:* Bob Williams. *CAST:* Allan ("Rocky") Lane, Eddy Waller, Roy Barcroft, Lyn Wilde, Clayton Moore, Gene Roth, Trevor Bardette, House Peters, Jr., Earle Hodgins, Edmund Cobb, John Hamilton, Steve Raines, Jack O'Shea, Dick Curtis, Lane Bradford, Stanley Price, "Black Jack." *SYN:* A Federal Marshal (Lane), trailing an escaped convict (Moore), who was convicted of the theft of a gold shipment five years previously, meets the daughter (Wilde) of a murdered major, who was also accused in the theft of the gold shipment, and agrees to help her find her father's murderer and clear his name.

**725. Shine on Harvest Moon** (12/30/38) B&W 57 mins. (Western). *DIR:* Joseph Kane. *A-PRO:* Charles E. Ford. *SP:* Jack Natteford. *CAST:* Roy Rogers, Mary Hart, Stanley Andrews, William Farnum, Frank Jaquet, Chester Gunnels, Matty Roubert, Pat Henning, Jack Rockwell, Joe Whitehead, David Sharpe, George Letz, Lulu Belle and Scotty, "Trigger." *SYN:* A range war erupts when a rancher (Andrews) has a falling out with his partner (Farnum), and it is up to Roy to restore peace. *NOTES:* The first screen appearance of Lulu Belle and Scotty, who were imported from the WLS National Barn Dance radio show in Chicago. Re-edited for TV at 54 mins.

**The Shop at Sly Corner** (G.B. title) *see* **Code of Scotland Yard**

**726. Should Husbands Work?** (7/26/39) B&W 71 mins. (Comedy). *DIR:* Gus Meins. *A-PRO:* Sol C. Siegel. *SP:* Jack Townley, Taylor Caven. *CAST:* James Gleason, Lucille Gleason, Russell Gleason, Harry Davenport, Berton Churchill, Marie Wilson, Mary Hart, Tommy Ryan, Henry Kolker, Arthur Hoyt, Barry Norton, Mary Forbes, William Brisbane, Harry C. Bradley. *SYN:* Joe Higgins (James Gleason) is about to be promoted until his wife Lil (Lucille Gleason) lets out a business secret that mars a merger and she ends up with his job and he stays at home and does the housework. *NOTES:* The 3rd entry in the "Higgins Family" series.

**727. The Showdown** (8/15/50) B&W 86 mins. (Western). *DIR/SP:* Dorrell McGowan, Stuart McGowan. *A-PRO:* William J. O'Sullivan. Based on the *Esquire* magazine story by Richard

Wormser, Dan Gordon. *CAST:* Bill Elliott, Walter Brennan, Marie Windsor, Henry (Harry) Morgan, Rhys Williams, Jim Davis, William Ching, Nacho Galindo, Leif Erickson, Henry Rowland, Charles Stevens, Victor Kilian, Yakima Canutt, Guy Teague, William Steele, Jack Sparks. *SYN:* An ex-lawman (Elliott) joins up with a wagon train as trail-herd boss to find his brother's killer, knowing that one of the men traveling with it is the guilty party. *NOTES:* Bill Elliott's last film for Republic.

**728. Sierra Sue** (11/12/41) B&W 64 mins. (Western). *DIR:* William Morgan. *A-PRO:* Harry Grey. *SP:* Earl Felton, Julian Zimet. *CAST:* Gene Autry, Smiley Burnette, Fay McKenzie, Frank M. Thomas, Robert E. Homans, Earle Hodgins, Dorothy Christy, Kermit Maynard, Jack Kirk, Eddie Dean, Budd Buster, Rex Lease, Hugh Prosser, Vince Barnett, Hal Price, Syd Saylor, Roy Butler, Sammy Stein, Eddie Cherkose, Bob McKenzie, Marin Sais, Bud Brown, Gene Eblen, Buel Bryant, Ray Davis, Art Dillard, Frankie Marvin, "Champion." *SYN:* Gene is a government inspector investigating a poisonous weed that's killing the ranchers' cattle. The ranchers want to burn the area, but Gene thinks a chemical spraying via airplane is in order. A cattle stampede is set off when a hired gunman shoots down the plane. *NOTES:* Re-edited for TV at 54 mins.

**729. Silent Partner** (6/9/44) B&W 55 mins. (Crime). *DIR/A-PRO:* George Blair. *SP:* Gertrude Walker. Additional dialogue by Dane Lussier. *CAST:* William (Bill) Henry, Beverly Lloyd, Grant Withers, Ray Walker, Joan Blair, Roland Drew, George Meeker, Wally Vernon, John Harmon, Dick Elliott, Eddy Fields, Patricia Knox. *SYN:* A newspaper reporter (Henry), who finds a murder victim's address book, attempts to make contact with five people listed in the book, and after numerous attempts on his life, succeeds in finding the killer.

**730. Silver City Bonanza** (3/1/51) B&W 67 mins. (Western). *DIR:* George Blair. *A-PRO:* Melville Tucker. *SP:* Bob Williams. *CAST:* Rex Allen, Buddy Ebsen, Mary Ellen Kay, Billy Kimbley, Alix Ebsen, Bill Kennedy, Gregg Barton, Clem Bevans, Frank Jenks, Hank Patterson, Harry Lauter, Harry Harvey, Tom Steele, Edmund Cobb, Marshall Reed, Ted Mapes, "Koko." *SYN:* When a killer murders a blind man and tries to force a woman (Kay) off of her ranch so he can get to the silver which is on the bottom of her land's lake, a cowboy (Allen) and his sidekick (Buddy Ebsen) go after the killer using the blind man's dog to track him down.

**731. Silver City Kid** (7/20/44) B&W 56 mins. (Western). *DIR:* John English. *A-PRO:* Stephen Auer. *SP:* Taylor Caven. Story by Bennett Cohen. *CAST:* Allan ("Rocky") Lane, Peggy Stewart, Wally Vernon, Twinkle Watts, Frank Jaquet, Harry Woods, Glenn Strange, Lane Chandler, Bud Geary, Tom London, Tom Steele, Jack Kirk, Sam Flint, Frank McCarroll, Hal Price, Edward Peil, Sr., Fred Graham, Frank O'Connor, Horace B. Carpenter, "Feather." *SYN:* The foreman (Lane) of a silver mine sets out to find the gang that has been stealing valuable ore.

**732. Silver Spurs** (8/12/43) B&W 65 mins. (Western). *DIR:* Joseph Kane. *A-PRO:* Harry Grey. *SP:* John K. Butler, J. Benton Cheney. CAST: Roy Rogers, Smiley Burnette, John Carradine, Phyllis Brooks, Jerome Cowan, Joyce Compton, Dick Wessel, Hal Taliaferro, Forrest Taylor, Charles Wilson, Byron Foulger, Jack Kirk, Kermit Maynard, Pat Brady, Jack O'Shea, Slim Whitaker, Arthur Loft, Eddy Waller, Tom London, Bud Osborne, Fred Burns, Henry Wills, Bob Nolan and the Sons of the Pioneers, "Trigger." SYN: A ranch foreman (Rogers) is framed for the murder of his boss (Cowan) by a swindler (Carradine), who wants the rancher's land for a railroad right-of-way, and sets out to clear his name and bring the swindler to justice. NOTES: Re-edited for TV at 54 mins.

**733. Sing Dance, Plenty Hot** (8/10/40) B&W 70 mins. (Musical). DIR: Lew Landers. A-PRO: Robert North. SP: Bradford Ropes, Gordon Rigby. Story by Vera Caspary, Bradford Ropes. Special material by Stanley Davis, Carl Herzinger. Story title by Duane Decker. CAST: Ruth Terry, Johnny Downs, Barbara Jo Allen (Vera Vague), Billy Gilbert, Claire Carleton, Mary Lee, Elisabeth Risdon, Lester Matthews, Leonard Carey. SYN: A phony promoter of charity shows (Matthews) runs off with the money he's gathered for three clients (Allen, Risdon, and Terry) who want to raise money for an orphanage, but is eventually turned in by his assistant (Downs). NOTES: After buying a story from *Collier's* magazine for the grand sum of $500, Republic threw out the original plot but kept the title for what was to be one of their big musicals for 1940. Screen writer Gordon Rigby, and special material writers Stanley Davis and Carl Herzinger were uncredited. [British title: *Melody Girl*].

**734. Sing, Neighbor, Sing** (8/12/44) B&W 70 mins. (Musical). DIR: Frank McDonald. A-PRO: Donald H. Brown. SP: Dorrell McGowan, Stuart McGowan. CAST: Brad Taylor, Ruth Terry, Virginia Brissac, Beverly Lloyd, Charles Irwin, Olin Howlin, Maxine Doyle, Mary Kenyon, Harry Cheshire, Roy Acuff and His Smoky Mountain Boys, Rachel, Lulu Belle and Scotty, The Milo Twins, Carolina Cotton. SYN: A lothario (Taylor) comes to a small college town and poses as an older and quite distinguished English psychologist until the real psychologist (Irwin) turns up.

**735. The Singing Cowboy** (5/13/36) B&W 56 mins. (Western). DIR: Mack V. Wright. PRO: Nat Levine. SP: Dorrell McGowan, Stuart McGowan. Story by Tom Gibson. CAST: Gene Autry, Smiley Burnette, Lois Wilde, Creighton Chaney, Ann Gillis, Earle Hodgins, Harvey Clark, John Van Pelt, Earl Eby, Ken Cooper, Harrison Greene, Wes Warner, Jack Rockwell, Tracy Layne, Oscar Gahan, Frankie Marvin, Jack Kirk, Audry Davis, George Pearce, Charles McAvoy, Alfred P. James, Fred "Snowflake" Toones, Patricia Caron, "Champion." SYN: Gene heads for the city, where he talks a coffee company into sponsoring a broadcast to raise some money for a little girl (Gillis) who needs an operation so that she won't be crippled for life, and in order to attract a bigger audience, they decide to use the then-infant medium of television.

**736. Singing Guns** (2/28/50) Trucolor 91 mins. (Western). DIR: R. G. Springsteen. A-PRO: Melville Tucker. PRO: Abe Lyman. SP: Dorrell McGowan, Stuart McGowan. Based on a novel by Max Brand. A Palomar Production. A Republic Presentation. CAST: Vaughn Monroe, Ella Raines, Walter Brennan, Ward Bond, Jeff Corey, Barry Kelley, Harry Shannon, Tom Fadden, Ralph Dunn, Rex Lease, George Chandler, Billy Gray, Mary Bear, Jimmie Dodd, John Doucette, Mary Eleanor Donahue, Denver Pyle, Richard Emory, VOICE OF: Roy Barcroft. SYN: When a cowboy (Monroe) has his lands stolen by a mining company, he robs stages of their gold shipments, and when the sheriff (Bond), who is after him is shot, he takes him to a doctor (Brennan) for patching up and is given the job of deputy sheriff. When a mine cave-in occurs, he redeems himself by helping the trapped miners, returning the gold, and defeating the corrupt mine owner (Corey). NOTES: Vaughn Monroe's first film for Republic. Academy Award Nominee — Best Song.

737. **The Singing Hill** (4/26/41) B&W 75 mins. (Western). DIR: Lew Landers. A-PRO: Harry Grey. SP: Olive Cooper. Story by Richard Murphy, Jesse Lasky, Jr. CAST: Gene Autry, Smiley Burnette, Virginia Dale, Mary Lee, Spencer Charters, Gerald Oliver Smith, George Meeker, Wade Boteler, Harry Stubbs, Cactus Mack, Jack Kirk, Chuck Morrison, Monte Montague, Forrest Taylor, Frankie Marvin, Dan White, Hal Price, Fred Burns, Herman Hack, Jack O'Shea, "Champion." SYN: Gene sets out to stop a young woman (Dale) from selling her ranch, which would mean a loss of free grazing land for local ranchers. NOTES: The above running time is the theatrical release running time. Other running times given are 65 mins, and 57 mins. Re-edited for TV at 54 mins. [Alternate title: *The Singing Hills*.]

**The Singing Hills** *see* **The Singing Hill**

738. **The Singing Vagabond** (12/11/35) B&W 54 mins. (Western). DIR: Carl Pierson. A-PRO: Armand Schaefer. PRO: Nat Levine. SP: Oliver Drake, Betty Burbridge. Story by Oliver Drake. CAST: Gene Autry, Smiley Burnette, Ann Rutherford, Barbara Pepper, Warner Richmond, Frank LaRue, Grace Goodall, Niles Welch, Tom Brower, Robinson Neeman, Ray Benard, Henry Roquemore, Allan Sears, Chief John Big Tree, Bob Burns, Charles King, Chief Thunder Cloud, June Thompson, Janice Thompson, Marion O'Connell, Marie Quillan, Elaine Shepard, Edmund Cobb, George Letz, Celia McCanon, "Champion." SYN: Captain Tex Autry (Gene) is framed for horse stealing and must prove his innocence. He escapes from prison, finds the guilty party who framed him, and stops a wagon train attack.

739. **Sioux City Sue** (11/21/46) B&W 69 mins. (Western). DIR: Frank McDonald. A-PRO: Armand Schaefer. SP: Olive Cooper. CAST: Gene Autry, Lynn Roberts, Sterling Holloway, Richard Lane, Ralph Sanford, Ken Lundy, Helen Wallace, Pierre Watkin, Kenne Duncan, Edwin Wills, Minerva Urecal, Frank Marlowe, LeRoy Mason, Harry Cheshire, George Carleton, Sam Flint, Michael Hughes, Tex Terry, Tristram Coffin, Frankie Marvin, Forest Burns, Tommy Coats, The Cass County Boys, "Champion, Jr." SYN: Gene is recruited by a talent scout (Roberts) to go to Hollywood to be a singing cowboy, but it turns out that he is to be the voice for an animated singing donkey. NOTES: Gene Autry's first film for Republic after returning from service

in World War II. Re-edited for TV at 54 mins.

**740. Sis Hopkins** (4/12/41) B&W 98 mins. (Musical-Comedy). *DIR:* Joseph Santley. *A-PRO:* Robert North. *SP:* Jack Townley, Milt Gross, Edward Eliscu, Ralph Spence, Melville Shavelson, Milt Josephson. Story by F. McGrew Willis. Based on the play by Carroll Fleming, George A. Nichols. *CAST:* Judy Canova, Bob Crosby, Charles Butterworth, Jerry Colonna, Susan Hayward, Katherine Alexander, Elvia Allman, Carol Adams, Lynn Merrick, Mary Ainslee, Charles Coleman, Andrew Tombes, Charles Lane, Byron Foulger, Betty Blythe, Frank Darien, Joe Devlin, Elliott Sullivan, Hal Price, Anne O'Neal, Bob Crosby and His Orchestra with the Bobcats. *SYN:* A country girl (Canova) mistakenly believes her uncle (Butterworth) is down on his luck so she invites him and his family to her farm, but on their arrival they discover her house has burned to the ground so they take in the country girl and send her to the same college as her cousin (Hayward) where she becomes a hit. *NOTES:* Screenwriters Ralph Spence, Melville Shavelson, and Milt Josephson were uncredited. Based on an old Broadway play and filmed first in 1919 with Mabel Normand.

**741. Sitting on the Moon** (9/11/36) B&W 76 mins. (Musical). *DIR:* Ralph Staub. *A-PRO:* Albert E. Levoy. *PRO:* Nat Levine. *SP:* Raymond L. Schrock. Adapted by Rex Taylor, Sidney Sutherland. Story by Julian Field. *CAST:* Roger Pryor, Grace Bradley, William Newell, Henry Kolker, Pert Kelton, Henry Wadsworth, Joyce Compton, Pierre Watkin, William Janney, June Martel, Jimmy Ray, Harvey Clark, George Cooper, The Theodores. *SYN:* A pair of songwriters (Pryor, Newell) fall for an ex-film star (Bradley) and her friend (Kelton), but problems arise when a professional blackmailer (Compton) arrives and claims one of them married her while he was drunk. *NOTES:* The directorial debut of Ralph Staub.

**742. Sleepy Lagoon** (9/5/43) B&W 65 mins. (Musical-Comedy). *DIR:* Joseph Santley. *A-PRO:* Albert J. Cohen. *SP:* Frank Gill, Jr., George Carleton Brown. Story by Prescott Chaplin. *CAST:* Judy Canova, Dennis Day, Ruth Donnelly, Joe Sawyer, Ernest Truex, Douglas Fowley, Will Wright, Herbert Corthell, Forrest Taylor, Eddy Chandler, Kitty McHugh, Ellen Lowe, Margaret Reid, Sammy Stein, Jack Kenney, Jay Novello, Eddie Gribbon, Jack Raymond, Larry Stewart, Emil Van Horn, Rondo Hatton, Frank Austin, John Walsh, James Farley, Frank Graham (Narrator). *SYN:* A woman (Canova) runs for office to restore law and order in the town of Sleepy Lagoon; she wins, and then proceeds to take on the town's crooked politicians headed by the mayor (Wright).

**743. Sleepytime Gal** (3/5/42) B&W 84 mins. (Musical-Comedy). *DIR:* Albert S. Rogell. *A-PRO:* Albert J. Cohen. *SP:* Art Arthur, Albert Duffy, Max Lief. Story by Mauri Grashin, Robert T. Shannon. *CAST:* Judy Canova, Tom Brown, Ruth Terry, Mildred Coles, Billy Gilbert, Harold Huber, Fritz Feld, Jay Novello, Skinnay Ennis, Jerry Lester, Jimmy Ames, Elisha Cook, Jr., Frank Sully, Thurston Hall, Paul Fix, Vicki Lester, Lester Dorr, Walter Merrill, Pat Gleason, Fred Santley, Mady Lawrence, Edward Earle, Hillary Brooke, Rick Vallin, Cyril Ring, William Forrest, Carl Leviness, Gertrude Astor, Marguerite Whitten, Dwight Frye, Eddie Acuff, Eugene Borden. *SYN:* A girl (Canova) is mistaken for a nightclub singer who is on the mob's hit list.

**744. Slippy McGee** (1/15/48) B&W 65 mins. (Crime). *DIR:* Albert Kelley. *A-PRO:* Lou Brock. *SP:* Norman S. Hall, Jerry Gruskin. Based on the novel *Slippy McGee: Sometimes Known as the Butterfly Man* by Marie Conway Oemler. *CAST:* Don ("Red") Barry, Dale Evans, Tom Brown, Harry Cheshire, James Seay, Murray Alper, Dick Elliott, Maude Eburne, Raymond Largay, Eddie Acuff, Michael Carr. *SYN:* When a safecracker (Barry) breaks his leg trying to save a young child from a speeding truck, his life is changed forever, mainly through the efforts of a priest (Brown), and he resorts to return the stolen money back to the bank and turn in his own gang. *NOTES:* First filmed as a silent in 1923.

**Small Town Lawyer** (G.B. title) *see* **Main Street Lawyer**

**745. Smuggled Cargo** (8/21/39) B&W 62 mins. (Drama). *DIR/A-PRO:* John H. Auer. *SP:* Michel Jacoby, Earl Felton. *CAST:* Barry Mackay, Rochelle Hudson, George Barbier, Ralph Morgan, Cliff Edwards, John Wray, Arthur Loft, Wallis Clark, Robert E. Homans. *SYN:* A Britisher (Mackay) and the daughter (Hudson) of a millionaire fruit financier, expose a corrupt distributor (Loft) who is attempting to get orange growers to sell their crops for less than it is worth.

**746. The Sombrero Kid** (7/31/42) B&W 56 mins. (Western). *DIR/A-PRO:*

George Sherman. *SP:* Norman S. Hall. Story by Doris Schroeder, Edward J. White. *CAST:* Don ("Red") Barry, Lynn Merrick, John James, Joel Friedkin, Rand Brooks, Robert E. Homans, Stuart Hamblen, Bob McKenzie, Lloyd "Slim" Andrews, I. Stanford Jolley, Frank Brownlee, Anne O'Neal, Kenne Duncan, Bud Geary, Bill Nestell, Hank Bell, Curley Dresden, Jack O'Shea, Pascale Perry, Griff Barnette, Chick Hannon, Merrill McCormick, Edward Cassidy. *SYN:* A man (Barry), who finds himself accused of murder is arrested by his own brother (James) and sets out to prove his innocence.

**747. Someone to Remember** (8/21/43) B&W 80 mins. (Drama). *DIR:* Robert Siodmak. *A-PRO:* Robert North. *SP:* Frances Hyland. Based on *Prodigal's Mother* by Ben Ames Williams. *CAST:* Mabel Paige, Harry Shannon, John Craven, Dorothy Morris, Charles Dingle, David Bacon, Peter Lawford, Tom Seidel, Richard Crane, Chester Clute, Elizabeth Dunne, Vera Lewis, John Good, Susan Levine, Buz Buckley, Harry C. Bradley, Edward Keane, George Lessey, Flo Buzby, James Carlisle, Wilbur Mack, George Reed, Jesse Graves, Virginia Brissac, Jimmy Butler, Michael Owen, Selmer Jackson, Irene Shirley, Frank Jaquet, Ann Evers, Lynette Bryant, Ada Ellis, Russell Hicks, Madeline Grey, Edward Earle, Leona Maricle, Henri DeSoto, Georgia Davis, Leo White, Broderick O'Farrell. *SYN:* An elderly widow (Paige),who lives in an apartment building that has been purchased by a neighboring university in order to construct dorms for the boys, takes a liking to a student (Craven) who shares the same name as her son, helping him with his studies and even playing a part in his romance with another student (Morris). She is secretly convinced that he is her grandson, fathered by her missing son. Before she is able to learn if she is correct, she dies not knowing that her son died in prison some 20 years earlier, news that killed her husband. *NOTES:* The starring debut of Mabel Paige. Remade in 1957 by Warner Bros. as *Johnny Trouble*, starring Ethel Barrymore. Working title was *The Prodigal's Mother*.

**748. Son of God's Country** (9/15/48) B&W 60 mins. (Western). *DIR:* R. G. Springsteen. *A-PRO:* Melville Tucker. *SP:* Paul Gangelin, Bob Williams. *CAST:* Monte Hale, Pamela Blake, Paul Hurst, Jim Nolan, Jay Kirby, Steve Darrell, Francis McDonald, Jason Robards, Sr., Fred Graham, Herman Hack. *SYN:* After the Civil War, a lawman (Hale) poses as an outlaw to infiltrate a gang of land grabbers.

**749. A Song for Miss Julie** (2/19/45) B&W 69 mins. (Musical). *DIR:* William Rowland. *PRO:* William Rowland, Carley Harriman. *E-PRO:* Howard Sheehan. *SP:* Rowland Leigh. Adapted by Leighton K. Brill. Story by Michael Foster. A Pre-Em Pictures, Inc. Production. A Republic Presentation. *CAST:* Shirley Ross, Barton Hepburn, Jane Farrar, Roger Clark, Cheryl Walker, Elisabeth Risdon, Lillian Randolph, Peter Garey, Renie Riano, Harry Crocker, Alicia Markova, Anton Dolin, Vivian Fay, The Robertos. *SYN:* Two playwrights (Hepburn, Clark), working on an operetta about a Southern gentleman in the 1850s who has something hidden in his past, try to persuade the man's only living relative (Risdon) to give her approval for the operetta. *NOTES:* The final film of Shirley Ross—she retired after this film.

750. **Song of Arizona** (3/9/46) B&W 68 mins. (Western). *DIR:* Frank McDonald. *A-PRO:* Edward J. White. *SP:* M. Coates Webster. Story by Bradford Ropes. *CAST:* Roy Rogers, George "Gabby" Hayes, Dale Evans, Lyle Talbot, Tommy Cook, Johnny Calkins, Sarah Edwards, Tommy Ivo, Michael Chapin, Dick Curtis, Edmund Cobb, Tom Quinn, Noble "Kid" Chissell, Little Brown Jug (Don Kay Reynolds), Robert Mitchell Boy Choir, Bob Nolan and the Sons of the Pioneers, "Trigger." *SYN:* At a ranch for homeless youths, a boy (Cook), whose father (Talbot) is a bank robber, leaves stolen money with his son before being killed. The other members of his gang learn the boy has the money and show up to take it. Roy arrives with the Sons of the Pioneers and brings the outlaws to justice. *NOTES:* Re-edited for TV at 54 mins.

751. **Song of Mexico** (12/28/45) B&W 57 mins. (Musical). *DIR/PRO/SP:* James A. Fitzpatrick. A James A. Fitzpatrick Production. A Republic Presentation. *CAST:* Adele Mara, Edgar Barrier, George J. Lewis, Jacqueline Dalya, Jose Pulido, Raquel de Alva, Margaret Falkenberg, Elizabeth Waldo, Carmen Molina, The Tipica Orchestra. *SYN:* A bride-to-be (Mara) learns that her fiancé is more interested in his career than in her. *NOTES:* This was the only feature to be directed by James A. Fitzpatrick, who also produced, directed, and narrated *Travel Talks* for MGM.

752. **Song of Nevada** (8/5/44) B&W 75 mins. (Western). *DIR:* Joseph Kane. *A-PRO:* Harry Grey. *SP:* Gordan Kahn, Olive Cooper. *CAST:* Roy Rogers, Dale Evans, Mary Lee, Lloyd Corrigan, Thurston Hall, John Eldredge, Forrest Taylor, George Meeker, Emmett Vogan, LeRoy Mason, William B. Davidson, Kenne Duncan, Si Jenks, Frank McCarroll, Henry Wills, Jack O'Shea, Helen Talbot, Jack Perrin, Tom Steele, Bob Nolan and the Sons of the Pioneers, "Trigger." *SYN:* Roy meets a rich ranch owner (Hall) who is believed to be dead after his plane crashes, and while he is in hiding, he hires Roy to straighten out his high society daughter (Evans) who has taken on Eastern ways and has come west to sell his ranch to make money for herself and her big-city boyfriend (Eldridge). *NOTES:* The final Roy Rogers film to be directed by Joseph Kane. Re-edited for TV at 54 mins.

753. **Song of Texas** (6/14/43) B&W 69 mins. (Western). *DIR:* Joseph Kane. *A-PRO:* Harry Grey. *SP:* Winston Miller. *CAST:* Roy Rogers, Sheila Ryan, Barton MacLane, Harry Shannon, Arline Judge, William Haade, Eve March, Hal Taliaferro, Pat Brady, Yakima Canutt, Tom London, Forrest Taylor, Maxine Doyle, Jack O'Shea, Alex Nahera Dancers, Bob Nolan and the Sons of the Pioneers, "Trigger." *SYN:* Roy sets out to help a ranch hand (Shannon) convince his visiting daughter (Ryan) that he owns the ranch he is working on, but when she sells part of the ranch, Roy has to win a chuckwagon race to get it back. *NOTES:* Re-edited for TV at 54 mins.

**Song of the Sierra** *see* **Springtime in the Sierras**

754. **Sons of Adventure** (9/1/48) B&W 68 mins. (Crime-Western). *DIR:* Yakima Canutt. *A-PRO:* Franklin Adreon. *SP:* Franklin Adreon, Sol Shor. *CAST:* Lynn Roberts, Russell Hayden, Gordon Jones, Grant Withers, George Chandler, Roy Barcroft, John Newland,

Stephanie Bachelor, John Holland, Gilbert Frye, Richard Irving, Joan Blair, John Crawford, Keith Richards, James Dale. *SYN:* When a western stuntman is killed on the set and blame falls on his fellow stuntman (Jones), another stuntman (Hayden) turns detective to prove him innocent and bring the real killer to justice. *NOTES:* Filmed inside Republic studios.

**755. Sons of the Pioneers** (7/2/42) B&W 61 mins. (Western). *DIR/A-PRO:* Joseph Kane. *SP:* M. Coates Webster, Mauri Grashin, Robert T. Shannon. Story by Mauri Grashin, Robert T. Shannon. *CAST:* Roy Rogers, George "Gabby" Hayes, Maris Wrixon, Forrest Taylor, Minerva Urecal, Bradley Page, Hal Taliaferro, Chester Conklin, Fred Burns, Jack O'Shea, Frank Ellis, Tom London, Bob Woodward, Fern Emmett, Ken Cooper, Karl Hackett, Frank Brownlee, Sarah Edwards, George Kesterson, Pascale Perry, Neal Hart, Horace B. Carpenter, Bud Osborne, Bob Nolan and the Sons of the Pioneers (Bob Nolan, Tim Spencer, Ken Carson, George "Shug" Fisher, Hugh Farr, Karl Farr), "Trigger." *SYN:* Roy is asked to return to his hometown to aid "Gabby," who is the sheriff, and help him get rid of a gang of landgrabbers who have been terrorizing the area. *NOTES:* Although the title refers to the singing group, they have little to do in this film. Re-edited for TV at 54 mins.

**756. SOS Coast Guard** (4/16/42) B&W 71 mins. (Action). *SYN:* Feature version of the 12 chapter serial. See **1003. SOS Coast Guard.**

**757. S.O.S. Tidal Wave** (6/2/39) B&W 62 mins. (Drama). *DIR:* John H. Auer. *A-PRO:* Armand Schaefer. *SP:* Maxwell Shane, Gordon Kahn. Story by James R. Webb. *CAST:* Ralph Byrd, George Barbier, Kay Sutton, Frank Jenks, Marc Lawrence, Dorothy Lee, Oscar O'Shea, Mickey Kuhn, Ferris Taylor, Don ("Red") Barry, Raymond Bailey. *SYN:* A news reporter (Byrd) exposes a crooked candidate (Taylor) and his political boss (Lawrence), who, in order to keep voters away from the polls, airs via television, the destruction of New York by a tidal wave and earthquake. *NOTES:* This film showed television's potential as a powerful medium and also treated television as part of everyday life. Scenes of the destruction of New York are from the 1933 RKO feature, *Deluge,* which was purchased by Republic to be used in several features and serials. [British title: *Tidal Wave*].

**758. South of Caliente** (10/15/51) B&W 67 mins. (Western). *DIR:* William Witney. *A-PRO:* Edward J. White. *SP:* Eric Taylor. *CAST:* Roy Rogers, Dale Evans, Pinky Lee, Douglas Fowley, Ric Roman, Leonard Penn, Willie Best, Lillian Molieri, Charlita, Pat Brady, Frank Richards, Marguerite McGill, George J. Lewis, Lillian Molieri, The Roy Rogers Riders, "Trigger," "Bullet." *SYN:* Roy sets out to nab the thieves who steal a rancher's (Evans) prize racing horse that she must sell to keep her ranch.

**759. South of Rio** (7/27/49) B&W 60 mins. (Western). *DIR:* Philip Ford. *A-PRO:* Melville Tucker. *SP:* Norman S. Hall. *CAST:* Monte Hale, Kay Christopher, Paul Hurst, Roy Barcroft, Douglas Kennedy, Don Haggerty, Rory Mallinson, Lane Bradford, Emmett Vogan, Myron Healey, Tom London, Edmund Cobb. *SYN:* An ex-ranger (Hale) goes after a gang of outlaws terrorizing the frontier.

**760. South of Santa Fe** (2/17/42) B&W 56 mins. (Western). *DIR/A-PRO:* Joseph Kane. *SP:* James R. Webb. *CAST:* Roy Rogers, George "Gabby" Hayes, Linda Hayes, Paul Fix, Pat Brady, Judy Clark, Bobby Beers, Arthur Loft, Charles Miller, Sam Flint, Jack Kirk, Jack Ingram, Hank Bell, Carleton Young, Lynton Brent, Robert Strange, Henry Wills, Jack O'Shea, Merrill McCormick, Spade Cooley, Bob Nolan and the Sons of the Pioneers, "Trigger." *SYN:* When Roy gets blamed for the kidnapping of three industrialists he has brought to town to invest in the opening of a gold mine, he sets out to rescue them and has to fight gangsters with machine guns and airplanes. *NOTES:* Re-edited for TV at 54 mins.

**761. South of the Border** (12/15/39) B&W 71 mins. (Western). *DIR:* George Sherman. *A-PRO:* William Berke. *SP:* Betty Burbridge, Gerald Geraghty. Story by Dorrell McGowan, Stuart McGowan. *CAST:* Gene Autry, Smiley Burnette, June Storey, Lupita Tovar, Mary Lee, Duncan Renaldo, Frank Reicher, Alan Edwards, Claire DuBrey, Dick Botiller, William Farnum, Selmer Jackson, Sheila Darcy, Rex Lease, Charles King, Reed Howes, Jack O'Shea, Slim Whitaker, Hal Price, Julian Rivero, Curley Dresden, Art Wenzel, The Checkerboard Band, "Champion." *SYN:* Gene and Frog (Burnette) journey down to Mexico as agents of the U.S. government to end a possible revolution instigated by foreign agents, headquartered at a submarine base. *NOTES:* Re-edited for TV at 54 mins.

**762. South Pacific Trail** (10/20/52) B&W 60 mins. (Western). *DIR:* William Witney. *A-PRO:* Edward J. White. *SP:* Arthur E. Orloff. *CAST:* Rex Allen, Estelita Rodriguez, Slim Pickens, Nestor Paiva, Roy Barcroft, Douglas Evans, Joe McGuinn, Forrest Taylor, The Republic Rhythm Riders, (Michael Barton, George Bamby, Darol Rice, Slim Duncan, Buddy Dooley), "Koko." *SYN:* When the grandfather (Paiva) of a ranch owner (Rodriguez) takes off on a trip, his foreman (Barcroft) plots a gold hijacking by wrecking the train the grandfather is on. Presumed dead, the foreman and his partner (Evans) try to take over the ranch, but are thwarted by a cowboy (Allen) and the grandfather who had gotten off the train before it was wrecked.

**763. Southward Ho!** (3/19/39) B&W 57 mins. (Western). *DIR/A-PRO:* Joseph Kane. *SP:* Gerald Geraghty. Story by Jack Natteford, John Rathmell. *CAST:* Roy Rogers, Mary Hart, George "Gabby" Hayes, Wade Boteler, Arthur Loft, Lane Chandler, Tom London, Charles Moore, Ed Brady, Fred Burns, Frank Ellis, Jack Ingram, Frank McCarroll, Curley Dresden, Jim Corey, Rudy Bowman, George Chesebro, Nicodemus Stewart, Harry Strang, Earl Dwire, Art Dillard, Bob Woodward, "Trigger." *SYN:* In post Civil War Texas, Roy and "Gabby" make claim to partial ownership of a ranch, while the other half belongs to a Union Colonel (Boteler), who is now the territory governor. They learn that a group of renegade Yankee soldiers, who are thought to be working for the governor, are terrorizing the ranchers. Roy sets out to stop them with the help of the other ranchers, and prove the governor innocent. *NOTES:* The first film teaming of Roy and "Gabby." Re-edited for TV at 54 mins.

**764. The Spanish Cape Mystery** (10/9/35) B&W 65 mins. (Mystery).

*DIR:* Lewis D. Collins. *PRO:* M. H. Hoffman. *SP:* Albert DeMond. Based on the novel by Ellery Queen (Manfred B. Lee, Frederic Dannay). A Liberty/Republic Picture. *CAST:* Helen Twelvetrees, Donald Cook, Berton Churchill, Frank Sheridan, Harry Stubbs, Guy Usher, Huntley Gordon, Betty Blythe, Olaf Hytten, Ruth Gillette, Jack LaRue, Frank Leigh, Barbara Bedford, Donald Kerr, George Cleveland, George Baxter, Katherine Morrow, Arnold Gray, Lee Prather. *SYN:* Ellery Queen (Cook), together with his friend (Churchill), are on vacation near Spanish Cape and come across a murder victim wearing a Spanish cape. Ellery, his father (Usher) and a sheriff (Stubbs) set out to solve the murder, with Ellery finally nabbing the killer. *NOTES:* This was the first appearance on screen of the "Ellery Queen" character, and the first of only two appearances by sleuth Ellery Queen in films of the 1930s; the other was *The Mandarin Mystery*, 1936, also by Republic.

**765. Specter of the Rose** (7/5/46) B&W 90 mins. (Dance-Comedy-Thriller). *DIR/PRO/SP:* Ben Hecht. Based in part on the ballet *Spectre de la Rose*. A Republic Presentation. *CAST:* Judith Anderson, Michael Chekhov, Ivan Kirov, Viola Essen, Lionel Stander, Charles "Red" Marshall, George Shadnoff, Billy Gray, Juan Panalle, Lew Hearn, Ferike Boros, Constantine, Ferdinand Pollina, Polly Rose, Jim Moran, Frieda Filer, Miriam Schiller, Miriam Golden, Grace Mann, Allan Cooke, Alice Cavers, Nina Haven, John Stanley, Arleen Claire, Celene Radding. *SYN:* A ballerina (Essen) falls in love and marries a mad, deranged dancing genius (Kirov), because the ballet "Spectre de la Rose" invokes strange images in his mind, and tries to cure him of his affliction. *NOTES:* The film debut of Ivan Kirov. Polly Rose was the daughter of showman, Billy Rose.

**Spies at Work** (G.B. title) *see* **Sabotage**

**766. Spoilers of the Forest** (4/5/57) Trucolor/Naturama 68 mins. (Drama). *DIR/A-PRO:* Joseph Kane. *E-PRO:* Herbert J. Yates. *SP:* Bruce Manning. *CAST:* Rod Cameron, Vera Ralston, Ray Collins, Hillary Brooke, Edgar Buchanan, Carl Benton Reid, Sheila Bromley, Hank Worden, John Compton, John Alderson, Angela Greene, Paul Stader, Mary Alan Hokanson, Raymond Greenleaf, Eleanor Audley, Don Haggerty, William Haade, Jo Ann Lilliquist, Bucko Stafford, Robert Karnes, Kem Dibbs, Rory Mallinson, Virginia Carroll, John Patrick, Bob Swan, Mack Williams, Theresa Harris, Helen Wallace, Pauline Moore, Judd Holdren. *SYN:* Set in Montana, the owner (Ralston) of 64,000 acres of rich timberland battles the efforts of two loggers (Collins, Cameron) who want to harvest her trees.

**767. Spoilers of the North** (4/24/47) B&W 66 mins. (Drama). *DIR:* Richard Sale. *A-PRO:* Donald H. Brown. *SP:* Milton Raison. *CAST:* Paul Kelly, Adrian Booth, Evelyn Ankers, James Millican, Roy Barcroft, Louis Jean Heydt, Ted Hecht, Harlan Briggs, Francis McDonald, Maurice Cass, Neyle Morrow. *SYN:* A salmon fisherman (Kelly) cons an unsuspecting woman (Ankers) into loaning him money to build a new fish cannery, and then gets his Indian girl (Booth) to draft illegal Indian labor to work at his canning plant. *NOTES:* The directorial debut of Richard Sale.

**768. Spoilers of the Plains** (2/2/51) B&W 68 mins. (Western). *DIR:* William Witney. *A-PRO:* Edward J. White. *SP:* Sloan Nibley. *CAST:* Roy Rogers, Penny Edwards, Gordon Jones, Grant Withers, William Forrest, Don Haggerty, Fred Kohler, Jr., House Peters, Jr., George Meeker, Keith Richards, Rex Lease, James Craven, Foy Willing and the Riders of the Purple Sage, "Trigger," "Bullet." *SYN:* Roy sets out to stop a gang of foreign spies who are intent on stealing an experimental weather payload.

**769. A Sporting Chance** (6/4/45) B&W 55 mins. (Comedy). *DIR:* George Blair. *A-PRO:* Rudolph E. Abel. *SP:* Dane Lussier. Additional dialogue by Jerry Sackheim. Story by Paul Gangelin. *CAST:* Jane Randolph, John O'Malley, Stephen Barclay, Edward Gargan, Isabel Withers, Janet Martin, Maxine Semon, Selmer Jackson, Robert Middlemass, Kenne Duncan. *SYN:* A spoiled young woman (Randolph) must find a job and support herself before she can inherit the family fortune. *NOTES:* Dialogue writer Jerry Sackheim was uncredited.

**770. Springtime in the Rockies** (11/15/37) B&W 60 mins. (Western). *DIR:* Joseph Kane. *A-PRO:* Sol C. Siegel. *SP:* Gilbert Wright, Betty Burbridge. *CAST:* Gene Autry, Smiley Burnette, Polly Rowles, Ula Love, Ruth Bacon, Jane Hunt, George Chesebro, Alan Bridge, Tom London, Edward Hearn, Frankie Marvin, William Hole, Edmund Cobb, Fred Burns, Art Davis, Lew Meehan, Jack Kirk, Frank Ellis, George Letz, Robert Dudley, Jack Rockwell, Oscar Gahan, Victor Cox, Jim Corey, Jimmy LeFeur and his Saddle Pals, "Champion." *SYN:* Gene is foreman on a cattle ranch whose owner (Rowles), a recent grad from animal husbandry school, decides to bring in a flock of sheep and Gene must try to keep the peace between her and the local cattlemen.

**771. Springtime in the Sierras** (7/15/47) Trucolor 75 mins. (Western). *DIR:* William Witney. *A-PRO:* Joseph Kane. *SP:* Sloan Nibley. *CAST:* Roy Rogers, Jane Frazee, Andy Devine, Stephanie Bachelor, Harold Landon, Harry Cheshire, Roy Barcroft, Chester Conklin, Hank Patterson, Whitey Christy, Pascale Perry, Bob Woodward, Bob Nolan and the Sons of the Pioneers, "Trigger." *SYN:* Roy sets out to stop a gang of professional hunters, led by a woman (Bachelor), that have been illegally shooting game out of season, and have murdered a game warden. *NOTES:* Re-edited for TV at 54 mins. [TV title: *Song of the Sierra*].

**772. The Square Ring** (1/28/55) B&W 73 mins. (Sports). *DIR:* Michael Relph. *PRO:* Basil Dearden. *SP:* Robert Westerby, Peter Myers, Alec Grahame. Based on the play by Ralph W. Peterson. An Ealing Production. A Republic Presentation. *CAST:* Jack Warner, Robert Beatty, Bill Owen, Maxwell Reed, George Rose, Bill Travers, Alfie Bass, Ronald Lewis, Sydney James, Joan Collins, Kay Kendall, Bernadette O'Farrell, Eddie Byrne, Vic Wise, Michael Golden, Joan Sims, Sidney Tafler, Alexander Gauge, Kid Berg, Madoline Thomas, Ben Williams, Harry Herbert, C. H. Nichols, Ivan Staff, Alf Hines, Joe Bloom, Michael Ingrams, Vernon Kelso. *SYN:* Five different stories that concentrates on the characters who have taken to the boxing ring for one reason or another, and what the night's fights mean to them. *NOTES:* Released in Britain in 1953 at a running time of 83 mins.

**The Stadium Murders** *see* **Hollywood Stadium Mystery**

773. **Stagecoach Express** (3/6/42) B&W 57 mins. (Western). *DIR/A-PRO:* George Sherman. *SP:* Arthur V. Jones. Story by Doris Schroeder. *CAST:* Don ("Red") Barry, Lynn Merrick, Al St. John, Robert Kent, Emmett Lynn, Guy Kingsford, Ethan Laidlaw, Eddie Dean, Charles King, Wheaton Chambers, Tommy Coats, Eddie Phillips, Francis Sayles, Al Taylor, Mary MacLaren, Bill Nestell, Frank O'Connor, Freddie Steele, Martin Faust. *SYN:* A cowboy (Barry) helps a woman (Merrick) run her stageline and learns that her partner (Kingsford) and a saloon owner (Kent) are out to steal gold shipments from the miners and prevent her from renewing her stagecoach contract.

774. **Stagecoach to Denver** (12/23/46) B&W 56 mins. (Western). *DIR:* R. G. Springsteen. *A-PRO:* Sidney Picker. *SP:* Earle Snell. Based on the comic strip created by Fred Harman. *CAST:* Allan ("Rocky") Lane, Bobby (Robert) Blake, Martha Wentworth, Roy Barcroft, Peggy Stewart, Emmett Lynn, Ted Adams, Edmund Cobb, Tom Chatterton, Bobby Hyatt, George Chesebro, Edward Cassidy, Wheaton Chambers, Forrest Taylor, Britt Wood, Tom London, Stanley Price, Marin Sais, Frank O'Connor, Budd Buster, Herman Hack, Cactus Mack, Tom Steele. *SYN:* While investigating a stagecoach wreck, Red Ryder (Lane) uncovers a kidnapping, murder, and land-grabbing plot. *NOTES:* Re-edited for TV at 54 mins. The 18th entry in the "Red Ryder" feature series.

775. **Stagecoach to Monterey** (9/15/44) B&W 55 mins. (Western). *DIR:* Lesley Selander. *A-PRO:* Stephen Auer. *SP:* Norman S. Hall. *CAST:* Allan ("Rocky") Lane, Peggy Stewart, Wally Vernon, Twinkle Watts, Tom London, Roy Barcroft, LeRoy Mason, Kenne Duncan, Bud Geary, Carl Sepulveda, Jack O'Shea, Jack Kirk, Fred Graham, Henry Wills, Cactus Mack, Robert Wilke, Herman Hack, Jim Mitchell, Al Taylor. *SYN:* An undercover treasury man (Lane) goes after a gang of Eastern con men who are counterfeiters.

776. **Stardust on the Sage** (5/25/42) B&W 65 mins. (Western). *DIR:* William Morgan. *A-PRO:* Harry Grey. *SP:* Betty Burbridge. Story by Dorrell McGowan, Stuart McGowan. *CAST:* Gene Autry, Smiley Burnette, William (Bill) Henry, Edith Fellows, Louise Currie, Emmett Vogan, George Ernest, Vince Barnett, Betty Farrington, Roy Barcroft, Tom London, Rex Lease, Frank Ellis, Edward Cassidy, Fred Burns, Frank LaRue, Franklyn Farnum, Edmund Cobb, Jerry Jerome, Merrill McCormick, Bert LeBaron, Monte Montague, George DeNormand, Bill Jamison, Jimmy Fox, George Sherwood, Bill Nestell, Frank O'Connor, Griff Barnette, Frankie Marvin, Lee Shumway, "Champion." *SYN:* Gene and Frog (Burnette) set out to find if a mine operation is legitimate when Gene learns that his name has been used in advising people to buy stock in the mine.

777. **Steppin' in Society** (7/9/45) B&W 72 mins. (Crime-Comedy). *DIR:* Alexander Esway. *PRO:* Joseph Bercholz. *E-PRO:* Howard Sheehan. *SP:* Bradford Ropes. Based on the novel by Marcel Arnac. *CAST:* Edward Everett Horton, Gladys George, Ruth Terry, Robert Livingston, Jack LaRue, Lola Lane, Isabel Jewell, Frank Jenks, Paul

Hurst, Harry Barris, Iris Adrian, Tom Herbert, Monte Hale. *SYN:* A judge (Horton), while on vacation, takes refuge in an underworld nightclub during a storm, and the mobsters mistakenly believe him to be one of them; eventually he converts them all to the side of law and order.

**778. Storm Over Bengal** (11/14/38) B&W 65 mins. (Adventure-War). *DIR:* Sidney Salkow. *A-PRO:* Armand Schaefer. *SP:* Garrett Fort. *CAST:* Patric Knowles, Richard Cromwell, Rochelle Hudson, Douglass Dumbrille, Colin Tapley, Gilbert Emery, Douglas Walton, Halliwell Hobbes, John Burton, Clyde Cook, Claud Allister, Pedro de Cordoba, Edward Van Sloan. *SYN:* Set during the conflict between British troops and Indians in Bengal, a brother (Cromwell), who is always in trouble, proves himself in battle and saves his brother (Knowles) and the entire British regiment from defeat. *NOTES:* Academy Award Nominee — Best Score.

**779. Storm Over Lisbon** (10/16/44) B&W 86 mins. (Spy). *DIR/A-PRO:* George Sherman. *SP:* Doris Gilbert. Adapted by Dane Lussier. Story by Elizabeth Meehan. *CAST:* Vera Hruba Ralston, Richard Arlen, Erich Von Stroheim, Robert Livingston, Otto Kruger, Eduardo Ciannelli, Mona Barrie, Frank Orth, Sarah Edwards, Alice Fleming, Leon Belasco, Vincent Gironda, Bud Geary, Kenne Duncan, Roy Barcroft, Ruth Roman, Karen Randle, Annyse Sherman, Marie Day, Lucien Prival, Muni Seroff, Lester Sharpe, Kirk Alyn, Gino Corrado, Jack George, Willy Kaufman, Almeda Fowler, Alphonse Martell, Louis Ludwig Lowy, Manuel Paris, Georgia Davis, Charles Wagenheim, Eula Guy, George Derrick, Victor Travers, Fred Rapport, Richard Alexander, George Humbert, Georges Renavent, Jack Kirk, The Aida Broadbent Girls. *SYN:* A Nazi sympathizer (Von Stroheim) and his henchman (Ciannelli) try to prevent an American correspondent (Arlen) from leaving Lisbon with important secret documents. [Alternate title: *Inside the Underworld*].

**780. Stormbound** (12/15/51) B&W 60 mins. (Drama). *DIR:* Luigi Capuano. *PRO:* Aldo Raciti. *SP:* Comenico Meccoli, Fulvio Palmieri, Corrado Pavolini. Story by Luigi Capuano. A Republic Presentation. *CAST:* Constance Dowling, Andrea Checchi, Aldo Silvani, Bianca Doria, Mirko Ellis, Tino Buazzelli, Paola Quattrini. *SYN:* A news reporter (Dowling) gets stuck in a shack during a storm with an infamous bandit (Silvani) who grants her an interview. *NOTES:* Filmed in Italy.

**781. A Strange Adventure** (8/24/56) B&W 56 mins. (Crime). *DIR:* William Witney. *A-PRO:* William J. O'Sullivan. *SP:* Houston Branch. *CAST:* Joan Evans, Ben Cooper, Marla English, Jan Merlin, Nick Adams, Peter Miller, Paul Smith, Emlen Davies, Frank Wilcox, Thomas Browne Henry, John Maxwell, Steve Wayne. *SYN:* A young man's (Cooper) love for hot rods and life in the fast lane gets him in trouble when he gets mixed up with a girl (Evans) and her friends (Merlin, Adams) when he is forced to drive them to their mountain hideout after they've knocked off an armored car.

**782. Strange Case of Dr. Manning** (3/21/58) B&W 75 mins. (Mystery). *DIR:* Arthur Crabtree. *PRO:* Derek Winn, Bill Luckwell. *SP:* Paul Tabori, Bill Luckwell, Tom Waldron. Story by

Leo Townsend. A Winwell Production. A Republic Presentation. CAST: Ron Randell, Greta Gynt, Bruce Seton, Charles Farrell, Virginia Keiley, Garard Green, Wally Patch, Peter Noble, Peter Fontaine, Brian Summers, David Lander, John Watson, Robert Raglan. SYN: When Dr. Manning (Lander) is kidnapped, his wife (Gynt) calls in a private eye (Randell) and Scotland Yard investigator (Seton) to find her husband. NOTES: U.S. sources credit John Bash and Alfred Strauss as producers, though their names were simply tagged on in place of the film's actual British producers. Released in Britain in 1957. [Original British title: *Morning Call*].

**783. Strange Impersonation** (3/16/46) B&W 68 mins. (Mystery). DIR: Anthony Mann. PRO: W. Lee Wilder. SP: Mindret Lord. Story by Anne Wigton, Lewis Herman. CAST: Brenda Marshall, William Gargan, Hillary Brooke, George Chandler, Ruth Ford, H. B. Warner, Lyle Talbot, Mary Treen, Cay Forester, Dick Scott. SYN: A chemist (Marshall), who plans to try out her newly invented anesthesia on herself with the help of her assistant (Brooke), is injected with the drug when something goes wrong and her fiance (Gargan) jilts her, she is blackmailed, and then disfigured in an accident.

**784. Stranger at My Door** (4/6/56) B&W 85 mins. (Western). DIR: William Witney. A-PRO: Sidney Picker. SP: Barry Shipman. CAST: Macdonald Carey, Patricia Medina, Skip Homeier, Stephen Wootton, Louis Jean Heydt, Howard Wright, Slim Pickens, Malcolm Atterbury, Fred Sherman. SYN: A fugitive (Homeier) comes to the farm of a minister (Carey) looking for a hideout, but soon finds that he is learning a set of morals and shows kindness to the preacher's wife (Medina) and son (Wootton).

**785. Strangers in the Night** (9/12/44) B&W 56 mins. (Drama-Mystery). DIR: Anthony Mann. A-PRO: Rudolph E. Abel. SP: Bryant Ford, Paul Gangelin. Story by Philip MacDonald. CAST: William Terry, Virginia Grey, Helene Thimig, Edith Barrett, Anne O'Neal. SYN: A Marine sergeant (Terry) returns stateside and tries to track down the girl he had sent love letters to while stationed in the South Pacific.

**786. Street Bandits** (11/15/51) B&W 54 mins. (Crime). DIR: R. G. Springsteen. A-PRO: William Lackey. SP: Milton Raison. CAST: Penny Edwards, Robert Clarke, Ross Ford, Roy Barcroft, John Eldredge, Helen Wallace, Arthur Walsh, Harry Hayden, Emmett Vogan, Jane Adams, Charles Wagenheim, Richard H. Bartlett, Norman Field, Robert Long, Dick Cogan. SYN: A lawyer (Clarke) learns his lesson when he takes on the case of a mobster (Barcroft) and gets wounded when the mobster kills his partner. Eventually, he is able to clear his name and vows never to take on another racketeering case.

**787. Street of Darkness** (6/11/58) B&W 60 mins. (Adventure). DIR: Robert Walker. PRO: Robert Keys. SP: Malvin Wald, Maurice Tombragel. CAST: Robert Keys, John Close, James Seay, Julie Gibson, Sheila Ryan, Dub Taylor, Henry Rowland, Dick Crockett, Val Winter, Ed Nelson, Walter Hamlin, Steve Raines, Pork Chops and Kidney Stew. SYN: A group of former Army buddies reunite in New Orleans and decide to track down a buried treasure.

*NOTES:* Burt Reynolds appeared in a similar picture in 1969 titled *Impasse.*

**788. Street of Missing Men** (4/28/39) B&W 63 mins. (Crime). *DIR:* Sidney Salkow. *A-PRO:* Armand Schaefer. *SP:* Frank Dolan, Leonard Lee. Story by Eleanore Griffin, William Rankin. *CAST:* Charles Bickford, Harry Carey, Sr., Tommy Ryan, Mabel Todd, Guinn "Big Boy" Williams, Nana Bryant, Ralph Graves, John Gallaudet, Regis Toomey. *SYN:* A man (Bickford) leaves prison after five years and seeks vengeance against the newspaper editor (Carey) whose efforts resulted in his conviction, but once he meets him face to face, he changes his mind, decides to work with him on the paper, becomes a protector of a newsboy (Ryan), and loses his life as he saves the newspaper from organized crime.

**789. Streets of San Francisco** (4/15/49) B&W 60 mins. (Crime). *DIR:* George Blair. *A-PRO:* Sidney Picker. *SP:* John K. Butler. Story by Adele Buffington, Gordan Kahn. *CAST:* Robert Armstrong, Mae Clarke, Gary Gray, Wally Cassell, Richard Benedict, John Harmon, J. Farrell MacDonald, Ian MacDonald, Charles Meredith, Eve March, Denver Pyle, Charles Cane, William (Bill) Henry, Claire DuBrey, Martin Garralaga. *SYN:* A policeman (Armstrong) takes the son (Gray) of a dead mobster (Ian MacDonald) into his home and tries to raise him as he would his own, showing him the difference between right and wrong.

**790. Suicide Squadron** (4/20/42) B&W 83 mins. (War-Music). *DIR:* Brian Desmond Hurst. *PRO:* William Sistrom. *SP:* Shaun Terence Young, Brian Desmond Hurst, Rodney Ackland. Story by Shaun Terence Young. An RKO-British Production. A Republic Presentation. *CAST:* Anton Walbrook, Sally Gray, Derrick DeMarney, Kenneth Kent, Percy Parsons, J. H. Roberts, Cecil Parker, Guy Middleton, John Laurie, Frederick Valk, Philip Friend, Michael Rennie, Robert Beatty, Marian Spencer, Lesley Gordon, Conway Palmer, Cynthia Heppner, Alan Keith. *SYN:* A Polish flying officer (Walbrook), wanting to fly during the German invasion of Poland at the onset of World War II, is tricked by his flying companions into journeying to Rumania and safety, because they regard him as more valuable for his musical talents than for his aerial skills, and figure he can do more for Poland in the concert halls than in the air. *NOTES:* First released by RKO in early 1942, RKO executives had little hope for successful U.S. distribution for this film; so they leased domestic rights—for a restricted period ending in 1947—to Republic Pictures, whose executives had more faith in it. It did reasonably well; the "Warsaw Concerto" was the making of the movie and was a milestone in cinema history: the record made from the soundtrack was the first soundtrack blockbuster in history. After Republic's lease ran out to release this film, it was again picked up by RKO and they reissued the film. Released in Britain in 1941 at a running time of 98 mins. [Original British title: *Dangerous Moonlight*].

**791. The Sun Shines Bright** (5/2/53) B&W 90 mins. (Drama). *DIR:* John Ford. *PRO:* John Ford, Merian C. Cooper. *SP:* Laurence Stallings. Based on *The Sun Shines Bright, The Mob from Massac,* and *The Lord Provides* by Irvin S. Cobb. An Argosy Production. *CAST:*

Charles Winninger, Arleen Whelan, John Russell, Stepin Fetchit, Russell Simpson, Ludwig Stossel, Francis Ford, Paul Hurst, Mitchell Lewis, Grant Withers, Milburn Stone, Dorothy Jordan, Elzie Emanuel, Henry O'Neill, Slim Pickens, James Kirkwood, Ernest Whitman, Trevor Bardette, Eve March, Hal Baylor, Jane Darwell, Ken Williams, Clarence Muse, Mae Marsh, Jack Pennick, Patrick Wayne. *SYN:* The story of a well-meaning southern judge (Winninger) whose honest attitudes and simple ways prove more powerful than the prejudice he is up against. *NOTES:* Stepin Fetchit repeats his role of "Jeff Poindexter" from the 1934 film. A remake of his 1934 Fox film, *Judge Priest*, which starred Will Rogers in the title role. John Ford calls this his favorite film.

**792. Sun Valley Cyclone** (5/10/46) B&W 56 mins. (Western). *DIR:* R. G. Springsteen. *A-PRO:* Sidney Picker. *SP:* Earle Snell. Based on the comic strip created by Fred Harman. *CAST:* Bill Elliott, Bobby (Robert) Blake, Alice Fleming, Roy Barcroft, Monte Hale, Kenne Duncan, Eddy Waller, Tom London, Edmund Cobb, Edward Cassidy, George Chesebro, Rex Lease, Hal Price, Jack Kirk, Frank O'Connor, Jack Sparks, "Thunder." *SYN:* Red Ryder (Elliott) sets out to capture rustlers who have been stealing army horses. *NOTES:* Re-edited for TV at 54 mins. The 15th entry in the "Red Ryder" feature series.

**Sundown Fury** *see* **Jesse James, Jr.**

**793. Sundown in Santa Fe** (11/5/48) B&W 60 mins. (Western). *DIR:* R. G. Springsteen. *A-PRO:* Melville Tucker. *SP:* Norman S. Hall. *CAST:* Allan ("Rocky") Lane, Eddy Waller, Roy Barcroft, Trevor Bardette, Jean Dean, Rand Brooks, Russell Simpson, Lane Bradford, B. G. Norman, Minerva Urecal, Joseph Crehan, Kenne Duncan, Robert Wilke, "Black Jack." *SYN:* An Army intelligence officer (Lane) sets out to capture the man who planned the assassination of President Lincoln.

**794. The Sundown Kid** (12/28/42) B&W 59 mins. (Western). *DIR:* Elmer Clifton. *A-PRO:* Edward J. White. *SP:* Norman S. Hall. *CAST:* Don ("Red") Barry, Ian Keith, Helen MacKellar, Linda Johnson, Emmett Lynn, Wade Crosby, Ted Adams, Fern Emmett, Bud Geary, Robert Kortman, Kenne Duncan, Kenneth Harlan, Jack Ingram, Jack Rockwell, Joe McGuinn, Cactus Mack, "Cyclone." *SYN:* A Pinkerton agent (Barry) goes undercover to capture a gang of counterfeiters, and with the help of a girl reporter (Johnson), locates his long lost mother (MacKellar).

**795. Sunset in El Dorado** (9/29/45) B&W 65 mins. (Western). *DIR:* Frank McDonald. *A-PRO:* Louis Gray. *SP:* John K. Butler. Story by Leon Abrams. *CAST:* Roy Rogers, George "Gabby" Hayes, Dale Evans, Hardie Albright, Margaret Dumont, Roy Barcroft, Tom London, Stanley Price, Robert Wilke, Edward Cassidy, Dorothy Granger, Edmund Cobb, Hank Bell, Jack Kirk, Gino Corrado, Frank Ellis, Tex Cooper, Bert Moorhouse, Joe McGuinn, Tex Terry, Bud Osborne, Bob Reeves, Bob Nolan and the Sons of the Pioneers, "Trigger." *SYN:* A woman (Evans) quits her job and heads to an old ghost town where her grandmother had been a notorious dancehall queen, and in a dream sequence, sees herself as her famous ancestor and meets the various characters of her Old West life. *NOTES:* Re-edited for TV at 54 mins.

**796. Sunset in the West** (9/25/50) Trucolor 67 mins. (Western). *DIR:* William Witney. *A-PRO:* Edward J. White. *SP:* Gerald Geraghty. *CAST:* Roy Rogers, Estelita Rodriguez, Penny Edwards, Gordon Jones, Will Wright, Pierre Watkin, Charles LaTorre, William Tannen, Steve Pendleton, Paul E. Burns, Dorothy Ann White, Foy Willing and the Riders of the Purple Sage, "Trigger." *SYN:* A sheriff (Wright) and his deputy (Rogers) set out to stop a gang of gunrunners who are wrecking trains as they smuggle their weapons out of the country.

**797. Sunset in Wyoming** (7/15/41) B&W 65 mins. (Western). *DIR:* William Morgan. *A-PRO:* Harry Grey. *SP:* Ivan Goff, Anne Morrison Chapin. Story by Joe Blair. *CAST:* Gene Autry, Smiley Burnette, Maris Wrixon, George Cleveland, Robert Kent, Sarah Edwards, Monte Blue, Dick Elliott, John Dilson, Stanley Blystone, Eddie Dew, Fred Burns, Reed Howes, Ralph Peters, Syd Saylor, Tex Terry, Lloyd Whitlock, Herman Hack, Bob Woodward, "Champion." *SYN:* Gene sets out to teach a logging company about conservation.

**798. Sunset on the Desert** (4/1/42) B&W 63 mins. (Western). *DIR/A-PRO:* Joseph Kane. *SP:* Gerald Geraghty. *CAST:* Roy Rogers, George "Gabby" Hayes, Lynne Carver, Frank M. Thomas, Beryl Wallace, Glenn Strange, Douglas Fowley, Fred Burns, Roy Barcroft, Henry Wills, Forrest Taylor, Bob Woodward, Edward Cassidy, Pat Brady, Cactus Mack, Bob Nolan and the Sons of the Pioneers, "Trigger." *SYN:* A group of outlaws mistake Roy as their leader, since he looks like him, and it is up to Roy to play along until he can bring them to justice. *NOTES:* Roy Rogers plays a dual role in this film. Re-edited for TV at 54 mins.

**799. Sunset Serenade** (9/14/42) B&W 58 mins. (Western). *DIR/A-PRO:* Joseph Kane. *SP:* Earl Felton. Story by Robert Yost. *CAST:* Roy Rogers, George "Gabby" Hayes, Helen Parrish, Onslow Stevens, Joan Woodbury, Frank M. Thomas, Roy Barcroft, Jack Kirk, Dick Wessel, Rex Lease, Jack Ingram, Fred Burns, Budd Buster, Jack Rockwell, Bob Nolan and the Sons of the Pioneers, "Trigger." *SYN:* When an Easterner (Parrish) arrives at her recently purchased ranch, it is up to Roy to see that she is not cheated out of it by a con man (Stevens). *NOTES:* Re-edited for TV at 54 mins.

**800. Surrender** (9/15/50) B&W 90 mins. (Drama). *DIR:* Allan Dwan. *PRO:* Herbert J. Yates. *SP:* James Edward Grant, Sloan Nibley. Story by James Edward Grant. *CAST:* Vera Ralston, John Carroll, Walter Brennan, Francis Lederer, William Ching, Maria Palmer, Jane Darwell, Roy Barcroft, Paul Fix, Esther Dale, Edward Norris, Howland Chamberlin, Norman Budd, Nacho Galindo, Jeff York, Mickey Simpson, Dick Elliott, Ralph Dunn, Virginia Farmer, J. Louis Johnson, Elizabeth Dunne, Cecil Elliott, Glenn Strange, Kenne Duncan, Paul Stader, Wesley Hopper, Tex Terry, Charles Morton, Doris Cole, Al Rhein, Al Murphy, Tina Menard, Frank Dae, Petra Silva, Tony Roux, Shelby Bacon, Fred Hoose. *SYN:* In a small town near the Mexican border, a wanted woman (Ralston) marries an important newspaperman (Ching) to escape the law, and when her other husband (Lederer) shows up and claims bigamy, she kills him. When she tries to escape across the border with a gambling hall owner (Carroll), they are shot by the sheriff (Brennan).

**Susanna** (G.B. title) *see* **Shepherd of the Ozarks**

**801. Susanna Pass** (4/29/49) Trucolor 67 mins. (Western). *DIR:* William Witney. *A-PRO:* Edward J. White. *SP:* Sloan Nibley, John K. Butler. *CAST:* Roy Rogers, Dale Evans, Estelita Rodriguez, Martin Garralaga, Robert Emmett Keane, Lucien Littlefield, Douglas Fowley, David Sharpe, Robert Bice, Foy Willing and the Riders of the Purple Sage, "Trigger," "Bullet." *SYN:* When a fish hatchery suffers a series of explosions, a game warden (Rogers) investigates and finds out that crooks are after the oil deposits beneath the hatchery's lake. *NOTES:* Dale Evans' first Roy Rogers film since 1947.

**802. Sweethearts on Parade** (7/15/53) Trucolor 90 mins. (Musical). *DIR:* Allan Dwan. *E-PRO:* Herbert J. Yates. *SP:* Houston Branch. *CAST:* Ray Middleton, Lucille Norman, Eileen Christy, Bill Shirley, Estelita Rodriguez, Clinton Sundberg, Harry Carey, Jr., Irving Bacon, Leon Tyler, Marjorie Wood, Mara Corday, Ann McCrea, Tex Terry, Emory Parnell. *SYN:* A young girl (Christy) becomes interested in the glamour of a traveling medicine show, especially her father's (Middleton) partner (Shirley).

**803. Swing Your Partner** (5/20/43) B&W 72 mins. (Musical). *DIR:* Frank

McDonald. *A-PRO:* Armand Schaefer. *SP:* Dorrell McGowan, Stuart McGowan. *CAST:* Roger Clark, Esther Dale, Judy Clark, Charles Judels, Rosemary LaPlanche, Sam Flint, Forbes Murray, Elmer Jerome, Vera Vague (Barbara Jo Allen), Dale Evans, Ransom Sherman, Harry Cheshire, Richard Lane, George "Shug" Fisher, Lulu Belle and Scotty, Peppy & Peanuts, The Tennessee Ramblers. *SYN:* The owner of a dairy (Dale) poses as worker to find out why the employees can't stand her.

**804. Swingin' on a Rainbow** (9/1/45) B&W 72 mins. (Comedy). *DIR:* William Beaudine. *A-PRO:* Edward J. White. *E-PRO:* Armand Schaefer. *SP:* Olive Cooper, John Grey. Story by Olive Cooper. *CAST:* Jane Frazee, Brad Taylor, Harry Langdon, Minna Gombell, Amelita Ward, Tim Ryan, Paul Harvey, Wendell Niles, Richard Davies, Helen Talbot. *SYN:* A songwriter (Frazee) goes to New York to find the man that stole her song and winds up falling in love and writing songs with a lyricist (Taylor). *NOTES:* The final film appearance of Harry Langdon — he died in 1944.

**805. Tahiti Honey** (4/6/43) B&W 69 mins. (Musical-Romance). *DIR/A-PRO:* John H. Auer. *SP:* Lawrence Kimble, Frederick Kohner, H. W. Hanemann. Story by Frederick Kohner. *CAST:* Simone Simon, Dennis O'Keefe, Michael Whalen, Lionel Stander, Wally Vernon, Tommye Adams (Abigail Adams), Tom Seidel, Dan Seymour. *SYN:* A pianist (O'Keefe), abandoned in Tahiti, takes on a singer (Simon), much to the dismay of the other band members, and when they head to San Francisco, they bomb in their first few engagements. When she suggests changing the type of music they play, they are a hit.

**The Tall Trouble** (G.B. title) *see* **Hell Canyon Outlaws**

**806. Taming Sutton's Gal** (9/15/57) B&W/Naturama 71 mins. (Drama). *DIR:* Lesley Selander. *A-PRO:* William J. O'Sullivan. *SP:* Thames Williamson, Frederic Louis Fox. Story by Thames Williamson. A Variety Production. *CAST:* John Lupton, Gloria Talbott, Jack Kelly, May Wynn, Verna Felton. *SYN:* A hunter (Lupton) must prove his innocence when he is accused of murdering a woman's (Wynn) husband (Kelly).

**807. Tarnished** (2/28/50) B&W 60 mins. (Drama). *DIR:* Harry Keller. *A-PRO:* Sidney Picker. *SP:* John K. Butler. Based on *Tarnished* by Eleanor R. Mayo. *CAST:* Dorothy Patrick, Arthur Franz, Barbara Fuller, James Lydon, Harry Shannon, Don Beddoe, Byron Barr, Alex Gerry, Hal Price, Stephen Chase, Esther Somers, Paul E. Burns, Ethel Wales, Michael Vallon. *SYN:* A Marine (Franz) returns to his small Maine home town, and based on his past exploits as a youth, most of the people assume he has been in jail, and only his girl (Patrick) stands by him.

**808. Tears for Simon** (1/4/57) Eastmancolor 91 mins. (Mystery). *DIR:* Guy Green. *PRO:* Vivian A. Cox, Sidney Box. *SP:* Janet Green. A Rank Film Production. A Republic Presentation. *CAST:* David Farrar, David Knight, Julia Arnall, Anthony Oliver, Thora Hird, Eleanor Summerfield, Anne Paige, Marjorie Rhodes, Anna Turner, Everley Gregg, Meredith Edwards, Irene Prador, Anita Sharp Bolster, Beverley Brooks, Brenda Hogan, Joan Sims, Shirley Ann Field, Eileen Peel, Barbara Shotter, Alma Taylor, Robert Brown,

Harry Brunning, Fanny Carby, Cyril Chamberlain, Peggy Ann Clifford, Glenda Davies, Guy Deghy, Michael Ward, Dorothy Gordon, Fred Griffiths, Joan Hickson, Glyn Houston, Ray Jackson, Shirley Jenkins, Freda Bamford, Jack Lambert, Margot Lister, Arthur Lovegrove, William Lucas, Barry McCormick, Jack McNaughton, Charlotte Mitchell, Hugh Morton, Dandy Nichols, Grace Denbigh Russell, Ewen Solon, Marianne Stone, Ronald Ward, Mona Washbourne, John Welsh, Leonard White, Barbara Windsor, George Woodbridge. *SYN:* The baby son of a U.S. Embassy official (Knight) and his wife (Arnall) is kidnapped, and a detective (Farrar) is assigned to find the baby, with almost no clues to go on. *NOTES:* Released in Britain in 1956. [Original British title: *Lost.*]

**809. Tell It to a Star** (8/16/45) B&W 67 mins. (Musical). *DIR:* Frank McDonald. *A-PRO:* Walter H. Goetz. *E-PRO:* Armand Schaefer. *SP:* John K. Butler. Story by Gerald Drayson Adams, John W. Krafft. *CAST:* Ruth Terry, Robert Livingston, Alan Mowbray, Franklin Pangborn, Isabel Randolph, Eddie Marr, Adrian Booth, Frank Orth, Tom Dugan, George Chandler, Mary McCarthy, William B. Davidson, Aurora Miranda. *SYN:* A cigarette girl (Terry), with singing aspirations, tries to get a bandleader (Livingston) to give her a job singing; a broke financier (Mowbray), who pretends to be her uncle, manages to get her a solo with his gift of gab.

**810. Tenth Avenue Kid** (8/22/38) B&W 60 mins. (Crime). *DIR:* Bernard

Vorhaus. *A-PRO:* Harry Grey. *SP:* Gordan Kahn. Story by Gordan Kahn, Adele Buffington. *CAST:* Bruce Cabot, Beverly Roberts, Tommy Ryan, Ben Welden, Horace MacMahon, John Wray, Jay Novello, Charles Wilson, Paul Bryar, Walter Sande, Ralph Dunn, Julian Petruzzi, Billy Wayne, Byron Foulger. *SYN:* A boy (Ryan) is orphaned when his dad is gunned down by a private detective (Cabot); the detective feels responsible for the kid and befriends him, but also tries to get him to reveal the whereabouts of money stolen by his dad during a bank robbery. *NOTES:* The film debut of Jay Novello.

**811. Terror at Midnight** (4/27/56) B&W 70 mins. (Crime). *DIR:* Franklin Adreon. *A-PRO:* Rudy Ralston. *SP:* John K. Butler. Story by John K. Butler, Irving Shulman. *CAST:* Scott Brady, Joan Vohs, Frank Faylen, John Dehner, Virginia Gregg, Ric Roman, John Gallaudet, Kem Dibbs, Percy Helton, Francis DeSales, John Maxwell. *SYN:* A newly promoted police sergeant (Brady) discovers that his girlfriend (Vohs) may be involved in a stolen car ring.

**Texas Legionnaires** *see* **466. Man from Music Mountain**

**Texas Manhunt** *see* **Phantom of the Plains**

**Texas Serenade** (G.B. title) *see* **The Old Corral**

**812. Texas Terrors** (11/22/40) B&W 57 mins. (Western). *DIR/A-PRO:* George Sherman. *SP:* Doris Schroeder, Anthony Coldeway. *CAST:* Don ("Red") Barry, Julie Duncan, Arthur Loft, Al St. John, Eddy Waller, William Ruhl, Ann Pennington, Sammy McKim, Reed Howes, Robert Fiske, Fred "Snowflake" Toones, Hal Taliaferro, Edmund Cobb, Al Haskell, Jack Kirk, Ruth Robinson, Blackjack Ward, Jimmy Wakely and His Rough Riders (Jimmy Wakely, Johnny Bond, Dick Rinehart). *SYN:* A lawyer (Barry) sets out to avenge the murders of his parents who were killed by a claim jumper when he was a baby. *NOTES:* Re-edited for TV at 54 mins.

**813. That Brennan Girl** (12/23/46) B&W 95 mins. (Drama). *DIR/PRO:* Alfred Santell. *SP:* Doris Anderson. Story by Adela Rogers St. John. *CAST:* James Dunn, Mona Freeman, William Marshall, June Duprez, Frank Jenks, Dorothy Vaughan, Charles Arnt, Rosalind Ivan, Fay Helm, Bill Kennedy, Connie Leon, Edythe Elliott, Sarah Padden, Jean Stevens, Lucien Littlefield, Marian Martin, Earle Hodgins. *SYN:* An unhappy young woman (Freeman), raised by her thoughtless mother (Duprez) to take what she wants out of life without regard for others, learns that this philosophy brings her unhappiness until she reforms her outlook. *NOTES:* The final film of director Alfred Santell—he retired after this film.

**814. That's My Baby** (9/14/44) B&W 68 mins. (Comedy-Drama). *DIR:* William Berke. *A-PRO:* Walter Colmes. *SP:* Nicholas Barrows, William Tunberg. Story by Irving Wallace. *CAST:* Richard Arlen, Ellen Drew, Leonid Kinskey, Richard Bailey, Minor Watson, Marjorie Manners, Madeline Grey, Alex Callam, Patrick J. Kelly, William Benedict, Jack Chefe, Fred Fisher, Gene Rodgers, Frank Mitchell, Lyle Latell, Alphonse Berge, Doris Duane, Adia Kuznetzoff, Chuy Reyes, Al Mardo, Isabelita (Lita Baron), Dewey "Pigmeat" Markham,

Peppy and Peanuts, Mike Riley and His Musical Maniacs. *SYN:* An engaged couple (Arlen, Drew) struggle with the problem of snapping her father (Watson) out of a deep depression, amid a strange brew of animation, live-action, seriousness, and music. *NOTES: Popeye* animator Dave Fleischer created the cartoons.

**815. That's My Gal** (5/15/47) Trucolor 66 mins. (Musical-Comedy). *DIR:* George Blair. *A-PRO:* Armand Schaefer. *SP:* Joseph Hoffman. Story by Frances Hyland, Bernard Feins. *CAST:* Lynn Roberts, Don ("Red") Barry, Pinky Lee, Frank Jenks, Edward Gargan, Judy Clark, Paul Stanton, John Hamilton, Ray Walker, Marian Martin, Elmer Jerome, George Carleton, Jan Savitt and His Top Hatters, Isabelita (Lita Baron), The Guadalajara Trio, The Four Step Brothers, St. Clair and Vilova, Dolores and Don Graham. *SYN:* A gang of con men raise money from a group of foolish investors to back a bad musical revue that will most certainly bomb leaving them to skip out with the money. Unfortunately, when one of the investors dies, his executrix (Roberts) makes sure that the show is a hit.

**816. That's My Man** (6/1/47) B&W 104 mins. (Drama-Sports). *DIR/PRO:* Frank Borzage. *SP:* Steve Fisher, Bradley King. *CAST:* Don Ameche, Catherine McLeod, Roscoe Karns, John Ridgely, Kitty Irish, Joe Frisco, Gregory Marshall, Dorothy Adams, Frankie Darro, Hampton J. Scott, John Miljan, William B. Davidson, Joe Hernandez, "Gallant Man." *SYN:* A professional gambler (Ameche), who lets his obsession with gambling nearly ruin his life, buys a colt and raises it to be a champion racehorse in the hopes that this will turn his life around. [Alternate title: *Will Tomorrow Ever Come?*]

**817. This is Korea!** (8/10/51) Trucolor 50 mins.(War). *PRO:* U. S. Navy. Supervised by John Ford. Filmed by U.S. Navy and U.S. Marine photographers. *CAST:* Narrated by John Ireland. *SYN:* A documentary on the First Marine Division and Seventh Fleet during the Korean War offensive.

**818. Thoroughbreds** (12/23/44) B&W 56 mins. (Sports). *DIR:* George Blair. *A-PRO:* Lester Sharpe. *SP:* Wellyn Totman. Story by Lester Sharpe. *CAST:* Tom Neal, Adele Mara, Roger Pryor, Paul Harvey, Gene Garrick, Doodles Weaver, Eddie Hall, Tom London, Charles Sullivan, Alan Edwards, Sam Bernard, Buddy Gorman, John Crawford, Jack Gardner, Robert Strange, Richard Bartell, Timothy Mahen, Nolan Leary, Michael Owen, Howard Mitchell, Harrison Greene, Kenne Duncan. *SYN:* A Cavalry sergeant (Neal), released from the Army at the same time that his beloved horse is sold to a society woman (Mara) to run in steeplechases, gets a job as trainer to the horse and eventually ends up riding him in the big race.

**819. Thou Shalt Not Kill** (12/30/39) B&W 67 mins. (Drama). *DIR:* John H. Auer. *A-PRO:* Robert North. *SP:* Robert Presnell. Story by George Carleton Brown. *CAST:* Charles Bickford, Owen Davis, Jr., Doris Day, Paul Guilfoyle, Granville Bates, Charles Waldron, Sheila Bromley, George Chandler, Charles Middleton, Emmett Vogan, Leona Roberts, Ethel May Halls, Edmund Elton, Elsie Prescott. *SYN:* A young minister (Bickford), who tries to reform a convicted murderer (Davis, Jr.), learns through confession that another man is the killer. NOTES: The Doris Day that appears in this film is *not* the well-known actress/vocalist. Working title was *Woman Who Dared.*

**820. Three Faces West** (7/12/40) B&W 79 mins. (Drama). *DIR:* Bernard Vorhaus. *A-PRO:* Sol C. Siegel. *SP:* F. Hugh Herbert, Joseph Moncure March, Samuel Ornitz, Doris Anderson. *CAST:* John Wayne, Charles Coburn, Sigrid Gurie, Spencer Charters, Roland Varno, Trevor Bardette, Helen MacKellar, Sonny Bupp, Wade Boteler, Russell Simpson, Charles Waldron, Wendell Niles, Dewey Robinson. *SYN:* A Viennese surgeon (Coburn) and his daughter (Gurie) come to the U.S. to set up a practice, settle in a small North Dakota town, and when drought forces them to move, they aid a local farmer (Wayne) in relocating the community to Oregon. NOTES: Screenwriter Doris Anderson was uncredited. [Alternate title: *The Refugee.*]

**821. Three Little Sisters** (7/31/44) B&W 69 mins. (Romance). *DIR:* Joseph Santley. *A-PRO:* Harry Grey. *SP:* Olive Cooper. Story by Olive Cooper, Maurice Clark. *CAST:* Mary Lee, Ruth Terry, Cheryl Walker, William Terry, Jackie Moran, Charles Arnt, Frank Jenks, Bill Shirley, Tom Fadden, Tom London, Milton Kibbee, Addison Richards, Lillian Randolph, Sam McDaniel, Forrest Taylor. *SYN:* A G.I. (William Terry) falls for a girl he's never seen after writing to her and hearing about the luxurious life she leads but, in reality, the girl (Lee) is confined to a wheelchair and her two sisters (Walker, Ruth Terry) barely make enough money as scrub-girls to get by.

**822. The Three Mesquiteers** (9/22/36) B&W 61 mins. (Western). *DIR:* Ray Taylor. *PRO:* Nat Levine. *SP:* Jack Natteford. Story by Charles Condon. Based on characters created by William Colt MacDonald. *CAST:* Robert Livingston, Ray ("Crash") Corrigan, Syd Saylor, Kay Hughes, J. P. McGowan, Alan Bridge, Frank Yaconelli, John Merton, Jean Marvey, Milburn Stone, Duke York, Nena Quartaro, Allen Connor, Stanley Blystone, Wally West, George Plues, Rose Plummer. *SYN:* The Three Mesquiteers (Livingston, Corrigan, Saylor) find themselves in the middle of a feud with rival cattlemen. NOTES: Syd Saylor's only appearance as a "Mesquiteer." Two other previous "Three Mesquiteer" features had been released the year before—*Law of the 45's*, a Normandy/First Division production, which starred Guinn "Big Boy" Williams as Tucson Smith, and Al St. John as Stony Brooke, with the part of Lullaby Joslin being removed; *Powdersmoke Range*, an RKO production, which starred Harry Carey, Sr., as Tucson Smith, Hoot Gibson as Stony Brooke, and Guinn "Big Boy" Williams as Lullaby Joslin, and co-starred two future "Mesquiteers," Tom Tyler and Bob Steele. The 1st entry in Republic's "Three Mesquiteers" series. Re-edited for TV at 54 mins.

**823. Three Texas Steers** (5/12/39) B&W 59 mins. (Western). *DIR:* George Sherman. *A-PRO:* William Berke. *SP:* Betty Burbridge, Stanley Roberts. Based on characters created by William Colt MacDonald. *CAST:* John Wayne, Ray ("Crash") Corrigan, Max Terhune, Carole Landis, Ralph Graves, Roscoe Ates, Collette Lyons, Billy Curtis, Ted Adams, Stanley Blystone, David Sharpe, Ethan Laidlaw, Lew Kelly, John Merton,

Dave Willock, Ted Mapes. "Naba," the Gorilla (Ray Benard). *SYN:* The Three Mesquiteers (Wayne, Corrigan, Terhune) help the owner (Landis) of a circus when her manager (Graves) tries to drive her off the land she inherited because the government wants it for a water improvement project. *NOTES:* This was ventriloquist Terhune's final appearance in the series. Re-edited for TV at 54 mins. The 22nd entry in the "Three Mesquiteers" series and the final appearance of Max Terhune as a "Mesquiteer." [British title: *Danger Rides the Range.*]

**824. Three's a Crowd** (5/23/45) B&W 58 mins. (Mystery). *DIR:* Lesley Selander. *A-PRO:* Walter H. Goetz. *SP:* Dane Lussier. Based on *Hasty Wedding* by Mignon G. Eberhart. *CAST:* Pamela Blake, Charles Gordon, Gertrude Michael, Pierre Watkin, Virginia Brissac, Ted Hecht, Grady Sutton, Tom London, Roland Varno, Anne O'Neal, Bud Geary, Nanette Vallon. *SYN:* Two newlyweds (Blake, Gordon) find themselves accused of murdering the wife's former boyfriend and set out to prove their innocence.

**825. Thumbs Up** (7/5/43) B&W 67 mins. (Musical). *DIR:* Joseph Santley. *A-PRO:* Albert J. Cohen. *SP:* Frank Gill, Jr. Story by Ray Golden, Henry Moritz. *CAST:* Brenda Joyce, Richard Fraser, Elsa Lanchester, Arthur Margetson, Pat O'Malley, Queenie Leonard, Molly Lamont, Gertrude Niesen, George Byron, Charles Irwin, Andre Charlot, The Hot Shots. *SYN:* A woman (Joyce) falls in love with an RAF captain (Fraser) while exploiting her friendship with a theatrical producer (Margetson) to further her career.

**Thunder Across the Pacific** (G.B. title) *see* **The Wild Blue Yonder**

**826. Thunder in God's Country** (4/8/51) B&W 67 mins. (Western). *DIR:* George Blair. *A-PRO:* Melville Tucker. *SP:* Arthur E. Orloff. *CAST:* Rex Allen, Mary Ellen Kay, Buddy Ebsen, Ian MacDonald, Paul Harvey, Harry Lauter, John Doucette, Harry Cheshire, John Ridgely, Frank Ferguson, Wilson Wood, "KoKo." *SYN:* A cowboy (Allen) and his sidekick (Ebsen) set out to stop a crooked gambler (MacDonald), who is an escaped criminal, from taking advantage of a community.

**827. Thunder in the Desert** (3/7/38) B&W 60 mins. (Western). *DIR:* Sam Newfield. *PRO:* A. W. Hackel. *SP:* George Plympton. *CAST:* Bob Steele, Louise Stanley, Don Barclay, Ed Brady, Charles King, Horace Murphy, Steve Clark, Lew Meehan, Ernie Adams, Richard Cramer, Budd Buster, Sherry Tansey. *SYN:* A cowboy (Steele) inherits a ranch from his murdered uncle, and with help from his sidekick (Barclay), sets out to find his uncle's killer.

**828. Thunder Over Arizona** (8/4/56) Trucolor/Naturama 75 mins. (Western). *DIR/A-PRO:* Joseph Kane. *SP:* Sloan Nibley. *CAST:* Skip Homeier, Kristine Miller, George Macready, Wallace Ford, Jack Elam, Nacho Galindo, Gregory Walcott, George Keymas, John Doucette, John Compton, Bob Swan, Julian Rivero, Francis McDonald, Fred Graham. *SYN:* When silver is discovered in a small town, a cowboy (Homeier) sets out to stop a crooked politician (Macready) from grabbing it all himself.

**829. Thunder Over Tangier** (11/25/57) B&W 66 mins. (Crime). *DIR:* Lance Comfort. *PRO:* W. G. Chalmers. *SP:* Paddy Manning O'Brine. A Sunset Palisades Production. A Republic Presentation. *CAST:* Robert Hutton, Lisa Gastoni, Martin Benson, Derek Sydney, Jack Allen, Leonard Sachs, Robert Raglan, Harold Berens, Emerton Court, Richard Shaw, Michael Balfour, Frank Forsyth, Reginald Hearne, Fred Lake, Alex Gallier, Marianne Stone, Adeeb Assaly, James Lomas, Frank Singuineau, Ronald Clark, Victor Beaumont. *SYN:* A movie stuntman (Hutton) becomes entangled with a gang of passport forgers in post-World War II Algeria, and when framed for murder, he sets out to clear himself with the help of a girl (Gastoni). *NOTES:* Released in Britain in July, 1957. [British title: *Man from Tangier.*]

**830. Thunderbirds** (11/27/52) B&W 98 mins. (War). *DIR/A-PRO:* John H. Auer. *SP:* Mary C. McCall, Jr. Story by Kenneth Gamet. *CAST:* John Derek, John Drew Barrymore, Mona Freeman, Gene Evans, Eileen Christy, Ward Bond, Barton MacLane, Wally Cassell, Ben Cooper, Robert Neil, Slim Pickens, Armando Silvestre, Benny Baker, Norman Budd, Mae Clarke, Sammy McKim, Allene Roberts, Richard Simmons, Walter Reed, Suzanne D'Albert, Barbara Pepper, Pepe Hern, Victor Millan. *SYN:* Two Oklahoma National Guard fliers (Derek, Barrymore) are called into active service in 1940 and battle their way through the Italian campaign and, eventually, Germany.

**831. Thundering Caravans** (6/20/52) B&W 54 mins. (Western). *DIR:* Harry Keller. *A-PRO:* Rudy Ralston. *SP:* M. Coates Webster. *CAST:* Allan ("Rocky") Lane, Eddy Waller, Mona Knox, Roy Barcroft, Isabel Randolph, Richard Crane, William (Bill) Henry, Edward Clark, Pierre Watkin, Stanley Andrews, Boyd "Red" Morgan, Marshall Reed, Tex Terry, Art Dillard, Dale Van Sickel, "Black Jack." *SYN:* A U.S. Marshal (Lane) helps a sheriff (Waller) solve a series of gold ore robberies.

**832. Thundering Trails** (1/25/43) B&W 56 mins. (Western). *DIR:* John English. *A-PRO:* Louis Gray. *SP:* Norman S. Hall, Robert Yost. Story by Robert Yost. based on characters created by William Colt MacDonald. *CAST:* Bob Steele, Tom Tyler, Jimmie Dodd, Nell O'Day, Sam Flint, Karl Hackett, Charles Miller, John James, Forrest Taylor, Edward Cassidy, Forbes Murray, Reed Howes, Bud Geary, Budd Buster, Vince Barnett, Lane Bradford, Cactus Mack, Eddie Parker, Al Taylor, Art Mix, Jack O'Shea, John Carpenter. *SYN:* The Three Mesquiteers (Steele, Tyler Dodd) set out to rescue the brother of a Texas Ranger who has gotten mixed up with outlaws. *NOTES:* The 48th entry in the "Three Mesquiteers" series.

**833. Ticket to Paradise** (6/25/36) B&W 70 mins. (Comedy). *DIR:* Aubrey Scotto. *PRO:* Nat Levine. *SP:* Jack Natteford, Nathanael West, Ray Harris. Story by David Silverstein. *CAST:* Roger Pryor, Wendy Barrie, Claude Gillingwater, Andrew Tombes, Luis Alberni, E. E. Clive, John Sheehan, Theodore Von Eltz, Russell Hicks, Earle Hodgins, Grace Hyle, Harry Woods, Charles Lane, Herbert Rawlinson, Gavin Gordon, Harry Harvey, Duke York, Eric Mayne, Bud Jamison, Harrison Greene, Stanley Fields, Wallace Gregory, Fern Emmett, Eleanor Huntley. *SYN:* When an amnesia victim (Pryor) runs off with a young girl (Barrie), her father (Gillingwater) hires a detective (Tombes) to track them down.

**Tidal Wave** (G.B. title) *see* **S.O.S. Tidal Wave**

**The Tiger Man** *see* **The Lady and the Monster**

834. **The Tiger Woman** (11/16/45) B&W 57 mins. (Crime). *DIR:* Philip Ford. *A-PRO:* Dorrell McGowan, Stuart McGowan. *SP:* George Carleton Brown. Based on the radio play by John A. Dunkel. *CAST:* Adele Mara, Kane Richmond, Richard Fraser, Peggy Stewart, Cy Kendall, Beverly Lloyd, Gregory Gay, John Kelly, Addison Richards, Donia Bussey, Frank Reicher, Garry Owen. *SYN:* A private detective (Richmond) goes after a nightclub singer (Mara) who has killed her husband for his insurance money and then kills her lover. *NOTES:* This feature bears no relation to the 1944 Republic serial of the same title.

835. **The Timber Trail** (6/15/48) Trucolor 67 mins. (Western). *DIR:* Philip Ford. *A-PRO:* Melville Tucker. *SP:* Bob Williams. *CAST:* Monte Hale, Lynn Roberts, James Burke, Roy Barcroft, Francis Ford, Robert Emmett Keane, Steve Darrell, Fred Graham, Wade Crosby, Eddie Acuff, Foy Willing and the Riders of the Purple Sage. *SYN:* A cowboy (Hale) stops in a town run by outlaws to help the daughter (Roberts) of a stagecoach operator (Ford) who is being driven out of business.

836. **Timberjack** (2/18/55) Trucolor 92 mins. (Western). *DIR/A-PRO:* Joseph Kane. *E-PRO:* Herbert J. Yates. *SP:* Allen Rivkin. Based on the novel by Dan Cushman. *CAST:* Sterling Hayden, Vera Ralston, David Brian, Adolphe Menjou, Hoagy Carmichael, Chill Wills, Jim Davis, Howard Petrie, Ian MacDonald, Elisha Cook, Jr., Karl Davis, Wally Cassell, Tex Terry, George Marshall, Chuck Roberson. *SYN:* A man (Hayden) returns to the timber country to claim his inheritance in a logging company from the owner (Brian) who murdered his father. While there he renews his romance with his girl (Ralston), who tries to talk him out of revenge, but, when her father (Menjou) is killed by the owner of the logging company, she joins in the fight to defeat him.

837. **Time Is My Enemy** (5/24/57) B&W 64 mins. (Crime). *DIR:* Don Chaffey. *PRO:* Roger Proudlock. *SP:* Allan Mackinnon. Based on the play *Second Chance* by Ella Adkins. A Vandyke Production. A Republic Presentation. *CAST:* Dennis Price, Renee Asherson, Susan Shaw, Patrick Barr, Bonar Colleano, Duncan Lamont, Brenda Hogan, Alfie Bass, Agnes Laughlan, William Franklyn, Bruce Beeby, Mavis Villiers, Barbara Grayley, Dandy Nichols, Nigel Neilson, Neil Wilson, Alistair Hunter, Erik Chitty, Audrey Hessey, Ian Wilson. *SYN:* A man (Price) tries to cover up a murder he committed by framing his ex-wife (Asherson) into firing a gun loaded with blanks at him so that she will confess to the murder of the man she thinks he is, the man he had killed. *NOTES:* Released in Britain in 1954.

838. **Tobor the Great** (9/1/54) B&W 77 mins. (Science-Fiction). *DIR:* Lee Sholem. *PRO:* Richard Goldstone. *SP:* Richard Goldstone, Philip MacDonald. Story by Carl Dudley. A Dudley Pictures

Production. A Republic Presentation. CAST: Charles Drake, Karin Booth, Billy Chapin, Taylor Holmes, Steven Geray, Henry Kulky, Franz Roehn, Hal Baylor, Alan Reynolds, Peter Brocco, Norman Field, Robert Shayne, Lyle Talbot, Emmett Vogan, William Schallert, Helen Winston, Jack Daly, Maury Hill. SYN: A boy (Chapin) becomes attached to a robot, designed for deep space exploration and named "Tobor," (or robot spelled backwards), invented by his grandfather (Holmes). The robot is endowed with human emotions and mind-linked to its creator, and when Communists kidnap the boy and his grandfather, the robot comes to their rescue.

**Tomorrow We Live** (G. B. title) *see* **At Dawn We Die**

**839. The Topeka Terror** (1/26/45) B&W 55 mins. (Western). *DIR:* Howard Bretherton. *A-PRO:* Stephen Auer. *SP:* Patricia Harper, Norman S. Hall. Story by Patricia Harper. *CAST:* Allan ("Rocky") Lane, Linda Stirling, Roy Barcroft, Earle Hodgins, Twinkle Watts, Bud Geary, Frank Jaquet, Jack Kirk, Tom London, Eva Novak, Hank Bell, Robert Wilke, Monte Hale, Jess Cavan, Fred Graham, Herman Nolan, Tom Smith, Herman Hack, Bill Wolfe, Jack O'Shea, Horace B. Carpenter, "Feather." *SYN:* When a man (London) and his two daughters (Stirling, Watts) are cheated out of their land by a land grabber (Barcroft), a federal agent (Lane) come to their aid.

**840. Toughest Man in Arizona** (10/10/52) Trucolor 90 mins. (Western). *DIR:* R. G. Springsteen. *A-PRO:* Sidney Picker. *SP:* John K. Butler. *CAST:* Vaughn Monroe, Joan Leslie, Edgar Buchanan, Victor Jory, Jean Parker, Henry (Harry) Morgan, Ian MacDonald, Lee MacGregor, Diana Christian, Bobby Hyatt, Charlita, Nadene Ashdown, Francis Ford, Paul Hurst, John Doucette, Rex Lease, Edmund Cobb, Cliff Clark, Sheb Wooley. *SYN:* A U.S. Marshal (Monroe) leads the survivors of an Indian attack back to Tombstone, and included in the party is the gun smuggler (Jory) who sold the warring Indians the guns. *NOTES:* Singer Vaughn Monroe's second and final film for Republic.

**841. Track the Man Down** (1/27/56) B&W 75 mins. (Crime). *DIR:* R. G. Springsteen. *A-PRO:* William N. Boyle. *SP:* Paul Erickson, Kenneth R. Hayles. *CAST:* Kent Taylor, Petula Clark, Renee Houston, Walter Rilla, George Rose, Mary MacKenzie, Kenneth Griffith, Ursula Howells, Lloyd Lamble, John Sanger, Bartlett Mullins, Frank Atkinson, John Welsh, Iris Vandeleur, Mona Lilian, Brian Franklin, Jack Lambert, Hugh Cameron, Eric Lander, Ted Palmer, Ned Hood, Charles Lloyd Pack, Arthur Lane, Michael Balfour, Michael Golden, Graeme Ashley. *SYN:* When a man (Rose) double-crosses his pals after a dog track robbery, he takes the money, tosses it into a suitcase, which he gives to his girl (Howells), who passes it to her sister (Clark), who boards a bus to take the money to the seashore and arouses the suspicions of a reporter (Taylor) taking the same coach. *NOTES:* Released in Britain in 1954.

**842. Traffic in Crime** (6/28/46) B&W 56 mins. (Crime). *DIR:* Lesley Selander. *A-PRO:* Donald H. Brown. *SP:* David Lang. Story by Leslie T. White. *CAST:* Kane Richmond, Adele

Mara, Anne Nagel, Wilton Graff, Roy Barcroft, Arthur Loft, Wade Crosby, Dick Curtis, Harry Cheshire, Robert Wilke, Charles Sullivan. *SYN:* An undercover policeman (Richmond) is out to break up two gambling rings in a small West Coast community, and also expose the corruption in his own precinct. *NOTES:* The plot line of this film appears to have been lifted whole from Dashiell Hammett's novel, *Red Harvest.*

**843. A Tragedy at Midnight** (2/2/42) B&W 69 mins. (Mystery). *DIR:* Joseph Santley. *A-PRO:* Robert North. *SP:* Isabel Dawn. Story by Hal Hudson, Sam Duncan. *CAST:* John Howard, Margaret Lindsay, Roscoe Karns, Mona Barrie, Keye Luke, Hobart Cavanaugh, Paul Harvey, Lilian Bond, Miles Mander, William Newell, Wendell Niles, Archie Twitchell. *SYN:* When a married couple (Howard, Lindsay), who like to solve murders that stump the police, take over a friend's apartment and find a girl murdered there, they leave just one step ahead of the police, and he broadcasts the crime's solution and all the background of the case on his radio show.

**844. The Trail Blazers** (11/11/40) B&W 58 mins. (Western). *DIR:* George Sherman. *A-PRO:* Harry Grey. *SP:* Barry Shipman. Story by Earle Snell. Based on characters created by William Colt MacDonald. *CAST:* Robert Livingston, Bob Steele, Rufe Davis, Pauline Moore, Weldon Heyburn, Carroll Nye, Tom Chatterton, Si Jenks, Mary Field, John Merton, Rex Lease, Robert Blair, Barry Hays, Pascale Perry, Harry Strang, Jack Kirk, Forrest Taylor, Horace B. Carpenter, Harrison Greene, Bud Osborne, Ray Teal, Cactus Mack, Bill Nestell, Chuck Baldra, Curley Dresden, Tom Smith, Matty Roubert, Herman Hack. *SYN:* The Three Mesquiteers (Livingston, Steele, Davis) work undercover as they bring the telegraph to town and stop an outlaw gang who are trying to sabotage it. *NOTES:* Re-edited for TV at 54 mins. The 33rd entry in the "Three Mesquiteers" series.

**845. Trail of Kit Carson** (7/11/45) B&W 57 mins. (Western). *DIR:* Lesley Selander. *A-PRO:* Stephen Auer. *SP:* Jack Natteford, Albert DeMond. Story by Jack Natteford. *CAST:* Allan ("Rocky") Lane, Helen Talbot, Tom London, Twinkle Watts, Roy Barcroft, Kenne Duncan, Jack Kirk, Bud Geary, Tom Dugan, George Chesebro, Robert Wilke, Freddie Chapman, Dickie Dillon, Herman Hack, John Carpenter, Henry Wills, Tom Steele, "Feather." *SYN:* Kit Carson (Lane) is determined to find out if his partner's death was murder or suicide.

**846. Trail of Robin Hood** (12/15/50) Trucolor 67 mins. (Western). *DIR:* William Witney. *A-PRO:* Edward J. White. *SP:* Gerald Geraghty. *CAST:* Roy Rogers, Penny Edwards, Gordon Jones, Jack Holt, Emory Parnell, Clifton Young, James Magill, Carol Nugent, Edward Cassidy, George Chesebro, Stanley Blystone, Lane Bradford, Ken Terrell, Foy Willing and the Riders of the Purple Sage, "Trigger," "Bullet." *GUEST STARS:* Rex Allen, Allan ("Rocky") Lane, Monte Hale, William Farnum, Tom Tyler, Ray ("Crash") Corrigan, Kermit Maynard, Tom Keene. *SYN:* Roy, with the help of several guest stars, helps retired B-western star Jack Holt, keep his Christmas tree business. *NOTES:* Roy Rogers' last feature done in color. Jack Holt and character actor George Chesebro play themselves in this film, and a highlight of the film occurs when longtime screen bad-guy Chesebro, shunned by the other old-time players, states: "I've been a villain in pictures for 20 years; now I'd like to be on the right side for a change."

**847. Trail of Vengeance** (3/29/37) B&W 60 mins. (Western). *DIR:* Sam Newfield. *PRO:* A. W. Hackel. *SP:* George Plympton, Fred Myton. Story by E. B. Mann. *CAST:* Johnny Mack Brown, Iris Meredith, Warner Richmond, Karl Hackett, Earle Hodgins, Frank LaRue, Frank Ellis, Lew Meehan, Frank Ball, Dick Curtis, Jim Corey, Horace Murphy, Richard Cramer, Steve Clark, Budd Buster, Jack C. Smith, Jack Kirk, Francis Walker, Tex Palmer, Wally West, Clyde McClary, Herman Hack, Horace B. Carpenter, Merrill McCormick, Ray Henderson. *SYN:* A cowboy (Brown) becomes involved in a range war as he searches for the killer of his brother.

**848. Trail to San Antone** (1/25/47) B&W 67 mins. (Western). *DIR:* John English. *A-PRO:* Armand Schaefer. *SP:* Jack Natteford, Luci Ward. *CAST:* Gene Autry, Peggy Stewart, Sterling Holloway, William (Bill) Henry, John Duncan, Tristram Coffin, Dorothy Vaughan, Edward Keane, Ralph Peters, The Cass County Boys, "Champion, Jr." *SYN:* Gene sets out to help in the rehabilitation of a crippled jockey (Duncan) so he can ride Gene's horse in the big race. *NOTES:* Re-edited for TV at 54 mins.

**849. Train to Alcatraz** (6/28/48) B&W 60 mins. (Prison). *DIR:* Philip Ford. *A-PRO:* Lou Brock. *SP:* Gerald Geraghty. *CAST:* Don ("Red") Barry, Janet Martin, William Phipps, Roy Barcroft, June Storey, Jane Darwell, Milburn Stone, Chester Clute, Ralph Dunn, Richard Irving, John Alvin, Michael Carr, Marc Krah, Denver Pyle, Iron Eyes Cody, Kenneth MacDonald, Harry Harvey, Steven Baron, Bobby Stone, Don Haggerty, John Doucette. *SYN:* Told via flashback, a group of prisoners headed for Alcatraz plan a big escape, but before it is over, all prisoners are killed with the exception of one (Phipps).

**850. The Traitor Within** (12/16/42) B&W 62 mins. (Drama). *DIR:* Frank McDonald. *A-PRO:* Armand Schaefer. *SP:* Jack Townley. Story by Charles G. Booth. *CAST:* Don ("Red") Barry, Jean Parker, George Cleveland, Ralph Morgan, Jessica Newcombe, Bradley Page, Dick Wessel, Emmett Vogan, Edward Keane, Eddie Acuff, Sam McDaniel, Eddie Johnson, Marjorie Cooley. *SYN:* When a truck driver (Barry) learns that the mayor (Morgan) of a town is not a World War I hero, he sets out to blackmail him which leads to tragic consequences.

**Transcontinent Express** (G.B. title) *see* **Rock Island Trail**

**851. Trent's Last Case** (9/22/53) B&W 90 mins. (Mystery). *DIR/PRO:* Herbert Wilcox. *SP:* Pamela Bower. Based on the novel by E. C. Bentley. A Wilcox-Neagle Production. A British Lion film. A Republic Presentation. *CAST:* Margaret Lockwood, Michael Wilding, Orson Welles, John McCallum, Miles Malleson, Hugh McDermott, Sam Kydd, Jack McNaughton, Henry Edwards, Kenneth Williams, Eileen Joyce. *SYN:* An investigative reporter (Wilding) sets out to prove that the death of an international financier (Welles) was murder, not suicide. *NOTES:* Two versions were previously filmed: one in 1920, and one in 1929, directed by Howard Hawks. Released in Britain in 1952.

**852. The Trespasser** (7/3/47) B&W 71 mins. (Mystery). *DIR:* George Blair. *A-PRO:* William J. O'Sullivan. *SP:* Jerry Gruskin. Adapted by Dorrell McGowan, Stuart McGowan. Story by Jerry Sackheim, Erwin Gelsey. *CAST:* Dale Evans, Warren Douglas, Janet Martin, Douglas Fowley, Adele Mara, Gregory Gay, Grant Withers, William Bakewell, Vince Barnett, Francis Pierlot, Joy Barlowe, Fred Graham, Dale Van Sickel, Betty Alexander, Joseph Crehan. *SYN:* A rookie reporter (Martin) and a veteran reporter (Fowley) set out to expose a book forging racket.

**The Trial of Portia Merriman** (G.B. title) *see* **Portia on Trial**

**853. Trial Without Jury** (7/8/50) B&W 60 mins. (Mystery). *DIR:* Philip Ford. *A-PRO:* Stephen Auer. *SP:* Albert DeMond. Adapted by Lawrence Goldman. Story by Rose Simon Kohn. *CAST:* Robert Rockwell, Barbara Fuller, Kent Taylor, Audrey Long, K. Elmo Lowe, Stanley Waxman, John Whitney, Barbara Billingsley, Ruthelma Stevens, William Grueneberg, Christine Larson, James Craven, William Haade, Bill Baldwin, Theodore Von Eltz, Sid Marion. *SYN:* A playwright (Taylor) is accused of murdering his producer (Von Eltz), and his girl (Long) suggests he rewrite his play to include the killing. Her brother (Rockwell), a police Lieutenant goes along with it, and when the play debuts, the killer is unmasked.

**854. Trigger, Jr.** (6/30/50) Trucolor 68 mins. (Western). *DIR:* William Witney. *A-PRO:* Edward J. White. *SP:* Gerald Geraghty. *CAST:* Roy Rogers, Dale Evans, Pat Brady, Gordon Jones, Grant Withers, Peter Miles, George Cleveland, Frank Fenton, I. Stanford Jolley, Stanley Andrews, Dale Van Sickel, Tom Steele, Jack Ingram, Foy Willing and the Riders of the Purple Sage, The Raynor Lehr Circus, "Trigger." *SYN:* Roy sets out to stop a crooked official (Withers) from extorting money from the local ranchers.

**855. The Trigger Trio** (10/18/37) B&W 60 mins. (Western). *DIR:* William Witney. *A-PRO:* Sol C. Siegel. *SP:* Oliver Drake, Joseph F. Poland. Story by Houston Branch, Joseph F. Poland. Based on characters created by William Colt MacDonald. *CAST:* Ray ("Crash") Corrigan, Max Terhune, Ralph Byrd, Sandra Corday, Robert Warwick, Cornelius Keefe, Hal Taliaferro, Willie Fung, Sammy McKim, Jack Ingram, Art Davis, Bob Burns, Fred Burns, Jerry Frank, Tex Billings, Harry Semels, "Buck." *SYN:* The Three Mesquiteers (Corrigan, Terhune, Byrd) track down the killer of a range inspector after he finds an outbreak of hoof and mouth disease. *NOTES:* Ralph Byrd's only appearance as a "Mesquiteer," substituting for Robert Livingston, hurt in a real-life swimming accident. The first feature film to be directed by William Witney. Re-edited for TV at 54 mins. The 10th entry in the "Three Mesquiteers" series.

**856. Trocadero** (4/24/44) B&W 74 mins. (Musical). *DIR:* William Nigh. *A-PRO:* Walter Colmes. *SP:* Allen Gale. Story by Charles F. Chaplin, Garrett Holmes. *CAST:* Rosemary Lane, Johnny

Downs, Ralph Morgan, Dick Purcell, Sheldon Leonard, Marjorie Manners, Emmett Vogan, Charles Calvert, Dewey Robinson, Ruth Hilliard, Eddie Bartell, Ida James, Patricia Kay, Betty Bradley, Jane Ellison, Wingy Mannone, The Stardusters, The Radio Rogues, Bob Chester and His Orchestra, Eddie LeBaron and His Orchestra, Matty Malneck and His Orchestra, Gus Arnheim and His Orchestra, *GUEST STARS*: Cliff Nazarro, Erskine Johnson, Dave Fleischer. *SYN:* A couple of youngsters (Downs, Lane) inherit a nightclub and make a success of it when they hire a swing band. *NOTES:* Eddie LeBaron was the real-life owner of the Trocadero.

**857. Tropical Heat Wave** (10/1/52) B&W 74 mins. (Crime). *DIR:* R. G. Springsteen. *A-PRO:* Sidney Picker. *SP:* Arthur T. Horman. *CAST:* Estelita Rodriguez, Robert Hutton, Grant Withers, Kristine Miller, Edwin Max, Lou Lubin, Martin Garralaga, Earl Lee, Lennie Bremen, Jack Kruschen. *SYN:* A professor of criminology (Hutton) poses as a gangster in order to help a singer (Rodriguez) and her uncle (Garralaga) when real gangsters threaten to take over their nightclub. *NOTES:* The famed song that shares this film's title is never sung in this film.

**858. Trouble in Store** (1/12/55) B&W 85 mins. (Comedy). *DIR:* John Paddy Carstairs. *PRO:* Maurice Cowan. *SP:* John Paddy Carstairs, Maurice Cowan, Ted Willis. A Two Cities Rank Production. A Republic Presentation. *CAST:* Norman Wisdom, Margaret Rutherford, Moira Lister, Derek Bond, Lana Morris, Jerry Desmonde, Megs Jenkins, Joan Sims, Michael Brennan, Joan Ingram, Eddie Leslie, Michael Ward, John Warwick, Perlita Neilson, Hamlyn Benson, Cyril Chamberlain, Ronan O'Casey, John Warren. *SYN:* When a clerk (Wisdom) begins working at a department store, he causes nothing but trouble for his boss (Desmonde), but ends up the hero when he thwarts a robbery. *NOTES:* Released in Britain in 1953.

**859. Trouble in the Glen** (12/1/54) Trucolor 91 mins. (Comedy). *DIR:* Herbert Wilcox. *PRO:* Herbert Wilcox, Herbert J. Yates. *SP:* Frank S. Nugent. Story by Maurice Walsh. An Everest Production. A Republic Presentation. *CAST:* Margaret Lockwood, Orson Welles, Forrest Tucker, Victor McLaglen, John McCallum, Janet Barrow, Eddie Byrne, Albert Chevalier, George Cormack, Dorothea Dell, Archie Duncan, Ann Gudrun, Grizelda Hervey, Alistair Hunter, William Kelly, Moultrie Kelsall, Stevenson Lang, Robin Lloyd, Margaret McCourt, Alex McCrindle, Jack Watling, Peter Sinclair, Mary MacKenzie, Duncan McIntyre, Jock McKay, Michael Shepley, Jack Stewart, F. A. Vinyals. *SYN:* A South American tycoon (Welles) arrives in Scotland to take possession of his inherited land, but he quickly antagonizes the locals by closing a highway that runs through the estate, evicting some tinkers who have long lived on the land, and upsetting a crippled girl (McCourt), who asks a visiting U.S. Air Force major, (Tucker), to help settle the matter. *NOTES:* Released in Britain in June, 1954.

**860. The Trusted Outlaw** (5/4/37) B&W 60 mins. (Western). *DIR:* Robert North Bradbury. *PRO:* A. W. Hackel. *SP:* George Plympton, Fred Myton. Story by Johnston McCulley. *CAST:*

Bob Steele, Lois January, Joan Barclay, Earl Dwire, Charles King, Richard Cramer, Hal Price, Budd Buster, Frank Ball, Oscar Gahan, George Morrell, Chick Hannon, Sherry Tansey, Clyde McClary, Jack Rockwell, Wally West, Ray Henderson, Fred Parker, Jack C. Smith, Al Taylor. *SYN:* An outlaw (Steele) decides to reform and go on the side of law and order but his former outlaw pals try to keep him in the gang.

**861. Tucson Raiders** (5/14/44) B&W 55 mins. (Western). *DIR:* Spencer G. Bennet. *A-PRO:* Edward J. White. *SP:* Anthony Coldeway. Story by Jack O'Donnell. Based on the comic strip created by Fred Harman. *CAST:* Bill Elliott, Bobby (Robert) Blake, George "Gabby" Hayes, Alice Fleming, Ruth Lee, Peggy Stewart, LeRoy Mason, Stanley Andrews, John Whitney, Bud Geary, Karl Hackett, Tom Steele, Tom Chatterton, Edward Cassidy, Edward Howard, Fred Graham, Frank McCarroll, Marshall Reed, Fred Pershing, Bert LeBaron, Joe Yrigoyen, Charles Sullivan, Neal Hart, Ted Wells, Carey Loftin, Foxy O'Callahan, Ken Terrell, Tommy Coats, *VOICES OF*: Roy Barcroft, Kenne Duncan, Tom London, Jack Kirk. *SYN:* The Duchess (Fleming) sends for her nephew Red Ryder (Elliott) and Little Beaver (Blake) when the territorial governor (Mason) threatens Painted Valley with crime and corruption. *NOTES:* This was the 1st entry in the "Red Ryder" feature series. Since Republic could not make another serial based on the "Red Ryder" character, but could make features, they were required by contractual agreement to carry the credit line on each feature "Based on Fred Harman's famous NEA comic, by special arrangement with Stephen Slesinger." With Bobby Blake as his sidekick, Elliott blazed his way out of the pages of a giant Red Ryder book to open the feature. Donald "Red" Barry played "Red Ryder" in the 1940 serial, *Adventures of Red Ryder.*

**862. The Tulsa Kid** (8/16/40) B&W 57 mins. (Western). *DIR/A-PRO:* George Sherman. *SP:* Oliver Drake, Anthony Coldeway. *CAST:* Don ("Red") Barry, Noah Beery, Sr., Luana Walters, David Durand, George Douglas, Ethan Laidlaw, Stanley Blystone, John Elliott, Jack Kirk, Fred "Snowflake" Toones, Charles Murphy, Joe Delacruz, Charles Thomas, Art Dillard, Cactus Mack, Jimmy Wakely and His Rough Riders (Jimmy Wakely, Johnny Bond, Dick Rinehart). *SYN:* A cowboy (Barry), who was taught all his tricks in the gunslinging trade by his foster father (Beery), must now face him in a showdown. *NOTES:* Re-edited for TV at 54 mins.

**863. Tumbling Tumbleweeds** (9/5/35) B&W 61 mins. (Western). *DIR:* Joseph Kane. *PRO:* Nat Levine. *SP:* Ford Beebe. Story by Alan Ludwig. *CAST:* Gene Autry, Smiley Burnette, Lucille Browne, Norma Taylor, George "Gabby" Hayes, Edward Hearn, Jack Rockwell, Frankie Marvin, George Chesebro, Eugene Jackson, Charles King, Slim Whitaker, George Burton, Tom London, Cornelius Keefe, Tommy Coats, Cliff Lyons, Bud Pope, Tracy Layne, Bud McClure, George Morrell, Oscar Gahan, Joe Girard, Henry Hall, Bart Carre, Tom Smith, Iris Meredith, Horace B. Carpenter, "Champion." *SYN:* When Gene returns home after a five-year absence to find his father has been murdered and his childhood companion (Browne) is accused of the crime, he sets out with two friends (Burnette, Hayes) from his medicine show to bring the killers to justice. NOTES: Gene Autry's first starring feature film and his first film for Republic. The directorial debut of Joseph Kane. Running times for this film vary between 57 and 61 mins. Re-edited for TV at 54 mins.

**864. Tuxedo Junction** (12/4/41) B&W 71 mins. (Comedy). DIR: Frank McDonald. A-PRO: Armand Schaefer. SP: Dorrell McGowan, Stuart McGowan. CAST: Leon Weaver, June Weaver, Frank Weaver, Thurston Hall, Frankie Darro, Sally Payne, Clayton Moore, Lorna Gray, William Benedict, Ken Lundy, Howard Hickman, Leonard Carey, Betty Blythe, Sam Flint, The Little Vagabonds. SYN: The Weavers (Leon, Frank, June) try to put together a winning float for the Rose Parade. NOTES: The title has nothing to do with the plot. The 8th entry in the "Weaver Brothers and Elviry" series. [British title: *The Gang Made Good*.]

**865. Twilight in the Sierras** (3/22/50) Trucolor 67 mins. (Western). DIR: William Witney. A-PRO: Edward J. White. SP: Sloan Nibley. CAST: Roy Rogers, Dale Evans, Estelita Rodriguez, Pat Brady, Russ Vincent, George Meeker, Fred Kohler, Jr., Edward Keane, House Peters, Jr., Pierce Lyden, Don Frost, Joseph Garro, William Lester, Bob Burns, Robert Wilke, Foy Willing and the Riders of the Purple Sage, "Trigger." SYN: A parole officer (Rogers), working on a ranch which employs parolees, is framed for murder when he comes upon a bunch of counterfeiters making gold certificates, and sets out to prove his innocence. NOTES: Re-edited for TV at 54 mins.

**866. Twilight on the Rio Grande** (4/1/47) B&W 71 mins. (Western). DIR: Frank McDonald. A-PRO: Armand Schaefer. SP: Dorrell McGowan, Stuart McGowan. CAST: Gene Autry, Sterling Holloway, Adele Mara, Bob Steele, Charles Evans, Martin Garralaga, Howard J. Negley, George J. Lewis, Nacho Galindo, Tex Terry, George Magrill, Bob Burns, Enrique Acosta, Frankie Marvin, Barry Norton, Gil Perkins, Nina Campana, Kenne Duncan, Tom London, Alberto Morin, Keith Richards, Ana Camargo, Donna Martell, Jack O'Shea, Steve Soldi, Bud Osborne, Frank McCarroll, Robert Wilke, Alex Montoya, Connie Menard, Joaquin Elizondo, The Cass County Boys, "Champion, Jr." SYN: Gene goes after the murderer of his partner (Steele) and uncovers a smuggling ring. NOTES: Re-edited for TV at 54 mins.

**867. The Twinkle in God's Eye** (10/13/55) B&W 73 mins. (Western). DIR: George Blair. A-PRO: Maurice Duke. PRO: Mickey Rooney. E-PRO: Herbert J. Yates. SP: P. J. Wolfson. CAST: Mickey Rooney, Coleen Gray, Hugh O'Brian, Joey Forman, Don ("Red") Barry, Touch (Mike) Connors, Jil Jarmyn, Kem Dibbs, Tony Garcen, Raymond Hatton, Ruta Lee, Clem Bevans. SYN: Fresh out of the seminary, a new preacher (Rooney) arrives in town to rebuild a church destroyed in an Indian raid and gains a following among the townspeople, despite some opposition from a gambling-hall owner (O'Brian).

**Two Black Sheep** (G.B. title) see **Two Sinners**

**868. Two-Gun Sheriff** (4/10/41) B&W 56 mins. (Western). DIR/A-PRO: George Sherman. SP: Doris Schroeder, Bennett Cohen. Story by Bennett Cohen. CAST: Don ("Red") Barry, Lynn

Merrick, Jay Novello, Lupita Tovar, Milton Kibbee, Fred Kohler, Jr., Marin Sais, Fred "Snowflake" Toones, Dirk Thane, Archie Hall (Arch Hall, Sr.), Charles Thomas, Lee Shumway, John Merton, Carleton Young, Curley Dresden, Buck Moulton, Bud McClure, Tex Parker, Herman Nolan, George Plues, Slim Whitaker, Jack O'Shea, John James, Pascale Perry, Al Taylor, Stanley Price, Forrest Taylor, Herman Hack, Frank Ellis, Rose Plummer. *SYN:* An outlaw (Barry), masquerades as the sheriff (Barry) of a town when he is kidnapped so that the outlaws can get their stolen cattle to market, but when the outlaws kill his girl (Tovar), he rescues his brother and they have a final showdown with the outlaws. *NOTES:* Don "Red" Barry plays a dual role in this film.

**869. Two Sinners** (9/14/35) B&W 72 mins. (Romance-Drama). *DIR:* Arthur Lubin. *PRO:* Trem Carr. *SP:* Jefferson Parker. Based on *Two Black Sheep* by Warwick Deeping. *CAST:* Otto Kruger, Martha Sleeper, Minna Gombell, Ferdinand Munier, Cora Sue Collins, Harrington Reynolds, Olaf Hytten, C. Montague Shaw, William P. Carleton, Harold Entwistle. *SYN:* When a man (Kruger) is paroled from prison, his life takes a change for the better when he meets a governess (Sleeper), but then complications arise when he meets her employer (Gombell) and daughter (Collins). [British title: *Two Black Sheep*.]

**870. Two Wise Maids** (2/15/37) B&W 70 mins. (Drama). *DIR:* Phil Rosen. *PRO:* Nat Levine. *SP:* Samuel Ornitz. Story by Endre Bohem. *CAST:* Alison Skipworth, Polly Moran, Hope Manning, Donald Cook, Jackie Searl, Lila Lee, Luis Alberni, Marcia Mae Jones, Maxie Rosenbloom, Harry Burns, Clarence Wilson, Selmer Jackson, John Hamilton, Theresa Maxwell Conover, Raymond Brown, James C. Morton, Stanley Blystone. *SYN:* Two old schoolteachers (Skipworth, Moran) try to reach their students, while the young principal (Cook) falls for a substitute teacher (Manning).

**Under California Skies** *see* **Under California Stars**

**871. Under California Stars** (5/1/48) Trucolor 70 mins. (Western). *DIR:* William Witney. *A-PRO:* Edward J. White. *SP:* Sloan Nibley, Paul Gangelin. Story by Paul Gangelin. *CAST:* Roy Rogers, Jane Frazee, Andy Devine, George Lloyd, Wade Crosby, Michael Chapin, House Peters, Jr., Steve Clark, Joseph Garro, Paul Power, John Wald, Bob Nolan and the Sons of the Pioneers, "Trigger." *SYN:* When Trigger is kidnapped and held for ransom, Roy and his ranch hands set out to retrieve him and bring the kidnappers to justice. *NOTES:* Re-edited for TV at 54 mins. [Alternate title: *Under California Skies*.]

**872. Under Colorado Skies** (12/15/47) Trucolor 65 mins. (Western). *DIR:* R. G. Springsteen. *A-PRO:* Melville Tucker. *SP:* Louise Rousseau. *CAST:* Monte Hale, Adrian Booth, Paul Hurst, William Haade, John Alvin, LeRoy Mason, Tom London, Steve Darrell, Gene Evans, Ted Adams, Steve Raines, Hank Patterson, Foy Willing and the Riders of the Purple Sage. *SYN:* A medical student (Hale) and part-time bank employee, accused of working with bank-robbers, uses his medical knowledge to track them down and clear his name.

**873. Under Cover Man** (9/24/36) B&W 57 mins. (Western). *DIR:* Albert

Ray. PRO: A. W. Hackel. SP: Andrew Bennison. CAST: Johnny Mack Brown, Suzanne Kaaren, Ted Adams, Lloyd Ingraham, Horace Murphy, Edward Cassidy, Frank Ball, Margaret Mann, Frank Darien, Dick Morehead, George Morrell, Art Dillard, Jim Corey, Ray Henderson. SYN: A Wells Fargo agent (Brown) goes undercover to catch a gang of outlaws. NOTES: Johnny Mack Brown's first Republic feature.

**874. Under Fiesta Stars** (8/25/41) B&W 64 mins. (Western). DIR: Frank McDonald. A-PRO: Harry Grey. SP: Karl Brown, Eliot Gibbons. Story by Karl Brown. CAST: Gene Autry, Smiley Burnette, Carol Hughes, Frank Darien, Joe Strauch, Jr., Pauline Drake, Ivan Miller, Sam Flint, Elias Gamboa, John Merton, Jack Kirk, Inez Palange, Curley Dresden, Hal Taliaferro, Frankie Marvin, Pascale Perry, "Champion." SYN: Gene and a girl (Hughes) inherit a gold mine. She wants to sell and he doesn't, so she hires some men to convince Gene to sell. NOTES: Re-edited for TV at 54 mins.

**Under Mexicali Skies** see **Under Mexicali Stars**

**875. Under Mexicali Stars** (11/20/50) B&W 67 mins. (Western). DIR: George Blair. A-PRO: Melville Tucker. SP: Bob Williams. CAST: Rex Allen, Dorothy Patrick, Roy Barcroft, Buddy Ebsen, Percy Helton, Walter Coy, Steve Darrell, Alberto Morin, Ray Walker, Frank Ferguson, Stanley Andrews, Robert Bice, "Koko." SYN: A treasury agent (Allen) and his sidekick (Ebsen) go after a gang of counterfeiters smuggling gold across the border into Mexico via helicopter. [Alternate title: Under Mexicali Skies.]

**876. Under Nevada Skies** (8/26/46) B&W 69 mins. (Western). DIR: Frank McDonald. A-PRO: Edward J. White. SP: Paul Gangelin, J. Benton Cheney. Story by M. Coates Webster. CAST: Roy Rogers, George "Gabby" Hayes, Dale Evans, Douglass Dumbrille, Leland Hodgson, Tristram Coffin, Rudolph Andres, LeRoy Mason, George Lynn, George J. Lewis, Tom Quinn, Iron Eyes Cody, Bob Nolan and the Sons of the Pioneers, "Trigger." SYN: When a gang of outlaws steal a secret map, which indicates the location of pitchblende deposits, Roy leads a posse of Indians against the outlaws. NOTES: This was the last in a long series of Rogers' westerns to be directed by Frank McDonald, to be replaced by William Witney. Re-edited for TV at 54 mins.

**877. Under Texas Skies** (9/20/40) B&W 57 mins. (Western). DIR: George Sherman. A-PRO: Harry Grey. SP: Anthony Coldeway, Betty Burbridge. Based on characters created by William Colt MacDonald. CAST: Robert Livingston, Bob Steele, Rufe Davis, Lois Ranson, Henry Brandon, Wade Boteler, Rex Lease, Walter Tetley, Yakima Canutt, Earle Hodgins, Curley Dresden, Jack Ingram, Jack Kirk, Ted Mapes, Vester Pegg, Charles King, Fred Burns, Al Haskell, Herman Hack, Silver Tip Baker, Forrest Taylor, Bob Burns, Jim Corey, Frank Ellis. SYN: The Three Mesquiteers (Livingston, Steele, Davis) set out to investigate the murder of a sheriff. NOTES: Rufe Davis and Bob Steele make their first appearances as Mesquiteers. Re-edited for TV at 54 mins. The 32nd entry in the "Three Mesquiteers" series.

**878. Under Western Stars** (4/20/38) B&W 65 mins. (Western). DIR: Joseph

Kane. A-PRO: Sol C. Siegel. SP: Dorrell McGowan, Stuart McGowan, Betty Burbridge. Story by Dorrell McGowan, Stuart McGowan. CAST: Roy Rogers, Smiley Burnette, Carol Hughes, Guy Usher, Tom Chatterton, Kenneth Harlan, Alden Chase, Brandon Beach, Earl Dwire, Jean Fowler, Dora Clement, Dick Elliott, Burr Caruth, Slim Whitaker, Jack Rockwell, Frankie Marvin, Earle Hodgins, Jack Kirk, Fred Burns, Curley Dresden, Jack Ingram, Tex Cooper, Bill Wolfe, The Maple City Four, "Trigger." SYN: Roy is elected congressman from a dust-bowl state who journeys to Washington, D.C., after being elected by fellow ranchers and cowpokes, to advocate public ownership of utilities, specifically, water, and gains support of his fellow congressmen to get his bill passed by showing them a documentary film on dust bowl conditions. NOTES: Originally scheduled to star Gene Autry, this was Roy Rogers' first starring feature. Re-edited for TV at 54 mins. Academy Award Nominee — Best Song.

**879. Undercover Woman** (4/11/46) B&W 56 mins. (Mystery-Comedy). DIR: Thomas Carr. A-PRO: Rudolph E. Abel. SP: Jerry Sackheim, Sherman L. Lowe. Adapted by Robert Metzler. Based on a play by Sylvia G. L. Dannet. CAST: Stephanie Bachelor, Robert Livingston, Richard Fraser, Isabel Withers, Helene Heigh, Edythe Elliott, John Dehner, Elaine Lange, Betty Blythe, Tom London, Larry J. Blake. SYN: At a local dude ranch, a private eye (Bachelor) and a local sheriff (Livingston), together with her assistant (Blythe) and a newspaperman (Dehner), set out to find the killer of an adulterous husband (Blake) she was shadowing.

**Underground Spy** see **The Red Menace**

**880. The Unearthly** (6/28/57) B&W 73 mins. (Horror). DIR/PRO: Brooke L. Peters. A-PRO: Robert A. Terry. SP: Geoffrey Dennis, Jane Mann. Story by Jane Mann. An AB-PT Pictures Production. A Republic Presentation. CAST: John Carradine, Allison Hayes, Myron Healey, Sally Todd, Marilyn Buferd, Arthur Batanides, Tor Johnson, Raymond Guta, Gloria Petroff, Harry Fleer, Roy Gordon, Guy Prescott, Paul McWilliams. SYN: A scientist (Carradine) is driven to find the secret of eternal youth by operating on humans and is assisted by a mutant named Lobo (Johnson), but his experiments are failures and the humans are doomed to live their lives as mutants in the laboratory's secret cellar. NOTES: Double-billed in some areas with Beginning of the End.

**Unforgotten Crime** see **The Affairs of Jimmy Valentine**

**881. Unmasked** (1/30/50) B&W 60 mins. (Crime). DIR: George Blair. A-PRO: Stephen Auer. SP: Albert DeMond, Norman S. Hall. Story by Manuel Seff, Paul Yawitz. CAST: Robert Rockwell, Barbara Fuller, Raymond Burr, Hillary Brooke, Paul Harvey, Norman Budd, John Eldredge, Emory Parnell, Russell Hicks, Grace Gillern, Lester Sharpe, Charles Quigley, Barbara Pepper, Charles Trowbridge, Harry Harvey. SYN: A scandal sheet editor (Burr), who kills a lady he's been blackmailing, finds himself in the clear when her husband (Paul Harvey), framed for the crime, kills himself, but the dead man's daughter (Fuller), who doesn't believe her father was a murderer, and a cop (Rockwell) search for the truth.

**882. Untamed Heiress** (4/12/54) B&W 70 mins. (Musical-Comedy). *DIR:* Charles Lamont. *A-PRO:* Sidney Picker. *E-PRO:* Herbert J. Yates. *SP:* Barry Shipman. Story by Jack Townley. *CAST:* Judy Canova, Don ("Red") Barry, George Cleveland, Taylor Holmes, Chick Chandler, Jack Kruschen, Hugh Sanders, Douglas Fowley, William Haade, Ellen Corby, Dick Wessel, James Flavin, Tweeny Canova. *SYN:* A gold prospector (Cleveland), searches for his lost love, who has since died, and locates her daughter (Canova), who has gotten mixed up with some gangsters; when the prospector gets into trouble, she and her gangster friends come to his rescue.

**883. Utah** (3/21/45) B&W 78 mins. (Western). *DIR:* John English. *A-PRO:* Donald H. Brown. *SP:* Jack Townley, John K. Butler. Story by Gilbert Wright, Betty Burbridge. *CAST:* Roy Rogers, George "Gabby" Hayes, Dale Evans, Peggy Stewart, Beverly Loyd, Grant Withers, Jill Browning, Vivien Oakland, Hal Taliaferro, Jack Rutherford, Emmett Vogan, Edward Cassidy, Ralph Colby, Forrest Taylor, Horace B. Carpenter, Bob Nolan and the Sons of the Pioneers, "Trigger." *SYN:* Roy tries to convince a showgirl (Evans) not to sell her ranch to sheepmen to finance her show in Chicago. *NOTES:* A reworking of the 1937 Republic feature, *Springtime in the Rockies.* Re-edited for TV at 54 mins.

**884. Utah Wagon Train** (10/15/51) B&W 67 mins. (Western). *DIR:* Philip Ford. *A-PRO:* Melville Tucker. *SP:* John K. Butler. *CAST:* Rex Allen, Penny Edwards, Buddy Ebsen, Roy Barcroft, Sarah Padden, Grant Withers, Arthur Space, Edwin Rand, Robert Karnes, William Holmes, Stanley Andrews, Frank Jenks, Forrest Taylor, "Koko." *SYN:* A wagonmaster (Allen) leads a modern day wagon train along an ancient wagon trail and searches for the killer of his father among the group.

**885. Valley of Hunted Men** (11/13/42) B&W 60 mins. (Western). *DIR:* John English. *A-PRO:* Louis Gray. *SP:* Albert DeMond, Morton Grant. Story by Charles Tetford. Based on characters created by William Colt MacDonald. *CAST:* Bob Steele, Tom Tyler, Jimmie Dodd, Anna Marie Stewart, Edward Van Sloan, Roland Varno, Edythe Elliott, Arno Frey, Dick French, Bob Stevenson, George Neise, Louis (Duke) Adlon, Budd Buster, Hal Price, William Benedict, Charles Flynn, Rand Brooks, Kenne Duncan, Jack Kirk, Kermit Maynard. *SYN:* The Three Mesquiteers (Steele, Tyler, Dodd) expose a Nazi posing as the nephew of a trusted German refugee (Van Sloan) who has developed a system to obtain valuable rubber from culebra plants. *NOTES:* The 47th entry in the "Three Mesquiteers" series.

**886. Valley of the Zombies** (5/24/46) B&W 56 mins. (Horror). *DIR:* Philip Ford. *A-PRO/SP:* Dorrell McGowan, Stuart McGowan. Story by Royal K. Cole, Sherman L. Lowe. *CAST:* Robert Livingston, Adrian Booth, Ian Keith, Thomas E. Jackson, Charles Trowbridge, Earle Hodgins, LeRoy Mason, William Haade, Wilton Graff, Charles Cane, Russ Clark, Chuck Hamilton. *SYN:* A mad undertaker (Keith) returns from the dead to get revenge on those who had him committed to an insane asylum. *NOTES:* Double-billed in some areas with *The Catman of Paris.*

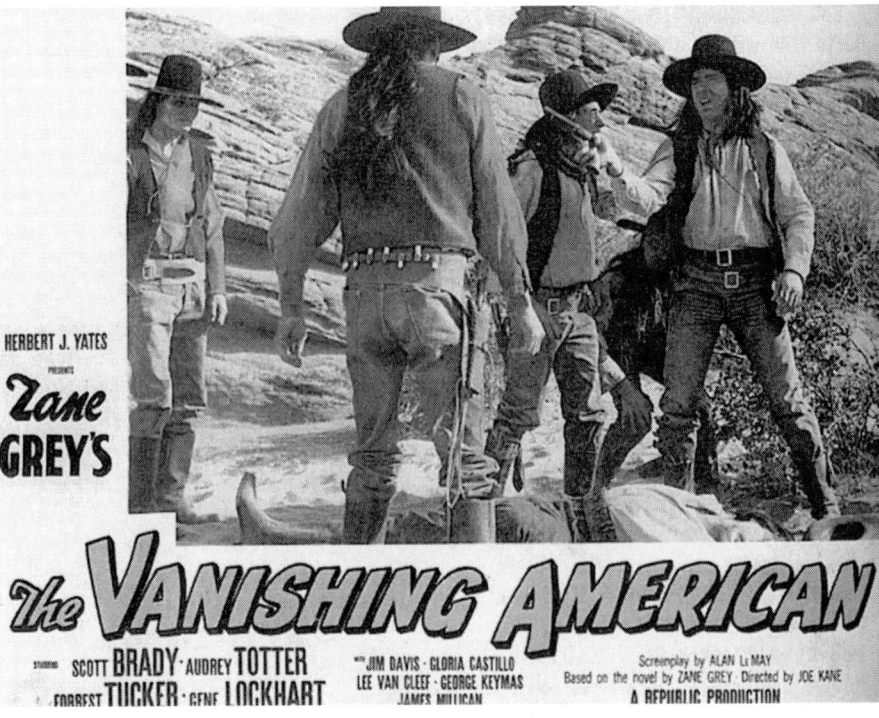

**887. The Vampire's Ghost** (5/21/45) B&W 59 mins. (Horror). *DIR:* Lesley Selander. *A-PRO:* Rudolph E. Abel. *SP:* Leigh Brackett, John K. Butler. Story by Leigh Brackett. Suggested by *The Vampyre* by Polidori. *CAST:* John Abbott, Charles Gordon, Peggy Stewart, Grant Withers, Adele Mara, Emmett Vogan, Roy Barcroft, Martin Wilkins, Frank Jaquet, Jimmy Aubrey, Zack Williams, Floyd Shackelford, George Carlton, Frederick Howard, Constantine Romanoff, Jim Thorpe, Tom Steele, Charles Sullivan, Pedro Regas. *SYN:* A 400-year-old zombie-vampire (Abbott), who lives and rules on the west coast of Africa, has been condemned to wander the Earth forever due to an ancient curse laid on his head back in 1588. *NOTES:* Double-billed in some areas with *The Phantom Speaks*.

**888. The Vanishing American** (11/17/55) B&W 90 mins. (Western). *DIR/A-PRO:* Joseph Kane. *E-PRO:* Herbert J. Yates. *SP:* Alan LeMay. Based on the novel by Zane Grey. *CAST:* Scott Brady, Audrey Totter, Forrest Tucker, Gene Lockhart, Jim Davis, John Dierkes, Gloria Castillo, Julian Rivero, Lee Van Cleef, George Keymas, Charles Stevens, Jay Silverheels, James Millican, Glenn Strange. *SYN:* A Navajo brave (Brady) teams up with a lady rancher (Totter) to stand up to the evil whites and turncoat Apaches who are trying to drive her and his people off their land. *NOTES:* A remake of the 1926 Paramount film, which starred Richard Dix in the title role.

**889. The Vanishing Westerner** (3/31/50) B&W 60 mins. (Western). *DIR:* Philip Ford. *A-PRO:* Melville Tucker. *SP:* Bob Williams. *CAST:*

Monte Hale, Paul Hurst, Aline Towne, Roy Barcroft, Arthur Space, Richard Anderson, William Phipps, Don Haggerty, Dick Curtis, Rand Brooks, Edmund Cobb, Harold Goodwin, Dale Van Sickel, Art Dillard, Cactus Mack, Bob Reeves, Bob Burns, Dudley Rose. *SYN:* A cowboy (Hale) is falsely accused of murdering a sheriff (Space) who pretends to be his own twin brother from England. *NOTES:* Arthur Space plays a dual role in this film. A remake of the 1946 Universal film, *Lawless Breed.*

**890. Vigilante Hideout** (8/6/50) B&W 60 mins. (Western). *DIR:* Fred C. Brannon. *A-PRO:* Gordon Kay. *SP:* Richard Wormser. *CAST:* Allan ("Rocky") Lane, Eddy Waller, Roy Barcroft, Virginia Herrick, Cliff Clark, Don Haggerty, Paul Campbell, Guy Teague, Art Dillard, Chick Hannon, Bob Woodward, "Black Jack." *SYN:* A cowboy (Lane) helps an eccentric inventor (Waller) find water for his town which is threatening to fold up due to drought.

**891. Vigilantes of Boomtown** (2/15/47) B&W 56 mins. (Western). *DIR:* R. G. Springsteen. *A-PRO:* Sidney Picker. *SP:* Earle Snell. Based on the comic strip created by Fred Harman. *CAST:* Allan ("Rocky") Lane, Bobby (Robert) Blake, Martha Wentworth, Roscoe Karns, Roy Barcroft, Peggy Stewart, George Turner, Eddie Simms, George Chesebro, Bobby Barber, George Lloyd, Ted Adams, John Dehner, Earle Hodgins, Harlan Briggs, Budd Buster, Jack O'Shea, Tom Steele, Herman Hack, Pascale Perry, Herman Nolan, LeRoy Mason (Narrator). *SYN:* In Carson City, Red Ryder (Lane) must protect the box office receipts during a championship boxing match between James J. Corbett (Turner) and Bob Fitzsimmons (Dehner). *NOTES:* This picture is loosely based on an actual heavyweight championship match that took place between champion James J. Corbett and challenger Bob Fitzsimmons in Carson City, Nevada, in 1897. The 19th entry in the "Red Ryder" feature series.

**892. Vigilantes of Dodge City** (11/15/44) B&W 54 mins. (Western). *DIR:* Wallace A. Grissel. *A-PRO:* Stephen Auer. *SP:* Norman S. Hall, Anthony Coldeway. Story by Norman S. Hall. Based on the comic strip created by Fred Harman. *CAST:* Bill Elliott, Bobby (Robert) Blake, Alice Fleming, Linda Stirling, LeRoy Mason, Hal Taliaferro, Tom London, Stephen Barclay, Bud Geary, Kenne Duncan, Robert Wilke, Horace B. Carpenter, Stanley Andrews. *SYN:* Red Ryder (Elliott) sets out to stop a gang of crooks from taking over the Duchess' freight and stage line. *NOTES:* The 5th entry in the "Red Ryder" feature series.

**893. Village Barn Dance** (1/30/40) B&W 74 mins. (Musical-Romance). *DIR:* Frank McDonald. *A-PRO:* Armand Schaefer. *SP:* Dorrell McGowan, Stuart McGowan. *CAST:* Richard Cromwell, Doris Day, George Barbier, Esther Dale, Robert Baldwin, Andrew Tombes, Barbara Jo Allen (Vera Vague), Don Wilson, Helen Troy, Frank Cook, Lulu Belle and Scotty, The Kidoodlers, The Texas Wanderers. *SYN:* A woman (Day) decides to save her community by marrying a rich industrialist (Baldwin) who has promised to bring jobs to the area if she will do so, but her intended (Cromwell), with the townsfolk, has been working up a radio program that will save the town and stop her marriage. *NOTES:* The Doris Day who appears in this film is *not* the well-known actress/vocalist.

894. **The Wac from Walla Walla** (10/10/52) B&W 83 mins. (Comedy). DIR: William Witney. A-PRO: Sidney Picker. SP: Arthur T. Horman. CAST: Judy Canova, Stephen Dunne, George Cleveland, June Vincent, Irene Ryan, Roy Barcroft, Allen Jenkins, George Chandler, Elizabeth Slifer, Thurston Hall, Sarah Spencer, Dick Wessel, Pattee Chapman, Dick Elliott, Carl "Alfalfa" Switzer, Tom Powers, Jarma Lewis, Emlen Davies, Virginia Carroll, Evelynne Smith, Phyllis Kennedy, The Republic Rhythm Riders. SYN: A woman (Canova) accidentally enlists in the Women's Army Corps and foils the attempt of enemy agents trying to steal the plans for a guided missile. [British title: *Army Capers*.]

895. **Wagon Tracks West** (10/28/43) B&W 55 mins. (Western). DIR: Howard Bretherton. A-PRO: Louis Gray. SP: William Lively. CAST: Bill Elliott, George "Gabby" Hayes, Tom Tyler, Anne Jeffreys, Rick Vallin, Robert Frazer, Roy Barcroft, Charles Miller, Tom London, Cliff Lyons, Jack Rockwell, Kenne Duncan, Minerva Urecal, Hal Price, Bill Nestell, Frank Ellis, Hank Bell, Jack O'Shea, Ray Jones, Jack Ingram, Curley Dresden, Frank McCarroll, Marshall Reed, Ben Corbett, Jack Montgomery, Tom Steele, J. W. Cody, Roy Butler, "Sonny." SYN: Bill and "Gabby" help to get rid of a crooked Indian commissioner (Frazier) who is trying to run the Indians off their land by poisoning their water.

896. **Wagon Wheels Westward** (12/21/ 45) B&W 56 mins. (Western). DIR: R. G. Springsteen. A-PRO: Sidney Picker. SP: Earle Snell. Story by Gerald Geraghty. Based on the comic strip created by Fred Harman. CAST: Bill Elliott, Bobby (Robert) Blake, Alice Fleming, Linda Stirling, Roy Barcroft, Emmett Lynn, Jay Kirby, Dick Curtis, George J. Lewis, Bud Geary, Tom London, Kenne Duncan, George Chesebro, Tom Chatterton, Frank Ellis, Bob McKenzie, Jack Kirk, "Thunder." SYN: Red Ryder (Elliott) has to deal with a crooked land swindler (Barcroft) when he leads a wagon train of settlers in search of buying land. NOTES: The 12th entry in the "Red Ryder" feature series.

897. **Wagons Westward** (6/19/40) B&W 70 mins. (Western). DIR: Lew Landers. A-PRO: Armand Schaefer. SP: Harrison Jacobs, Joseph Moncure March. CAST: Chester Morris, Anita Louise, Buck Jones, Ona Munson, George "Gabby" Hayes, Guinn "Big Boy" Williams, Douglas Fowley, Edmund Cobb, John Gallaudet, Virginia Brissac, Trevor Bardette, Selmer Jackson, Charles Stevens, Joe McGuinn, Tex Cooper, Art Dillard, Horace B. Carpenter, Tom Smith, The Hull Twins. SYN: A twin (Morris), protected by a crooked sheriff (Jones), gets arrested and his twin brother (Morris), who is an undercover government agent, assumes his outlaw brother's identity to bring his brother's gang to justice. NOTES: Chester Morris plays a dual role in this film. This film was not well received by the public because Buck Jones was cast as a crooked sheriff. Buck Jones' only film for Republic. Re-edited for TV at 54 mins.

898. **Wake of the Red Witch** (3/1/ 49) B&W 106 mins. (Adventure). DIR: Edward Ludwig. A-PRO: Edmund Grainger. SP: Harry Brown, Kenneth Gamet. Based on the novel by Garland Roark. CAST: John Wayne, Gail Russell, Gig Young, Adele Mara, Luther

GARLAND ROARK'S FAMOUS SEA STORY!
JOHN WAYNE
GAIL RUSSELL
IN
WAKE OF THE RED WITCH
with
GIG YOUNG
ADELE MARA • LUTHER ADLER
and
EDUARD FRANZ • GRANT WITHERS • HENRY DANIEL
PAUL FIX • JEFF COREY
Directed by EDWARD LUDWIG
Associate Producer—EDMUND GRAINGER
A REPUBLIC PICTURE

Adler, Eduard Franz, Grant Withers, Henry Daniell, Paul Fix, Dennis Hoey, Jeff Corey, Erskine Sanford, Duke Kahanamoku, John Wengraf, Henry Brandon, Myron Healey, John Pickard, Harlan Warde, Fernando Alvarado, Jose Alvarado, Carlos Thompson, Mickey Simpson, Grant Means, Jim Nolan, Harry Vejar, David Clarke, Fred Fox, Al Kikume, Leo C. Richmond, Harold Lishman, Fred Libby, Robert W. Wood, Fred Graham, Rory Mallinson, Norman Rainey, Wallace Scott, Kuka Tuitama, George Pliz. *SYN:* A ship's captain (Wayne) incurs the wrath of a shipping tycoon (Adler) over pearls and a woman's (Russell) love. *NOTES:* The first part of the film is a flashback, and the film's final image is of John Wayne and Gail Russell aboard the "Red Witch" as it sails into the world of their afterlife. John Wayne would use the fictitious company name "Batjac" for his production company in the fifties. Released in a "Computer-colorized" version in the 1980s by the new Republic studios.

**899. Wall Street Cowboy** (8/6/39) B&W 66 mins. (Western). *DIR/A-PRO:* Joseph Kane. *SP:* Gerald Geraghty, Norman S. Hall. Story by Doris Schroeder. *CAST:* Roy Rogers, George "Gabby" Hayes, Raymond Hatton, Ann Baldwin, Pierre Watkin, Craig Reynolds, Ivan Miller, George Letz, Reginald Barlow, Adrian Morris, Jack Roper, Jack Ingram, Fred Burns, Paul Fix, George Chesebro, Ted Mapes, Louisiana Lou (Eva Greenwood), "Trigger." *SYN:* Roy, "Gabby" and Chuckwalla (Hatton) leave their ranch and head to New York to stop a powerful Wall Street conglomerate from stripping their ranch land, because a valuable mineral, Molybdenum, a mineral used in the mining of steel, has been discovered on the property. *NOTES:* Re-edited for TV at 54 mins.

**War Brides** (G.B. title) *see* **G. I. War Brides**

**War of the Wildcats** (G.B. and Re-release title) *see* **In Old Oklahoma**

**War Shock** (G.B. title) *see* **A Woman's Devotion**

**Washington Cowboy** *see* **Rovin' Tumbleweeds**

**900. The Wayward Girl** (9/22/57) B&W/Naturama 71 mins. (Drama). *DIR:* Lesley Selander. *A-PRO:* William J. O'Sullivan. *SP:* Houston Branch, Frederic Louis Fox. A Vanity Production. A Republic Presentation. *CAST:* Marcia Henderson, Peter Walker, Katherine Barrett, Whit Bissell, Rita Lynn, Peg Hillias, Tracey Roberts, Ray Teal, Ric Roman, Barbara Eden, Grandon Rhodes, Francis DeSales, John Maxwell. *SYN:* A girl (Henderson) becomes the victim of an unkind stepmother (Barrett) when she defends herself against her stepmother's boyfriend and is charged with murder. The stepmother eventually confesses to the murder, but the girl ends up paroled in the care of lonely-hearts club operator (Bissell), who actually runs a white slavery ring.

**901. The Weapon** (5/17/57) B&W 80 mins. (Thriller). *DIR:* Val Guest. *PRO:* Hal E. Chester, Frank Bevis. *SP:* Fred Freiberger. Story by Fred Freiberger, Hal E. Chester. A Periclean Production. A Republic Presentation. *CAST:* Steve Cochran, Lizabeth Scott, Herbert Marshall, Nicole Maurey, Jon Whiteley, George Cole, Laurence Naismith, Stanley Maxted, Denis Shaw, Fred Johnson,

**SHE FOUGHT For The Right To Love...In A City Of Violence And Terror!**

# The WAYWARD GIRL
NATURAMA

Starring
**MARCIA HENDERSON · PETER WALKER**
**KATHARINE BARRETT · WHIT BISSELL**

with RITA LYNN · PEG HILLIAS · TRACEY ROBERTS · RAY TEAL · Written by HOUSTON BRANCH and FREDERIC LOUIS FOX
Produced by WILLIAM J. O'SULLIVAN · Directed by LESLEY SELANDER · REPUBLIC PICTURES presents A VARIETY PRODUCTION

John Horsley, Basil Dignam, Richard Goolden, Arthur Lovegrove, Felix Felton, Joan Schofield, Myrtle Reed, Roland Brand, Ryck Rydon, Vivian Matalon, Peter Augustine, George Bradford, Peter Godsell, Frazer Hines, Aston and Renee. *SYN:* A youngster (Whiteley) accidentally shoots his playmate with a gun he finds and then hides the weapon and runs away, but the gun turns out to be the murder weapon in a case involving a U.S. Army officer 10 years earlier, and a C.I.D. officer (Cochran) is in pursuit of the boy, as is the murderer of the Army man.

902. **Web of Danger** (6/10/47) B&W 58 mins. (Drama). *DIR:* Philip Ford. *A-PRO:* Donald H. Brown. *SP:* David Lang, Milton Raison. *CAST:* Adele Mara, Bill Kennedy, Damian O'Flynn, Richard Loo, Victor Sen Yung, Roy Barcroft, William Hall, J. Farrell MacDonald, Michael Branden, Edward Gargan, Chester Clute, Ralph Sanford, Russell Hicks. *SYN:* Two construction workers (Kennedy, O'Flynn) put aside their differences as they try to finish a bridge to help refugees flee a flooded valley.

903. **Wells Fargo Gunmaster** (5/15/51) B&W 60 mins. (Western). *DIR:* Philip Ford. *A-PRO:* Gordon Kay. *SP:* M. Coates Webster. *CAST:* Allan ("Rocky") Lane, Chubby Johnson, Mary Ellen Kay, Michael Chapin, Roy Barcroft, Walter Reed, Stuart Randall, William Bakewell, George Meeker, Anne O'Neal, James Craven, Forrest Taylor, Lee Roberts, Jack Perrin, "Black Jack." *SYN:* A special investigator (Lane) is hired by Wells Fargo to stop a rash of holdups and bring those responsible to justice.

904. **West of Cimarron** (12/15/41) B&W 56 mins. (Western). *DIR:* Les Orlebeck. *A-PRO:* Louis Gray. *SP:* Albert DeMond, Don Ryan. Based on characters created by William Colt MacDonald. *CAST:* Bob Steele, Tom Tyler, Rufe Davis, Lois Collier, James Bush, Guy Usher, Hugh Prosser, Cordell Hickman, Roy Barcroft, Budd Buster, Mickey Rentschler, John James, Bud Geary, Cactus Mack, Stanley Blystone. *SYN:* The Three Mesquiteers (Steele, Tyler, Davis) take on carpetbaggers robbing the populace in post-Civil War Texas. *NOTES:* A remake of the 1936 Republic feature, *The Lonely Trail*. Republic's 41st entry in the "Three Mesquiteers" series.

**West of Suez** (G.B. title) *see* **The Fighting Wildcats**

**West of the Badlands** *see* **The Border Legion**

**West of the Great Divide** *see* **North of the Great Divide**

905. **The West Side Kid** (8/23/43) B&W 57 mins. (Drama). *DIR/A-PRO:* George Sherman. *SP:* Albert Beich, Anthony Coldeway. *CAST:* Don ("Red") Barry, Henry Hull, Dale Evans, Chick Chandler, Matt McHugh, Nana Bryant, Walter Catlett, Edward Gargan, Chester Clute, Peter Lawford, George Metaxa. *SYN:* A newspaper publisher (Hull), unhappy with his family full of ingrates, offers a gangster (Barry) the princely sum of $25 to kill him. *NOTES:* This was Dale Evans' first dramatic role after appearing in musicals. The following year she teamed for the first time with Roy Rogers.

906. **Western Jamboree** (12/2/38) B&W 56 mins. (Western). *DIR:* Ralph Staub. *A-PRO:* Harry Grey. *SP:* Gerald

Geraghty. Story by Patricia Harper. *CAST:* Gene Autry, Smiley Burnette, Jean Rouverol, Esther Muir, Joe Frisco, Frank Darien, Margaret Armstrong, Harry Holman, Edward Raquello, Bentley Hewlett, Kermit Maynard, George Walcott, Ray Teal, Frank Ellis, Eddie Dean, Davison Clark, Jack Perrin, Jack Ingram, "Champion." *SYN:* Gene is after a gang of crooks who secretly lay pipeline to tap the well of valuable helium gas which lies beneath a ranch owner's land. *NOTES:* The German dirigible *Hindenberg* which used inflammable hydrogen in its gas bags had burst into flames during its landing approach in New Jersey the previous year, thus causing interest in non-inflammable helium. The film debut of Ray Teal. Re-edited for TV at 54 mins.

**907. Westward Ho!** (8/19/35) B&W 60 mins. (Western). *DIR:* Robert North Bradbury. *PRO:* Paul Malvern. *E-PRO:* Trem Carr. *SP:* Lindsley Parsons, Robert Emmett. Continuity by Harry Friedman. Story by Lindsley Parsons, Robert Emmett. A Republic-Lone Star Production. *CAST:* John Wayne, Sheila Mannors, Frank McGlynn, Jr., Jack Curtis, Yakima Canutt, Bradley Metcalfe, Hank Bell, Mary MacLaren, James Farley, Dick Jones, Glenn Strange, Lloyd Ingraham, Frank Ellis, Earl Dwire, Fred Burns, Jack Kirk, Tex Palmer, Chuck Baldra, Charles Sargent, Henry Hall, Ray Henderson, Charles Brinley, Edward Hearn, Al Taylor, Herman Hack, Silver Tip Baker, Fred Parker, Eddie Parker, The Singing Riders. *SYN:* A cowboy (Wayne) sets out to catch the gang of outlaws that murdered his parents not knowing that his long lost brother (McGlynn, Jr.), who was kidnapped by the outlaws, is a member of the gang. *NOTES:* Republic's first feature release and John Wayne's first film for Republic.

**908. Westward Ho** (4/24/42) B&W 56 mins. (Western). *DIR:* John English. *A-PRO:* Louis Gray. *SP:* Morton Grant, Doris Schroeder. Story by Morton Grant. Based on characters created by William Colt MacDonald. *CAST:* Bob Steele, Tom Tyler, Rufe Davis, Evelyn Brent, Donald Curtis, Lois Collier, Emmett Lynn, John James, Tom Seidel, Jack Kirk, Budd Buster, Kenne Duncan, Milton Kibbee, Edmund Cobb, Monte Montague, Al Taylor, Bud Osborne, Jack Montgomery, Horace B. Carpenter, John Cason, Jack O'Shea, Ray Jones, Tex Palmer, Curley Dresden. *SYN:* The Three Mesquiteers (Steele, Tyler, Davis) go after a town banker who is the leader of a gang of thieves. *NOTES:* The 44th entry in the "Three Mesquiteers" series. [TV title: *Riders for Justice.*]

**Wheel of Fortune** see **462 A Man Betrayed**

**909. When Gangland Strikes** (3/15/56) B&W 70 mins. (Crime). *DIR:* R. G. Springsteen. *A-PRO:* William J. O'Sullivan. *SP:* John K. Butler, Frederic Louis Fox. *CAST:* Raymond Greenleaf, Marjie Millar, John Hudson, Anthony Caruso, Marian Carr, Slim Pickens, Mary Treen, Ralph Dumke, Morris Ankrum, Robert Emmett Keane, Addison Richards, John Gallaudet, Paul Birch, Richard Deacon, James Best, Jim Hayward, Peter Mamakos, Fred Siterman, Dick Elliott, Norman Leavitt, Jack Perrin. *SYN:* A country prosecutor (Greenleaf) puts aside his duties and devotes his energy to saving his blackmailed daughter (Millar) from a murder charge. *NOTES:* A remake of the 1939 Republic feature, *Main Street Lawyer.*

**When We Look Back** *see* **Frisco Waterfront**

**910. Whispering Footsteps** (12/20/43) B&W 54 mins. (Thriller). *DIR:* Howard Bretherton. *A-PRO:* George Blair. *SP:* Gertrude Walker, Dane Lussier. Story by Gertrude Walker. *CAST:* John Hubbard, Rita Quigley, Joan Blair, Charles Halton, Cy Kendall, Juanita Quigley, Mary Gordon, William Benedict, Matt McHugh, Marie Blake. *SYN:* A bank clerk (Hubbard) is suspected of murdering several young girls in his home town.

**911. Who Killed Aunt Maggie?** (11/1/40) B&W 70 mins. (Mystery-Comedy). *DIR:* Arthur Lubin. *A-PRO:* Albert J. Cohen. *SP:* Stuart Palmer. Additional dialogue by Frank Gill, Jr., Hal Fimberg. Based on the novel by Medora Field. *CAST:* John Hubbard, Wendy Barrie, Edgar Kennedy, Elizabeth Patterson, Onslow Stevens, Joyce Compton, Walter Abel, Mona Barrie, Willie Best, Daisy Lee Mothershed, Milton Parsons, Tom Dugan, William Haade, Joel Friedkin. *SYN:* A private detective (Hubbard) sets out to investigate murders in an old house. *NOTES:* Frank Gill, Jr. and Hal Fimberg were uncredited.

**912. The Wild Blue Yonder** (12/5/51) B&W 98 mins. (War). *DIR:* Allan Dwan. *E-PRO:* Herbert J. Yates. *SP:* Richard Tregaskis. Story by Andrew Geer, Charles Grayson. *CAST:* Wendell Corey, Vera Ralston, Forrest Tucker, Phil Harris, Walter Brennan, William Ching, Ruth Donnelly, Harry Carey, Jr., Penny Edwards, Wally Cassell, James

Brown, Richard Erdman, Phillip Pine, Martin Kilburn, Hal Baylor, Joe Brown, Jr., Jack Kelly, Bob Beban, Peter Coe, Hall Bartlett, William Witney, David Sharpe, Paul Livermore, Jay Silverheels, Glenn Vernon, Joel Allen, Don Garner, Gayle Kellogg, Gil Herman, Freeman Lusk, Reed Hadley, Richard Avonde, Robert Karnes, Kathleen Freeman, Jim Leighton, Ray Hyke, John Hart, Paul McGuire, Robert Kent, Amy Iwanabe, Walter (Andy) Brennan, Jr., Bob Morgan, Steve Wayne, Stan Holbrook, Jack Sherman, Myron Healey. *SYN:* A pair of Army Air Corps officers (Corey, Tucker) and their crew are assigned to bomb a South Pacific target using the new B-29 Superfortress, while on the ground each vies for the affection of an Army nurse (Ralston). [British title: *Thunder Across the Pacific.*]

913. **The Wild Frontier** (10/1/47) B&W 59 mins. (Western). *DIR:* Philip Ford. *A-PRO:* Gordon Kay. *SP:* Albert DeMond. *CAST:* Allan ("Rocky") Lane, Jack Holt, Eddy Waller, Pierre Watkin, John James, Roy Barcroft, Tom London, Sam Flint, Ted Mapes, Budd Buster, Wheaton Chambers, Bob Burns, Art Dillard, Bud McClure, Silver Harr, "Black Jack." *SYN:* A man (Lane) sets out to find his father's (Watkin) killer (Holt), who is secretly heading an outlaw gang. *NOTES:* The first of Allan ("Rocky") Lane's films in which he used his own name for his character, marking the demise of the *Red Ryder* series.

914. **Wild Horse Ambush** (4/15/52) B&W 54 mins. (Western). *DIR:* Fred C. Brannon. *A-PRO:* Rudy Ralston. *SP:* William Lively. *CAST:* Michael Chapin,

Eilene Janssen, James Bell, Richard Avonde, Roy Barcroft, Julian Rivero, Movita Castenada, Drake Smith, Scott Lee, Alex Montoya, John Daheim, Ted Cooper, Wayne Burson. *SYN:* The "Rough Ridin' Kids" (Chapin, Janssen) help to foil a gang of counterfeiters who are capturing wild horses and smuggling counterfeit money under the animals' manes. *NOTES:* Republic's 4th and final entry in the "Rough-Ridin' Kids" series.

**915. Wild Horse Rodeo** (12/6/37) B&W 55 mins. (Western) *DIR:* George Sherman. *A-PRO:* Sol C. Siegel. *SP:* Betty Burbridge. Story by Oliver Drake, Gilbert Wright. Based on characters created by William Colt MacDonald. *CAST:* Robert Livingston, Ray ("Crash") Corrigan, Max Terhune, June Martel, Walter Miller, Edmund Cobb, William Gould, Jack Ingram, Dick Weston (Roy Rogers), Henry Isabell, Art Dillard, Ralph Robinson, Jack Kirk, Kermit Maynard, Fred "Snowflake" Toones, "Cyclone." *SYN:* The Three Mesquiteers (Livingston, Corrigan, Terhune) capture a wild horse (Cyclone) to be used as the main attraction in a rodeo and must stop the crooks trying to steal the animal. *NOTES:* This film includes a plea for freedom for wild horses, features an early appearance by Roy Rogers, and was George Sherman's first film as a director. The 11th entry in the "Three Mesquiteers" series.

**Will Tomorrow Ever Come?** (G.B. title) *see* **That's My Man**

**916. Winds of the Wasteland** (6/15/36) B&W 58 mins. (Western). *DIR:* Mack V. Wright. *PRO:* Nat Levine. *SP:* Joseph F. Poland. *CAST:* John Wayne, Phyllis Fraser, Yakima Canutt, Douglas Cosgrove, Lane Chandler, Sam Flint, Lew Kelly, Robert Kortman, Edward Cassidy, Merrill McCormick, Charles Locher, Joe Yrigoyen, Christian J. Frank, Bud McClure, Jack Ingram, Art Mix, Jack Rockwell, Arthur Millett, Tracy Layne, Lloyd Ingraham, Horace B. Carpenter, Bob Burns, Clyde McClary. *SYN:* Two former Pony Express riders (Wayne, Chandler) buy a dilapidated stagecoach and compete for a chance at a $25,000 mail contract by racing a rival coach line.

**917. Winter Wonderland** (5/17/47) B&W 71 mins. (Romance-Sports). *DIR:* Bernard Vorhaus. *A-PRO:* Walter Colmes, Henry Sokal. *SP:* Peter Goldbaum, David Chandler, Arthur Marx, Gertrude Purcell. Story by Fred Schiller. *CAST:* Lynn Roberts, Charles Drake, Roman Bohnen, Eric Blore, Mary Eleanor Donahue, Renee Godfrey, Janet Warren, Harry Tyler, Renie Riano, Diana Mumby, Alvin Hammer. *SYN:* Wintertime romance blossoms for a farm girl (Roberts) and ski instructor (Drake).

**918. Wolf of New York** (1/25/40) B&W 69 mins. (Crime). *DIR:* William McGann. *A-PRO:* Robert North. *SP:* Gordan Kahn, Lionel Houser. Additional dialogue by Charles Belden. Story by Leslie T. White, Arnold Belgard. *CAST:* Edmund Lowe, Rose Hobart, James Stephenson, Jerome Cowan, William Demarest, Maurice Murphy, Charles D. Brown, Edward Gargan, Andrew Tombes, Ben Welden, Ann Baldwin, Roy Gordon. *SYN:* When a criminal attorney (Lowe), who has made his mark defending mobsters, loses a case, and learns that his client was truly innocent of murder, he proceeds to turn his talents to the pursuit of true justice, is appointed district attorney, and proceeds to prosecute his former client (Stephenson). *NOTES:* Charles Belden was uncredited.

**919. Woman Doctor** (2/6/39) B&W 65 mins. (Drama). *DIR:* Sidney Salkow. *A-PRO:* Sol C. Siegel. *SP:* Joseph Moncure March. Story by Alice Altschuler, Miriam Geiger. *CAST:* Frieda Inescort, Henry Wilcoxon, Claire Dodd, Sybil Jason, Cora Witherspoon, Frank Reicher, Gus Glassmire, Dick Jones, Joan Howard, Spencer Charters, Virginia Brissac. *SYN:* A physician (Inescort) deserts her husband (Wilcoxon) and daughter (Jason) to practice her surgical skills, but a near-tragedy reunites the family.

**Woman from Headquarters** *see* **Women from Headquarters**

**920. Woman in the Dark** (11/15/52) B&W 60 mins. (Crime). *DIR:* George Blair. *A-PRO:* Stephen Auer. *SP:* Albert DeMond. Based on the play by Nicholas Cosentino. *CAST:* Penny Edwards, Ross Elliott, Rick Vallin, Richard Benedict, Argentina Brunetti, Martin Garralaga, Edit Angold, Peter Brocco, Barbara Billingsley, John Doucette, Richard Irving, Luther Crockett, Carlos Thompson, Charles Sullivan. *SYN:* A lawyer (Vallin) takes on the mob when his brother (Benedict) is gunned down.

**921. Woman of the North Country** (9/5/52) Trucolor 92 mins. (Western). *DIR/A-PRO:* Joseph Kane. *SP:* Norman Reilly Raine. Story by Charles Marquis Warren. Adapted by Prescott Chaplin. *CAST:* Ruth Hussey, Rod Cameron, John Agar, Gale Storm, J. Carrol Naish,

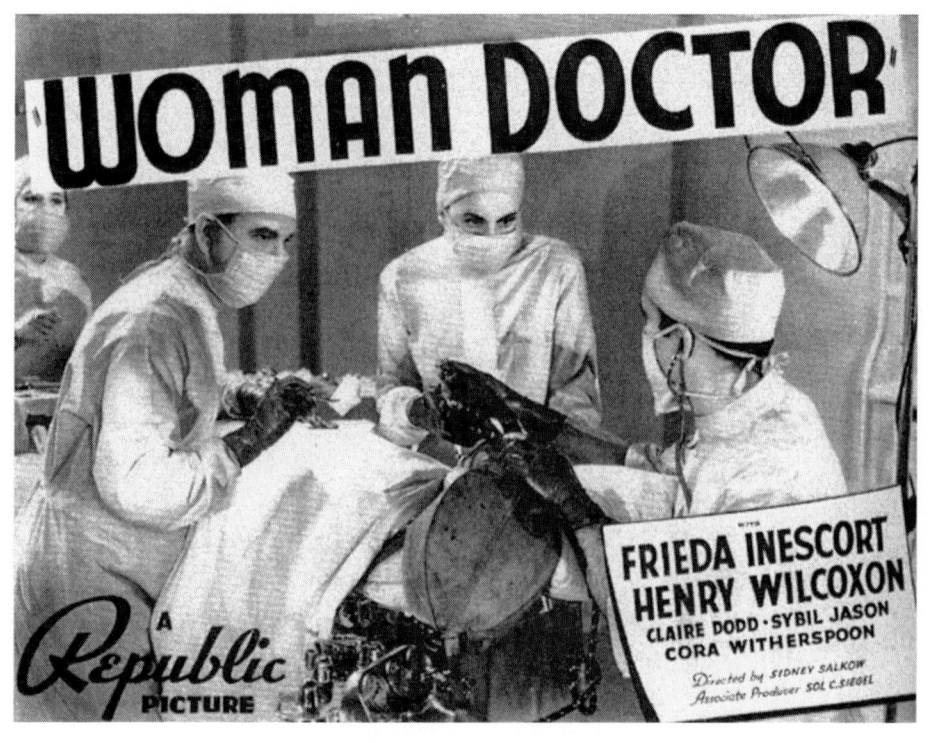

Jim Davis, Jay C. Flippen, Taylor Holmes, Barry Kelley, Grant Withers, Stephen Bekassy, Howard Petrie, Hank Worden, Virginia Brissac, Dub Taylor, Richard Alexander, Raphael Bennett, Stanley Andrews. *SYN:* In Minnesota, a mine owner (Cameron) is tricked into marriage only to discover that his bride (Hussey) is after his fortune. *NOTES:* Prescott Chaplin was uncredited.

**922. Woman They Almost Lynched** (3/20/53) B&W 90 mins. (Western). *DIR:* Allan Dwan. *PRO:* Herbert J. Yates. *SP:* Steve Fisher. From the *Saturday Evening Post* story by Michael Fessier. *CAST:* John Lund, Brian Donlevy, Audrey Totter, Joan Leslie, Ben Cooper, Nina Varela, James Brown, Ellen Corby, Fern Hall, Minerva Urecal, Jim Davis, Reed Hadley, Ann Savage, Virginia Christine, Marilyn Lindsey, Nacho Galindo, Richard Simmons, Gordon Jones, Frank Ferguson, Post Park, Tom McDonough, Ted Ryan, Richard Crane, Carl Pitti, Joe Yrigoyen, Jimmy Hawkins, James Kirkwood, Paul Livermore, Lee Roberts. *SYN:* During the Civil War, in a small town on the Arkansas-Missouri border, a woman saloon owner (Leslie) is suspected of being a Confederate spy.

**923. The Woman Who Came Back** (12/13/45) B&W 68 mins. (Mystery). *DIR/A-PRO:* Walter Colmes. *SP:* Lee Willis, Dennis Cooper. Based on an idea by Philip Yordan. Story by John Kafka. *CAST:* John Loder, Nancy Kelly, Otto Kruger, Ruth Ford, Harry Tyler, Jeanne Gail, Almira Sessions, J. Farrell MacDonald, Emmett Vogan. *SYN:* A young woman (Kelly) returns to her New England town where she is suspected of being a witch. With the help of a doctor (Loder) and minister (Kruger), she is able to convince the townspeople that she is not a witch.

**924. A Woman's Devotion** (11/16/56) B&W 88 mins. (Thriller). *DIR:* Paul Henreid. *PRO:* John Bash. *SP:* Robert Hill. A Republic Presentation. *CAST:* Ralph Meeker, Janice Rule, Paul Henreid, Rosenda Monteros, Fanny Schiller, Jose Torvay, Yerye Beirute, Tony Carbajal, Jamie Gonzalez, Carlos Riquelme. *SYN:* While on his honeymoon with his wife (Rule) in Acapulco, a World War II veteran and artist (Meeker), still mentally disturbed from his war experiences, sets out to prove himself innocent of the murder of a Mexican model and a maid. *NOTES:* One of the more effective low-budget films directed by actor Paul Henreid. [Alternate title: *Battleshock.*] [British title: *War Shock.*]

**925. Women from Headquarters** (5/1/50) B&W 60 mins. (Crime). *DIR:* George Blair. *A-PRO:* Stephen Auer. *SP:* Gene Lewis. *CAST:* Virginia Huston, Robert Rockwell, Barbara Fuller, Norman Budd, Frances Charles, K. Elmo Lowe, Otto Waldis, Grandon Rhodes, Jack Kruschen, Bert Conway, Marlo Dwyer, Sid Marion, John DeSimone, Gil Herman, Leonard Penn. *SYN:* The life of a woman police officer, (Huston) as she tries to reform a wayward girl (Fuller), and assist a police sergeant (Rockwell) in smashing a drug ring. [Alternate title: *Woman from Headquarters.*]

**926. Women in War** (6/6/40) B&W 71 mins. (War-Drama). *DIR:* John H. Auer. *A-PRO:* Sol C. Siegel. *SP:* F. Hugh Herbert, Doris Anderson. *CAST:* Elsie Janis, Wendy Barrie, Patric Knowles, Mae Clarke, Dennis Moore, Dorothy Peterson, Billy Gilbert, Colin Tapley, Stanley Logan, Barbara Pepper, Pamela Randell, Lawrence Grant, Lester Matthews, Marian Martin, Holmes Herbert, Vera Lewis, Charles D. Brown, Peter Cushing. *SYN:* In London, a woman (Barrie) joins an auxiliary nursing service rather than go to jail, and is unaware that the head of the nursing unit (Janis) is actually her mother. *NOTES:* This film was one of the earliest to use involvement in the war as a background to nurse training. Academy Award Nominee — Best Visual Effects.

**927. The Wrong Road** (10/11/37) B&W 62 mins. (Crime). *DIR:* James Cruze. *A-PRO:* Colbert Clark. *SP:* Gordon Rigby, Eric Taylor. Story by Gordon Rigby. *CAST:* Richard Cromwell, Helen Mack, Lionel Atwill, Horace MacMahon, Russ Powell, Billy Bevan, Marjorie Main, Rex Evans, Joseph Crehan, Arthur Hoyt, Syd Saylor, Selmer Jackson, Chester Clute, Gordon Hart, Sidney Bracey, Gladden James, Harry Wilson, Forbes Murray, James Marcus, Jack Perrin, Ferris Taylor, Frank O'Connor, Larry Steers. *SYN:* A couple (Cromwell, Mack) decide to steal a large sum of money from the bank where she works as a teller. On the run, they hide the money in a music box, get caught, and serve time in prison. But when they get out, they can't seem to locate the music box.

**928. Wyoming** (7/28/47) B&W 84 mins. (Western). *DIR/A-PRO:* Joseph Kane. *SP:* Lawrence Hazard, Gerald Geraghty. *CAST:* Bill Elliott, Vera Ralston, John Carroll, George "Gabby" Hayes, Albert Dekker, Virginia Grey,

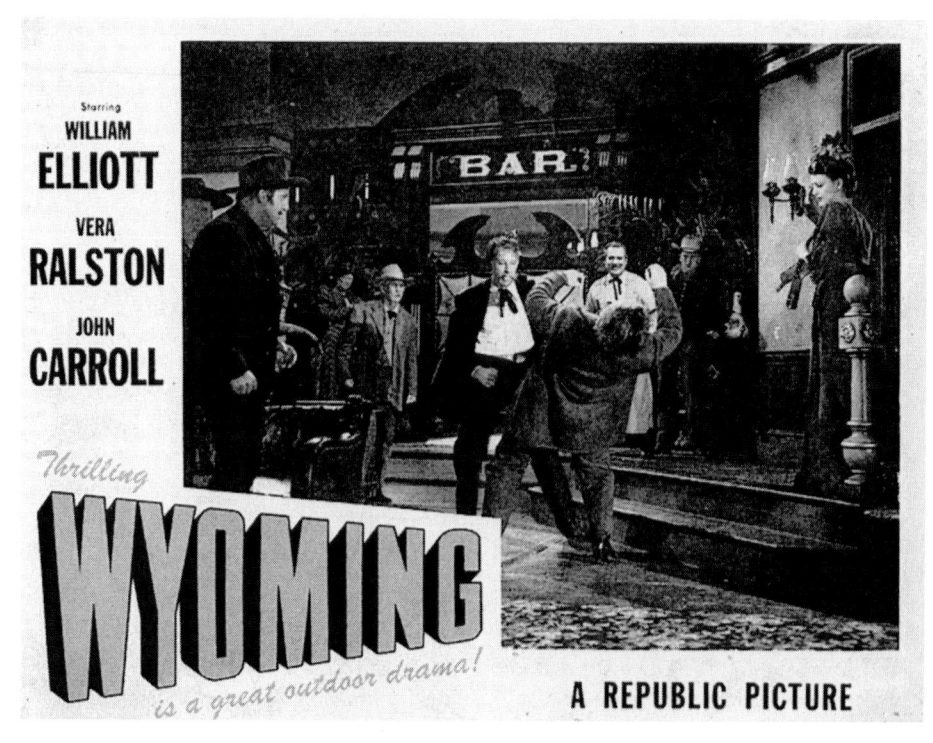

Maria Ouspenskaya, Grant Withers, Harry Woods, Minna Gombell, Dick Curtis, Roy Barcroft, Trevor Bardette, Paul Harvey, Louise Kane, Linda Green, Tom London, George Chesebro, Jack O'Shea, Tex Cooper, Charles Middleton, Eddy Waller, Olin Howlin, Charles King, Glenn Strange, Eddie Acuff, Ben Johnson, Marshall Reed, Rex Lease, Charles Morton, Tex Terry, Dale Fink, Edward Peil, Sr., Roque Ybarra, James Archuletta, David Williams, Lee Shumway. SYN: A pioneer (Elliott) becomes Wyoming's top cattle rancher and when the Homestead Act is introduced, he tries to keep the homesteaders from settling on his land.

**929. The Wyoming Bandit** (7/15/49) B&W 60 mins. (Western). DIR: Philip Ford. A-PRO: Gordon Kay. SP: M. Coates Webster. CAST: Allan ("Rocky") Lane, Eddy Waller, Trevor Bardette, Victor Kilian, Rand Brooks, William Haade, Harold Goodwin, Lane Bradford, Robert Wilke, John Hamilton, Edmund Cobb, Reed Hadley, "Black Jack." SYN: A U.S. Marshal (Lane), on the trail of a gang of outlaws, gets assistance in his search from a former outlaw (Bardette) who learns that the outlaws killed his son.

**930. Wyoming Outlaw** (6/27/39) B&W 62 mins. (Western). DIR: George Sherman. A-PRO: William Berke. SP: Betty Burbridge, Jack Natteford. Story by Jack Natteford. Based on characters created by William Colt MacDonald. CAST: John Wayne, Ray ("Crash") Corrigan, Raymond Hatton, Don ("Red") Barry, Adele Pearce (Pamela Blake), LeRoy Mason, Charles Middleton, Katherine Kenworthy, Elmo Lincoln, Jack

Ingram, David Sharpe, Jack Kenney, Yakima Canutt, Dave O'Brien, Curley Dresden, Tommy Coats, Ralph Peters, Jack Kirk, Al Taylor, Bud McTaggart, Budd Buster, Ed Payson. *SYN:* The Three Mesquiteers (Wayne, Corrigan, Hatton) are forced to hunt down a young man (Barry) who is forced to turn to crime after his involvement with a corrupt politician (Mason) who demands campaign money in exchange for employment. *NOTES:* This role launched Barry into a career as a western star. Elmo Lincoln was the screen's first Tarzan. The 23rd entry in the "Three Mesquiteers" series.

**931. Wyoming Wildcat** (1/6/41) B&W 56 mins. (Western). *DIR/A-PRO:* George Sherman. *SP:* Bennett Cohen, Anthony Coldeway. Story by Bennett Cohen. *CAST:* Don ("Red") Barry, Julie Duncan, Syd Saylor, Frank M. Thomas, Dick Botiller, Edmund Cobb, Ed Brady, Edward Cassidy, George Sherwood, Ethan Laidlaw, Al Haskell, Frank Ellis, Curley Dresden, Art Dillard, Cactus Mack, Kermit Maynard, Frank O'Connor, Fred Burns. *SYN:* An ex-outlaw (Barry) becomes a guard on the Wells Fargo line and then is hunted by the law when the stage is robbed. *NOTES:* Re-edited for TV at 54 mins.

**932. X Marks the Spot** (11/4/42) B&W 55 mins. (Crime). *DIR/A-PRO:* George Sherman. *SP:* Stuart Palmer, Richard Murphy. Story by Mauri Grashin, Robert T. Shannon. *CAST:* Damian O'Flynn, Helen Parrish, Dick Purcell, Jack LaRue, Neil Hamilton, Robert E. Homans, Anne Jeffreys, Dick Wessel, Esther Muir, Joseph Kirk, Edna Harris, Fred Kelsey, Vince Barnett. *SYN:* A private investigator (O'Flynn) and a girl (Parrish) go after the killers of his police sergeant father (Homans). *NOTES:* No relation to the 1931 Tiffany Picture of the same name.

**933. Yankee Fakir** (4/1/47) B&W 71 mins. (Western-Mystery). *DIR/PRO:* W. Lee Wilder. *SP:* Richard S. Conway. Story by Mindret Lord. A W. W. Production. A Republic Presentation. *CAST:* Douglas Fowley, Joan Woodbury, Clem Bevans, Ransom Sherman, Frank Reicher, Marc Lawrence, Walter Soderling, Eula Guy, Forrest Taylor, Elinor Appleton, Peter Michael, Elspeth Dudgeon, Ernie Adams, Tom Bernard. *SYN:* A salesman (Fowley) heads west, falls in love with a border patrolman's (Taylor) daughter (Woodbury), and when the patrolman is murdered, sets out to find his killer.

**934. The Yellow Rose of Texas** (6/24/44) B&W 69 mins. (Western). *DIR:* Joseph Kane. *A-PRO:* Harry Grey. *SP:* Jack Townley. *CAST:* Roy Rogers, Dale Evans, Grant Withers, Harry Shannon, George Cleveland, William Haade, Weldon Heyburn, Hal Taliaferro, Tom London, Dick Botiller, Janet Martin, Robert Wilke, Jack O'Shea, Rex Lease, Emmett Vogan, John Dilson, William Desmond, Horace B. Carpenter, Chester Conklin, Fred "Snowflake" Toones, Little Brown Jug (Don Kay Reynolds), Bob Nolan and the Sons of the Pioneers, "Trigger." *SYN:* An insurance investigator (Rogers) becomes an entertainer on a showboat so he can recover some lost funds, and clear the name of the man (Shannon) who was wrongly convicted of the crime. *NOTES:* Re-edited for TV at 54 mins.

**935. Yellowneck** (3/22/55) Trucolor 83 mins. (Adventure — War). *DIR:* John R. Hugh. *PRO:* Harlow G. Frederick.

*SP:* Nat S. Linden, John R. Hugh. Story by John R. Hugh. An Empire Production. A Republic Presentation. *CAST:* Lin McCarthy, Stephen Courtleigh, Berry Kroeger, Harold Gordon, Bill Mason, Jose Billie, Roy Osceola, Al Tamez. *SYN:* Five Confederate Army deserters, known as "Yellownecks," make their way through the Florida Everglades in the hope of reaching a ship bound for Cuba.

**936. Yodelin' Kid from Pine Ridge** (6/14/37) B&W 60 mins. (Western). *DIR:* Joseph Kane. *A-PRO:* Armand Schaefer. *SP:* Dorrell McGowan, Stuart McGowan, Jack Natteford. Story by Jack Natteford. *CAST:* Gene Autry, Smiley Burnette, Betty Bronson, LeRoy Mason, Charles Middleton, Russell Simpson, Jack Dougherty, Guy Wilkerson, Frankie Marvin, Henry Hall, Fred "Snowflake" Toones, Jack Kirk, Bob Burns, Al Taylor, George Morrell, Lew Meehan, Jim Corey, Jack Ingram, Art Dillard, Art Mix, Bud Osborne, Oscar Gahan, Herman Hack, Tom Smith, Charles Brinley, Jack Montgomery, Jack Evans, Bill Nestell, The Tennessee Ramblers (Dick Hartman, W. J. Blair, Elmer Warren, Happy Morris, Pappy Wolf), "Champion." *SYN:* Gene returns home to the turpentine forests of Georgia and Florida and enlists the aid of his Wild West show to stop a range war. *NOTES:* A reworking of the 1935 feature, *Tumbling Tumbleweeds*. Includes stock footage from the 1935 R-K-O film, *Annie Oakley*. [British title: *The Hero of Pine Ridge*.]

**937. Yokel Boy** (3/13/42) B&W 69 mins. (Musical-Comedy). *DIR:* Joseph Santley. *A-PRO:* Robert North. *SP:* Isabel Dawn. Story by Russell Crouse. Adapted by Arthur V. Jones. Based on the musical play by Samuel Stept, Charles Tobias, and Lew Brown. *CAST:* Joan Davis, Albert Dekker, Eddie Foy, Jr., Alan Mowbray, Roscoe Karns, Mikhail Rasumny, Lynne Carver, Tom Dugan, Marc Lawrence, Florence Wright, Pierre Watkin, Charles Lane, Cyril Ring, Betty Blythe, Lois Collier, Tim Ryan, Harry Hayden, Anne Jeffreys, Mady Lawrence, Rod Bacon, Arthur O'Connell, Emmett Vogan, Charles Quigley, James C. Morton, Marilyn Hare. *SYN:* A country boy (Foy, Jr.), who has seen so many movies that he can foresee how much money any given film will bring in, is brought to Hollywood by the employee (Karns) of a failing Hollywood studio, where he gets into trouble when he convinces the studio to cast a real gangster (Dekker) in the role of a gangster. *NOTES:* After paying five thousand dollars for the musical play, which starred Judy Canova on stage, Republic changed their minds, decided not to star Judy Canova, threw out the original plot, and just kept the title. [British title: *Hitting the Headlines*.]

**938. Young and Wild** (4/24/58) B&W/Naturama 69 mins. (Action-Crime). *DIR:* William Witney. *PRO:* Sidney Picker. *SP:* Arthur T. Horman. An Esla Production. A Republic Presentation. *CAST:* Gene Evans, Scott Marlowe, Carolyn Kearney, Robert Arthur, James Kevin, Tom Gilson, Ken Lynch, Emlen Davies, Morris Ankrum, Wendell Holmes, John Zaremba. *SYN:* A young couple (Arthur, Kearney) witness a hit-and-run accident and find themselves the victims of intense harassment as they try to hold off the teenagers responsible for the accident. *NOTES:* William Witney's last directed feature at Republic. The film debut of Carolyn Kearney. Double-billed in some areas with *Juvenile Jungle*.

**939. Young Bill Hickok** (10/21/40) B&W 59 mins. (Western). *DIR/A-PRO:* Joseph Kane. *SP:* Norton S. Parker, Olive Cooper. *CAST:* Roy Rogers, George "Gabby" Hayes, Jacqueline Wells, John Miljan, Sally Payne, Archie Twitchell, Monte Blue, Hal Taliaferro, Ethel Wales, Jack Ingram, Monte Montague, Iron Eyes Cody, Fred Burns, Frank Ellis, Slim Whitaker, Jack Kirk, Hank Bell, Henry Wills, Dick Elliott, William Desmond, John Elliott, Jack Rockwell, Bill Wolfe, Tom Smith, "Trigger." *SYN:* Bill Hickok (Rogers) and Calamity Jane (Payne) set out to defeat a guerrilla band that is plotting with a foreign agent (Miljan) to build an empire in the American Southwest. *NOTES:* Re-edited for TV at 54 mins.

**940. Young Buffalo Bill** (4/12/40) B&W 59 mins. (Western). *DIR/A-PRO:* Joseph Kane. *SP:* Harrison Jacobs, Robert Yost, Gerald Geraghty. Story by Norman Houston. *CAST:* Roy Rogers, George "Gabby" Hayes, Pauline Moore, Hugh Sothern, Chief Thunder Cloud, Julian Rivero, Trevor Bardette, Steve Pendleton, Wade Boteler, Anna Demetrio, Estelita Zarco, Hank Bell, William Kellogg, Iron Eyes Cody, Jack O'Shea, George Chesebro, "Trigger." *SYN:* Bill Cody (Rogers) aids settlers and Indians who are being defrauded by Spanish land grant claimants. *NOTES:* Re-edited for TV at 54 mins.

**941. Youth on Parade** (10/24/42) B&W 72 mins. (Musical-Comedy). *DIR:* Albert S. Rogell. *A-PRO:* Albert J. Cohen. *SP:* George Carleton Brown. Additional dialogue by Frank Gill, Jr. *CAST:* John Hubbard, Martha O'Driscoll, Bruce Langley, Ruth Terry, Charles Smith, Nana Bryant, Ivan Simpson, Chick Chandler, Paul Fix, Lynn Merrick, John Boyle, Jr., Marlyn Schild, Eddie Acuff, Bud Jamison, Sue Robin, Ruth Daye, Edward Earle, Betty Atkinson, Harry Hayden, Walter Soderling, Boyd Irwin, Walter Fenner, Alfred Hall, Elmer Jerome, Maurice Cass, Barbara Slater, Rick Vallin, Ben Lessy, Warren Ashe, Frank Coghlan, Jr., Yvonne DeCarlo, Jack Boyle, Ivan Miller. *SYN:* A group of collegians, faced with expulsion by their psychology professor (Hubbard) unless they produce their perfect fictional student, hire a New York actress (Terry) to impersonate her. *NOTES:* This marked the first film pairing for the songwriting team of Sammy Cahn and Jule Styne. Academy Award Nominee—Best Song.

**942. Youth on Parole** (10/4/37) B&W 60 mins. (Crime-Romance). *DIR/A-PRO:* Phil Rosen. *SP:* Henry Blankfort, Hershel Rebaus. *CAST:* Marian Marsh, Gordon Oliver, Margaret Dumont, Peggy Shannon, Miles Mander, Sarah Padden, Wade Boteler, Joe Caits, Mary Kornman, Milburn Stone, Harry Tyler, Ranny Weeks, Theodore Von Eltz, Ula Love, Paul Stanton. *SYN:* After being paroled from jail, two youths (Marsh, Oliver), because of their past, must prove their innocence when they are suspected of committing a crime.

**943. Yukon Patrol** (4/30/42) B&W 68 mins. (Western-Spy). *SYN:* Feature version of the 12 chapter serial, *King of the Royal Mounted.* See **985. King of the Royal Mounted.**

**944. Zanzabuka** (4/13/56) Trucolor 64 mins. (Travelogue). *DIR/PRO:* Louis

Cotlow. Narration written by Ronald Davidson. *CAST:* Narrated by Bob Danvers-Walker. *SYN:* The story of Louis Cotlow's eight-month expedition through Tanganyika, Kenya, and the Belgian Congo. *NOTES:* The title translates to "Dangerous Safari" in the pygmy language.

**945. The Zero Hour** (5/26/39) B&W 62 mins. (Drama). *DIR:* Sidney Salkow. *A-PRO:* Sol C. Siegel. *SP:* Garrett Fort. *CAST:* Frieda Inescort, Otto Kruger, Adrienne Ames, Don Douglas, Jane Darwell, J. M. Kerrigan, Ann E. Todd, Leonard Carey, Sarah Padden, Ferris Taylor, Willard Parker, Landers Stevens. *SYN:* A former Broadway star (Inescort) and her paralyzed husband (Kruger) decide to adopt a child (Todd), but when she falls in love with a widower (Douglas), who also wants to adopt the child, her invalid husband commits suicide, feeling that he is in the way of their happiness.

**946. Zorro Rides Again** (9/22/38, 1/16/59) B&W 68 mins. (Western). *SYN:* Feature version of the 12 chapter serial of the same name. *NOTES:* This was the only feature version of a Republic serial to be released twice. *See* **1010. Zorro Rides Again.**

# Serials (1936–1955)

Following is a complete list of serials produced and distributed by Republic Pictures Corporation. Climaxing almost twenty years of serial production, Republic produced forty-four 12-chapter serials, seventeen 15-chapter serials, four 13-chapter serials, and one 14-chapter serial, for a total of 849 episodes at a total running time of 224 hours, 10 minutes, and 52 seconds.

Release dates given are approximate, and credits from other sources are given as they appeared on screen. Re-release dates and alternate titles are also given.

In 1966, 26 serials were re-titled and edited to 100 minutes, and sold to television as the **Century 66** package. Their names are included here for the sake of completeness.

Omitted from this listing is the 1935 Mascot serial "The Fighting Marines," since it bore the Mascot logo, but was released through Republic exchanges.

947. **Adventures of Captain Marvel** (3/28/41) B&W 216 mins. 12 chapters. (Adventure). *DIR:* William Witney, John English. *A-PRO:* Hiram S. Brown, Jr. *SP:* Ronald Davidson, Norman S. Hall, Arch B. Heath, Joseph F. Poland, Sol Shor. CHAPTER TITLES: (1) Curse of the Scorpion, (2) The Guillotine, (3) Time Bomb, (4) Death Takes the Wheel, (5) The Scorpion Strikes, (6) Lens of Death, (7) Human Targets, (8) Boomerang, (9) Dead Man's Trap, (10) Doom Ship, (11) Valley of Death, (12) Captain Marvel's Secret. *CAST:* Tom Tyler, Frank Coghlan, Jr., William Benedict, Louise Currie, Robert Strange, Harry Worth, Bryant Washburn, John Davidson, George Pembroke, Peter George Lynn, Reed Hadley, Jack Mulhall, Kenne Duncan, Nigel de Brulier,

John Bagni, Carleton Young, Leland Hodgson, Jimmy Fawcett, Stanley Price, Ernest Sarracino, Tetsu Komai, Paul Lopez, Wilson Benge, Jerry Jerome, Dick Crockett, Chuck Morrison, Francis Sayles, Eddie Dew, Loren Riebe, Earl Bunn, George Suzanne, Edward Cassidy, Ted Mapes, Frank Marlowe, Armand Cortes, Ken Terrell, Major Sam Harris, Duke Taylor, Lynton Brent, Augie Gomez, Al Taylor, Curley Dresden, Henry Wills, Steve Clemente, Al Kikume, Bud Geary, Marten Lamont, Carl Zwolsman, Frank Wayne, Ray Hanson, Victor Cox, Joe Delacruz, David Sharpe, *VOICE OF*: Gerald Mohr. *SYN*: Billy Batson (Coghlan, Jr.) becomes Captain Marvel (Tyler) as he sets out to stop the "Scorpion" from securing the five lenses of the Golden Scorpion. *NOTES*: Working title was *Captain Marvel*. Republic's only superhero serial. Re-released in 1953 as *Return of Captain Marvel*.

**948. Adventures of Frank and Jesse James** (10/30/48) B&W 180 mins. 13 chapters. (Western). *DIR*: Fred C. Brannon, Yakima Canutt. *A-PRO*: Franklin Adreon. *SP*: Franklin Adreon, Basil Dickey, Sol Shor, Robert G. Walker. *CHAPTER TITLES*: (1) Agent of Treachery, (2) The Hidden Witness, (3) The Lost Tunnel, (4) Blades of Death, (5) Roaring Wheels, (6) Passage to Danger, (7) The Secret Code, (8) Doomed Cargo, (9) The Eyes of the Law, (10) The Stolen Body, (11) The Death Trap, (12) Talk or Die!, (13) Unmasked. *CAST*: Clayton Moore, Steve Darrell, Noel Neill, George J. Lewis, Stanley Andrews, John Crawford, Sam Flint, House Peters, Jr., Dale Van Sickel, Tom Steele, James Dale, I. Stanford Jolley, Gene Stutenroth, Lane Bradford, George Chesebro, Jack Kirk, Steve Clark, Duke Taylor, Carey Loftin, Duke Green, Frank Ellis, Roy Bucko, Art Dillard, Ralph Bucko, Victor Cox, Fred Graham, Guy Teague, Frank O'Connor, Joe Yrigoyen, Augie Gomez, Eddie Parker, Bud Osborne, Bud Wolfe, Rosa Turich, David Sharpe, Bob Reeves, Ken Terrell, Joe Phillips. *SYN*: Jesse (Moore) joins his brother Frank (Darrell) at the home of Jim Powell (Andrews) and his daughter Judy (Neill), and there, they plan to make restitution to the past victims of the James gang with the help of Jim Powell's silver mine. When a vein of gold is also discovered by mining engineer Amos Ramsey (Crawford) he murders Jim to gain control of the mine and Frank and Jesse vow to bring Jim's killer to justice. *NOTES*: Screen writer Robert G. Walker was uncredited. The correct title to Chapter 12 is *Talk or Die!*, NOT *Suspicion*. Re-released in 1956 under the same title.

**949. Adventures of Red Ryder** (6/28/40) B&W 212 mins. 12 chapters. (Western). *DIR*: William Witney, John English. *A-PRO*: Hiram S. Brown, Jr. *SP*: Franklyn Adreon, Ronald Davidson, Norman S. Hall, Barney A. Sarecky, Sol Shor. Based upon the famous NEA newspaper feature. *CHAPTER TITLES*: (1) Murder on the Santa Fe Trail, (2) Horsemen of Death, (3) Trail's End, (4) Water Rustlers, (5) Avalanche, (6) Hangman's Noose, (7) Framed, (8) Blazing Walls, (9) Records of Doom, (10) One Second to Live, (11) The Devil's Marksman, (12) Frontier Justice. *CAST*: Don ("Red") Barry, Noah Beery, Sr., Tommy Cook, Maude Pierce Allen, Vivian Coe, Harry Worth, Hal Taliaferro, William Farnum, Robert Kortman, Carleton Young, Ray Teal, Gene Alsace, Gayne Whitman, Hooper Atchley, John Dilson, Lloyd Ingraham, Charles Hutchison, Gardner James, Wheaton Chambers, Lynton Brent, Joe Yrigoyen, Joe Delacruz, Jimmy Fawcett, Bill Nestell, Bud Geary, James Carlisle, Augie Gomez, Max Waizman, Charles Murphy, Eddie Jauregui, Ernest Sarracino, Bob Jamison, Ray Adams, Jack Kirk, Fred Burns, Duke Green, Roy Brent, Budd Buster, Bob Burns, Curley Dresden, Chester Conklin, Walter James, Edward Hearn, Jack O'Shea, Ed Brady, Gus Shindle, Walter Stiritz, Dan White, Matty Roubert, Post Park, Reed Howes, Al Taylor, Art Dillard, Robert Wilke, Bill Yrigoyen, Ken Terrell, Charles Thomas, Chick Hannon, Barry Hays, Bill Wilkus, Frankie Marvin, Jack Rockwell, William Benedict, Edward Cassidy, Victor Cox, Merrill McCormick, Rose Plummer, David Sharpe, Art Mix. *SYN:* Red Ryder (Barry) and Little Beaver (Cook) must stop banker Calvin Drake (Worth) and his gang from illegally acquiring the settlers' land for a railroad right-of-way. *NOTES:* This was the first entry in the "Red Ryder" character for Republic Studios, but it would be four more years before a feature series was developed.

**The Baron's African War** *see* **Secret Service in Darkest Africa**

**Bat Men of Africa** *see* **Darkest Africa**

**Black Dragon of Manzanar** *see* **G-Men Vs. the Black Dragon**

950. **The Black Widow** (11/1/47) B&W 180 mins. 13 chapters. (Mystery-Crime). *DIR:* Spencer G. Bennet, Fred C. Brannon. *A-PRO:* Mike J. Frankovich. *SP:* Franklin Adreon, Basil Dickey, Jesse Duffy, Sol Shor. *CHAPTER TITLES:* (1) Deadly Prophecy, (2) The Stolen Formula, (3) Hidden Death, (4) Peril in the Sky, (5) The Spider's Lair, (6) Glass Guillotine, (7) Wheels of Death, (8) False Information, (9) The Spider's Venom, (10) The Stolen Corpse, (11) Death Dials a Number, (12) The Talking Mirror, (13) A Life for a Life. *CAST:* Bruce Edwards, Virginia Lindley, Carol Forman, Anthony Warde, Ramsay Ames, I. Stanford Jolley, Theodore Gottlieb, Virginia Carroll, Gene Stutenroth, Sam Flint, Tom Steele, Dale Van Sickel, LeRoy Mason, Forrest Taylor, Ernie Adams, Keith Richards, Hal Landon, Gil Perkins, Robert Wilke, George Chesebro, Bob Reeves, Jack O'Shea, Maxine Doyle, Bud Wolfe, Stanley Price, Larry Steers, George Douglas, Frank O'Connor, Frank Lackteen, Frank White, Robert Barron, Peggy Wynne, John Phillips, Ken Terrell, Duke Green, Bill Bailey, Charles Sullivan, Dave Anderson, Jerry Jerome, Richard Gordon, Ted Mapes, Carey Loftin, Arvon Dale, John Alban, Laura Stevens. *SYN:* Madame Sombra (Forman), also known as "The Black Widow," together with her gang, Nick Ward (Warde) and Dr. Z. V. Jaffa (Jolley), plan to steal the secret of a new atomic rocket engine from Professor Henry Weston (Flint) for her father, Hitomu (Gottlieb), as part of his plan for world domination. Mystery writer and criminologist Steven Colt (Edwards) and reporter Joyce Winters (Lindley) set out to stop Sombra and her gang and recover the rocket engine. *NOTES:* Beginning with this serial and continuing on, the Republic "Eagle" logo preceded the main title with the words, "A Republic Serial." Ernie Adams' final screen appearance—he died 11/26/47. [TV version: Six 26½-min. chapters.] [Century 66 feature version: *Sombra, the Spider Woman.*]

**951. Canadian Mounties Vs. Atomic Invaders** (7/8/53) B&W 167 mins. 12 chapters. (Adventure-Crime). DIR/*A-PRO:* Franklin Adreon. *SP:* Ronald Davidson. *CHAPTER TITLES:* (1) Arctic Intrigue, (2) Murder or Accident?, (3) Fangs of Death, (4) Underground Inferno, (5) Pursuit to Destruction, (6) The Boat Trap, (7) Flame Versus Gun, (8) Highway of Horror, (9) Doomed Cargo, (10) Human Quarry, (11) Mechanical Homicide, (12) Cavern of Revenge. *CAST:* William (Bill) Henry, Susan Morrow, Arthur Space, Dale Van Sickel, Pierre Watkin, Mike Ragan, Stanley Andrews, Harry Lauter, Hank Patterson, Edmund Cobb, Gayle Kellogg, Tom Steele, Jean Wright, Jeane Wood, Bob Reeves, Joe Yrigoyen, Carey Loftin, Duane Thorsen, Fred Graham, Drew Cahill, William Fawcett, Kenner G. Kemp, Gordon Armitage, George DeNormand, Paul Palmer, Earl Bunn, Jimmy Fawcett, David Sharpe, Bob Jamison, Duke Taylor. *SYN:* Sergeant Don Roberts (Henry) and Canadian undercover agent Kay Conway (Morrow) journey to the frozen wilderness of Taniak in the Yukon territory to stop Marlof (Space) and his foreign agents from establishing a missile launching site in order to reign guided missiles on key American cities in preparation for his country's invasion of the United States. *NOTES:* Republic's fourth and final serial tribute to the Royal Canadian Mounted Police. Michael Fox, a Columbia serial player, and Roy Barcroft were considered for the role of "Marlof" before Arthur Space was signed. [Century 66 feature version: *Missile Base at Taniak.*]

**952. Captain America** (2/5/44) B&W 243 mins. 15 chapters. (Adventure). *DIR:* John English, Elmer Clifton. *A-PRO:* William J. O'Sullivan. *SP:* Royal K. Cole, Ronald Davidson, Basil Dickey, Jesse Duffy, Harry Fraser, Grant Nelson, Joseph F. Poland. Based on the character appearing in *Captain America Comics*. *CHAPTER TITLES:* (1) The Purple Death, (2) Mechanical Executioner, (3) Scarlet Shroud, (4) Preview of Murder, (5) Blade of Wrath, (6) Vault of Vengeance, (7) Wholesale Destruction, (8) Cremation in the Clouds, (9) Triple Tragedy, (10) The Avenging Corpse, (11) The Dead Man Returns, (12) Horror on the Highway, (13) Skyscraper Plunge, (14) The Scarab Strikes, (15) The Toll of Doom. *CAST:* Dick Purcell, Lorna Gray, Lionel Atwill, Charles Trowbridge, Russell Hicks, George J. Lewis, John Davidson, Norman Nesbitt, Frank Reicher, Hugh Sothern, Tom Chatterton, Robert Frazer, John Hamilton, Crane Whitley, Edward Keane, John Bagni, Jay Novello, Paul Marion, Lynton Brent, Duke Green, LeRoy Mason, Fred Graham, Joe Yrigoyen, Ben Erway, Stanley Price, Howard Hickman, George Sherwood, George Byron, Post Park, Al Ferguson, Ben Taggart, Jerry Jerome, Frank O'Connor, Herb Lytton, Jack Kirk, Jack O'Shea, Brooks Benedict, Sam Ash, Robert Wilke, Lorn Courdaye, Gil Perkins, Kenne Duncan, Edward Van Sloan, Edward Cassidy, Robert Strange, Ken Terrell, Wilson Benge, Bud Geary, Tom Steele, John Daheim, Tom London, Harry Strang, George Magrill, Charles Hutchison, Glenn Knight, Roy Brent, Jeffrey Sayre, Dale Van Sickel, Hal Craig, Bert LeBaron, George DeNormand, Terry Frost, Ralf Harolde, Allen Pomeroy, James Carlisle, Helen Thurston. *SYN:* District Attorney Grant Gardner (Purcell) becomes Captain America (Purcell) as he sets out to put an end to the reign of terror of Dr.

Cyrus Maldor (Atwill), also known as "The Scarab." *NOTES:* Dick Purcell plays a dual role in this serial. Republic's last serial to feature a comic book character. Re-released in 1953 as *Return of Captain America.*

**Captain Mephisto and the Transformation Machine** *see* **Manhunt on Mystery Island**

**The Claw Monsters** *see* **Panther Girl of the Kongo**

**Code 645** *see* **G-Men Never Forget**

953. **The Crimson Ghost** (10/26/46) B&W 167 mins. 12 chapters. (Mystery-Science Fiction). *DIR:* William Witney, Fred C. Brannon. *A-PRO:* Ronald Davidson. *SP:* Albert DeMond, Basil Dickey, Jesse Duffy, Sol Shor. *CHAPTER TITLES:* (1) Atomic Peril, (2) Thunderbolt, (3) The Fatal Sacrifice, (4) The Laughing Skull, (5) Flaming Death, (6) Mystery of the Mountain, (7) Electrocution, (8) The Slave Collar, (9) Blazing Fury, (10) The Trap that Failed, (11) Double Murder, (12) The Invisible Trail. *CAST:* Charles Quigley, Linda Stirling, Clayton Moore, I. Stanford Jolley, Kenne Duncan, Forrest Taylor, Emmett Vogan, Sam Flint, Joe Forte, Stanley Price, Wheaton Chambers, Tom Steele, Dale Van Sickel, Rex Lease, Fred Graham, Bud Wolfe, Bill Wilkus, Ken Terrell, Duke Taylor, George Magrill, Eddie Rocco, John Daheim, Loren Riebe, Rose Plummer, Bill Yrigoyen, Virginia Carroll, Carey Loftin, Dick Rush, Rod Bacon, Robert Wilke, Eddie Parker, Joe Yrigoyen, Polly Burson. *SYN:* Criminologist Duncan Richards (Quigley) and secretary Diana Farnsworth (Stirling) set out to stop "The Crimson Ghost" from stealing the Cyclotrode, a counter-atomic device which has the power to stop all electric current within the radius of its rays. *NOTES:* Working title was *The Scarlet Shadow.* This was the only serial to be directed by William Witney following his World War II tour of duty. Viewers of this serial should look at the license plate of the car to understand Witney's opinion of serial production after the war. Released in a "Computer-colorized" version in the 1990s by the new Republic studios. [TV version: Six 26½-min. chapters.] [Century 66 feature version: *Cyclotrode "X."*]

**Cyclotrode "X"** *see* **The Crimson Ghost**

**D-Day on Mars** *see* **The Purple Monster Strikes**

954. **Dangers of the Canadian Mounted** (4/24/48) B&W 167 mins. 12 chapters. (Adventure-Crime). *DIR:* Fred C. Brannon, Yakima Canutt. *A-PRO:* Mike J. Frankovich. *SP:* Franklin Adreon, Basil Dickey, Sol Shor, Robert G. Walker, Jesse Duffy. *CHAPTER TITLES:* (1) Legend of Genghis Khan, (2) Key to the Legend, (3) Ghost Town, (4) Terror in the Sky, (5) Pursuit, (6) Stolen Cargo, (7) The Fatal Shot, (8) False Testimony, (9) The Prisoner Spy, (10) The Secret Meeting, (11) Secret of the Altar, (12) Liquid Jewels. *CAST:* Jim Bannon, Virginia Belmont, Anthony Warde, Dorothy Granger, Bill Van Sickel, Tom Steele, Dale Van Sickel, I. Stanford Jolley, Phil Warren, Lee Morgan, James Dale, Ted Adams, John Crawford, Jack Clifford, Eddie Parker, Frank O'Connor, James Carlisle, Ken Terrell, Eddie Phillips, Robert Wilke, Carey Loftin, Marshall Reed, House Peters, Jr., Tom McDonough, Holly

Bane, Paul Gustine, Ted Mapes, Charles Regan, Jack Kirk, Al Taylor, Harry Cording, Bud Wolfe, Arvon Dale, Roy Bucko, David Sharpe, VOICES OF: Roy Barcroft, Don ("Red") Barry. *SYN:* When an ancient Chinese junk, purported to be one of the treasure ships of Genghis Khan and believed to hold a clue to a vast hidden fortune, is discovered near the town of Alcana on the Canada-Alaska border, an outlaw gang headed by Mort Fowler (Warde), who takes his orders from the mysterious "Chief," begins a campaign of terror to secure the riches and it is up to Mountie Christopher Royal (Bannon) and flying-service owner Roberta Page (Belmont) to stop them. *NOTES:* The correct title to Chapter 8 is *False Testimony,* NOT *Fatal Testimony.* Script writer Jesse Duffy, who worked on the screenplay for five days, was uncredited. Eddie Parker's name was listed in the credits as "Eddy Parker." Bill Van Sickel is the son of Dale Van Sickel. Re-released in 1956 under the same title. [Century 66 feature version: *R.C.M.P. and the Treasure of Genghis Khan.*]

**955. Daredevils of the Red Circle** (6/10/39) B&W 211 mins. 12 chapters. (Mystery-Crime). *DIR:* William Witney, John English. *A-PRO:* Robert Beche. *SP:* Barry Shipman, Franklyn Adreon, Rex Taylor, Ronald Davidson, Sol Shor. *CHAPTER TITLES:* (1) The Monstrous Plot, (2) The Mysterious Friend, (3) The Executioner, (4) Sabotage, (5) The Ray of Death, (6) Thirty Seconds to Live, (7) The Flooded Mine, (8) S.O.S., (9) Ladder of Peril, (10) The Infernal Machine, (11) The Red Circle Speaks, (12) Flight to Doom. *CAST:* Charles Quigley, Herman Brix, David Sharpe, Carole Landis, Miles Mander, Charles Middleton, C. Montague Shaw, Ben Taggart, William Pagan, Corbet Morris, Raymond Bailey, Fred "Snowflake" Toones, George Chesebro, Ray Miller, Robert Winkler, Al Taylor, Bob Robinson, Truda Marson, Roy Brent, Bernard Suss, Bert LeBaron, Lee Frederick, Eddie Cherkose, Frank Wayne, John Merton, Loren Riebe, Reed Howes, Howard Mitchell, Reginald Barlow, Lloyd Whitlock, Joe McGuinn, Edmund Cobb, Earl Bunn, Yakima Canutt, Duke Taylor, Mike Jeffers, George DeNormand, Robert Wilke, Ken Terrell, Bill Wilkus, Broderick O'Farrell, Earle Hodgins, Jack Chapin, Bud Wolfe, Forrest Dillon, Buel Bryant, Earl Askam, Forest Burns, Jerry Jerome, Dave Wengren, Sailor Vincent, Jerry Frank, Norman Nesbitt, George Turner, Fred Schaefer, Bill Nestell, Harry Strang, Eddie Parker, Walter Merrill, Raymond Largay, Joe Yrigoyen, Cy Slocum, Wally West, Bud Geary, Charles Thomas, Stanley Price, Arthur Fowler, Jack Kenney, Dick Scott, Bob Thom, Curley Dresden, Roy Barcroft, Max Marx, Oscar Hendrian, George Plues, Monte Montague, Harry Anderson, Edward Foster, Jimmy Fawcett, Ted Mapes, Millard McGowan, Charles Soderberg, "Tuffie." *SYN:* Three circus daredevils (Brix, Quigley, Sharpe), with the help of the mysterious "Red Circle," set out to stop escaped prisoner Harry Crowell (Middleton), also known as "39013," from destroying the Granville empire, and killing Horace Granville (Mander) and his daughter (Landis). [TV version: Six 26½-min. chapters.]

**956. Daredevils of the West** (5/1/43) B&W 196 mins. 12 chapters. (Western). *DIR:* John English. *A-PRO:* William J. O'Sullivan. *SP:* Ronald Davidson, Basil Dickey, William Lively, Joseph O'Donnell, Joseph F. Poland. *CHAPTER TITLES:* (1) Valley of Death, (2) Flaming Prison, (3) The Killer Strikes, (4) Tunnel of Terror, (5) Fiery Tomb, (6) Redskin Raiders, (7) Perilous Pursuit, (8) Dance of Doom, (9) Terror Trail, (10) Suicide Showdown, (11) Cavern of Cremation, (12) Frontier Justice. *CAST:* Allan ("Rocky") Lane, Kay Aldridge, Eddie Acuff, William Haade, Robert Frazer, Ted Adams, George J. Lewis, Stanley Andrews, Jack Rockwell, Charles Miller, John Hamilton, Budd Buster, Kenneth Harlan, Kenne Duncan, Rex Lease, Chief Thunder Cloud, Duke Green, Eddie Parker, Ray Jones, Joe Yrigoyen, Ken Terrell, Bill Yrigoyen, Chief Many Treaties, Tom Steele, Jack O'Shea, George Magrill, Earl Bunn, Pierce Lyden, George Plues, Al Taylor, Ralph Bucko, Edmund Cobb, Frank McCarroll, Augie Gomez, Rodd Redwing, Harry Smith, Crane Whitley, Tom London, George Pembroke, Allen Pomeroy, Edward Cassidy, Herbert Rawlinson, Tex Cooper, Babe DeFreest, Charles Bruner, Art Dillard, Warren Fiske, George Sky Eagle, Charles Soldani, George Sowards, Bryan Topetchy. *SYN:* A cattle broker (Frazer), desiring the unopened Comanche Strip range as grazing land, plots to stop June Foster (Aldridge), her foreman Red Kelly (Acuff) and Duke Cameron (Lane) from opening a road through the Comanche Strip for a stage line. *NOTES:* One of Republic's "lost" serials. Only chapters 2, 4, 5, and 12 are known to exist at this writing. The correct title to Chapter 7 is *Perilous Pursuit*, NOT *Perilous Plunge*.

**957. Darkest Africa** (2/15/36) B&W 269 mins. 15 chapters. (Adventure-Jungle). *DIR:* B. Reeves Eason, Joseph Kane. *PRO:* Nat Levine. *SUP:* Barney A. Sarecky. *SP:* John Rathmell, Barney A. Sarecky, Ted Parsons. Story by John Rathmell, Tracy Knight. *CHAPTER TITLES:* (1) Baru—Son of the Jungle, (2) The Tiger-Men's God, (3) Bat-Men of Joba, (4) The Hunter Lions of Joba, (5) Bonga's Courage, (6) Prisoners of the High Priest, (7) Swing for Life, (8) Fang and Claw, (9) When Birdmen Strike, (10) Trial by Thunder-Rods, (11) Jars of Death, (12) Revolt of the Slaves, (13) Gauntlet of Destruction, (14) The Divine Sacrifice, (15) The Prophecy of Gorn. *CAST:* Clyde Beatty, Manuel King, Elaine Shepard, Lucien Prival, Wheeler Oakman, Edward McWade, Edmund Cobb, Ray Turner, Ray Benard, Donald Reed, Harrison Greene, Joe Delacruz, Joseph Boyd, Eddie Parker, Henry Sylvester, Prince Modupe, "Naba," the Gorilla (Ray Benard), The Bat-Men, The Tiger-Men. *SYN:* Clyde Beatty joins forces with Baru (King) to rescue his sister (Shepard) from the lost city of Joba. *NOTES:* The correct titles to Chapters 8 and 11 are *Fang and Claw* and *Jars of Death*, NOT *Jaws of the Tiger* and *Jaws of Death*. This serial was Republic's first released serial. It was originally planned as a Mascot Production sequel to their 1934 serial, *The Lost Jungle*, which is included as stock footage in this serial, before Mascot was consolidated into Republic Pictures Corp. Working title was *Dark Continent*. Re-released in 1948 as *King of Jungleland*. [Century 66 feature version: *Bat Men of Africa*.]

**958. Daughter of Don Q** (7/27/46) B&W 167 mins. 12 chapters. (Mystery-Crime). *DIR:* Spencer G. Bennet, Fred C. Brannon. *A-PRO:* Ronald Davidson. *SP:* Albert DeMond, Basil Dickey, Jesse Duffy, Lynn Perkins. *CHAPTER TITLES:* (1) Multiple Murder, (2) Vendetta, (3)

Under the Knives, (4) Race to Destruction, (5) Blackout, (6) Forged Evidence, (7) Execution by Error, (8) Window to Death, (9) The Juggernaut, (10) Cremation, (11) Glass Guillotine, (12) Dead Man's Vengeance. *CAST:* Adrian Booth, Kirk Alyn, LeRoy Mason, Roy Barcroft, Claire Meade, Kernan Cripps, Jimmy Ames, Eddie Parker, Tom Steele, Dale Van Sickel, Fred Graham, Tom Quinn, John Daheim, Ted Mapes, I. Stanford Jolley, Buddy Roosevelt, Frederick Howard, George Chesebro, Michael Gaddis, Charles Sullivan, Arvon Dale, Maxine Doyle, Virginia Carroll, Jack O'Shea, George Magrill, Eddie Rocco, Matty Roubert, Joe Yrigoyen, Ken Terrell, Robert Wilke, Bud Wolfe, D'Arcy Miller, Betty Danko. *SYN:* Carlos Manning (Mason), a descendent of Don Quantaro, locates a Spanish land grant that gave Don Quantaro a large tract of land that is now the business district in a city. He enlists the aid of Mel Donovan (Barcroft) to kill off the Quantaro heirs so he will be sole surviving heir, but his plans are thwarted by reporter Cliff Roberts (Alyn) and Dolores Quantaro (Booth). *NOTES:* Associate producer Ronald Davision, noted for his wit, was a script writer on the serial *Daredevils of the Red Circle* and managed to incorporate the numerical name of the villain — 39013 — of that serial, on the mug shot of Roy Barcroft. The correct titles to Chapters 3 and 12 are *Under the Knives* and *Dead Man's Vengeance*, NOT *Under the Knife* and *Dead Man's Revenge*.

**959. Desperadoes of the West** (8/2/50) B&W 167 mins. 12 chapters. (Western). *DIR:* Fred C. Brannon. *A-PRO:* Franklin Adreon. *SP:* Ronald Davidson. *CHAPTER TITLES:* (1) Tower of Jeopardy, (2) Perilous Barrier, (3) Flaming Cargo, (4) Trail of Terror, (5) Plunder Cave, (6) Six-Gun Hijacker, (7) The Powder Keg, (8) Desperate Venture, (9) Stagecoach to Eternity, (10) Hidden Desperado, (11) Open Warfare, (12) Desperate Gamble. *CAST:* Richard Powers, Judy Clark, Roy Barcroft, I. Stanford Jolley, Lee Phelps, Lee Roberts, Cliff Clark, Edmund Cobb, Hank Patterson, Dale Van Sickel, Tom Steele, Sandy Sanders, John Cason, Guy Teague, Bud Osborne, Stanley Blystone, Chuck Hayward, Bert LeBaron, Frank O'Connor, George Chesebro, Art Dillard, Holly Bane, Duke Taylor, Cactus Mack, Ken Cooper, Dennis Moore, Steve Clark, Chick Hannon, Mauritz Hugo, Jack Harden, Ace Hudkins, Al Taylor, Bob Reeves, Tom McDonough, Eddie Parker, John Daheim, Paul Gustine, Fred Kohler, Jr., Ralph Bucko, Harold Goodwin, Jack Ingram, Forest Burns, Jim Rinehart, Billy Dix, Ray Morgan, Wayne Burson, Augie Gomez, Merrill McCormick, Joe Phillips. *SYN:* An Eastern promoter (Jolley) and his gang of outlaws set out to stop a group of ranchers, led by Colonel Arnold (Cliff Clark) and Ward Gordon (Powers), from striking oil before their lease expires so he can secure the lease for himself. *NOTES:* Working titles were *Bandit King of Oklahoma* and *Desperado Kings of the West*. The correct title to Chapter 11 is *Open Warfare*, NOT *Open Waters*.

**960. Dick Tracy** (2/20/37) B&W 290 mins. 15 chapters. (Mystery-Crime). *DIR:* Ray Taylor, Alan James. *PRO:* Nat Levine. *A-PRO:* J. Laurence Wickland. *SP:* Barry Shipman, Winston Miller. Story by Morgan B. Cox, George Morgan. Based on the cartoon strip by Chester Gould. *CHAPTER TITLES:* (1) The Spider Strikes, (2) The Bridge of

Terror, (3) The Fur Pirates, (4) Death Rides the Sky, (5) Brother Against Brother, (6) Dangerous Waters, (7) The Ghost Town Mystery, (8) Battle in the Clouds, (9) The Stratosphere Adventure, (10) The Gold Ship, (11) Harbor Pursuit, (12) The Trail of the Spider, (13) The Fire Trap, (14) The Devil in White, (15) Brothers United. *CAST:* Ralph Byrd, Kay Hughes, Smiley Burnette, Lee Van Atta, John Picorri, Carleton Young, Fred Hamilton, Francis X. Bushman, John Dilson, Richard Beach, Wedgewood Nowell, Theodore Lorch, Edwin Stanley, Harrison Greene, Herbert Weber, Buddy Roosevelt, George DeNormand, Byron Foulger, Oscar and Elmer, Nicholas Nelson, Bruce Mitchell, Sam Flint, John Holland, Monte Montague, Mary Kelley, Ann Ainslee, Forbes Murray, Hal Price, Henry Sylvester, Milburn Morante, George DeNormand, Loren Riebe, Leander de Cordova, John Ward, Kit Guard, William Stahl, Edward J. LeSaint, Al Taylor, Wally West, Al Ferguson, Jane Keckley, I. Stanford Jolley, William Humphrey, John Bradford, Jack Gardner, Harry Strang, Jack Cheatham, Jack Stewart, John Butler, Bob Reeves, Lester Dorr, Harry Anderson, Kernan Cripps, Louis Morrell, Henry Hale, Andre Cheron, Donald Kerr, Jack Ingram, Charley Phillips, Alice Fleming, Eva McKenzie, Lorin Raker, Wilfrid Lucas, Roscoe Gerall, Walter Long, Burr Caruth, Ray Henderson, Roy Barcroft, Brooks Benedict, John Mills (American actor), Harold DeGarro, Henry Guttman, Edgar Allan, Buddy Williams, Philip Mason. *SYN:* Dick Tracy (Byrd) is assigned to capture the "Lame One," also known as "The Spider," and his Spider Gang, and put an end to their activities. *NOTES:* The last Republic serial to be produced by Nat Levine.

This was the second consecutive serial in which John Picorri's name was misspelled "John Piccori." Working titles were *Adventures of Dick Tracy* and *The Spider Ring.*

**961. Dick Tracy Returns** (8/20/38) B&W 254 mins. 15 chapters. (Crime). *DIR:* William Witney, John English. *PRO:* Sol C. Siegel. *A PRO:* Robert Beche. *SP:* Barry Shipman, Franklyn Adreon, Ronald Davidson, Rex Taylor, Sol Shor. Based on the cartoon strip by Chester Gould. *CHAPTER TITLES:* (1) The Sky Wreckers, (2) The Runway of Death, (3) Handcuffed to Doom, (4) Four Seconds to Live, (5) Death in the Air, (6) Stolen Secrets, (7) Tower of Death, (8) Cargo of Destruction, (9) The Clock of Doom, (10) High Voltage!, (11) The Missing Witness, (12) The Runaway Torpedo, (13) Passengers to Doom, (14) In the Hands of the Enemy, (15) G-Men's Drag-Net. *CAST:* Ralph Byrd, Lynn Roberts, Charles Middleton, Jerry Tucker, David Sharpe, Lee Ford, Michael Kent, John Merton, Raphael Bennett, Jack Roberts, Ned Glass, Edward Foster, Alan Gregg, Reed Howes, Robert Terry, Tom Seidel, Jack Ingram, Dick Bitgood, Roy Darmour, Duke Green, Pat O'Shea, Tom Steele, Bob Thom, James Blaine, Lynton Brent, Maston Williams, Archie Hall, Eddie Cherkose, Douglas Evans, Eddie Parker, Gordon Hart, William Stahl, Ralph Bowman, Ian Rayo, Eddie Dew, Frank Wayne, Jack Montgomery, Walter Jones, Pat McKee, Willard Kent, Sherry Hall, Jerry Frank, Millard McGowan, Frank Hall Crane, Wedgewood Nowell, Charles McMurphy, Larry Steers, Earl Bunn, Harry Tenbrook, George Magrill, Malcolm Graham, Henry Otho, Bruce Mitchell, Allen Pomeroy, Budd Buster, Jack Mack, Forrest Taylor,

Henry Sylvester, Sam Lufkin, Sid Troy, Dan Wolheim, Gloria Rich, Duke York, Bud Wolfe, Charles Sherlock, Oscar Hendrian, Charles Martin, Al Taylor, Richmond Lynch, Harrison Greene, J. P. McGowan, Charles McAvoy, Frank O'Connor, Herbert Weber, James Carlisle, Douglas Meins, Jenifer Gray, Kernan Cripps, Ralph McCullough, Charles Sullivan, John Gustin, Allan Cavan, Loren Riebe, Ted Wells, Buddy Mason, William Mitchell, Jack Egan, Edward Coke, Walter Low, Pat Gleason, King Mojave, Monte Montague, Frank Marlowe, Bill Hunter, Buel Bryant, Frank Hagney, Charley Phillips, Richard Parker, Virginia Carroll, Frank LaRue, Warren Jackson, Francis Sayles, Charles Emerson, Hal Cooke, Earl Askam, Harry Anderson, Brian Burke, John P. Wade, Walter Wills, Yakima Canutt, Art Dillard, Bert White, Wesley Hopper, Charles Regan. *SYN:* Dick Tracy (Byrd) and Steve Lockwood (Kent) set out to capture the notorious Pa Stark (Middleton) and his sons, Champ (Merton), Trigger (Bennett), Dude (Jack Roberts) Slasher (Ingram) and Kid (Glass). *NOTES:* Working title was *Return of Dick Tracy*. First draft screenplay was by George Worthing Yates and John Rathmell, who were uncredited. The correct title to Chapter 11 is *The Missing Witness*, NOT *The Kidnapped Witness*. Re-released in 1948 under the same title.

**962. Dick Tracy Vs. Crime, Inc.** (12/27/41) B&W 263 mins. 15 chapters. (Mystery-Crime). *DIR:* William Witney, John English. *A-PRO:* William J. O'Sullivan. *SP:* Ronald Davidson, Norman S. Hall, William Lively, Joseph O'Donnell, Joseph F. Poland. Based on the cartoon strip by Chester Gould. *CHAPTER TITLES:* (1) The Fatal Hour, (2) The Prisoner Vanishes, (3) Doom Patrol, (4) Dead Man's Trap, (5) Murder at Sea, (6) Besieged, (7) Sea Racketeers, (8) Train of Doom, (9) Beheaded, (10) Flaming Peril, (11) Seconds to Live, (12) Trial by Fire, (13) The Challenge, (14) Invisible Terror, (15) Retribution. *CAST:* Ralph Byrd, Michael Owen, Jan Wiley, John Davidson, Ralph Morgan, Kenneth Harlan, John Dilson, Howard Hickman, Robert Frazer, Robert Fiske, Jack Mulhall, Hooper Atchley, Anthony Warde, Chuck Morrison, Archie Twitchell, Frank Meredith, Jack Kenney, John Merton, Raphael Bennett, Jacques Lory, Joseph Kirk, Forrest Taylor, Dick Lamarr, Pat O'Shea, Barry Hays, Bill Wilkus, Marjorie "Babe" Kane, Charles McAvoy, Bert LeBaron, Richard Kipling, Edward Hearn, John James, Fred Schaefer, Frank Alten, Terry Frost, George Peabody, Nora Lane, Sam Bernard, Bud Wolfe, Charles Miller, Robert Wilke, Wheaton Chambers, Eddie Parker, Fred Kohler, Jr., John Webb Dillon, William Hamner, Stanley Price, Walter McGrail, Harry Tenbrook, Warren Jackson, Edmund Cobb, Al Taylor, C. Montague Shaw, Walter Miller, Benny Burt, Carol Adams, Frances Morris, Hugh Prosser, John Bagni, David Sharpe, George Allen, Buddy Roosevelt, Jimmy Fawcett, Ken Terrell, Bob Robinson, Duke Taylor, Bud Geary, Al Seymour, Evan Thomas, Charley Phillips, Douglas Evans, Julian Madison, Howard Mitchell, Wally Rose, Lynton Brent, Sid Troy, Alexander Lockwood, Max Waizman, Ray Hanson, Dick Rush, Selmer Jackson, Griff Barnette, Charles McMurphy. *SYN:* Dick Tracy (Byrd) and Bill Carr (Owen) set out to stop the "Ghost" from murdering members of the Secret Council of Eight. *NOTES:* Republic's last serial utilizing the *Dick Tracy* character. Working titles were *Dick Tracy Strikes Again* and *Dick Tracy's Revenge*. Ralph Byrd would go on to portray *Dick Tracy* in 2 RKO features, *Dick Tracy's Dilemma* and *Dick Tracy Meets Gruesome*, and also star in a *Dick Tracy* television series Re-released in 1952 as *Dick Tracy Vs. Phantom Empire*.

**Dick Tracy Vs. Phantom Empire** *see* **Dick Tracy Vs. Crime, Inc.**

**963. Dick Tracy's G-Men** (9/2/39) B&W 263 mins. 15 chapters. (Crime). *DIR:* William Witney, John English. *A-PRO:* Robert Beche. *SP:* Barry Shipman, Franklyn Adreon, Rex Taylor, Ronald Davidson, Sol Shor. Based on the cartoon strip by Chester Gould. *CHAPTER TITLES:* (1) The Master Spy, (2) Captured, (3) The False Signal, (4) The Enemy Strikes, (5) Crack-Up!, (6) Sunken Peril, (7) Tracking the Enemy, (8) Chamber of Doom, (9) Flames of Jeopardy, (10) Crackling Fury, (11) Caverns of Peril, (12) Fight in the Sky, (13) The Fatal Ride, (14) Getaway, (15) The Last Stand. *CAST:* Ralph Byrd, Irving Pichel, Ted Pearson, Phylis Isley (Jennifer Jones), Walter Miller, George Douglas, Kenneth Harlan, Robert Carson, Julian Madison, Ted Mapes, William Stahl, Robert Wayne, Joe McGuinn, Ken Terrell, Harry Humphrey, Harrison Greene, Earl Bunn, Jack Ingram, Merrill McCormick, Ray Johnson, David Sharpe, Harry Lang, Bud Geary, Robert Terry, Bud Wolfe, Curley Dresden, Charley Phillips, Monte Montague, Charles Hutchison, Charles Sullivan, Lee Shumway, George DeNormand, Budd Buster, Edward Cassidy, Jim Cassidy, Al Taylor, Bert LeBaron, Bill Wilkus, Joe Yrigoyen, George Allen, Charles Regan, Bigelow Sayre, Russell Coller, Eddie Parker, Allen Pomeroy, Fred Schaefer, Frank Meredith, Jack Raymond, Eddie Cherkose, Bill Lally, Peter Von Ziegler, Bruce Mitchell, Robert Hartford, Ken Cooper, Reginald Barlow, Millard McGowan, Cy Slocum, Jimmy Fawcett, Tom Steele, Bill Yrigoyen, Frank O'Connor, Sailor Vincent, Jerry Frank, Louis Caits, Gilman Shelton, Barry Hays, Ed Brady, Walter Merrill, Robert Brister, Bernard Suss, Allan Davis, Ray Harper, Josef Swickard, John Locke, Milton Frome, Ethan Laidlaw, Edward Peil, Sr., Edward Hearn, Edmund Cobb, Raymond Largay, Herbert Weber, Stanley Price, Jack Roberts, Reed Howes, Joe Forte, Forrest Taylor, Lloyd Ingraham, Charles Murphy, Perry Ivins, John Moloney, Bob Jamison, Charles Sherlock, Carey Loftin, Charles K. French, Broderick O'Farrell, Wally West, Alan Gregg, Bill Nestell, Jack Kenney, Allan Cavan, Sammy McKim, George Cleveland, Tristram Coffin, George Burton, Sid Troy. *SYN:* Dick Tracy (Byrd) and Steve Lockwood (Pearson) set out to stop master spy Zarnoff (Pichel) from sabotaging America's defenses. *NOTES:* Working title was *Dick Tracy and His G-Men*. Re-released in 1955 under the same title.

**Doctor Satan's Robot** *see* **Mysterious Doctor Satan**

**964. Don Daredevil Rides Again** (4/11/51) B&W 167 mins. 12 chapters. (Western). *DIR:* Fred C. Brannon. *A-PRO:* Franklin Adreon. *SP:* Ronald Davidson. *CHAPTER TITLES:* (1) Return of the Don, (2) Double Death, (3) Hidden Danger, (4) Retreat to Destruction, (5) Cold Steel, (6) Flaming Juggernaut, (7) Claim Jumper, (8) Perilous Combat, (9) Hostage of Destiny, (10) Marked for Murder, (11) Captive Witness, (12) Flames of Vengeance. *CAST:* Ken Curtis, Aline Towne, Roy Barcroft, Lane Bradford, Robert Einer, John Cason, I. Stanford Jolley, Hank Patterson, Lee Phelps, Sandy Sanders, Guy Teague, Tom Steele, Mike Ragan, Cactus Mack, Art Dillard, Joe Phillips, Roy Bucko, Bud Osborne, Saul Gorss, Gene Stutenroth, James Magill, David Sharpe, Charles Horvath, Frank McCarroll, Dale Van Sickel, Jack Ingram, George Lloyd, Jack Harden, Carey Loftin, Carlie Taylor, Forrest Taylor, Bert LeBaron, James Linn, Gene Christopher, Tony DeMario, Don C. Harvey, Frank Meredith, Tex Terry, Bob Reeves, Chick Hannon, Herman Hack. *SYN:* Lee Hadley (Curtis) becomes "Don Daredevil" as he helps his cousin Patricia Doyle (Towne) and the neighboring ranchers thwart the attempts of outlaws, led by Doug Stratton (Barcroft), to gain control of their land through a Spanish land grant. *NOTES:* Due to rising serial costs, Republic created the "Don Daredevil" character to utilize stock footage from *Zorro's Black Whip*. Although, the title of this serial was *Don Daredevil Rides Again*, there was no original *Don Daredevil* serial.

**965. Drums of Fu Manchu** (3/15/40) B&W 269 mins. 15 chapters. (Mystery). *DIR:* William Witney, John English. *A-PRO:* Hiram S. Brown, Jr. *SP:* Franklyn Adreon, Morgan B. Cox, Ronald Davidson, Norman S. Hall, Barney A. Sarecky, Sol Shor, Rex Taylor, R. P. Thompson. Suggested by stories by Sax Romer. *CHAPTER TITLES:* (1) Fu Manchu Strikes, (2) The Monster, (3) Ransom in the Sky, (4) The Pendulum of Doom, (5) The House of Terror, (6) Death Dials a Number, (7) Vengeance of the Si Fan, (8) Danger Trail, (9) The Crystal of Death, (10) Drums of Doom, (11) The Tomb of Ghengis Khan, (12) Fire of Vengeance, (13) The Devil's Tattoo, (14) Satan's Surgeon, (15) Revolt. *CAST:* Henry Brandon, William Royle, Robert Kellard, Gloria Franklin, Olaf Hytten, Tom Chatterton, Luana Walters, Lal Chand Mehra, George Cleveland, John Dilson, John Merton, Dwight Frye, Wheaton Chambers, George Pembroke, Guy D'Ennery, Merrill McCormick, Walter Stritz, Charley Phillips, Lowden Adams, John Lester Johnson, Evan Thomas, Philip Ahn, Jamiel Hasson, James B. Leong, Lee Shumway, John Bagni, Bert LeBaron, Ann Baldwin, John Meredith, Joseph DeStefani, Bill Yrigoyen, Tofik Mickey, Paul Renay, Francis Walker, John Picorri, Paul Marion, Kam Tong, Eric Lansdale, Robert Blair, Jenifer Gray, Frank Ellis, Henry Wills, Victor Cox, Bob Stevenson, George Bruggeman, Bill Nind, Michael Vallon, Tony Paton, Akim Dobrynin, Carl Sepulveda, Jack Montgomery, Bob Woodward, Harry Strang, Norman Nesbitt, John Ward, David Sharpe, Hector V. Sarno, Budd Buster, Eddie Kaye, Bob Jamison, Alan Gregg, James Flatley, Art Dillard, Al Taylor, Ernest Sarracino, Jack Roper, Vinegar Roan, Bill Wilkus, Tommy Coats, Frank Wayne, Ted Wells, Burt Dillard, Johnny Judd, Jimmy Fawcett, Augie Gomez, Duke Green, George Suzanne, Duke Taylor, Ken Terrell, Joe Yrigoyen. *SYN:* Sir Denis Nayland Smith (Royle) and Allan Parker (Kellard) vow to stop Fu Manchu (Brandon), leader of the sinister Si Fan, and his Dacoits from locating and stealing the Sacred Sceptre of Genghis Khan in order to bring war to Central Asia and secure his position as new world conqueror. *NOTES:* Republic's only serial in which the villain survives at the end. The screenplay was based on elements from seven different novels plus original ideas. Screen writers Rex Taylor and R. P. Thompson were uncredited. The correct title to Chapter 10 is *Drums of Doom*, NOT *Drums of Death*.

**FBI-99** see **Federal Operator 99**

**966. Federal Agents Vs. Underworld, Inc.** (1/29/49) B&W 167 mins. 12 chapters. (Crime). *DIR:* Fred C. Brannon. *A-PRO:* Franklin Adreon. *SP:* Royal K. Cole, Basil Dickey, William Lively, Sol Shor. *CHAPTER TITLES:* (1) The Golden Hands, (2) Criminals' Lair, (3) Death in Disguise, (4) Fatal Evidence, (5) The Trapped Conspirator, (6) Wheels of Disaster, (7) The Hidden Key, (8) The Enemy's Mouthpiece, (9) The Stolen Hand, (10) Unmasked, (11) Tombs of the Ancients, (12) The Curse of Kurigal. *CAST:* Kirk Alyn, Rosemary LaPlanche, Roy Barcroft, Carol Forman, James Dale, Bruce Edwards, James Craven, Tristram Coffin, Tom Steele, Dale Van Sickel, Jack O'Shea, Marshall Reed, Robert Wilke, Robert St. Angelo, Dave Anderson, Carey Loftin, Post Park, Joe Yrigoyen, Bud Wolfe, Saul Gorss, Loren Riebe, James Carlisle, John Daheim, Bert LeBaron, Duke Taylor, Ken Terrell, Art Dillard, David Sharpe. *SYN:* Professor James Clayton (Craven), discoverer of the famous Golden Hands of Kurigal, which hold the key to a vast fortune, is kidnapped by Spade Gordon (Barcroft) who joins Nila (Forman), an international thief, who has one of the Hands and seeks to secure the other Hand in order to form an organization known as Underworld, Incorporated. Federal agents Dave Worth (Alyn) and Steve Evans (Dale) are assigned to locate Professor Clayton and the missing Hands and to put an end to Underworld, Incorporated.

*NOTES:* Working title was *Crime Fighters Vs. Underworld, Inc.* The correct titles to Chapters 2 and 3 are *Criminals' Lair* and *Death in Disguise*, NOT *The Floating Coffin* and *Death in the Skies*. [Century 66 feature version: *Golden Hands of Kurigal*.]

**967. Federal Operator 99** (7/7/45) B&W 169 mins. 12 chapters. (Crime). *DIR:* Spencer G. Bennet, Wallace A. Grissell, Yakima Canutt. *A-PRO:* Ronald Davidson. *SP:* Albert DeMond, Basil Dickey, Jesse Duffy, Joseph F. Poland. *CHAPTER TITLES:* (1) The Case of the Crown Jewels, (2) The Case of the Stolen Ransom, (3) The Case of the Lawful Counterfeit, (4) The Case of the Telephone Code, (5) The Case of the Missing Expert, (6) The Case of the Double Trap, (7) The Case of the Golden Car, (8) The Case of the Invulnerable Criminal, (9) The Case of the Torn Blueprint, (10) The Case of the Hidden Witness, (11) The Case of the Stradivarius, (12) The Case of the Musical Clue. *CAST:* Marten Lamont, Helen Talbot, George J. Lewis, Lorna Gray, Hal Taliaferro, LeRoy Mason, Bill Stevens, Maurice Cass, Kernan Cripps, Elaine Lange, Frank Jaquet, Forrest Taylor, Jay Novello, Tom London, Jack Ingram, Frederick Howard, Craig Lawrence, Jack O'Shea, Harry Strang, Michael Gaddis, Rex Lease, Jack George, Dale Van Sickel, Nolan Leary, Duke Green, Ken Terrell, Edmund Cobb, Tom Steele, Jack Kirk, Fred Graham, Walter Shumway, Frank Marlowe, Stanley Price, Jimmy Zaner, Curt Barrett, George Chesebro, Ernie Adams. *SYN:* Federal Operator 99, Jerry Blake (Lamont), and secretary Joyce Kingston (Talbot), set out to stop master criminal Jim Belmont (Lewis) and his gang. *NOTES:* Republic's only serial to begin each chapter-title printed on a file folder with the words "*The Case of the....*" This serial also marked the beginning of presenting full cast and technical credits at the beginning of each chapter, not done since *Hawk of the Wilderness*. Re-released in 1956 under the same title. [Century 66 feature version: *FBI-99*.]

**968. The Fighting Devil Dogs** (5/28/38) B&W 204 mins. 12 chapters. (Adventure-Mystery). *DIR:* William Witney, John English. *PRO:* Sol C. Siegel. *A-PRO:* Robert Beche. *SP:* Barry Shipman, Franklyn Adreon, Ronald Davidson, Sol Shor. *CHAPTER TITLES:* (1) The Lightning Strikes, (2) The Mill of Disaster, (3) The Silenced Witness, (4) Cargo of Mystery, (5) Undersea Bandits, (6) The Torpedo of Doom, (7) The Phantom Killer, (8) Tides of Trickery, (9) Attack from the Skies, (10) In the Camp of the Enemy, (11) The Baited Trap, (12) Killer at Bay. *CAST:* Lee Powell, Herman Brix, Eleanor Stewart, Montagu Love, Hugh Sothern, Lester Dorr, Sam Flint, Perry Ivins, Forrest Taylor, John Picorri, Carleton Young, John Davidson, Henry Otho, Reed Howes, Tom London, Edmund Cobb, Alan Gregg, Allan Mathews, Fred Schaefer, Harry Strang, Sherry Hall, Thomas Carr, Howard Chase, Lloyd Whitlock, Lee Baker, Jack Ingram, Robert Kortman, Bud Osborne, F. Herrick Herrick, Ken Cooper, Jerry Frank, Jack O'Shea, Millard McGowan, Dirk Thane, Theodore Lorch, Al Taylor, Robert Wilbur, Harry Anderson, Jack Daley, Monte Montague, George Magrill, Larry Steers, William Stahl, Bruce Lane, Lee Frederick, Buel Bryant, Tom Steele, Victor Wong, Joe Delacruz, John Hiestand, James Carlisle, Edward Cassidy, Buddy Roosevelt, Wesley Hopper, Edward Foster, Earl Douglas, Eddie Dew, Jack Roberts, Frederick Freeman, Francis Sayles, George DeNormand, Duke York, Ray Hanson, Frank Baker, Robert Wilke, Joe Yrigoyen, John Merton, Edward Argyle, Duke Green, Ray Henderson, Eddie Parker, *VOICES OF:* Stanley Price, Edwin Stanley. *SYN:* Two Marines (Powell, Brix) set out to stop "The Lightning" and his artificial thunderbolts of electricity, as he seeks world domination. *NOTES:* The correct title to Chapter 3 is *The Silenced Witness*, NOT *Silent Witness*. [TV version: Six 26½-min. chapters.] [Century 66 feature version: *The Torpedo of Doom*.]

**969. Flying Disc Man from Mars** (10/25/50) B&W 167 mins. 12 chapters. (Science Fiction). *DIR:* Fred C. Brannon. *A-PRO:* Franklin Adreon. *SP:* Ronald Davidson. *CHAPTER TITLES:* (1) Menace from Mars, (2) The Volcano's Secret, (3) Death Rides the Stratosphere, (4) Execution by Fire, (5) The Living Projectile, (6) Perilous Mission, (7) Descending Doom, (8) Suicidal Sacrifice, (9) The Funeral Pyre, (10) Weapons of Hate, (11) Disaster on the Highway, (12) Volcanic Vengeance. *CAST:* Walter Reed, Lois Collier, Gregory Gay, James Craven, Harry Lauter, Richard Irving, Sandy Sanders, Michael Carr, Dale Van Sickel, Tom Steele, George Sherwood, Jimmy O'Gatty, John DeSimone, Lester Dorr, Dick Cogan, Clayton Moore, Dick Crockett, John Daheim, Bill Wilkus, Chuck Hamilton, Saul Gorss, Barry Brooks, Ken Terrell, Carey Loftin, David Sharpe, Paul Gustine, Guy Teague. *SYN:* Kent Fowler (Reed) sets out to stop scientist Dr. Bryant (Craven) and Martian invader Mota (Gay) from building atomic-powered planes and bombs and placing Earth under supreme Martian dictatorship. *NOTES:* Working titles were *Atom Man from Mars, Disc Man from Mars, Disc Men of the Skies, Flying Planet Men,* and *Jet Man from Mars.*

**970. Ghost of Zorro** (3/24/49) B&W 167 mins. 12 chapters. (Western). *DIR:* Fred C. Brannon. *A-PRO:* Franklin Adreon. *SP:* Royal K. Cole, William Lively, Sol Shor. *CHAPTER TITLES:* (1) Bandit Territory, (2) Forged Orders, (3) Robber's Agent, (4) Victims of Vengeance, (5) Gun Trap, (6) Deadline at Midnight, (7) Tower of Disaster, (8) Mob Justice, (9) Money Lure, (10) Message of Death, (11) Runaway Stagecoach, (12) Trail of Blood. *CAST:* Clayton Moore, Pamela Blake, Roy Barcroft, George J. Lewis, Gene Stutenroth, John Crawford, I. Stanford Jolley, Steve Clark, Steve Darrell, Dale Van Sickel, Tom Steele, Alex Montoya, Marshall Reed, Frank O'Connor, Jack O'Shea, Holly Bane, Bob Reeves, John Daheim, Eddie Parker, Post Park, Stanley Blystone, Joe Yrigoyen, George Chesebro, Charles King, Roger Creed, Ken Terrell, Robert Wilke, Roy Bucko, Art Dillard, Frank Ellis, Bob Robinson. *SYN:* Ken Mason (Moore) is hired by Jonathan White (Clark) and his daughter Rita (Blake) to extend telegraph lines from St. Joseph to Twin Bluffs. When Jonathan is killed, Rita vows to continue building the telegraph, and Ken, learning that his grandfather was Don Diego Vega, the original Zorro, vows to ride as Zorro to help Rita and bring the killers of Jonathan White to justice. *NOTES:* This was Republic's last use of the Zorro character.

**Ghost Riders of the West** *see* **The Phantom Rider**

**971. G-Men Never Forget** (1/31/48) B&W 167 mins. 12 chapters. (Crime). *DIR:* Fred C. Brannon, Yakima Canutt. *A-PRO:* Mike J. Frankovich. *SP:* Franklin Adreon, Basil Dickey, Jesse Duffy, Sol Shor. *CHAPTER TITLES:* (1) Death Rides the Torrent, (2) 100,000 Volts, (3) Code Six Four Five, (4) Shipyard Saboteurs, (5) The Dead Man Speaks, (6) Marked Evidence, (7) Hot Cargo, (8) The Fatal Letter, (9) The Death Wind, (10) The Innocent Victim, (11) Counter-Plot, (12) Exposed. *CAST:* Clayton Moore, Roy Barcroft, Ramsay Ames, Drew Allen, Tom Steele, Dale Van Sickel, Edmund Cobb, Stanley Price, Jack O'Shea, Barry Brooks, Doug Aylesworth, Frank O'Connor, Dian Fauntelle, Eddie Acuff, George Magrill, Ken Terrell, Tom McDonough, James Linn, Russ Whitman, John Crawford, Glenn Turner, Gil Perkins, Matty Roubert, Bud Wolfe, Robert Barron, George Douglas, Charles Regan, Carey Loftin, Tom Monroe, John Daheim, Arvon Dale, Charles Sullivan, Duke Green, Phil Warren, Robert Wilke, David Sharpe. *SYN:* Vic Murkland (Barcroft) escapes from prison and has plastic surgery which makes him into Police Commissioner Angus Cameron (Barcroft). Murkland captures Cameron and assumes his place, and it is up to federal agent Ted O'Hara (Moore) and Detective Sergeant Frances Blake (Ames) to expose Murkland and stop his reign of crime. *NOTES:* The correct titles to Chapters 2 and 6 are *100,000 Volts* and *Marked Evidence,* NOT *The Flaming Doll House* and *Marked Money.* Roy Barcroft plays a dual role in this serial. [Century 66 feature version: *Code 645.*]

**972. G-Men Vs. the Black Dragon** (1/16/43) B&W 243 mins. 15 chapters.

(Adventure-War). *DIR:* William Witney. *A-PRO:* William J. O'Sullivan. *SP:* Ronald Davidson, William Lively, Joseph O'Donnell, Joseph F. Poland. *CHAPTER TITLES:* (1) Yellow Peril, (2) Japanese Inquisition, (3) Arsenal of Doom, (4) Deadly Sorcery, (5) Celestial Murder, (6) Death and Destruction, (7) The Iron Monster, (8) Beast of Tokyo, (9) Watery Grave, (10) The Dragon Strikes, (11) Suicide Mission, (12) Dead on Arrival, (13) Condemned Cargo, (14) Flaming Coffin, (15) Democracy in Action. *CAST:* Rod Cameron, Roland Got, Constance Worth, Nino Pipitone, Noel Cravat, George J. Lewis, Maxine Doyle, Donald Kirke, Ivan Miller, Walter Fenner, C. Montague Shaw, Harry Burns, Forbes Murray, Hooper Atchley, Robert E. Homans, Allen Jung, Norman Nesbitt, John Daheim, Lawrence Grant, Crane Whitley, Eddie Parker, Ken Terrell, Kenneth Harlan, Harry Tauvera, Tom Steele, Peter George Lynn, Stanley Price, Pat O'Malley, Edward Keane, Walter Low, George DeNormand, Charley Phillips, Charles Flynn, Gil Perkins, William Forrest, Paul Fung, Ray Parsons, Sam Bernard, Robert Strange, Eddie Phillips, Bill Cody, Duke Taylor, John Hamilton, Mary Bayless, Martin Faust, Bud Geary, John Wallace, Charles LaTorre, Dick French, Virginia Carroll, Dale Van Sickel, Arvon Dale, John James, Tom Seidel, Edmund Cobb, Norman Willis, Elliott Sullivan, Bud Wolfe, Eddie Dew, Otto Metzetti, *VOICES OF:* Baron Lichter, Walter Thiel, Buddy Roosevelt. *SYN:* Rex Bennett (Cameron), American special investigator, Vivian Marsh (Worth), British secret agent, and Chang Sing (Got) of the Chinese secret service, join forces to search out and destroy the Black Dragon Society, led by Oyama Haruchi (Pipitone). *NOTES:* William Witney's last directed serial before entering service during World War II. He entered service before filming was completed and the serial was completed by John English, who was uncredited. Released by European distributors as *Haruchi, Son of Fu Manchu.* [Century 66 feature version: *Black Dragon of Manzanar.*]

**Golden Hands of Kurigal** *see* **Federal Agents Vs. Underworld, Inc.**

973. **Government Agents Vs. Phantom Legion** (7/4/51) B&W 167 mins. 12 chapters. (Crime). *DIR:* Fred C. Brannon. *A-PRO:* Franklin Adreon. *SP:* Ronald Davidson. *CHAPTER TITLES:* (1) River of Fire, (2) The Stolen Corpse, (3) The Death Drop, (4) Doorway to Doom, (5) Deadline for Disaster, (6) Mechanical Homicide, (7) Flaming Highway, (8) Sea Saboteurs, (9) Peril Underground, (10) Execution by Accident, (11) Perilous Plunge, (12) Blazing Retribution. *CAST:* Walter Reed, Mary Ellen Kay, Dick Curtis, John Pickard, Fred Coby, Pierce Lyden, George Meeker, John Phillips, Mauritz Hugo, Edmund Cobb, Eddie Dew, George Lloyd, Dale Van Sickel, Tom Steele, Arthur Space, Norval Mitchell, Frank Meredith, Gene Christopher, Frank Alten, Terry Frost, Dick Crockett, Roy Barcroft, George Volk, Ben Taggart, Richard Grant, Dean Henson, Jay Merrick, Duke Taylor, Buddy Thorpe, Ralph Dunn, Joe Phillips, Eddie Parker, Frank O'Connor, David Sharpe. *SYN:* A mysterious criminal, known as the "Voice," is sabotaging trucking shipments in order to obtain their shipments to sell on the black market. Government agent Hal Duncan (Reed) suspecting that one of four men, Armstrong (Lyden), Willard (Meeker), Thompson (Hugo), and

Crandall (Space), of the Interstate Truck Owners' Association, is the mysterious "Voice," sets out to stop him and put an end to his criminal activities. NOTES: Working title was *Government Agents Vs. Phantom Underground*. The last of Republic's serials to utilize a mystery villain until their final serial release in 1955, *King of the Carnival*.

974. **Haunted Harbor** (8/26/44) B&W 243 mins. 15 chapters. (Adventure). DIR: Spencer G. Bennet, Wallace A. Grissell. A-PRO: Ronald Davidson. SP: Royal K. Cole, Basil Dickey, Jesse Duffy, Grant Nelson, Joseph F. Poland. From the novel by Dayle Douglas (Ewart Adamson). CHAPTER TITLES: (1) Wanted for Murder, (2) Flight to Danger, (3) Ladder of Death, (4) The Unknown Assassin, (5) Harbor of Horror, (6) Return of the Fugitive, (7) Journey into Peril, (8) Wings of Doom, (9) Death's Door, (10) Crimson Sacrifice, (11) Jungle Jeopardy, (12) Fire Trap, (13) Monsters of the Deep, (14) High Voltage, (15) Crucible of Justice. CAST: Kane Richmond, Kay Aldridge, Roy Barcroft, Clancy Cooper, Marshall Reed, Oscar O'Shea, Forrest Taylor, Hal Taliaferro, Edward Keane, George J. Lewis, Kenne Duncan, Bud Geary, Robert E. Homans, Duke Green, Dale Van Sickel, Tom Steele, Rico de Montez, Robert Wilke, Fred Graham, Bud Wolfe, Carey Loftin, Charles Hayes, Nick Thompson, Dick Botiller, Fred Cordova, Pietro Sosso, Jack O'Shea, Kit Guard, Ken Terrell, Herbert Evans, Eddie Parker, Harry Smith, Harry Wilson. SYN: Jim Marsden (Richmond), framed for the murder of an island banker (Keane) by the banker's partner, Kane (Barcroft), sets out to prove his innocence and also to find the gold bullion that was lost when his schooner sank. NOTES: Republic's last serial to use first chapter opticals and also the last serial to be adapted from another medium. Re-released in 1951 as *Pirates' Harbor*.

975. **Hawk of the Wilderness** (12/3/38) B&W 213 mins. 12 chapters. (Adventure). DIR: William Witney, John English. PRO: Sol C. Siegel. A-PRO: Robert Beche. SP: Barry Shipman, Rex Taylor, Norman S. Hall, Sol, Shor, Reginald "Reggie" Callow. Based on the book of the same name by William L. Chester. CHAPTER TITLES: (1) Mysterious Island, (2) Flaming Death, (3) Tiger Trap, (4) Queen's Ransom, (5) Pendulum of Doom, (6) The Dead Fall, (7) White Man's Magic, (8) Ambushed, (9) Marooned, (10) Caves of Horror, (11) Valley of Skulls, (12) Trail's End. CAST: Herman Brix, (Ray) Mala, Monte Blue, Jill Martin, Noble Johnson, William Royle, Tom Chatterton, George Eldredge, Patrick J. Kelly, Dick Wessel, Fred "Snowflake" Toones, Lane Chandler, Ann Evers, Earl Askam, Jerry Sheldon, Fred Miller, George Letz, Harry Tenbrook, William Stahl, Loren Riebe, Ted Mapes, Jack O'Shea, Art Felix, Frank Hill, Jerry Frank, Henry Wills, Jerome DeNuccio, Iron Eyes Cody, John Roy, Joe Garcia, Moe Malulo, Jack Minton, Jimmy Dime, Tony Urchel, Phillip Armenta, Chief John Big Tree, Charley P. Randolph, Art Miles, Jim I. Spencer, Joe Draper, Alex Montoya, Gertrude Chorre, Cy Shindall, L. Y. Maxwell, Clarence Chorre, Sonny Chorre, Wally Rose, "Tuffie." SYN: A group of smugglers led by Salerno (Royle) find a bottle with a message in it addressed to Dr. Edward Munro (Chatterton) telling of a lost island and treasure. Together, these

travelers journey to an uncharted island in the Arctic Circle, seeking Lincoln Rand, Jr. (Brix), also known as Kioga, and a race from which the American Indians descended, and the lost treasure. NOTES: Screen writers Sol Shor and Reginald "Reggie" Callow were uncredited. The correct title to Chapter 10 is *Caves of Horror*, NOT *Camp of Horror*. [TV version: Six 26½-min. chapters.] [Century 66 feature version: *Lost Island of Kioga*.]

**976. The Invisible Monster** (5/10/50) B&W 167 mins. 12 chapters. (Mystery-Crime). DIR: Fred C. Brannon. A-PRO: Franklin Adreon. SP: Ronald Davidson. CHAPTER TITLES: (1) Slaves of the Phantom, (2) The Acid Clue, (3) The Death Car, (4) Highway Holocaust, (5) Bridge to Eternity, (6) Ordeal by Fire, (7) Murder Train, (8) Window of Peril, (9) Trail to Destruction, (10) High Voltage Danger, (11) Death's Highway, (12) The Phantom Meets Justice. CAST: Richard Webb, Aline Towne, Lane Bradford, Stanley Price, John Crawford, George Meeker, Keith Richards, Dale Van Sickel, Tom Steele, Marshall Reed, Forest Burns, Eddie Parker, Frank O'Connor, Charles Sullivan, Howard Mitchell, Bud Wolfe, Guy Teague, Carey Loftin, Tom Monroe, David Sharpe, George Volk, Douglas Evans, Ken Terrell, Harold Goodwin, Edward Keane, John Hamilton, Roy Gordon, Duke Taylor, George Magrill, Mark Strong, Bert LeBaron. SYN: Insurance investigator Lane Carson (Webb) and his assistant Carol Richards (Towne) set out to stop a master criminal, known as "The Phantom Ruler" (Price), from equipping an invisible army and dominating the world. NOTES: Working title was *The Phantom Ruler*. [Century 66 feature version: *Slaves of the Invisible Monster*.]

**977. The James Brothers of Missouri** (8/31/49) B&W 167 mins. 12 chapters. (Western). DIR: Fred C. Brannon. A-PRO: Franklin Adreon. SP: Royal K. Cole, William Lively, Sol Shor. CHAPTER TITLES: (1) Frontier Renegades, (2) Racing Peril, (3) Danger Road, (4) Murder at Midnight, (5) Road to Oblivion, (6) Missouri Manhunt, (7) Hangman's Noose, (8) Coffin on Wheels, (9) Dead Man's Return, (10) Galloping Gunslingers, (11) The Haunting Past, (12) Fugitive's Code. CAST: Keith Richards, Robert Bice, Noel Neill, Roy Barcroft, Patricia Knox, Lane Bradford, Gene Stutenroth, John Hamilton, Edmund Cobb, Hank Patterson, Dale Van Sickel, Tom Steele, Lee Roberts, Frank O'Connor, Marshall Reed, Wade Ray, Nolan Leary, David Sharpe, Art Dillard, Duke Green, John Crawford, Jim Rinehart, Ray Morgan, Post Park, Duke Taylor, Al Ferguson, Cactus Mack, Joe Phillips, Tommy Coats, Bert LeBaron, Ken Terrell, Ted Hubert, Robert Wilke, Roy Bucko, Ralph Bucko, Forest Burns, Helen Griffith, Herman Hack, Chick Hannon, Chuck Roberson, Bud Wolfe, Frosty Royce, Rocky Shahan. SYN: Pledging to clear their names and re-establish themselves as members of society, Frank James (Bice) and Jesse James (Richards) travel to Rimrock, Missouri where they meet former gang member Lon Royer (Hamilton) and his daughter Peg (Neill), and agree to help him secure a federal contract for his stage line. When Lon is murdered by rival stage line owner Ace Marlin (Barcroft), Frank and Jesse vow to help Peg secure the federal contract for the stage line and bring Lon's murderer to justice. NOTES: The correct title to Chapter 12 is *Fugitive's Code*, NOT *Fugitive Code*.

**978. Jesse James Rides Again** (8/2/47) B&W 180 mins. 13 chapters. (Western). *DIR:* Fred C. Brannon, Thomas Carr. *A-PRO:* Mike J. Frankovich. *SP:* Franklin Adreon, Basil Dickey, Jesse Duffy, Sol Shor. *CHAPTER TITLES:* (1) The Black Raiders, (2) Signal for Action, (3) The Stacked Deck, (4) Concealed Evidence, (5) The Corpse of Jesse James, (6) The Traitor, (7) Talk or Die!, (8) Boomerang, (9) The Captured Raider, (10) The Revealing Torch, (11) The Spy, (12) Black Gold, (13) Deadline at Midnight. *CAST:* Clayton Moore, Linda Stirling, Roy Barcroft, John Compton, Tristram Coffin, Tom London, Holly Bane, Edmund Cobb, Gene Stutenroth, Fred Graham, LeRoy Mason, Edward Cassidy, Dave Anderson, Eddie Parker, Tom Steele, Dale Van Sickel, Robert Blair, Ted Mapes, Tex Terry, Gil Perkins, Tex Palmer, Casey MacGregor, Emmett Lynn, Charles Morton, Watson Downs, Duke Taylor, Monte Montague, Lee Shumway, Carey Loftin, Loren Riebe, Frank Marlowe, Herman Hack, Chuck Roberson, Carl Sepulveda, Ken Terrell, Bert LeBaron, Pascale Perry, Nellie Walker, Chester Conklin, Tommy Coats, George Chesebro, Bud Wolfe, Tom Chatterton, Charles King, Robert Riordan, Howard Mitchell, Richard Alexander, Keith Richards, Victor Cox, Helen Griffith, Don Summers. *SYN:* Falsely accused of the Northfield, Minnesota bank robbery, Jesse James (Moore) and his friend Steve Lane (Compton) leave Missouri and stop in Peaceful Valley, Tennessee, where they help the townspeople battle and defeat the Black Raiders and their leader (Coffin) who are after their oil rich land. *NOTES:* The first serial to use the Republic "Eagle" logo and the only serial to use the logo with the words, "A Republic Production," instead of "A Republic Serial." Chapter 5 is unique in that the cliffhanger was not resolved until midway through the chapter. Re-released in 1955 under the same title.

**979. Jungle Drums of Africa** (1/21/53) B&W 167 mins. 12 chapters. (Adventure-Jungle). *DIR:* Fred C. Brannon. *A-PRO:* Franklin Adreon. *SP:* Ronald Davidson. *CHAPTER TITLES:* (1) Jungle Ambush, (2) Savage Strategy, (3) The Beast-Fiend, (4) Voodoo Vengeance, (5) The Lion Pit, (6) Underground Tornado, (7) Cavern of Doom, (8) The Water Trap, (9) Trail to Destruction, (10) The Flaming Ring, (11) Bridge of Death, (12) The Avenging River. *CAST:* Clay Moore, Phyllis Coates, Johnny Spencer, Roy Glenn, Sr., John Cason, Henry Rowland, Steve Mitchell, Bill Walker, Don Blackman, Felix Nelson, Joel Fluellen, Bill Washington, Tom Steele, Robert Davis, Roy Engel, Bob Johnson, DeForest Covan, Walter Smith, Maxie Thrower, Joe Yrigoyen, "Chiquita." *SYN:* Sent to Africa by the Ameranium Development Company to obtain a uranium concession from Chief Douanga (Walker), engineer Alan King (Moore) and his assistant Bert Hadley (Spencer), join forces with medical missionary Dr. Carol Bryant (Coates) as they set out to stop trading-post operator Kurgan (Rowland) from securing the uranium deposits for a foreign government. *NOTES:* Working title was *Robin Hood of Darkest Africa*. Clayton Moore's ninth and final Republic serial; for this serial he shortened his name to Clay Moore. Much of the wild-animal footage came from Republic's 1950 documentary feature, *Jungle Stampede*. [Century 66 feature version: *U-238 and the Witch Doctor*.]

**980. Jungle Girl** (6/21/41) B&W 265 mins. 15 chapters. (Adventure-Jungle). *DIR:* William Witney, John English. *A-PRO:* Hiram S. Brown, Jr. *SP:* Ronald Davidson, Norman S. Hall, William Lively, Joseph O'Donnell, Joseph F. Poland, Alfred Batson. Based on the famous novel *Jungle Girl* by Edgar Rice Burroughs. *CHAPTER TITLES:* (1) Death by Voodoo, (2) Queen of Beasts, (3) River of Fire, (4) Treachery, (5) Jungle Vengeance, (6) Tribal Fury, (7) The Poison Dart, (8) Man Trap, (9) Treasure Tomb, (10) Jungle Killer, (11) Dangerous Secret, (12) Trapped, (13) Ambush, (14) Diamond Trail, (15) Flight to Freedom. *CAST:* Frances Gifford, Tom Neal, Trevor Bardette, Gerald Mohr, Eddie Acuff, Frank Lackteen, Tommy Cook, Robert Barron, Al Kikume, Bud Geary, Al Taylor, Joe McGuinn, Jerry Frank, Ken Terrell, Yakima Canutt, Duke Green, David Sharpe, Harry Smith, Tom Steele, Duke Taylor, Helen Thurston. *SYN:* Nyoka (Gifford) and Jack Stanton (Neal) must prevent her uncle (Bardette) and Slick Latimer (Mohr) from stealing the sacred Nakros diamonds and starting a native uprising. *NOTES:* Republic's first serial heroine serial. Re-released in 1947 under the same title.

**Jungle Gold** *see* **The Tiger Woman**

**King of Jungleland** *see* **Darkest Africa**

**981. King of the Carnival** (6/27/55) B&W 167 mins. 12 chapters. (Crime). *DIR/A-PRO:* Franklin Adreon. *SP:* Ronald Davidson. *CHAPTER TITLES:* (1) Daredevils of the Air, (2) Death Takes the Wheel, (3) The Trap that Failed, (4) Operation Murder, (5) The Mechanical Bloodhound, (6) Undersea Peril, (7) High Hazard, (8) Death Alley, (9) Cave of Doom, (10) The Masked Executioner, (11) Undersea Warfare, (12) Vengeance Under the Big Top. *CAST:* Harry Lauter, Fran Bennett, Keith Richards, Robert Shayne, Gregory Gay, Rick Vallin, Robert Clarke, Terry Frost, Mauritz Hugo, Lee Roberts, Chris Mitchell, Stuart Whitman, Tom Steele, George DeNormand, Bill Scully, Tom McDonough, Harry Hollins, Bert LeBaron, Eddie Parker, Jean Harvey, Brick Sullivan, Richard Alexander, Ray Spiker, Guy Teague, Dorothy Andre, John Cason, Duke Taylor, Godfrey Wainwright. *SYN:* Bert King (Lauter), trapeze artist, and his partner June Edwards (Bennett) work together with treasury agent Art Kerr (Vallin) to help ferret out counterfeiters working at the circus, who taking orders from a mysterious voice known as "V." *NOTES:* Working title was *King of the Circus*. The correct title to Chapter 11 is *Undersea Warfare* NOT *Undersea Warrior*. After almost 20 years of serial production, this was Republic's final serial.

**982. King of the Forest Rangers** (4/27/46) B&W 167 mins. 12 chapters. (Crime). *DIR:* Spencer G. Bennet, Fred C. Brannon. *A-PRO:* Ronald Davidson. *SP:* Albert DeMond, Basil Dickey, Jesse Duffy, Lynn Perkins. *CHAPTER TITLES:* (1) The Mystery of the Towers, (2) Shattered Evidence, (3) Terror by Night, (4) Deluge of Destruction, (5) Pursuit into Evil, (6) Brink of Doom, (7) Design for Murder, (8) The Flying Coffin, (9) S.O.S. Ranger, (10) The Death Detector, (11) The Flaming Pit, (12) Tower of Vengeance. *CAST:* Larry Thompson, Helen Talbot, Stuart Hamblen, Anthony Warde, LeRoy Mason, Scott Elliott, Tom London, Walter Soderling, Bud Geary, Harry Strang,

Ernie Adams, Eddie Parker, Jack Kirk, Tom Steele, Dale Van Sickel, Stanley Blystone, Marin Sais, Buddy Roosevelt, Robert Wilke, Sam Ash, Carey Loftin, Sailor Vincent, Jay Kirby, Joe Yrigoyen, Nick Warwick, Ken Terrell, Bud Wolfe, Wheaton Chambers, James Martin, Rex Lease, Charles Sullivan, David Sharpe. *SYN:* Forest Ranger Steve King (Thompson) and trading post proprietress Marion Brennan (Talbot) seek to find the secret of Antelope Towers and to stop Professor Carver (Hamblen) and his henchman Burt Spear (Warde) from murdering the owners of the land on which the Towers reside. *NOTES:* David Sharpe, in his first new serial appearance since *Perils of Nyoka*, played a cast member and also doubled Stuart Hamblen. Filming was done at Big Bear Lake in Northern California and, because of rising production costs, this was the last serial to use extensive location photography. [TV version: Six 26½-min. chapters.]

**983. King of the Mounties** (10/17/42) B&W 196 mins. 12 chapters. (Crime-War). *DIR:* William Witney. *A-PRO:* William J. O'Sullivan. *SP:* Taylor Caven, Ronald Davidson, William Lively, Joseph O'Donnell, Joseph F. Poland. Based on Zane Grey's *King of the Royal Mounted*. *CHAPTER TITLES:* (1) Phantom Invaders, (2) Road to Death, (3) Human Target, (4) Railroad Saboteurs, (5) Suicide Dive, (6) Blazing Barrier, (7) Perilous Plunge, (8) Electrocuted, (9) Reign of Terror, (10) The Flying Coffin, (11) Deliberate Murder, (12) On to Victory. *CAST:* Allan ("Rocky") Lane, Gilbert Emery, Russell Hicks, Peggy Drake, George Irving, Abner Biberman, William Vaughn, Nestor Paiva, Bradley Page, Douglass Dumbrille, William Bakewell, Duncan Renaldo, Francis Ford, Jay Novello, Anthony Warde, Norman Nesbitt, John Hiestand, Allen Jung, Paul Fung, Arvon Dale, Ken Terrell, John Roy, Bud Weiser, Duke Taylor, Frank Wayne, Pete Katchenaro, Harry Cording, Carleton Young, Tom Steele, Kam Tong, Earl Bunn, Hal Taliaferro, Duke Green, Stanley Price, Tommy Coats, Bob Jamison, Jack Kenney, Sam Serrano, King Kong, Joe Chambers, Jimmy Fawcett, Forrest Taylor, David Sharpe. *SYN:* Sergeant Dave King (Lane) of the Mounties sets out to stop the Axis Fifth Column in Canada, led by Admiral Yamata (Biberman), Marshal Von Horst (Vaughn), and Count Baroni (Paiva). *NOTES:* Working titles were *King of the Royal Mounted Rides Again*, *King of the Royal Mounted Strikes Again*, *King of the Royal Mounted Strikes Back*, and *King of the Northwest Mounted Strikes Again*.

**984. King of the Rocket Men** (6/8/49) B&W 167 mins. 12 chapters. (Science Fiction). *DIR:* Fred C. Brannon. *A-PRO:* Franklin Adreon. *SP:* Royal K. Cole, William Lively, Sol Shor. *CHAPTER TITLES:* (1) Dr. Vulcan — Traitor, (2) Plunging Death, (3) Dangerous Evidence, (4) High Peril, (5) Fatal Dive, (6) Mystery of the Rocket Man, (7) Molten Menace, (8) Suicide Flight, (9) Ten Seconds to Live, (10) The Deadly Fog, (11) Secret of Dr. Vulcan, (12) Wave of Disaster. *CAST:* Tristram Coffin, Mae Clarke, Don Haggerty, House Peters, Jr., James Craven, I. Stanford Jolley, Douglas Evans, Ted Adams, Stanley Price, Dale Van Sickel, Tom Steele, David Sharpe, Eddie Parker, Michael Ferro, Frank O'Connor, Buddy Roosevelt, Arvon Dale, Bud Wolfe, Marshall Bradford, Bert LeBaron, Art Gilmore, Carey Loftin,

Jack O'Shea. *SYN:* Dr. Vulcan (?????), a member of Science Associates, is murdering the other members of Science Associates to gain control of atomic secrets. Professor Millard (Craven), who pretends to be dead, summons Jeff King (Coffin) and gives him a jet-propelled flying suit. King then becomes Rocket Man as he tracks down Dr. Vulcan and his gang. *NOTES:* The only serial in which the mystery villain was revealed in Chapter 11 and not the last chapter. Re-released in 1956 under the same title.

**985. King of the Royal Mounted** (9/20/40) B&W 211 mins. 12 chapters. (Crime-Spies). *DIR:* William Witney, John English. *A-PRO:* Hiram S. Brown, Jr. *SP:* Franklyn Adreon, Norman S. Hall, Joseph F. Poland, Barney A. Sarecky, Sol Shor. *CHAPTER TITLES:* (1) Manhunt, (2) Winged Death, (3) Boomerang, (4) Devil Doctor, (5) Sabotage, (6) False Ransom, (7) Death Tunes In, (8) Satan's Cauldron, (9) Espionage, (10) Blazing Guns, (11) Master Spy, (12) Code of the Mounted. *CAST:* Allan ("Rocky") Lane, Robert Strange, Robert Kellard, Lita Conway, Herbert Rawlinson, Harry Cording, Bryant Washburn, Budd Buster, Stanley Andrews, John Davidson, John Dilson, Paul McVey, Lucien Prival, Norman Willis, Tony Paton, Ken Terrell, Charles Thomas, Bill Wilkus, Ted Mapes, Major Sam Harris, George Plues, Frank Wayne, Richard Simmons, Loren Riebe, Wallace Reid, Jr., William Justice, William Stahl, John Bagni, Earl Bunn, Curley Dresden, George DeNormand, Bud Geary, Dave Marks, Robert Wayne, William Kellogg, Tommy Coats, Alan Gregg, Denny Sullivan, Walter Low, George Ford, Bob Jamison, Dale Van Sickel, Al Taylor, Cy Slocum, Douglas Evans, Duke Taylor, Jimmy Fawcett, David Sharpe, Duke Green. *SYN:* Sergeant Dave King (Lane) of the Mounties must stop foreign agents from stealing "Compound X," a substance, that not only cures infantile paralysis, but, because of its magnetic properties, would benefit the agents' country in the production of mines to use against Allied shipping.

**986. King of the Texas Rangers** (10/4/41) B&W 215 mins. 12 chapters. (Crime). *DIR:* William Witney, John English. *A-PRO:* Hiram S. Brown, Jr. *SP:* Ronald Davidson, Norman S. Hall, William Lively, Joseph O'Donnell, Joseph F. Poland. *CHAPTER TITLES:* (1) The Fifth Column Strikes, (2) Dead End, (3) Man Hunt, (4) Trapped, (5) Test Flight, (6) Double Danger, (7) Death Takes the Witness, (8) Counterfeit Trail, (9) Ambush, (10) Sky Raiders, (11) Trail of Death, (12) Code of the Rangers. *CAST:* "Slingin' Sammy" Baugh, Neil Hamilton, Pauline Moore, Duncan Renaldo, Charles Trowbridge, Herbert Rawlinson, Frank Darien, Robert O. Davis, Monte Blue, Stanley Blystone, Kermit Maynard, Roy Barcroft, Kenne Duncan, Jack Ingram, Robert Barron, Frank Bruno, Monte Montague, Joe Forte, Lucien Prival, Paul Gustine, Henry Hall, William Kellogg, Richard Simmons, Alan Gregg, Iron Eyes Cody, Forrest Taylor, Lee Shumway, Ernest Sarracino, Bud Geary, Bob Jamison, John James, Dick Scott, Bud Wolfe, Barry Hays, Earl Bunn, George Barrows, Pat O'Shea, Bert Lebaron, Jerry Jerome, Bobby Barber, Forest Burns, Max Waizman, Slim Whitaker, Jack Chapin, Howard Hughes, Michael Owen, Ken Terrell, Hooper Atchley, Otto Reichow, Chick Hannon, Herman Hack, Tommy Coats, Charles

Thomas, Bob Robinson, Carlie Taylor, Edward Cassidy, Buddy Roosevelt, John Bagni, Eddie Dew, George Allen, Jimmy Fawcett, Al Taylor, Duke Green, Merlyn Nelson, Loren Riebe, David Sharpe, Cy Slocum, Tom Steele, Duke Taylor, Bill Wilkus, Joe Yrigoyen. *SYN:* Tom King, Jr. (Baugh) of the Texas Rangers sets out to solve his father's murder and bring to justice a group of fifth column saboteurs. *NOTES:* Sammy Baugh's only screen appearance. He did not consider himself an actor but a football player. He was All-American at Texas Christian University, 1934–1936, and was All-Pro for the Washington Redskins, 1937–1952. This serial was shot during the summer of 1941, Sammy's off season with the Redskins. [TV version: Six 26½-min. chapters.]

**987. The Lone Ranger** (2/12/38) B&W 264 mins. 15 chapters. (Western) *DIR:* William Witney, John English. *A-PRO:* Sol C. Siegel. *SUP:* Robert Beche. *SP:* Barry Shipman, George Worthing Yates, Franklyn Adreon, Ronald Davidson, Lois Eby. Based on the radio serial "The Lone Ranger" by Fran Striker. *CHAPTER TITLES:* (1) Hi-Yo Silver!, (2) Thundering Earth, (3) The Pitfall, (4) Agent of Treachery, (5) The Steaming Cauldron, (6), Red Man's Courage, (7) Wheels of Disaster, (8) Fatal Treasure, (9) The Missing Spur, (10) Flaming Fury, (11) The Silver Bullet, (12) Escape, (13) The Fatal Plunge, (14) Messengers of Doom, (15) The Last of the Rangers. *CAST:* Lee Powell, Chief Thunder Cloud, Lynn Roberts, Stanley Andrews, George Cleveland, William Farnum, Hal Taliaferro, Herman Brix, Lane Chandler, George Letz, John Merton, Sammy McKim, Tom London, Raphael Bennett, Maston Williams, Charles Thomas, Allan Cavan, Reed Howes, Walter James, Francis Sayles, Murdock MacQuarrie, Jane Keckley, Phillip Armenta, Ted Adams, Jimmy Hollywood, Jack Kirk, Art Dillard, Millard McGowan, Frank Ellis, Carl Stockdale, Bud Osborne, Fred Burns, Inez Cody, Duke Green, Forbes Murray, Edna Lawrence, Charles King, Jack Perrin, Frank Leyva, George Mari, Slim Whitaker, Edmund Cobb, Jack Rockwell, J. W. Cody, Carl Saxe, George Magrill, Iron Eyes Cody, John Bacca, John Bacon, Griff Barnette, Hank Bell, Leon Bellas, Bill Carrasco, Frank Chrysler, Roy Cline, Tex Cooper, Ed Diaz, Bruce Galbreth, Wendle Gill, Oscar Hancock, Buck Hires, Roy Kennedy, Al Lorenzen, Harry Mack, Frankie Marvin, Lafe McKee, Henry Olivas, Perry Pratt, Charles Williams, Wally Wilson, Ben Wright, John Brehme, John Bristol, Jerry Brown, Forest Burns, Yakima Canutt, Jack Casey, Gunner Johnson, Bill Jones, Robert Kortman, Ralph LeFever, Ike Lewin, Ken Cooper, Les Cooper, Al Delmar, Curley Dresden, Ray Elliott, Art Felix, Elmer Napier, Post Park, George Plues, Loren Riebe, Al Rimpau, Vinegar Roan, Jerry Frank, John Goodwin, Jack Hendricks, Wesley Hopper, Jack Ingram, Henry Isabell, Eddie Jauregui, Chuck Jennings, Glen Johnson, John Slater, George St. Leon, Burl Tatum, Al Taylor, Duke Taylor, Bobby Thompson, Blackie Whiteford, Shorty Woods, Joe Yrigoyen, Bill Yrigoyen, "Silver Chief," *VOICE OF:* Billy Bletcher. *SYN:* During the period of Reconstruction following the Civil War, five Texans (Brix, Powell, Letz, Chandler, Taliaferro), vow to stop Captain Mark Smith (Andrews), who has assumed the identity Marcus Jeffries, from becoming dictator of Texas. One of these Texans is a mysterious masked rider known as "The Lone Ranger" who rides with an Indian companion, Tonto (Chief Thunder Cloud). NOTES: Lois Eby was Republic's only female serial writer. Although a sequence involving President Abraham Lincoln (Frank McGlynn, Sr.) and George Blanchard (George Cleveland) was excised from Chapter 1 due to a time problem, Frank McGlynn, Sr. received screen credit in the serial. This sequence was later reinstated in the 1940 feature version of the serial, *Hi-Yo-Silver!*

**988. The Lone Ranger Rides Again** (2/25/39) B&W 263 mins. 15 chapters. (Western). *DIR:* William Witney, John English. *A-PRO:* Robert Beche. *SP:* Franklyn Adreon, Ronald Davidson, Sol Shor, Barry Shipman. Story by Gerald Geraghty. Based on the radio serial "The Lone Ranger" by Fran Striker. *CHAPTER TITLES:* (1) The Lone Ranger Returns, (2) Masked Victory, (3) The Black Raiders Strike, (4) The Cavern of Doom, (5) Agents of Deceit, (6) The Trap, (7) Lone Ranger at Bay, (8) Ambush, (9) Wheels of Doom, (10) The Dangerous Captive, (11) Death Below, (12) Blazing Peril, (13) Exposed, (14) Besieged, (15) Frontier Justice. *CAST:* Robert Livingston, Chief Thunder Cloud, Duncan Renaldo, Jinx Falken (Jinx Falkenburg), Ralph Dunn, J. Farrell MacDonald, William Gould, Rex Lease, Ted Mapes, Henry Otho, John Beach, Glenn Strange, Stanley Blystone, Eddie Parker, Al Taylor, Carleton Young, Slim Whitaker, Bob Robinson, Ralph LeFever, Charles Regan, Fred Schaefer, David Sharpe, Art Felix, Chick Hannon, Eddie Dean, Bob McClung, Betty Roadman, Duke Lee, Howard Chase, Ernie Adams, Nelson McDowell, Walter Wills, Jack Kirk, Fred Burns, Buddy Mason, Lew Meehan, Wheeler Oakman, Forrest Taylor, Frank Ellis, Herman Hack, Bill Yrigoyen, Wesley Hopper, Bud Wolfe, Joe Yrigoyen, Duke Taylor, Forest Burns, George DeNormand, George Burton, Tommy Coats, Howard Hickey, Barry Hays, Ted Wells, Burt Dillard, Cecil Kellogg, Carl Sepulveda, Buddy Messenger, Jerome Ward, Roger Williams, Buddy Roosevelt, Jack Montgomery, Post Park, Art Dillard, Horace B. Carpenter, Cactus Mack, Lafe McKee, Augie Gomez, Charles Hutchison, Monte Montague, Griff Barnette, Joe Perez, "Silver Chief," *VOICE OF:* Billy Bletcher. *SYN:* The Lone Ranger (Livingston), Tonto (Chief Thunder Cloud), and Juan Vasquez (Renaldo) are enlisted to help the settlers of San Ramon Valley in New Mexico stop Bart Dolan (Dunn) and his Black Raiders gang from taking their land. *NOTES:* Working title was *The Lone Ranger Returns*. In keeping with the radio show alteration at that time, Tonto's horse's name was changed from *White Fella* to *Scout*. Story writer Gerald Geraghty was uncredited.

**Lost Island of Kioga** *see* **Hawk of the Wilderness**

**989. Man with the Steel Whip** (7/19/54) B&W 167 mins. 12 chapters. (Western). *DIR/A-PRO:* Franklin Adreon. *SP:* Ronald Davidson. *CHAPTER TITLES:* (1) The Spirit Rider, (2) Savage Fury, (3) Mask of El Latigo, (4) The Murder Cave, (5) The Stone Guillotine, (6) Flame and Battle, (7) Double Ambush, (8) The Blazing Barrier, (9) The Silent Informer, (10) Window of Death, (11) The Fatal Masquerade, (12) Redskin Raiders. *CAST:* Richard Simmons, Barbara Bestar, Dale Van Sickel, Mauritz Hugo, Lane Bradford, Pat Hogan, Roy Barcroft, Stuart Randall, Edmund Cobb, I. Stanford Jolley, Guy Teague, Alan Wells, Tom Steele, Art Dillard, Chuck Hayward, Charles Stevens, Jerry Brown,

Harry Harvey, Bob Clark, Charles Sullivan, Robert Henry, Tom Monroe, Chris Mitchell, Gregg Barton, George Eldredge, Tex Terry, Walt LaRue, Herman Hack. *SYN:* Saloon owner Barnet (Hugo) and his gang want to drive the Indians off their reservation so he may obtain the rich vein of gold discovered there. Jerry Randall (Simmons), a young rancher, becomes "El Latigo" as he and Nancy Cooper (Bestar), former Indian reservation schoolteacher, vow to help the Indians keep their land and bring Barnet and his gang to justice. *NOTES:* Working title was *Man with a Whip*. Republic's final western serial.

**Manhunt in the African Jungles** *see* **Secret Service in Darkest Africa**

990. **Manhunt of Mystery Island** (3/17/45) B&W 219 mins. 15 chapters. (Mystery-Crime). *DIR:* Spencer G. Bennet, Wallace A. Grissell, Yakima Canutt. *A-PRO:* Ronald Davidson. *SP:* Albert DeMond, Basil Dickey, Jesse Duffy, Alan James, Grant Nelson, Joseph F. Poland. *CHAPTER TITLES:* (1) Secret Weapon, (2) Satan's Web, (3) The Murder Machine, (4) The Lethal Chamber, (5) Mephisto's Mantrap, (6) Ocean Tomb, (7) The Death Drop, (8) Bombs Away, (9) The Fatal Flood, (10) The Sable Shroud, (11) Satan's Shadow, (12) Cauldron of Cremation, (13) Bridge to Eternity, (14) Power Dive to Doom, (15) Fatal Transformation. *CAST:* Richard Bailey, Linda Stirling, Roy Barcroft, Kenne Duncan, Forrest Taylor, Forbes Murray, Jack Ingram, Harry Strang, Edward Cassidy, Frank Alten, Lane Chandler, Russ Vincent, Dale Van Sickel, Tom Steele, Duke Green, Si Jenks, Fred Graham, Eddie Parker, Duke Taylor, Frederick Howard. *SYN:* Claire Forrest (Stirling) enlists the aid of famous criminologist Lance Reardon (Bailey) as they search for her missing father, Professor Forrest (Taylor), on Mystery Island, which is owned by four men, Henry Hargraves (Murray), Edward Armstrong (Ingram), Fred Braley (Strang) and Paul Melton (Cassidy), each of whom is a direct descendent of a Captain Mephisto who once governed the island. One of these men, using a transformation machine, is able to transform himself into Captain Mephisto (Barcroft) as he tries to stop Claire and Lance from locating Professor Forrest and his invention. *NOTES:* Working titles were *Manhunt* and *Mystery Island*. Unit manager on this serial was director R. G. Springsteen. Beginning with Chapter 9 of this serial, and continuing until the end of Republic's serial production, a running time of 13 minutes and 20 seconds for Chapters 2 through 12 (or 15) was to become the standard for the remaining 30 serials. [Century 66 feature version: *Captain Mephisto and the Transformation Machine*.]

991. **The Masked Marvel** (11/6/43) B&W 197 mins. 12 chapters.(Crime-Spies). *DIR:* Spencer G. Bennet. *A-PRO:* William J. O'Sullivan. *SP:* Royal K. Cole, Ronald Davidson, Basil Dickey, Jesse Duffy, Grant Nelson, George Plympton, Joseph F. Poland. *CHAPTER TITLES:* (1) The Masked Crusader, (2) Death Takes the Helm, (3) Dive to Doom, (4) Suspense at Midnight, (5) Murder Meter, (6) Exit to Eternity, (7) Doorway to Destruction, (8) Destined to Die, (9) Danger Express, (10) Suicide Sacrifice, (11) The Fatal Mistake, (12) The Man Behind the Mask. *CAST:* William Forrest, Louise Currie, Johnny Arthur, Rod Bacon, Richard Clarke, Anthony Warde, David Bacon, Tom Steele, Bill Healy, Howard Hickman, Kenneth Harlan, Thomas Louden, Eddie Parker, Duke Green, Dale Van

Sickel, Wendell Niles, Lester Dorr, George Pembroke, Stanley Price, John Daheim, Eddie Phillips, Ken Terrell, Allen Pomeroy, Crane Whitley, Forbes Murray, Robert Wilke, Nolan Leary, Bill Cody, Carey Loftin, Lynton Brent, Lee Roberts, Joe Yrigoyen, Fred Graham, Roy Barcroft, Herbert Rawlinson, Edward Van Sloan, George J. Lewis, Sam Bernard, Harry Woods, Brooks Benedict, George Suzanne, Sam Flint, Sam Ash, Jack O'Shea, Nora Lane, Pat O'Shea, Harold Kruger, Bud Geary, Tom London, Frank O'Connor, Ernie Adams, Charles Hutchison, Thom Metzetti, Betty Miles, Preston Peterson, *VOICE OF*: Gayne Whitman. *SYN*: One of four insurance investigators (David Bacon, Rod Bacon, Clarke, Healy) becomes the "Masked Marvel" to stop Mura Sakima (Arthur) as he tries to sabotage America's war industries. *NOTES*: The last war-related serial produced by Republic. The voice of Tom Steele was dubbed by radio actor Gayne Whitman. Tom Steele received no screen credit as the man behind the mask, "The Masked Marvel." His first-chapter, first-character optical was prepared reading "Tom Steele as the Masked Marvel." Republic, believing that this would remove the key element of mystery by making such a disclosure, decided to remove his first-chapter optical and have his name head the second cast card. Through an oversight his name was omitted altogether, allowing second lead player, William Forrest, to advance to top billing. This was unusual in a Republic serial since Forrest was neither hero, nor lead heavy, the only such occurrence in a Republic serial. David Bacon, no relation to Rod Bacon, was fatally stabbed in a tavern brawl on September 12, 1943, less than a month after filming had been completed. [Century 66 feature version: *Sakima and the Masked Marvel*.]

**Missile Base at Taniak** *see* **Canadian Mounties Vs. Atomic Invaders**

**992. Mysterious Dr. Satan** (12/13/40) B&W 267 mins. 15 chapters. (Crime). *DIR:* William Witney, John English. *A-PRO:* Hiram S. Brown, Jr. *SP:* Franklyn Adreon, Ronald Davidson, Norman S. Hall, Joseph F. Poland, Sol Shor. *CHAPTER TITLES:* (1) Return of the Copperhead, (2) Thirteen Steps, (3) Undersea Tomb, (4) The Human Bomb, (5) Doctor Satan's Man of Steel, (6) Double Cross, (7) The Monster Strikes, (8) Highway of Death, (9) Double Jeopardy, (10) Bridge of Peril, (11) Death Closes In, (12) Crack-Up, (13) Disguised, (14) The Flaming Coffin, (15) Doctor Satan Strikes. *CAST:* Edward (Eduardo) Ciannelli, Robert Wilcox, William Newell, C. Montague Shaw, Ella Neal, Dorothy Herbert, Charles Trowbridge, Jack Mulhall, Edwin Stanley, Walter McGrail, Joe McGuinn, Bud Geary, Paul Marion, Archie Twitchell, Lynton Brent, Ken Terrell, Al Taylor, Jimmy Fawcett, Edward Cassidy, William Stahl, Frank Conklin, Eddie Parker, James Bush, Harry Strang, Duke Green, Bert LeBaron, Eddie Dew, Ted Stanhope, John Bagni, Jerry Jerome, Jack O'Shea, Al Seymour, Kenneth Harlan, Ernest Sarracino, Virginia Carroll, Floyd Criswell, Wally West, Frank Brownlee, Robert Wayne, Frank Ellis, Patrick J. Kelly, Charles Hutchison, Alan Gregg, Yakima Canutt, Bud Wolfe, Hal Price, George Allen, Marten Lamont, Tom Steele, Bill Wilkus, Davison Clark, Duke Taylor, Tristram Coffin, Lloyd Whitlock, Sam Garrett, Bob Rogers, Cy Slocum, Fred Schaefer, David Sharpe, Helen Thurston, Bill

Yrigoyen. *SYN:* "The Copperhead" (Wilcox) must stop Doctor Satan (Ciannelli) from securing a remote control device for his mechanical robot and building an army of robots to rob and terrorize the nation. *NOTES:* Working title was *Dr. Satan*. This serial was planned as *Adventures of Superman*, but negotiations broke down and Republic had to revamp the serial. Barney A. Sarecky worked on the *Superman* script, but not the *Mysterious Dr. Satan* script. [TV version: Seven 26½-min. chapters.] [Century 66 feature version: *Dr. Satan's Robot.*]

**Nyoka and the Lost Secrets of Hippocrates** *see* **Perils of Nyoka**

**Nyoka and the Tigermen** *see* **Perils of Nyoka**

**993. The Painted Stallion** (6/5/37) B&W 212 mins. 12 chapters. (Western). *DIR:* William Witney, Alan James, Ray Taylor. *A-PRO:* J. Laurence Wickland. *SP:* Barry Shipman, Winston Miller. Story by Morgan B. Cox, Ronald Davidson. Based on an idea by Hal G. Evarts. *CHAPTER TITLES:* (1) Trail to Empire, (2) The Rider of the Stallion, (3) The Death Leap, (4) Avalanche, (5) Valley of Death, (6) Thundering Wheels, (7) Trail Treachery, (8) The Whistling Arrow, (9) The Fatal Message, (10) Ambush, (11) Tunnel of Terror, (12) Human Targets. *CAST:* Ray ("Crash") Corrigan, Hoot Gibson, LeRoy Mason, Duncan Renaldo, Sammy McKim, Hal Taliaferro, Jack Perrin, Oscar and Elmer, Julia Thayer, Yakima Canutt, Maston Williams, Duke Taylor, Loren Riebe, George DeNormand, Gordon DeMain, Charles King, Vinegar Roan, Lafe McKee, Frank Leyva, Frankie Marvin, Curley Dresden, Chief John Big Tree, Pascale Perry, Don Orlando, Henry Hale, Edward Peil, Sr., Horace B. Carpenter, Lee "Lasses" White, Joe Yrigoyen, Paul Lopez, Monte Montague, Greg Star Whitespear, Ralph Bucko, Roy Bucko, Leo Dupee, Babe DeFreest, Joe Dominguez, Jack Padjan, Al Haskell, Augie Gomez, "Minister." *SYN:* The former Mexican governor (Mason) of Santa Fe plots to sabotage the treaty between the United States and Mexico by destroying the first American wagon train headed to Santa Fe, but is thwarted in his attempts by a mysterious female rider (Thayer) on a painted stallion. *NOTES:* [TV version: Six 26½-min. chapters.]

**994. Panther Girl of the Kongo** (1/3/55) B&W 167 mins. 12 chapters. (Adventure-Jungle). *DIR/A-PRO:* Franklin Adreon. *SP:* Ronald Davidson. *CHAPTER TITLES:* (1) The Claw Monster, (2) Jungle Ambush, (3) The Killer Beast, (4) Sands of Doom, (5) Test of Terror, (6) High Peril, (7) Double Trap, (8) Crater of Flame, (9) River of Death, (10) Blasted Evidence, (11) Double Danger, (12) House of Doom. *CAST:* Phyllis Coates, Myron Healey, Arthur Space, John Day, Mike Ragan, Morris Buchanan, Roy Glenn, Sr., Archie Savage, Ramsay Hill, Naaman Brown, Dan Ferniel, James Logan, Gene Stutenroth, Fred Graham, Charles Sullivan, Steve Calvert, Keith McConnell, DeForest Covan, Walter Smith, Daniel Elam, Wesley Gale, Don Carlos, Alan Reynolds, Martin Wilkins, Tom Steele. *SYN:* Jean Evans (Coates), the Panther Girl, and big-game hunter Larry Sanders (Healey) set out to stop Dr. Morgan (Space), who is using a hormone compound causing ordinary crayfish to grow to enormous size, and his cohorts Cass (Day) and Rand

(Ragan), from scaring off the natives in the region in order to operate an illegal diamond mine. *NOTES:* Working title was *Panther Woman of the Kongo*. The correct title to Chapter 7 is *Double Trap*, NOT *Timber Trap*. Although Tom Steele had a minor acting part in this serial and was also stuntman and double for Myron Healey, for some unknown reason he was denied screen credit in this serial. For this serial, John Daheim changed his name to John Day. The crayfish, which are the central characters to the story, are found in fresh waters of all the continental land masses except the Dark Continent. [Century 66 feature version: *The Claw Monsters*.]

**995. Perils of Nyoka** (6/27/42) B&W 261 mins. 15 chapters. (Adventure). *DIR:* William Witney. *A-PRO:* William J. O'Sullivan. *SP:* Ronald Davidson, Norman S. Hall, William Lively, Joseph O'Donnell, Joseph F. Poland. *CHAPTER TITLES:* (1) Desert Intrigue, (2) Death's Chariot, (3) Devil's Crucible, (4) Ascending Doom, (5) Fatal Second, (6) Human Sacrifice, (7) Monster's Clutch, (8) Tuareg Vengeance, (9) Burned Alive, (10) Treacherous Trail, (11) Unknown Peril, (12) Underground Tornado, (13) Thundering Death, (14) Blazing Barrier, (15) Satan's Fury. *CAST:* Kay Aldridge, Clayton Moore, William Benedict, Lorna Gray, Charles Middleton, Tristram Coffin, Forbes Murray, Robert Strange, George Pembroke, Georges Renavent, John Davidson, George J. Lewis, Ken Terrell, John Bagni, Kenne Duncan, Arvon Dale, Duke Taylor, Tom Steele, Iron Eyes Cody, Augie Gomez, John Bleifer, Joe Garcia, Loren Riebe, Henry Wills, Art Dupuis, Pedro Regas, Al Kikume, Herbert Rawlinson, Robert Barron, Forrest Taylor, Bud Wolfe, Leonard Hampton, Babe DeFreest, Helen Thurston, Yakima Canutt, Steve Clemente, Art Dillard, John Daheim, Jerry Frank, Duke Green, Carey Loftin, Jack O'Shea, George Plues, Cy Slocum, David Sharpe, Harry Smith, George Suzanne, Dirk Thane, "Ace," "Professor," "Satan," the gorilla. *SYN:* Nyoka (Aldridge), seeking to find her missing father (Strange), joins Larry Grayson (Moore), and his party as they search for the lost Tablets of Hippocrates. *NOTES:* Script writer Taylor Caven, who worked on the screenplay for one month, was uncredited. Emil Van Horn played "Satan," the gorilla. Re-released in 1952 as *Nyoka and the Tigermen*. [Century 66 feature version: *Nyoka and the Lost Secrets of Hippocrates*.]

**Perils of the Darkest Jungle** *see* **The Tiger Woman**

**996. The Phantom Rider** (1/26/46) B&W 167 mins. 12 chapters. (Western). *DIR:* Spencer G. Bennet, Fred C. Brannon. *A-PRO:* Ronald Davidson. *SP:* Albert DeMond, Basil Dickey, Jesse Duffy, Lynn Perkins, Barney A. Sarecky. *CHAPTER TITLES:* (1) The Avenging Spirit, (2) Flaming Ambush, (3) Hoofs of Doom, (4) Murder Masquerade, (5) Flying Fury, (6) Blazing Peril, (7) Gantlet of Guns, (8) Behind the Mask, (9) The Captive Chief, (10) Beasts at Bay, (11) The Death House, (12) The Last Stand. *CAST:* Robert Kent, Peggy Stewart, LeRoy Mason, George J. Lewis, Kenne Duncan, Hal Taliaferro, Chief Thunder Cloud, Tom London, Roy Barcroft, Monte Hale, John Hamilton, Hugh Prosser, Jack Kirk, Rex Lease, Tommy Coats, Bill Yrigoyen, Joe Yrigoyen, Jack O'Shea, Walt LaRue, Cliff Parkinson, Carl Sepulveda, Art Dillard, Bud Bailey, George Carleton,

Tom Steele, Dale Van Sickel, George Chesebro, Wayne Burson, Post Park, Fred Graham, Bob Duncan, Augie Gomez, Robert Wilke, John Roy, Cactus Mack, Eddie Parker, Ted Mapes, Duke Taylor, Hal Price, James Linn, Tex Cooper, Henry Wills, Cliff Lyons. *SYN:* Dr. James Stirling (Kent) becomes "The Phantom Rider," a spirit of just causes sent to the Indians in time of danger, as he helps Blue Feather (Lewis) and Yellow Wolf (Thunder Cloud) to establish an Indian police force to cope with outlaws and renegades who use the Indian reservation as a safe haven. Fred Carson (Mason), an outlaw posing as an Indian Agent, seeks to employ any means to stop the police force from becoming a reality. *NOTES:* Beginning with this serial, Chapter 1 had a running time of 20 minutes and all subsequent chapters had a running time of 13 minutes 20 seconds, a standard adhered to by the remaining 27 serials. The correct title to Chapter 7 is *Ganlet of Guns,* NOT *Gauntlet of Guns.* Re-released in 1954 as *Ghost Riders of the West.*

**Pirates' Harbor** *see* **Haunted Harbor**

**997. The Purple Monster Strikes** (10/6/45) B&W 209 mins. 15 chapters. (Science Fiction). *DIR:* Spencer G. Bennet, Fred C. Brannon. *A-PRO:* Ronald Davidson. *SP:* Royal K. Cole, Albert DeMond, Basil Dickey, Lynn Perkins, Joseph F. Poland, Barney A. Sarecky, Jesse Duffy. *CHAPTER TITLES:* (1) The Man in the Meteor, (2) The Time Trap, (3) Flaming Avalanche, (4) The Lethal Pit, (5) Death on the Beam, (6) The Demon Killer, (7) The Evil Eye, (8) Descending Doom, (9) The Living Dead, (10) House of Horror, (11) Menace from Mars, (12) Perilous Plunge, (13) Fiery Shroud, (14) The Fatal Trial, (15) Takeoff to Destruction. *CAST:* Dennis Moore, Linda Stirling, Roy Barcroft, James Craven, Bud Geary, Mary Moore, John Davidson, Joe Whitehead, Emmett Vogan, George Carleton, Kenne Duncan, Rosemonde James, Monte Hale, Wheaton Chambers, Frederick Howard, Anthony Warde, Ken Terrell, Fred Graham, John Daheim, Tom Steele, Cliff Lyons, Robert Blair, Carey Loftin, Henry Wills, Dale Van Sickel, George Chesebro, Robert Wilke, Polly Burson, Babe DeFreest. *SYN:* The Purple Monster (Barcroft), a visitor from Mars, murders and assumes the identity of Dr. Cyrus Layton (Craven) to gain control of his plans for an interstellar spacecraft so that Mars can conquer the Earth. Attorney Craig Foster (Moore) and Dr. Layton's niece Sheila (Stirling) set out to stop the Purple Monster and his henchman Hodge Garrett (Geary) from carrying out their plans of invasion. *NOTES:* Working title was *The Purple Shadow Strikes, The Purple Ghost Strikes, The Purple Menace Strikes,* and the present title, *The Purple Monster Strikes.* Mary Moore was the wife of Clayton Moore. Screen writer Jesse Duffy was uncredited. Re-released in 1957 under the same title. [Century 66 feature version: *D-Day on Mars.*]

**998. Radar Men from the Moon** (1/9/52) B&W 167 mins. 12 chapters. (Science Fiction). *DIR:* Fred C. Brannon. *A-PRO:* Franklin Adreon. *SP:* Ronald Davidson. *CHAPTER TITLES:* (1) Moon Rocket, (2) Molten Terror, (3) Bridge of Death, (4) Flight to Destruction, (5) Murder Car, (6) Hills of Death, (7) Camouflaged Destruction, (8) The Enemy Planet, (9) Battle in the Stratosphere, (10) Mass Execution, (11) Planned Pursuit, (12) Death of the Moon Man. *CAST:* George Wallace, Aline Towne, William Bakewell, Roy Barcroft, Clayton Moore, Peter Brocco, Bob Stevenson, Don Walters, Tom Steele, Dale Van Sickel, Wilson Wood, Noel Cravat, Baynes Barron, Paul McGuire, Ted Thorpe, Dick Cogan, Stephen Gregory, Paul Palmer, Harry Hollins, Carey Loftin, Jack Shea, Billy Dix, William Marke, Claude Dunkin, Sam Sebby, Arthur Walsh, Guy Teague, Joe Bailey, Dick Rich, Tony Merrill, John Marshall, Ken Terrell. *SYN:* Commando Cody (Wallace), Sky Marshal of the Universe, together with his assistants, Ted Richards (Bakewell) and Joan Gilbert (Towne), set out to stop Retik (Barcroft), ruler of the Moon, from conquering Earth. *NOTES:* Working title was *Planet Men from Mars*. Republic's only serial to feature earthlings traveling in outer space and landing on a celestial body. The correct titles to Chapters 7 and 12 are *Camouflaged Destruction* and *Death of the Moon Man*, NOT *Human Targets* and *Take Off to Eternity*. Re-released in 1957 under the same title. [Century 66 feature version: *Retik, the Moon Menace*.]

**999. Radar Patrol Vs. Spy King** (11/23/49) B&W 167 mins. 12 chapters. (Crime). *DIR:* Fred C. Brannon. *A-PRO:* Franklin Adreon. *SP:* Royal K. Cole, William Lively, Sol Shor. *CHAPTER TITLES:* (1) The Fatal Fog, (2) Perilous Trail, (3) Rolling Fury, (4) Flight of the Spy King, (5) Trapped Underground, (6) Wheels of Disaster, (7) Electrocution, (8) Death Rings the Phone, (9) Tomb of Terror, (10) Death Dive, (11) Desperate Mission, (12) Day of Reckoning. *CAST:* Kirk Alyn, Jean Dean, Anthony Warde, George J. Lewis, Eve Whitney, John Merton, John Crawford, Tristram Coffin, Harold Goodwin, Dale Van Sickel, Tom Steele, Eddie Parker, Forbes Murray, Frank O'Connor, Stephen Gregory, Frank Dae, Arvon Dale, Carey Loftin, David Sharpe, Charles Flynn, John Daheim, Bud Wolfe, Duke Taylor, Bert LeBaron, Ken Terrell, Art Dillard, Helen Thurston, Louise Volding, Buddy Joe Hooker, *VOICE OF:* Roy Barcroft. *SYN:* Former O.S.S. agent Chris Calvert (Alyn), research scientist Joan Hughes (Dean) and Lieutenant Manuel Agura (Lewis) of the Border Patrol join forces as they set out to stop Spy King John Baroda (Merton) and his gang from sabotaging construction of an experimental radar station. *NOTES:* This was the last Republic serial to use multiple writers.

**R.C.M.P. and the Treasure of Genghis Khan** see **Dangers of the Canadian Mounted**

**Retik, the Moon Menace** see **Radar Men from the Moon**

**Return of Captain America** see **Captain America**

**Return of Captain Marvel** see **Adventures of Captain Marvel**

**1000. Robinson Crusoe of Clipper Island** (11/14/36) B&W 256 mins. 14 chapters. (Adventure-Mystery). *DIR:* Mack V. Wright, Ray Taylor. *PRO:* Nat Levine. *A-PRO:* Sol C. Siegel. *SUP:* J. Laurence Wickland. *SP:* Morgan B. Cox, Barry Shipman, Maurice Geraghty. *CHAPTER TITLES:* (1) The Mysterious Island, (2) Flaming Danger, (3) Fathoms Below, (4) Into the Enemy's Camp, (5) Danger in the Air, (6) The God of the Volcano, (7) Trail's End, (8) The Jaws of the Beast, (9) The Cave of the Winds, (10) Wings of Fury, (11) Agents of Disaster, (12) The Sea Trap,

(13) Mutiny, (14) Thunder Mountain. CAST: (Ray) Mala, Mamo Clark, Herbert Rawlinson, William Newell, John Ward, John Dilson, Selmer Jackson, John Picorri, George Chesebro, Robert Kortman, George Cleveland, Lloyd Whitlock, Tiny Roebuck, Tracy Layne, Herbert Weber, Anthony Pawley, Allen Connor, Evan Thomas, Larry Thompson, Allen Cavan, Ralph McCullough, David Horsey, Edmund Cobb, Edward Cassidy, Bud Osborne, Henry Sylvester, Jack Mack, Harry Strang, Oscar Hendrian, Val Duran, Loren Riebe, Allan Mathews, Al Taylor, Henry Hale, Lester Dorr, Eddie Phillips, Roscoe Gerall, Don Brodie, Frank Ellis, Charles McMurphy, Jack Stewart, Francis Walker, Frazer Acosta, F. Herrick Herrick, Jerry Jerome, Buddy Roosevelt, Jimmy Fawcett, Clarence Morrow, Loni Ornellas, "Zane," "Buck." SYN: Intelligence operative Mala is sent to Clipper Island, along with his "man Friday" Hank (Newell), to find the head of an international espionage ring, the mysterious "H. K." NOTES: Republic's only 14 chapter serial. John Picorri's name was misspelled in the credits as "John Piccori." [TV version: Six 26-min. chapters.] [Century 66 feature version: *Robinson Crusoe of Mystery Island.*]

**Robinson Crusoe of Mystery Island** see **Robinson Crusoe of Clipper Island**

**1001. Secret Service in Darkest Africa** (7/24/43) B&W 243 mins. 15 chapters. (Adventure-War). *DIR:* Spencer G. Bennet. *A-PRO:* William J. O'Sullivan. *SP:* Royal K. Cole, Basil Dickey, Jesse Duffy, Ronald Davidson, Joseph O'Donnell, Joseph F. Poland. *CHAPTER TITLES:* (1) North African Intrigue, (2) The Charred Witness, (3) Double Death, (4) The Open Grave, (5) Cloaked in Flame, (6) Dial of Doom, (7) Murder Dungeon, (8) Funeral Arrangements Completed, (9) Invisible Menace, (10) Racing Peril, (11) Lightning Terror, (12) Ceremonial Execution, (13) Fatal Leap, (14) Victim of Villainy, (15) Nazi Treachery Unmasked. *CAST:* Rod Cameron, Joan Marsh, Duncan Renaldo, Lionel Royce, Kurt Krueger, Frederic Brunn, Sigurd Tor, Georges Renavent, Kurt Katch, Ralf Harolde, William Vaughn, William Yetter, Hans von Morhart, Erwin Goldi, Frederic Worlock, Paul Marion, Ken Terrell, Duke Green, Joe Yrigoyen, Reed Howes, Carey Loftin, Eddie Phillips, Bud Geary, Harry Semels, Leonard Hampton, Tom Steele, Eddie Parker, John Daheim, George Sorel, George DeNormand, Walter Fenner, Jacques Lory, Ed Agresti, Jack Chefe, John Royce, Jack LaRue, George J. Lewis, John Bleifer, Augie Gomez, Jack O'Shea, Norman Nesbitt, Anthony Warde, Frank Alten, John Davidson, Buddy Roosevelt, Charles LaTorre, Nino Bellini, George Magrill, Emily LaRue. *SYN:* Rex Bennett (Cameron), American undercover agent, joins forces in Casablanca with Janet Blake (Marsh), newspaper journalist and secret United Nations agent, and Pierre LaSalle (Renaldo), a French Diplomatic Headquarters Captain, as they set out to stop Nazi agent Baron Von Rommler (Royce), who is secretly posing as Sultan Abou Ben Ali (Royce), from bringing the Arabs to the Axis cause. *NOTES:* Working title was *Secret Service in North Africa*. Rod Cameron reprised his role of Rex Bennett from *G-Men Vs. the Black Dragon*. Lionel Royce played a dual role in this serial. Director Spencer G. Bennet's first serial assignment for

Republic. Republic's only serial to feature the recurrence of an original character. This serial was released outside of the United States as *Desert Agent*. Re-released in 1954 as *Manhunt in the African Jungles*. The re-release lobby cards and one-sheets carried the title as *Man Hunt in the African Jungle*, whereas the actual on-screen title was the above re-release title. [Century 66 feature version: *The Baron's African War*.]

**Sakima and the Masked Marvel** *see* **The Masked Marvel**

**Sharad of Atlantis** *see* **Undersea Kingdom**

**Slaves of the Invisible Monster** *see* **The Invisible Monster**

**Sombra, the Spider Woman** *see* **The Black Widow**

**1002. Son of Zorro** (1/18/47) B&W 180 mins. 13 chapters. (Western). *DIR:* Spencer G. Bennet, Fred C. Brannon. *A-PRO:* Ronald Davidson. *SP:* Franklin Adreon, Basil Dickey, Jesse Duffy, Sol Shor. *CHAPTER TITLES:* (1) Outlaw County, (2) The Deadly Millstone, (3) Fugitive from Injustice, (4) Buried Alive, (5) Water Trap, (6) Volley of Death, (7) The Fatal Records, (8) Third Degree, (9) Shoot to Kill, (10) Den of the Beast, (11) The Devil's Trap, (12) Blazing Walls, (13) Check Mate. *CAST:* George Turner, Peggy Stewart, Roy Barcroft, Edward Cassidy, Ernie Adams, Stanley Price, Edmund Cobb, Ken Terrell, Wheaton Chambers, Fred Graham, Eddie Parker, Si Jenks, Jack O'Shea, Jack Kirk, Tom Steele, Dale Van Sickel, Mike J. Frankovich, Pierce Lyden, Rocky Shahan, Ted Adams, Gil Perkins, Tex Terry, Tom London, Art Dillard, Joe Phillips, George Bell, Duke Taylor, Charles King, Post Park, Cactus Mack, Bud Wolfe, Newton House, Frank O'Connor, Ted Mapes, Al Ferguson, Tommy Ryan, Carl Sepulveda, Herman Hack, George Chesebro, John Daheim, Howard Mitchell, Doc Adams, Ralph Bucko, Roy Bucko, Joe Balch, Tommy Coats, Frank Ellis, Silver Harr, Pascale Perry. *SYN:* Returning home to Box County after the Civil War, lawyer Jeffrey Stewart (Turner) finds that Box County has been taken over by a group of crooked politicians and outlaws. Assuming the guise of his ancestor "Zorro," Stewart, working together with his foreman Pancho (Price) and postmistress Kate Wells (Stewart), sets out to bring the politicians and outlaws to justice. *NOTES:* Working title was *Zorro Strikes Again*. Tom London, who plays the outlaw mastermind, received no screen billing. His name was inadvertently omitted from the second cast card. Dale Van Sickel's name was misspelled on the cast card reading "Dale Van Sickle." The correct title to Chapter 3 is *Fugitive from Injustice*, NOT *Fugitive from Justice*. Re-released in 1956 under the same title. [TV version: Six 26-min. chapters.]

**1003. SOS Coast Guard** (8/28/37) B&W 224 mins. 12 chapters. (Crime-Mystery). *DIR:* William Witney, Alan James. *A-PRO:* Sol C. Siegel. *SUP:* Robert Beche. *SP:* Barry Shipman, Franklyn Adreon, Winston Miller, Edward Lynn. Story by Morgan B. Cox, Ronald Davidson, Lester Scott. *CHAPTER TITLES:* (1) Disaster at Sea, (2) Barrage of Death, (3) The Gas Chamber, (4) The Fatal Shaft, (5) The Mystery Ship, (6) Deadly Cargo, (7) Undersea Terror, (8) The Crash!, (9) Wolves at Bay, (10) The Acid Trail, (11) The Sea Battle, (12) The Deadly Circle. *CAST:* Ralph Byrd, Bela Lugosi, Maxine Doyle,

Richard Alexander, Lee Ford, John Picorri, Lawrence Grant, Thomas Carr, Carleton Young, Allen Connor, George Chesebro, Ranny Weeks, Joe Mack, Herbert Weber, Dick Sheldon, Bob Walker, Gene Marvey, Eddie Phillips, Reed Sheffield, Frank Wayne, Warren Jackson, Dick Scott, Herbert Rawlinson, Jack Clifford, Jack Daley, Tom Ung, Lee Frederick, King Mojave, Curley Dresden, Henry Morris, Vinegar Roan, James Millican, Alexander Leftwich, Roy Barcroft, Joe Girard, Lester Dorr, Edward Cassidy, Jack Roberts, Earl Bunn, Kit Guard, Frank Ellis, Henry Hale, Duke Taylor, Harry Strang, Charles McMurphy, Edwin Mordant, Michael Morgan, Floyd Criswell, Billie Van Every, Rex Lease, Alan Gregg, Loren Riebe, Frank Fanning, Frank Meredith, John Gustin, Pat Mitchell, Henry Otho, Jerry Frank, Buddy Roosevelt, Duke York, Forrest Dillon, Jack Ingram, Dan Wolheim, Roger Williams, Frankie Marvin, Robert Dudley, Audrey Gaye, Richard Beach, Yakima Canutt, Baldy Cook, Leon Davidson, Bobbie Koshay, Norwood Edwards, Clarke Jennings, Jerry Larkin, Jack Long, Robert Wilke, Teddy Mangean. *SYN:* Terry Kent (Byrd) of the Coast Guard tries to stop mad scientist Boroff (Lugosi) and his assistant Thorg (Alexander) from developing and using a new disintegration gas. *NOTES:* Screen writers Winston Miller and Edward Lynn, along with story writer Lester Scott, were uncredited. Was Bela Lugosi's screen character's name, *Boroff*, possibly a homage to his friend, *Boris* Karl*off*?

**1004. Spy Smasher** (4/4/42) B&W 214 mins. 12 chapters. (Adventure-War). *DIR:* William Witney. *A-PRO:* William J. O'Sullivan. *SP:* Ronald Davidson, Norman S. Hall, William Lively, Joseph O'Donnell, Joseph F. Poland. Suggested by the character "Spy Smasher" appearing in *Whiz Comics* and *Spy Smasher Magazines*. Publications respectively copyrighted by Fawcett Publications, Inc. *CHAPTER TITLES:* (1) America Beware, (2) Human Target, (3) Iron Coffin, (4) Stratosphere Invaders, (5) Descending Doom, (6) The Invisible Witness, (7) Secret Weapon, (8) Sea Raiders, (9) Highway Racketeers, (10) 2700° Fahrenheit, (11) Hero's Death, (12) V...-. *CAST:* Kane Richmond, Marguerite Chapman, Sam Flint, Hans Schumm, Tristram Coffin, Franco Corsaro, Hans von Morhart, Georges Renavent, Robert O. Davis, Henry Zynda, Paul Bryar, Tom London, Richard Bond, Crane Whitley, John James, Yakima Canutt, Max Waizman, Howard Hughes, Charley Phillips, Martin Faust, Tom Steele, Eddie Jauregui, John Daheim, Bob Jamison, Walter Low, Jerry Jerome, Jack Arnold, Martin Garralaga, Robert Wilke, Buddy Roosevelt, William Forrest, Nick Vehr, Duke Taylor, Sid Troy, Lee Phelps, Lowden Adams, George Sherwood, Ken Terrell, Louis Tomei, Carey Loftin, Jimmy Fawcett, Leonard St. Leo, Ray Parsons, Duke Green, Charles Regan, Bert LeBaron, Bill Wilkus, Loren Riebe, Bud Wolfe, Dudley Dickerson, Carleton Young, Cy Slocum, John Peters, Al Seymour, David Sharpe, Roy Brent, Ray Hanson, Ray Jones, Tommy Coats, Hugh Prosser, Frank Alten, George J. Lewis, Arvon Dale, Bob Stevenson, Gil Perkins, Pat Moran, John Buckley, James Dale, Jack O'Shea. *SYN:* Spy Smasher (Richmond) and his twin brother Jack (Richmond) join forces as they try to stop the "Mask" (Schumm) and his enemy agents from flooding the United States with counterfeit currency and destroying America's defenses. *NOTES:* Kane Richmond plays a dual role in this serial. [Century 66 feature version: *Spysmasher Returns.*]

**Spysmasher Returns** *see* **Spy Smasher**

**Target: Sea of China** *see* **Trader Tom of the China Seas**

**1005. The Tiger Woman** (5/27/44) B&W 196 mins. 12 chapters. (Adventure-Jungle). *DIR:* Spencer G. Bennet, Wallace A. Grissell. *A-PRO:* William J. O'Sullivan. *SP:* Royal K. Cole, Ronald Davidson, Basil Dickey, Jesse Duffy, Grant Nelson, Joseph F. Poland. *CHAPTER TITLES:* (1) Temple of Terror, (2) Doorway to Death, (3) Cathedral of Carnage, (4) Echo of Eternity, (5) Two Shall Die, (6) Dungeon of the Doomed, (7) Mile a Minute Murder, (8) Passage to Peril, (9) Cruise to Cremation, (10) Target for Murder, (11) The House of Horror, (12) Triumph Over Treachery. *CAST:* Allan ("Rocky") Lane, Linda Stirling, Duncan Renaldo, George J. Lewis, LeRoy Mason, Crane Whitley, Robert Frazer, Rico de Montez, Stanley Price, Nolan Leary, Kenne Duncan, Tom Steele, Duke Green, Eddie Parker, Ken Terrell, Cliff Lyons, Charles Hayes, Bud Geary, John Daheim, Frank Marlowe, Georges Renavent, Tom London, Dale Van Sickel, Marshall Reed, Fred Graham, Robert Wilke, Al Ferguson, Rex Lease, Roy Darmour, Bert LeBaron, Paul Gustine, Carey Loftin, Walt LaRue, Bud Wolfe, Herman Hack, Babe DeFreest, Augie Gomez, Harry Smith, Catherine McLeod, Joe Molina. *SYN:* Allen Saunders (Lane) joins forces with a mysterious white queen of the jungle known as "The Tiger Woman" (Stirling), as they investigate the cause in the delay of developing a new oil field. *NOTES:* Working title was *Tiger Woman of the Amazon.* Linda Stirling's serial debut. This serial bears no relation to the 1945 Republic feature, *The Tiger Woman.* Re-released in 1951 as *Perils of the Darkest Jungle.* [Century 66 feature version: *Jungle Gold.*]

**The Torpedo of Doom** *see* **The Fighting Devil Dogs**

**1006. Trader Tom of the China Seas** (1/11/54) B&W 167 mins. 12 chapters. (Adventure). *DIR/A-PRO:* Franklin Adreon. *SP:* Ronald Davidson. *CHAPTER TITLES:* (1) Sea Saboteurs, (2) Death Takes the Deck, (3) Five Fathoms Down, (4) On Target, (5) The Fire Ship, (6) Collision, (7) War in the Hills, (8) Native Execution, (9) Mass Attack, (10) Machine Murder, (11) Underground Ambush, (12) Twisted Vengeance. *CAST:* Harry Lauter, Aline Towne, Lyle Talbot, Robert Shayne, Fred Graham, Richard Reeves, Tom Steele, John Crawford, Dale Van Sickel, Victor Sen Yung, Jan Arvan, Ramsay Hill, George Selk, Charley Phillips, Bill Hudson, Bert LeBaron, Richard Alexander, Duane Thorsen, Ken Terrell, Saul Gorss, Steve Conte, Robert Bice, Charles Sullivan, Bill Chandler, Budd Buster, Rush Williams, Jerry Brown. *SYN:* Tom Rogers (Lauter), recruited by American undercover agent Major Conroy (Shayne) to prevent a native uprising in a United Nations South China Sea country, joins forces with Vivian Wells (Towne) as they try to stop foreign agents Barent (Talbot) and Daley (Graham) from smuggling guns and poison gas to the natives in order to foment a revolution and make the country a protectorate of their own foreign government. *NOTES:* All scenes involving Richard Alexander were taken from *S.O.S. Coastguard.* Ramsay

Hill's name was misspelled in the credits as "Ramsey Hill." [Century 66 feature version: *Target: Sea of China*.]

**U-238 and the White Witch Doctor** *see* **Jungle Drums of Africa**

**1007. Undersea Kingdom** (5/30/36) B&W 226 mins. 12 chapters. (Science Fiction) *DIR:* B. Reeves Eason, Joseph Kane. *PRO:* Nat Levine. *SUP:* Barney A. Sarecky. *SP:* John Rathmell, Maurice Geraghty, Oliver Drake. Story by John Rathmell, Tracy Knight. *CHAPTER TITLES:* (1) Beneath the Ocean Floor, (2) The Undersea City, (3) Arena of Death, (4) Revenge of the Volkites, (5) Prisoners of Atlantis, (6) The Juggernaut Strikes, (7) The Submarine Trap, (8) Into the Metal Tower, (9) Death in the Air, (10) Atlantis Destroyed, (11) Flaming Death, (12) Ascent to the Upperworld. *CAST:* Ray ("Crash") Corrigan, Lois Wilde, Monte Blue, William Farnum, Boothe Howard, Raymond Hatton, C. Montague Shaw, Lee Van Atta, Smiley Burnette, Frankie Marvin, Lon Chaney, Jr., Lane Chandler, Jack Mulhall, John Bradford, Malcolm McGregor, Ralph Holmes, John Merton, Ernie Smith, Lloyd Whitlock, Everett Kibbons, Millard McGowan, William Stahl, Bill Yrigoyen, Kenneth Lawton, Eddie Parker, Al Seymour, George DeNormand, Alan Curtis, Tom Steele, Wes Warner, Dan Rowan, Rube Schaeffer, David Horsley, Tracy Layne, Jack Ingram. *SYN:* Ray "Crash" Corrigan accompanies Professor Norton (Shaw), and his party as they descend the ocean depths to locate the lost continent of Atlantis, and once there, find two warring factions, the White Robes, led by the true ruler of Atlantis, Sharad (Farnum), and the Black Robes, led by the tyrant ruler Unga Khan (Blue). *NOTES:* Re-released in 1950 under the same title. [Century 66 feature version: *Sharad of Atlantis*.]

**1008. The Vigilantes Are Coming** (8/22/36) B&W 229 mins. 12 chapters. (Western). *DIR:* Mack V. Wright, Ray Taylor. *PRO:* Nat Levine. *SUP:* J. Laurence Wickland. *SP:* John Rathmell, Maurice Geraghty, Winston Miller. Story by Maurice Geraghty, Leslie Swabacker. *CHAPTER TITLES:* (1) The Eagle Strikes, (2) Birth of the Vigilantes, (3) Condemned by Cossacks, (4) Unholy Gold, (5) Treachery Unmasked, (6) A Tyrant's Trickery, (7) Wings of Doom, (8) A Treaty with Treason, (9) Arrow's Flight, (10) Prison of Flame, (11) A Race with Death, (12) Fremont Takes Command. *CAST:* Robert Livingston, Kay Hughes, Guinn "Big Boy" Williams, Raymond Hatton, Fred Sr. Kohler, Robert Warwick, William Farnum, Robert Kortman, John Merton, Lloyd Ingraham, William Desmond, Yakima Canutt, Tracy Layne, Bud Pope, Steve Clemente, Bud Osborne, Phillip Armenta, Ray ("Crash") Corrigan, John O'Brien, Henry Hall, Stanley Blystone, Joe Delacruz, Fred Burns, Tommy Coats, Ken Cooper, Frank Ellis, Sam Garrett, Herman Hack, Jack Ingram, Bob Jamison, Jack Kenney, Jack Kirk, Frankie Marvin, Pascale Perry, Vinegar Roan, Lloyd Saunders, John Slater, Al Taylor, Jerome Ward, Len Ward, Wes Warner, Wally West. *SYN:* In 1844 California, Don Loring (Livingston) becomes the masked avenger, "The Eagle," as he tries to stop General Jason Burr (Kohler) from conspiring with the Russian emissary (Warwick) to become supreme dictator of California. *NOTES:* Working title was *The Vigilantes*. [TV version: Six 26-min. chapters.]

**1009. Zombies of the Stratosphere** (7/16/52) B&W 167 mins. 12 chapters. (Science Fiction). *DIR:* Fred C. Brannon. *A-PRO:* Franklin Adreon. *SP:* Ronald Davidson. *CHAPTER TITLES:* (1) The Zombie Vanguard, (2) Battle of the Rockets, (3) Undersea Agents, (4) Contraband Cargo, (5) The Iron Executioner, (6) Murder Mine, (7) Death on the Waterfront, (8) Hostage for Murder, (9) The Human Torpedo, (10) Flying Gas Chamber, (11) Man Vs. Monster, (12) Tomb of the Traitors. *CAST:* Judd Holdren, Aline Towne, Wilson Wood, Lane Bradford, Stanley Waxman, John Crawford, Craig Kelly, Ray Boyle, Leonard Nimoy, Tom Steele, Dale Van Sickel, Roy Engel, Jack Harden, Paul Stader, Gayle Kellogg, Jack Shea, Robert Garabedian, Jack Mack, Robert Strange, Floyd Criswell, Davison Clark, Paul Gustine, Henry Rowland, Clifton Young, Norman Willis, George Magrill, Frank Alten, John Daheim, Ken Terrell, *VOICE OF:* Roy Barcroft. *SYN:* Larry Martin (Holdren) and his assistants Bob Wilson (Wood) and Sue Davis (Towne) must stop invading Martians, Marex (Bradford) and Narab (Nimoy), and scientist Dr. Harding (Waxman), from using a hydrogen bomb to send Earth spinning off into space so that Mars may be relocated in its orbit. *NOTES:* Released in a "Computer-colorized" version in the 1990s by the new Republic studios.

**1010. Zorro Rides Again** (11/20/37) B&W 212 mins. 12 chapters. (Western). *DIR:* William Witney, John English. *A-PRO:* Sol C. Siegel. *SUP:* Robert Beche. *SP:* Barry Shipman, John Rathmell, Franklyn Adreon, Ronald Davidson, Morgan B. Cox, Sherman L. Lowe. *CHAPTER TITLES:* (1) Death from the Sky, (2) The Fatal Minute, (3) Juggernaut, (4) Unmasked, (5) Sky Pirates, (6) The Fatal Shot, (7) Burning Embers, (8) Plunge of Peril, (9) Tunnel of Terror, (10) Trapped, (11) Right of Way, (12) Retribution. *CAST:* John Carroll, Helen Christian, Reed Howes, Duncan Renaldo, Noah Beery, Sr., Richard Alexander, Nigel de Brulier, Robert Kortman, Jack Ingram, Roger Williams, Edmund Cobb, Mona Rico, Tom London, Harry Strang, Jerry Frank, George Mari, Paul Lopez, Frank Leyva, Dirk Thane, Murdock MacQuarrie, Hector V. Sarno, Lane Chandler, Josef Swickard, Chris-Pin Martin, Ray Teal, Tony Martelli, Henry Isabell, Al Taylor, Merrill McCormick, Jack Hendricks, Loren Riebe, Vinegar Roan, Forest Burns, Art Felix, Duke Taylor, Brooks Benedict, Rosa Turich, Yakima Canutt, Frank Ellis, Al Haskell, Bob Jamison, Frankie Marvin, Jack Kirk, Frank McCarroll, "Pair O'Dice." *SYN:* James Vega (Carroll) assumes the guise of his ancestor "Zorro," as he sets out to stop El Lobo (Alexander) and Marsden (Beery) from destroying the California Yucatan Railroad. *NOTES:* Screen writer Sherman L. Lowe was uncredited. The only Republic serial to have a feature version released twice to theatres, in 1938 and again in 1959. Working title was *Mysterious Don Miguel.* [TV version: Six 26-min. chapters.]

**1011. Zorro's Black Whip** (11/16/44) B&W 182 mins. 12 chapters. (Western). *DIR:* Spencer G. Bennet, Wallace A. Grissell. *A-PRO:* Ronald Davidson. *SP:* Basil Dickey, Jesse Duffy, Grant Nelson, Joseph F. Poland. "Zorro" character created by Johnston McCulley. *CHAPTER TITLES:* (1) The Masked Avenger, (2) Tomb of Terror, (3) Mob Murder, (4) Detour to Death, (5) Take Off that Mask!, (6) Fatal Gold, (7) Wolf Pack,

(8) The Invisible Victim, (9) Avalanche, (10) Fangs of Doom, (11) Flaming Juggernaut, (12) Trail of Tyranny. *CAST:* George J. Lewis, Linda Stirling, Lucien Littlefield, Francis McDonald, Hal Taliaferro, John Merton, John Hamilton, Tom Chatterton, Tom London, Jack Kirk, Jay Kirby, Si Jenks, Stanley Price, Tom Steele, Duke Green, Dale Van Sickel, Cliff Lyons, Roy Brent, Bill Yrigoyen, Forrest Taylor, Fred Graham, Marshall Reed, Augie Gomez, Carl Sepulveda, Horace B. Carpenter, Herman Hack, Carey Loftin, Cliff Parkinson, Ken Terrell, Duke Taylor, Nolan Leary, Post Park, Robert Wilke, Vinegar Roan, Babe DeFreest. *SYN:* Barbara Meredith (Stirling) becomes "The Black Whip" when her brother (Kirby) is killed and, together with special agent Vic Gordon (Lewis), fight the sinister forces opposed to Idaho statehood. *NOTES:* Working title was *The Black Whip*. Beginning with this serial, Republic removed the first chapter opticals, which had been a part of every Republic serial, with the exception of *Hawk of the Wilderness*, and brought back the re-cap chapter. Although the name "Zorro" is never mentioned in the serial, this was the only one of Republic's five Zorro serials to give Johnston McCulley screen credit. Re-released in 1957 under the same title.

**1012. Zorro's Fighting Legion** (11/20/39) B&W 211 mins. 12 chapters. (Western). *DIR:* William Witney, John English. *A-PRO:* Hiram S. Brown, Jr. *SP:* Ronald Davidson, Franklyn Adreon, Morgan B. Cox, Sol Shor, Barney A. Sarecky. *CHAPTER TITLES:* (1) The Golden God, (2) The Flaming "Z," (3) Descending Doom, (4) The Bridge of Peril, (5) The Decoy, (6) Zorro to the Rescue, (7) The Fugitive, (8) Flowing Death, (9) The Golden Arrow, (10) Mystery Wagon, (11) Face to Face, (12) Unmasked. *CAST:* Reed Hadley, Sheila Darcy, William Corson, Leander de Cordova, Edmund Cobb, John Merton, C. Montague Shaw, Budd Buster, Carleton Young, Guy D'Ennery, Paul Marion, Joe Molina, Jim Pierce, Helen Mitchel, Curley Dresden, Charles King, Al Taylor, Joe Delacruz, Jason Robards, Sr., Theodore Lorch, Jack O'Shea, Jerome Ward, Millard McGowan, Augie Gomez, Cactus Mack, Bud Geary, Jack Moore, George Plues, Jack Carrington, Victor Cox, Robert Wilbur, John Wallace, Burt Dillard, Jimmy Fawcett, Martin Faust, Ken Terrell, Wylie Grant, Carl Sepulveda, Eddie Cherkose, Charles Murphy, Max Marx, Buel Bryant, Norman Lane, Ralph Faulkner, Alan Gregg, Ernest Sarracino, Yakima Canutt, Reed Howes, Barry Hays, Joe McGuinn, Bill Yrigoyen, Jerry Frank, Gordon Clark, Frank Ellis, Ted Mapes, Henry Wills, Joe Yrigoyen, *VOICE OF:* Billy Bletcher. *SYN:* Zorro (Hadley) and his fighting legion vow to stop "Don del Oro," a member of the San Mendolito council, and his Yaqui Indians from raiding the gold trains bound for the Republic of Mexico's treasury. *NOTES:* Working title was *Return of Zorro*. Paul Marion's name was misspelled in the credits. He was listed as "Paul Marian." Re-released in 1958 under the same title. [TV version: Six 26-min. chapters.]

# Cartoons (1947–1949)

*Following is a complete list of cartoons distributed by Republic Pictures Corporation between 1947 and 1949.*

**1013. It's a Grand Old Nag** (1947) Trucolor 7 mins. *DIR/PRO:* Bob Clampett. *CAST:* Narrated by Stan Freberg. *SYN:* Unknown. *NOTES:* Republic Picture's first cartoon release.

**1014. Jerky Journeys — Beyond Civilization to Texas** (3/15/49) Trucolor 7 mins. An Impossible Picture. A Republic Presentation. *DIR:* Unknown. *PRO:* Art Hineman. *CAST:* Narrated by Kenny Delmar. *SYN:* Unknown.

**1015. Jerky Journeys — Bungle in the Jungle** (5/15/49) Trucolor 7 mins. An Impossible Picture. A Republic Presentation. *DIR:* Unknown. *PRO:* Art Hineman. *CAST:* Narrated by Frank Nelson. *SYN:* Unknown.

**1016. Jerky Journeys — Romantic Rumbolia** (6/15/49) Trucolor 7 mins. An Impossible Picture. A Republic Presentation. *DIR:* Unknown. *PRO:* Art Hineman. *CAST:* Narrated by Frank Nelson. *SYN:* Unknown.

**1017. Jerky Journeys — The 3 Minnies: Sota, Tonka, & Ha Ha!** (4/15/49) Trucolor 7 mins. An Impossible Picture. A Republic Presentation. *DIR:* Unknown. *PRO:* Art Hineman. *CAST:* Narrated by Frank Nelson. *SYN:* Unknown.

# Short Subjects (1940–1955)

Following is a complete list of short subjects produced and/or distributed by Republic Pictures Corporation. Credits and cast lists are given, where known.

**1018. The Battle for Korea** (7/1/50) (Documentary-War). B&W 9 mins. *DIR/PRO:* Unknown. *CAST:* Unknown. *SYN:* Unknown.

**1019. Commando Cody — Sky Marshal of the Universe.** (2/17/53) B&W 26½ mins. per episode. 12 episodes. (Science Fiction). *DIR:* Fred C. Brannon, Harry Keller, Franklin Adreon. *A-PRO:* Franklin Adreon. *SP:* Ronald Davidson, Barry Shipman. *EPISODES:* (1) Enemies of the Universe, (2) Atomic Peril, (3) Cosmic Vengeance, (4) Nightmare Typhoon, (5) War of the Space Giants, (6) Destroyers of the Sun, (7) Robot Monster from Mars, (8) The Hydrogen Hurricane, (9) Solar Sky Raiders, (10) S.O.S. Ice Age, (11) Lost in Outer Space, (12) Captives of the Zero Hour. *CAST:* Judd Holdren, Aline Towne, William Schallert, Richard Crane, Craig Kelly, Gregory Gay, Dale Van Sickel, Edward Foster, Joanne Jordan, Peter Brocco, John Daheim, Zon Murray, Tom Steele, Stanley Waxman, Riley Hill, I. Stanford Jolley, John Crawford, William Fawcett, Paul Livermore, Gloria Pall, Lyle Talbot, William (Bill) Henry, Keith Richards, Rick Vallin, Kenneth MacDonald, Marshall Reed, Grant Withers, Sydney Mason, Sandy Sanders, Peter Ortiz, Denver Pyle, Lane Bradford, Fred Graham, Mauritz Hugo, Lee Roberts, *VOICE OF:* Roy Barcroft. *SYN:* Commando Cody (Holdren) and his associates, Mr. Henderson (Kelly), Joan Albright (Towne), Ted Richards (Schallert), and Dick Preston (Crane), set out to stop "The Ruler" (Gay) from conquering and enslaving the peoples of earth. *NOTES:* Unlike the earlier serial that featured Commando Cody, *Radar Men from the Moon*, (1952), Commando Cody wore a mask and uniform throughout this series. The picture on the wall in episode 1 is that of Roy Barcroft. William Schallert appeared in episodes 1–3 and was replaced by Richard Crane for the remainder of the series. This series was unusual for its time in that it was released to theatres prior to its TV syndication. It was first shown in theatres beginning with the above release date and theater owners reserved the right to show this series with each episode complete or as a serial with a cliffhanger ending. The series was telecast on NBC from July 16, 1955 to October 8, 1955.

**1020. Fights — Marciano Vs. LaStarza** (9/28/53) (Sports). *DIR/PRO:* Unknown. *CAST:* Narrated by Bill Corum. *SYN:* The heavyweight championship fight between Rocky Marciano and Roland LaStarza on Sept. 24, 1953 in which Marciano won by a TKO in 11 rounds.

**1021. Fights — Robinson Vs. Turpin** (6/20/51) (Sports). *DIR/PRO:* Unknown. *CAST:* Narrated by Jimmy Powers. *SYN:* The middleweight championship fight between Sugar Ray Robinson and Randy Turpin on June 10, 1951, in which Turpin won by a decision in 15 rounds.

**1022. Henry Browne, Farmer** (12/2/42) B&W 11 mins. (Documentary). *DIR:* Roger Barlow. *PRO:* U.S. Department of Agriculture. *CAST:* Narrated by Canada Lee. *SYN:* This was the first Government film showing the part American Negroes played in World War II.

**1023. Land of Opportunity — The American Rodeo** (1949) (Travelogue). B&W 9 mins. *DIR/PRO:* Unknown. *CAST:* Allan "Rocky" Lane, "Black Jack." Narrated by Gerald Courtemarsh. *SYN:* Unknown.

**1024. Land of Opportunity — The Mardi Gras** (2/24/50) (Travelogue). B&W 9 mins. *DIR/PRO:* Unknown. *CAST:* Selmer Jackson, Anna May Slaughter. *SYN:* Unknown.

**1025. Land of Opportunity — The Sponge Diver** (1949) (Travelogue). B&W 9 mins. *DIR/PRO:* Unknown. *CAST:* Robert Rockwell, Billy Gray. *SYN:* Unknown.

**1026. Land of Opportunity — Tillers of the Soil** (1/19/50) (Travelogue). B&W 9 mins. *DIR/PRO:* Unknown. *CAST:* Will Wright, Sammy McKim. *SYN:* Unknown.

**1027. Meet the Stars — Baby Stars** (1941) (Variety). B&W 20 mins. *DIR/PRO:* Harriet Parsons. *CAST:* Joan Blondell, Eleanor Bordman, Evelyn Brent, Ella Bryan, Sue Carol, Lucia Carroll, June Collyer, Dolores Del Rio, Peggy Diggins, Sally Eilers, Lorraine Elliott, Helen Ferguson, Janet Gaynor, Carmelita Geraghty, Jayne Hazard, Evalyn Knapp, Joan Leslie, Kay Leslie, Anita Louise, Marilyn Merrick, Gay Parkes, Tobyna Ralston, Sheila Ryan, Patricia Van Cleve, Tanya Widrin, Lois Wilson, Claire Windsor. *SYN:* Unknown.

**1028. Meet the Stars — Chinese Garden Festival** (1940) (Variety). B&W 20 mins. *DIR/PRO:* Harriet Parsons. *CAST:* Kay Aldredge, William Bakewell, Armanda Berela, Beulah Bondi, Doris Bouden, Gloria Brewster, Barbara Brewster, Slavina Brown, Suzanne Carnahan, Georgia Carroll, Charles Coburn, Dolores Del Rio, John Garfield, Jane Hamilton, Rita Hayworth, Mary Healy, Rose Hobart, Mary Beth Hughes, Ann Hunter, King Kennedy, Dorothy

Lamour, Herta Margot, Mary Martin, Patricia Morison, Ona Munson, Cliff Nazarro, Gertrude Niesen, Maria Ouspenskaya, Mary Pickford, Walter Pidgeon, Charles "Buddy" Rogers, Cesar Romero, Rosland Russell, Tom Rutherford, Margaret Tallichet, Heather Thatcher, Vera Vague (Barbara Jo Allen), Jane Withers, Anna May Wong. *SYN:* Unknown.

**1029. Meet the Stars — Hollywood Visits the Navy** (1941) (Variety). B&W 20 mins. *DIR/PRO:* Harriet Parsons. *CAST:* Richard Barthelmess, Charles Butterworth, Olympe Bradna, Henry Fonda, Carole Landis, Mary Lee, Carmen Miranda, George Murphy, Anne Nagel. George O'Brien. *SYN:* Unknown.

**1030. Meet the Stars — Los Angeles Examiner Benefit** (1941) (Variety). B&W 20 mins. *DIR/PRO:* Harriet Parsons. *CAST:* Bud Abbott, The Andrews Sisters, Baby Dumpling, Milton Berle, Butch and Buddy, Lou Costello, Topsy Duncan, Eva Duncan Reginald Gardner, Judy Garland, Mary Beth Hughes, Lorraine Krueger, Arthur Lake, Mary Martin, Constance Moore, Buddy Pepper, Mickey Rooney, Bob Williams and "Red Dust." *SYN:* Unknown.

**1031. Meet the Stars — Meet Roy Rogers** (1941) (Variety). B&W 20 mins. *DIR/PRO:* Harriet Parsons. *CAST:* Roy Rogers, Roscoe Ates, Gene Autry, Bob Baker, Judy Canova, Bill Elliott, Billy Gilbert, George "Gabby" Hayes, Mary Lee. *SYN:* Unknown.

**1032. Meet the Stars — Stars at Play** (1941) (Variety). B&W 20 mins. *DIR/PRO:* Harriet Parsons. *CAST:* Annabella, Desi Arnaz, Gene Autry, Lucille Ball, Binnie Barnes, Joe E. Brown, June Collyer, Bing Crosby, William Demarest, Stu Erwin, Virginia Field, Rita Hayworth, Jack Holt, Jeanne Howlett, Jackie Hughes, Roscoe Karns, Andrea Leeds, Edmund Lowe, Tony Martin, Mary McCarthy, Constance Moore, Patricia Morison, J. Carrol Naish, Gail Patrick, Buddy Pepper, George Raft, The Ritz Brothers, Cesar Romero, Randolph Scott, Lana Turner, Jane Withers. *SYN:* Unknown.

**1033. Meet the Stars — Stars Past and Present** (1941) (Variety) B&W 20 mins. *DIR/PRO:* Harriet Parsons. *CAST:* Walter Abel, Gene Autry, Binnie Barnes, Richard Bennett, Jack Buetel, Smiley Burnette, Mae Busch, Judy Canova, Chester Conklin, Minta Durfee, Sally Eilers, William Farnum, Eddie Gribbon, George "Gabby" Hayes, Brenda Joyce, Edgar Kennedy, The Keystone Kops, Mary Lee, Mary Martin, Ilona Massey, Walter McGrail, Ann Miller, Patricia Morison, Jack Mulhall, Charlie Murray, Sr., William T. Orr, Eddie Quillan, Charles Ray, Cesar Romero, Wesley Ruggles, Jane Russell, Mack Sennett, Eddie Sutherland. *SYN:* Unknown.

**1034. Meet the Stars — Variety Reel No. 4** (1941) (Variety). B&W 20 mins. *DIR/PRO:* Harriet Parsons. *CAST:* Edward Arnold, Mary Astor, Gene Autry, Fay Bainter, Binnie Barnes, Billy Benedict, Joan Benny, Beulah Bondi, George Burns, Sandra Burns, Judy Canova, June Collyer, Frank Craven, Donald Crisp, Doris Davenport, Bette Davis, Deanna Durbin, Jimmy Durante, Stu Erwin, Glenn Ford, Greer Garson, Porter Hall, George "Gabby" Hayes, William Holden, Brenda Joyce, Guy Kibbee, Mary Livinston, Gene Markey,

Melinda Markey, Ilona Massey, Ann Miller, William T. Orr, Louella Parsons, Gail Patrick, Walter Pidgeon, Juanita Quigley, Rita Quigley, Bob Ross, Shirley Ross, Ann Rutherford, Martha Scott, Robert Stack, Kathryn Stevens, Ruth Tobey, Ann E. Todd, Cobina Wright, Jr. *SYN:* Unknown.

**1035. This World of Ours — Bali** (1954) (Travelogue). Trucolor 9 mins. A Vistarama Travel Series. *DIR/PRO:* Carl Dudley.

**1036. This World of Ours — Belgium** (1951) (Travelogue). Trucolor 9 mins. A Vistarama Travel Series. *DIR/PRO:* Carl Dudley.

**1037. This World of Ours — Caribbean Sky Cruise** (1955) (Travelogue). Trucolor 9 mins. A Vistarama Travel Series. *DIR/PRO:* Carl Dudley.

**1038. This World of Ours — Ceylon** (1953) (Travelogue). Trucolor 9 mins. A Vistarama Travel Series. *DIR/PRO:* Carl Dudley.

**1039. This World of Ours — Chile** (1952) (Travelogue). Trucolor 9 mins.. A Vistarama Travel Series. *DIR/PRO:* Carl Dudley.

**1040. This World of Ours — City of Destiny** (1953) (Travelogue). Trucolor 9 mins. A Vistarama Travel Series. *DIR/PRO:* Carl Dudley.

**1041. This World of Ours — Denmark** (1950) (Travelogue). Trucolor 9 mins. A Vistarama Travel Series. *DIR/PRO:* Carl Dudley.

**1042. This World of Ours — Egypt** (1951) (Travelogue). Trucolor 9 mins. A Vistarama Travel Series. *DIR/PRO:* Carl Dudley.

**1043. This World of Ours — England** (1951) (Travelogue). Trucolor 9 mins. A Vistarama Travel Series. *DIR/PRO:* Carl Dudley.

**1044. This World of Ours — Formosa** (1954) Trucolor 9 mins. A Vistarama Travel Series. *DIR/PRO:* Carl Dudley.

**1045. This World of Ours — France** (1950) Trucolor 9 mins. A Vistarama Travel Series. *DIR/PRO:* Carl Dudley.

**1046. This World of Ours — Germany** (1953) (Travelogue). Trucolor 9 mins. A Vistarama Travel Series. *DIR/PRO:* Carl Dudley.

**1047. This World of Ours — Glacier National Park** (1950) (Travelogue). Trucolor 9 mins. A Vistarama Travel Series. *DIR/PRO:* Carl Dudley.

**1048. This World of Ours — Greece** (1951) (Travelogue). Trucolor 9 mins. A Vistarama Travel Series. *DIR/PRO:* Carl Dudley.

**1049. This World of Ours — Hawaii** (1951) (Travelogue). Trucolor 9 mins. A Vistarama Travel Series. *DIR/PRO:* Carl Dudley.

**1050. This World of Ours — Holland** (1950) (Travelogue). Trucolor 9 mins. A Vistarama Travel Series. *DIR/PRO:* Carl Dudley.

**1051. This World of Ours — Hong Kong** (1954) (Travelogue). Trucolor 9 mins. A Vistarama Travel Series. *DIR/PRO:* Carl Dudley.

**1052. This World of Ours — India** (1952) (Travelogue). Trucolor 9 mins. A Vistarama Travel Series. *DIR/PRO:* Carl Dudley.

**1053. This World of Ours — Ireland** (1954) (Travelogue). Trucolor 9 mins. A Vistarama Travel Series. *DIR/PRO:* Carl Dudley.

**1054. This World of Ours — Israel** (1952) (Travelogue). Trucolor 9 mins. A Vistarama Travel Series. *DIR/PRO:* Carl Dudley.

**1055. This World of Ours — Italy** (1951) (Travelogue). Trucolor 9 mins. A Vistarama Travel Series. *DIR/PRO:* Carl Dudley.

**1056. This World of Ours — Japan** (1953) (Travelogue). Trucolor 9 mins. A Vistarama Travel Series. *DIR/PRO:* Carl Dudley.

**1057. This World of Ours — London** (1951) (Travelogue). Trucolor 9 mins. A Vistarama Travel Series. *DIR/PRO:* Carl Dudley.

**1058. This World of Ours — Norway** (1950) (Travelogue). Trucolor 9 mins. A Vistarama Travel Series. *DIR/PRO:* Carl Dudley.

**1059. This World of Ours — The Philippines** (1952) (Travelogue). Trucolor 9 mins. A Vistarama Travel Series. *DIR/PRO:* Carl Dudley.

**1060. This World of Ours — Portugal** (1951) (Travelogue). Trucolor 9 mins. A Vistarama Travel Series. *DIR/PRO:* Unknown.

**1061. This World of Ours — Puerto Rico** (1952) (Travelogue). Trucolor 9 mins. A Vistarama Travel Series. *DIR/PRO:* Unknown.

**1062. This World of Ours — Singapore** (1953) (Travelogue). Trucolor 9 mins. A Vistarama Travel Series. *DIR/PRO:* Unknown.

**1063. This World of Ours — Spain** (1951) (Travelogue). Trucolor 9 mins. A Vistarama Travel Series. *DIR/PRO:* Unknown.

**1064. This World of Ours — Sweden** (1950) (Travelogue). Trucolor 9 mins. A Vistarama Travel Series. *DIR/PRO:* Carl Dudley.

**1065. This World of Ours — Switzerland** (1951) (Travelogue). Trucolor 9 mins. A Vistarama Travel Series. *DIR/PRO:* Carl Dudley.

**1066. This World of Ours — Thailand** (1954) (Travelogue). Trucolor 9 mins. A Vistarama Travel Series. *DIR/PRO:* Carl Dudley.

**1067. This World of Ours — Turkey** (1955) (Travelogue). Trucolor 9 mins. A Vistarama Travel Series. *DIR/PRO:* Carl Dudley.

**1068. This World of Ours — Venezuela** (1955) (Travelogue). Trucolor 9 mins. A Vistarama Travel Series. *DIR/PRO:* Carl Dudley.

# *Training Films (1941–1945)*

*Following is a complete list of training films produced by Republic Pictures Corporation for the Army and Navy. Credits and cast lists are given, where known.*

1069. Army — Maintenance for LVT's (1945) *DIR:/PRO:* Unknown. *CAST:* Unknown. *SYN:* Unknown.

1070. Army 101 — Equipment Maintenance (1944) *DIR:/PRO:* Unknown. *CAST:* Carey Loftin, Cliff Lyons, Helen Thurston, Dale Van Sickel, Bud Wolfe. *SYN:* Unknown.

1071. Army 102 — Trench Foot (1944) *DIR:/PRO:* Unknown. *CAST:* Louis Jean Heydt. *SYN:* Unknown.

1072. Army 146 — 60mm Mortar (1941) *DIR:/PRO:* Unknown. *CAST:* Unknown. *SYN:* Unknown.

1073. Army 147 — 60mm Mortar (1941) *DIR:/PRO:* Unknown. *CAST:* Unknown. *SYN:* Unknown.

1074. Army 148 — 60mm Mortar (1941) *DIR:/PRO:* Unknown. *CAST:* Unknown. *SYN:* Unknown.

1075. Army 150 — National Labor (1944) *DIR:/PRO:* Unknown. *CAST:* Unknown. *SYN:* Unknown.

1076. Army 156 — Horsemanship (1942) *DIR:/PRO:* Unknown. *CAST:* Alan Baxter, Richard Crane, Kane Richmond. *SYN:* Unknown.

1077. Army 220 — Cavalry Rifle Platoon (1942) *DIR:/PRO:* Unknown. *CAST:* Narrated by Gayne Whitman. *SYN:* Unknown.

1078. Army 220A — Cavalry Rifle Platoon (1943) *DIR:/PRO:* Unknown. *CAST:* Narrated by Gayne Whitman. *SYN:* Unknown.

**1079. Army 681—Keep It Clean** (1942) *DIR:/PRO:* Unknown. *CAST:* Don "Red" Barry. *SYN:* Unknown.

**1080. Army 682—Cracking Tanks** (1942) *DIR:/PRO:* Unknown. *CAST:* Unknown. *SYN:* Unknown.

**1081. Army 7167—Frequency Modulation** (1944) *DIR:/PRO:* Unknown. *CAST:* Unknown. *SYN:* Unknown.

**1082. Army 828—First Aid** (1943) *DIR:/PRO:* Unknown. *CAST:* Keene Duncan. Narrated by Gayne Whitman. *SYN:* Unknown.

**1083. Army 9652—Car Sharing** (1944) *DIR:/PRO:* Unknown. *CAST:* Narrated by Gayne Whitman. *SYN:* Unknown.

**1084. Navy MN3387—Your Weapons** (1944) *DIR:/PRO:* Unknown. *CAST:* Keefe Brasselle, Lane Chandler, LeRoy Mason, Joe McGuinn, Michael Owen, Marshall Reed, Robert Wilke. *SYN:* Unknown.

# Appendix A: Films Listed by Release Date

*After each title and release date (month/day or just month) is a reference to the entry number. Unknown release dates are given as (??). Re-releases are omitted.*

## 1935

Westward Ho! (8/19) 907
Tumbling Tumbleweeds (9/5) 863
Cappy Ricks Returns (9/10) 100
Two Sinners (9/14) 869
The Crime of Dr. Crespi (9/24) 148
Melody Trail (9/24) 489
Born to Gamble (10/4) 77
The New Frontier (10/5) 523
The Spanish Cape Mystery (10/9) 764
$1,000 a Minute (10/22) 552
Lawless Range (11/4) 434
Racing Luck (11/19) 617
Sagebrush Troubador (11/19) 681
Forced Landing (11/26) 246
Frisco Waterfront (12/3) 254
The Singing Vagabond (12/11) 738

## 1936

Hitch Hike Lady (1/3) 347
The Leavenworth Case (1/6) 439
The Oregon Trail (1/15) 554
Dancing Feet (1/20) 158
The Return of Jimmy Valentine (2/1) 639
The Bold Caballero (2/3) 67
The Lawless Nineties (2/15) 433
Darkest Africa (2/15) 957
The Leathernecks Have Landed (2/17) 438
Red River Valley (3/2) 632
Laughing Irish Eyes (3/4) 429
King of the Pecos (3/9) 411
Comin' Round the Mountain (3/31) 135
The House of a Thousand Candles (4/3) 360

Federal Agent (4/14) 223
The Girl from Mandalay (4/14) 282
The Harvester (4/18) 313
The Singing Cowboy (5/13) 735
Darkest Africa (5/21) 163
Burning Gold (5/22) 85
The Lonely Trail (5/25) 448
Hearts in Bondage (5/26) 322
Down to the Sea (5/30) 196
Undersea Kingdom (5/30) 1007
Navy Born (6/2) 521
Winds of the Wasteland (6/15) 916
Guns and Guitars (6/22) 306
Frankie and Johnnie (6/25) 250
Ticket to Paradise (6/25) 833
Follow Your Heart (8/11) 244
The Gentleman from Louisiana (8/15) 272
Oh, Susanna! (8/19) 537
The Vigilantes are Coming (8/22) 1008
Sitting on the Moon (9/11) 741
Bulldog Edition (9/20) 83
The Three Mesquiteers (9/22) 822
Under Cover Man (9/24) 873
The President's Mystery (9/28) 603
Ride, Ranger, Ride (9/30) 642
Cavalry (10/5) 110
Go-Get-'Em Haines (10/22) 289
Country Gentlemen (10/24) 140
Forbidden Heaven (10/26) 245
Ghost-Town Gold (10/26) 276
Robinson Crusoe of Clipper Island (11/14) 1000
The Big Show (11/16) 56
Happy-Go-Lucky (12/5) 311
Roarin' Lead (12/9) 655
The Old Corral (12/21) 543
The Mandarin Mystery (12/23) 476

## 1937

Riders of the Whistling Skull (1/4) 647
A Man Betrayed (1/8) 461
Larceny on the Air (1/11) 421
Beware of Ladies (1/12) 53

Robinson Crusoe of Clipper Island (1/15) 658
Join the Marines (1/25) 400
The Gun Ranger (2/9) 303
The Gambling Terror (2/15) 261
Two Wise Maids (2/15) 870
Dick Tracy (2/20) 960
Paradise Express (2/22) 576
Circus Girl (3/1) 117
Hit the Saddle (3/3) 346
Bill Cracks Down (3/22) 59
"Lightnin' " Crandall (3/24) 440
Git Along Little Dogies (3/27) 286
Trail of Vengeance (3/29) 847
Jim Hanvey, Detective (4/5) 396
Lawless Land (4/6) 432
Navy Blues (4/19) 520
Bar-Z Bad Men (4/22) 41
Round-Up Time in Texas (4/22) 673
The Hit Parade (4/26) 341
The Trusted Outlaw (5/4) 860
Gunsmoke Ranch (5/5) 308
Rootin' Tootin' Rhythm (5/12) 667
Guns in the Dark (5/13) 307
Michael O'Halloran (5/15) 493
Gun Lords of Stirrup Basin (5/18) 302
Affairs of Cappy Ricks (5/24) 5
Come On, Cowboys! (5/24) 132
It Could Happen to You (5/28) 388
The Painted Stallion (6/5) 993
Border Phantom (6/7) 72
Dangerous Holiday (6/7) 159
Yodelin' Kid from Pine Ridge (6/14) 936
A Lawman Is Born (6/21) 435
Rhythm in the Clouds (6/21) 640
Range Defenders (6/30) 624
Doomed at Sundown (7/7) 190
Meet the Boy Friend (7/12) 485
The Red Rope (7/19) 634
Bulldog Drummond at Bay (7/31) 82
Boothill Brigade (8/2) 69
All Over Town (8/8) 12
Sea Racketeers (8/20) 705
Public Cowboy No. 1 (8/23) 611
S O S Coast Guard (8/28) 1003
Escape By Night (9/1) 210
Heart of the Rockies (9/6) 319

The Sheik Steps Out (9/6) 717
The Arizona Gunfighter (9/24) 23
Youth on Parole (10/4) 942
Boots and Saddles (10/11) 70
The Wrong Road (10/11) 927
The Trigger Trio (10/18) 855
Ridin' the Lone Trail (11/1) 650
Portia on Trail (11/8) 598
Manhattan Merry-Go-Round (11/13) 477
Springtime in the Rockies (11/15) 770
Zorro Rides Again (11/20) 1010
The Duke Comes Back (11/29) 200
The Colorado Kid (12/6) 127
Wild Horse Rodeo (12/6) 915
Glamorous Night (12/15) 287
Exiled to Shanghai (12/20) 212
Lady, Behave! (12/22) 414
Mama Runs Wild (12/22) 459
Dick Tracy (12/27) 183

## 1938

Paroled — to Die (1/11) 578
The Purple Vigilantes (1/24) 615
The Old Barn Dance (1/29) 542
Outside of Paradise (2/7) 568
The Painted Stallion (2/11) 571
The Lone Ranger (2/12) 987
Born to be Wild (2/16) 76
Hollywood Stadium Mystery (2/21) 349
Prison Nurse (3/1) 609
Call the Mesquiteers (3/7) 95
Thunder in the Desert (3/7) 827
King of the Newsboys (3/18) 410
Arson Gang Busters (3/28) 29
The Higgins Family (3/29) 339
Invisible Enemy (4/4) 385
Outlaws of Sonora (4/14) 567
Call of the Yukon (4/18) 94
The Feud Maker (4/18) 226
Under Western Stars (4/20) 878
Romance on the Run (5/11) 664
Gangs of New York (5/23) 263
The Fighting Devil Dogs (5/28) 968
Desert Patrol (6/6) 177
Ladies in Distress (6/13) 412

Riders of the Black Hills (6/15) 645
Gold Mine in the Sky (7/5) 291
Army Girl (7/15) 28
Heroes of the Hills (7/29) 331
A Desperate Adventure (8/6) 180
Come On, Leathernecks (8/8) 133
Man from Music Mountain (8/15) 465
Dick Tracy Returns (8/20) 961
Durango Valley Raiders (8/22) 202
Tenth Avenue Kid (8/22) 810
Pals of the Saddle (8/28) 574
Billy the Kid Returns (9/4) 60
Overland Stage Raiders (9/20) 570
Zorro Rides Again (9/22) 946
The Night Hawk (10/1) 525
Prairie Moon (10/7) 601
Down in "Arkansaw" (10/8) 193
I Stand Accused (10/28) 365
Rhythm of the Saddle (11/5) 641
Storm Over Bengal (11/14) 778
Santa Fe Stampede (11/18) 693
Come On, Rangers (11/25) 134
Western Jamboree (12/2) 906
Hawk of the Wilderness (12/3) 975
Orphans of the Street (12/5) 557
Red River Range (12/22) 629
Shine on Harvest Moon (12/30) 725

## 1939

Fighting Thoroughbreds (1/6) 232
The Mysterious Miss X (1/10) 515
Pride of the Navy (1/23) 606
Federal Man-Hunt (2/2) 225
Home on the Prairie (2/3) 352
Woman Doctor (2/6) 919
The Lone Ranger Rides Again (2/25) 988
I Was a Convict (3/6) 366
Rough Riders' Round-Up (3/13) 672
Southward Ho! (3/19) 763
Mexacali Rose (3/29) 491
Frontier Pony Express (4/12) 256
The Night Riders (4/12) 526
Forged Passport (4/24) 247
Street of Missing Men (4/28) 788
Blue Montana Skies (5/4) 66

APPENDIX A

Three Texas Steers (5/12) 823
Man of Conquest (5/15) 473
My Wife's Relatives (5/20) 514
The Zero Hour (5/26) 945
S. O. S. Tidal Wave (6/2) 757
Daredevils of the Red Circle (6/10) 955
In Old Caliente (6/19) 372
Wyoming Outlaw (6/27) 930
Mountain Rhythm (6/29) 508
Mickey, the Kid (7/3) 494
She Married a Cop (7/12) 715
Should Husbands Work? (7/26) 726
Colorado Sunset (7/31) 130
Wall Street Cowboy (8/6) 899
New Frontier (8/10) 524
In Old Monterey (8/14) 376
Smuggled Cargo (8/21) 745
Flight at Midnight (8/28) 240
Dick Tracy's G-Men (9/2) 963
Calling All Marines (9/20) 96
The Arizona Kid (9/29) 24
The Kansas Terrors (10/6) 406
Sabotage (10/13) 677
Jeepers Creepers (10/27) 393
Main Street Lawyer (11/3) 457
The Covered Trailer (11/10) 141
Rovin' Tumbleweeds (11/16) 674
Saga of Death Valley (11/17) 680
Zorro's Fighting Legion (11/20) 1012
Cowboys from Texas (11/29) 146
South of the Border (12/15) 761
Days of Jesse James (12/20) 167
Thou Shalt Not Kill (12/30) 819
Money to Burn (12/31) 503

## 1940

Heroes of the Saddle (1/12) 332
Wolf of New York (1/25) 918
Village Barn Dance (1/30) 893
Pioneers of the West (3/12) 590
Forgotten Girls (3/15) 248
Drums of Fu Manchu (3/15) 965
Rancho Grande (3/22) 623
Ghost Valley Raiders (3/26) 277
Hi-Yo-Silver (4/10) 334
Young Buffalo Bill (4/12) 940

Dark Command (4/15) 162
In Old Missouri (4/17) 375
Grandpa Goes to Town (4/19) 296
Covered Wagon Days (4/22) 142
The Crooked Road (5/10) 151
Gaucho Serenade (5/10) 266
Gangs of Chicago (5/19) 262
Rocky Mountain Rangers (5/24) 660
Women in War (6/6) 926
Wagons Westward (6/19) 897
Grand Ole Opry (6/25) 295
Adventures of Red Ryder (6/28) 949
One Man's Law (6/29) 551
The Carson City Kid (7/1) 106
Three Faces West (7/12) 820
Carolina Moon (7/15) 104
Scatterbrain (7/20) 699
Girl from God's Country (7/30) 280
The Ranger and the Lady (7/30) 625
Sing Dance, Plenty Hot (8/10) 733
The Tulsa Kid (8/16) 862
Oklahoma Renegades (8/29) 541
Earl of Puddlestone (8/31) 205
Ride, Tenderfoot, Ride (9/6) 643
Girl from Havana (9/11) 281
Colorado (9/15) 126
Under Texas Skies (9/20) 877
King of the Royal Mounted (9/20) 985
Frontier Vengeance (10/10) 257
Melody and Moonlight (10/11) 487
Hit Parade of 1941 (10/15) 342
Young Bill Hickok (10/21) 939
Who Killed Aunt Maggie? (11/1) 911
Friendly Neighbors (11/7) 252
The Trail Blazers (11/11) 844
Melody Ranch (11/15) 488
Texas Terrors (11/22) 812
Meet the Missus (11/29) 486
The Border Legion (12/5) 71
Barnyard Follies (12/6) 42
Mysterious Dr. Satan (12/13) 992
Behind the News (12/20) 45
Lone Star Raiders (12/23) 445
Bowery Boy (12/30) 78
Meet the Stars—Chinese Garden Festival (??) 1028

## 1941

Wyoming Wildcat (1/6) 931
Robin Hood of the Pecos (1/14) 657
Ridin' On a Rainbow (1/24) 649
Arkansas Judge (1/28) 27
Petticoat Politics (1/31) 582
The Phantom Cowboy (2/14) 583
Prairie Pioneers (2/16) 602
The Great Train Robbery (2/28) 299
A Man Betrayed (3/7) 462
Back in the Saddle (3/14) 34
Mr. District Attorney (3/26) 500
In Old Cheyenne (3/28) 374
Adventures of Captain Marvel (3/28) 947
Pals of the Pecos (4/8) 573
Two-Gun Sheriff (4/10) 868
Sis Hopkins (4/12) 740
Rookies on Parade (4/17) 666
Lady from Louisiana (4/22) 416
The Singing Hill (4/26) 737
Country Fair (5/5) 139
Sheriff of Tombstone (5/7) 723
The Gay Vagabond (5/12) 270
Saddlemates (5/16) 679
Desert Bandit (5/24) 175
Nevada City (6/20) 522
Jungle Girl (6/21) 980
Kansas Cyclone (6/24) 405
Puddin' Head (6/25) 613
Angels with Broken Wings (6/27) 19
Poison Pen (6/30) 596
Gangs of Sonora (7/10) 264
Mountain Moonlight (7/12) 507
Sunset in Wyoming (7/15) 797
Hurricane Smith (7/20) 361
Citadel of Crime (7/24) 119
Rags to Riches (7/31) 618
Doctors Don't Tell (8/20) 187
Ice-Capades (8/20) 367
Under Fiesta Stars (8/25) 874
The Pittsburgh Kid (8/29) 592
Bad Man of Deadwood (9/5) 35
Outlaws of Cherokee Trail (9/10) 564
The Apache Kid (9/12) 20
Death Valley Outlaws (9/26) 172
Sailors on Leave (9/30) 682
King of the Texas Rangers (10/4) 986
Mercy Island (10/10) 490
Down Mexico Way (10/15) 195
Jesse James at Bay (10/17) 394
Gauchos of Eldorado (10/24) 267
Public Enemies (10/30) 612
The Devil Pays Off (11/10) 182
Sierra Sue (11/12) 728
A Missouri Outlaw (11/25) 498
Tuxedo Junction (12/4) 864
Red River Valley (12/12) 633
West of Cimarron (12/15) 904
Mr. District Attorney in the Carter Case (12/18) 501
Dick Tracy Vs. Crime, Inc. (12/27) 962
Meet the Stars — Baby Stars (??) 1027
Meet the Stars — Hollywood Visits the Navy (??) 1029
Meet the Stars — Los Angeles Examiner Benefit (??) 1030
Meet the Stars — Meet Roy Rogers (??) 1031
Meet the Stars — Stars at Play (??) 1032
Meet the Stars — Stars Past and Present (??) 1033
Meet the Stars — Variety Reel No. 4 (??) 1034
Army 146 — 60mm Mortar (??) 1072
Army 147 — 60mm Mortar (??) 1073
Army 148 — 60mm Mortar (??) 1074

## 1942

Lady for a Night (1/5) 415
Arizona Terrors (1/6) 26
Man from Cheyenne (1/16) 463
Cowboy Serenade (1/22) 145
Pardon My Stripes (1/26) 577
Code of the Outlaw (1/30) 123
A Tragedy at Midnight (2/2) 843
South of Santa Fe (2/17) 760
Sleepytime Gal (3/5) 743
Stagecoach Express (3/6) 773
Heart of the Rio Grande (3/11) 318
Yokel Boy (3/13) 937

Raiders of the Range (3/18) 621
Affairs of Jimmy Valentine (3/25) 7
Jesse James, Jr. (3/25) 395
Shepherd of the Ozarks (3/26) 718
Sunset on the Desert (4/1) 798
Spy Smasher (4/4) 1004
The Girl from Alaska (4/16) 279
S O S Coast Guard (4/16) 756
Suicide Squadron (4/20) 790
Westward Ho (4/24) 908
Home in Wyomin' (4/29) 351
Yukon Patrol (4/30) 943
Remember Pearl Harbor! (5/18) 636
Romance on the Range (5/18) 663
Stardust on the Sage (5/25) 776
The Cyclone Kid (5/31) 154
Moonlight Masquerade (6/10) 504
In Old California (6/11) 373
The Phantom Plainsman (6/16) 585
Perils of Nyoka (6/27) 995
Sons of the Pioneers (7/2) 755
Hi, Neighbor! (7/27) 333
The Sombrero Kid (7/31) 746
Joan of Ozark (8/1) 397
Call of the Canyon (8/17) 91
The Old Homestead (8/17) 545
Sunset Serenade (9/14) 799
Bells of Capistrano (9/15) 48
Shadows on the Sage (9/24) 712
Moscow Strikes Back (10/1) 506
Flying Tigers (10/8) 243
King of the Mounties (10/17) 983
Youth on Parade (10/24) 941
Outlaws of Pine Ridge (10/27) 565
X Marks the Spot (11/4) 932
Valley of Hunted Men (11/13) 885
Heart of the Golden West (11/16) 317
Henry Browne, Farmer (12/2) 1022
The Traitor Within (12/16) 850
Secrets of the Underground (12/18) 710
Ice-Capades Revue (12/24) 368
The Sundown Kid (12/28) 794
Ridin' Down the Canyon (12/30) 648
Johnny Doughboy (12/31) 398
Army 156 — Horsemanship (??) 1076
Army 220 — Cavalry Rifle Platoon (??) 1077
Army 681 — Keep It Clean (??) 1079
Army 682 — Cracking Tanks (??) 1080

## 1943

Mountain Rhythm (1/8) 509
London Blackout Murders (1/15) 444
G-Men Vs. the Black Dragon (1/16) 972
Thundering Trails (1/25) 832
The Fighting Devil Dogs (1/29) 229
Dead Man's Gulch (2/12) 169
Carson City Cyclone (3/3) 105
Idaho (3/10) 369
The Blocked Trail (3/12) 64
The Purple V (3/12) 614
At Dawn We Die (3/20) 30
The Alibi (3/24) 11
Hit Parade of 1943 (3/26) 343
Tahiti Honey (4/6) 805
King of the Cowboys (4/9) 408
The Mantrap (4/13) 478
Santa Fe Scouts (4/16) 692
Shantytown (4/20) 714
Chatterbox (4/27) 112
Calling Wild Bill Elliott (4/30) 97
Daredevils of the West (5/1) 956
A Gentle Gangster (5/10) 271
Days of Old Cheyenne (5/15) 168
Swing Your Partner (5/20) 803
Riders of the Rio Grande (5/21) 646
False Faces (5/28) 220
The Man from Thunder River (6/11) 470
Song of Texas (6/14) 753
Fugitive from Sonora (7/1) 258
Thumbs Up (7/5) 825
Secret Service in Darkest Africa (7/24) 1001
The Saint Meets the Tiger (7/29) 683
Silver Spurs (8/12) 732
The Black Hills Express (8/15) 62
Someone to Remember (8/21) 747
The West Side Kid (8/23) 905
Headin' for God's Country (8/26) 315
Nobody's Darling (8/27) 532
Sleepy Lagoon (9/5) 742
Hoosier Holiday (9/15) 358

Beyond the Last Frontier (9/18) 54
Bordertown Gunfighters (10/1) 74
A Scream in the Dark (10/15) 702
The Man from the Rio Grande (10/18) 469
Wagon Tracks West (10/28) 895
Man from Music Mountain (10/30) 466
The Masked Marvel (11/6) 991
Here Comes Elmer (11/15) 330
Overland Mail Robbery (11/20) 569
Deerslayer (11/22) 173
Mystery Broadcast (11/23) 517
Canyon City (11/24) 99
Death Valley Manhunt (11/24) 171
Drums of Fu Manchu (11/27) 198
In Old Oklahoma (12/6) 377
Pistol Packin' Mama (12/15) 591
Whispering Footsteps (12/20) 910
California Joe (12/29) 89
Raiders of Sunset Pass (12/30) 620
O, My Darling Clementine (12/31) 536
Army 220A — Cavalry Rifle Platoon (??) 1078
Army 828 — First Aid (??) 1082

## 1944

Hands Across the Border (1/5) 310
Pride of the Plains (1/5) 607
Captain America (2/5) 952
Casanova in Burlesque (2/19) 108
Beneath Western Skies (3/3) 52
The Fighting Seabees (3/10) 231
Mojave Firebrand (3/19) 502
My Best Gal (3/28) 511
Hidden Valley Outlaws (4/2) 337
The Laramie Trail (4/3) 420
Outlaws of Santa Fe (4/4) 566
Call of the South Seas (4/7) 93
Rosie, the Riveter (4/9) 669
The Lady and the Monster (4/17) 413
Trocadero (4/24) 856
Jamboree (5/5) 391
Cowboy and the Senorita (5/13) 144
Tucson Raiders (5/14) 861

The Tiger Woman (5/27) 1005
Silent Partner (6/9) 729
Goodnight Sweetheart (6/17) 293
The Yellow Rose of Texas (6/24) 934
Man from Frisco (7/1) 464
Marshal of Reno (7/2) 483
Call of the Rockies (7/14) 92
Silver City Kid (7/20) 731
Secrets of Scotland Yard (7/26) 709
Three Little Sisters (7/31) 821
The Girl Who Dared (8/5) 284
Song of Nevada (8/5) 752
Bordertown Trail (8/11) 75
Sing, Neighbor, Sing (8/12) 734
Port of 40 Thieves (8/13) 597
The San Antonio Kid (8/16) 687
Haunted Harbor (8/26) 974
Strangers in the Night (9/12) 785
That's My Baby (9/14) 814
Atlantic City (9/15) 31
San Fernando Valley (9/15) 688
Stagecoach to Monterey (9/15) 775
Cheyenne Wildcat (9/30) 115
Code of the Prairie (10/6) 124
My Buddy (10/12) 512
Storm Over Lisbon (10/16) 779
Lights of Old Santa Fe (11/6) 442
Sheriff of Sundown (11/7) 722
End of the Road (11/10) 209
Vigilantes of Dodge City (11/15) 892
Zorro's Black Whip (11/16) 1011
Brazil (11/30) 79
Faces in the Fog (11/30) 218
Firebrands of Arizona (12/1) 234
Lake Placid Serenade (12/23) 419
Thoroughbreds (12/23) 818
The Big Bonanza (12/30) 55
Sheriff of Las Vegas (12/31) 720
Army 101— Equipment Maintenance (??) 1070
Army 102 — Trench Foot (??) 1071
Army 150 — National Labor (??) 1075
Army 7167 — Frequency Modulation (??) 1081
Army 9652 — Car Sharing (??) 1083
Navy MN3387 — Your Weapons (??) 1084

APPENDIX A

## 1945

Grissly's Millions (1/16) 301
The Big Show-Off (1/22) 57
The Topeka Terror (1/26) 839
Great Stagecoach Robbery (2/15) 298
A Song for Miss Julie (2/19) 749
Sheriff of Cimarron (2/28) 719
Manhunt of Mystery Island (3/17) 990
Utah (3/21) 883
The Great Flamarion (3/30) 297
Identity Unknown (4/2) 370
Earl Carroll Vanities (4/5) 204
Corpus Christi Bandits (4/20) 138
The Phantom Speaks (5/10) 586
Lone Texas Ranger (5/20) 446
The Vampire's Ghost (5/21) 887
Three's a Crowd (5/23) 824
Flame of Barbary Coast (5/28) 236
Santa Fe Saddlemates (6/2) 691
A Sporting Chance (6/4) 769
Bells of Rosarita (6/19) 50
The Chicago Kid (6/29) 116
Gangs of the Waterfront (7/3) 265
Federal Operator 99 (7/7) 967
Steppin' In Society (7/9) 777
Road to Alcatraz (7/10) 653
Trail of Kit Carson (7/11) 845
Oregon Trail (7/14) 555
The Cheaters (7/15) 113
Hitchhike to Happiness (7/16) 348
Jealousy (7/23) 392
The Man from Oklahoma (8/1) 467
Tell It to a Star (8/16) 809
Swingin' on a Rainbow (9/1) 804
Phantom of the Plains (9/7) 584
Behind City Lights (9/10) 44
Bandits of the Badlands (9/14) 39
The Fatal Witness (9/15) 222
Love, Honor and Goodbye (9/15) 450
Sunset in El Dorado (9/29) 795
Scotland Yard Investigator (9/30) 701
The Purple Monster Strikes (10/6) 997
Marshal of Laredo (10/7) 482
Don't Fence Me In (10/20) 189
Rough Riders of Cheyenne (11/1) 670
Girls of the Big House (11/2) 285

Colorado Pioneers (11/14) 128
Mexicana (11/15) 492
The Tiger Woman (11/16) 834
Captain Tugboat Annie (11/17) 101
An Angel Comes to Brooklyn (11/27) 16
The Cherokee Flash (12/13) 114
The Woman Who Came Back (12/13) 923
Along the Navajo Trail (12/15) 13
Wagon Wheels Westward (12/21) 896
Dakota (12/25) 155
Song of Mexico (12/28) 751
Army — Maintenance for LVT's (??) 1069

## 1946

Gay Blades (1/25) 268
The Phantom Rider (1/26) 996
A Guy Could Change (1/27) 309
California Gold Rush (2/4) 88
Days of Buffalo Bill (2/8) 166
The Madonna's Secret (2/16) 453
Crime of the Century (2/28) 149
Song of Arizona (3/9) 750
Strange Impersonation (3/16) 783
Sheriff of Redwood Valley (3/29) 721
Murder in the Music Hall (4/10) 510
Undercover Woman (4/11) 879
Alias Billy the Kid (4/17) 9
Home on the Range (4/18) 353
The Catman of Paris (4/20) 109
The Glass Alibi (4/27) 288
King of the Forest Rangers (4/27) 982
Rainbow Over Texas (5/9) 622
Sun Valley Cyclone (5/10) 792
Passkey to Danger (5/11) 579
The French Key (5/18) 251
The El Paso Kid (5/22) 207
Valley of the Zombies (5/24) 886
In Old Sacramento (5/31) 378
One Exciting Week (6/8) 550
The Man from Rainbow Valley (6/15) 468
Traffic in Crime (6/28) 842
Specter of the Rose (7/5) 765
My Pal Trigger (7/10) 513

Night Train to Memphis (7/12) 529
Rendezvous With Annie (7/22) 637
Red River Renegades (7/23) 630
Daughter of Don Q (7/27) 958
Conquest of Cheyenne (7/29) 137
The Inner Circle (8/7) 380
The Last Crooked Mile (8/9) 424
G. I. War Brides (8/12) 278
The Invisible Informer (8/19) 386
Earl Carroll Sketchbook (8/22) 203
Under Nevada Skies (8/26) 876
The Mysterious Mr. Valentine (9/3) 516
Rio Grande Raiders (9/9) 652
Roll on Texas Moon (9/12) 662
The Crimson Ghost (10/26) 953
Home in Oklahoma (11/8) 350
Plainsman and the Lady (11/11) 593
Santa Fe Uprising (11/15) 694
Affairs of Geraldine (11/18) 6
Sioux City Sue (11/21) 739
I've Always Loved You (12/2) 389
Out California Way (12/5) 559
The Fabulous Suzanne (12/15) 216
Heldorado (12/15) 323
Stagecoach to Denver (12/23) 774
That Brennan Girl (12/23) 813

Oregon Trail Scouts (5/5) 556
That's My Gal (5/15) 815
Winter Wonderland (5/17) 917
That's My Man (6/1) 816
Saddle Pals (6/6) 678
Web of Danger (6/10) 902
Northwest Outpost (6/25) 534
Rustlers of Devil's Canyon (7/1) 675
The Trespasser (7/3) 852
Robin Hood of Texas (7/15) 656
Springtime in the Sierras (7/15) 771
Blackmail (7/24) 63
Wyoming (7/28) 928
Jesse James Rides Again (8/2) 978
Marshal of Cripple Creek (8/15) 481
The Pretender (8/16) 604
Along the Oregon Trail (8/30) 14
Exposed (9/8) 213
Driftwood (9/15) 197
The Wild Frontier (10/1) 913
On the Old Spanish Trail (10/15) 549
The Black Widow (11/1) 950
The Fabulous Texan (11/9) 217
The Flame (11/24) 235
Bandits of Dark Canyon (12/15) 38
Under Colorado Skies (12/15) 872
It's a Grand Old Nag (??) 1013

## 1947

Son of Zorro (1/18) 1002
The Pilgrim Lady (1/22) 588
Trail to San Antone (1/25) 848
Calendar Girl (1/31) 86
Last Frontier Uprising (2/1) 425
Angel and the Badman (2/15) 15
Apache Rose (2/15) 21
The Magnificent Rogue (2/15) 455
Vigilantes of Boomtown (2/15) 891
The Ghost Goes Wild (3/8) 274
Hit Parade of 1947 (3/22) 344
Homesteaders of Paradise Valley (4/1) 354
Twilight on the Rio Grande (4/1) 866
Yankee Fakir (4/1) 933
Bells of San Angelo (4/15) 51
Spoilers of the North (4/24) 767

## 1948

The Main Street Kid (1/1) 456
The Gay Ranchero (1/10) 269
Slippy McGee (1/15) 744
G-Men Never Forget (1/31) 971
Campus Honeymoon (2/1) 98
Oklahoma Badlands (2/22) 540
Madonna of the Desert (2/23) 452
The Inside Story (3/14) 381
Lightnin' in the Forest (3/26) 441
Bill and Coo (3/28) 58
California Firebrand (4/1) 87
The Bold Frontiersman (4/15) 68
Dangers of the Canadian Mounted (4/24) 954
Heart of Virginia (4/25) 321
Old Los Angeles (4/25) 546
Under California Stars (5/1) 871

King of the Gamblers (5/10) 409
Carson City Raiders (5/13) 107
The Gallant Legion (5/24) 260
I, Jane Doe (5/25) 364
Secret Service Investigator (5/31) 706
The Timber Trail (6/15) 835
Train to Alcatraz (6/28) 849
Eyes of Texas (7/15) 214
Marshal of Amarillo (7/25) 479
Daredevils of the Clouds (8/10) 161
Sons of Adventure (9/1) 754
Angel in Exile (9/3) 17
Night Time in Nevada (9/5) 528
Out of the Storm (9/11) 560
Desperadoes of Dodge City (9/15) 178
Son of God's Country (9/15) 748
The Denver Kid (10/1) 174
Macbeth (10/1) 451
Moonrise (10/1) 505
Code of Scotland Yard (10/24) 122
Adventures of Frank and Jesse James (10/30) 948
Angel on the Amazon (11/1) 18
Grand Canyon Trail (11/5) 294
Sundown in Santa Fe (11/5) 793
Renegades of Sonora (11/24) 638
The Plunderers (12/1) 594
Homicide for Three (12/8) 355
The Far Frontier (12/29) 221

## 1949

Rose of the Yukon (1/5) 668
Sheriff of Wichita (1/22) 724
Federal Agents Vs. Underworld, Inc. (1/29) 966
Daughter of the Jungle (2/8) 164
The Last Bandit (2/25) 422
Wake of the Red Witch (3/1) 898
Hideout (3/8) 338
Duke of Chicago (3/15) 201
Jerky Journeys — Beyond Civilization to Texas (3/15) 1014
Ghost of Zorro (3/24) 970
The Red Pony (3/28) 628
Death Valley Gunfighter (3/29) 170
Prince of the Plains (4/8) 608

Streets of San Francisco (4/15) 789
Jerky Journeys — The 3 Minnies: Sota, Tonka, & Ha Ha! (4/15) 1017
Susanna Pass (4/29) 801
Frontier Investigator (5/2) 255
Law of the Golden West (5/9) 430
Jerky Journeys — Bungle in the Jungle (5/15) 1015
Outcasts of the Trail (6/8) 563
King of the Rocket Men (6/8) 984
Jerky Journeys — Romantic Rumbolia (6/15) 1016
Hellfire (6/26) 326
The Wyoming Bandit (7/15) 929
South of Rio (7/27) 759
Flaming Fury (7/28) 239
The Red Menace (8/1) 627
Brimstone (8/15) 80
Bandit King of Texas (8/29) 37
The James Brothers of Missouri (8/31) 977
Post Office Investigator (9/1) 599
The Kid from Cleveland (9/5) 407
Down Dakota Way (9/9) 192
Flame of Youth (9/22) 238
San Antone Ambush (10/1) 686
The Fighting Kentuckian (10/5) 230
Alias the Champ (10/15) 10
Navajo Trail Raiders (10/15) 519
Ranger of Cherokee Strip (11/4) 626
The Golden Stallion (11/15) 292
Radar Patrol Vs. Spy King (11/23) 999
Pioneer Marshal (11/24) 589
Powder River Rustlers (11/25) 600
Land of Opportunity — The Sponge Diver (??) 1025
Land of Opportunity — The American Rodeo (??) 1023

## 1950

Bells of Coronado (1/8) 49
The Blonde Bandit (1/11) 65
Land of Opportunity — Tillers of the Soil (1/19) 1026
Unmasked (1/30) 881
Gunmen of Abilene (2/6) 305

Land of Opportunity — The Mardi Gras (2/24) 1024
Singing Guns (2/28) 736
Tarnished (2/28) 807
Belle of Old Mexico (3/1) 47
Sands of Iwo Jima (3/1) 689
Federal Agent at Large (3/12) 224
Twilight in the Sierras (3/22) 865
Code of the Silver Sage (3/25) 125
House by the River (3/25) 359
Harbor of Missing Men (3/26) 312
The Vanishing Westerner (3/31) 889
The Arizona Cowboy (4/1) 22
Salt Lake Raiders (5/1) 684
Women from Headquarters (5/1) 925
The Invisible Monster (5/10) 976
Rock Island Trail (5/18) 659
The Savage Horde (5/22) 697
Destination Big House (6/1) 181
Hills of Oklahoma (6/1) 340
The Avengers (6/26) 33
Covered Wagon Raid (6/30) 143
Trigger, Jr. (6/30) 854
The Battle for Korea (7/1) 1018
Trial Without Jury (7/8) 853
Jungle Stampede (7/29) 403
The Old Frontier (7/29) 544
Desperadoes of the West (8/2) 959
Vigilante Hideout (8/6) 890
The Showdown (8/15) 727
Lonely Heart Bandits (8/29) 447
Surrender (9/15) 800
Prisoners in Petticoats (9/18) 610
Redwood Forest Trail (9/18) 635
Sunset in the West (9/25) 796
Frisco Tornado (10/1) 253
Hit Parade of 1951 (10/15) 345
Rustlers on Horseback (10/23) 676
Flying Disc Man from Mars (10/25) 969
North of the Great Divide (11/15) 533
Rio Grande (11/15) 651
Under Mexicali Stars (11/20) 875
The Missourians (11/25) 499
California Passage (12/15) 90
Trail of Robin Hood (12/15) 846
This World of Ours — Denmark (??) 1041
This World of Ours — France (??) 1045
This World of Ours — Glacier National Park (??) 1047
This World of Ours — Holland (??) 1050
This World of Ours — Norway (??) 1058
This World of Ours — Sweden (??) 1063

## 1951

Pride of Maryland (1/20) 605
Belle LeGrand (1/27) 46
Rough Riders of Durango (1/30) 671
Spoilers of the Plains (2/2) 768
Missing Women (2/23) 496
Night Riders of Montana (2/28) 527
Silver City Bonanza (3/1) 730
Oh! Susanna (3/3) 538
Cuban Fireball (3/5) 153
Insurance Investigator (3/23) 382
Heart of the Rockies (3/30) 320
Thunder in God's Country (4/8) 826
Don Daredevil Rides Again (4/11) 964
Buckaroo Sheriff of Texas (5/1) 81
Bullfighter and the Lady (5/15) 84
In Old Amarillo (5/15) 371
Wells Fargo Gunmaster (5/15) 903
Million Dollar Pursuit (5/30) 495
Fighting Coast Guard (6/1) 228
Fights — Robinson Vs. Turpin (6/20) 1021
Secrets of Monte Carlo (6/20) 708
The Dakota Kid (7/1) 157
Government Agents Vs. Phantom Legion (7/4) 973
Fugitive Lady (7/15) 259
Rodeo King and the Senorita (7/15) 661
Lost Planet Airmen (7/25) 449
This is Korea! (8/10) 817
Fort Dodge Stampede (8/24) 249
Arizona Manhunt (9/15) 25
Havana Rose (9/15) 314
Adventures of Captain Fabian (10/6) 3
South of Caliente (10/15) 758
Utah Wagon Train (10/15) 884

Honeychile (10/20) 356
The Sea Hornet (11/6) 703
Pals of the Golden West (11/15) 572
Street Bandits (11/15) 786
Desert of Lost Men (11/19) 176
The Wild Blue Yonder (12/5) 912
Stormbound (12/15) 780
This World of Ours — Belgium (??) 1036
This World of Ours — Egypt (??) 1042
This World of Ours — England (??) 1043
This World of Ours — Greece (??) 1048
This World of Ours — Hawaii (??) 1049
This World of Ours — Italy (??) 1055
This World of Ours — London (??) 1057
This World of Ours — Portugal (??) 1059
This World of Ours — Spain (??) 1062
This World of Ours — Switzerland (??) 1064

## 1952

Radar Men from the Moon (1/9) 998
Captive of Billy the Kid (1/22) 102
A Lady Possessed (1/26) 417
Colorado Sundown (2/8) 129
The Last Musketeer (3/1) 426
Leadville Gunslinger (3/22) 437
Oklahoma Annie (3/24) 539
The Fabulous Senorita (4/1) 215
Border Saddlemates (4/15) 73
Hoodlum Empire (4/15) 357
Wild Horse Ambush (4/15) 914
Gobs and Gals (5/1) 290
Black Hills Ambush (5/20) 61
Bal Tabarin (6/1) 36
I Dream of Jeanie (6/15) 363
Thundering Caravans (6/20) 831
Zombies of the Stratosphere (7/16) 1009
Old Oklahoma Plains (7/25) 547
Woman of the North Country (9/5) 921

The Quiet Man (9/14) 616
Tropical Heat Wave (10/1) 857
Desperadoes' Outpost (10/8) 179
Toughest Man in Arizona (10/10) 840
The Wac from Walla Walla (10/10) 894
South Pacific Trail (10/20) 762
Woman in the Dark (11/15) 920
Thunderbirds (11/27) 830
The Flying Squadron (??) 242
This World of Ours — Chile (??) 1039
This World of Ours — India (??) 1052
This World of Ours — Israel (??) 1054
This World of Ours — Puerto Rico (??) 1060
This World of Ours — The Philippines (??) 1066

## 1953

Ride the Man Down (1/1) 644
Jungle Drums of Africa (1/21) 979
Marshal of Cedar Rock (2/1) 480
San Antone (2/15) 685
Commando Cody, Sky Marshal of the Universe (2/17) 1019
Old Overland Trail (2/25) 548
Woman They Almost Lynched (3/20) 922
The Lady Wants Mink (3/30) 418
A Perilous Journey (4/5) 581
Fair Wind to Java (4/28) 219
The Sun Shines Bright (5/2) 791
Iron Mountain Trail (5/8) 387
Savage Frontier (5/15) 696
City That Never Sleeps (6/12) 121
Canadian Mounties Vs. Atomic Invaders (7/8) 951
Sweethearts on Parade (7/15) 802
Down Laredo Way (8/5) 194
Bandits of the West (8/8) 40
Champ for a Day (8/15) 111
El Paso Stampede (9/8) 208
Trent's Last Case (9/22) 851
Shadows of Tombstone (9/28) 711
Fights — Marciano Vs. LaStarza (9/28) 1020
Red River Shore (12/15) 631

This World of Ours — Ceylon (??) 1038
This World of Ours — City of Destiny (??) 1040
This World of Ours — Germany (??) 1046
This World of Ours — Japan (??) 1056
This World of Ours — Singapore (??) 1061

## 1954

Trader Tom of the China Seas (1/11) 1006
Sea of Lost Ships (2/1) 704
The Phantom Stallion (2/10) 587
Crazylegs (2/15) 147
Flight Nurse (3/1) 241
Geraldine (4/1) 273
Untamed Heiress (4/12) 882
Jubilee Trail (5/15) 402
Hell's Half Acre (6/1) 328
Laughing Anne (7/1) 428
Man with the Steel Whip (7/19) 989
Make Haste to Live (8/1) 458
The Outcast (8/15) 561
Johnny Guitar (8/23) 399
Roogie's Bump (8/25) 665
The Shanghai Story (9/1) 713
Tobor the Great (9/1) 838
The She Wolf (11/15) 716
Trouble in the Glen (12/1) 859
The Atomic Kid (12/8) 32
Hell's Outpost (12/15) 329
This World of Ours — Bali (??) 1035
This World of Ours — Formosa (??) 1044
This World of Ours — Hong Kong (??) 1051
This World of Ours — Ireland (??) 1053
This World of Ours — Thailand (??) 1065

## 1955

Panther Girl of the Kongo (1/3) 994
African Manhunt (1/5) 8
Trouble in Store (1/12) 858
Carolina Cannonball (1/28) 103
The Square Ring (1/28) 772
Doctor in the House (2/2) 186
Timberjack (2/18) 836
Yellowneck (3/22) 935
A Day to Remember (3/29) 165
The Eternal Sea (5/5) 211
Santa Fe Passage (5/12) 690
I Cover the Underworld (5/19) 362
Don Juan's Night of Love (5/26) 188
City of Shadows (6/2) 120
The Road to Denver (6/15) 654
Double Jeopardy (6/23) 191
King of the Carnival (6/27) 981
Lay That Rifle Down (7/7) 436
The Green Buddha (7/9) 300
The Last Command (8/3) 423
The Divided Heart (8/11) 184
Headline Hunters (9/15) 316
Cross Channel (9/29) 152
The Twinkle in God's Eye (10/13) 867
A Man Alone (10/17) 460
Mystery of the Black Jungle (10/20) 518
No Man's Woman (10/27) 530
Secret Venture (11/10) 707
The Vanishing American (11/17) 888
The Fighting Chance (12/15) 227
In Old Vienna (??) 379
This World of Ours — Caribbean Sky Cruise (??) 1037
This World of Ours — Turkey (??) 1067
This World of Ours — Venezuela (??) 1068

## 1956

Flame of the Islands (1/6) 237
Jaguar (1/20) 390
Track the Man Down (1/27) 841
Hidden Guns (1/30) 335
Doctor at Sea (2/23) 185
Come Next Spring (3/9) 131
When Gangland Strikes (3/15) 909
Magic Fire (3/29) 454

Stranger at My Door (4/6) 784
Zanzabuka (4/13) 944
Circus Girl (4/20) 118
Terror at Midnight (4/27) 811
The Maverick Queen (5/3) 484
Dakota Incident (7/23) 156
Thunder Over Arizona (8/4) 828
Lisbon (8/17) 443
A Strange Adventure (8/24) 781
Daniel Boone, Trail Blazer (10/5) 160
Scandal Incorporated (10/12) 698
The Man is Armed (10/19) 472
Above Us the Waves (10/26) 1
A Woman's Devotion (11/16) 924
Accused of Murder (12/21) 2

## 1957

Tears for Simon (1/4) 808
The Congress Dances (1/11) 136
Duel at Apache Wells (1/25) 199
Affair in Reno (2/15) 4
Hell's Crossroads (3/8) 327
Spoilers of the Forest (4/5) 766
The Man in the Road (4/12) 471
The Weapon (5/17) 901
Time Is My Enemy (5/24) 837
The Lawless Eighties (5/31) 431
Journey to Freedom (6/21) 401
Beginning of the End (6/28) 43
The Unearthly (6/28) 880
Last Stagecoach West (7/15) 427
Pawnee (9/7) 580
Taming Sutton's Gal (9/15) 806
The Wayward Girl (9/22) 900
Operation Conspiracy (9/27) 553

Hell Canyon Outlaws (10/6) 324
Panama Sal (10/18) 575
Raiders of Old California (11/1) 619
The Crooked Circle (11/11) 150
Eighteen and Anxious (11/15) 206
Thunder Over Tangier (11/25) 829
Hell Ship Mutiny (12/6) 325
Gunfire at Indian Gap (12/13) 304
The Fighting Wildcats (12/27) 233

## 1958

Outcasts of the City (1/10) 562
Scotland Yard Dragnet (2/7) 700
International Counterfeiters (2/14) 383
The Notorious Mr. Monks (2/28) 535
Strange Case of Dr. Manning (3/21) 782
Missile Monsters (3/28) 497
Satan's Satellites (3/28) 695
Young and Wild (4/24) 938
Juvenile Jungle (4/24) 404
Man or Gun (5/30) 474
Girl in the Woods (6/1) 283
The Man Who Died Twice (6/6) 475
Street of Darkness (6/11) 787
No Place to Land (10/3) 531
Invisible Avenger (12/2) 384

## 1959

Zorro Rides Again (1/16) 946
Plunderers of Painted Flats (1/23) 595
O. S. S. 117 Is Not Dead (2/13) 558
Hidden Homicide (2/25) 336
Ghost of Zorro (6/30) 275

# Appendix B: Academy Award Nominations and Winners

*An asterisk (\*) indicates a winner.*

### Best Picture
1952 The Quiet Man

### Best Actor
1949 John Wayne — Sands of Iwo Jima

### Best Supporting Actor
1952 Victor McLaglen — The Quiet Man

### Best Director
*1952 John Ford — The Quiet Man

### Writing — Motion Picture Story
1949 Harry Brown — Sands of Iwo Jima

1951 Budd Boetticher, Ray Nazarro — The Bullfighter and the Lady

### Writing — Screenplay
1952 Frank S. Nugent — The Quiet Man

### Cinematography — B&W
1938 Ernest Miller, Harry Wild — Army Girl

### Cinematography — Color
*1952 Winton C. Hoch, Archie Stout — The Quiet Man

## Art Decoration/ Set Decoration — B&W

1937 John Victor Mackay — Manhattan Merry-Go-Round
1939 John Victor Mackay — Man of Conquest
1940 John Victor Mackay — Dark Command

## Art Decoration/ Set Decoration — Color

1952 Frank Hotaling, John McCarthy, Jr., Charles Thompson — The Quiet Man

## Sound

1935 Republic Sound Department — $1,000 Dollars a Minute
1938 Charles Lootens — Army Girl
1939 Charles Lootens — Man of Conquest
1940 Charles Lootens — Behind the News
1941 Charles Lootens — The Devil Pays Off
1942 Daniel J. Bloomberg — Flying Tigers
1943 Daniel J. Bloomberg — In Old Oklahoma
1944 Daniel J. Bloomberg — Brazil
1945 Daniel J. Bloomberg — Flame of Barbary Coast
1948 Republic Sound Department — Moonrise
1949 Republic Sound Department — Sands of Iwo Jima
1952 Republic Sound Department: Daniel J. Bloomberg, Director — The Quiet Man

## Film Editing

1949 Richard L. Van Enger — Sands of Iwo Jima
1953 Irvine "Cotton" Warburton — Crazylegs

## Music — Best Score

1937 Alberto Colombo — Portia On Trial
1938 Cy Feur — Storm Over Bengal
1939 Cy Feur — She Married a Cop
1940 Cy Feur — Hit Parade of 1941

## Music — Original Score

1938 Victor Young — Army Girl
1939 Victor Young — Man of Conquest
1940 Victor Young — Dark Command

## Music — Scoring — Drama or Comedy

1941 Cy Feur, Walter Scharf — Mercy Island
1942 Victor Young — Flying Tigers
1943 Walter Scharf — In Old Oklahoma
1944 Walter Scharf, Roy Webb — The Fighting Seabees
1945 Dale Butts, Morton Scott — Flame of Barbary Coast

## Music — Scoring — Musical

1941 Cy Feur — Ice-Capades
1942 Walter Scharf — Johnny Doughboy
1943 Walter Scharf — Hit Parade of 1943
1944 Walter Scharf — Brazil
1945 Morton Scott — Hitchhike to Happiness

## Best Song

1938 "Dust" from *Under Western Stars*. Music and lyrics by Johnny Marvin.

1940 "Who Am I?" from *Hit Parade of 1941*. Music by Jule Styne, lyrics by Walter Bullock.
1941 "Be Honest With Me" from *Ridin' on a Rainbow*. Music and lyrics by Gene Autry and Fred Rose.
1942 "It Seems I Heard That Song Before" from *Youth on Parade*. Music by Jule Styne, lyrics by Sammy Cahn.
1943 "Change of Heart" from *Hit Parade of 1943*. Music by Jule Styne, lyrics by Harold Adamson.
1944 "Rio De Janeiro" from *Brazil*. Music by Ary Barroso, lyrics by Ned Washington.
1945 "Endlessly" from *Earl Carroll Vanities*. Music by Walter Kent, lyrics by Kim Gannon.
1950 "Mule Train" from *Singing Guns*. Music and lyrics by Fred Glickman, Hy Heath, and Johnny Lange.

## Documentary

1942 U.S. Dept. of Agriculture—Henry Browne, Farmer
*1942 Artinko Pictures—Moscow Strikes Back (*see Note*)

## Special Effects

1940 Photography: Howard J. Lydecker, William Bradford, Ellis J. Thackery; Sound: Herbert Norsch—Women in War
1942 Photography: Howard J. Lydecker; Sound: Daniel J. Bloomberg—Flying Tigers

## Honorary Award (Certificate)

*1945 Daniel J. Bloomberg, Republic Studio, and the Republic Sound Department for the building of an outstanding musical scoring auditorium which provides optimum recording conditions and combines all elements of acoustic and engineering design.

## Special Award (Plaque)

*1947 *Bill and Coo*, in which artistry and patience blended in a novel and entertaining use of the medium of motion pictures (*see Note*)

## Scientific or Technical, Class III

*1941 Charles Lootens and the Republic Studio Sound Department for pioneering the use of and for the first practical application to motion picture production of Class B push-pull variable area recording.
*1942 Daniel J. Bloomberg and the Republic Studio Sound Department for the design and application to motion picture production of a device for marking action negative for pre-selection purposes.
*1943 Daniel J. Bloomberg and the Republic Studio Sound Department for the design and development of an inexpensive method of converting Moviolas to Class B push-pull reproduction.
*1944 Daniel J. Bloomberg and the Republic Studio Sound Department for the design and development of a multi-interlock selector switch.
*1956 Daniel J. Bloomberg, John Pond, William Wade and the Engineering and Camera Departments of Republic Studio for the Naturama adaptation to the Mitchell Camera.

*Note: Although not produced by Republic Pictures, these two entries were released by Republic Pictures and are included for the sake of completeness.*

# Appendix C: Movie Series

Following is a complete listing of Republic's film series, produced using either a title only (e.g., Hit Parade), which did not have a continuing character, or using the same character (e.g., Cappy Ricks, Dick Tracy), played by different actors or the same actor, in a group of films.

**Cappy Ricks — (F)**
(Robert McWade)

Cappy Ricks Returns (1935)

**Cappy Ricks — (F)**
(Walter Brennan)

Affairs of Cappy Ricks (1937)

**Commando Cody — (S)**
(George Wallace)

Radar Men from the Moon (1952)

**Commando Cody — (SS)**
(Judd Holdren)

Commando Cody — Sky Marshal of the Universe (1953)

**Dick Tracy — (S)**
(Ralph Byrd)

Dick Tracy (1937)
Dick Tracy Returns (1938)
Dick Tracy's G-Men (1939)
Dick Tracy Vs. Crime, Inc. (1941)

**Earl Carroll — (F)**

Earl Carroll Vanities (1945)
Earl Carroll Sketchbook (1946)

**Ellery Queen — (F)**
(Donald Cook)

The Spanish Cape Mystery (1935)

**Ellery Queen — (F)**
(Eddie Quillan)

The Mandarin Mystery (1936)

## The Higgins Family — (F)
(James Gleason, Lucille Gleason, Russell Gleason, Harry Davenport)

The Higgins Family (1938)
My Wife's Relatives (1939)
Should Husbands Work? (1939)
The Covered Trailer (1939)
Money to Burn (1939)
Grandpa Goes to Town (1940)
Earl of Puddlestone (1940)

## The Higgins Family — (F)
(Roscoe Karns, Ruth Donnelly, George Ernest, Spencer Charters)

Meet the Missus (1940)
Petticoat Politics (1941)

## The Hit Parade — (F)

The Hit Parade (1937)
Hit Parade of 1941 (1940)
Hit Parade of 1943 (1943)
Hit Parade of 1947 (1947)
Hit Parade of 1950 (1951)

## Ice-Capades — (F)

Ice-Capades (1941)
Ice-Capades Revue (1942)

## Jerky Journeys — (A)

Beyond Civilization to Texas (1949)
The 3 Minnies: Sota, Tonka & Ha Ha! (1949)
Romantic Rumbolia (1949)
Bungle in the Jungle (1949)

## King of the Royal Mounted — (S)
(Allan "Rocky" Lane)

King of the Royal Mounted (1940)
King of the Mounties (1942)

## Land of Opportunity — (SS)

The American Rodeo (1949)
The Sponge Diver (1949)
Tillers of the Soil (1950)
The Mardi Gras (1950)

## Meet the Stars — (SS)

Chinese Garden Festival (1940)
Wampas Baby Stars (1941)
Variety Reel (1941)
Los Angeles Examiner Benefit (1941)
Hollywood Visits the Navy (1941)
Stars at Play (1941)
Meet Roy Rogers (1941)
Stars Past and Present (1941)

## Mr. District Attorney — (F)
(Dennis O'Keefe)

Mr. District Attorney (1941)

## Mr. District Attorney — (F)
(James Ellison)

Mr. District Attorney in the Carter Case (1941)

## Mr. District Attorney — (F)
(John Hubbard)

Secrets of the Underground (1942)

## Nyoka — (S)
(Francis Gifford)

Jungle Girl (1941)

## Nyoka — (S)
(Kay Aldridge)

Perils of Nyoka (1942)

## Olsen & Johnson — (F)

Country Gentlemen (1936)
All Over Town (1937)

## Rex Bennett — (S)
(Rod Cameron)

G-Men Vs. the Black Dragon (1943)
Secret Service in Darkest Africa (1943)

## This World of Ours — (SS)
Norway (1950)
Denmark (1950)
Glacier National Park (1950)
Sweden (1950)
France (1950)
Holland (1950)
London (1951)
Portugal (1951)
Spain (1951)
England (1951)
Hawaii (1951)
Greece (1951)
Belgium (1951)
Switzerland (1951)
Italy (1951)
Egypt (1951)
Puerto Rico (1952)
Chile (1952)
Israel (1952)
India (1952)
The Philippines (1952)
Ceylon (1953)
City of Destiny (1953)
Singapore (1953)
Germany (1953)
Japan (1953)
Hong Kong (1954)
Formosa (1954)
Ireland (1954)
Thailand (1954)
Bali (1954)
Venezuela (1955)
Caribbean Sky Cruise (1955)
Turkey (1955)

## Weaver Brothers and Elviry — (F)
(Leon Weaver, Frank Weaver, June Weaver)

Down in "Arkansaw" (1938)
Jeepers Creepers (1939)
In Old Missouri (1940)
Grand Ole Opry (1940)
Friendly Neighbors (1940)
Arkansas Judge (1941)
Mountain Moonlight (1941)
Tuxedo Junction (1941)
Shepherd of the Ozarks (1942)
The Old Homestead (1942)
Mountain Rhythm (1943)

# Appendix D: Western Stars and Western Series

Following is a complete listing of Republic's western stars and their films (excluding their series films, which, if any, are listed separately), followed by the western film series, beginning with the character Jesse James *and continuing through* Zorro. *The western film series consisted of using the same character (e.g., Jesse James, Red Ryder), played by different actors or the same actor, in a group of films.*
\* = Serial     \*\* = Short Subject

## Rex Allen

The Arizona Cowboy (1950)
Hills of Oklahoma (1950)
Redwood Forest Trail (1950)
Under Mexicali Stars (1950)
Silver City Bonanza (1951)
Thunder in God's Country (1951)
Rodeo King and the Senorita (1951)
Utah Wagon Train (1951)
Colorado Sundown (1952)
The Last Musketeer (1952)
Border Saddlemates (1952)
Old Oklahoma Plains (1952)
South Pacific Trail (1952)
Old Overland Trail (1953)
Iron Mountain Trail (1953)
Down Laredo Way (1953)
Shadows of Tombstone (1953)
Red River Shore (1953)
Phantom Stallion (1954)

## Rex Allen
(as guest star)

Trail of Robin Hood (1950)

## Gene Autry

Tumbling Tumbleweeds (1935)
Melody Trail (1935)

## Appendix D

Sagebrush Troubadour (1935)
The Singing Vagabond (1936)
Red River Valley (1936)
Comin' Round the Mountain (1936)
The Singing Cowboy (1936)
Guns and Guitars (1936)
Oh, Susanna! (1936)
Ride, Ranger, Ride (1936)
The Big Show (1936)
The Old Corral (1936)
Round-Up Time in Texas (1937)
Git Along Little Dogies (1937)
Rootin' Tootin' Rhythm (1937)
Yodelin' Kid from Pine Ridge (1937)
Public Cowboy No. 1 (1937)
Boots and Saddles (1937)
Springtime in the Rockies (1937)
The Old Barn Dance (1938)
Gold Mine in the Sky (1938)
Man from Music Mountain (1938)
Prairie Moon (1938)
Rhythm of the Saddle (1938)
Western Jamboree (1938)
Home on the Prairie (1939)
Mexicali Rose (1939)
Blue Montana Skies (1939)
Mountain Rhythm (1939)
Colorado Sunset (1939)
In Old Monterey (1939)
Rovin' Tumbleweeds (1939)
South of the Border (1939)
Rancho Grande (1940)
Gaucho Serenade (1940)
Carolina Moon (1940)
Ride, Tenderfoot, Ride (1940)
Melody Ranch (1940)
Ridin' on a Rainbow (1941)
Back in the Saddle (1941)
The Singing Hill (1941)
Sunset in Wyoming (1941)
Under Fiesta Stars (1941)
Down Mexico Way (1941)
Sierra Sue (1941)
Cowboy Serenade (1942)
Heart of the Rio Grande (1942)
Home in Wyomin' (1942)

Stardust on the Sage (1942)
Call of the Canyon (1942)
Bells of Capistrano (1942)
Sioux City Sue (1946)
Trail to San Antone (1947)
Twilight on the Rio Grande (1947)
Saddle Pals (1947)
Robin Hood of Texas (1947)

### Gene Autry
(as guest star)

Manhattan Merry-Go-Round (1937)
**Variety Reel (1941)
**Stars at Play (1941)
**Meet Roy Rogers (1941)
**Stars Past and Present (1941)

### Don "Red" Barry

Ghost Valley Raiders (1940)
*Adventures of Red Ryder (1940)
One Man's Law (1940)
The Tulsa Kid (1940)
Frontier Vengeance (1940)
Texas Terrors (1940)
Wyoming Wildcat (1941)
The Phantom Cowboy (1941)
Two Gun Sheriff (1941)
Desert Bandit (1941)
Kansas Cyclone (1941)
The Apache Kid (1941)
Death Valley Outlaws (1941)
A Missouri Outlaw (1941)
Arizona Terrors (1942)
Stagecoach Express (1942)
Jesse James, Jr. (1942)
The Cyclone Kid (1942)
The Sombrero Kid (1942)
Outlaws of Pine Ridge (1942)
The Sundown Kid (1942)
Dead Man's Gulch (1943)
Carson City Cyclone (1943)
Days of Old Cheyenne (1943)
Fugitive from Sonora (1943)
The Black Hills Express (1943)
The Man from the Rio Grande (1943)
Canyon City (1943)

California Joe (1943)
Outlaws of Santa Fe (1944)

## Don "Red" Barry
(as co-star)

Wyoming Outlaw (1939)
Saga of Death Valley (1939)
Days of Jesse James (1939)
Plainsman and the Lady (1946)
The Twinkle in God's Eye (1955)

## Don "Red" Barry
(as guest star)

Bells of Rosarita (1945)
Out California Way (1946)

## Johnny Mack Brown

Under Cover Man (1936)
Lawless Land (1936)
Bar-Z Bad Men (1937)
The Gambling Terror (1937)
Trail of Vengeance (1937)
Guns in the Dark (1937)
A Lawman is Born (1937)
Boothill Brigade (1937)

## Rod Cameron

The Plunderers (1948)
Brimstone (1949)
Oh! Susanna (1951)
Woman of the North Country (1952)
Ride the Man Down (1953)
San Antone (1953)
Hell's Outpost (1954)
Santa Fe Passage (1955)

## Sunset Carson

Call of the Rockies (1944)
Bordertown Trail (1944)
Code of the Prairie (1944)
Firebrands of Arizona (1944)
Sheriff of Cimarron (1945)
Santa Fe Saddlemates (1945)
Oregon Trail (1945)
Bandits of the Badlands (1945)
Rough Riders of Cheyenne (1945)
The Cherokee Flash (1945)
Days of Buffalo Bill (1946)
Alias Billy the Kid (1946)
The El Paso Kid (1946)
Red River Renegades (1946)
Rio Grande Raiders (1946)

## Sunset Carson
(as guest star)

Bells of Rosarita (1945)

## Bill Elliott

Calling Wild Bill Elliott (1943)
The Man from Thunder River (1943)
Bordertown Gunfighters (1943)
Wagon Tracks West (1943)
Overland Mail Robbery (1943)
Death Valley Manhunt (1943)
Mojave Firebrand (1944)
Hidden Valley Outlaws (1944)
In Old Sacramento (1946)
Plainsman and the Lady (1946)
Wyoming (1947)
The Fabulous Texan (1947)
Old Los Angeles (1948)
The Gallant Legion (1948)
The Last Bandit (1949)
Hellfire (1949)
The Savage Horde (1950)
The Showdown (1950)

## Bill Elliott
(as co-star)

Boots and Saddles (1937)

## Bill Elliott
(as guest star)

**Meet Roy Rogers (1941)
Bells of Rosarita (1945)

## Monte Hale

Home on the Range (1946)
Sun Valley Cyclone (1946)

Man from Rainbow Valley (1946)
Out California Way (1946)
Last Frontier Uprising (1947)
Along the Oregon Trail (1947)
Under Colorado Skies (1947)
California Firebrand (1948)
The Timber Trail (1948)
Son of God's Country (1948)
Prince of the Plains (1949)
Law of the Golden West (1949)
Outcasts of the Trail (1949)
South of Rio (1949)
San Antone Ambush (1949)
Ranger of Cherokee Strip (1949)
Pioneer Marshal (1949)
The Vanishing Westerner (1950)
The Old Frontier (1950)
The Missourians (1950)

## Monte Hale
(as co-star)

The Topeka Terror (1945)
Oregon Trail (1945)
Bandits of the Badlands (1945)
Rough Riders of Cheyenne (1945)
Colorado Pioneers (1945)
The Phantom Rider (1946)
California Gold Rush (1946)
Sun Valley Cyclone (1946)

## Monte Hale
(as guest star)

Trail of Robin Hood (1950)

## Allan "Rocky" Lane

*Daredevils of the West (1943)
Silver City Kid (1944)
Stagecoach to Monterey (1944)
Sheriff of Sundown (1944)
The Topeka Terror (1945)
Corpus Christi Bandits (1945)
Trail of Kit Carson (1945)
The Wild Frontier (1947)
Bandits of Dark Canyon (1947)
Oklahoma Badlands (1948)

The Bold Frontiersman (1948)
Carson City Raiders (1948)
Marshal of Amarillo (1948)
Desperadoes of Dodge City (1948)
The Denver Kid (1948)
Sundown in Santa Fe (1948)
Renegades of Sonora (1948)
Sheriff of Wichita (1949)
Death Valley Gunfighter (1949)
Frontier Investigator (1949)
The Wyoming Bandit (1949)
Bandit King of Texas (1949)
Navajo Trail Raiders (1949)
Powder River Rustlers (1949)
Gunmen of Abilene (1950)
Code of the Silver Sage (1950)
Salt Lake Raiders (1950)
Covered Wagon Raid (1950)
Vigilante Hideout (1950)
Frisco Tornado (1950)
Rustlers on Horseback (1950)
Rough Riders of Durango (1951)
Night Riders of Montana (1951)
Wells Fargo Gunmaster (1951)
Fort Dodge Stampede (1951)
Desert of Lost Men (1951)
Captive of Billy the Kid (1952)
Leadville Gunslinger (1952)
Black Hills Ambush (1952)
Thundering Caravans (1952)
Desperadoes' Outpost (1952)
Marshal of Cripple Creek (1953)
Savage Frontier (1953)
Bandits of the West (1953)
El Paso Stampede (1953)

## Allan "Rocky" Lane
(as guest star)

Bells of Rosarita (1945)
Out California Way (1946)
**Land of Opportunity (1949)
Trail of Robin Hood (1950)

## Roy Rogers

Under Western Stars (1938)
Billy the Kid Returns (1938)

Come On, Rangers (1938)
Shine on Harvest Moon (1938)
Rough Riders' Round-Up (1939)
Frontier Pony Express (1939)
Southward, Ho! (1939)
In Old Caliente (1939)
Wall Street Cowboy (1939)
The Arizona Kid (1939)
Saga of Death Valley (1939)
Days of Jesse James (1939)
Young Buffalo Bill (1940)
The Carson City Kid (1940)
The Ranger and the Lady (1940)
Colorado (1940)
Young Bill Hickok (1940)
The Border Legion (1940)
Robin Hood of the Pecos (1941)
In Old Cheyenne (1941)
Sheriff of Tombstone (1941)
Nevada City (1941)
Bad Man of Deadwood (1941)
Jesse James at Bay (1941)
Red River Valley (1941)
Man from Cheyenne (1942)
South of Santa Fe (1942)
Sunset on the Desert (1942)
Romance on the Range (1942)
Sons of the Pioneers (1942)
Sunset Serenade (1942)
Heart of the Golden West (1942)
Ridin' Down the Canyon (1942)
Idaho (1943)
King of the Cowboys (1943)
Song of Texas (1943)
Silver Spurs (1943)
Man from Music Mountain (1943)
Hands Across the Border (1943)
Cowboy and the Senorita (1944)
The Yellow Rose of Texas (1944)
Song of Nevada (1944)
San Fernando Valley (1944)
Lights of Old Santa Fe (1944)
Utah (1945)
Bells of Rosarita (1945)
Man from Oklahoma (1945)
Sunset in El Dorado (1945)

Don't Fence Me In (1945)
Along the Navajo Trail (1945)
Song of Arizona (1946)
Rainbow Over Texas (1946)
My Pal Trigger (1946)
Under Nevada Skies (1946)
Roll on Texas Moon (1946)
Home in Oklahoma (1946)
Heldorado (1946)
Apache Rose (1947)
Bells of San Angelo (1947)
Springtime in the Sierras (1947)
On the Old Spanish Trail (1947)
The Gay Ranchero (1948)
Under California Stars (1948)
Eyes of Texas (1948)
Night Time in Nevada (1948)
Grand Canyon Trail (1948)
The Far Frontier (1948)
Susanna Pass (1949)
Down Dakota Way (1949)
The Golden Stallion (1949)
Bells of Coronado (1950)
Twilight in the Sierras (1950)
Trigger, Jr. (1950)
Sunset in the West (1950)
North of the Great Divide (1950)
Trail of Robin Hood (1950)
Spoilers of the Plains (1951)
Heart of the Rockies (1951)
In Old Amarillo (1951)
South of Caliente (1951)
Pals of the Golden West (1951)

## Roy Rogers (Leonard Slye)
(as co-star)

The Big Show (1936)
The Old Corral (1936)

## Roy Rogers (Dick Weston)
(as co-star)

Wild Horse Rodeo (1937)
The Old Barn Dance (1938)

## Roy Rogers
(as co-star)

Jeepers Creepers (1939)
Dark Command (1940)
Arkansas Judge (1941)

## Roy Rogers
(as guest star)

**Meet Roy Rogers (1941)
Brazil (1944)
Lake Placid Serenade (1944)
Out California Way (1946)
Hit Parade of 1947 (1947)

## Bob Steele

Cavalry (1936)
The Gun Ranger (1936)
Border Phantom (1936)
The Trusted Outlaw (1937)
"Lightnin'" Crandall (1937)
Gun Lords of Stirrup Basin (1937)
Doomed at Sundown (1937)
The Red Rope (1937)
The Arizona Gunfighter (1937)
Ridin' the Lone Trail (1937)
The Colorado Kid (1937)
Paroled — to Die (1938)
Thunder in the Desert (1938)
The Feud Maker (1938)
Desert Patrol (1938)
Durango Valley Raiders (1938)

## Bob Steele
(as co-star)

The Carson City Kid (1940)
Sheriff of Redwood Valley (1946)
Rio Grande Raiders (1946)
Twilight on the Rio Grande (1947)
Bandits of Dark Canyon (1947)
The Savage Horde (1950)
San Antone (1953)
Savage Frontier (1953)
The Outcast (1954)
Duel at Apache Wells (1957)

## John Wayne

Westward Ho! (1935)
The New Frontier (1935)
Lawless Range (1935)
The Oregon Trail (1936)
The Lawless Nineties (1936)
King of the Pecos (1936)
The Lonely Trail (1936)
Winds of the Wasteland (1936)
Dark Command (1940)
In Old California (1942)
In Old Oklahoma (1943)
Flame of Barbary Coast (1945)
Dakota (1945)
Angel and the Badman (1947)
The Fighting Kentuckian (1949)
Rio Grande (1950)

## Jesse James
(Don "Red" Barry)

Days of Jesse James (1939)

## Jesse James
(Roy Rogers)

Jesse James at Bay (1941)

## Jesse James
(Clayton Moore)

*Jesse James Rides Again (1947)
*Adventures of Frank and Jesse James (1948)

## Jesse James
(Keith Richards)

*The James Brothers of Missouri (1949)

## Jesse James
(Henry Brandon)

Hell's Crossroads (1957)

## Johnny Rapidan
(Robert Livingston)

The Laramie Trail (1944)

## John Paul Revere
(Eddie Dew)

Beyond the Last Frontier (1943)
Raiders of Sunset Pass (1943)

## John Paul Revere
(Robert Livingston)

Pride of the Plains (1944)
Beneath Western Skies (1944)

## The Lone Ranger
(Lee Powell)

*The Lone Ranger (1938)

## The Lone Ranger
(Robert Livingston)

*The Lone Ranger Rides Again (1939)

## Red Ryder
(Don "Red" Barry)

*Adventures of Red Ryder (1940)

## Red Ryder
(Bill Elliott)

Tucson Raiders (1944)
Marshal of Reno (1944)
The San Antonio Kid (1944)
Cheyenne Wildcat (1944)
Vigilantes of Dodge City (1944)
Sheriff of Las Vegas (1944)
Great Stagecoach Robbery (1945)
Lone Texas Ranger (1945)
Phantom of the Plains (1945)
Marshal of Laredo (1945)
Colorado Pioneers (1945)
Wagon Wheels Westward (1945)
California Gold Rush (1946)
Sheriff of Redwood Valley (1946)
Sun Valley Cyclone (1946)
Conquest of Cheyenne (1946)

## Red Ryder
(Allan "Rocky" Lane)

Santa Fe Uprising (1946)
Stagecoach to Denver (1946)
Vigilantes of Boomtown (1947)
Homesteaders of Paradise Valley (1947)
Oregon Trail Scouts (1947)
Rustlers of Devil's Canyon (1947)
Marshal of Cripple Creek (1947)

## Rough-Ridin' Kids
(Michael Chapin, Eilene Janssen)

Buckaroo Sheriff of Texas (1951)
The Dakota Kid (1951)
Arizona Manhunt (1951)
Wild Horse Ambush (1952)

## The Three Mesquiteers
(Robert Livingston,
Ray Corrigan, Syd Saylor)

The Three Mesquiteers (1936)

## The Three Mesquiteers
(Robert Livingston,
Ray Corrigan, Max Terhune)

Ghost Town Gold (1936)
Roarin' Lead (1936)
The Riders of the Whistling Skull (1937)
Hit the Saddle (1937)
Gunsmoke Ranch (1937)
Come on, Cowboys! (1937)
Range Defenders (1937)
Heart of the Rockies (1937)

## The Three Mesquiteers
(Ralph Byrd, Ray Corrigan,
Max Terhune)

The Trigger Trio (1937)

## The Three Mesquiteers
(Robert Livingston,
Ray Corrigan, Max Terhune)

Wild Horse Rodeo (1937)
The Purple Vigilantes (1938)

Call the Mesquiteers (1938)
Outlaws of Sonora (1938)
Riders of the Black Hills (1938)
Heroes of the Hills (1938)

## The Three Mesquiteers
(John Wayne, Ray Corrigan, Max Terhune)

Pals of the Saddle (1938)
Overland Stage Raiders (1938)
Santa Fe Stampede (1938)
Red River Range (1938)
The Night Riders (1939)
Three Texas Steers (1939)

## The Three Mesquiteers
(John Wayne, Ray Corrigan, Raymond Hatton)

Wyoming Outlaw (1939)
New Frontier (1939)

## The Three Mesquiteers
(Robert Livingston, Duncan Renaldo, Raymond Hatton)

The Kansas Terrors (1939)
Cowboys from Texas (1939)
Heroes of the Saddle (1940)
Pioneers of the West (1940)
Covered Wagon Days (1940)
Rocky Mountain Rangers (1940)
Oklahoma Renegades (1940)

## The Three Mesquiteers
(Robert Livingston, Bob Steele, Rufe Davis)

Under Texas Skies (1940)
The Trail Blazers (1940)
Lone Star Raiders (1940)
Prairie Pioneers (1941)
Pals of the Pecos (1941)
Saddlemates (1941)
Gangs of Sonora (1941)

## The Three Mesquiteers
(Tom Tyler, Bob Steele, Rufe Davis)

Outlaws of Cherokee Trail (1941)
Gauchos of Eldorado (1941)
West of Cimarron (1941)
Code of the Outlaw (1942)
Raiders of the Range (1942)
Westward Ho (1942)
The Phantom Plainsman (1942)

## The Three Mesquiteers
(Tom Tyler, Bob Steele, Jimmie Dodd)

Shadows on the Sage (1942)
Valley of Hunted Men (1942)
Thundering Trails (1943)
The Blocked Trail (1943)
Santa Fe Scouts (1943)
Riders of the Rio Grande (1943)

## Zorro
(Robert Livingston)

The Bold Caballero (1937)

## Zorro
(John Carroll)

*Zorro Rides Again (1937)

## Zorro
(Reed Hadley)

*Zorro's Fighting Legion (1939)

## Zorro
(George Turner)

*Son of Zorro (1947)

## Zorro
(Clayton Moore)

*Ghost of Zorro (1949)

# Bibliography

Adams, Les, and Buck Rainey. *Shoot-Em-Ups*. New Rochelle, N.Y.: Arlington House, 1978.
Alicoate, Jack, ed. *Film Daily Yearbook of Motion Pictures*. New York: Film Daily, 1947–1970.
Baer, Richard D. *The Filmbuff's Checklist of Motion Pictures (1912–1979)*. Hollywood Film Archive, 1979.
Barbour, Alan G. *The Serials of Republic*. New York: Screen Facts Press, 1967.
Carr, Robert E., and Hayes, R. M. *Wide Screen Movies — A History and Filmography of Wide Gauge Filmmaking*. Jefferson, N.C.: McFarland, 1988.
Cline, William C. *In the Nick of Time*. Jefferson, N.C.: McFarland, 1984.
Cross, Robin. *2000 Movies: The 1940's*. New York: Arlington House, 1985.
\_\_\_\_\_. *2000 Movies: The 1950's*. New York: Arlington House, 1988.
Dimmitt, Richard B. *A Title Guide to the Talkies (1927–1963)*. New York: Scarecrow, 1965.
Dixon, Wheeler W. *The "B" Directors: A Biographical Directory*. Metuchen, N.J.: Scarecrow, 1985.
Eyles, Allen. *John Wayne*. New York: A.S. Barnes & Co., 1979.
Fetrow, Alan G. *Feature Films, 1940–1949: A United States Filmography*. Jefferson, N.C.: McFarland, 1994.
\_\_\_\_\_. *Sound Films, 1927–1939: A United States Filmography*. Jefferson, N.C.: McFarland, 1992.
Gifford, Denis. *The British Film Catalogue 1895–1985, A Reference Guide* New York: Facts on File, 1986.
Hayes, R. M. *The Republic Chapterplays*. Jefferson, N.C.: McFarland, 1991.
Hurst, Richard Maurice. *Republic Studios: Between Poverty Row and the Majors*. Metuchen, N.J.: Scarecrow, 1979.
Krasfur, Richard P., ed. *American Film Institute Catalog of Motion Pictures: Feature Films 1931–1940*. New York: R. Bowker, 1976.

Lenburg, Jeff. *The Encyclopedia of Animated Cartoon Series.* Westport, Connecticut: Arlington House, 1981.
Maltin, Leonard. *Selected Short Subjects.* New York: Da Capo Press, 1972.
_____. *TV Movies and Video Guide.* New American Library, 1967–1989.
Mathis, Jack. *Valley of the Cliffhangers.* Jack Mathis Advertising, 1975.
_____. *Republic Confidential: The Players, Vol. 2.* Jack Mathis Advertising, 1992.
_____. *Valley of the Cliffhangers, Supplement.* Jack Mathis Advertising, 1995.
Miller, Don. *B Movies.* New York: Ballantine, 1973.
Nash, Jay Robert, and Stanley Ralph Ross. *The Motion Picture Guide: 9 Vols.* Evanston, Ill.: Cinebooks, 1986.
*The New York Times Directory of the Film.* New York: Arno Press/Random House, 1971.
*The New York Times Film Reviews 1913–1968: 6 Vols.* New York: Arno Press/New York Times, 1971.
Parish, James Robert. *Hollywood Character Actors.* Westport, CT.: Arlington House, 1978.
Pitts, Michael R. *Western Movies: A TV and Video Guide to 4200 Genre Films.* Jefferson, N.C.: McFarland, 1986.
_____. *Poverty Row Studios, 1929–1940.* Jefferson, N.C.: McFarland, 1997.
Quigley, Martin, Jr., ed. *International Motion Picture Almanac.* New York: Quigley, 1959–1967.
Rainey, Buck. *Saddle Aces of the Cinema.* New York: A.S. Barnes & Co., 1980.
Rothel, David. *The Gene Autry Book.* Madison, N.C.: Empire Publishing, 1988.
Shale, Richard. *Academy Awards: An Unger Reference Index.* New York: Unger, 1978.
Warren, Bill. *Keep Watching the Skies!: American Science Fiction Movies of the Fifties.* 2 Vols. Jefferson, N.C.: McFarland, 1982, 1986.
Weiss, Ken, and Ed Goodgold. *To Be Continued.* New York: Crown, 1972.
Zinman, David. *Saturday Afternoon at the Bijou.* New Rochelle, N.Y.: Arlington House, 1973.

# Chapter Title Index

This index to entry number is a complete listing of the 849 chapter titles for the 66 Republic serials. The number in parentheses is the chapter number.

The Acid Clue (2) 976
The Acid Trail (10) 1003
Agent of Treachery (1) 948
Agent of Treachery (4) 987
Agents of Deceit (5) 988
Agents of Disaster (11) 1000
Ambush (13) 980
Ambush (9) 986
Ambush (8) 988
Ambush (10) 993
Ambushed (8) 975
America Beware (1) 1004
Arctic Intrigue (1) 951
Arena of Death (3) 1007
Arrow's Flight (9) 1008
Arsenal of Doom (3) 972
Ascending Doom (4) 995
Ascent to the Upperworld (12) 1007
Atlantis Destroyed (10) 1007
Atomic Peril (1) 953
Attack from the Skies (9) 968
Avalanche (5) 949
Avalanche (4) 993
Avalanche (9) 1011
The Avenging Corpse (10) 952
The Avenging River (12) 979
The Avenging Spirit (1) 996

The Baited Trap (11) 968
Bandit Territory (1) 970
Barrage of Death (2) 1003
Baru — Son of the Jungle (1) 957
Bat-Men of Joba (3) 957
Battle in the Clouds (8) 960
Battle in the Stratosphere (9) 998
Battle of the Rockets (2) 1009
Beast of Tokyo (8) 972
The Beast-Fiend (3) 979
Beasts at Bay (10) 996
Beheaded (9) 962
Behind the Mask (8) 996
Beneath the Ocean Floor (1) 1007
Besieged (6) 962
Besieged (14) 988
Birth of the Vigilantes (2) 1008
Black Gold (12) 978
The Black Raiders (1) 978
The Black Raiders Strike (3) 988
Blackout (5) 958
Blade of Wrath (5) 952
Blades of Death (4) 948
Blasted Evidence (10) 994
Blazing Barrier (6) 983

Blazing Barrier (14) 995
The Blazing Barrier (8) 989
Blazing Fury (9) 953
Blazing Guns (10) 985
Blazing Peril (12) 988
Blazing Peril (6) 996
Blazing Retribution (12) 973
Blazing Walls (8) 949
Blazing Walls (12) 1002
The Boat Trap (6) 951
Bombs Away (8) 990
Bonga's Courage (5) 957
Boomerang (8) 947
Boomerang (8) 978
Boomerang (3) 985
Bridge of Death (11) 979
Bridge of Death (3) 998
Bridge of Peril (10) 992
The Bridge of Peril (4) 1012
The Bridge of Terror (2) 960
Bridge to Eternity (5) 976
Bridge to Eternity (13) 990
Brink of Doom (6) 982
Brother Against Brother (5) 960
Brothers United (15) 960
Buried Alive (4) 1002
Burned Alive (9) 995
Burning Embers (7) 1010

# Chapter Title Index

Camouflaged Destruction (7) 998
Captain Marvel's Secret (12) 947
The Captive Chief (9) 996
Captive Witness (11) 964
Captured (2) 963
The Captured Raider (9) 978
Cargo of Destruction (8) 961
Cargo of Mystery (4) 968
The Case of the Crown Jewels (1) 967
The Case of the Double Trap (6) 967
The Case of the Golden Car (7) 967
The Case of the Hidden Witness (10) 967
The Case of the Invulnerable Criminal (8) 967
The Case of the Lawful Counterfeit (3) 967
The Case of the Missing Expert (5) 967
The Case of the Musical Clue (12) 967
The Case of the Stolen Ransom (2) 967
The Case of the Stradivarius (11) 967
The Case of the Telephone Code (4) 967
The Case of the Torn Blueprint (9) 967
Cathedral of Carnage (3) 1005
Cauldron of Cremation (12) 990
Cave of Doom (9) 981
The Cave of the Winds (9) 1000
Cavern of Cremation (11) 956
Cavern of Doom (7) 979
The Cavern of Doom (4) 988
Cavern of Revenge (12) 951
Caverns of Peril (11) 963
Caves of Horror (10) 975
Celestial Murder (5) 972
Ceremonial Execution (12) 1001
The Challenge (13) 962
Chamber of Doom (8) 963
The Charred Witness (2) 1001
Check Mate (13) 1002

Claim Jumper (7) 964
The Claw Monster (1) 994
Cloaked in Flame (5) 1001
The Clock of Doom (9) 961
Code of the Mounted (12) 985
Code of the Rangers (12) 986
Code Six Four Five (3) 971
Coffin on Wheels (8) 977
Cold Steel (5) 964
Collision (6) 1006
Concealed Evidence (4) 978
Condemned by Cossacks (3) 1008
Condemned Cargo (13) 972
Contraband Cargo (4) 1009
The Corpse of Jesse James (5) 978
Counterfeit Trail (8) 986
Counter-Plot (11) 971
Crackling Fury (10) 963
Crack-Up (12) 992
Crack-Up! (5) 963
The Crash! (8) 1003
Crater of Flame (8) 994
Cremation (10) 958
Cremation in the Clouds (8) 952
Criminals' Lair (2) 966
Crimson Sacrifice (10) 974
Crucible of Justice (15) 974
Cruise to Cremation (9) 1005
The Crystal of Death (9) 965
The Curse of Kurigal (12) 966
Curse of the Scorpion (1) 947

Dance of Doom (8) 956
Danger Express (9) 991
Danger in the Air (5) 1000
Danger Road (3) 977
Danger Trail (8) 965
The Dangerous Captive (10) 988
Dangerous Evidence (3) 984
Dangerous Secret (11) 980
Dangerous Waters (6) 960
Daredevils of the Air (1) 981
Day of Reckoning (12) 999
Dead End (2) 986
The Dead Fall (6) 975
The Dead Man Returns (11) 952
The Dead Man Speaks (5) 971
Dead Man's Return (9) 977

Dead Man's Trap (9) 947
Dead Man's Trap (4) 962
Dead Man's Vengeance (12) 958
Dead on Arrival (12) 972
Deadline at Midnight (6) 970
Deadline at Midnight (13) 978
Deadline for Disaster (5) 973
Deadly Cargo (6) 1003
The Deadly Circle (12) 1003
The Deadly Fog (10) 984
The Deadly Millstone 1002 (2)
Deadly Prophecy (1) 950
Deadly Sorcery (4) 972
Death Alley (8) 981
Death and Destruction (6) 972
Death Below (11) 988
Death by Voodoo (1) 980
The Death Car (3) 976
Death Closes In (11) 992
The Death Detector (10) 982
Death Dials a Number (11) 950
Death Dials a Number (6) 965
Death Dive (10) 999
The Death Drop (3) 973
The Death Drop (7) 990
Death from the Sky (1) 1010
The Death House (11) 996
Death in Disguise (3) 966
Death in the Air (5) 961
Death in the Air (9) 1007
The Death Leap (3) 993
Death of the Moon Man (12) 998
Death on the Beam (5) 997
Death on the Waterfront (7) 1009
Death Rides the Sky (4) 960
Death Rides the Stratosphere (3) 969
Death Rides the Torrent (1) 971
Death Rings the Phone (8) 999
Death Takes the Deck (2) 1006
Death Takes the Helm (2) 991
Death Takes the Wheel (4) 947

# Chapter Title Index

Death Takes the Wheel (2)  981
Death Takes the Witness (7)  986
The Death Trap (11)  948
Death Tunes In (7)  985
The Death Wind (9)  971
Death's Chariot (2)  995
Death's Door (9)  974
Death's Highway (11)  976
The Decoy (5)  1012
Deliberate Murder (11)  983
Deluge of Destruction (4)  982
Democracy in Action (15)  972
The Demon Killer (6)  997
Den of the Beast (10)  1002
Descending Doom (7)  969
Descending Doom (8)  997
Descending Doom (5)  1004
Descending Doom (3)  1012
Desert Intrigue (1)  995
Design for Murder (7)  982
Desperate Gamble (12)  959
Desperate Mission (11)  999
Desperate Venture (8)  959
Destined to Die (8)  991
Detour to Death (4)  1011
Devil Doctor (4)  985
The Devil in White (14)  960
Devil's Crucible (3)  995
The Devil's Marksman (11)  949
The Devil's Tattoo (13)  965
The Devil's Trap (11)  1002
Dial of Doom (6)  1001
Diamond Trail (14)  980
Disaster at Sea (1)  1003
Disaster on the Highway (11)  969
Disguised (13)  992
Dive to Doom (3)  991
The Divine Sacrifice (14)  957
Doctor Satan Strikes (15)  992
Doctor Satan's Man of Steel (5)  992
Dr. Vulcan — Traitor (1)  984
Doom Patrol (3)  962
Doom Ship (10)  947
Doomed Cargo (8)  948
Doomed Cargo (9)  951
Doorway to Death (2)  1005
Doorway to Destruction (7)  991
Doorway to Doom (4)  973

Double Ambush (7)  989
Double Cross (6)  992
Double Danger (6)  986
Double Danger (11)  994
Double Death (2)  964
Double Death (3)  1001
Double Jeopardy (9)  992
Double Murder (11)  953
Double Trap (7)  994
The Dragon Strikes (10)  972
Drums of Doom (10)  965
Dungeon of the Doomed (6)  1005

The Eagle Strikes (1)  1008
Echo of Eternity (4)  1005
Electrocuted (8)  983
Electrocution (7)  953
Electrocution (7)  999
The Enemy Planet (8)  998
The Enemy Strikes (4)  963
The Enemy's Mouthpiece (8)  966
Escape (12)  987
Espionage (9)  985
The Evil Eye (7)  997
Execution by Accident (10)  973
Execution by Error (7)  958
Execution by Fire (4)  969
The Executioner (3)  955
Exit to Eternity (6)  991
Exposed (12)  971
Exposed (13)  988
The Eyes of the Law (9)  948

Face to Face (11)  1012
False Information (8)  950
False Ransom (6)  985
The False Signal (3)  963
False Testimony (8)  954
Fang and Claw (8)  957
Fangs of Death (3)  951
Fangs of Doom (10)  1011
Fatal Dive (5)  984
Fatal Evidence (4)  966
The Fatal Flood (9)  990
The Fatal Fog (1)  999
Fatal Gold (6)  1011
The Fatal Hour (1)  962
Fatal Leap (13)  1001
The Fatal Letter (8)  971
The Fatal Masquerade (11)  989
The Fatal Message (9)  993
The Fatal Minute (2)  1010
The Fatal Mistake (11)  991

The Fatal Plunge (13)  987
The Fatal Records (7)  1002
The Fatal Ride (13)  963
The Fatal Sacrifice (3)  953
Fatal Second (5)  995
The Fatal Shaft (4)  1003
The Fatal Shot (7)  954
The Fatal Shot (6)  1010
Fatal Transformation (15)  990
Fatal Treasure (8)  987
The Fatal Trial (14)  997
Fathoms Below (3)  1000
Fiery Shroud (13)  997
Fiery Tomb (5)  956
The Fifth Column Strikes (1)  986
Fight in the Sky (12)  963
Fire of Vengeance (12)  965
The Fire Ship (5)  1006
Fire Trap (12)  974
The Fire Trap (13)  960
Five Fathoms Down (3)  1006
Flame and Battle (6)  989
Flame Versus Gun (7)  951
Flames of Jeopardy (9)  963
Flames of Vengeance (12)  964
Flaming Ambush (2)  996
Flaming Avalanche (3)  997
Flaming Cargo (3)  959
Flaming Coffin (14)  972
The Flaming Coffin (14)  992
Flaming Danger (2)  1000
Flaming Death (5)  953
Flaming Death (2)  975
Flaming Death (11)  1007
Flaming Fury (10)  987
Flaming Highway (7)  973
Flaming Juggernaut (6)  964
Flaming Juggernaut (11)  1011
Flaming Peril (10)  962
The Flaming Pit (11)  982
Flaming Prison (2)  956
The Flaming Ring (10)  979
The Flaming "Z" (2)  1012
Flight of the Spy King (4)  999
Flight to Danger (2)  974
Flight to Destruction (4)  998
Flight to Doom (12)  955
Flight to Freedom (15)  980
The Flooded Mine (7)  955
Flowing Death (8)  1012
The Flying Coffin (8)  982
The Flying Coffin (10)  983
Flying Fury (5)  996

# Chapter Title Index

Flying Gas Chamber (10) 1009
Forged Evidence (6) 958
Forged Orders (2) 970
Four Seconds to Live (4) 961
Framed (7) 949
Fremont Takes Command (12) 1008
Frontier Justice (12) 949
Frontier Justice (12) 956
Frontier Justice (15) 988
Frontier Renegades (1) 977
Fu Manchu Strikes (1) 965
The Fugitive (7) 1012
Fugitive from Injustice (3) 1002
Fugitive's Code (12) 977
Funeral Arrangements Completed (8) 1001
The Funeral Pyre (9) 969
The Fur Pirates (3) 960

Galloping Gunslingers (10) 977
Gantlet of Guns (7) 996
The Gas Chamber (3) 1003
Gauntlet of Destruction (13) 957
Getaway (14) 963
Ghost Town (3) 954
The Ghost Town Mystery (7) 960
Glass Guillotine (6) 950
Glass Guillotine (11) 958
G-Men's Drag-Net (15) 961
The God of the Volcano (6) 1000
The Gold Ship (10) 960
The Golden Arrow (9) 1012
The Golden God (1) 1012
The Golden Hands (1) 966
The Guillotine (2) 947
Gun Trap (5) 970

Handcuffed to Doom (3) 961
Hangman's Noose (6) 949
Hangman's Noose (7) 977
Harbor of Horror (5) 974
Harbor Pursuit (11) 960
The Haunting Past (11) 977
Hero's Death (11) 1004
Hidden Danger (3) 964
Hidden Death (3) 950
Hidden Desperado (10) 959
The Hidden Key (7) 966
The Hidden Witness (2) 948
High Hazard (7) 981

High Peril (4) 984
High Peril (6) 994
High Voltage (14) 974
High Voltage! (10) 961
High Voltage Danger (10) 976
Highway Holocaust (4) 976
Highway of Death (8) 992
Highway of Horror (8) 951
Highway Racketeers (9) 1004
Hills of Death (6) 998
Hi-Yo Silver! (1) 987
Hoofs of Doom (3) 996
Horror on the Highway (12) 952
Horsemen of Death (2) 949
Hostage for Murder (8) 1009
Hostage of Destiny (9) 964
Hot Cargo (7) 971
House of Doom (12) 994
House of Horror (10) 997
The House of Horror (11) 1005
The House of Terror (5) 965
The Human Bomb (4) 992
Human Quarry (10) 951
Human Sacrifice (6) 995
Human Target (3) 983
Human Target (2) 1004
Human Targets (7) 947
Human Targets (12) 993
The Human Torpedo (9) 1009
The Hunter Lions of Joba (4) 957

In the Camp of the Enemy (10) 968
In the Hands of the Enemy (14) 961
The Infernal Machine (10) 955
The Innocent Victim (10) 971
Into the Enemy's Camp (4) 1000
Into the Metal Tower (8) 1007
Invisible Menace (9) 1001
Invisible Terror (14) 962
The Invisible Trail (12) 953
The Invisible Victim (8) 1011
The Invisible Witness (6) 1004
Iron Coffin (5) 1004
Iron Executioner (5) 1009
The Iron Monster (7) 972

Japanese Inquisition (2) 972
Jars of Death (11) 957
The Jaws of the Beast (8) 1000
Journey into Peril (7) 974
Juggernaut (3) 1010
The Juggernaut (9) 958
The Juggernaut Strikes (6) 1007
Jungle Ambush (1) 979
Jungle Ambush (2) 994
Jungle Jeopardy (11) 974
Jungle Killer (10) 980
Jungle Vengeance (5) 980

Key to the Legend (2) 954
Killer at Bay (12) 968
The Killer Beast (3) 994
The Killer Strikes (3) 956

Ladder of Death (3) 974
Ladder of Peril (9) 955
The Last of the Rangers (15) 987
The Last Stand (15) 963
The Last Stand (12) 996
The Laughing Skull (4) 953
Legend of Genghis Khan (1) 954
Lens of Death (6) 947
The Lethal Chamber (4) 990
The Lethal Pit (4) 997
A Life for a Life (13) 950
The Lightning Strikes (1) 968
Lightning Terror (11) 1001
The Lion Pit (5) 979
Liquid Jewels (12) 954
The Living Dead (9) 997
The Living Projectile (5) 969
Lone Ranger at Bay (7) 988
The Lone Ranger Returns (1) 988
The Lost Tunnel (3) 948

Machine Murder (10) 1006
The Man Behind the Mask (12) 991
Man Hunt (3) 986
The Man in the Meteor (1) 997
Man Trap (8) 980
Man Vs. Monster (11) 1009
Manhunt (1) 985
Marked Evidence (6) 971
Marked for Murder (10) 964
Marooned (9) 975

# Chapter Title Index

Mask of El Latigo (3) 989
The Masked Avenger (1) 1011
The Masked Crusader (1) 991
The Masked Executioner (10) 981
Masked Victory (2) 988
Mass Attack (9) 1006
Mass Execution (10) 998
Master Spy (11) 985
The Master Spy (1) 963
The Mechanical Bloodhound (5) 981
Mechanical Executioner (2) 952
Mechanical Homicide (11) 951
Mechanical Homicide (6) 973
Menace from Mars (1) 969
Menace from Mars (11) 997
Mephisto's Mantrap (5) 990
Message of Death (10) 970
Messengers of Doom (14) 987
Mile a Minute Murder (7) 1005
The Mill of Disaster (2) 968
The Missing Spur (9) 987
The Missing Witness (11) 961
Missouri Manhunt (6) 977
Mob Justice (8) 970
Mob Murder (3) 1011
Molten Menace (7) 984
Molten Terror (2) 998
Money Lure (9) 970
The Monster (2) 965
The Monster Strikes (7) 992
Monster's Clutch (7) 995
Monsters of the Deep (13) 974
The Monstrous Plot (1) 955
Moon Rocket (1) 998
Multiple Murder (1) 958
Murder at Midnight (4) 977
Murder at Sea (5) 962
Murder Car (5) 998
The Murder Cave (4) 989
Murder Dungeon (7) 1001
The Murder Machine (3) 990
Murder Masquerade (4) 996
Murder Meter (5) 991
Murder Mine (6) 1009
Murder on the Santa Fe Trail (1) 949
Murder or Accident? (2) 951

Murder Train (7) 976
Mutiny (13) 1000
The Mysterious Friend (2) 955
Mysterious Island (1) 975
The Mysterious Island (1) 1000
Mystery of the Mountain (6) 953
Mystery of the Rocket Man (6) 984
The Mystery of the Towers (1) 982
The Mystery Ship (5) 1003
Mystery Wagon (10) 1012

Native Execution (8) 1006
Nazi Treachery Unmasked (15) 1001
North African Intrigue (1) 1001

Ocean Tomb (6) 990
On Target (4) 1006
On to Victory (12) 983
100,000 Volts (2) 971
One Second to Live (10) 949
The Open Grave (4) 1001
Open Warfare (11) 959
Operation Murder (4) 981
Ordeal by Fire (6) 976
Outlaw County (1) 1002

Passage to Danger (6) 948
Passage to Peril (8) 1005
Passengers to Doom (13) 961
Pendulum of Doom (5) 975
The Pendulum of Doom (4) 965
Peril in the Sky (4) 950
Peril Underground (9) 973
Perilous Barrier (2) 959
Perilous Combat (8) 964
Perilous Mission (6) 969
Perilous Plunge (11) 973
Perilous Plunge (7) 983
Perilous Plunge (12) 997
Perilous Pursuit (7) 956
Perilous Trail (2) 999
Phantom Invaders (1) 983
The Phantom Killer (7) 968
The Phantom Meets Justice (12) 976
The Pitfall (3) 987
Planned Pursuit (11) 998
Plunder Cave (5) 959
Plunge of Peril (8) 1010

Plunging Death (2) 984
The Poison Dart (7) 980
The Powder Keg (7) 959
Power Dive to Doom (14) 990
Preview of Murder (4) 952
Prison of Flame (10) 1008
The Prisoner Spy (9) 954
The Prisoner Vanishes (2) 962
Prisoners of Atlantis (5) 1007
Prisoners of the High Priest (6) 957
The Prophecy of Gorn (15) 957
The Purple Death (1) 952
Pursuit (5) 954
Pursuit into Evil (5) 982
Pursuit to Destruction (5) 951

Queen of Beasts (2) 980
Queen's Ransom (4) 975

Race to Destruction (4) 958
A Race with Death (11) 1008
Racing Peril (2) 977
Racing Peril (10) 1001
Railroad Saboteurs (4) 983
Ransom in the Sky (3) 965
The Ray of Death (5) 955
Records of Doom (9) 949
The Red Circle Speaks (11) 955
Red Man's Courage (6) 987
Redskin Raiders (6) 956
Redskin Raiders (12) 989
Reign of Terror (9) 983
Retreat to Destruction (4) 964
Retribution (15) 962
Retribution (12) 1010
Return of the Copperhead (1) 992
Return of the Don (1) 964
Return of the Fugitive (6) 974
The Revealing Torch (10) 978
Revenge of the Volkites (4) 1007
Revolt (15) 965
Revolt of the Slaves (12) 957
The Rider of the Stallion (2) 993
Right of Way (11) 1010

# Chapter Title Index

River of Death (9)  994
River of Fire (1)  973
River of Fire (3)  980
Road to Death (2)  983
Road to Oblivion (5)  977
Roaring Wheels (5)  948
Robber's Agent (3)  970
Rolling Fury (3)  999
Runaway Stagecoach (11)  970
The Runaway Torpedo (12)  961
The Runway of Death (2)  961

The Sable Shroud (10)  990
Sabotage (4)  955
Sabotage (5)  985
Sands of Doom (4)  994
Satan's Cauldron (8)  985
Satan's Fury (15)  995
Satan's Shadow (11)  990
Satan's Surgeon (14)  965
Satan's Web (2)  990
Savage Fury (2)  989
Savage Strategy (2)  979
The Scarab Strikes (14)  952
Scarlet Shroud (3)  952
The Scorpion Strikes (5)  947
The Sea Battle (11)  1003
Sea Racketeers (7)  962
Sea Raiders (8)  1004
Sea Saboteurs (8)  973
Sea Saboteurs (1)  1006
The Sea Trap (12)  1000
Seconds to Live (11)  962
The Secret Code (7)  948
The Secret Meeting (10)  954
Secret of Dr. Vulcan (11)  984
Secret of the Altar (11)  954
Secret Weapon (1)  990
Secret Weapon (7)  1004
Shattered Evidence (2)  982
Shipyard Saboteurs (4)  971
Shoot to Kill (9)  1002
Signal for Action (2)  978
The Silenced Witness (3)  968
The Silent Informer (9)  989
The Silver Bullet (11)  987
Six-Gun Hijacker (6)  959
Sky Pirates (5)  1010
Sky Raiders (10)  986
The Sky Wreckers (1)  961
Skyscraper Plunge (13)  952
The Slave Collar (8)  953
Slaves of the Phantom (1)  976

S. O. S. (8)  955
S. O. S. Ranger (9)  982
The Spider Strikes (1)  960
The Spider's Lair (5)  950
The Spider's Venom (9)  950
The Spirit Rider (1)  989
The Spy (11)  978
The Stacked Deck (3)  978
Stagecoach to Eternity (9)  959
The Steaming Cauldron (5)  987
The Stolen Body (10)  948
Stolen Cargo (6)  954
The Stolen Corpse (10)  950
The Stolen Corpse (2)  973
The Stolen Formula (2)  950
The Stolen Hand (9)  966
Stolen Secrets (6)  961
The Stone Guillotine (5)  989
The Stratosphere Adventure (9)  960
Stratosphere Invaders (4)  1004
The Submarine Trap (7)  1007
Suicidal Sacrifice (8)  969
Suicide Dive (5)  983
Suicide Flight (8)  984
Suicide Mission (11)  972
Suicide Sacrifice (10)  991
Suicide Showdown (10)  956
Sunken Peril (6)  963
Suspense at Midnight (4)  991
Swing for Life (7)  957

Take Off that Mask! (5)  1011
Takeoff to Destruction (15)  997
Talk or Die! (12)  948
Talk or Die! (7)  978
The Talking Mirror (12)  950
Target for Murder (10)  1005
Temple of Terror (1)  1005
Ten Seconds to Live (9)  984
Terror by Night (3)  982
Terror in the Sky (4)  954
Terror Trail (9)  956
Test Flight (5)  986
Test of Terror (5)  994
Third Degree (8)  1002
Thirteen Steps (2)  992
Thirty Seconds to Live (6)  955
Thunder Mountain (14)  1000

Thunderbolt (2)  953
Thundering Death (13)  995
Thundering Earth (2)  987
Thundering Wheels (6)  993
Tides of Trickery (8)  968
Tiger Trap (3)  975
The Tiger-Men's God (2)  957
Time Bomb (3)  947
The Time Trap (2)  997
The Toll of Doom (15)  952
The Tomb of Ghengis Khan (11)  965
Tomb of Terror (9)  999
Tomb of Terror (2)  1011
Tomb of the Traitors (12)  1009
Tombs of the Ancients (11)  966
The Torpedo of Doom (6)  968
Tower of Death (7)  961
Tower of Disaster (7)  970
Tower of Jeopardy (1)  959
Tower of Vengeance (12)  982
Tracking the Enemy (7)  963
Trail of Blood (12)  970
Trail of Death (11)  986
Trail of Terror (4)  959
The Trail of the Spider (12)  960
Trail of Tyranny (12)  1011
Trail to Destruction (9)  976
Trail to Destruction (9)  979
Trail to Empire (1)  993
Trail Treachery (7)  993
Trail's End (3)  949
Trail's End (12)  975
Trail's End (7)  1000
Train of Doom (8)  962
The Traitor (6)  978
The Trap (6)  988
The Trap that Failed (10)  953
The Trap that Failed (3)  981
Trapped (12)  980
Trapped (4)  986
Trapped (10)  1010
The Trapped Conspirator (5)  966
Trapped Underground (5)  999
Treacherous Trail (10)  995
Treachery (4)  980
Treachery Unmasked (5)  1008
Treasure Tomb (9)  980

## Chapter Title Index

A Treaty with Treason (8) 1008
Trial by Fire (12) 962
Trial by Thunder-Rods (10) 957
Tribal Fury (6) 980
Triple Tragedy (9) 952
Triumph Over Treachery (12) 1005
Tuareg Vengeance (8) 995
Tunnel of Terror (4) 956
Tunnel of Terror (11) 993
Tunnel of Terror (9) 1010
2700° Fahrenheit (10) 1004
Twisted Vengeance (12) 1006
Two Shall Die (5) 1005
A Tyrant's Trickery (6) 1008

Under the Knives (3) 958
Underground Ambush (11) 1006
Underground Inferno (4) 951
Underground Tornado (6) 979
Underground Tornado (12) 995
Undersea Agents (3) 1009
Undersea Bandits (5) 968
The Undersea City (2) 1007
Undersea Peril (6) 981
Undersea Terror (7) 1003

Undersea Tomb (3) 992
Undersea Warfare (11) 981
Unholy Gold (4) 1008
The Unknown Assassin (4) 974
Unknown Peril (11) 995
Unmasked (13) 948
Unmasked (10) 966
Unmasked (4) 1010
Unmasked (12) 1012

V...- (12) 1004
Valley of Death (11) 947
Valley of Death (1) 956
Valley of Skulls (11) 975
Vault of Vengeance (6) 952
Vendetta (2) 958
Vengeance of the Si Fan (7) 965
Vengeance Under the Big Top (12) 981
Victim of Villainy (14) 1001
Victims of Vengeance (4) 970
Volcanic Vengeance (12) 969
The Volcano's Secret (2) 969
Volley of Death (5) 993
Volley of Death (6) 1002
Voodoo Vengeance (4) 979

Wanted for Murder (1) 974
War in the Hills (7) 1006

Water Rustlers (4) 949
Water Trap (5) 1002
The Water Trap (8) 979
Watery Grave (9) 972
Wave of Disaster (12) 984
Weapons of Hate (10) 969
Wheels of Death (7) 950
Wheels of Disaster (6) 966
Wheels of Disaster (7) 987
Wheels of Disaster (6) 999
Wheels of Doom (9) 988
When Birdmen Strike (9) 957
The Whistling Arrow (8) 993
White Man's Magic (7) 975
Wholesale Destruction (7) 952
Window of Death (10) 989
Window of Peril (8) 976
Window to Death (8) 958
Winged Death (2) 985
Wings of Doom (8) 974
Wings of Doom (7) 1008
Wings of Fury (10) 1000
Wolf Pack (7) 1011
Wolves at Bay (9) 1003

Yellow Peril (1) 972

The Zombie Vanguard (1) 1009
Zorro to the Rescue (6) 1012

# Name Index

*References are to entry numbers.*

Abbott, Anthony  603
Abbott, Bud  1030
Abbott, John  209, 444, 709, 887
Abel, Rudolph E.  222, 284, 285, 424, 769, 785, 879, 887
Abel, Walter  598, 911, 1033
Abrams, Leon  795
Aby, Earl  322
"Ace," the Wonder Dog  280, 557, 995
Ackland, Rodney  11, 790
Acosta, Enrique  866
Acosta, Frazer  1000
Acosta, Rodolfo  84, 685
Acuff, Eddie  35, 38, 48, 51, 71, 167, 236, 315, 323, 412, 501, 515, 618, 641, 657, 672, 743, 744, 835, 850, 928, 941, 956, 971, 980
Acuff, Roy and His Smoky Mountain Boys  230, 295, 333, 529, 536, 734
Adair, Jack  477
Adair, Phyllis  288
Adams, Carol  35, 270, 367, 649, 740, 962
Adams, Cleve F.  222
Adams, Doc  1002
Adams, Dorothy  380, 816
Adams, Ernie  23, 35, 41, 54, 127, 132, 162, 202, 256, 302, 303, 315, 419, 440, 516, 566, 604, 615, 624, 650, 827, 933, 950, 967, 982, 988, 991, 1002
Adams, Eustace  196
Adams, Frank R.  117
Adams, Gerald Drayson  4, 260, 386, 455, 546, 594, 703, 809
Adams, Jane  786
Adams, Jill  185
Adams, Lowden  272, 965, 1004
Adams, Nick  781
Adams, Peter  237
Adams, Ray  949
Adams, Samuel Hopkins  603
Adams, Stanley  32, 325
Adams, Ted  23, 50, 127, 177, 202, 253, 261, 266, 307, 340, 432, 519, 527, 574, 630, 774, 794, 823, 872, 873, 891, 954, 956, 984, 987, 1002
Adams, Tommye (Abigail Adams)  504, 805
Adams, Victor  200
Adamson, Ewart  205, 270, 486, 582; *see also* Dayle Douglas
Adkins, Ella  837
Adler, Luther  357, 898
Adlon, Louis (Duke)  57, 885
Adreon, Franklin  22, 164, 327, 340, 472, 530, 635, 754, 811, 948, 950, 951, 954, 959, 964, 966, 969, 970, 971, 973, 976, 977, 978, 979, 981, 984, 989, 994, 998, 999, 1002, 1006, 1009, 1019; *see also* Franklyn Adreon
Adreon, Franklyn  949, 955, 961, 963, 965, 968, 985, 987, 988, 992, 1003, 1010, 1012; *see also* Franklin Adreon
Adrian, Iris  560, 653, 777
Agar, John  689, 921
Agay, Irene  216
Agnew, Charles  377
Agresti, Ed  1001
Aguglia, Mimi  153
Ahearn, Danny  83
Ahern, Will and Gladys  286
Aherne, Brian  18
Ahn, Philip  219, 328, 708, 713, 965
Ainley, Joe  160
Ainslee, Ann  960
Ainslee, Mary  205, 682, 740
Ainsworth, Cupid  291
Airaldi, Roberto  33
Alan, Robert  451
Alaniz, Rico  402
Alban, John  950
Alberghetti, Anna Maria  199, 423

Alberni, Luis 244, 330, 477, 699, 833, 870
Albert, Eddie 344, 637
Albertson, Frank 45, 119, 268, 330, 517, 536, 669, 718
Albright, Hardie 101, 104, 795
Albright, John 235, 364, 409
Albright, Lola 580
Albright, Wally 491, 612
Alden, Bob 586
Alden, Eric 397, 419
Alderson, Erville 322, 464
Alderson, John 427, 766
Aldrich, Alden 581
Aldridge, Kay 956, 974, 995, 1028
Alexander, Ben 77, 322
Alexander, Betty 852
Alexander, Jim 204, 666
Alexander, Katherine 19, 740
Alexander, Richard 93, 123, 142, 162, 326, 373, 406, 408, 464, 534, 581, 621, 659, 663, 693, 779, 921, 978, 981, 1003, 1006, 1010
Alexis, Demetrius 419
Allan, Edgar 960
Alland, William 451
Allen, Barbara Jo 367, 368, 419, 487, 488, 733, 893; *see also* Vera Vague
Allen, Chris 465
Allen, Cliff 16
Allen, Corey 404
Allen, Drew 971
Allen, Edgar 476
Allen, Francis K. 653
Allen, George 962, 963, 986, 992
Allen, Harry 282, 568
Allen, Jack 829
Allen, Jane 397
Allen, Joel 912
Allen, Joseph, Jr. 478, 509
Allen, Judith 53, 59, 70, 85, 286
Allen, Lester 297
Allen, Maude Pierce 949
Allen, Patrick 152
Allen, Rex 22, 73, 129, 194, 340, 363, 387, 426, 547, 548, 587, 631, 635, 661, 711, 730, 762, 826, 846, 875, 884
Allen, Rick 595
Allen, Robert 232

Allen, Victor 132
Allister, Claud 82, 778
Allman, Elvia 740
Allwyn, Astrid 262, 343, 388, 486, 613
Alper, Murray 195, 210, 744
Alsace, Gene 949
Alten, Frank 962, 973, 990, 1001, 1004, 1009
Altschuler, Alice 494, 677, 919
Alvarado, Don 223
Alvarado, Fernando 898
Alvarado, Jose 898
Alvin, John 68, 497, 713, 849, 872
Alyn, Kirk 92, 144, 284, 469, 569, 591, 779, 958, 966, 999
Ameche, Don 816
The American G.I. Chorus 534
Ames, Adrienne 945
Ames, Jimmy 743, 958
Ames, Leon 96, 133, 366, 473
Ames, Marlene 13
Ames, Ramsay 950, 971
Andelin, James 121
Anders, Luana 475, 535
Anderson, Cap 632
Anderson, Cornie 673
Anderson, Daphne 428
Anderson, Dave 364, 950, 966, 978
Anderson, Doris 813, 820, 926
Anderson, Eddie 59
Anderson, George 76, 409
Anderson, Harry 955, 960, 961, 968
Anderson, James 426
Anderson, Judith 765
Anderson, Richard 889
Anderson, Rick 145, 394
Anderson, Robert 128, 475
Andre, Dorothy 981
Andre, Gwili 485
Andre, Joyce 206
Andre, Lona 277
Andres, Rudolph 876; *see also* Robert O. Davis
Andrews, Lloyd "Slim" 145, 154, 746
Andrews, Robert D. 366
Andrews, Stanley 22, 31, 80, 99, 208, 217, 311, 377, 419, 422, 464, 601, 656, 684,

725, 831, 854, 861, 875, 884, 892, 921, 948, 951, 956, 985, 987
The Andrews Sisters 1030
Angel, Heather 28, 67, 200, 598
Angold, Edit 920
Ankers, Evelyn 222, 251, 767
Ankrum, Morris 43, 211, 228, 327, 423, 530, 909, 938
Annabella 1032
Anstead, Melva 467
Anthony, Stuart 85, 625, 680
Anys, Georgette 165
Apfel, Oscar 83, 100, 322, 396
Apostolof, Stephen C. 401
Appel, Sam 195
Appleby, Dorothy 576
Appleton, Elinor 933
Archainbaud, George 55, 285
Archard, Marcel 11
Archer, John 4, 333, 507, 530, 614, 714; *see also* Ralph Bowman
Archuletta, James 928
Arco, Louis 709
Ardell, Maxine 397, 488
Arden, Eve 204, 343, 418
Arden, Mary 88, 392, 482
Argyle, Edward 968
Arledge, John 609
Arlen, Richard 55, 71, 94, 335, 370, 413, 586, 779, 814
Arliss, Leslie 683
Armenta, Phillip 975, 987, 1008
Armetta, Henry 477
Armida 667
Armitage, Gordon 951
Armontel, Roland 188
Arms, Russell 161
Armstrong, Antony 471
Armstrong, Gary 128, 505
Armstrong, Henry 592
Armstrong, Louis, and His Orchestra 31
Armstrong, Margaret 415, 906
Armstrong, Mary 112
Armstrong, Paul, Jr. 639
Armstrong, Robert 45, 119, 150, 181, 213, 240, 248, 265, 268, 278, 473, 525, 789
Arnac, Beatrice 558
Arnac, Marcel 777

# NAME INDEX

Arnall, Julia 808
Arnaud, Yvonne 30
Arnaz, Desi 1032
Arness, James 46, 237
Arnheim, Gus, and His Orchestra 856
Arnold, Edward 121, 1034
Arnold, Jack 1004
Arnold, Melvyn 147
Arnold, Phil 323, 456
Arnova, Alba 259
Arnt, Charles 86, 377, 500, 678, 813, 821
Arruza, Carlos 84
Arslan, Sylvia 298, 719
Arthur, Art 450, 682, 743
Arthur, Henry 514
Arthur, Johnny 212, 341, 393, 507, 718, 991
Arthur, Louise 404
Arthur, Robert 485, 938
Arthur, Victor 340
Arundell, Dennis 683
Arvan, Jan 1006
Asbury, Herbert 263
Ash, Sam 50, 189, 323, 461, 678, 952, 982, 991
Ashdown, Nadene 840
Ashe, Warren 173, 941
Asherson, Renee 837
Ashley, Edward 268, 450, 453
Ashley, Graeme 841
Ashley, June 152
Ashton, Marcia 300
Askam, Earl 590, 629, 955, 961, 975
Askin, Leon 103
Assaly, Adeeb 829
Asther, Nils 392, 450, 517
Aston and Renee 901
Astor, Gertrude 12, 415, 743
Astor, Mary 1034
Astor Pictures 652
Atchley, Hooper 62, 322, 373, 377, 508, 521, 523, 542, 598, 639, 655, 680, 681, 949, 962, 972, 986
Ates, Roscoe 7, 131, 340, 356, 507, 623, 645, 657, 823, 1031
Atkinson, Betty 941
Atkinson, Frank 300, 841
Atterbury, Malcolm 156, 784
Atwater, Gladys 373
Atwell, Roy 313
Atwill, Lionel 709, 927, 952

Atwood, Donna 368
Aubert, Lenore 109
Aubrey, Jimmy 67, 289, 887
Audley, Eleanor 766
Auer, John H. 18, 33, 96, 117, 121, 148, 180, 182, 211, 235, 247, 250, 328, 342, 345, 364, 365, 385, 398, 461, 462, 504, 557, 568, 577, 640, 745, 757, 805, 819, 830, 926
Auer, Mischa 360
Auer, Stephen 10, 138, 161, 201, 224, 355, 409, 447, 452, 453, 495, 497, 668, 687, 720, 722, 731, 775, 839, 845, 853, 881, 892, 920, 925
Auerbach, Artie 330
Augustine, Peter 901
Aumont, Genevieve 401
Austin, Charlotte 580
Austin, Frank 742
Austin, Lois 278
Austin, William 274, 510, 552
Autry, Gene 34, 48, 56, 66, 70, 91, 104, 130, 135, 145, 195, 266, 286, 291, 306, 318, 351, 352, 376, 465, 477, 488, 489, 491, 508, 537, 542, 543, 601, 611, 623, 632, 641, 642, 643, 649, 656, 667, 673, 674, 678, 681, 728, 735, 737, 738, 739, 761, 770, 776, 797, 848, 863, 866, 874, 906, 936, 1031, 1032, 1033, 1034
Avco-Embassy Pictures 84
Avonde, Richard 696, 711, 912, 914
Axman, Hanne 627
Aylesworth, Arthur 210, 246, 411, 603
Aylesworth, Doug 971
Aylmer, Felix 287
Ayres, Lew 322, 410, 438

Babb, Dorothy 203
Babcock, Dwight V. 653, 696
Baby Dumpling 1030
Bacca, John 987
Bachelor, Stephanie 63, 98, 149, 204, 265, 274, 278, 355, 389, 409, 419, 455, 464, 579, 597, 701, 709, 754, 771, 879

Backus, George 505
Backus, Jim 206, 273
Bacon, David 747, 991
Bacon, Irving 156, 176, 335, 348, 356, 377, 408, 505, 529, 678, 802
Bacon, John 987
Bacon, Rod 270, 612, 937, 953, 991
Bacon, Ruth 770
Bacon, Shelby 138, 800
Badel, Alan 454
Baer, Buddy 219, 324, 402
Baer, John 25, 120
Bagni, John 221, 323, 512, 604, 947, 952, 962, 965, 985, 986, 992, 995
Bagues, Salvador 325
Bailer, Dorothy 467
Bailey, Bill 950
Bailey, Bud 996
Bailey, Claude 683
Bailey, Joe 357, 998
Bailey, Raymond 240, 757, 955
Bailey, Richard 814, 990
Bailey, William Norton 641, 656
Baine, Enid 698
Bainter, Fay 1034
Bair, David 2
Baird, John 410
Baird, Michael 156, 327
Bakalyan, Richard 404
Baker, Art 46, 601
Baker, Belle 31
Baker, Benny 355, 668, 715, 830
Baker, Bob 1031
Baker, Eddie 370
Baker, Frank 616, 968
Baker, Kenny 86, 342
Baker, Lee 968
Baker, Silver Tip 23, 537, 660, 877, 907
Baker, Tommy 680
Bakewell, William 159, 212, 339, 852, 903, 983, 998, 1028
Balch, Joe 1002
Baldra, Chuck 71, 126, 130, 302, 352, 433, 434, 522, 523, 542, 583, 590, 601, 602, 623, 625, 633, 657, 723, 844, 907
Baldwin, Ann 248, 623, 899, 918, 965

# Name Index

Baldwin, Bill  853
Baldwin, Faith  598
Baldwin, Robert  457, 893
Baldwin, Walter  671
Balenda, Carla  587
Balfour, Michael  707, 829, 841
Ball, Betty  357
Ball, Frank  23, 41, 69, 72, 127, 202, 226, 261, 302, 303, 432, 523, 578, 634, 650, 847, 860, 873
Ball, Lucille  1032
Ballard, Todhunter  561
Ballew, Smith  266
Ballou, Marion  598
Balter, Sam  592
Bamby, George  762
Bamford, Freda  808
Bane, Holly  107, 221, 528, 533, 608, 638, 954, 959, 970, 978; see also Mike Ragan
Banning, Leslye  61
Bannon, Jim  164, 481, 954
Barber, Bobby  891, 986
Barbier, George  745, 757, 893
Barclay, Don  72, 827
Barclay, Joan  615, 860
Barclay, Stephen  189, 285, 297, 607, 769, 892
Barcroft, Roy  9, 13, 14, 22, 25, 38, 40, 50, 55, 61, 63, 68, 73, 74, 93, 97, 99, 102, 103, 105, 112, 114, 115, 124, 125, 128, 138, 155, 157, 176, 178, 179, 192, 194, 208, 214, 217, 221, 224, 234, 249, 255, 260, 284, 294, 305, 310, 326, 331, 337, 353, 356, 357, 371, 377, 382, 387, 394, 420, 425, 427, 430, 437, 441, 442, 446, 452, 456, 464, 466, 469, 479, 480, 481, 482, 483, 491, 499, 513, 527, 529, 533, 539, 540, 546, 547, 548, 556, 560, 563, 564, 569, 572, 573, 586, 589, 593, 594, 600, 608, 620, 623, 626, 638, 644, 646, 648, 659, 661, 663, 675, 676, 684, 686, 691, 696, 697, 706, 711, 722, 723, 724, 736, 754, 759, 762, 767, 771, 774, 775, 776,
779, 786, 792, 793, 795, 798, 799, 800, 831, 835, 839, 842, 845, 849, 861, 875, 884, 887, 889, 890, 891, 894, 895, 896, 902, 903, 904, 913, 914, 928, 951, 954, 955, 958, 959, 960, 964, 966, 970, 971, 973, 974, 977, 978, 986, 989, 990, 991, 996, 997, 998, 999, 1002, 1003, 1009, 1019
Bardette, Trevor  40, 162, 173, 249, 260, 281, 326, 340, 399, 479, 481, 581, 631, 633, 686, 706, 724, 791, 793, 820, 897, 928, 929, 940, 980
Bardot, Brigitte  185
Bari, Lynn  363, 407
Baringer, Barry  223
Barker, Abe  185
Barker, Lex  518
Barker, Reginald  245
Barkley, Lucille  25
Barlow, Reginald  282, 524, 674, 899, 955, 963
Barlowe, Joy  852
Barnes, Binnie  19, 259, 373, 1032, 1033, 1034
Barnes, Jane  489
Barnes, Pinky  110
Barnes, Rayford  631
Barnett, Antonina  534
Barnett, Vince  158, 196, 235, 332, 585, 613, 728, 776, 832, 852, 932
Barnette, Griff  172, 257, 264, 564, 693, 712, 746, 776, 962, 987, 988
Baron, Steven  849
Barr, Byron  143, 192, 456, 807
Barr, Patrick  837
Barr, Tony  153
Barrat, Robert  130, 155, 217, 279, 301, 473, 605
Barrett, Claudia  179, 527, 544, 676
Barrett, Curt  967
Barrett, Edith  415, 785
Barrett, Katherine  206, 900
Barrett, Michael  325
Barrett, Tony  238, 610
Barrie, Mona  779, 843, 911
Barrie, Wendy  612, 833, 911, 926
Barrier, Edgar  451, 751
Barris, Harry  777
Barron, Baynes  998
Barron, Robert  34, 470, 592, 950, 971, 980, 986, 995
Barrow, Janet  859
Barrows, George  986
Barrows, Nicholas  159, 814
Barry, Don ("Red")  20, 26, 50, 62, 89, 96, 99, 105, 116, 154, 167, 168, 169, 172, 175, 257, 258, 277, 395, 405, 424, 441, 452, 469, 498, 512, 551, 559, 565, 566, 583, 593, 636, 680, 744, 746, 757, 773, 794, 812, 815, 849, 850, 861, 862, 867, 868, 882, 905, 930, 931, 949, 954, 1079
Barry, Hilda  700
Barry, Phyllis  5, 245
Barrymore, Ethel  505, 747
Barrymore, John Drew  830
Bartell, Eddie  856
Bartell, Harry  4
Bartell, Richard  818
Barthelmess, Richard  1029
Bartlett, Bennie  321, 532
Bartlett, Hall  147, 912
Bartlett, Michael  244
Bartlett, Richard H.  786
Bartlett, Sy  423
Bartlett, William  94
Barton, Anne  580
Barton, George  50
Barton, Gregg  243, 730, 989
Barton, Joan  15
Barton, Joy  91
Barton, Michael  61, 323, 418, 762
Bascon, Joaquin  323
Bash, John  665, 782, 924
Basie, Count, and His Orchestra  343
Bass, Alfie  772, 837
Batanides, Arthur  880
Bates, Florence  47, 314, 381
Bates, Granville  421, 664, 819
The Bat-Men  957
Batson, Alfred  980
Battle, John Tucker  443, 460
Baugh, "Slingin' Sammy"  986
Baum, Vicki  44, 297
Bautista, Joe  282
Baxley, Jack  512

# Name Index

Baxter, Alan  263, 388, 592, 618, 1076
Baxter, George  764
Bay, Vivian  33
Bayless, Mary  972
Bayley, Eleanor  397
Baylor, Hal  111, 241, 791, 838, 912; *see also* Hal Fieberling
Bayne, Al  349
Beach, Brandon  92, 581, 878
Beach, Guy  593
Beach, John  66, 277, 491, 331, 352, 570, 988
Beach, Rex  33
Beach, Richard  56, 400, 476, 960, 1003
Beal, John  187
Bear, Mary  736
Bearden, Gene  407
Beaton, Rodney Betzi  16
Beatty, Clyde  957
Beatty, Robert  772, 790
Beauchamp, D. D.  46
Beaudine, William  153, 314, 550, 804
Beaumont, Victor  829
Beavers, Louise  129, 363
Beban, Bob  912
Beban, George, Jr.  201, 217
Beche, Robert  955, 961, 963, 968, 975, 987, 988, 1003, 1010
Beck, George  248
Beck, John  411
Beck, Thomas  365
Beckett, Scotty  167, 494
Beddoe, Don  46, 238, 338, 357, 402, 495, 661, 807
Bedell, Patsy  397
Bedford, Barbara  246, 764
Bedoya, Alfonso  17, 18
Beebe, Ford  863
Beebe, Jane  144
Beeby, Bruce  471, 837
Beecher, Elizabeth  670
Beecher, Janet  333, 366, 473
Beers, Bobby  760
Beery, Noah, Jr.  106, 240, 697
Beery, Noah, Sr.  105, 296, 491, 498, 565, 590, 862, 949, 1010
Beich, Albert  116, 209, 265, 268, 905
Beirute, Yerye  924

Bekassy, Stephen  219, 708, 921
Belasco, Leon  153, 204, 215, 273, 290, 314, 364, 779
Belden, Charles  918
Beldon, Eileen  596
Belgard, Arnold  575, 918
Belita  367
Bell, George  138, 1002
Bell, Hank  13, 50, 80, 106, 114, 124, 135, 162, 195, 234, 236, 256, 260, 298, 317, 394, 422, 466, 522, 541, 563, 569, 583, 593, 594, 620, 632, 633, 660, 670, 672, 688, 746, 760, 795, 839, 895, 907, 939, 940, 987
Bell, James  25, 81, 157, 197, 364, 436, 644, 914
Bell, Mostyn  379
Bell, Rodney  16, 46, 418
Bellah, James Warner  651
Bellak, George  384
Bellas, Leon  987
Bellen, Robert Leslie  63
Bellini, Nino  1001
Bellis, Guy  605
Belmont, Virginia  954
Belmore, Daisy  282
Belmore, Lionel  246, 347, 634
Beltran, Alma  402
Benaderet, Bea  595
Benard, Ray  438, 738, 957; *see also* Ray ("Crash") Corrigan; "Naba" the gorilla
Benedict, Billy  1034
Benedict, Brooks  510, 559, 952, 960, 991, 1010
Benedict, Richard  43, 181, 357, 472, 599, 789, 920
Benedict, William  119, 293, 351, 374, 394, 410, 413, 473, 488, 588, 706, 814, 864, 885, 910, 947, 949, 995
Benge, Wilson  158, 947, 952
Bennet, Spencer G.  52, 89, 97, 99, 124, 446, 502, 861, 950, 958, 967, 974, 982, 990, 991, 996, 997, 1001, 1002, 1005, 1011
Bennett, Ann  132
Bennett, Bruce  160, 335; *see also* Herman Brix

Bennett, Constance  18
Bennett, Fran  981
Bennett, Lee  157
Bennett, Marjorie  436
Bennett, Raphael  8, 91, 267, 408, 498, 542, 601, 611, 921, 961, 962, 987
Bennett, Richard  1033
Bennison, Andrew  432, 873
Benny, Joan  1034
The Benoits  367, 368
Benson, George  186
Benson, Hamlyn  858
Benson, James  1
Benson, Martin  185, 829
Bentley, Arthur  707
Bentley, E. C.  851
Beradino, John  407
Bercholz, Joseph  44, 777
Berela, Armanda  1028
Berens, Harold  829
Berg, Kid  772
Berg, Dr. Louis  609
Berge, Alphonse  814
Berke, William  59, 95, 104, 130, 159, 266, 331, 461, 524, 526, 567, 570, 574, 623, 629, 643, 645, 674, 693, 761, 814, 823, 930
Berkes, John  145
Berkova, Saundra  101
Berland, Jacques  558
Berle, Milton  1030
Berlin, Patsy  148
Berliner, Martin  379
Bernard, Barry  222
Bernard, Bert  290
Bernard, George  290
Bernard, Joelle  558
Bernard, Sam  368, 464, 512, 612, 818, 962, 972, 991
Bernard, Tom  933
Besbas, Peter  401
Besser, Joe  316, 595
Best, James  131, 909
Best, Willie  141, 284, 758, 911
Bestar, Barbara  519, 989
Bevan, Billy  444, 717, 927
Bevans, Clem  102, 280, 301, 457, 505, 730, 867, 933
The Beverly Hill Billies  56, 485
Bevis, Frank  901
Biberman, Abner  182, 270, 281, 983
Biby, Edward  709

Bice, Robert 37, 40, 49, 516, 801, 875, 977, 1006
Bickford, Charles 263, 280, 788, 819
The Big Broadcast 341
Big Tree, Chief John 332, 738, 975, 993
Bikel, Theodore 1, 165, 184
Bilbrook, Lydia 591
Bildt, Paul 383
"Bill," the Dog 210
Billie, Jose 935
Billings, Tex 855
Billingsley, Barbara 418, 853, 920
Bilson, George 325
Bing, Herman 429, 552
Birch, Paul 227, 909
Bird, Billie 575
Bird, Richard 82
Birell, Tala 285, 355, 385
Birgel, Willy 118
Bishop, Julie 316, 510, 689; see also Jacqueline Wells
Bissell, Whit 32, 156, 357, 713, 900
Bitgood, Dick 961
Black, Maurice 429
"Black Jack," the Horse 37, 38, 40, 61, 68, 102, 107, 125, 174, 176, 178, 179, 208, 249, 253, 255, 305, 437, 479, 480, 519, 527, 540, 600, 638, 671, 676, 684, 696, 724, 793, 831, 890, 903, 913, 929, 1023
Blackman, Don 979
Blackmer, Sidney 2, 19, 195, 246, 377, 413, 493, 557, 603, 666
Blackwell, Carlyle, Jr. 588
Blagoi, George 534
Blaine, James 961
Blair, Bob 425
Blair, George 6, 10, 161, 164, 181, 201, 209, 213, 224, 239, 265, 268, 274, 278, 355, 382, 390, 409, 441, 447, 452, 499, 599, 668, 701, 708, 709, 729, 730, 769, 789, 815, 818, 826, 852, 875, 881, 910, 920, 925
Blair, Joan 301, 500, 618, 729, 754, 910
Blair, Joe 797
Blair, Robert 660, 844, 965, 978, 997

Blair, W. J. 936
Blake, Bobby (Robert) 88, 115, 128, 137, 155, 298, 309, 353, 354, 378, 446, 481, 482, 483, 556, 559, 584, 675, 687, 694, 720, 721, 774, 792, 861, 891, 892, 896
Blake, Gladys 503
Blake, Larry J. 43, 65, 181, 472, 562, 879
Blake, Marie 910
Blake, Oliver 329, 505
Blake, Pamela 101, 748, 824, 970 see also Adele Pearce
Blake, Richard 151
Blakeney, Olive 155, 597, 665
Blanchard, Mari 531
Blandick, Clara 366
Blankfort, Henry 942
Blatty, William Peter 531
Blees, Robert 227
Bleifer, John 280, 315, 534, 995, 1001
Bletcher, Billy 112, 488, 615, 987, 988, 1012
Blin, Roger 3
Blomfield, Derek 11
Blondell, Joan 415, 1027
Bloom, Joe 772
Blore, Eric 180, 205, 917
Blount, Marguerite 688
Blue, Ben 244
Blue, Monte 27, 35, 65, 167, 256, 299, 433, 626, 642, 667, 703, 797, 939, 975, 986, 1007
Blystone, Stanley 34, 70, 214, 356, 364, 368, 373, 395, 581, 600, 629, 797, 822, 823, 846, 862, 870, 904, 959, 970, 982, 986, 988, 1008
Blythe, Betty 205, 452, 740, 764, 864, 879, 937
Boddey, Martin 186, 707
Boddy, Philip L. 121
Boehnel, William 246
Boetticher, Budd 84
Bogarde, Dirk 185, 186
Bohem, Endre 282, 311, 360, 421, 580, 870
Bohn, John 148
Bohnen, Roman 7, 917
Boland, Eddie 647
Boland, Mary 342, 459
Bollmann, Hannelore 136
Bolster, Anita 291, 444

Bolster, Anita Sharp 808
Bolton, Muriel Roy 301
Bonanova, Fortunio 18, 79, 314, 390, 511
Bond, Derek 858
Bond, Johnny 318, 680, 812, 862
Bond, Lilian 843
Bond, Ray 640
Bond, Richard 1004
Bond, Tommy 464
Bond, Ward 76, 155, 156, 187, 210, 399, 438, 460, 462, 616, 736, 830
Bondi, Beulah 1028, 1034
Bonner, Priscilla 488
Bonney, Gail 418
Boone, Ray 407
Booth, Adrian 14, 80, 87, 155, 213, 260, 338, 353, 422, 425, 441, 468, 538, 559, 594, 659, 697, 703, 767, 809, 872, 886, 958; see also Lorna Gray
Booth, Charles G. 361, 850
Booth, Karin 8, 838
Borchers, Cornell 184
Borden, Eddie 628
Borden, Eugene 109, 155, 402, 743
Bordman, Eleanor 1027
Borell, Louis 444
Borg, Sven Hugo 512, 709
Borg, Veda Ann 27, 45, 216, 220, 284, 450, 488, 581, 588, 592
Borgaze, Frank 389
Borgnine, Ernest 399, 423
Boros, Ferike 280, 765
Borzage, Bill 505
Borzage, Frank 505, 816
Bosworth, Hobart 598
Boteler, Wade 60, 140, 159, 167, 266, 396, 476, 489, 515, 603, 639, 677, 737, 763, 820, 877, 940, 942
Botiller, Dick 67, 135, 406, 491, 761, 931, 934, 974
Bouchey, Willis 362, 427
Bouden, Doris 1028
Boudreau, Lou 407
Bouer, John 282
Boulton, Matthew 709
Bovard, Mary 461, 476
Bowen, Harry 313, 639
Bower, Aubrey 3
Bower, Pamela 428, 851

# Name Index

Bowers, William 216
Bowland, Ed 346
Bowman, Empsie 596
Bowman, Lee 359
Bowman, Ralph 42, 570, 961; *see also* John Archer
Bowman, Rudy 115, 763
Box, Betty E. 165, 185, 186
Box, Sidney 1, 808
Boxer, John 707
Boyd, Beverly 532
Boyd, Joseph 957
Boyd, William 85, 223, 289, 617
Boylan, Malcolm Stuart 182, 280, 281, 490, 500, 633, 636, 682
Boyle, Jack 511, 941
Boyle, John, Jr. 941
Boyle, Ray 1009
Boyle, Walden 364
Boyle, William N. 152, 300, 707, 841
The Boys Choir of Saint Joseph's School 623
Bracey, Sidney 927
Brackett, Leigh 887
Bradbury, Robert North 110, 303, 434, 860, 907
Bradford, George 901
Bradford, John 543, 960, 1007
Bradford, Lane 22, 37, 49, 125, 170, 179, 221, 253, 340, 430, 482, 499, 544, 608, 626, 686, 696, 724, 759, 793, 832, 846, 929, 948, 964, 976, 977, 989, 1009, 1019
Bradford, Marshall 527, 984
Bradley, Betty 856
Bradley, Curley 376
Bradley, Grace 421, 664, 741
Bradley, Harry C. 158, 552, 726, 747
Bradley, PM-3/C John H. 689
Bradna, Olympe 1029
Brady, Alice 313
Brady, Buff 661
Brady, Ed 71, 373, 680, 763, 827, 931, 949, 963
Brady, Pat 13, 49, 91, 192, 292, 463, 466, 633, 648, 663, 732, 753, 758, 760, 798, 854, 865

Brady, Scott 399, 484, 581, 811, 888
Brady, William 205
Braham, Lionel 451
Branch, Houston 36, 120, 227, 285, 315, 592, 781, 802, 855, 900
Brand, Frank 709
Brand, George 495
Brand, Max 622, 736
Brand, Roland 901
Branden, Michael 6, 189, 251, 505, 656, 902; *see also* Archie Twitchell
Brandon, Henry 35, 327, 361, 534, 546, 625, 877, 898, 965
Brannan, Carol 238
Brannon, Fred C. 25, 37, 102, 125, 255, 305, 527, 671, 676, 684, 890, 914, 948, 950, 953, 954, 958, 959, 964, 966, 969, 970, 971, 973, 976, 977, 978, 979, 982, 984, 996, 997, 998, 999, 1002, 1009, 1019
Brasselle, Keefe 233, 1084
Brauner, Arthur 383
Braus, Mortimer 181
Breakston, George 403
Brecher, Egon 385
Breen, Bobby 398
Breen, Joe 698
Brehme, John 987
Bremen, Lennie 857
Bren, J. Robert 373
Brennan, Michael 858
Brennan, Ruth 90, 329, 538
Brennan, Walter 5, 80, 131, 155, 197, 704, 727, 736, 800, 912
Brennan, Walter, Jr. (Andy) 357, 402, 685, 912
Brent, Evelyn 603, 908, 1027
Brent, George 18, 407
Brent, Linda 377, 420, 545, 702
Brent, Lynton 35, 97, 144, 158, 167, 286, 408, 512, 543, 633, 760, 947, 949, 952, 961, 962, 991, 992
Brent, Roy 105, 470, 551, 565, 949, 952, 955, 1004, 1011
Bressart, Felix 389
Bretherton, Howard 54, 57, 74, 105, 258, 282, 337, 370,
438, 469, 566, 646, 687, 692, 839, 895, 910
The Brewer Kids 623
Brewster, Barbara 1028
Brewster, Carol 484
Brewster, Gloria 1028
Brian, David 2, 581, 836
Brian, Eddie 232
Brian, Mary 5, 520
Brice, Monte 397
Bridge, Alan 48, 66, 90, 162, 193, 329, 371, 387, 402, 426, 433, 470, 489, 513, 523, 538, 656, 770, 822
Bridge, Loie 536
Bridges, Beau 628
Bridges, Lloyd 338, 505, 706
Brier, Audren 397
Brierre, Maurice 322
Briggs, Harlan 240, 311, 513, 515, 767, 891
Bright, John 407
Brill, Leighton K. 749
Brinley, Charles 434, 907, 936
Brisbane, William 726
Briskin, Mort 460
Brissac, Virginia 219, 422, 516, 546, 734, 747, 824, 897, 919, 921
Brister, Robert 963
Bristol, John 987
Bristow, Gwen 402
Britt, May 716
Britton, Barbara 216, 644
Brix, Herman 955, 968, 975, 987; *see also* Bruce Bennett
The Aida Broadbent Girls 779
Brocco, Peter 32, 46, 239, 305, 359, 599, 838, 920, 998, 1019
Brock, Lou 238, 610, 744, 849
Broderick, Helen 450
Brodie, Buster 50
Brodie, Don 329, 521, 1000
Brodie, Steve 36, 150, 228, 668, 704
Bromberg, J. Edward 182, 361
Bromley, Sheila 410, 431, 766, 819; *see also* Sheila Mannors
Bronson, Betty 936
Bronson, Lillian 510, 653
Brook, Claude 160

# Name Index

Brook, Lyndon 1
Brook, Patrick 398
Brook, Terence 707
Brooke, Clifford 453
Brooke, Hillary 203, 382, 418, 743, 766, 783, 881
Brooke, Hugh 287
The Brooklyn Dodgers 665
Brooks, Barry 969, 971
Brooks, Beverley 808
Brooks, Howard 5
Brooks, Louise 570
Brooks, Phyllis 732
Brooks, Ralph 402
Brooks, Rand 7, 145, 320, 746, 793, 885, 889, 929
Brooks, Richard 511
Brophy, Edward 133, 341, 396, 552, 664, 702
Brower, Tom 433, 738
Brown, Beth 382
Brown, Boots 512
Brown, Bud 728
Brown, Charles D. 182, 248, 424, 918, 926
Brown, Donald H. 189, 348, 516, 550, 586, 734, 767, 842, 883, 902
Brown, George Carleton 19, 31, 71, 112, 464, 742, 819, 834, 941
Brown, Harry 689, 898
Brown, Helen 500
Brown, Hiram S., Jr. 947, 949, 965, 980, 985, 986, 992, 1012
Brown, James 80, 147, 217, 241, 260, 497, 689, 703, 704, 912, 922
Brown, Jerry 987, 989, 1006
Brown, Joe, Jr. 912
Brown, Joe E. 108, 112, 397, 1032
Brown, John 147
Brown, Johnny Mack 41, 69, 261, 307, 432, 435, 847, 873
Brown, Karl 116, 262, 281, 322, 400, 493, 500, 602, 666, 874
Brown, Lew 937
Brown, Melville 246
Brown, Naaman 994
Brown, Norma 656
Brown, Phil 505
Brown, Raymond 135, 870
Brown, Robert 808
Brown, Slavina 1028

Brown, Tom 201, 396, 535, 743, 744
Brown, Vanessa 389
Browne, Charles A. 117, 223
Browne, Lucille 863
Browne, Michael 149
Browning, Jill 883
Brownlee, Frank 20, 26, 169, 368, 395, 463, 498, 663, 712, 746, 755, 992
Bruce, David 243
Bruce, Gary 112, 258
Bruce, Lorraine 558
Bruce, Nigel 244
Bruce, Virginia 79, 450
Bruggeman, George 965
Brundige, Bill 147
Brune, Gabrielle 30
Bruner, Charles 956
Brunetti, Argentina 65, 199, 685, 920
Brunius, Jacques 428
Brunn, Frederic 364, 1001
Brunning, Harry 808
Bruno, Frank 986
Bruno, Leo 384
Bryan, Arthur Q. 329
Bryan, Ella 1027
Bryant, Buel 728, 955, 961, 968, 1012
Bryant, Lynette 747
Bryant, Nana 65, 214, 273, 338, 561, 612, 788, 905, 941
Bryar, Paul 656, 810, 1004
Bryde, June (June Gittleson) 467
Buazzelli, Tino 780
Buchanan, Edgar 131, 458, 766, 840
Buchanan, Elsa 385
Buchanan, Morris 402, 994
Buchel, Brian 82
"Buck," the Dog 1000
"Buck," the Great Dane 855
"Buck," the Wonder Dog 94, 489
Buck and Bubbles 31
Buckley, Buz 680, 747
Buckley, John 1004
Bucko, Ralph 34, 51, 74, 114, 266, 488, 948, 956, 959, 977, 993, 1002
Bucko, Roy 23, 34, 52, 92, 114, 166, 261, 408, 652, 948, 954, 964, 970, 977, 993, 1002

Budd, Norman 495, 627, 800, 830, 881, 925
Buetel, Jack 1033
Buferd, Marilyn 880
Buffington, Adele 117, 200, 493, 609, 717, 717, 789, 810
"Bullet," the Dog 214, 320, 371, 533, 572, 758, 768, 801, 846
Bunn, Earl 947, 951, 955, 956, 961, 963, 983, 985, 986, 1003
Bupp, Sonny 820
Bupp, Tommy 655
Burbridge, Betty 9, 114, 130, 132, 266, 291, 331, 353, 406, 465, 468, 489, 524, 526, 555, 559, 567, 574, 576, 601, 615, 623, 629, 643, 645, 674, 692, 693, 738, 761, 770, 776, 823, 877, 878, 883, 915, 930
Burgess, Dorothy 415
Burke, Billie 113
Burke, Brian 961
Burke, James 158, 254, 438, 557, 835
Burke, Kathleen 717
Burke, Larry 512
Burke, Michael 612
Burkett, James S. 101
Burnett, Dana 244
Burnett, W. R. 2, 162
Burnette, Smiley 34, 48, 52, 54, 56, 60, 66, 70, 75, 91, 92, 104, 124, 130, 135, 145, 195, 234, 266, 286, 291, 306, 317, 318, 322, 349, 351, 352, 369, 376, 408, 420, 421, 461, 465, 477, 485, 489, 491, 508, 537, 542, 543, 601, 607, 611, 620, 623, 632, 641, 642, 643, 649, 667, 673, 674, 681, 728, 732, 735, 737, 738, 761, 770, 776, 797, 863, 874, 878, 906, 936, 960, 1007, 1033
Burniston, Shirley 186
Burns, Bob 34, 89, 91, 115, 234, 276, 286, 306, 346, 448, 466, 502, 524, 566, 590, 602, 611, 615, 633, 657, 671, 674, 675, 678, 738, 855, 865, 866, 877, 889, 913, 916, 936, 949
Burns, Forest 694, 739, 955,

# NAME INDEX

959, 976, 977, 986, 987, 988, 1010
Burns, Fred  24, 35, 60, 71, 126, 130, 167, 195, 256, 266, 277, 308, 317, 352, 372, 374, 376, 378, 394, 434, 463, 466, 483, 522, 537, 567, 570, 601, 620, 625, 643, 652, 660, 674, 680, 723, 732, 737, 755, 763, 770, 776, 797, 798, 799, 855, 877, 878, 899, 907, 931, 939, 949, 987, 988, 1008
Burns, George  1034
Burns, Harry  408, 870, 972
Burns, Paul E.  155, 213, 338, 436, 452, 513, 588, 678, 796, 807
Burns, Robert E.  635, 643
Burns, Sandra  1034
Burnstine, Norman  29, 385
Burr, Raymond  205, 460, 881
Burroughs, Edgar Rice  980
Burrows, Bob  402
Burrud, Billy  525
Burson, Polly  953, 997
Burson, Wayne  914, 959, 996
Burt, Benny  705, 962
Burt, Frank  238
Burtis, Billy  564
Burtis, James  158, 552, 639
Burtis, Thomson  377
Burton, Frederick  78, 200, 310
Burton, George  58, 132, 863, 963, 988
Burton, John  778
Burton, Julian  474
Burton, Robert  436, 474, 654
Burton, Sam  115
Burton, Val  205, 486, 699
Busch, Mae  1033
Busch, Paul, Jr.  118
Bush, James  133, 369, 408, 904, 992
Bush, Maurice  428
Bushman, Francis X.  960
Bushman, Lenore  629
Busse, Enright  468
Bussey, Donia  356, 386, 455, 579, 834
Buster, Budd  13, 23, 41, 52, 64, 72, 88, 91, 110, 127, 130, 154, 162, 177, 190, 202, 226,

234, 261, 264, 302, 303, 307, 318, 337, 346, 353, 394, 435, 446, 578, 607, 620, 692, 721, 728, 774, 799, 827, 832, 847, 860, 885, 891, 904, 908, 913, 930, 949, 956, 961, 963, 965, 985, 1006, 1012
Butch and Buddy  398, 1030
Butler, Jimmy  747
Butler, John  960
Butler, John K.  4, 6, 54, 64, 65, 87, 125, 189, 192, 239, 260, 278, 284, 312, 316, 321, 327, 337, 338, 362, 441, 456, 467, 497, 513, 530, 550, 560, 561, 586, 599, 605, 607, 620, 656, 661, 706, 708, 732, 789, 795, 801, 807, 809, 811, 840, 883, 884, 887, 909
Butler, Roy  234, 351, 368, 466, 728, 895
Butterworth, Charles  740, 1029
Buzby, Flo  747
Byington, Spring  27
Byrd, Ralph  28, 76, 193, 232, 494, 757, 855, 960, 961, 962, 963, 1003
Byrne, Eddie  184, 772, 859
Byron, George  112, 358, 368, 391, 825, 952
Byron, Kathleen  707
Byron, Richard  218

The Cabin Kids  286, 673
Cabot, Bruce  15, 260, 494, 659, 810
Caesar, Arthur  31, 591
Cahill, Drew  951
Cahn, Sammy  666
Caine, Georgia  5, 59, 649
Cairns, Jessica  700
Cairns, Sally  397
Caits, Joe  296, 942
Caits, Louis  963
Calhern, Louis  532, 628
Calkins, Johnny  505, 750
Callahan, George E.  101, 610
Callam, Alex  154, 585, 814
Callard, Kay  233, 700
Callegari, Gian Paolo  518
Callow, Reginald "Reggie"  975
Calloway, Cab, and His Cotton Club Orchestra  477

Calvert, Charles  856
Calvert, E. H.  554
Calvert, Steve  994
Calvet, Corinne  595
Camargo, Ana  432, 866
Camax, Valentine  3
Cameron, Hugh  841
Cameron, Rod  80, 191, 227, 316, 329, 475, 538, 594, 644, 685, 690, 703, 766, 921, 972, 1001
Campan, Zanie  3
Campana, Nina  94, 388, 667, 866
Campanella, Roy  665
Campbell, Colin  213, 222, 701
Campbell, Louise  78
Campbell, Muriel  715
Campbell, Paul  890
Campbell, Reginald  282
Campbell, William  206
Candido, Candy  595
Cane, Charles  46, 48, 65, 80, 230, 413, 581, 789, 886
Canel, Leon  558
Cannon, Esma  596
Canova, Judy  103, 112, 356, 397, 436, 539, 613, 699, 740, 742, 743, 882, 894, 937, 1031, 1033, 1034
Canova, Tweeny  436, 882
Cansino, Carmela  195
Cansino, Rita (Rita Hayworth)  346
Cansino, Vernon  452
Canty, Marietta  46, 419
Canutt, Yakima  35, 97, 106, 107, 132, 146, 155, 162, 257, 267, 276, 277, 299, 308, 319, 337, 346, 377, 405, 406, 408, 411, 434, 448, 522, 526, 540, 541, 554, 570, 590, 602, 607, 624, 625, 647, 655, 675, 692, 693, 712, 719, 727, 753, 754, 877, 907, 916, 930, 948, 954, 955, 961, 967, 971, 980, 987, 990, 992, 993, 995, 1003, 1004, 1008, 1010, 1012
Cap, Franz  383
Capon, Paul  336
Cappella and Patricia  144
Cappo, Joe  16
Capuano, Luigi  242, 780
Carbajal, Tony  924

Carby, Fanny  808
Card, Bob  34, 60, 71, 526
Card, Ken  394
Cardwell, James  22, 161, 164, 192, 409, 656, 686
Carey, Ed  440
Carey, Harry, Jr.  505, 561, 651, 685, 802, 912
Carey, Harry, Sr.  15, 788, 822
Carey, Leonard  375, 507, 709, 733, 864, 945
Carey, Macdonald  474, 784
Carle, Richard  640
Carleton, Claire  2, 36, 151, 281, 295, 299, 356, 402, 487, 582, 644, 733
Carleton, George  6, 44, 164, 350, 482, 528, 608, 739, 815, 996, 997
Carleton, William P.  639, 869
Carlisle, James  678, 747, 949, 952, 954, 961, 966, 968
Carlisle, Mary  232, 618, 674
Carlos, Don  994
Carlson, Richard  423
Carlson, Shorty  376
Carlton, George  887
Carlyle, David  485, 640; *see also* Robert Paige
Carmen, Jean  23
Carmichael, Hoagy  836
Carmichael, Patsy  332
Carnahan, Suzanne  1028
Carney, Alan  338, 604
Carney, Bob  2, 581
Carol, Sue  1027
Caron, Patricia  735
Carpenter, Horace B.  23, 35, 41, 56, 72, 92, 105, 110, 115, 124, 127, 128, 134, 138, 167, 190, 234, 267, 286, 298, 302, 303, 308, 317, 373, 397, 410, 411, 433, 446, 448, 465, 467, 483, 537, 551, 555, 565, 578, 623, 624, 634, 641, 674, 680, 691, 693, 712, 719, 722, 731, 755, 839, 844, 847, 863, 883, 892, 897, 908, 916, 934, 988, 993, 1011
Carpenter, Jeanne  287
Carpenter, John  207, 531, 691, 832, 845
Carpenter, Ken  517
Carpenter, Paul  185, 700
Carr, Harry  675

Carr, Jack  78, 412
Carr, Jane  11
Carr, Marian  909
Carr, Mary  555
Carr, Michael  238, 340, 610, 744, 849, 969
Carr, Nat  598
Carr, Thomas  9, 39, 114, 166, 207, 555, 624, 630, 652, 670, 691, 719, 879, 968, 978, 1003
Carr, Trem  100, 245, 254, 434, 523, 869, 907
Carradine, John  325, 335, 399, 732, 880
Carrasco, Bill  987
Carre, Bart  863
Carrell, Anita  238
Carrier, Albert  575
Carrillo, Leo  477, 492
Carrington, Jack  1012
Carroll, Ann  654
Carroll, Curt  685
Carroll, Georgia  1028
Carroll, John  17, 33, 46, 217, 235, 243, 273, 343, 345, 364, 546, 595, 800, 928, 1010
Carroll, June  16
Carroll, Lucia  1027
Carroll, Martha  155
Carroll, Virginia  278, 316, 323, 419, 464, 510, 583, 766, 894, 950, 953, 958, 961, 972, 992
Carson, Charles  287
Carson, Ken  376, 755
Carson, Robert  963
Carson, Sunset  9, 39, 50, 75, 92, 114, 124, 166, 207, 234, 555, 630, 652, 670, 691, 719
Carstairs, John Paddy  858
Carter, Ben  205
Carter, Harrison  96
Carter, William  389
Cartledge, Billy  50
Caruso, Anthony  109, 120, 221, 424, 431, 572, 610, 690, 909
Caruth, Burr  97, 134, 276, 308, 313, 352, 524, 583, 629, 649, 660, 878, 960
Carver, Lynne  373, 463, 501, 798, 937
Carver, Peter  336
Cary, Falkland  700
Cary, Lucian  200, 201

Case, Robert Ormand  279
Casey, Jack  987
Casey, Sue  708
Casey, Taggart  404
Caskey, Ted  617
Cason, John  20, 61, 172, 621, 631, 635, 676, 696, 712, 908, 959, 964, 979, 981
Caspary, Vera  416, 733
Cass, Maurice  109, 139, 180, 212, 263, 678, 767, 941, 967
Cass, Monty  632
The Cass County Boys  656, 678, 739, 848, 866
Cassell, Wally  2, 121, 538, 689, 789, 830, 836, 912
Cassidy, Edward  9, 13, 24, 46, 50, 61, 68, 69, 81, 105, 110, 126, 128, 130, 132, 138, 146, 166, 178, 179, 207, 217, 266, 337, 346, 354, 408, 432, 465, 470, 495, 508, 549, 556, 585, 586, 615, 629, 634, 649, 662, 674, 688, 692, 697, 719, 746, 774, 776, 792, 795, 798, 832, 846, 861, 873, 883, 916, 931, 947, 949, 952, 956, 963, 968, 978, 986, 990, 992, 1000, 1002, 1003
Cassidy, Jim  963
Cassidy, John F.  693
Cassity, James C.  474
Castaine, Robert B.  31
Castel, Colette  558
Castelot, Jacques  188
Casteneda, Movita  914
Castile, Lynn  479
Castillo, Gloria  888
Castle, Dolores  628
Castle, Don  452
Castle, Mary  427
Castle, Peggie  43, 327
Catlett, Walter  244, 317, 343, 356, 419, 905
Caudebec, Al  644
Cavan, Allan  66, 134, 346, 410, 523, 526, 615, 961, 963, 987, 1000
Cavan, Jess  34, 88, 128, 166, 234, 377, 502, 565, 680, 723, 839
Cavanagh, Paul  345
Cavanaugh, Hobart  141, 197, 381, 557, 702, 843
Caven, Taylor  26, 270, 391, 395, 483, 486, 503, 582,

# NAME INDEX

726, 731, 983, 995
Cavendish, Constance 417
Cavers, Alice 765
Cawthorn, Joseph 699
The CBS-KMBC Texas
  Rangers 130
Cecil, Fusty 75
Centa, Antonio 259
Central Newsreel Studios of
  Moscow 506
Cey, Jacques 152, 165
Chaffey, Don 837
Chalmers, W. G. 829
Chamberlain, Cyril 185, 186,
  596, 808, 858
Chamberlin, Howland 17,
  197, 359, 800
Chambers, Joe 983
Chambers, Wheaton 54, 62,
  74, 207, 482, 510, 549, 565,
  602, 773, 774, 913, 949,
  953, 962, 965, 982, 997,
  1002
"Champion," the Horse 34,
  48, 56, 66, 70, 91, 104, 130,
  135, 145, 195, 266, 286, 291,
  306, 318, 351, 352, 376,
  465, 488, 489, 491, 508,
  537, 542, 543, 601, 611,
  623, 632, 641, 642, 643,
  649, 667, 673, 674, 681,
  728, 735, 737, 738, 761,
  770, 776, 797, 863, 874,
  906, 936
"Champion, Jr.," the Horse
  656, 678, 739, 848, 866
Chandler, Bill 1006
Chandler, Chick 116, 351,
  515, 598, 613, 682, 882,
  905, 941
Chandler, David 917
Chandler, Eddy 101, 710, 742
Chandler, Fletcher 338
Chandler, George 96, 288,
  309, 323, 377, 424, 441,
  467, 488, 507, 678, 710,
  736, 754, 783, 809, 819,
  894
Chandler, Lane 134, 322,
  377, 413, 433, 473, 590,
  639, 680, 705, 731, 763,
  916, 975, 987, 990, 1007,
  1010, 1084
Chandler, Tanis 6, 109
Chaney, Creighton 735; see
  also Lon Chaney, Jr.
Chaney, Lon, Jr. 160, 543,

1007; see also Creighton
  Chaney
Chanslor, Roy 369, 399
Chantler, David 454
Chapin, Anne Morrison 797
Chapin, Billy 838
Chapin, Jack 955, 986
Chapin, Michael 25, 81, 157,
  750, 871, 903, 914
Chapin, Robert 78
Chaplin, Charles F. 856
Chaplin, Prescott 236, 512,
  742, 921
Chaplin, Saul 666
Chapman, Edward 165, 443,
  596
Chapman, Freddie 88, 128,
  138, 298, 720, 845
Chapman, Marguerite 1004
Chapman, Pattee 894
Chapman, Tedwell 216
Charles, Frances 925
Charlita 80, 758, 840
Charlot, Andre 825
Charney, Kim 283
Charteris, Leslie 683
Charters, Spencer 7, 141, 252,
  280, 313, 414, 486, 501,
  552, 582, 737, 820, 919
Chase, Alden 878
Chase, Borden 231, 236, 389
Chase, Frank 43
Chase, Howard 465, 968,
  988
Chase, Stephen 10, 46, 208,
  238, 253, 402, 547, 807
Chatterton, Tom 9, 107, 115,
  124, 128, 137, 142, 175, 321,
  353, 446, 464, 479, 482,
  483, 564, 586, 621, 674,
  692, 721, 774, 844, 861,
  878, 896, 952, 965, 975,
  978, 1011
Cheatham, Jack 960
Checchi, Andrea 242, 780
The Checkerboard Band 761
Chefe, Jack 410, 814, 1001
Chekhov, Michael 765
Cheney, J. Benton 87, 310,
  408, 420, 441, 466, 470,
  660, 663, 712, 732, 876
Cherkose, Eddie 291, 728,
  955, 961, 963, 1012
Cheron, Andre 960
Cherry, Robert 397
Chesebro, George 56, 80,
  114, 128, 166, 170, 253, 260,

305, 354, 378, 395, 422,
  433, 482, 483, 488, 524,
  527, 567, 573, 590, 615,
  622, 632, 639, 655, 672,
  684, 691, 693, 697, 719,
  763, 770, 774, 792, 845,
  846, 863, 891, 896, 899,
  928, 940, 948, 950, 955,
  958, 959, 967, 970, 978,
  996, 997, 1000, 1002, 1003
Cheshire, Harry 6, 22, 42,
  80, 217, 235, 333, 447, 505,
  536, 588, 734, 739, 744,
  771, 803, 826, 842
Chester, Bob, and His
  Orchestra 856
Chester, Hal E. 901
Chester, William L. 975
Chevalier, Albert 859
Chevie, Edmond 206
Ching, William 36, 46, 538,
  703, 727, 800, 912
Chinita 343
Chiquita 390
"Chiquita," the monkey 979
Chirello, George "Shorty"
  451
Chissell, Noble "Kid" 392,
  512, 750
Chitty, Erik 837
Chivers, David 336
Chodorov, Jerome 12, 158,
  272
Chorre, Clarence 975
Chorre, Gertrude 975
Chorre, Sonny 642, 975
Christian, Diana 840
Christian, Helen 1010
Christine, Virginia 285, 380,
  516, 584, 922
Christopher, Gene 964, 973
Christopher, Kay 125, 759
Christy, Dorothy 144, 155,
  455, 588, 672, 728
Christy, Eileen 363, 581, 802,
  830
Christy, Ken 48, 710
Christy, Whitey 771
Chrysler, Frank 987
Chrystal, Belle 596
Chuman, Howard 219, 708
Church, Claire 521, 552
Churchill, Berton 193, 412,
  726, 764
Ciannelli, Eduardo 248, 259,
  779; see also Edward Cian-
  nelli

Ciannelli, Edward 992; see also Eduardo Ciannelli
Cisar, George 698
Claire, Arleen 189, 765
Claire, Willis 375
Clampett, Bob 1013
Clark, Barbara 397
Clark, Bob 989
Clark, Cliff 176, 239, 364, 599, 600, 840, 890, 959
Clark, Colbert 158, 341, 429, 485, 927
Clark, Dane 472, 505
Clark, Davison 76, 171, 265, 602, 625, 906, 992, 1009
Clark, Edward 208, 329, 495, 831
Clark, Ernest 186
Clark, Gloria 581
Clark, Gordon 1012
Clark, Harry 367
Clark, Harvey 159, 735, 741
Clark, John 562
Clark, Judy 760, 803, 815, 959
Clark, Mamo 280, 1000
Clark, Maurice 821
Clark, Petula 841
Clark, Roger 218, 749, 803
Clark, Ronald 829
Clark, Roydon 644
Clark, Russ 886
Clark, Steve 23, 37, 67, 69, 102, 115, 135, 177, 202, 226, 261, 302, 305, 307, 422, 433, 435, 519, 578, 650, 827, 847, 871, 948, 959, 970
Clark, Wallis 210, 339, 413, 457, 745
Clarke, David 65, 689, 898
Clarke, Mae 131, 161, 243, 322, 347, 360, 682, 789, 830, 926, 984
Clarke, Richard 991
Clarke, Robert 215, 786, 981
Clauser, Al, and His Oklahoma Outlaws 667
Clavering, Eric 683
Cleary, Leo 49, 176, 627
Clement, Clay 29, 322, 347, 438, 439
Clement, Dora 878
Clement, Greta 604
Clemente, Steve 947, 995, 1008
Clements, John 30
Clements, Stanley 605

Cleveland, George 155, 246, 352, 464, 466, 511, 522, 551, 567, 576, 590, 594, 685, 764, 797, 850, 854, 882, 894, 934, 963, 965, 987, 1000
Clifford, Charles L. 28
Clifford, Jack 364, 411, 954, 1003
Clifford, Peggy Ann 808
Clift, Denison 209, 709
Clifton, Elmer 64, 168, 794, 952
Clifton, Herbert 413, 643
Cline, Roy 987
Clinton, Walter 65
Clive, E. E. 833
Close, John 43, 46, 562, 787
Cloutier, Suzanne 186
Clute, Chester 46, 112, 129, 204, 220, 330, 344, 366, 397, 419, 520, 550, 747, 849, 902, 905, 927
Clyde, Andy 103, 593, 654
Clyde, David 282
Clyde, Jean 596
Clyde, June 139
Coates, Phyllis 208, 480, 979, 994
Coats, Tommy 20, 114, 166, 258, 294, 395, 526, 537, 555, 570, 686, 719, 739, 773, 861, 863, 930, 965, 977, 978, 983, 985, 986, 988, 996, 1002, 1004, 1008
Cobb, Edmund 22, 34, 49, 66, 68, 89, 92, 107, 114, 143, 154, 162, 166, 207, 221, 253, 267, 318, 321, 335, 340, 425, 436, 467, 470, 473, 483, 488, 551, 556, 566, 586, 608, 630, 652, 656, 686, 691, 694, 724, 730, 738, 750, 759, 770, 774, 776, 792, 795, 812, 840, 889, 897, 908, 915, 929, 931, 951, 955, 956, 957, 959, 962, 963, 967, 968, 971, 972, 973, 977, 978, 987, 989, 1000, 1002, 1010, 1012
Cobb, Irvin S. 791
Cobb, Lee J. 654
Cobbledock, Gordon 407
Coburn, Charles 820, 1028
Coby, Fred 156, 973
Cochran, Steve 131, 901

Cochrane, Frank 82
Cochrane, Nick 330
Cody, Bill 972, 991
Cody, Inez 987
Cody, Iron Eyes 90, 260, 533, 564, 593, 642, 647, 679, 849, 876, 939, 940, 975, 986, 987, 995
Cody, J. W. 895, 987
Cody, Joe 154
Coe, Peter 325, 689, 912
Coe, Vivian 949
Coen, Franklin 232, 247
Coffin, Tristram 48, 63, 81, 87, 145, 178, 217, 386, 427, 462, 484, 516, 544, 652, 661, 739, 848, 876, 963, 966, 978, 984, 992, 995, 999, 1004
Cogan, Dick 786, 969, 998
Coghlan, Frank, Jr. 941, 947
Cohen, Albert J. 19, 31, 108, 112, 182, 187, 204, 231, 343, 385, 415, 464, 577, 613, 636, 666, 742, 743, 825, 911, 941
Cohen, Bennett 9, 39, 114, 166, 175, 207, 257, 277, 551, 555, 630, 652, 670, 691, 719, 731, 868, 931
Cohen, Octavus Roy 396, 592
Coke, Edward 961
Colby, Ralph 883
Coldeway, Anthony 97, 124, 171, 483, 702, 812, 861, 862, 877, 892, 905, 931
Cole, Doris 800
Cole, George 901
Cole, Lester 5, 244, 347, 603
Cole, Mildred 479
Cole, Royal K. 63, 213, 886, 952, 966, 970, 974, 977, 984, 991, 997, 999, 1001, 1005
Colebrook, Edward 388
Coleman, Caryl 456
Coleman, Charles 294, 455, 588, 740
Coleman, Claudia 521
Coleman, Robert 217
Coleman, Ruth 568
Coles, Mildred 178, 540, 743
Colleano, Bonar 837
Coller, Russell 963
Collier, Lois 180, 267, 560,

564, 585, 621, 692, 904, 908, 937, 969
Collins, Cora Sue 313, 398, 869
Collins, G. Pat 239
Collins, Joan 772
Collins, Lewis D. 196, 439, 481, 639, 764
Collins, Ray 338, 766
Collyer, June 1027, 1032, 1034
Colmans, Edward 316, 402
Colmes, Walter 251, 370, 407, 814, 856, 917, 923
Colonna, Jerry 31, 367, 368, 487, 740
Colteaux, Juanita 377
Comandini, Adele 237
Comfort, Lance 471, 829
Companeez, Jacques 11
Compson, Betty 83, 117, 146, 429
Compton, Fay 417
Compton, John 538, 766, 828, 978
Compton, Joyce 140, 213, 271, 283, 313, 348, 640, 705, 732, 741, 911
Comstock, William 330
Conden and Bohland 510
Condon, Charles 541, 822
Condos, Nick 158
Conklin, Chester 292, 293, 373, 394, 464, 663, 755, 771, 934, 949, 978, 1033
Conklin, Frank 225, 992
Conlan, Paul 699
Conley, Onest 617
Conlin, Jimmy 16, 368, 464, 649
Conn, Billy 592
Connor, Allen 308, 822, 1000, 1003
Connor, Frank 43
Connor, Kenneth 596
Connors, Touch (Mike) 390, 867
Conover, Theresa Maxwell 870
Conrad, Charles 32
Conrad, Eddie 45, 376
Conrad, Jack 288, 428
Conrad, Mikel 357, 495
Considine, Bob 357
Constantine 765
Conte, Steve 1006
Conway, Bert 610, 925

Conway, Lita 985
Conway, Morgan 48, 99
Conway, Richard S. 933
Conway, Robert 112, 545
Conway, Russ 610
Coogan, Jackie 206, 531
Coogan, Robert 398
Cook, Clyde 605, 778
Cook, Donald 53, 117, 282, 439, 764, 870
Cook, Elisa, Jr. 2, 743, 836
Cook, Frank 893
Cook, Judy 464
Cook, Tommy 407, 750, 949, 980
Cook, Baldy 1003
Cooke, Allan 765
Cooke, Hal 961
Cooke, Victor Ray 410
Cookson, Peter 44, 284
Cooley, Marjorie 850
Cooley, Spade 112, 351, 760
Coontz, Bill 335, 531, 619
Cooper, Ben 199, 211, 227, 241, 316, 329, 399, 423, 561, 581, 704, 781, 830, 922
Cooper, Bobby 709
Cooper, Clancy 169, 173, 974
Cooper, Dee 719
Cooper, Dennis 923
Cooper, George 200, 223, 239, 598, 741
Cooper, Georgia 470
Cooper, Jack 428
Cooper, James Fenimore 173
Cooper, Jeanne 711
Cooper, Ken 135, 145, 306, 351, 395, 632, 647, 673, 735, 755, 959, 963, 968, 987, 1008
Cooper, Les 987
Cooper, Melville 343
Cooper, Merian C. 616, 651, 791
Cooper, Olive 7, 37, 71, 91, 145, 158, 195, 244, 299, 311, 322, 340, 367, 369, 374, 396, 400, 408, 414, 429, 511, 515, 521, 532, 557, 563, 639, 640, 657, 699, 714, 715, 723, 737, 739, 752, 804, 821, 939
Cooper, Ted 25, 914
Cooper, Tex 162, 166, 473, 488, 489, 721, 795, 878, 897, 928, 956, 987, 996
Coote, Robert 717

Copland, Aaron 628
Coplen, Yorke 403
Corbett, Ben 24, 67, 134, 291, 374, 895
Corby, Ellen 378, 703, 882, 922
Corday, Mara 418, 802
Corday, Sandra 855
Cording, Harry 162, 258, 469, 954, 983, 985
Cordova, Fred 974
Corey, Jeff 235, 338, 364, 582, 659, 736, 898
Corey, Jim 60, 69, 132, 135, 175, 266, 291, 302, 306, 307, 372, 374, 376, 395, 483, 488, 551, 567, 583, 602, 615, 657, 673, 693, 723, 763, 770, 847, 873, 877, 936
Corey, Joseph 2
Corey, Wendell 328, 428, 912
Cormack, George 859
Corrado, Gino 46, 109, 464, 554, 779, 795
Correll, Mady 385
Corrigan, D'Arcy 12
Corrigan, Lloyd 274, 293, 335, 355, 408, 414, 419, 442, 444, 478, 532, 669, 710, 752
Corrigan, Ray ("Crash") 95, 132, 140, 276, 308, 319, 331, 346, 400, 438, 524, 526, 567, 570, 574, 615, 624, 629, 645, 647, 655, 693, 822, 823, 846, 855, 915, 930, 993, 1007, 1008; see also Ray Benard; "Naba," the gorilla
Corsaro, Franco 1004
Corson, William 1012
Cortes, Armand 947
Cortese, Valentina 454
Cortez, Arthur 184
Cortez, Ricardo 63, 380
Corthell, Herbert 158, 742
Corum, Bill 1020
Cosentino, Nicholas 920
Cosgrove, Douglas 916
Cosgrove, Luke 394
Cosmopolitan Pictures 5
Costa, Robert 328
Costello, Don 298, 482
Costello, Grace 398
Costello, Lou 1030
Costello, Maurice 416, 674

Costello, Willy 489
Coster, Nicolas 120, 561
Cota, David 13
Cotlow, Louis 944
Cotner, Carl 488
Cotton, Carolina 734
Coulouris, George 165, 185, 186
Courdaye, Lorn 952
Court, Emerton 829
Courtemarsh, Gerald 1023
Courtleigh, Stephen 935
Courtney, Inez 341
Covan, DeForest 979, 994
Cowan, Ashley 235
Cowan, Jerome 44, 197, 279, 348, 397, 488, 510, 550, 618, 715, 732, 918
Cowan, Maurice 858
Cowan, Sada 245
Cox, Morgan B. 59, 960, 965, 993, 1000, 1003, 1010, 1012
Cox, Victor 34, 71, 234, 376, 625, 770, 947, 948, 949, 965, 978, 1012
Cox, Vivian A. 808
Coy, Johnny 203
Coy, Walter 404, 875
Coyle, John T. 94
Crabbe, Larry "Buster" 130, 431
Crabtree, Arthur 233, 782
Craig, Catherine 604
Craig, Hal 952
Craig, James 474
Craig, May 616
Craig, Yvonne 206
Cram, Mildred 521
Cramer, Richard 54, 281, 307, 339, 440, 634, 827, 847, 860
Crane, Frank Hall 961
Crane, Jimmy 505
Crane, Richard 18, 98, 211, 243, 437, 530, 585, 747, 831, 922, 1019, 1076
Cravat, Noel 972, 998
Craven, Frank 313, 511, 1034
Craven, James 166, 178, 510, 685, 721, 768, 853, 903, 966, 969, 984, 997
Craven, John 747
Cravens, Mozelle 620
Crawford, Broderick 235
Crawford, Joan 399
Crawford, John 356, 447,
480, 547, 754, 818, 948, 954, 970, 971, 976, 977, 999, 1006, 1009, 1019
Crawford, Oliver 283
Creed, Roger 50, 970
Crehan, Joseph 10, 22, 60, 101, 116, 126, 147, 187, 200, 201, 220, 260, 266, 309, 310, 355, 422, 459, 462, 517, 522, 528, 529, 593, 605, 606, 793, 852, 927
Crichton, Charles 184
Cripps, Kernan 101, 266, 346, 958, 960, 961, 967
Crisp, Donald 1034
Criswell, Floyd 992, 1003, 1009
Crocker, Harry 749
Crockett, Dick 787, 947, 969, 973
Crockett, Luther 153, 920
Croft-Cooke, Rupert 222
Cromwell, Richard 133, 778, 893, 927
Crosby, Bing 1032
Crosby, Bob 666, 740; see also Bob Crosby and His Orchestra
Crosby, Bob, and His Orchestra with the Bobcats 740; see also Bob Crosby
Crosby, Wade 14, 39, 119, 315, 345, 373, 377, 378, 418, 548, 668, 670, 718, 794, 835, 842, 871
Crosman, Henrietta 244
Crosson, Robert 362
Crouse, Russell 937
Crowe, Eileen 616
Crowe, Lt. Col. H. P. 689
Crowell, William 53
Crowley, David 428
Crowley, Kathleen 120
Croy, Homer 313
Cruze, James 133, 263, 609, 927
Culler, Sid 488
Culver, Roland 700
Cummings, Billy 50, 128, 556
Cummings, Robert 365
Cunard, Grace 234, 298
Cunningham, Cecil 145, 377
Cunningham, Joe 7, 140, 410
Curci, Gennaro 477
Currie, Finlay 287
Currie, Louise 776, 947, 991

Currier, Mary 17, 149
Curtis, Alan 636, 1007
Curtis, Billy 355, 823
Curtis, Dick 41, 69, 88, 143, 261, 307, 435, 519, 617, 659, 694, 724, 750, 842, 847, 889, 896, 928, 973
Curtis, Donald 123, 237, 373, 397, 908
Curtis, Jack 434, 907
Curtis, Keene 451
Curtis, Ken 616, 651, 964
Curwood, James Oliver 94
Cusack, Cyril 471
Cusanelli, Peter 155
Cushing, Peter 454, 926
Cushman, Dan 836
Cuthbertson, Allan 553
"Cyclone," the Horse 50, 794, 915

Dae, Frank 141, 800, 999
Daheim, John 129, 914, 952, 953, 958, 959, 966, 969, 970, 971, 972, 991, 995, 997, 999, 1001, 1002, 1004, 1005, 1009, 1019; see also John Day
Dahlen, Armin 184
Dainton, Noel 683
D'Albert, Suzanne 830
Dale, Arvon 950, 954, 958, 971, 972, 983, 984, 995, 999, 1004
Dale, Esther 44, 800, 803, 893
Dale, Frank 104
Dale, James 364, 754, 948, 954, 966, 1004
Dale, Michael 562
Dale, Virginia 315, 737
Daley, Jack 968, 1003
Dalmas, Herbert 679, 682
Dalroy, Rube 67
D'Alvarez, Marguerite 16
Daly, Jack 838
Dalya, Jacqueline 416, 751
d'Ambricourt, Adrienne 36
Damler, John 2, 227
Danceil, Linda 402
Dandridge, Dorothy 31, 343, 416
Dandridge, Ruby 350
Danieli, Luciana 259
Daniell, Henry 116, 898
Daniels, Bette 686
Daniels, Hank 378

## Name Index

Daniels, Harold  190, 541
Daniels, Keith  360
Daniels, Mark  384
Daniely, Lisa  471
Danko, Betty  958
Dann, Roger  364
Dannay, Frederic  476, 764; see also Ellery Queen
Dannet, Sylvia G. L.  879
Dano, Royal  399
Dano, Steve  384
Dante, Tony  357
Danvers-Walker, Bob  944
DaPron, Louis  666
Darcy, Sheila  761, 1012
Dare, Midgie  397
Darien, Frank  27, 216, 361, 396, 677, 740, 873, 874, 906, 986
Darling, W. Scott  246, 639
Darmour, Roy  75, 364, 464, 512, 961, 1005
Darnell, Linda  156
Darrell, Steve  22, 107, 109, 323, 528, 549, 563, 662, 671, 748, 835, 872, 875, 948, 970
Darrin, Michael  335
Darrin, Sonia  224, 364
Darro, Frankie  321, 605, 816, 864
Darwell, Jane  101, 635, 791, 800, 849, 945
DaSilva, Henry  79
Davenport, Doris  45, 1034
Davenport, E. L.  364
Davenport, Harry  141, 205, 217, 278, 296, 315, 339, 361, 503, 514, 557, 576, 714, 726
Davenport, Havis  698
Davidson, John  947, 952, 962, 968, 985, 995, 997, 1001
Davidson, Leon  1003
Davidson, Ronald  61, 161, 403, 944, 947, 949, 951, 952, 953, 955, 956, 958, 959, 961, 962, 963, 964, 965, 967, 968, 969, 972, 973, 974, 976, 979, 980, 981, 982, 983, 986, 987, 988, 989, 990, 991, 992, 993, 994, 995, 996, 997, 998, 1001, 1002, 1003, 1004, 1005, 1006, 1009, 1010, 1011, 1012, 1019

Davidson, William B.  5, 378, 593, 752, 809, 816
Davies, Emlen  781, 894, 938
Davies, Glenda  808
Davies, Jack  185
Davies, Lloyd G.  627
Davies, Richard  804
Davis, Allan  963
Davis, Art  306, 667, 681, 770, 855
Davis, Audry  306, 735
Davis, Bette  1034
Davis, Elaine  32
Davis, Gail  170, 221, 255, 430
Davis, George  109, 708
Davis, Georgia  358, 747, 779
Davis, Jim  80, 90, 199, 217, 326, 329, 402, 423, 427, 484, 538, 561, 619, 644, 697, 703, 727, 836, 888, 921, 922
Davis, Joan  937
Davis, Karl  474, 654, 836
Davis, Owen, Jr.  388, 819
Davis, Ray  728
Davis, Robert  979
Davis, Robert O.  585, 986, 1004; see also Rudolph Andres
Davis, Rufe  42, 123, 264, 267, 391, 445, 564, 573, 585, 602, 621, 679, 844, 877, 904, 908
Davis, Shirley  608
Davis, Stanley  330, 733
Davis, Wee Willie  628
Davray, Jo  558
Dawn, Isabel  45, 187, 293, 367, 415, 462, 636, 843, 937
Dawson, Billy  532
Dawson, Hal K.  235
Day, Dennis  742
Day, Doris  680, 819, 893
Day, John  678, 994; see also John Daheim
Day, Marie  779
Daye, Ruth  941
Dea, Marie  558
Deacon, Richard  4, 436, 909
de Alva, Raquel  751
Dean, Eddie  195, 267, 405, 408, 541, 573, 728, 773, 906, 988
Dean, Ivor  553
Dean, Jean  793, 999

Dean, Jo Ann  622
Dean, Marga  108
Dean, William  397
Deane, Shirley  601
Deans, Herbert  36
Dearden, Basil  772
Dearing, Edgar  189, 560
Dearing, Sayre  402
DeBanzie, Brenda  165, 185
deBriac, Jean  109
De Bruce, Jean  558
de Brulier, Nigel  196, 947, 1010
DeCarlo, Yvonne  173, 237, 454, 941
Deckers, Eugene  185
de Cordoba, Pedro  153, 473, 778
de Cordova, Leander  420, 583, 960, 1012
de Corsia, Ted  431
Dee, Frances  462
Deems, Douglas  332, 612
Deeping, Warwick  869
DeFreest, Babe  956, 993, 995, 997, 1005, 1011
DeGarro, Harold  960
DeGaw, Boyce  45, 367, 415
Deghy, Guy  184, 808
DeGolyer, Mary  627
de Grunwald, Anatole  30
Dehner, John  109, 419, 424, 559, 811, 879, 891
Dein, Edward  591
Dekker, Albert  217, 251, 373, 377, 604, 928, 937
Delacruz, Joe  862, 947, 949, 957, 968, 1008, 1012
De Laurentiis, Ponto  716
Delbat, Germaine  165
Delevanti, Cyril  101
Dell, Dorothea  859
Dell, Myrna  668
Delmar, Al  987
Delmar, Kenny  1014
Delmas, Herbert  573
de Loos, Janna  419
Del Rey, Nita  215
del Rey, Paquita  195
Del Rey, Pilar  402
Del Rio, Diana  636
Del Rio, Dolores  1027, 1028
Deltgen, Rene  118
Del Vando, Poppy  13
DeMain, Gordon  112, 993
Demarest, William  139, 341, 398, 418, 664, 666, 918, 1032

DeMario, Donna 21; see also
   Donna Martell
DeMario, Tony 964
DeMarney, Derrick 790
Demetrio, Anna 76, 93, 940
DeMille, Katherine 372
DeMond, Albert 10, 52, 63,
   73, 93, 124, 179, 201, 224,
   238, 264, 355, 409, 439,
   452, 480, 495, 521, 547,
   564, 608, 621, 627, 646,
   648, 679, 764, 845, 853,
   881, 885, 904, 913, 920,
   953, 958, 967, 982, 990,
   996, 997
DeMond, Robert 572
de Montez, Rico 79, 195,
   974, 1005
Demourelle, Vic 491
Denby, Emanuel 384
Dench and Stewart 367, 368
Denham, Maurice 185
Denison, Clift 709
Denison, Leslie 237
D'Ennery, Guy 142, 602,
   965, 1012
Denning, Richard 216, 312,
   368, 382
Dennis, Geoffrey 880
Dennis, Phil 189
Dennis, Robert C. 472
Denny, Reginald 400
DeNormand, George 489,
   776, 951, 952, 955, 960,
   960, 963, 968, 972, 981,
   985, 988, 993, 1001, 1007
DeNuccio, Jerome 975
DePalma, Walter 641
Depp, Harry 59, 101, 318,
   413, 574, 597, 653
deRavenne, Charles 360
Derek, John 704, 830
DeRita, Joe 251
Derr, E. B. 173
Derr, Richard 384
Derrick, George 779
Dertano, Robert C. 401
de Sa, Alfredo 18, 79
DeSales, Francis 811, 900
DeSimone, Bonnie 661
DeSimone, John 495, 925,
   969
Desmond, William 110, 234,
   934, 939, 1008
Desmonde, Jerry 858
Desney, Ivan 558
DeSoto, Henri 747

DeStefani, Joseph 623, 965
De Tolly, Lola 534
de Valdez, Carlos 67
Deverall, Helen 64
Devine, Andy 51, 214, 217,
   221, 260, 269, 294, 422,
   528, 546, 549, 771, 871
Devlin, Joe 462, 512, 718,
   740
Dew, Eddie 54, 408, 620,
   712, 797, 947, 961, 968,
   972, 973, 986, 992
Dewey, Earle S. 375, 509
Dewhurst, William 82
de Wit, Jacqueline 436
DeWolf, Karen 83, 159, 590,
   642, 679, 680
Dexter, Al 591
Dexter, Maury 550
DeZurik, Carolyn 42
DeZurik, Mary Jane 42
Diamond, Bobby 418
Diamond, Don 619
Diaz, Ed 987
Dibbs, Kem 160, 766, 811,
   867
Dickenson, Elizabeth 665
Dickerson, Dudley 415, 1004
Dickey, Basil 948, 950, 952,
   953, 954, 956, 958, 966,
   967, 971, 974, 978, 982,
   990, 991, 996, 997, 1001,
   1002, 1005, 1011
Dickinson, Angie 335
Dickson, Gloria 7, 490
Diebold, Leonard 121
Dierkes, John 199, 329, 451,
   581, 888
Dieterle, William 454
Diggins, Peggy 1027
Dignam, Basil 901
Dignam, Mark 186
Dill, Michael 505
Dillard, Art 34, 41, 54, 60,
   64, 71, 106, 168, 256, 261,
   291, 317, 352, 437, 463,
   502, 523, 526, 541, 567,
   574, 583, 590, 624, 625,
   638, 645, 648, 680, 694,
   696, 723, 728, 763, 831,
   862, 873, 889, 890, 897,
   913, 915, 931, 936, 948,
   949, 956, 959, 961, 964,
   965, 966, 970, 977, 987,
   988, 989, 995, 996, 999,
   1002
Dillard, Burt 965, 988, 1012

Dillaway, Donald 256, 305
Dillon, Bobby 298
Dillon, Dickie 88, 115, 138,
   234, 298, 719, 720, 845
Dillon, Forrest 167, 955, 1003
Dillon, John Webb 438, 962
Dillon, Josephine 413
Dilson, Clyde 200
Dilson, John 162, 193, 210,
   408, 590, 797, 934, 949,
   960, 962, 965, 985, 1000
Dilton, Dickie 112
DiMaggio, Joe 477
Dime, Jimmy 975
Dinelli, Mel 359
Dingle, Charles 747
Dinovitch, Abe 534
DiReda, Joe 404
Disney, Doris Miles 259
Dix, Billy 73, 81, 959, 998
Dix, Dorothy 306
Dix, Richard 473, 888
Dixon, Denver 306, 542; see
   also George Kesterson; Art
   Mix
Dixon, Jeanette 397
Dixon, Lee 15
Dobbins, Earl 75, 446
Dobkin, Lawrence 8, 619
Dobrynin, Akim 965
Dobson, James 363
Doby, Larry 407
Dockstader, George 329
Dodd, Claire 521, 919
Dodd, Jimmie 64, 161, 239,
   243, 599, 646, 692, 712,
   736, 832, 885
Dodge, Richard 402
Dolan, Frank 788
Dolgoruki, Igor 534
Dolin, Anton 749
Dolly, Tonyna Micky 417
Domergue, Faith 690
Dominguez, Frances 402
Dominguez, Joe 266, 402,
   406, 491, 993
Don, Jack 306
Donahue, Mary Eleanor 736,
   917
Donatt, Renee 452, 505
Doner, Jack 384
Doner, Maurice 238
Donlevy, Brian 228, 357,
   644, 922
Donnell, Jeff 241, 563, 599,
   635
Donnelly, Ruth 28, 217, 270,

# Name Index

274, 378, 398, 486, 582, 598, 682, 699, 742, 912
Donnini, Giulio  188
Donovan, Arthur  592
Donovan, Gloria  389
Dooley, Billy  94
Dooley, Buddy  762
Doran, Ann  407, 447
Dorety, Charles  52
Doria, Bianca  716, 780
Dorn, Philip  230, 389
Dorr, Lester  65, 143, 527, 656, 743, 960, 968, 969, 991, 1000, 1003
Dors, Diana  122
Doss, Tommy  651
Doucet, Catharine  396
Doucette, John  150, 156, 304, 431, 484, 736, 826, 828, 840, 849, 920
Dougherty, Jack  936
Douglas, Dayle  974; *see also* Ewart Adamson
Douglas, Don  301, 490, 515, 557, 677, 945
Douglas, Earl  968
Douglas, George  142, 351, 406, 445, 526, 574, 862, 950, 963, 971
Douglas, Robert  219
Douglas, Warren  153, 355, 380, 441, 455, 588, 599, 708, 852
Dowd, Kaye  16
Dowling, Constance  235, 780
Dowling, Patrick  707
Downing, Joseph  525
Downing, Marion  489
Downs, Cathy  40, 290
Downs, Johnny  340, 487, 733, 856
Downs, Watson  978
Doyle, Laird  534
Doyle, Maxine  77, 132, 234, 413, 464, 569, 620, 673, 688, 734, 753, 950, 958, 972, 1003
Drake, Charles  604, 838, 917
Drake, Dona  194
Drake, Oliver  70, 135, 146, 276, 308, 319, 346, 405, 537, 573, 607, 611, 615, 647, 647, 655, 673, 681, 738, 738, 855, 862, 915, 1007
Drake, Pauline  333, 710, 874
Drake, Peggy  983

Drake, Steve  260
Draper, Joe  975
Dresden, Curley  26, 34, 35, 54, 62, 66, 71, 95, 105, 106, 154, 171, 172, 175, 264, 277, 310, 331, 376, 377, 394, 406, 433, 470, 488, 498, 524, 551, 567, 570, 574, 602, 615, 624, 641, 643, 660, 667, 692, 693, 712, 746, 761, 763, 844, 868, 874, 877, 878, 895, 908, 930, 931, 947, 949, 955, 963, 985, 987, 993, 1003, 1012
Drew, Ellen  368, 814
Drew, Lillian  465
Drew, Roland  729
Driscoll, Bobby  55, 370
Driver, Edgar  700
Drysdale, Don Michael  357
Duane, Doris  814
Dublin, L. C.  53
DuBois, Diane  156
Dubov, Paul  32
DuBrey, Claire  48, 109, 155, 181, 386, 441, 442, 560, 761, 789
Duchin, Eddie, Orchestra  341
Dudgeon, Elspeth  933
Dudley, Carl  838, 1035, 1036, 1037, 1038, 1039, 1040, 1041, 1042, 1043, 1044, 1045, 1046, 1047, 1048, 1049, 1050, 1051, 1052, 1053, 1054, 1055, 1056, 1057, 1058, 1059, 1060, 1061, 1062, 1063, 1064, 1065, 1066, 1067, 1068
Dudley, Robert  770, 1003
Duering, Carl  184
Duff, Howard  237
Duff, Warren  423, 458
Duffield, Brainerd  451
Duffy, Albert  195, 743
Duffy, Jesse  75, 950, 952, 953, 954, 958, 967, 971, 974, 978, 982, 990, 991, 996, 997, 1001, 1002, 1005, 1011
DuFrane, Frank  421
Dugan, Tom  204, 588, 809, 845, 911, 937
Dugay, Yvette  713
Duke, Maurice  32, 390, 867
Duke, Robert  16

Dumbrille, Douglass  109, 217, 674, 697, 778, 876, 983
Dumke, Ralph  909
Dumont, Margaret  795, 942
Duna, Steffi  210, 281
Duncan Eva  1030
Duncan, Archie  859
Duncan, Bob  996
Duncan, John  91, 848
Duncan, Julie  812, 931
Duncan, Kenne  20, 50, 52, 88, 99, 115, 116, 123, 125, 127, 137, 138, 168, 209, 232, 258, 310, 337, 353, 377, 420, 464, 468, 469, 483, 498, 502, 513, 516, 529, 555, 566, 569, 607, 620, 622, 630, 652, 653, 662, 670, 688, 691, 692, 694, 709, 720, 721, 722, 739, 746, 752, 769, 775, 779, 792, 793, 794, 800, 818, 845, 861, 866, 885, 892, 895, 896, 908, 947, 952, 953, 956, 974, 986, 990, 995, 996, 997, 1005, 1082
Duncan, Sam  843
Duncan, Slim  179, 418, 762
Duncan, Topsy  1030
Dunham, Phil  53, 123, 234
Dunhill, Steve  81
Dunkel, John A.  834
Dunkin, Claude  998
Dunn, Eddie  46, 81, 235, 355, 441, 447
Dunn, Emma  117, 313, 358, 512, 529
Dunn, James  322, 606, 813
Dunn, Ralph  16, 60, 133, 409, 410, 450, 736, 800, 810, 849, 973, 988
Dunne, Elizabeth  18, 747, 800
Dunne, Stephen  417, 894
Dunning, Decla  364
Dupee, Leo  993
Dupont, E. A.  454
Duprez, June  813
Dupuis, Art  995
Duran, Val  400, 1000
Durand, David  862
Durante, Jimmy  488, 1034
Durbin, Deanna  1034
Durfee, Minta  1033
Durkin, Grace  56, 461, 476
Duryea, Dan  297, 464
Dvorak, Ann  236, 263, 477

# Name Index  340

Dwan, Allan 17, 46, 86, 197, 241, 363, 381, 534, 637, 689, 800, 802, 912, 922
Dwire, Earl 24, 110, 190, 261, 286, 291, 303, 411, 434, 440, 465, 523, 537, 542, 567, 615, 632, 763, 860, 878, 907
Dworshak, Lois 367, 368
Dwyer, Leslie 553
Dwyer, Marlo 497, 610, 925

Eagle-Lion Pictures 481
Eagles, James 331
Earl, June 397
Earle, Edward 74, 89, 101, 112, 162, 376, 408, 512, 645, 743, 747, 941
Early, Pearl 373, 377
Eason, B. Reeves 28, 66, 94, 508, 632, 957, 1007
Easton, Bob 314
Eaton, Shirley 186
Eben, Al 441
Eberhart, Mignon G. 824
Eblen, Gene 728
Ebsen, Alix 730
Ebsen, Buddy 661, 730, 826, 875, 884
Eburne, Maude 46, 71, 126, 141, 293, 348, 439, 467, 508, 514, 576, 594, 645, 669, 677, 744
Eby, Earl 735
Eby, Lois 987
Eddy, Helen Jerome 396
Eddy, Nelson 534
Eden, Barbara 900
Eden, Rob 158
Edmunds, William 173, 281, 709
Edwards, Alan 500, 761, 818
Edwards, Blake 32, 265, 483, 512
Edwards, Bruce 174, 249, 600, 689, 950, 966
Edwards, Cliff 252, 745
Edwards, Elaine 547
Edwards, Henry 851
Edwards, J. C., and Band 158
Edwards, James 8
Edwards, Joan 344
Edwards, Lee 384
Edwards, Meredith 165, 808
Edwards, Norwood 1003
Edwards, Penny 102, 320, 371, 495, 497, 533, 768, 786, 796, 846, 884, 912, 920
Edwards, Sarah 87, 285, 356, 456, 500, 750, 755, 779, 797
Edwards, Thornton 195
Egan, Jack 961
Eilers, Sally 414, 1027, 1033
Einer, Robert 964
Ekberg, Carl 709
Elam, Daniel 994
Elam, Jack 402, 828
Eldredge, George 397, 422, 975, 989
Eldredge, John 244, 251, 382, 447, 501, 579, 676, 752, 786, 881
Eliot, Kathleen 578
Eliscu, Edward 740
Eliscu, Fernanda 312
Elizondo, Joaquin 866
Elkins, Saul 606
Ellington, Duke, and His Orchestra 341
Elliott, Barbara 50
Elliott, Bill 50, 74, 88, 97, 115, 128, 137, 171, 217, 260, 298, 326, 337, 378, 422, 446, 470, 482, 483, 502, 546, 569, 584, 593, 687, 697, 720, 721, 727, 792, 861, 892, 895, 896, 928, 1031; *see also* Gordon Elliott
Elliott, Cecil 356, 800
Elliott, Dick 45, 46, 199, 265, 355, 356, 456, 462, 465, 488, 551, 592, 622, 659, 668, 729, 744, 797, 800, 878, 894, 909, 939
Elliott, Edythe 217, 354, 694, 813, 879, 885
Elliott, Gordon 70; *see also* Bill Elliott
Elliott, John 20, 22, 445, 693, 862, 939
Elliott, Keenan 326
Elliott, Lorraine 1027
Elliott, Ray 987
Elliott, Robert 101, 494
Elliott, Ross 8, 18, 103, 176, 920
Elliott, Scott 430, 982
Ellis, Ada 747
Ellis, Edward 457, 462, 473
Ellis, Frank 14, 34, 62, 69, 88, 95, 105, 115, 124, 135, 138, 234, 261, 286, 302, 307, 373, 374, 376, 434, 502, 524, 569, 573, 583, 602, 611, 615, 624, 647, 660, 672, 674, 694, 723, 755, 763, 770, 776, 795, 847, 868, 877, 895, 896, 906, 907, 931, 939, 948, 965, 970, 987, 988, 992, 1000, 1002, 1003, 1008, 1010, 1012
Ellis, Mary 287
Ellis, Mary Jo 397
Ellis, Mirko 780
Ellis, Patricia 640, 664
Ellis, Paul 360
Ellison, James 86, 274, 278, 347, 367, 438, 501
Ellison, Jane 856
Elston, Allan 576
Eltner, Don 43
Elton, Edmund 34, 819
Elwenspoek, Hans 184
Emanuel, Elzie 791
Emerson, Chares 961
Emerson, Hope 46, 111, 418
Emerson, Hope 581
Emery, Gilbert 778, 983
Emile, William 67
Emmett, Fern 85, 132, 158, 159, 313, 394, 489, 552, 554, 570, 576, 647, 680, 755, 794, 833
Emmett, Robert 523, 554, 907
Emory, Richard 37, 102, 125, 736
Endore, Guy 416
Engel, Roy 979, 1009
England, Sue 329
English, John 44, 62, 93, 95, 123, 169, 171, 189, 218, 264, 301, 420, 470, 510, 569, 585, 586, 597, 620, 621, 688, 731, 832, 848, 883, 885, 908, 947, 949, 952, 955, 956, 961, 962, 963, 965, 968, 972, 975, 980, 985, 986, 987, 988, 992, 1010, 1012
English, Marla 781
English, Richard 12, 79, 83, 339, 421
Ennis, Skinnay 743
Entwistle, Harold 869
Erdman, Richard 912
Erickson, Leif 581, 727

# NAME INDEX

Erickson, Louise 669
Erickson, Paul 300, 707, 841
Eristoff, Nestor 534
Ernest, George 414, 486, 507, 582, 617, 776
Erskine, Carl 665
Erskine, Chester 250
Erskine, Eileen 417
Erskine, John 603
Erway, Ben 509, 952
Erwin, Stu 1032, 1034
The Escalante Family 117
Eslava, Jose, Orchestra 266
Esmond, Annie 82
Esmond, Carl 109
Essen, Viola 765
Estabrook, Howard 155
Estrella, Esther 195, 602
Estridge, Robin 1, 165
Esway, Alexander 777
Eunson, Dale 206
Eunson, Katherine 206
Evans, Charles 179, 213, 581, 866
Evans, Clifford 683
Evans, Connie 710
Evans, Dale 13, 21, 49, 50, 51, 57, 108, 144, 189, 192, 292, 323, 330, 348, 350, 358, 377, 442, 467, 513, 559, 572, 622, 662, 688, 744, 750, 752, 758, 795, 801, 803, 852, 854, 865, 876, 883, 905, 934
Evans, Douglas 22, 87, 292, 338, 456, 533, 600, 611, 616, 676, 706, 762, 961, 962, 976, 984, 985
Evans, Gene 830, 872, 938
Evans, Herbert 974
Evans, Jack 302, 306, 624, 650, 936
Evans, Jacqueline 160
Evans, Joan 561, 781
Evans, Madge 28
Evans, Muriel 411, 523
Evans, Rex 927
Evarts, Hal G. 993
Everest, Barbara 222
Evers, Ann 645, 747, 975
Everton, Paul 557
Ewell, Tom 175
Eyer, Richard 131

Fadden, Tom 381, 505, 736, 821
Fain, Elmer 673

Fain, Matty 83, 357, 421
Fairey, Tommy Gene 681
Falk, Norbert 136
Falken, Jinx (Jinx Falkenburg) 988
Falkenberg, Margaret 751
The Falkner Orchestra 398
Fallows, Ruth 520
Fanchon 98
Fanning, Frank 189, 586, 1003
Faragoh, Francis 416
Farber, Jerry 451
Fargo, Peter 24
Farley, Dot 615, 688
Farley, James 510, 742, 907
Farley, Morgan 451
Farmer, Virginia 222, 267, 800
Farnum, Franklyn 92, 115, 217, 776
Farnum, Geraldine 467
Farnum, William 130, 264, 286, 491, 611, 674, 693, 725, 761, 846, 949, 987, 1007, 1008, 1033
Farr, Audrey 238
Farr, Derek 122, 471
Farr, Hugh 56, 543, 648, 651, 755
Farr, Karl 56, 543, 648, 651, 755
Farr, Patricia 414
Farrar, David 808
Farrar, Jane 749
Farrell, Charles 245, 336, 782
Farrell, Marian 554
Farrington, Betty 351, 368, 776
Faulkner, Carl 138
Faulkner, Ralph 1012
Fauntelle, Dian 971
Faust, Louis R. 326, 422, 594
Faust, Martin 679, 773, 972, 1004, 1012
Fawcett, Charles 3
Fawcett, Jimmy 947, 949, 951, 955, 962, 963, 965, 983, 985, 986, 992, 1000, 1004, 1012
Fawcett, William 156, 356, 436, 539, 951, 1019
Fawcett Publications Inc. 1004
Fax, Jesslyn 475
Fay, Vivian 749

Fay, William 111
Faye, Randall 115, 216, 234, 274, 298, 701
Faylen, Frank 811
"Feather," the Horse 50, 731, 839, 845
Feins, Bernard 815
Feld, Fritz 47, 101, 109, 389, 497, 743
Feldary, Eric 364
Feldman, Charles K. 451, 628
Feldmar, Emil 379
Felix, Art 440, 975, 987, 988, 1010
Felix and His Martiniques 314
Feller, Bob 407
Fellows, Edith 318, 776
Felton, Earl 18, 96, 317, 511, 525, 557, 592, 609, 728, 745, 799
Felton, Felix 185, 186, 901
Felton, Verna 285, 806
Fenner, Walter 141, 508, 941, 972, 1001
Fenton, Frank 251, 292, 293, 344, 626, 638, 669, 702, 854
Fenwick, Jean 418, 503
Ference, Ilona 184
Ferguson, Al 134, 217, 673, 952, 960, 977, 1002, 1005
Ferguson, Frank 120, 211, 217, 381, 399, 431, 539, 561, 713, 826, 875, 922
Ferguson, Helen 1027
Fernandez, Freddy 160
Ferniel, Dan 994
Ferrari, Mario 242
Ferreau, Janine 713
Ferrell, Tony 297
Ferro, Michael 984
Fessier, Michael 922
Fetchit, Stepin 791
Fetherston, Eddie 45, 189, 612
Fieberling, Hal 689; *see also* Hal Baylor
Field, Alexander 707
Field, Julian 741
Field, Margaret 157
Field, Mary 418, 510, 597, 637, 844
Field, Medora 284, 911
Field, Norman 147, 181, 786, 838

Field, Shirley Ann 808
Field, Sylvia 532
Field, Virginia 1032
Fields, Darlene 472
Fields, Eddy 209, 216, 729
Fields, Joseph 272, 552
Fields, Leonard 7, 12, 388, 500, 501, 710
Fields, Stanley 12, 341, 717, 833
Fierro, Paul 581, 685
Filauri, Antonio 709
Filer, Frieda 765
Filmer, Robert 207
Fimberg, Hal 911
Fink, Dale 928
Finlayson, James 12, 294
Finn, Mickey 283
Finn, Sam 477
Firehouse Five Plus Two 345
Fisher, Clay 690
Fisher, Feddie, and His Schnickelfritz Band 391
Fisher, Fred 814
Fisher, George "Shug" 50, 323, 358, 391, 651, 755, 803
Fisher, Steve 121, 328, 685, 704, 713, 816, 922
Fiske, Robert 20, 104, 126, 169, 615, 812, 962
Fiske, Warren 956
Fitzgerald, Barry 616
Fitzgerald, Johnny Lang 645
Fitzgerald, Tim 700
Fitzmaurice, Michael 360
Fitzpatrick, James A. 751
Fitzroy, Emily 67
Fitzsimmons, Cortland 204, 476
FitzSimons, Charles 616
Fix, Paul 17, 90, 119, 151, 155, 195, 219, 230, 231, 236, 301, 326, 377, 399, 498, 521, 525, 535, 594, 612, 644, 743, 760, 800, 898, 899, 941
Fix, Peter Paul 535
Flagg, Steve (Michael St. Angel) 345, 495
Flaherty, Pat 322, 349, 357
Flanagan, Bud 85; *see also* Dennis O'Keefe
Flash, Gerry 696
"Flash," the Dog 95
Flateau, Georges 3
Flatley, James 965
Flavin, James 96, 228, 494,
538, 594, 656, 697, 706, 882
Fleer, Harry 880
Fleischer, Dave 814, 856
Fleming, Alice 88, 115, 128, 137, 298, 446, 478, 482, 483, 517, 569, 584, 687, 720, 721, 779, 792, 861, 892, 896, 960
Fleming, Carroll 740
Fleming, Rhonda 377
Flint, Sam 13, 46, 101, 112, 413, 433, 434, 442, 448, 464, 467, 509, 513, 523, 632, 659, 731, 739, 760, 803, 832, 864, 874, 913, 916, 948, 950, 953, 960, 968, 991, 1004
Flippen, Jay C. 921
Florey, Robert J. 464
Flournoy, Elizabeth 357
Fluellen, Joel 979
Flynn, Charles 91, 238, 364, 885, 972, 999
Flynn, Errol 3
Flynn, Joe 575
Foley, Romey 128
Fonda, Henry 628, 1029
Fontaine, Frank 345
Fontaine, Joan 473
Fontaine, Peter 782
Foote, Bradbury 355, 409, 453, 495, 610
Forbes, Mary 204, 568, 726
Ford, Bryant 785
Ford, Charles E. 60, 134, 291, 465, 725
Ford, Dorothy 581, 689
Ford, Francis 38, 130, 197, 214, 221, 255, 565, 594, 616, 791, 835, 840, 983
Ford, George 985
Ford, Glenn 1034
Ford, John 616, 629, 651, 791, 817
Ford, Lee 961, 1003
Ford, Philip 17, 36, 38, 68, 81, 87, 149, 157, 174, 178, 179, 338, 380, 386, 424, 430, 479, 497, 516, 544, 563, 589, 600, 605, 608, 610, 626, 635, 661, 686, 759, 834, 835, 849, 853, 884, 886, 889, 902, 903, 913, 929
Ford, Ross 253, 671, 786
Ford, Ruth 783, 923
Ford, Wallace 212, 309, 462, 484, 637, 699, 828
Ford, Whitey 139
Foreman, Carl 155
Forester, Cay 155, 604, 688, 783
Forman, Carol 950, 966
Forman, Joey 32, 867
Forrest, John 370
Forrest, William 44, 48, 231, 249, 265, 285, 497, 653, 743, 768, 972, 991, 1004
Forsyth, Frank 829
Fort, Garrett 415, 778, 945
Forte, Joe 574, 661, 953, 963, 986
Fortune, Jan 162, 473
Foster, Bill 595
Foster, Edward 357, 955, 961, 968, 1019
Foster, Lewis R. 156
Foster, Michael 749
Foster, Norman 439
Foster, Preston 28
Foster, Royal 58
Fostini, John 259
Foulger, Byron 40, 76, 113, 200, 251, 270, 301, 332, 377, 410, 421, 560, 581, 593, 649, 684, 703, 732, 740, 810, 960
The Four Step Brothers 815
Fowler, Almeda 512, 779
Fowler, Arthur 955
Fowler, Harry 165, 233
Fowler, Jean 878
Fowley, Douglas 13, 174, 187, 189, 288, 501, 521, 619, 631, 638, 742, 758, 798, 801, 852, 882, 897, 933
Fox, Fred 898
Fox, Frederic Louis 156, 316, 806, 900, 909
Fox, Jimmy 776
Fox, Michael 951
Fox, Wallace 607
Fox Pictures 791
Foy, Bob 637
Foy, Eddie, Jr. 139, 356, 397, 504, 613, 666, 699, 937
Frago, Peter 680
Francen, Victor 3
Francia, Maria G. 242
Francis, Diana 283
Francis, Olin 352, 526, 570, 574, 629
Francis, Owen 59

# NAME INDEX

Francke, Peter 118
Frank, Christian J. 916
Frank, J. L., Golden West Cowboys 291
Frank, Jacquin 64
Frank, Jerry 70, 331, 693, 855, 955, 961, 963, 968, 975, 980, 987, 995, 1003, 1010, 1012
Franklin, Brian 841
Franklin, Gloria 270, 965
Franklin, Paul 352, 641
Franklyn, Hazel 417
Franklyn, William 1, 837
Frankovich, Mike J. 259, 950, 954, 971, 978, 1002
Franks, Jerome, Jr. 108
Franz, Arthur 241, 689, 807
Franz, Eduard 423, 898
Fraser, Elisabeth 340
Fraser, Harry 952
Fraser, Phyllis 313, 916
Fraser, Richard 63, 222, 701, 825, 834, 879
Frasher, Jim 635
Frassineti, Augusto S. 188
Frawley, William 231, 236, 344, 348, 380, 419, 612, 637
Frazee, Jane 19, 55, 86, 269, 294, 309, 487, 504, 549, 669, 771, 804, 871
Frazer, Alex 65
Frazer, Robert 35, 123, 169, 264, 551, 573, 895, 952, 956, 962, 1005
Freberg, Stan 273, 1013
Frederick, Harlow G. 935
Frederick, Howard 446
Frederick, Lee 955, 968, 1003
Fredericks, Charles 324
Freedman, Benedict 32, 390
Freeman, Devery 457
Freeman, Everett 552
Freeman, Frederick 968
Freeman, Helen 588
Freeman, Howard 492
Freeman, Kathleen 359, 447, 580, 581, 912
Freeman, Mona 654, 813, 830
Frees, Wolf 300
Freiberger, Fred 43, 901
French, Charles K. 674, 963
French, Dick 885, 972
Freshman, William 287, 596
Frey, Arno 885
Frey, Kathy 491

Freytag, Robert 454
Friedkin, Joel 88, 154, 564, 621, 678, 746, 911
Friedman, Harry 907
Friedman, Seymour 8
Friend, Philip 553, 790
Fries, Ted 635
Friml, Rudolph 534
Frisco, Joe 31, 643, 816, 906
Frohlich, Sig 32
Frome, Milton 32, 963
Frost, Don 865
Frost, Terry 21, 89, 267, 540, 952, 962, 973, 981
Frostova, Janina 419
Frye, Dwight 53, 148, 262, 385, 525, 743, 965
Frye, Gilbert 754
Frye, Katherine 318, 655
Frye, Theodore 655
Fuller, Barbara 10, 238, 312, 447, 627, 659, 697, 807, 853, 881, 925
Fuller, Samuel 78, 225, 263, 265
Fulton, Irving 50
Fulton, Rad 131
Fung, Paul 397, 636, 972, 983
Fung, Willie 132, 243, 286, 311, 612, 634, 855
Furneaux, Yvonne 152, 443
Furness, Betty 603

Gaddis, Michael 958, 967
Gaffney, Edwin 570
Gagnon, Betty 269
Gagnon, Pfc. Rene A. 689
Gahan, Oscar 23, 41, 60, 106, 261, 286, 303, 307, 435, 448, 524, 634, 723, 735, 770, 860, 863, 936
Gail, Jeanne 923
Gaines, Mel 474
Galbreth, Bruce 987
Gale, Allen 856
Gale, Gladys 158, 397, 521
Gale, Wesley 994
Galindo, Nacho 47, 314, 316, 390, 402, 561, 727, 800, 828, 866, 922
Gallagher, Carole 174
Gallagher, Skeets 119, 201
"Gallant Man," the Horse 816
Gallaudet, John 225, 497, 530, 563, 788, 811, 897, 909

Galli, Rosina 259, 267, 464, 618
Gallier, Alex 233, 829
Gallo, Maresa 716
Galvani, Dino 259
Gam, Rita 454
Gamboa, Elias 195, 874
Gamet, Kenneth 228, 243, 329, 431, 484, 697, 830, 898
Gan, Chester 106, 243
Gangelin, Paul 51, 55, 513, 662, 748, 769, 785, 871, 876
Gannaway, Albert C. 160, 335, 474, 531, 595, 619
Ganzer, Gerry 600
Garabedian, Robert 1009
Garber, Jan, and His Orchestra 330
Garcen, Tony 867
Garcia, Joe 687, 975, 995
Garden, Irina 383
Gardner, Gladys 318
Gardner, Gloria 318
Gardner, Jack 464, 512, 818, 960
Gardner, Reginald 1030
Garey, Peter 749
Garfield, John 1028
Gargan, Edward 47, 78, 98, 153, 161, 204, 213, 268, 274, 280, 322, 345, 377, 380, 396, 678, 688, 769, 815, 902, 905, 918
Gargan, William 510, 521, 783
Garland, Judy 1030
Garner, Don 912
Garner, Paul 341
Garralaga, Martin 215, 314, 373, 402, 420, 422, 452, 460, 464, 593, 685, 789, 801, 857, 866, 920, 1004
Garrett, Sam 992, 1008
Garrick, Gene 274, 818
Garro, Joseph 865, 871
Garson, Greer 1034
Gary, Gene 364, 668
Gastoni, Lisa 186, 829
Gates, Harvey 425
Gates, Maxine 539
Gates, Nancy 328, 530
Gateson, Marjorie 108, 272, 375, 514
Gauge, Alexander 772
Gay, Gregory 36, 63, 312,

579, 834, 852, 969, 981, 1019
Gay, Nancy 469, 569, 607
Gaye, Audrey 1003
Gaynor, Janet 1027
Geary, Bud 44, 52, 64, 74, 97, 99, 105, 114, 115, 124, 128, 145, 171, 234, 236, 253, 264, 298, 337, 351, 377, 408, 420, 446, 464, 468, 469, 470, 482, 483, 502, 555, 564, 566, 569, 584, 585, 607, 621, 687, 691, 692, 720, 721, 722, 731, 746, 775, 779, 794, 824, 832, 839, 845, 861, 892, 896, 904, 947, 949, 952, 955, 962, 963, 972, 974, 980, 982, 985, 986, 991, 992, 997, 1001, 1005, 1012
Gebuhr, Otto 118
Geer, Andrew 912
Geiger, Miriam 919
Geise, Sugar 108
Geldert, Clarence 289
Gelsey, Erwin 852
Genardi, Maria 452
George, Anthony 304
George, Gladys 532, 777
George, Jack 415, 709, 779, 967
George, Muriel 11
Geraghty, Carmelita 1027
Geraghty, Gerald 13, 21, 24, 40, 66, 106, 134, 194, 260, 294, 323, 350, 372, 376, 387, 491, 508, 549, 587, 590, 594, 622, 625, 627, 631, 696, 697, 711, 761, 763, 796, 798, 846, 849, 854, 896, 899, 906, 928, 940, 988
Geraghty, Maurice 346, 1000, 1007, 1008
Gerald, Helen 278
Gerald, Jim 3, 82
Gerall, Roscoe 960, 1000
Geray, Steven 36, 312, 417, 492, 838
Germaine, Mary 300
Gerry, Alex 143, 610, 807
Gerson, Betty Lou 627
Gerstle, Frank 362, 418
Gest, Inna 534
Geva, Tamara 477
Gibbons, Eliot 20, 175, 240, 874

Gibson, Helen 121
Gibson, Hoot 822, 993
Gibson, Julie 787
Gibson, Mimi 436
Gibson, Tom 735
Gibson, Tyler 397
Gibson, Wynne 248, 263, 493, 517
Giermann, Frederick 709
Gifford, Frances 980
Gifford, Ruth 488
Gilbert, Billy 19, 28, 247, 714, 733, 743, 926, 1031
Gilbert, Doris 31, 273, 419, 779
Gilbert, Jody 65, 326, 359, 524
Gill, Florence 421
Gill, Frank, Jr. 31, 79, 103, 108, 112, 203, 204, 273, 343, 492, 742, 825, 911, 941
Gill, Wendle 987
Gillern, Grace 881
Gillette, James 175
Gillette, Ruth 83, 272, 764
Gillie, Jean 683
Gillingwater, Claude 833
Gillis, Ann 113, 268, 466, 735
Gilmer, Helene 700
Gilmore, Art 984
Gilmore, Virginia 501
Gilson, Tom 938
Girard, Joe 554, 863, 1003
Giraud, Octavio 554
Gironda, Vincent 779
Givot, George 341
Glandbard, Max 324
Glass, Ned 961
Glassmire, Gus 919
Gleason, James 28, 141, 205, 296, 339, 474, 477, 503, 514, 726
Gleason, Lucille 141, 189, 205, 296, 339, 503, 514, 520, 726
Gleason, Pat 95, 397, 419, 461, 612, 743, 961
Gleason, Russell 141, 205, 296, 339, 503, 514, 726
Gleckler, Robert 263, 557
Glendon, J. Frank 411, 681
Glenn, Roy, Sr. 979, 994
Goddard, Alf 683
Godfrey, George 647
Godfrey, Renee 917
Godoy, Arturo 296
Godoy, Ledda 296

Godsell, Peter 901
Goetz, Walter H. 93, 149, 301, 597, 809, 824
Goff, Ivan 797
Goldbaum, Peter 917
Goldberg, Lou 250
Golden, Michael 152, 772, 841
Golden, Miriam 765
Golden, Ray 342, 488, 825
Golden Gate Quartet 343
Goldi, Erwin 1001
Goldie, Wyndham 186
Goldman, Lawrence 853
Goldschmidt, Robert 128
Goldsmith, Ken 438
Goldstone, Richard 838
Golubeff, Gregory 534
Gombell, Minna 422, 804, 869, 928
Gomboa, Elias 142
Gomez, Antonio 84
Gomez, Augie 66, 258, 260, 405, 483, 546, 672, 947, 948, 949, 956, 959, 965, 988, 993, 995, 996, 1001, 1005, 1011, 1012
Gomez, Thomas 17
Gonzalez-Gonzalez, Jose 575
Gonzalez, Jamie 924
Good, John 747
Goodall, Grace 738
Goodman, Jack 268
Goodrich, Marcus 521
Goodwin, Bill 32, 203, 344
Goodwin, Gary 102
Goodwin, Harold 68, 107, 430, 889, 929, 959, 976, 999
Goodwin, John 987
Goodwins, Leslie 16, 108
Goolden, Richard 901
Gorcey, David 251, 601
Gorcey, Leo 19, 598
Gordon, Bert 568
Gordon, Bert I. 43
Gordon, C. Henry 385, 473
Gordon, Charles 101, 653, 824, 887
Gordon, Dan 727
Gordon, Dorothy 808
Gordon, Gavin 439, 833
Gordon, Harold 935
Gordon, Homer King 303
Gordon, Huntley 598, 764
Gordon, Joe 407
Gordon, Kay 397

# NAME INDEX

Gordon, Leo  535, 690
Gordon, Lesley  790
Gordon, Mary  213, 414, 429, 485, 709, 715, 910
Gordon, Mildred  458
Gordon, Richard  185, 186, 950
Gordon, Roy  65, 595, 710, 880, 918, 976
Gordon, Vera  493
Gorman, Buddy  818
Gorman, Eric  616
Gorn, Lester  43
Gorog, Laszlo  510
Gorss, Saul  964, 966, 969, 1006
Got, Roland  525, 972
Gottlieb, Alex  29, 365, 385
Gottlieb, Theodore  950
Gould, Chester  960, 961, 962, 963
Gould, Sid  464
Gould, William  320, 408, 615, 915, 988
Gover, Mildred  162
Grady, Robert  482
Graff, Wilton  204, 265, 842, 886
Graham, Dolores and Don  815
Graham, Frank  413, 742
Graham, Fred  39, 55, 68, 114, 128, 129, 155, 230, 320, 377, 380, 483, 502, 513, 547, 549, 559, 566, 579, 581, 584, 654, 691, 731, 748, 775, 828, 835, 839, 852, 861, 898, 948, 951, 952, 953, 958, 967, 974, 978, 990, 991, 994, 996, 997, 1002, 1005, 1006, 1011, 1019
Graham, George  401
Graham, Jane  318
Graham, Jo  140
Graham, Lewis  148
Graham, Malcolm  961
Graham, Richard  377
Grahame, Alec  772
Grainger, Edmund  217, 243, 689, 898
Granach, Alexander  397, 462, 512
Granby, Joseph  46, 297, 586, 635
Granet, Bert  272
Granger, Dorothy  66, 447, 482, 577, 795, 954

Grant, Frances  110, 537, 632
Grant, Harvey  404
Grant, James Edward  15, 84, 90, 594, 659, 689, 800
Grant, Kirby  629
Grant, Lawrence  360, 474, 926, 972, 1003
Grant, Marshall  505
Grant, Morton  54, 692, 885, 908
Grant, Richard  973
Grant, Stephen  15
Grant, Wylie  1012
Grapewin, Charley  31, 677
Grashin, Mauri  368, 507, 577, 662, 743, 755, 755, 932
Grasso, Giovanni  242
Graves, Diana  417
Graves, Jesse  50, 747
Graves, Peter  43
Graves, Ralph  788, 823
Gray, Arnold  764
Gray, Billy  736, 765, 1025
Gray, Coleen  867
Gray, Dolores  415
Gray, Gary  789
Gray, Jenifer  961, 965
Gray, Judy  11
Gray, Lorna  284, 536, 629, 648, 864, 952, 967, 995; see also Adrian Booth
Gray, Louis  52, 54, 64, 75, 92, 115, 123, 124, 234, 264, 267, 298, 337, 353, 420, 425, 445, 446, 467, 468, 483, 564, 569, 573, 585, 602, 607, 620, 621, 646, 679, 692, 712, 795, 832, 885, 895, 904, 908
Gray, Roger  537
Gray, Sally  790
Gray, Vernon  165
Grayley, Barbara  837
Grayson, Charles  912
Green, Anna Katherine  439
Green, Danny  336, 428
Green, Duke  114, 565, 656, 722, 948, 949, 950, 952, 956, 961, 965, 967, 968, 971, 974, 977, 980, 983, 985, 986, 987, 990, 991, 992, 995, 1001, 1004, 1005, 1011
Green, Garard  782
Green, Gertrude  193
Green, Janet  808

Green, Linda  928
Greenberg, Hank  407
Greene, Angela  4, 418, 581, 766
Greene, Eve  397
Greene, Harrison  27, 35, 67, 76, 272, 306, 332, 368, 408, 464, 524, 624, 735, 818, 833, 844, 957, 960, 961, 963
Greene, Jaclynne  362
Greene, John  595
Greene, Joseph J.  44
Greenleaf, Raymond  316, 766, 909
Greenwood, Charlotte  197
Greer, Allen  23
Greer, Dabbs  580
Gregg, Alan  641, 961, 963, 965, 968, 985, 986, 992, 1003, 1012
Gregg, Everley  808
Gregg, Hubert  185
Gregg, Virginia  811
Gregory, Jackson  420
Gregory, Stephen  998, 999
Gregory, Wallace  833
Gregson, John  1
Greig, Robert  113, 204, 414, 450, 493
Grevier, Anna  417
Grey, Harry  34, 48, 66, 91, 97, 142, 144, 145, 146, 195, 310, 318, 332, 351, 352, 406, 408, 412, 419, 442, 450, 466, 470, 477, 491, 508, 511, 532, 541, 559, 590, 601, 641, 648, 649, 660, 714, 728, 732, 737, 752, 753, 776, 797, 810, 821, 844, 874, 877, 906, 934
Grey, John  804
Grey, Madeline  747, 814
Grey, Romer  484
Grey, Virginia  2, 48, 84, 211, 236, 301, 369, 412, 423, 581, 710, 785, 928
Grey, Zane  71, 484, 888, 983
Gribbon, Eddie  99, 742, 1033
Gries, Tom  283
Grieve, Bill  407
Griffin, Eleanore  377, 788
Griffin, Julia  434
Griffin, Robert E.  531, 580
Griffith, Edith M.  6

Griffith, Helen 977, 978
Griffith, James 362, 713
Griffith, Julia 246
Griffith, Kay 142
Griffith, Kenneth 122, 300, 841
Griffith, William 421
Griffiths, Fred 707, 808
Grimes, Karolyn 356, 651
Grinde, Nick 193, 212, 225, 252, 279, 507, 653
Grissel, Wallace A. 138, 483, 892, 967, 974, 990, 1005, 1011
Gromek, Steve 407
Gross, Charles 3
Gross, Jack J. 580
Gross, Milt 613, 666, 740
Grosskurth, Kurt 454
Groves, Jerry 18
Gruber, Frank 251, 378, 555
Gruen, James 438
Grueneberg, William 853
Grundei, Fred 379
Gruning, Ilka 510
Gruskin, Jerry 98, 744, 852
The Guadalajara Trio 815
Guard, Kit 13, 92, 106, 166, 331, 394, 960, 974, 1003
Gudrun, Ann 186, 859
Guebhard, Mark 184
Guest, Val 901
Guhl, George 291, 299, 521
Guilfoyle, Paul 148, 677, 819
Guizar, Tito 79, 269, 492, 549
Gullick, Bill 654
Gumley, Leonard 689
Gunnels, Chester 134, 725
Gurie, Sigrid 820
Gurs, Peter 534
Gustin, John 961, 1003
Gustine, Paul 954, 959, 969, 986, 1005, 1009
Guta, Raymond 880
Guttman, Henry 960
Guy, Eula 288, 604, 779, 933
Gwynne, Anne 274, 288
Gynt, Greta 30, 782

Haade, William 6, 81, 119, 155, 168, 175, 213, 309, 317, 318, 349, 374, 378, 381, 402, 405, 463, 464, 513, 538, 544, 584, 588, 631, 654, 657, 659, 682, 685, 702, 703, 718, 720, 753, 766, 853, 872, 882, 886, 911, 929, 934, 956
Haas, Charles F. 505
Haas, Hugo 155, 230, 392, 534
Hack, Herman 24, 26, 34, 52, 67, 88, 92, 97, 107, 114, 130, 142, 176, 261, 291, 302, 354, 434, 488, 489, 498, 523, 524, 585, 590, 600, 615, 625, 660, 687, 719, 722, 723, 737, 748, 774, 775, 797, 839, 844, 845, 847, 868, 877, 891, 907, 936, 964, 977, 978, 986, 988, 989, 1002, 1005, 1008, 1011
Hackel, A. W. 23, 41, 69, 72, 110, 127, 177, 190, 202, 226, 261, 271, 302, 303, 307, 432, 435, 440, 578, 634, 650, 827, 847, 860, 873
Hackett, Hal 98
Hackett, Karl 23, 35, 72, 74, 89, 110, 124, 127, 172, 193, 196, 202, 217, 226, 258, 292, 302, 311, 373, 394, 395, 498, 502, 564, 578, 634, 641, 667, 755, 832, 847, 861
Hadley, Reed 26, 217, 349, 382, 557, 912, 922, 929, 947, 1012
Hagens, William 149, 579
Hagerthy, Ron 121, 206, 458
Haggerty, Don 32, 150, 357, 402, 475, 587, 689, 759, 766, 768, 849, 889, 890, 984
Hagney, Frank 97, 162, 236, 276, 373, 460, 488, 581, 961
Haines, Patricia 553
Haines, William Wister 211
Hakins, Richard 341
Hale, Alan, Jr. 4, 356, 460
Hale, Grace 158
Hale, Henry 960, 993, 1000, 1003
Hale, Jonathan 155, 209, 212, 224, 263, 268, 274, 311, 376, 382, 390, 409, 487, 512, 532, 586, 592, 661, 668
Hale, Monte 14, 39, 55, 87, 88, 128, 353, 425, 430, 468, 499, 544, 555, 559, 563, 589, 608, 626, 670, 686, 748, 759, 777, 792, 835, 839, 846, 872, 889, 996, 997
Hale, Richard 685, 704
Hall, Alfred 941
Hall, Archie (Arch Hall, Sr.) 570, 641, 868, 961
Hall, Ben 617, 645, 649
Hall, Eddie 265, 818
Hall, Ellen 92
Hall, Fern 120, 530, 922
Hall, Genee 693
Hall, Henry 67, 433, 434, 584, 646, 667, 863, 907, 936, 986, 1008
Hall, Jon 325
Hall, Lois 164, 201, 708
Hall, Michael 61, 426
Hall, Norman S. 62, 74, 80, 89, 105, 138, 161, 168, 169, 171, 256, 258, 430, 469, 502, 565, 566, 630, 652, 668, 686, 687, 720, 722, 744, 746, 759, 775, 793, 794, 832, 839, 881, 892, 899, 947, 949, 962, 965, 975, 980, 985, 986, 992, 995, 1004
Hall, Porter 162, 1034
Hall, Sherry 5, 189, 491, 961, 968
Hall, Stuart 419
Hall, Thurston 4, 46, 47, 91, 224, 252, 293, 330, 358, 375, 393, 409, 503, 718, 743, 752, 864, 894
Hall, Virginia 548
Hall, William 210, 376, 902
Halligan, William 62, 205
Halloran, John 15, 219, 357, 402
Halls, Ethel May 332, 819
Halton, Charles 45, 225, 262, 274, 338, 373, 500, 910
Ham, Otto 145
Hamblen, Stuart 24, 105, 236, 376, 408, 593, 697, 746, 982
Hambling, Arthur 683
Hamilton, Chuck 364, 886, 969
Hamilton, Donna 305
Hamilton, Fred 960
Hamilton, Harry 457
Hamilton, J. Frank 315, 714
Hamilton, Jane 1028
Hamilton, John 10, 37, 38,

46, 49, 178, 208, 217, 247, 260, 284, 297, 353, 365, 387, 388, 419, 430, 453, 461, 464, 480, 495, 499, 527, 562, 589, 597, 720, 724, 815, 870, 929, 952, 956, 972, 976, 977, 996, 1011
Hamilton, Margaret 197, 270, 457, 628
Hamilton, Neil 28, 349, 414, 598, 710, 932, 986
Hamlin, Walter 787
Hammer, Alvin 216, 628, 917
Hammett, Dashiell 842
Hammond, Reid 698
Hamner, William 962
Hampton, Leonard 995, 1001
Hampton, Louise 683
Hancock, Oscar 987
Handl, Irene 122
Handley, Dorothy Curnor 669
Hanemann, H. W. 360, 805
Haney, Betty Jane 60
Hanley, Jack 665
Hanlon, Tom 332, 351
Hanna, Mark 73
Hanneford, Grace 628
Hanneford, Poodles 50, 628
Hannon, Chick 71, 75, 106, 114, 134, 307, 422, 463, 488, 489, 519, 547, 625, 657, 722, 746, 860, 890, 949, 959, 964, 977, 986, 988
Hansen, Nina 534
Hanson, Ray 947, 962, 968, 1004
Harari, Robert 367, 397
Harbord, Carl 444
Harden, Jack 484, 959, 964, 1009
Hardie, Russell 196, 313
Harding, Beritita 454
Harding, John 562
Hardy, Oliver 230
Hardy Family, The 339
Hare, Lumsden 444
Hare, Marilyn 19, 333, 368, 415, 718, 937
Harell, Marte 136
Hargreaves, Lance Z. 233
Harlan, Kenneth 100, 308, 794, 878, 956, 962, 963, 972, 991, 992
Harlan, Otis 347, 567

Harlan, Veit 118
The Harlem Sandman 343
Harley, Bonnie Jean 376
Harman, Fred 88, 115, 128, 137, 298, 354, 446, 481, 482, 483, 556, 584, 675, 687, 694, 720, 721, 774, 792, 861, 891, 892, 896
Harman, Gil 329
Harmer, Lillian 158
Harmon, John 10, 91, 181, 262, 366, 505, 592, 729, 789
Harmon, Marie 207; see also Marie Harmond
Harmon, Pat 523
Harmond, Marie 528; see also Marie Harmon
Harolde, Ralf 35, 246, 461, 586, 618, 649, 952, 1001
Harper, Patricia 839, 906
Harper, Ray 963
Harr, Silver 88, 913, 1002
Harrigan, William 212, 250, 665
Harriman, Carley 749
Harrington, James 627
Harris, Arlene 330, 348, 456, 550
Harris, Edna 932
Harris, Gordon 700
Harris, Larry 612
Harris, Phil 912
Harris, Ray 509, 833
Harris, Robert 428
Harris, Major Sam 230, 616, 648, 709, 947, 985
Harris, Sibyl 225
Harris, Theresa 766
Harris, Winifred 503
Harrison, Carey 91, 709
Harrison, Dorothy 42
Harrison, Jimmy 433
Harrison, Kathleen 122
Harrison, P. S. 173
Hart, Eddie 95, 641
Hart, Gordon 352, 465, 570, 674, 927, 961
Hart, John 46, 594, 912
Hart, Mary 60, 134, 256, 372, 514, 515, 672, 725, 726, 763; see also Lynn Roberts; Lynne Roberts
Hart, Moss 250
Hart, Neal 74, 75, 88, 138, 678, 722, 755, 861
Hartford, Robert 963

Hartley, John 252, 295
Hartman, Dick 936
Hartmann, Georg 379
Hartnell, William 700
Harvey, Clem 399
Harvey, Don C. 43, 46, 305, 527, 964
Harvey, Forrester 205, 490, 701, 709
Harvey, Harry 25, 35, 40, 129, 140, 170, 276, 465, 548, 554, 661, 730, 833, 849, 881, 989
Harvey, Jack 140
Harvey, Jean 981
Harvey, Paul 45, 116, 189, 201, 268, 317, 323, 339, 391, 441, 466, 501, 504, 517, 613, 804, 818, 826, 843, 881, 928
Haskell, Al 74, 162, 195, 406, 491, 672, 723, 812, 877, 931, 993, 1010
Hasse, O. E. 1
Hasson, Jamiel 717, 965
Hatswell, Don 616
Hatton, Raymond 134, 142, 146, 256, 279, 332, 334, 406, 429, 524, 541, 580, 590, 660, 672, 867, 899, 930, 1007, 1008
Hatton, Rondo 742
Hauser, Gilgi 184
Hauser, Philo 184
Haven, Nina 765
Havoc, June 108, 417
Hawkins, Frank 336
Hawkins, Jimmy 505, 627, 696, 922
Hawkins, Tim 505
Hawks, Howard 851
Hawks, Michael 453
Hay, George Dewey 295, 358
Hayden, Barbara 581
Hayden, Harry 240, 397, 413, 462, 507, 560, 786, 937, 941
Hayden, Russell 754
Hayden, Sterling 211, 399, 423, 836
Hayes, Allison 191, 880
Hayes, Barry 331
Hayes, Bernadene 270, 609
Hayes, Charles 974, 1005
Hayes, Douglas 700
Hayes, George "Gabby" 13, 24, 35, 50, 55, 71, 74, 97, 106, 126, 162, 167, 171, 189,

232, 317, 322, 323, 337, 347, 350, 372, 374, 376, 377, 394, 433, 442, 463, 467, 470, 473, 483, 488, 502, 513, 522, 552, 569, 622, 625, 633, 648, 657, 662, 663, 680, 723, 750, 755, 760, 763, 795, 798, 799, 861, 863, 876, 883, 895, 897, 899, 928, 939, 940, 1031, 1033, 1034
Hayes, Pfc. Ira H. 689
Hayes, Linda 119, 568, 648, 663, 760
Hayes, Lorraine (Laraine Day) 190
Hayes, Margaret 283
Hayle, Grace 313
Hayles, Kenneth R. 707, 841
Haynes, Roberta 325
Hays, Barry 142, 551, 844, 949, 962, 963, 986, 988, 1012
Hayter, James 165
Hayward, Chuck 219, 402, 959, 989
Hayward, Jim 909
Hayward, Lillie 318, 690
Hayward, Louis 359
Hayward, Susan 231, 343, 740
Haywood, Billi 16
Hayworth, Rita 1028, 1032
Hazard, Jayne 161, 1027
Hazard, Lawrence 155, 217, 928
Hazlett, Bill 679
Healey, Myron 8, 179, 327, 364, 527, 589, 684, 759, 880, 898, 912, 994
Healy, Bill 991
Healy, Eunice 244
Healy, Mary 1028
Hearn, Edward 56, 142, 162, 411, 433, 632, 770, 863, 907, 949, 962, 963
Hearn, Lew 765
Hearne, Reginald 829
Heath, Arch B. 947
Heath, Ariel 62
Heathcoate, Thomas 1, 185
Hebers, Jeannie 318
Hecht, Ben 765
Hecht, Ted 209, 767, 824
Hedloe, John 497
Hegan, Jim 407
Heigh, Helene 879

Heller, John G. 553
Helm, Fay 813
Helprin, M. 246
Helton, Percy 194, 312, 363, 427, 530, 811, 875
Henderson, Al C. 23
Henderson, Dell 347
Henderson, Douglas 531
Henderson, Kelo 427
Henderson, Marcia 900
Henderson, Ray 66, 261, 434, 602, 634, 847, 860, 873, 907, 960, 968
Hendrian, Oscar 955, 961, 1000
Hendricks, Ben, Jr. 76, 554
Hendricks, Jack 987, 1010
Hendriks, Jan 454
Hendrix, Wanda 704
Henning, Pat 725
Henreid, Paul 924
Henry, Carol 691, 719
Henry, Charlotte 245, 272, 322, 476, 639
Henry, Dee "Buzzy" 97, 320, 329, 402, 431, 505, 561, 648, 654
Henry, Diane 569
Henry, Frank 323, 678
Henry, Louise 341
Henry, Robert 989
Henry, Thomas Browne 43, 46, 357, 418, 460, 599, 781
Henry, William (Bill) 2, 93, 170, 174, 216, 220, 278, 386, 409, 413, 459, 480, 516, 544, 577, 638, 696, 729, 776, 789, 831, 848, 951, 1019
Henson, Dean 973
Hepburn, Barton 749
Heppner, Cynthia 790
Herald, Heinz 297
Herbert, Sir Alan P. 359
Herbert, Dorothy 992
Herbert, F. Hugh 162, 248, 309, 342, 488, 532, 820, 926
Herbert, Hans 419
Herbert, Harry 772
Herbert, Holmes 272, 392, 599, 926
Herbert, Hugh 314, 342
Herbert, Percy 300
Herbert, Tom 777
Herczeg, Geza 381
Herman, Al 477, 541

Herman, Gil 121, 357, 548, 689, 912, 925
Herman, Lewis 783
Herman, Woody, and His Orchestra 204, 344
Herman's Mountaineers 319
Hern, Pepe 320, 390, 402, 458, 830
Hernandez, Chiquita, Orchestra 432
Hernandez, Joe 816
The Herrara Sisters 195
Herrick, F. Herrick 276, 968, 1000
Herrick, Virginia 890
Hervey, Grizelda 859
Hervey, Irene 151
Herzinger, Carl 733
Hessey, Audrey 837
Heugly, Archie 451
Hewlett, Bentley 76, 906
Heyburn, Weldon 75, 123, 124, 171, 286, 464, 569, 705, 844, 934
Heydt, Louis Jean 211, 407, 475, 530, 619, 767, 784, 1071
Heyes, Herbert 97, 112, 171, 408, 566
Heywood, Herbert 76, 411
Hickey, Howard 988
Hickman, Cordell 55, 904
Hickman, Darryl 704
Hickman, Howard 48, 78, 133, 162, 187, 262, 311, 361, 365, 396, 400, 406, 410, 864, 952, 962, 991
Hicks, Chuck 304
Hicks, Russell 27, 46, 187, 213, 236, 260, 268, 278, 322, 366, 408, 429, 462, 547, 552, 588, 593, 594, 597, 612, 747, 833, 881, 902, 952, 983
Hickson, Joan 185, 186, 808
Hiess, Henriette 379
Hiestand, John 968, 983
The Higgins Family 339
Hildebrand, Rodney 448
Hill, Arthur 165
Hill, Betty 415
Hill, Ethel 377, 464
Hill, Frank 975
Hill, Maury 838
Hill, Paula 326
Hill, Peter Murray 596
Hill, Ramsay 994, 1006

# Name Index

Hill, Riley 719, 1019
Hill, Robert 924
Hilliard, Ernest 89, 397, 617
Hilliard, Ruth 856
Hillias, Peg 900
Hineman, Art 1014, 1015, 1016, 1017
Hines, Alf 772
Hines, Frazer 901
Hinton, Ed 437
Hinton, Mary 596
Hird, Thora 165, 808
Hires, Buck 987
Hirliman, George A. 289, 617
Hirsch, Elroy "Crazylegs" 147
Hirsch, Ray 364
Hirsch, Win 147
Hitchcock, Keith 444, 709
Ho, Andy 428
Hobart, Rose 918, 1028
Hobbes, Halliwell 778
Hodgins, Earle 12, 50, 64, 91, 95, 112, 234, 276, 306, 337, 352, 408, 424, 435, 456, 469, 537, 540, 542, 546, 555, 556, 584, 615, 624, 673, 687, 697, 724, 728, 735, 813, 833, 839, 847, 877, 878, 886, 891, 955
Hodgson, Leland 876, 947
Hoerl, Arthur 8
Hoey, Dennis 662, 898
Hoff, Carl, and Band 341
Hoffman, Bob 505
Hoffman, Gertrude W. 272
Hoffman, Joseph 140, 293, 606, 815
Hoffman, M. H. 77, 246, 764
Hoffman, Max, Jr. 667
Hoffman, Otto 12
Hogan, Brenda 808, 837
Hogan, Dick 623
Hogan, Michael 416
Hogan, Pat 377, 989
Hohl, Arthur 369
Hokanson, Mary Alan 418, 497, 766
Holbrook, Stan 912
Holden, James 241, 689
Holden, William 1034
Holdren, Judd 766, 1009, 1019
Hole, William 770
Holland, John 46, 91, 117,
400, 402, 409, 430, 573, 576, 659, 754, 960
Holland, Zeke 197
Holles, Antony 287
Holliday, Martha 235, 364
Hollins, Harry 981, 998
Holloway, Stanley 165
Holloway, Sterling 342, 400, 552, 656, 678, 739, 848, 866
Hollywood, Jimmy 987
Holman, Harry 612, 712, 906
Holmes, Garrett 856
Holmes, John Merrill 267
Holmes, Maynard 438, 636
Holmes, Phillips 360
Holmes, Ralph 1007
Holmes, Taylor 227, 329, 357, 484, 561, 594, 644, 838, 882, 921
Holmes, Wendell 938
Holmes, William 371, 884
Holt, David 6, 113
Holt, Jack 80, 260, 422, 513, 846, 913, 1032
Holt, Jennifer 620
Homans, Robert E. 42, 203, 291, 349, 373, 396, 429, 462, 469, 525, 586, 603, 633, 642, 714, 728, 745, 746, 932, 972, 974
Homeier, Skip 156, 595, 654, 784, 828
Homes, Geoffrey (Daniel Mainwaring) 710
Homolka, Oscar 122
Hood, Ned 841
Hooker, Buddy Joe 999
Hoose, Fred 46, 539, 800
The Hoosier Hot Shots 358, 376
Hope, Dorothy 30
Hopper, DeWolf (William Hopper) 421
Hopper, Hedda 159
Hopper, Wesley 800, 961, 968, 987, 988
Hopton, Russell 53, 254
Horman, Arthur T. 290, 404, 857, 894, 938
Horne, James W. 12
Horne, Victoria 153, 378, 450
Horsey, David 1000, 1007
Horsley, John 901
Horswell, Bert 137
Horton, Edward Everett 79, 203, 274, 777
Horton, Nigel 709
Horton, Robert 472
Horvath, Charles 156, 580, 964
Horwin, Jerry 348
The Hot Shots 825
Houcke, Gilbert 118
Hough, E. Morton 77
Hould, Ra (Ronald Sinclair) 70, 159
House, Newton 1002
Houser, Lionel 162, 677, 918
Housman, Arthur 612
Houston, Donald 186
Houston, Glyn 808
Houston, Norman 254, 372, 648, 940
Houston, Renee 841
Hoven, Adrian 118
Howard, Boothe 537, 632, 1007
Howard, David 349
Howard, Edward 861
Howard, Esther 297, 326, 640
Howard, Frederick 298, 887, 958, 967, 990, 997
Howard, Gordon 383
Howard, Joan 919
Howard, John 230, 364, 458, 843
Howard, Lewis 389
Howard, Mary 12
Howard, Shemp 550
Howard, William K. 309
Howat, Clark 121
Howe, James Wong 384
Howe, Wally 434
Howell, Helen 493
Howell, Jean 327
Howell, Kenneth 371
Howells, Ursula 233, 841
Howes, Reed 34, 105, 142, 172, 195, 332, 405, 408, 692, 697, 761, 797, 812, 832, 949, 955, 961, 963, 968, 987, 1001, 1010, 1012
Howland, Olin 140, 167; see also Olin Howlin
Howlett, Jeanne 1032
Howlin, Olin 15, 21, 140, 155, 215, 217, 228, 293, 326, 351, 373, 397, 464, 648, 659, 691, 710, 719,

734, 928; *see also* Olin
   Howland
Hoyos, Rodolfo  227, 402
Hoyt, Arthur  400, 552, 576,
   726, 927
Hruba, Vera  367, 368; *see
   also* Vera Ralston; Vera
   Hruba Ralston
Hubbard, John  84, 112, 144,
   710, 910, 911, 941
Hubbard, Tom  160, 324,
   335, 619, 619
Huber, Harold  139, 195, 263,
   368, 457, 462, 577, 743
Hubert, Ted  977
Hubner, Herbert  118
Hudis, Norman  233, 233
Hudkins, Ace  959
Hudman, Wesley  61, 249,
   437
Hudson, Bill  1006
Hudson, Hal  843
Hudson, John  704, 909
Hudson, Rochelle  606, 745,
   778
Hugh, John R.  935
Hughes, Anthony  94
Hughes, Carol  71, 291, 350,
   465, 485, 874, 878
Hughes, Charles Anthony
   412
Hughes, David  616
Hughes, Howard  986, 1004
Hughes, Jackie  1032
Hughes, Kay  56, 276, 461,
   476, 642, 822, 960, 1008
Hughes, Lloyd  461
Hughes, Mary Beth  141, 297,
   1028, 1030
Hughes, Michael  274, 739
Hughes, Richard  184
Hughes, Robin  708
Hughes, Roddy  596
Hughes, Rupert  603
Hughes, Whitey  531
Hugo, Mauritz  102, 157, 170,
   253, 354, 392, 638, 698,
   959, 973, 981, 989, 1019
Hulett, Otto  121
Hull, Henry  293, 905
Hull, Warren  493, 640, 643
The Hull Twins  897
Humbert, George  512, 779
Hummert, Frank  477
Humphrey, Harry  963
Humphrey, William  960
Hunnicutt, Arthur  423

Hunt, Eleanor  289
Hunt, Jane  770
Hunt, Jimmy  659
Hunt, Marsha  133, 381
Hunter, Alistair  837, 859
Hunter, Ann  1028
Hunter, Bill  961
Hunter, Ian  27
Hunter, N. C.  596
Huntley, Eleanor  833
Huntley, G. P., Jr.  493
Huntley, Raymond  185
Hurst, Brian Desmond  11,
   287, 790
Hurst, Paul  15, 57, 78, 87,
   155, 321, 378, 430, 452,
   495, 499, 510, 544, 563,
   577, 582, 589, 593, 608,
   626, 686, 748, 759, 777,
   791, 840, 872, 889
Hussey, Ruth  364, 418, 921
Huston, Virginia  925
Hutchison, Charles  949, 952,
   963, 988, 991, 992
Hutton, Robert  290, 562,
   698, 829, 857
Hyams, John  322
Hyams, Leila  552
Hyatt, Bobby  774, 840
Hyde-White, Wilfrid  82, 596
Hyde, Eva  614
Hyer, Martha  253, 684
Hyke, Ray  912
Hyland, Dick Irving  419, 450
Hyland, Frances  113, 343,
   373, 378, 510, 747, 815
Hyle, Grace  833
Hylton, Jane  707
Hymer, Warren  29, 96, 347,
   400, 414, 429, 439, 485,
   520, 705
Hytten, Olaf  51, 159, 266,
   360, 764, 869, 965

Imhof, Roger  108
Impossible Pictures  1014,
   1015, 1016, 1017
Ince, John  123, 135, 189, 425
Indrisano, John  34, 429
Inescort, Frieda  237, 598,
   919, 945
Infuhr, Teddy  98, 197
Ingham, Geoffrey  419
Ingraham, Lloyd  35, 60, 85,
   126, 226, 261, 289, 302,
   322, 394, 433, 440, 448,
   465, 488, 585, 625, 632,

697, 873, 907, 916, 949,
   963, 1008
Ingram, Jack  24, 39, 52, 66,
   95, 106, 123, 130, 167, 177,
   190, 202, 217, 249, 260,
   277, 299, 308, 352, 369,
   408, 448, 463, 470, 488,
   491, 502, 508, 512, 522,
   524, 526, 543, 551, 567,
   586, 602, 611, 620, 621,
   623, 645, 646, 674, 680,
   692, 719, 723, 760, 763,
   794, 799, 854, 855, 877,
   878, 895, 899, 906, 915,
   916, 930, 936, 939, 959,
   960, 961, 963, 964, 967,
   968, 986, 987, 990, 1003,
   1007, 1008, 1010
Ingram, Joan  858
Ingram, Rex  505
Ingrams, Michael  772
Ireland, John  531, 817
Irish, Kitty  816
Irish, Tom  121
Irving, George  322, 476, 521,
   983
Irving, Margaret  244
Irving, Richard  65, 754, 849,
   920, 969
Irwin, Boyd  98, 364, 378,
   941
Irwin, Charles  734, 825
Isabelita (Lita Baron)  814,
   815
Isabell, Henry  915, 987, 1010
Isbell, Jane  466
Isley, Phylis (Jennifer Jones)
   524, 963
Ivan, Rosalind  813
Ives, Douglas  186
Ivins, Perry  46, 499, 629,
   963, 968
Ivo, Tommy  204, 505, 563,
   706, 750
Iwanabe, Amy  912

Jackson, Eugene  306, 322,
   448, 632, 863
Jackson, Harry  575
Jackson, Jackie  628
Jackson, Joe, Jr.  368
Jackson, Peggy  222
Jackson, Ray  808
Jackson, Selmer  29, 78, 81,
   96, 155, 193, 200, 217, 251,
   288, 305, 409, 477, 485,
   604, 609, 663, 720, 747,

# NAME INDEX

761, 769, 870, 897, 927, 962, 1000, 1024
Jackson, Sherry 131, 143
Jackson, Thomas E. 53, 159, 280, 365, 461, 516, 886
Jackson, Warren 95, 961, 962, 1003
Jackson and Lynam 367, 368
Jacobs, Harrison 126, 394, 897, 940
Jacoby, Michel 745
Jacques, Ted 65, 600
Jaeckel, Richard 228, 357, 689, 703, 704, 713
Jaffe, Carl 152
Jaggberg, Kurt 379
Jagger, Dean 197, 210, 211, 212
James, Alan 960, 990, 993, 1003
James, Alfred P. 735
James, Edward 358, 416
James, Gardner 949
James, Gladden 927
James, Ida 856
James, John 52, 75, 154, 243, 298, 337, 354, 420, 470, 564, 646, 692, 746, 832, 868, 904, 908, 913, 962, 972, 986, 1004
James, Rosemonde 13, 50, 467, 997
James, Roy 570
James, Sydney 772
James, Walter 537, 949, 987
Jamieson, Harold 443
Jamison, Bill 776
Jamison, Bob 949, 951, 963, 965, 93, 985, 986, 1004, 1008, 1010
Jamison, Bud 397, 833, 941
Janis, Elsie 926
Janney, William 77, 741
Janssen, Eilene 25, 81, 157, 914
Janssen, Elsa 388
January, Lois 41, 440, 634, 860
Jaquet, Frank 52, 91, 92, 93, 114, 128, 236, 301, 368, 373, 555, 621, 691, 725, 731, 747, 839, 887, 967
Jara, Maurice 402, 572
Jarman, Claude, Jr. 219, 651
Jarmyn, Jil 436, 474, 530, 867
Jason, Leigh 415

Jason, Sybil 919
Jauregui, Eddie 48, 949, 987, 1004
Jayawardena, Sujata 118
Jeayes, Allan 30
Jeffers, Mike 955
Jeffrey, Michael 159
Jeffreys, Anne 74, 97, 112, 171, 337, 397, 470, 502, 545, 569, 895, 932, 937
Jeffries, Betty 384
Jeffries, James J. 42
Jenkins, Allen 381, 539, 894
Jenkins, Megs 596, 858
Jenkins, Polly, and Her Plowboys 465
Jenkins, Shirley 808
Jenks, Frank 487, 669, 714, 730, 757, 777, 813, 815, 821, 884
Jenks, Si 39, 67, 145, 244, 267, 280, 299, 368, 467, 539, 555, 603, 625, 643, 752, 844, 990, 1002, 1011
Jennings, Chuck 987
Jennings, Clarke 1003
Jennings, Maxine 278
Jenny, Jack, and His Orchestra 477
Jerome, Elmer 368, 408, 803, 815, 941
Jerome, Jerry 441, 612, 776, 947, 950, 952, 955, 986, 992, 1000, 1004
Jewell, Isabel 158, 438, 699, 777
Jimenez, Edwardo 572
Joby, Hans 72
Johnson, Ben 88, 651, 928
Johnson, Bob 979
Johnson, Brad 418
Johnson, Carter 361
Johnson, Chic 12, 140
Johnson, Chubby 249, 304, 316, 527, 903
Johnson, Eddie 850
Johnson, Edna 91
Johnson, Erskine 856
Johnson, Fred 408, 901
Johnson, Glen 987
Johnson, Gunner 987
Johnson, Hall, Choir 244, 317, 375, 415
Johnson, J. Louis 800
Johnson, John Lester 965
Johnson, June 56, 264, 445, 476, 573

Johnson, Linda 38, 794
Johnson, Noble 256, 260, 533, 593, 625, 975
Johnson, Ray 963
Johnson, Raymond 402
Johnson, Robert Lee 196, 280, 313
Johnson, Tor 401, 880
Johnston, Alva 209
Johnston, Barbara 341
Johnston, Oliver 700
Joiner, Patricia 497
Jolley, I. Stanford 37, 56, 90, 276, 376, 437, 466, 689, 746, 854, 948, 950, 953, 954, 958, 959, 960, 964, 970, 984, 989, 1019
Jolliffe, John 510
Jones, Arthur V. 773, 937
Jones, Bill 987
Jones, Buck 897
Jones, Carolyn 273, 458
Jones, Dick 18, 334, 509, 635, 689, 907, 919
Jones, Gordon 22, 47, 243, 281, 290, 320, 365, 533, 606, 754, 768, 796, 846, 854, 922
Jones, Griffith 336
Jones, Grover 162
Jones, Herb 484
Jones, Marcia Mae 414, 532, 870
Jones, Mary 700
Jones, Peter 165
Jones, Ray 48, 62, 267, 394, 569, 590, 723, 895, 908, 956, 1004
Jones, Stan 426, 651
Jones, Thomas 121
Jones, Tiny 488, 616
Jones, Trefor 287
Jones, Walter 961
The Jones Boys 56
The Jones Family 339
Jons, Beverly 107
Jope-Slade, Christine 245
Jordan, Bob 472
Jordan, Charles 370
Jordan, Dorothy 791
Jordan, Joanne 362, 1019
Jordan, Patrick 553
Jory, Victor 82, 281, 287, 427, 473, 840
Josefsberg, Milt 367
Josephson, Milt 740
Joslyn, Allyn 505

# Name Index

Journet, Marcel 599
Joyce, Brenda 825, 1033, 1034
Joyce, Eileen 851
Joyce, Jean 567, 664
Judd, Johnny 965
Judels, Charles 56, 378, 593, 640, 803
Judge, Arline 753
Jung, Allen 972, 983
Jurado, Katy 84, 685
Justice, James Robertson 1, 185, 186
Justice, William 985
Justine and Carter 11

Kaaren, Suzanne 491, 606, 618, 640, 873
Kacher, Bunny 121
Kafka, John 923
Kahanamoku, Duke 898
Kahn, Gordan 144, 365, 459, 494, 442, 752, 789, 810, 810, 520, 717, 757, 918
Kahn, Lilly 165
Kalili, Maiola 219
Kallman, Dick 324
Kane, Eddie 12, 13, 50, 323, 419, 467, 477, 674, 710
Kane, Joseph 2, 24, 29, 35, 60, 70, 71, 76, 80, 90, 106, 113, 126, 132, 134, 144, 150, 155, 167, 199, 219, 228, 236, 256, 260, 276, 291, 299, 304, 306, 308, 310, 317, 319, 329, 357, 369, 372, 374, 376, 378, 394, 402, 408, 411, 422, 427, 431, 433, 448, 463, 465, 466, 475, 484, 489, 522, 535, 537, 538, 542, 543, 546, 576, 593, 594, 611, 618, 625, 633, 642, 644, 648, 654, 657, 659, 663, 672, 673, 680, 681, 685, 697, 703, 704, 723, 725, 732, 752, 753, 755, 760, 763, 766, 770, 771, 798, 799, 828, 836, 863, 878, 888, 899, 921, 928, 934, 936, 939, 940, 957, 1007
Kane, Louise 538, 928
Kane, Marjorie "Babe" 464, 962
Kaplan, Marvin 215
Kaplan, Russ 155
Karabanova, Zoya 534

Karlan, Richard 2, 150, 475
Karloff, Boris 1003
Karnes, Robert 340, 766, 884, 912
Karns, Roscoe 270, 381, 486, 582, 816, 843, 891, 937, 1032
Kasket, Harold 185
Kasznar, Kurt 237
Katch, Kurt 614, 1001
Katchenaro, Pete 983
Kauffman, Tamara Lynn 655
Kaufman, Allan 324
Kaufman, Willy 779
Kaufmann, Maurice 707
Kay, Geraldine 148
Kay, Gordon 37, 38, 68, 107, 125, 143, 170, 174, 178, 253, 255, 305, 479, 519, 527, 540, 600, 638, 671, 676, 684, 724, 890, 903, 913, 929
Kay, Mary Ellen 73, 129, 176, 249, 426, 661, 730, 826, 903, 973
Kay, Patricia 856
Kaye, Darwood 332
Kaye, Eddie 965
Kaye, Lucie 396, 598
Kean, Betty 504
Kean, Jane 682
Keane, Edward 46, 74, 89, 171, 256, 326, 368, 413, 514, 559, 662, 678, 747, 848, 850, 865, 952, 972, 974, 976
Keane, Robert Emmett 32, 53, 60, 71, 76, 255, 340, 396, 519, 560, 622, 636, 801, 835, 909
Kearney, Carolyn 938
Keckley, Jane 308, 488, 655, 960, 987
Keefe, Cornelius 56, 543, 679, 855, 863
Keefer, Major Bill 679
Keekas, Harry 474
Keeler, Wee Willie 115, 143
Keen, Geoffrey 184, 185, 186
Keene, Mike 665
Keene, Richard 397, 715
Keene, Tom 846; *see also* Richard Powers
Keiley, Virginia 782
Keir, David 30
Keith, Alan 790
Keith, Brian 324

Keith, Ian 74, 108, 370, 470, 584, 636, 794, 886
Keith, Rosalind 29
Kellard, Robert 602, 965, 985
Keller, Harry 40, 61, 65, 102, 176, 208, 249, 437, 480, 587, 631, 696, 807, 831, 1019
Keller, Martin 184
Kelley, Albert 744
Kelley, Alice 81
Kelley, Barry 2, 111, 304, 713, 736, 921
Kelley, Bob 147
Kelley, Burt 5
Kelley, DeForest 201
Kelley, Mary 960
Kellino, Pamela 417
Kellino, Roy 417
Kellogg, Bruce 173; *see also* William Kellogg
Kellogg, Cecil 988
Kellogg, Frances 432
Kellogg, Gayle 912, 951, 1009
Kellogg, John 8, 656, 706
Kellogg, William 48, 351, 405, 551, 940, 985, 986; *see also* Bruce Kellogg
Kelly, Burt 520
Kelly, Carol 160
Kelly, Claire 698
Kelly, Craig 1009, 1019
Kelly, Don 150, 535
Kelly, Jack 191, 806, 912
Kelly, James L. 505
Kelly, Jeanne (Jean Brooks) 148
Kelly, Jimmie 312
Kelly, John 78, 272, 592, 598, 834
Kelly, Judy 30
Kelly, Lew 12, 71, 76, 291, 299, 465, 576, 680, 823, 916
Kelly, Nancy 510, 923
Kelly, Patrick J. 814, 975, 992
Kelly, Patsy 342, 373
Kelly, Paul 218, 243, 247, 288, 301, 400, 466, 767
Kelly, Tommy 217
Kelly, Walter C. 429
Kelly, William 859
Kelsall, Moultrie 859
Kelsey, Fred 12, 672, 681, 932
Kelso, Edmond 567, 570
Kelso, Vernon 772

# Name Index

Keltner, Ken 407
Kelton, Pert 341, 485, 641, 741
Kemmer, Edward 575
Kemp, Kenner G. 189, 951
Kemp, Matty 112
Kemper, Charles 16, 90
Kendall, Cy 83, 96, 158, 271, 288, 386, 411, 448, 485, 525, 657, 834, 910
Kendall, Kay 186, 772
Kennedy, Bill 730, 813, 902
Kennedy, Bob 407
Kennedy, Don 329
Kennedy, Douglas 211, 327, 357, 538, 626, 644, 685, 704, 759
Kennedy, Edgar 101, 373, 552, 577, 612, 639, 911, 1033
Kennedy, Fred 651
Kennedy, Jack 612, 632
Kennedy, King 1028
Kennedy, Madge 595
Kennedy, Phyllis 894
Kennedy, Ron 335
Kennedy, Roy 987
Kennedy, Tom 19, 141, 314, 330, 343, 536, 577, 604, 669, 682
Kenney, Jack 31, 542, 742, 930, 955, 962, 963, 983, 1008
Kenney, James 1, 185, 336
Kenny, Clyde 448
Kent, Crauford 222, 674
Kent, Dorothea 91, 408, 715
Kent, Keneth 790
Kent, Michael 180, 961
Kent, Robert 96, 224, 773, 797, 912, 996
Kent, Willard 961
Kenton, Erle C. 582
Kenworthy, Katherine 930
Kenyon, Charles 584
Kenyon, Mary 205, 688, 734
Kerima 716
Kerman, David 568
Kern, Grace 655
Kerr, Donald 31, 117, 605, 764, 960
Kerr, Laura 79
Kerrigan, J. M. 55, 231, 322, 429, 677, 945
Kerrigan, Marian 50
Kerwin, David 24
Kesterson, George 71, 394,
657, 663, 755; *see also* Art Mix; Denver Dixon
Kevin, James 938
Keyes, Evelyn 328
Keymas, George 304, 484, 690, 828, 888
Keys, Robert 787
The Keystone Kops 1033
Kibbee, Guy 396, 1034
Kibbee, Milton 62, 137, 318, 354, 373, 405, 512, 570, 821, 868, 908
Kibbons, Everett 1007
Kidd, John 595
The Kidoodlers 42, 487, 893
Kiffe, Karl 398
Kikume, Al 164, 219, 898, 947, 980, 995
Kilburn, Martin 912
Kilburn, Terry 490
Kilian, Victor 42, 44, 232, 544, 557, 727, 929
Killick, Robert 379
Kilpatrick, Tom 462
Kimble, Lawrence 18, 33, 48, 182, 235, 345, 364, 398, 504, 577, 612, 805
Kimbley, Billy 730
Kimmell, Leslie 359
King, Bradley 816
King, Charles 20, 55, 74, 89, 97, 124, 146, 175, 190, 256, 261, 291, 306, 408, 433, 435, 440, 470, 483, 551, 632, 634, 646, 650, 667, 693, 738, 761, 773, 827, 860, 863, 877, 928, 970, 978, 987, 993, 1002, 1012
King, Claude 311, 438, 552
King, Eugene 59
King, George 30, 122
King, Hugh 907
King, Manuel 957
King, Patty 628
King, Rex 56
King, Stanley 388
King, Walter Woolf 121
The King Cole Trio 330, 591
Kingsford, Guy 311, 773
Kingsford, Walter 250, 388, 709
Kinkead, Randal 184
Kinskey, Leonid 231, 290, 356, 415, 485, 568, 717, 814
Kipling, Richard 962
Kippen, Manart 236
Kiraly, Erno 419
Kirby, Jay 137, 166, 483, 540, 720, 748, 896, 982, 1011
Kirby, Newt 655
Kirby, Ralph 145
Kirk, Jack 9, 15, 23, 26, 35, 52, 54, 60, 67, 68, 71, 75, 88, 89, 92, 99, 104, 105, 106, 115, 123, 124, 128, 130, 132, 134, 137, 138, 142, 144, 146, 171, 172, 190, 234, 256, 260, 264, 266, 286, 302, 303, 306, 308, 310, 331, 337, 346, 351, 353, 354, 373, 374, 377, 394, 395, 405, 408, 411, 413, 433, 434, 442, 445, 446, 448, 463, 464, 469, 482, 483, 488, 502, 522, 523, 526, 537, 540, 551, 556, 566, 567, 569, 570, 573, 574, 584, 585, 590, 601, 602, 607, 615, 620, 624, 633, 641, 643, 647, 648, 650, 660, 663, 672, 673, 674, 679, 687, 692, 719, 720, 721, 722, 723, 728, 731, 732, 735, 737, 760, 770, 775, 779, 792, 795, 799, 812, 839, 844, 845, 847, 861, 862, 874, 877, 878, 885, 896, 907, 908, 915, 930, 936, 939, 948, 949, 952, 954, 967, 982, 987, 988, 996, 1002, 1008, 1010, 1011
Kirk, Joseph 591, 932, 962
Kirke, Donald 140, 537, 565, 576, 624, 698, 972
Kirkland, Jack 250
Kirkwood, James 46, 197, 363, 791, 922
Kirov, Ivan 765
Kirwin, Patrick 82
Kitchin, Laurence 596
Klauber, Marcel 268, 283
Kline, Bob 595
Kline, Herbert 407
Klingenberg, Heinz 454
Knaggs, Skelton 315
Knapp, Evalyn 83, 429, 1027
Knapp, Robert 698
Knight, Albert 673
Knight, Charles 574
Knight, David 808
Knight, Fuzzy 144, 340, 356, 535, 539
Knight, Glenn 952

Knight, Patricia 217
Knight, Red 91
Knight, Tracy 957, 1007
Knowles, Patric 530, 778, 926
Knox, Alexander 184
Knox, Elyse 723
Knox, Mickey 181
Knox, Mona 831
Knox, Patricia 108, 213, 382, 415, 464, 536, 597, 599, 729, 977
Kobliansky, Nick 534
Koenig, Mabelle 230
Kohler, Fred, Jr. 97, 160, 260, 357, 401, 522, 609, 621, 768, 865, 868, 959, 962
Kohler, Fred, Sr. 55, 60, 263, 1008
Kohn, Rose Simon 853
Kohner, Frederick 398, 413, 419, 419, 805
"Koko," the Horse 22, 73, 129, 194, 340, 387, 426, 547, 548, 587, 631, 635, 661, 711, 730, 762, 826, 875, 884
Kolb, Clarence 366, 588, 598, 653
Kolker, Henry 254, 295, 457, 726, 741
Komai, Tetsu 947
Kong, King 983
Kornman, Mary 410, 942
Kortman, Robert 52, 62, 89, 92, 168, 172, 276, 395, 434, 448, 466, 566, 794, 916, 949, 968, 987, 1000, 1008, 1010
Kortner, Fritz 614
Koshay, Bobbie 1003
Kosleck, Martin 149, 182, 265, 709
Koumani, Maya 233, 336
Krafft, John W. 173, 374, 507, 809
Krah, Marc 849
Kraly, Hans 180
Krasne, Philip N. 580
Kreig, Frank 447
Kreuger, Kurt 614
Kroeger, Berry 935
Kronman, Harry 78
Krueger, Kurt 1001
Krueger, Lorraine 550, 1030
Kruger, Alma 613
Kruger, Harold 991

Kruger, Otto 116, 204, 216, 287, 423, 490, 779, 869, 923, 945
Krumgold, Joseph 151, 396, 400, 414, 457
Kruschen, Jack 103, 153, 857, 882, 925
Kuhn, Hans 184
Kuhn, Mickey 757
Kulkovich, Henry "Bomber" 10; *see also* Henry Kulky
Kulky, Henry 290, 838; *see also* Henry "Bomber" Kulkovich
Kuller, Sid 342
Kuter, Kay E. 120
Kuznetzoff, Adia 814
Kydd, Sam 851
Kyne, Peter B. 5, 46, 100

Lacardo, Vic 56
Lace, Lentia 223
Lacey, Catherine 596
Lackey, William 181, 382, 605, 708, 786
Lackteen, Frank 135, 164, 281, 406, 556, 950, 980
Ladd, Alan 12, 133, 262, 375, 486, 582
Lafayette, Jeanne 56
Laffan, Patricia 336
Laidlaw, Ethan 95, 130, 145, 146, 217, 258, 352, 410, 473, 526, 641, 773, 823, 862, 931, 963
Laird, Effie 52, 359, 464
Lait, Jack, Jr. 172, 498
Lake, Arthur 57, 212, 1030
Lake, Fred 829
Lally, Bill 963
Lally, William J. 627
Lamal, Isabel 466
Lamarr, Dick 962
Lamas, Fernando 33
Lamb, Gil 344
Lambert, Jack 80, 152, 533, 593, 808, 841
Lamble, Lloyd 300, 841
Lamont, Charles 83, 103, 333, 436, 606, 882
Lamont, Duncan 837
Lamont, Marten 487, 635, 947, 967, 992
Lamont, Molly 271, 825
Lamour, Dorothy 1028
Lanchester, Elsa 328, 534, 825

Landau, Richard 472
Lander, David 782
Lander, Eric 841
Landers, Lew 34, 173, 281, 649, 733, 737, 897
Landis, Carole 146, 823, 955, 1029
Landon, Hal 107, 260, 519, 950
Landon, Harold 771
Landres, Paul 324
Lane, Allan ("Rocky") 37, 38, 40, 50, 61, 68, 93, 102, 107, 125, 138, 143, 170, 174, 176, 178, 179, 200, 208, 249, 253, 255, 268, 295, 305, 309, 354, 437, 479, 480, 481, 519, 527, 529, 540, 556, 559, 600, 638, 671, 675, 676, 684, 694, 696, 722, 724, 731, 774, 775, 793, 831, 839, 845, 846, 890, 891, 903, 913, 929, 956, 983, 985, 1005, 1023
Lane, Arthur 707, 841
Lane, Billy 397
Lane, Bruce 968
Lane, Charles 151, 243, 351, 386, 505, 560, 740, 833, 937
Lane, Lola 262, 370, 717, 777
Lane, Mike 324
Lane, Morgan 401
Lane, Nora 112, 318, 397, 419, 613, 710, 962, 991
Lane, Norman 1012
Lane, Richard 79, 344, 457, 739, 803
Lane, Rosemary 112, 856
Lane, Wade 595
Lang, David 842, 902
Lang, Fritz 359
Lang, Harold 101, 165, 428
Lang, Harry 963
Lang, June 247
Lang, Kathryn 238
Lang, Stevenson 859
Langdon, Harry 804
Lange, Elaine 109, 378, 467, 879, 967
Langford, Frances 341, 342
Langley, Bruce 630, 941
Langton, Paul 283
Lannes, Georges 558
Lansdale, Eric 965
LaPlanche, Rosemary 803, 966

Lardner, Ring, Jr. 27
Largay, Raymond 744, 955, 963
Larkin, Jerry 56, 1003
Larkin, John 250
Larkin, John Francis 476
LaRocque, Rod 254
LaRoy, Rita 476
Larsen, Peter 379
Larson, Bobby 635
Larson, Christine 853
Larson, Jack 635
LaRue, Emily 1001
LaRue, Frank 69, 127, 154, 435, 440, 498, 302, 567, 570, 611, 632, 738, 776, 847, 961
LaRue, Jack 29, 155, 159, 248, 271, 372, 378, 510, 591, 644, 694, 702, 764, 777, 932, 1001
LaRue, Walt 524, 989, 996, 1005
Lasky, Art 200
Lasky, Jesse, Jr. 34, 737
Lassani, Giorgio 188
Latell, Lyle 516, 814
The Lathrops 477
LaTorre, Charles 18, 312, 708, 796, 972, 1001
Lattuado, Alberto 716
Laughlan, Agnes 837
Laurel, Stan 230
Laurence, Charles 152
Laurenz, John 21
Laurie, John 790
Lauter, Harry 37, 255, 505, 608, 619, 730, 826, 951, 969, 981, 1006
Lavrencic, Dora 184
Lawford, Peter 614, 747, 905
Lawless, Kevin 616
Lawrence-Brown, Stan 403
Lawrence, Craig 50, 419, 967
Lawrence, Edna 623, 987
Lawrence, Hugh 404
Lawrence, Jack 257, 264
Lawrence, Mady 318, 743, 937
Lawrence, Marc 91, 189, 236, 560, 612, 757, 933, 937
Lawrence, Muriel 36, 46, 363
Lawrence, Sheldon 233
Lawrence, Ted 665
Lawrence, Walter 323
Lawson, Charles 17
Lawson, Kate 280, 408, 659

Lawson, Priscilla 331
Lawton, Alma 417
Lawton, Kenneth 272, 1007
Lay, Eugene 278
Layne, Tracy 56, 135, 306, 411, 433, 448, 489, 647, 735, 863, 916, 1000, 1007, 1008
Leary, Nolan 92, 124, 168, 364, 446, 464, 510, 512, 559, 566, 586, 678, 691, 722, 818, 967, 977, 991, 1005, 1011
Lease, Rex 26, 49, 50, 75, 92, 115, 124, 125, 129, 143, 144, 154, 155, 166, 169, 172, 177, 234, 236, 253, 260, 323, 340, 351, 369, 373, 376, 394, 408, 422, 445, 446, 464, 522, 528, 551, 555, 560, 564, 583, 593, 594, 623, 670, 691, 692, 711, 712, 722, 728, 736, 761, 768, 776, 792, 799, 840, 844, 877, 928, 934, 953, 956, 967, 982, 988, 996, 1003, 1005
Leaver, Philip 11
Leavitt, Norman 909
LeBaron, Bert 39, 776, 861, 952, 955, 959, 962, 963, 964, 965, 966, 976, 977, 978, 981, 984, 986, 992, 999, 1004, 1005, 1006
LeBaron, Eddie, and His Orchestra 856
LeBeal, Robert 165
LeBlanc, Andre 33
Lederer, Charles 451
Lederer, Francis 443, 453, 613, 800
Lee, Anna 243, 278
Lee, Billy 376, 393, 522
Lee, Canada 1022
Lee, Connie 104, 277, 491, 508, 623, 643
Lee, Dorothy 757
Lee, Duke 693, 988
Lee, Earl 273, 857
Lee, Eddie 49, 315, 470
Lee, Leonard 788
Lee, Lila 140, 870
Lee, Manfred B. 476, 764; see also Ellery Queen
Lee, Mary 19, 34, 42, 104, 144, 266, 487, 488, 623, 643, 649, 714, 733, 737,

752, 761, 821, 1029, 1031, 1033
Lee, Norman 82
Lee, Pinky 204, 371, 550, 572, 758, 815
Lee, Robin 368
Lee, Rudy 436
Lee, Ruta 867
Lee, Ruth 138, 329, 382, 455, 861
Lee, Scott 914
Leeds, Andrea 388, 1032
Leeds, Charles A. 471
Leeds, Lila 505
Leeds, Peter 32, 612
LeFeur, Jimmy, and his Saddle Pals 770
LeFever, Ralph 987, 988
Lefton, Abe 489, 543
Leftwich, Alexander 1003
LeGall, Andre 558
Lehman, Ernest 381
The Raynor Lehr Circus 854
Leiber, Fritz 51, 196, 322
Leigh, Frank 764
Leigh, George 222
Leigh, Nelson 370
Leigh, Patric Dennis 531
Leigh, Rowland 749
Leighton, Jim 912
Leighton, Melinda 123, 145
LeMay, Alan 241, 363, 888
Lemon, Bob 407
Lemont, John 300
Lemus, Conchita 21
Lenard, Grace 464
Lennon, James 10
Lenoir, Leon 79
Leo, Maurice 342
Leon, Connie 512, 813
Leon, Peggy 392
Leonard, Queenie 825
Leonard, Sheldon 164, 424, 452, 622, 856
Leong, James B. 315, 636, 965
Leontovitsch, Maria 184
LeSaint, Edward J. 83, 554, 960
Lescoulie, Jack 541
Leslie, Aleen 669
Leslie, Dudley 287
Leslie, Eddie 858
Leslie, Joan 241, 329, 402, 840, 922, 1027
Leslie, Kay 1027
Leslie, Maxine 577

# Name Index

Leslie, Nan  387, 589
Lessey, George  591, 747
Lessy, Ben  941
Lester, Bruce  708
Lester, Dan  300
Lester, Jan  318
Lester, Jerry  743
Lester, Vicki  743
Lester, William  865
Letz, George  60, 256, 291, 473, 672, 725, 738, 770, 899, 975, 987; *see also* George Montgomery
Levey, Gerry  553
Levine, Nat  53, 56, 67, 83, 85, 117, 135, 140, 196, 244, 272, 276, 282, 306, 311, 313, 322, 341, 346, 347, 360, 400, 421, 448, 476, 489, 521, 537, 543, 552, 554, 576, 603, 642, 647, 655, 673, 681, 735, 738, 741, 822, 833, 863, 870, 916, 957, 960, 1000, 1007, 1008
Levine, Susan  747
Leviness, Carl  50, 743
Levitte, Jean  558
Levoy, Albert E.  396, 414, 598, 640, 741
Levy, Parke  203, 344
Lewin, Ike  987
Lewis, Dorothy  367
Lewis, Franklin  407
Lewis, Gene  447, 925
Lewis, George J.  62, 63, 64, 172, 405, 420, 565, 579, 622, 638, 642, 751, 758, 866, 876, 896, 948, 952, 956, 967, 970, 972, 974, 991, 995, 996, 999, 1001, 1004, 1005, 1011
Lewis, Harry  2, 472
Lewis, Jarma  894
Lewis, Jean Ann  401
Lewis, Jimmy, and his Texas Cowboys  104
Lewis, Mitchell  791
Lewis, Ronald  772
Lewis, Ted, and His Band  477
Lewis, Vera  747, 926
Leyva, Frank  987, 993, 1010
Lezard, Cecile  33
Libby, Fred  898
Liberty Pictures  77, 148, 764
Libkov, Marek M.  109, 579

Libott, Robert  238
Lichter, Baron  972
Lie, Henry  510
Liebmann, Robert  136
Lief, Max  743
The Light Crust Doughboys  56, 537
Lilburn, James  329, 402, 616, 685
Lilian, Mona  841
Lillane and Mario  204
Lilliquist, Jo Ann  766
Linaker, Kay  282
Lincoln, Elmo  66, 130, 930
Linden, Eric  77
Linden, Nat S.  935
Linder, Leslie  300
Lindley, Virginia  950
Lindo, Olga  11
Lindsay, Margaret  843
Lindsey, Marilyn  922
Linn, Frank  721
Linn, James  9, 114, 189, 964, 971, 996
Linn, Ralph  101, 512
Lishman, Harold  898
Lister, Margot  808
Lister, Moira  858
Litel, John  153, 218, 364, 419, 453, 512
Little Brown Jug (Don Kay Reynolds)  481, 628, 750, 934
The Little Vagabonds  864
Littlefield, Lucien  48, 100, 108, 144, 293, 349, 378, 393, 441, 442, 503, 525, 637, 677, 801, 813, 1011
Lively, William  25, 129, 157, 164, 166, 225, 387, 895, 914, 956, 962, 966, 970, 972, 977, 980, 983, 984, 986, 995, 999, 1004
Livermore, Paul  357, 912, 922, 1019
Livingston, Robert  29, 50, 52, 55, 67, 79, 95, 113, 117, 132, 142, 146, 155, 161, 189, 225, 264, 276, 293, 294, 308, 319, 331, 332, 346, 406, 410, 412, 419, 420, 421, 445, 525, 541, 557, 567, 573, 590, 591, 602, 607, 615, 624, 645, 647, 655, 660, 679, 777, 779, 809, 822, 844, 877, 879, 886, 915, 988, 1008

Livinston, Mary  1034
Llewellyn, Richard  596
Lloyd, Beverly  204, 729, 734, 834
Lloyd, Doris  278, 701
Lloyd, Frank  423, 713
Lloyd, George  22, 35, 37, 83, 170, 174, 255, 266, 350, 373, 374, 387, 464, 512, 563, 639, 871, 891, 964, 973
Lloyd, Robin  859
Locher, Charles  916
Locher, Felix  325
Locke, Harry  186
Locke, John  963
Lockhart, Gene  357, 364, 381, 418, 464, 717, 888
Lockhart, Kathleen  473
Lockwood, Alexander  324, 962
Lockwood, Margaret  11, 428, 851, 859
Loder, John  392, 923
Lodge, John  82
Loeb, Lee  6, 86, 247, 247, 450
Loes, Billy  665
Loft, Arthur  34, 106, 126, 151, 167, 193, 195, 377, 442, 467, 512, 550, 576, 611, 641, 669, 702, 721, 732, 745, 760, 763, 812, 842
Loftin, Carey  861, 948, 950, 951, 953, 954, 963, 964, 966, 969, 971, 974, 976, 978, 982, 984, 991, 995, 997, 998, 999, 1001, 1004, 1005, 1011, 1070
Loftos, William  484
Logan, James  994
Logan, Stanley  605, 926
Lohan, Gerard  428
Lola and Fernando  593
Lomas, James  829
Lombard, Linda  505
London, Julie  227
London, Tom  9, 14, 26, 35, 41, 44, 50, 52, 88, 89, 92, 99, 105, 114, 115, 124, 128, 137, 138, 142, 145, 149, 162, 166, 189, 204, 218, 221, 234, 236, 255, 266, 277, 284, 298, 301, 306, 337, 354, 369, 377, 386, 413, 425, 433, 445, 464, 467, 468, 469, 479, 481, 482, 483, 488, 491, 502, 508, 510,

526, 544, 555, 559, 567, 569, 573, 579, 584, 601, 625, 630, 641, 645, 648, 649, 652, 662, 670, 671, 675, 678, 681, 686, 687, 692, 693, 694, 712, 719, 721, 722, 731, 732, 753, 755, 759, 763, 770, 774, 775, 776, 792, 795, 818, 821, 824, 839, 845, 861, 863, 866, 872, 879, 892, 895, 896, 913, 928, 934, 952, 956, 967, 968, 978, 982, 987, 991, 996, 1002, 1004, 1005, 1010, 1011
Long, Audrey 10, 201, 355, 382, 599, 853
Long, Hal 217, 408, 657
Long, Jack 1003
Long, Lotus 668
Long, Robert 786
Long, Walter 67, 960
Longstreet, Stephen 562
Lono, James 94
Loo, Richard 243, 713, 902
Loos, Mary 86, 197, 344, 381, 637
Loos, Theodor 118
Lopez, Manuel 402
Lopez, Paul 947, 993, 1010
Lopez, Perry 402
Lorch, Theodore 394, 629, 960, 968, 1012
Lord, Marjorie 194, 714
Lord, Mindret 288, 783, 933
Lord, Phillips H. 500, 501, 710
Lorenzen, Al 987
Lorimer, Louise 147
Loring, Teala 22
Lorraine, Guido 1
Lorre, Peter 325, 500
Lory, Jacques 962, 1001
Loser, Hanni 379
Louden, Thomas 991
Loughery, Jackie 206
Louis, Joe 592
Louise, Anita 457, 897, 1027
Louisiana Lou (Eva Greenwood) 899
Love, Montagu 415, 968
Love, Ula 770, 942
Lovegrove, Arthur 808, 901
Lovell, Raymond 11
Lovett, Dorothy 478
Lovsky, Celia 239
Low, Jack 162, 464

Low, Walter 961, 972, 985, 1004
Lowe, Edmund 151, 595, 918, 1032
Lowe, Edward T. 279, 612
Lowe, Ellen 75, 293, 597, 623, 669, 679, 742
Lowe, K. Elmo 407, 853, 925
Lowe, Sherman L. 109, 386, 455, 489, 543, 879, 886, 1010
Lowell, Monte 505
Lowery, Robert 321, 436, 653, 702
Lowy, Louis Ludwig 779
Loy, Myrna 628
Loyd, Beverly 883
Lubin, Arthur 254, 262, 360, 494, 869, 911
Lubin, Lou 857
Luby, S. Roy 72, 634
Lucas, Jimmy 91
Lucas, Wilfrid 960
Lucas, William 808
Luckwell, Bill 233, 336, 782
Luckwell, Kay 233
Luden, Jack 75, 670
Ludwig, Alan 863
Ludwig, Edward 217, 231, 237, 898
Luff, Beverly 655
Lufkin, Sam 172, 961
Lugosi, Bela 1003
Luke, Keye 219, 328, 843
Lulu Belle and Scotty (Myrtle and Scott Wiseman) 139, 333, 725, 734, 803, 893
Lund, John 4, 156, 922
Lundigan, William 315, 381, 682
Lundy, Ken 612, 739, 864
Lung, Charles 315, 708
Lupton, John 806
Lurie, Allan 595
Lusk, Freeman 912
Lussier, Dane 413, 418, 455, 517, 588, 597, 729, 769, 779, 824, 910
Luther, Lester 627
Lyden, Pierce 9, 62, 64, 89, 99, 112, 114, 143, 169, 171, 217, 234, 258, 566, 622, 662, 675, 688, 865, 956, 973, 1002
Lydon, James 6, 78, 181, 511, 538, 560, 807
Lydon, Richard 128

Lyman, Abe 736
Lynch, Ken 474, 938
Lynch, Richmond 961
Lynch, Sean 428
Lynd, Helen 240
Lynn, Edward 1003
Lynn, Emmett 57, 80, 105, 137, 168, 169, 293, 294, 296, 373, 397, 402, 420, 422, 468, 539, 556, 565, 566, 675, 694, 699, 773, 774, 794, 896, 908, 978
Lynn, George 200, 283, 355, 876
Lynn, Leni 19
Lynn, Peggy 564
Lynn, Peter George 679, 947, 972
Lynn, Rita 900
Lynne, Eve 236
Lyon, Ben 158, 196, 254
Lyon, Francis D. 147
Lyon, Therese 450
Lyons, Cliff 56, 155, 162, 230, 433, 651, 863, 895, 996, 997, 1005, 1011, 1070
Lyons, Collette 823
Lytton, Herb 480, 952

McArt, Don 401
MacAuley, Ed 407
McAvoy, Charles 612, 735, 961, 962
MacBride, Donald 153, 290, 342, 436
McCall, Bill 537, 691
McCall, Mary C., Jr. 644, 830
McCallum, John 851, 859
McCambridge, Mercedes 399
McCann, Doreen 505, 586
McCanon, Celia 738
McCarey, Ray 31
McCarroll, Frank 24, 50, 74, 92, 97, 102, 105, 134, 137, 138, 142, 234, 258, 317, 337, 470, 498, 566, 569, 602, 620, 657, 672, 720, 721, 731, 752, 763, 861, 866, 895, 956, 964, 1010
McCarthy, Dennis 700
McCarthy, Lin 935
McCarthy, Mary 809, 1032
McCarthy, Red 367, 510
McCarthy, Rod 368
McCarty, Mary 50, 368

McClary, Clyde 72, 261, 303, 624, 847, 860, 916
McClendon, Jack 16, 446
McClory, Sean 362, 616
McClung, Bob 576, 988
McClure, Bud 67, 570, 625, 693, 863, 868, 913, 916
McClure, Greg 292
McClure, M'Liss 382
McConnell, Keith 73, 994
McConville, Bernard 95, 276, 319, 353, 411, 448, 465, 542, 543, 570, 611, 625, 642, 645, 647, 679
McCormack, Meredith 465
McCormick, Barry 808
McCormick, Merrill 70, 132, 175, 260, 307, 372, 373, 374, 406, 488, 491, 543, 567, 601, 615, 624, 746, 760, 776, 847, 916, 949, 959, 963, 965, 1010
McCourt, Margaret 859
McCowen, Alec 184
McCoy, Horace 217, 410, 654
McCracken, Esther 596
McCrea, Ann 802
McCrindle, Alex 859
McCulley, Johnson 67, 634, 667, 860, 1011
McCullough, Philo 433
McCullough, Ralph 397, 576, 961, 1000
McDaniel, Etta 104, 220, 322, 398, 433, 448, 592
McDaniel, Hattie 235
McDaniel, Sam 286, 321, 706, 821, 850
McDermott, Hugh 851
McDonald, Angel (Super Swedish Angel) 10
MacDonald, Edmund 91, 243, 317, 478
McDonald, Francis 68, 75, 90, 106, 109, 115, 138, 164, 199, 279, 298, 386, 427, 513, 529, 580, 600, 662, 668, 678, 685, 748, 767, 828, 1011
McDonald, Frank 13, 27, 42, 50, 104, 116, 139, 248, 266, 295, 344, 358, 375, 393, 442, 467, 509, 513, 536, 545, 622, 623, 643, 718, 734, 739, 750, 795, 803, 809, 850, 864, 866, 874, 876, 893

MacDonald, Ian 2, 199, 399, 581, 789, 826, 836, 840
MacDonald, J. Farrell 134, 162, 252, 341, 347, 374, 494, 789, 902, 923, 988
McDonald, Jack "Sockeye" 10
MacDonald, Kenneth 176, 217, 224, 257, 326, 437, 480, 602, 607, 684, 696, 849, 1019
McDonald, Marie 345, 702
MacDonald, Philip 785, 838
McDonald, Ray 238
MacDonald, Wallace 322, 347
MacDonald, William Colt 13, 64, 95, 123, 142, 146, 264, 267, 276, 319, 331, 332, 346, 406, 445, 524, 526, 541, 564, 567, 570, 573, 574, 585, 590, 602, 615, 621, 624, 629, 645, 646, 647, 655, 660, 679, 692, 693, 712, 822, 823, 832, 844, 855, 877, 885, 904, 908, 915, 930
McDonough, Tom 922, 954, 959, 971, 981
McDowall, Roddy 451, 596
McDowell, Nelson 70, 319, 446, 642, 693, 988
MacFadden, Hamilton 210, 705
McFarland, Frank 224
McFarland, Spanky 144, 398
MacFarlane, Bruce 133, 134, 247
McGann, William 373, 918
McGill, Marguerite 758
McGinnis, Joel 218, 505
McGlynn, Frank, Jr. 434, 907
McGlynn, Frank, Sr. 322, 373, 987
McGowan, Dorrell 27, 42, 55, 56, 59, 133, 135, 139, 189, 193, 195, 252, 286, 295, 306, 326, 333, 349, 358, 375, 376, 380, 393, 411, 412, 461, 507, 509, 514, 529, 536, 545, 632, 642, 674, 678, 688, 705, 718, 727, 734, 735, 736, 761, 776, 803, 834, 852, 864, 866, 878, 886, 893, 936

McGowan, J. P. 306, 319, 346, 822, 961
McGowan, Millard 955, 961, 963, 968, 987, 1007, 1012
McGowan, Stuart 27, 42, 55, 56, 59, 133, 139, 189, 193, 195, 252, 286, 295, 306, 326, 333, 349, 358, 375, 376, 380, 393, 411, 412, 461, 507, 509, 514, 529, 536, 545, 632, 642, 674, 678, 688, 705, 718, 727, 734, 735, 736, 761, 776, 803, 834, 852, 864, 866, 878, 886, 893, 936
McGowan and Mack 419
MacGowran, Jack 616
McGrail, Walter 96, 962, 992, 1033
McGraw, Charles 549
MacGregor, Casey 505, 978
MacGregor, Lee 840
McGregor, Malcolm 1007
McGuinn, Joe 34, 48, 114, 154, 162, 590, 643, 762, 794, 795, 897, 955, 963, 980, 992, 1012, 1084
McGuinness, James Kevin 651
McGuire, Dorothy 458
McGuire, John 51, 224, 689
McGuire, Marion 101
McGuire, Paul 912, 998
Machaty, Gustav 392
McHugh, Kitty 702, 742
McHugh, Matt 201, 225, 272, 332, 512, 905, 910
McIntyre, Duncan 859
Mack, Cactus 20, 50, 54, 71, 114, 123, 260, 317, 337, 374, 405, 465, 467, 524, 526, 547, 551, 555, 564, 565, 569, 602, 621, 643, 670, 680, 722, 737, 774, 775, 794, 798, 832, 844, 862, 889, 904, 931, 959, 964, 977, 988, 996, 1002, 1012
Mack, Harry 987
Mack, Helen 96, 365, 410, 927
Mack, Irene 656
Mack, Jack 639, 961, 1000, 1009
Mack, Joe 1003
Mack, Wilbur 347, 421, 524, 747
Mackaill, Dorothy 82

# Name Index

Mackay, Barry  287, 745
McKay, Doreen  339, 526, 574
McKay, George  577
McKay, Jock  859
McKay, Wanda  173
McKee, Lafe  987, 988, 993
McKee, Pat  961
MacKellar, Helen  162, 195, 264, 299, 794, 820
McKenney, Eileen  76
MacKenzie, Aeneas  33, 231
McKenzie, Bob  60, 119, 135, 172, 256, 308, 373, 498, 629, 728, 746, 896
McKenzie, Eva  526, 960
McKenzie, Fay  145, 195, 318, 351, 510, 636, 728
MacKenzie, Mary  553, 841, 859
McKim, Harry  168, 373, 502
McKim, Sammy  95, 140, 308, 319, 346, 364, 447, 459, 524, 526, 542, 612, 629, 660, 674, 812, 830, 855, 963, 987, 993, 1026
McKinley, Ray, and Orchestra  343
McKinney, Florine  100, 541
McKinney, Mira  320, 601, 670
McKinney, Nina Mae  529
Macklin, James  531
McLaglen, Victor  86, 120, 219, 450, 616, 651, 859
MacLane, Barton  17, 262, 271, 283, 327, 329, 366, 390, 402, 472, 488, 694, 704, 753, 830
MacLaren, Ian  385, 598
MacLaren, Mary  411, 435, 523, 602, 773, 907
McLaughlin, Gibb  30
McLeay, Janet  96
McLeod, Catherine  217, 389, 546, 561, 816, 1005
McLeod, Gordon  683
McLeod, Mary  278, 444, 614
MacMahon, Horace  111, 225, 262, 366, 410, 412, 488, 520, 606, 666, 677, 715, 810, 927
McMurphy, Charles  961, 962, 1000, 1003
MacMurray, Fred  219
McNally, Stephen  327, 458

McNamara, James H.  351, 551
MacNamara, Major James H.  416
McNaughton, Jack  808, 851
McNear, Howard  4
McNeil, Ron  474
McNeile, H. C. "Sapper"  82
McNulty, Dorothy  705
Macollum, Barry  27
MacQuarrie, Murdock  130, 286, 465, 523, 987, 1010
McQueen, Butterfly  236
MacQuitty, William  1
Macready, George  304, 595, 828
McTaggart, Bud  169, 243, 264, 930
McVey, Paul  525, 985
McWade, Edward  957
McWade, Robert  100
McWilliams, Paul  880
Macy, Mike  419
Madden, Jeanne  705
Madeira, Humberto  443
Madison, Julian  177, 202, 307, 962, 963
Madison, Noel  714
Magill, James  73, 846, 964
Magrill, George  76, 555, 691, 866, 952, 953, 956, 958, 961, 968, 971, 976, 987, 1001, 1009
Mahen, Timothy  818
Main, Marjorie  162, 410, 927
Makeham, Eliot  186
Mala, (Ray)  94, 279, 280, 975, 1000
Malcolm, Robert  586
Malerba, Luigi  716
Malleson, Miles  851
Mallinson, Rory  90, 174, 249, 608, 661, 684, 759, 766, 898
Malloy, Doris  494, 649
Malneck, Matty, and His Orchestra  699, 714, 856
Maloney, James  324
Maltz, Albert  506
Malulo, Moe  975
Malvern, Paul  411, 433, 434, 448, 523, 554, 659, 907
Malyon, Eily  27, 301
Mamakos, Peter  150, 362, 909
Mamoulian, Rouben  84
Mandell, Harry L.  283

Mander, Miles  710, 843, 942, 955
Manero, Jose  195
Mangean, Teddy  1003
Mann, Anthony  297, 511, 532, 783, 785
Mann, E. B.  307, 440, 650, 847
Mann, Edward  698
Mann, Grace  765
Mann, Jane  880
Mann, Margaret  225, 873
Mann, Michael  665
Mann, Milton  698
Manners, David  322
Manners, Marjorie  57, 251, 370, 814, 856
Manni, Ettore  716
Manning, Bruce  237, 357, 402, 766
Manning, Hope  493, 543, 870
Manning, Knox  344
Mannone, Wingy  856
Mannors, Sheila  434, 907; see also Sheila Bromley
Manoff, Arnold  464, 512
Manoff, Yvonne  341
Manogoff, Bobby  10
Mansfield, Rankin  156
Manson, Helena  3
Many Treaties, Chief  173, 679, 956
Mapes, Ted  24, 66, 71, 97, 106, 137, 178, 217, 267, 351, 372, 374, 513, 563, 625, 633, 657, 730, 823, 877, 899, 913, 947, 950, 954, 955, 958, 963, 975, 978, 985, 988, 996, 1002, 1012
Maple, Christine  56, 461, 655
The Maple City Four  286, 542, 878
Mara, Adele  17, 31, 33, 50, 63, 90, 93, 98, 109, 213, 218, 236, 260, 285, 301, 309, 364, 380, 386, 389, 424, 455, 456, 528, 529, 579, 656, 659, 689, 703, 751, 818, 834, 842, 852, 866, 887, 898, 902
Maran, Francisco  196
March, Eve  97, 753, 789, 791
March, Hal  32
March, Joseph Moncure  248, 445, 699, 820, 897, 919

# Name Index

March, Sally 24
Marchetti, Giulio 259
Marcus, James 448, 927
Mardo, Al 814
Margetson, Arthur 825
Margot, Herta 1028
Mari, George 987, 1010
Maricle, Leona 747
Marion, Betty 310
Marion, Charles R. 215
Marion, Paul 109, 142, 239, 312, 372, 952, 965, 992, 1001, 1012
Marion, Sid 853, 925
Maris, Mona 33
Mark, Michael 297, 392, 534, 604
Marke, William 998
Markey, Gene 1034
Markey, Melinda 1034
Markham, Dewey "Pigmeat" 814
Markova, Alicia 749
Marks, Clarence E. 232
Marks, Dave 985
Marks, Joe E. 568
Markson, Ben 366, 606
Marle, Arnold 152, 300
Marlowe, Anthony 186
Marlowe, Don 401
Marlowe, Faye 637
Marlowe, Frank 370, 399, 464, 512, 739, 947, 961, 967, 978, 1005
Marlowe, Jo Ann 468
Marlowe, Scott 938
Marly, Florence 290
Marmont, Percy 443
Maron, Alfred 471
Marr, Eddie 809
Marriot, Robert 665
Marsh, Anthony 91, 570, 598
Marsh, Charles 31, 521
Marsh, Garry 122
Marsh, Joan 158, 1001
Marsh, Mae 230, 616, 791
Marsh, Marian 180, 609, 942
Marsh, Myra 406, 521
Marshal, Alan 385
Marshall, Brenda 783
Marshall, Charles "Red" 765
Marshall, Elizabeth 326
Marshall, George 836
Marshall, Gregory 38, 816
Marshall, Herbert 901
Marshall, John 998
Marshall, Tully 66

Marshall, William 3, 63, 86, 203, 510, 813
Marshe, Vera 599
Marson, Truda 955
Marston, Joel 147, 547
Martel, June 693, 741, 915
Martel, William 627
Martell, Alphonse 109, 410, 779
Martell, Donna 866; see also Donna DeMario
Martell, Gregg 627
Martell, Karl 118, 558
Martelli, Tony 1010
Martin, Al 271, 309
Martin, Charles 360, 961
Martin, Chris-Pin 22, 60, 70, 256, 644, 1010; see also King Martin
Martin, Don 191, 472, 530, 604
Martin, Freddy, and His Orchestra 343
Martin, James 982
Martin, Janet 50, 86, 93, 310, 321, 409, 413, 419, 456, 769, 849, 852, 934
Martin, Jill 975
Martin, King 67; see also Chris-Pin Martin
Martin, Lewis 427
Martin, Marian 265, 285, 539, 586, 813, 815, 926
Martin, Mary 1028, 1030, 1033
Martin, Nora Lou, and the Pals of the Golden West 623, 674
Martin, Tony 1032
Martin, Vivienne 707
Martinez, Tony 18
Martinson, Leslie H. 32
Marvey, Gene 1003
Marvey, Jean 822
Marvin, Frankie 34, 48, 56, 66, 70, 91, 130, 135, 145, 195, 266, 286, 291, 306, 318, 322, 465, 488, 508, 537, 542, 543, 601, 611, 623, 632, 641, 642, 643, 656, 667, 673, 680, 681, 728, 735, 737, 739, 770, 776, 863, 866, 874, 878, 936, 949, 987, 993, 1003, 1007, 1008, 1010
Marx, Arthur 917
Marx, Max 955, 1012

Marx, Neyle 583
Mascot Pictures 363, 957
Mason, Bill 935
Mason, Buddy 961, 988
Mason, James 11, 417
Mason, James (American actor) 376, 611, 641
Mason, LeRoy 14, 20, 21, 38, 52, 62, 87, 89, 99, 135, 234, 269, 276, 277, 289, 291, 310, 323, 331, 337, 353, 377, 446, 469, 483, 491, 502, 510, 513, 524, 529, 566, 569, 620, 625, 630, 641, 660, 673, 678, 687, 688, 693, 739, 752, 775, 861, 872, 876, 886, 891, 892, 930, 936, 950, 952, 958, 967, 978, 982, 993, 996, 1005, 1084
Mason, Louis 301
Mason, Philip 960
Mason, Sydney 357, 418, 1019
Massen, Osa 182, 562
Massey, Ilona 534, 594, 1033, 1034
Massey, Jim 74
Massis, Louis 558
Matalon, Vivian 901
Mather, Aubrey 205
Mathews, Allan 968, 1000
Mathews, Carl 64, 317, 670
Matray, Maria 510
Matthews, Lester 237, 266, 444, 733, 926
Matz, Johanna 136
Maude, Beatrice 27, 368
Maurey, Nicole 901
Mauu, Charles 325
Max, Edwin 857
Maxey, Paul 46, 120
Maxted, Stanley 901
Maxwell, Edwin 98, 461, 664
Maxwell, Jane 518
Maxwell, John 26, 211, 220, 399, 475, 781, 811, 900
Maxwell, L. Y. 975
May, Patsy 298
Mayer, Charles 667
Mayer, Ray 609
Maynard, Kermit 14, 26, 54, 64, 130, 249, 260, 332, 351, 371, 395, 423, 498, 526, 692, 697, 728, 732, 846, 885, 906, 915, 931, 986
Mayne, Eric 833

## Name Index

Mayne, Ferdy 184
Mayo, Eleanor R. 807
Mayo, Frank 85, 419
Mazurki, Mike 155, 251, 325, 475
Meade, Claire 958
Meader, George 582
Meadows, Dennis 448, 681; see also Dennis Moore
Means, Grant 898
Meccoli, Comenico 780
Medbury, John P. 140
Medina, Patricia 784
Medwin, Michael 1, 185
Meehan, Elizabeth 280, 313, 315, 534, 779
Meehan, Lew 23, 69, 146, 190, 226, 302, 303, 307, 433, 435, 440, 601, 634, 650, 770, 827, 847, 936, 988
Meek, Donald 6
Meeker, George 21, 53, 57, 174, 210, 269, 350, 409, 507, 597, 626, 672, 729, 737, 752, 768, 865, 903, 973, 976
Meeker, Ralph 924
The Meglin Kiddies 655
Megowan, Don 324, 475
Mehra, Lal Chand 360, 438, 965
Meichsner, Eberhard 118
Meinrad, Josef 136
Meins, Douglas 296, 503, 961
Meins, Gus 141, 205, 296, 339, 341, 412, 503, 514, 515, 664, 699, 726
Meisel, Kurt 383
The Merry Meisters 419
Mell, Joseph 418
Melton, Frank 5, 112, 161, 639, 645
Menacker, Sammy 10
Menard, Connie 866
Menard, Tina 402, 800
Mence, George 640
Menjou, Adolphe 836
Menken, Shepard 627
Mercedes, Maria 553
Mercer, Beryl 245, 347
Mercer, Freddie 712
Mercier, Louis 109, 364
Meredith, Charles 789
Meredith, Frank 962, 963, 964, 973, 1003

Meredith, Iris 261, 435, 847, 863
Meredith, John 965
Meremblum, Peter Junior, Orchestra 492
Merivale, Philip 415
Merlin, Jan 781
Merrall, Mary 300
Merrick, Doris 588
Merrick, Jay 973
Merrick, Lynn 20, 26, 105, 154, 168, 169, 172, 175, 258, 270, 395, 405, 498, 509, 565, 740, 746, 773, 868, 941
Merrick, Marilyn 1027
Merrill, Anthony 476
Merrill, Tony 998
Merrill, Walter 743, 955, 963
Merritt, George 11
Mersen, Anne-Marie 558
Merton, John 23, 26, 39, 67, 114, 127, 142, 162, 267, 303, 308, 445, 488, 498, 555, 624, 672, 822, 823, 844, 868, 874, 955, 961, 962, 965, 968, 987, 999, 1007, 1008, 1011, 1012
Messenger, Buddy 988
Messinger, Gertrude 489, 639
Metaxa, George 701, 905
Metcalfe, Bradley 411, 907
Metro-Goldwyn-Mayer 339, 751
Metzetti, Otto 972
Metzetti, Thom 991
Metzler, Robert 879
Meyer, Emile 484
Meyer, Greta 59
Meyer, Russ 665
Michael, Gertrude 218, 824
Michael, Peter 569, 604, 933
Michaels, Johnny 173
Michaels, Pat 694
Mickey, Tofik 965
Middlemass, Robert 24, 365, 485, 512, 769
Middleton, Charles 146, 422, 604, 819, 928, 930, 936, 955, 961, 995
Middleton, Guy 790
Middleton, Ray 262, 279, 361, 362, 363, 402, 415, 416, 490, 654, 802
Middleton, Robert 531
Mikhelson, Andre 184

Milan, Frank 574
Milasch, Robert 693
Miles, Art 155, 975
Miles, Betty 991
Miles, John 217
Miles, Peter 90, 628, 854
Milestone, Lewis 628
Miley, Jerry 46
Miljan, John 235, 272, 424, 816, 939
Mill, Robert R. 614
Millakowsky, Herman 36, 218, 510
Millan, Victor 830
Milland, Ray 443, 460
Millar, Marjie 909
Miller, Ann 342, 488, 1033, 1034
Miller, Charles 52, 54, 62, 64, 168, 337, 397, 585, 607, 620, 621, 760, 832, 895, 956, 962
Miller, D'Arcy 958
Miller, David 243
Miller, Doris 604
Miller, Fred 975
Miller, Hugh 82
Miller, Ivan 83, 94, 140, 146, 182, 193, 247, 257, 394, 415, 465, 542, 874, 899, 941, 972
Miller, Kristine 241, 273, 329, 828, 857
Miller, Lorraine 54, 646
Miller, Marvin 713
Miller, Peter 781
Miller, Ray 955
Miller, Seton I. 438, 713
Miller, Timmy 466
Miller, Walter 133, 193, 266, 296, 352, 915, 962, 963
Miller, Winston 104, 318, 463, 643, 753, 960, 993, 1003, 1008
Milletaire, Carl 36, 227
Millett, Arthur 916
Millhauser, Bertram 614
Millholland, Ray 280
Millican, James 147, 402, 497, 561, 637, 767, 888, 1003
Millot, Charles 558
Mills, Frank 318
Mills, Gordon 160
Mills, John 1
Mills, John (American actor) 960

The Mills Brothers 112
Milne, Peter 273, 623
Milner, Martin 228, 689
The Milo Twins 734
Milton, Gerald 475
Minevitch, Borrah, and His Harmonica Rascals 342
"Minister," the Horse 993
Minton, Jack 975
Miranda, Aurora 79, 809
Miranda, Carmen 79, 1029
Mitchel, Helen 1012
Mitchell, Barry (Brad Dexter) 323
Mitchell, Belle 439
Mitchell, Bruce 537, 576, 960, 961, 963
Mitchell, Charlotte 808
Mitchell, Chris 981, 989
Mitchell, Dale 407
Mitchell, Frank 814
Mitchell, Grant 414
Mitchell, Howard 46, 128, 235, 318, 364, 818, 955, 962, 976, 978, 1002
Mitchell, Jim 88, 775
Mitchell, Norval 973
Mitchell, Pat 1003
Mitchell, Robert, Boy Choir 50, 369, 750
Mitchell, Shirley 391
Mitchell, Steve 979
Mitchell, Stuart 553
Mitchell, William 961
Mitchell, Yvonne 184
Mitchum, John 472
Mitchum, Robert 54, 628
Mitrovich, Marta 364, 610
Mix, Art 56, 142, 373, 488, 522, 648, 674, 832, 916, 936, 949; *see also* Denver Dixon; George Kesterson
Moehring, Kansas 258, 469, 691
Moffitt, Jack 462
Moffitt, John C. 488
Mohr, Gerald 65, 109, 309, 386, 408, 455, 579, 947, 980
Mojave, King 611, 961, 1003
Molasses and January 341
Molieri, Lillian 758, 758
Molina, Carlos, and His Orchestra 47
Molina, Carmen 751
Molina, Joe 1005, 1012
Molinas, Richard 165, 184

Moloney, John 963
Monaghan, John 417
Mong, William V. 649
Monogram Pictures 647
Monroe, Tom 208, 357, 600, 676, 971, 976, 989
Monroe, Vaughn 736, 840
Montague, Monte 20, 71, 154, 192, 286, 426, 505, 574, 585, 621, 645, 663, 697, 737, 776, 908, 939, 955, 960, 961, 963, 968, 978, 986, 988, 993
Montana, Monte 464
Montana, Patsy 130
Monte, Lola 641
Monteros, Rosenda 924
Montes, Lola 413
Montgomery, Doreen 596
Montgomery, George 580; *see also* George Letz
Montgomery, Goodee 53
Montgomery, Jack 34, 71, 142, 162, 175, 261, 277, 488, 629, 663, 895, 908, 936, 961, 965, 988
Montgomery, Martha 380
Montgomery, Ray 40
Montoya, Alex 164, 866, 914, 970, 975
Moody, Ralph 580
Mooney, John 402
Moore, Charles 175, 394, 405, 582, 763
Moore, Clay 979; *see also* Clayton Moore
Moore, Clayton 14, 102, 194, 221, 255, 323, 479, 565, 594, 724, 864, 948, 953, 969, 970, 971, 978, 995, 998; *see also* Clay Moore
Moore, Constance 31, 203, 204, 344, 378, 492, 1030, 1032
Moore, Daniel 240
Moore, Dennis 269, 519, 573, 621, 660, 926, 959, 997; *see also* Dennis Meadows
Moore, Eva 701
Moore, Ida 285, 356
Moore, Jack 1012
Moore, Jacqueline 450
Moore, John 336
Moore, Mary 997
Moore, Pauline 27, 106, 126, 167, 766, 844, 940, 986

Moorehead, Agnes 3
Moorhouse, Bert 13, 397, 419, 795
Moran, Betty 257
Moran, Charles 213
Moran, Frank 464
Moran, Jackie 29, 493, 532, 821
Moran, Jim 765
Moran, Pat 1004
Moran, Patsy 355
Moran, Peggy 408, 641
Moran, Polly 412, 486, 582, 629, 870
Morante, Milburn 41, 132, 276, 291, 302, 543, 611, 624, 645, 667, 960
Moravia, Alberto 716
Mordant, Edwin 567, 1003
More, Kenneth 186
Morehead, Dick 873
Moreland, Mantan 101
The Morell Trio 688
Moreno, Antonio 71
Moreno, Rita 215
Moreno, Rosita 360
Morgan, Bob 912
Morgan, Boyd "Red" 156, 176, 426, 831
Morgan, Buck 261, 660
Morgan, Eula 16, 710
Morgan, Gene 225, 266, 280
Morgan, George 960
Morgan, Guy 471
Morgan, Helen 250
Morgan, Henry (Harry) 46, 111, 505, 727, 840
Morgan, Lee 89, 160, 954
Morgan, Michael 1003
Morgan, Ralph 28, 320, 473, 557, 745, 850, 856, 962
Morgan, Ray 959, 977
Morgan, Raymond L. 335
Morgan, Tracey 698
Morgan, William 48, 78, 145, 270, 315, 318, 351, 490, 500, 710, 728, 776, 797
Morie, Ruby 397
Morin, Alberto 18, 651, 866, 875
Morison, Patricia 1028, 1032, 1033
Morita, Miki 72
Moritz, Henry 714, 825
Morley, Karen 392
Morley, Kay 98
Morrell, George 13, 35, 41,

# NAME INDEX

128, 132, 261, 286, 303, 306, 346, 537, 570, 624, 632, 667, 673, 693, 860, 863, 873, 936
Morrell, Louis 960
Morris, Adrian 899
Morris, Aileen 397
Morris, Chester 250, 280, 897
Morris, Corbet 955
Morris, Dorothy 747
Morris, Frances 56, 410, 962
Morris, Happy 936
Morris, Henry 67, 1003
Morris, Lana 858
Morris, Michael 618
Morris, Wayne 152, 300
Morrison, Chuck 123, 394, 564, 573, 612, 621, 643, 674, 737, 947, 962
Morrow, Brad 356
Morrow, Clarence 1000
Morrow, Katherine 764
Morrow, Neyle 312, 626, 767
Morrow, Susan 951
Mortimer, Charles 596
Morton, Charles 115, 234, 337, 466, 566, 593, 800, 928, 978
Morton, Danny 157, 181, 214, 599
Morton, Hugh 808
Morton, James C. 205, 373, 416, 459, 611, 612, 640, 870, 937
Moser, Hans 136
Mosier, Enid 417
Moss, Jimmy 73
Mothershed, Daisy Lee 31, 618, 911
Moulton, Buck 20, 66, 868
Moultrie, Freddie 363
Mowbray, Alan 204, 367, 456, 588, 699, 809, 937
Mowbray, Henry 438
Muir, Esther 617, 906, 932
Mulhall, Jack 159, 352, 512, 567, 947, 962, 992, 1007, 1033
Mullen, Virginia 505
Muller, Paul 518
Mullin, Dan 384
Mulliner, Arthur 709
Mullins, Bartlett 300, 841
Mumby, Diana 917
Mundin, Herbert 385
Munier, Ferdinand 67, 419, 869

Munson, Ona 113, 155, 369, 416, 897, 1028
Murdock, Perry 72, 110
Murphy, Al 68, 155, 236, 345, 616, 800
Murphy, Bob 598
Murphy, Charles 524, 693, 862, 949, 963, 1012
Murphy, Dudley 457
Murphy, George 1029
Murphy, Horace 35, 41, 60, 69, 72, 127, 132, 146, 190, 202, 261, 276, 277, 302, 303, 432, 440, 488, 526, 578, 634, 650, 674, 680, 827, 847, 873
Murphy, Mary 458, 460, 484
Murphy, Maurice 141, 196, 247, 918
Murphy, Ralph 518, 518, 518
Murphy, Richard 20, 34, 154, 395, 737, 932
Murphy, William 219, 228, 357, 689
Murray, Charlie, Jr. 171
Murray, Charlie, Sr. 117, 1033
Murray, Dennis 550
Murray, Forbes 20, 50, 97, 99, 145, 146, 337, 375, 395, 464, 643, 679, 691, 803, 832, 927, 960, 972, 987, 990, 991, 995, 999
Murray, Jean 662
Murray, John Fenton 32, 390
Murray, Ken 58
Murray, Zon 73, 179, 194, 207, 294, 527, 548, 587, 1019
Muse, Clarence 244, 429, 791
The Music Maids 343, 358, 391
Mycroft, Walter C. 82, 287, 596
Myers, Carmel 415
Myers, Jerry Lynn 364
Myers, Peter 772
Myrtil, Odette 230, 417
Myton, Fred 62, 72, 171, 177, 190, 261, 302, 847, 860

"Naba," the Gorilla 823, 957; see also Ray ("Crash") Corrigan; Ray Benard
Nachmann, Kurt 136
Nader, George 676
Naefe, Jester 136

Nagel, Anne 210, 510, 842, 1029
Nagel, Conrad 282
Nagy, Bill 553
Nahera, Alex, Dancers 753
Naish, J. Carrol 423, 438, 639, 644, 651, 705, 921, 1032
Naismith, Laurence 901
Nalder, Reggie 3
Nandi 428
Napier, Alan 197, 451
Napier, Elmer 987
Napier, Russell 471
Napoli, Nicholas 506
Narciso, Grazia 452
Nash, Mary 413
Nash, Robert 580
Natheaux, Louis 289
Natteford, Jack 60, 70, 130, 134, 167, 291, 319, 331, 332, 406, 422, 448, 551, 552, 554, 576, 590, 639, 655, 667, 672, 725, 763, 822, 833, 845, 845, 848, 930, 936
Natwick, Mildred 616
Navarro, Anna 402
Navarro, George 402
Nazarro, Cliff 91, 180, 247, 296, 568, 577, 666, 682, 714, 856, 1028
Nazarro, Ray 84
Neal, Ella 992
Neal, Tom 243, 818, 980
Needham, Gordon 700
Neeman, Robinson 738
Negley, Howard J. 409, 418, 447, 460, 499, 866
Neher, Jeanne 384
Neil, Robert 363, 499, 830
Neill, Noel 948, 977
Neilson, Nigel 837
Neilson, Perlita 858
Neise, George 464, 562, 885
Nelson, Billy 220
Nelson, Bobby 69, 261, 302, 634
Nelson, Ed 787
Nelson, Felix 979
Nelson, Frank 1015, 1016, 1017
Nelson, Grant 952, 974, 990, 991, 1005, 1011
Nelson, Merlyn 986
Nelson, Nicholas 960

Nesbitt, Norman 464, 952, 955, 965, 972, 983, 1001
Nestell, Bill 34, 92, 234, 372, 397, 464, 526, 542, 625, 691, 746, 773, 776, 844, 895, 936, 949, 955, 963
Neubauer, Leonard 418
Neubert, Carl 109
Nevins, Frank J. 659
Newcombe, Jessica 850
Newell, Elsa 521
Newell, William 53, 56, 59, 83, 159, 311, 368, 421, 461, 476, 521, 640, 741, 843, 992, 1000
Newfield, Sam 23, 41, 69, 85, 127, 177, 190, 202, 223, 226, 261, 289, 302, 307, 435, 440, 578, 617, 650, 655, 827, 847
Newlan, Paul "Tiny" 270
Newland, John 355, 754
Newley, Anthony 1
Newman, Robert 370
Newton, Mary 285, 511
Newton, Robert 596
Nibert, Terry 104
Nibley, Sloan 49, 51, 192, 214, 221, 269, 292, 371, 528, 549, 572, 768, 771, 800, 801, 828, 865, 871
Niccolls, Herbert F. 401
Nicholls, George, Jr. 28, 473, 598
Nicholls, Jill 700
Nichols, C. H. 772
Nichols, Dandy 808, 837
Nichols, George A. 740
Nichols, Nellie V. 477
Nichols, Ray 60
Nichols, Robert 32
Nicholson, Meredith 360
Nicol, Alex 111
Nielsen, Hans 383
Niesen, Gertrude 666, 825, 1028
Nigh, William 59, 856
Niles, Ken 380
Niles, Wendell 266, 330, 613, 804, 820, 843, 991
Nilsson, Anna Q. 315
Nimoy, Leonard 548, 1009
Nind, Bill 709, 965
Noble, Peter 782
Noble, Ray, and His Orchestra 419
Noel, Hattie 415

Noel, Magali 558
Nolan, Bob 13, 21, 50, 51, 56, 91, 144, 189, 214, 228, 269, 310, 317, 323, 344, 350, 353, 369, 408, 442, 463, 466, 467, 513, 528, 543, 549, 622, 633, 648, 662, 663, 688, 732, 750, 752, 753, 755, 760, 771, 795, 798, 799, 871, 876, 883, 934
Nolan, Danni 37, 238, 610
Nolan, Herman 839, 868, 891
Nolan, Jeanette 451
Nolan, Jim 10, 37, 164, 170, 528, 748, 898
Nolan, Lloyd 45, 147, 262
Norfolk, Edgar 428
Noriega, Eduardo 160
Norman, B. G. 793
Norman, Lucille 802
Normand, Mabel 740
Normandy/First Division Pictures 822
Norrell, Wedgewood 56
Norris, Edward 19, 34, 187, 209, 510, 800
Norris, Jay 231, 512
North, Robert 45, 79, 151, 203, 248, 262, 270, 281, 361, 367, 368, 373, 377, 457, 486, 487, 582, 612, 733, 740, 747, 819, 843, 918, 937
North, Sheree 16
Northrup, Patsy Fay 318
Norton, Barry 726, 866
Norton, Edgar 59
Norton, Jack 101, 236, 368
Nova, Lou 86
Novak, Eva 63, 65, 138, 156, 326, 364, 656, 839
Novarese, Vittorio Nino 188
Novarro, Ramon 180, 717
Novello, Ivor 287
Novello, Jay 35, 48, 71, 96, 116, 119, 126, 281, 299, 390, 443, 466, 657, 723, 742, 743, 810, 868, 952, 967, 983
Nowell, Wedgewood 960, 961
Nugent, Carol 846
Nugent, Eddie 158, 246, 313, 461
Nugent, Frank S. 616, 859

Nugent, Judy 194
Nusser, James 324
Nye, Carroll 844
Nye, G. Raymond 286

Oakland, Dagmar 439
Oakland, Vivien 284, 883
Oakman, Wheeler 957, 988
O'Brian, Hugh 81, 228, 867
O'Brien-Moore, Erin 439, 704
O'Brien, Dave 440, 524, 930
O'Brien, Edmond 713
O'Brien, George 1029
O'Brien, John 1008
O'Brien, Pat 402
O'Brine, Paddy Manning 829
O'Callahan, Foxy 39, 74, 89, 722, 861
O'Casey, Ronan 858
O'Connell, Arthur 937
O'Connell, Hugh 613
O'Connell, Jean 397
O'Connell, Marion 738
O'Connor, Frank 13, 54, 60, 166, 337, 425, 446, 526, 615, 643, 645, 678, 693, 731, 773, 774, 776, 792, 927, 931, 948, 950, 952, 954, 959, 961, 963, 970, 971, 973, 976, 977, 984, 991, 999, 1002
O'Day, Nell 832
O'Dea, John 259
O'Dea, Joseph 616
O'Dell, Doye 323, 425, 468
Odlum, Jerome 378, 425, 702
O'Donnell, Jack 617, 861
O'Donnell, Joseph 956, 962, 972, 980, 983, 986, 995, 1001, 1004
O'Donnell, Paddy 616
O'Donnell, Spec 510
O'Dowd, Dan 401
O'Driscoll, Martha 941
Oemler, Marie Conway 744
O'Farrell, Bernadette 772
O'Farrell, Broderick 91, 368, 747, 955, 963
Offenbach, Rudolph 428
Offerman, George, Jr. 257
O'Flynn, Damian 160, 206, 228, 335, 357, 589, 678, 902, 932

O'Gatty, Jimmy 969
Ogg, Jimmy 46, 635
O'Hara, Barry 401
O'Hara, Brian 89
O'Hara, Maureen 443, 616, 628, 651
O'Herlihy, Dan 451
O'Keefe, Dennis 7, 78, 204, 231, 281, 418, 500, 504, 805; *see also* Bud Flanagan
Olaguivel, Juan 33
Oldham, Michael 428
Olivas, Henry 987
Oliver, Anthony 808
Oliver, Gordon 606, 677, 942
Olmstead, Edwin 148
Olmstead, Harry 23, 69, 127, 202, 226, 302, 435, 578
O'Locklin, Allen 698
Olsen, Larry 446
Olsen, Moroni 44, 189, 477
Olsen, Ole 12, 140
Olson, James P. 41
O'Malley, John 769
O'Malley, Pat 73, 573, 616, 660, 825, 972
O'Moore, Patrick 278
O'Neal, Anne 47, 373, 377, 740, 746, 785, 824, 903
O'Neil, Barbara 237
O'Neill, Henry 791
O'Neill, Maire 82, 287
Orlando, Don 574, 993
Orlebeck, Les 267, 564, 573, 590, 602, 679, 712, 904
Orloff, Arthur E. 81, 125, 179, 208, 426, 499, 631, 762, 826
Orloff, Orest 184
Ornellas, Loni 1000
Ornitz, Samuel 28, 244, 341, 388, 410, 598, 820, 870
O'Roarke, Brefni 30
Orr, Gertrude 94, 140, 313, 476
Orr, William T. 1033, 1034
Ortego, Artie 67, 406, 590, 670
Orth, Frank 510, 779, 809
Ortiz, Peter 402, 651, 1019
Osborne, Bud 26, 64, 70, 73, 88, 99, 105, 114, 115, 123, 129, 146, 167, 256, 260, 264, 276, 277, 373, 420, 445, 502, 524, 526, 527, 551, 555, 564, 570, 573, 583, 594, 601, 607, 622,
623, 645, 646, 660, 674, 693, 697, 732, 755, 795, 844, 866, 908, 936, 948, 959, 964, 968, 987, 1000, 1008
Osborne, Judy 417
Osborne, Lucille 117
Osborne, Vivienne 244
Oscar and Elmer (Ed Platt, Lou Fulton) 308, 341, 485, 543, 960, 993
Osceola, Roy 935
O'Shea, Jack 9, 34, 35, 48, 56, 75, 80, 89, 92, 105, 115, 124, 144, 146, 154, 175, 195, 234, 236, 256, 265, 310, 373, 374, 376, 378, 394, 402, 408, 422, 466, 469, 470, 482, 483, 484, 549, 556, 565, 566, 567, 569, 581, 583, 593, 624, 645, 646, 652, 663, 670, 687, 691, 697, 719, 722, 724, 732, 737, 746, 752, 753, 755, 760, 761, 775, 832, 839, 866, 868, 891, 895, 908, 928, 934, 940, 949, 950, 952, 956, 958, 966, 967, 968, 970, 971, 974, 975, 984, 991, 992, 995, 996, 1001, 1002, 1004, 1012
O'Shea, Michael 464
O'Shea, Oscar 410, 715, 757, 974
O'Shea, Pat 961, 962, 986, 991
Osta, Terrisita 48
Osten-Sacken, Maria 118
Osterloh, Robert 312, 399
O'Sullivan, William J. 63, 120, 213, 316, 326, 380, 386, 455, 561, 579, 581, 588, 727, 781, 806, 852, 900, 909, 952, 956, 962, 972, 983, 991, 995, 1001, 1004, 1005
Otho, Henry 491, 570, 961, 968, 988, 1003
Oulton, Brian 186
Ouspenskaya, Maria 389, 928, 1028
Overlander, Webb 616
Overman, Jack 706
Owen, Bill 165, 772
Owen, Garry 94, 235, 296, 586, 682, 834
Owen, Michael 172, 747, 818, 962, 986, 1084

Owens, Harry, and His Royal Hawaiians 419
Owsley, Monroe 341

The Pacemakers 643
Pack, Charles Lloyd 841
Padden, Sarah 155, 212, 248, 318, 359, 370, 445, 473, 482, 499, 564, 813, 884, 942, 945
Padilla, Ruben 84
Padjan, Jack 308, 993
Padula, Vincent 33, 324
Pagan, William 955
Page, Bradley 100, 246, 281, 501, 755, 850, 983
Page, Dorothy 459
Page, Joy 84
Page, Sam 384
Paige, Anne 808
Paige, Janis 259
Paige, LeRoy "Satchel" 407
Paige, Mabel 747
Paige, Robert 235, 365; *see also* David Carlyle
"Pair O'Dice," the Horse 1010
Paiva, Nestor 13, 215, 279, 424, 562, 698, 762, 983
Palange, Inez 410, 510, 598, 874
Paley, Stanley 16
Pall, Gloria 120, 1019
Pallette, Eugene 113, 378, 419
Palma, Pamela 518
Palmer, Conway 790
Palmer, Maria 241, 562, 800
Palmer, Paul 951, 998
Palmer, Stuart 349, 351, 577, 911, 932
Palmer, Ted 841
Palmer, Tex 23, 41, 69, 126, 142, 172, 177, 226, 261, 302, 303, 307, 411, 433, 434, 435, 440, 526, 574, 634, 847, 907, 908, 978
Palmieri, Fulvio 780
Pampanini, Silvana 188
Panalle, Juan 765
Pangborn, Franklin 12, 86, 159, 342, 476, 501, 504, 511, 552, 809
Pape, Lionel 568
Paramore, Edward E. 598
Paramore, Edward E., Jr. 151, 473
Paramount Pictures 341, 888
Paris, George 534

Paris, Manuel 18, 314, 402, 779
Park, Post 39, 71, 73, 207, 719, 922, 949, 952, 966, 970, 977, 987, 988, 996, 1002, 1011
Parker, Barnett 342, 462, 603, 715
Parker, Ben 384
Parker, Cecil 790
Parker, Eddie 166, 168, 236, 286, 380, 491, 586, 591, 600, 640, 832, 907, 948, 953, 954, 955, 956, 957, 958, 959, 961, 962, 963, 968, 970, 972, 973, 974, 976, 978, 981, 982, 984, 988, 990, 991, 992, 996, 999, 1001, 1002, 1005, 1007
Parker, Franklin 339, 639
Parker, Fred 434, 624, 634, 860, 907
Parker, Jean 173, 240, 279, 333, 592, 715, 840, 850
Parker, Jefferson 245, 271, 869
Parker, Joe 206
Parker, Norton S. 652, 939
Parker, Richard 961
Parker, Tex 868
Parker, Willard 945
Parkes, Gay 1027
Parkinson, Cliff 75, 97, 128, 138, 687, 693, 996, 1011
Parks, Eddie 536, 593
Parks, Larry 173
Parkyakarkus 204
Parnell, Emory 29, 46, 86, 94, 215, 290, 326, 338, 356, 535, 539, 659, 668, 711, 802, 846, 881
Parrish, Helen 373, 799, 932
Parrish, James 82
Parry, Harvey 201
Parsons, Harriet 397, 1027, 1028, 1029, 1030, 1031, 1032, 1033, 1034
Parsons, Lindsley 434, 554, 907
Parsons, Louella 1034
Parsons, Milton 45, 279, 563, 706, 911
Parsons, Patsy Lee 60, 332
Parsons, Percy 790
Parsons, Ray 112, 972, 1004
Parsons, Ted 957
Passante, Mario 716

Patch, Wally 596, 782
Patisson, Danik 558
Paton, Tony 965, 985
Patrick, Dorothy 47, 65, 181, 224, 359, 447, 696, 807, 875
Patrick, Gail 86, 343, 381, 453, 473, 593, 637, 1032, 1034
Patrick, Jack 160
Patrick, John 766
Patrick, Lee 218, 532
Patterson, Elizabeth 389, 911
Patterson, Hank 51, 125, 174, 207, 264, 528, 540, 563, 583, 656, 694, 730, 771, 872, 951, 959, 964, 977
Patterson, Lee 1
Patton, Bill 615
Paul, Elliott 506
Pavelec, Ted 495
Pavlow, Muriel 122, 186
Pavolini, Corrado 780
Pawley, Anthony 5, 576, 1000
Pawley, Edward 663
Pawley, William 601, 672
Paxton, Dick 357, 612
Payne, John 654, 690
Payne, Sally 35, 56, 212, 339, 374, 394, 463, 465, 509, 514, 522, 633, 657, 663, 723, 864, 939
Payson, Blanche 12
Payson, Ed 930
Payton, Lew 415
Peabody, George 962
Pearce, Adele 930 see also Pamela Blake
Pearce, Al 330, 348, 456, 550; see also Al Pearce and His Gang
Pearce, Al, and His Gang 341; see also Al Pearce
Pearce, George 319, 735
Pearson, Ted 963
Peary, Harold 139
Peck, Steven 505
Pedersen, Eric 228
Peel, Eileen 808
Pegg, Vester 126, 723, 877
Peil, Edward, Sr. 71, 99, 123, 132, 276, 308, 374, 394, 405, 408, 464, 526, 537, 551, 615, 633, 647, 678, 731, 928, 963, 993
Peluffo, Stelita 76, 567

Pembroke, George 324, 947, 956, 965, 991, 995
Pembroke, Scott 433, 554
Pendleton, Ann 667
Pendleton, Steve 81, 176, 651, 796, 940
Penn, Leonard 412, 447, 758, 925
Pennick, Jack 228, 230, 357, 410, 416, 508, 651, 659, 703, 791
Pennington, Ann 812
Pepito 28
Pepper, Barbara 28, 130, 240, 246, 248, 254, 349, 598, 681, 738, 830, 881, 926
Pepper, Buddy 1030, 1032
Peppy and Peanuts 397, 803, 814
Percy, Edward 122
Perez, Ismael 84
Perez, Joe 988
Perez, Paul 576
Perkins, Gil 50, 866, 950, 952, 971, 972, 978, 1002, 1004
Perkins, Lynn 958, 982, 996, 997
Perkins, Peter 260, 479
Perkins, Valentine 610, 659
Perrin, Jack 80, 260, 586, 615, 631, 752, 903, 906, 909, 927, 987, 993
Perrins, Leslie 82
Perry, Barbara 16
Perry, Bob 477, 616
Perry, Pascale 35, 67, 71, 88, 105, 166, 167, 175, 214, 234, 306, 394, 434, 483, 537, 541, 602, 655, 660, 667, 680, 687, 712, 746, 755, 771, 844, 868, 874, 891, 978, 993, 1002, 1008
Perryman, Lloyd 648, 651
Pershing, Fred 861
Peters, Brooke L. 880
Peters, House, Jr. 157, 178, 256, 539, 540, 546, 611, 638, 724, 768, 865, 871, 948, 954, 984
Peters, John 534, 1004
Peters, Ralph 48, 95, 130, 277, 373, 397, 408, 567, 674, 693, 797, 848, 930
Peters, Robert 359
Peterson, Dorothy 218, 677, 926

Peterson, Preston 991
Peterson, Ralph W. 772
Petit, Albert 109
Petrie, Howard 219, 484, 836, 921
Petroff, Boris L. 562
Petroff, Gloria 880
Petruzzi, Julian 810
Phelps, Lee 189, 340, 413, 510, 539, 552, 612, 959, 964, 1004
Phelps, Tex 411, 448, 465, 523
Philipp, Gunther 136
Phillippe, Michele 188
Phillippi, Patti 510
Phillips, Arnold 392, 510
Phillips, Arthur 450
Phillips, Charley 621, 960, 961, 962, 963, 965, 972, 1004, 1006
Phillips, Eddie 67, 171, 773, 954, 972, 991, 1000, 1001, 1003
Phillips, Howard 263
Phillips, Joe 112, 948, 959, 964, 973, 977, 1002
Phillips, John 323, 357, 950, 973
Phipps, Nicholas 185, 186
Phipps, William 178, 631, 696, 849, 889
Picerni, Paul 475, 713
Pichel, Irving 53, 196, 200, 272, 322, 360, 400, 421, 717, 963
Pick and Pat 341
Pickard, John 237, 357, 538, 898, 973
Pickard, Obed 257
Pickens, Slim 73, 129, 194, 387, 423, 426, 547, 548, 561, 587, 631, 690, 711, 762, 784, 791, 830, 909
Picker, Sidney 4, 65, 88, 103, 128, 137, 153, 239, 273, 290, 312, 314, 321, 338, 354, 356, 404, 436, 441, 456, 481, 482, 539, 556, 560, 599, 653, 656, 675, 678, 690, 694, 706, 721, 774, 784, 789, 792, 807, 840, 857, 882, 891, 894, 896, 938
Pickford, Mary 1028
Picorri, John 196, 960, 965, 968, 1000, 1003

Pidgeon, Walter 162, 1028, 1034
Pierce, Jim 1012
Pierlot, Francis 109, 278, 301, 357, 364, 517, 612, 852
Pierreux, Jacqueline 558
Pierson, Carl 523, 738
Pietrangeli, Antonio 716
Piltz, George 164
Pine, Phillip 357, 382, 912
Piper, Frederick 185, 471
Pipitone, Nino 972
Pitti, Carl 922
Pittman, Montgomery 131
Pitts, ZaSu 494
Plank, Tom 50
Platt, Louise 248
Platt, Victor 300
Pliz, George 898
Plues, George 67, 132, 291, 306, 346, 524, 570, 611, 655, 822, 868, 955, 956, 985, 987, 995, 1012
Plummer, Rose 74, 154, 286, 302, 584, 674, 691, 822, 868, 949, 953
Plympton, George 23, 41, 69, 110, 190, 202, 226, 261, 302, 303, 435, 578, 634, 827, 847, 860, 991
Poe, Edgar Allan 148
The Poison Gardner Trio 512
Poland, Joseph F. 137, 433, 543, 624, 681, 855, 916, 947, 952, 956, 962, 967, 972, 974, 980, 983, 985, 986, 990, 991, 992, 995, 997, 1001, 1004, 1005, 1011
Polidori 887
Pollard, Snub 272
Pollina, Ferdinand 765
Pollock, Ellen 700
"Pom Pom," the Dog 582
Pomeroy, Allen 952, 956, 961, 963, 991
Poncin, Marcel 165
Pope, Bud 411, 448, 642, 681, 863, 1008
Pops and Louie 343
Porcasi, Paul 71, 187, 196, 438, 618
Pork Chops and Kidney Stew 787
Porter, George 318
Porter, Jean 318, 351, 688
Porter, William 338
Poston, Tom 121

Potel, Victor 101, 196, 280, 288, 323, 674
Potter, Peter 601
Powell, Charles Arthur 352
Powell, Joe 428
Powell, Lee 134, 968, 987
Powell, Russ 346, 693, 927
Power, Hartley 11
Power, Paul 50, 871
Powers, Jimmy 1021
Powers, Mala 121, 273
Powers, Richard 285, 442, 597, 959; *see also* Tom Keene
Powers, Tom 15, 17, 36, 116, 215, 228, 424, 586, 704, 894
Prack, Rudolf 136
Prador, Irene 808
Praskins, Leonard 55
Prather, Lee 764
Pratt, Perry 987
Pratt, Purnell 130, 134, 158, 254, 295, 400, 514, 552
Pratt, Theodore 490
Prescott, Elsie 819
Prescott, Guy 698, 880
Presle, Micheline 3
Presnell, Robert 55, 361, 819
Press, Marvin 534
Presson, Jay 16
Price, Alonzo 520
Price, Dennis 837
Price, Hal 20, 23, 46, 64, 95, 106, 110, 129, 138, 145, 154, 253, 264, 351, 352, 368, 376, 445, 446, 464, 465, 483, 502, 521, 524, 526, 539, 601, 611, 621, 650, 671, 719, 728, 731, 737, 740, 761, 792, 807, 860, 885, 895, 960, 992, 996
Price, Peter 587
Price, Stanley 9, 326, 551, 565, 724, 774, 795, 868, 947, 950, 952, 953, 955, 962, 963, 967, 968, 971, 972, 976, 983, 984, 991, 1002, 1005, 1011
Price, Vincent 3
Prickett, Maude 291
Priest, Bobbie 467
Prima, Louis, and His Band 477
"Prince," the Great Dane 140
Prince Modupe 957
Prival, Lucien 77, 779, 957, 985, 986

"Professor," the monkey  995
Prosser, Hugh  161, 236, 526, 728, 904, 962, 996, 1004
Proter, Jean  266
Proudlock, Roger  837
Prouse, Peter  181
Prouty, Jed  7, 42, 159, 311, 504, 545
Pryor, Maureen  186
Pryor, Roger  78, 370, 467, 552, 639, 741, 818, 833
Puente, Laurita  135
Puglia, Frank  2, 79, 83, 199, 224, 247, 372, 402, 713
Puig, Eva  593
Pulido, Jose  751
Pullen, William  324
Purcell, Bob  239
Purcell, Dick  369, 373, 520, 545, 592, 856, 932, 952
Purcell, Gertrude  27, 368, 373, 917
Purcell, Noel  185
Purcell, Robert  627
Purdy, Constance  512
Pyle, Denver  224, 238, 326, 399, 479, 495, 539, 544, 581, 671, 736, 789, 849, 1019

Qualen, John  46, 494
Quartaro, Nena  822
Quattrini, Paola  780
Queen, Ellery  476, 764; *see also* Frederic Dannay; Manfred B. Lee
Quentin, Patrick  355
Quest, Hans  454
Quigley, Charles  6, 881, 937, 953, 955
Quigley, Juanita  413, 910, 1034
Quigley, Rita  910, 1034
Quillan, Eddie  272, 309, 476, 1033
Quillan, Marie  489, 738
Quilland, Diane  189
Quinlan, William  628
Quinn, Tom  750, 876, 958
Quinn, Tony  683

Raaf, Vici  418
Rachel  734
Raciti, Aldo  780
Rackin, Martin  443
Radding, Celene  765
The Radio Rogues  536, 856

Rafferty, Frances  713
Raft, George  357, 1032
Ragan, Mike  157, 951, 964, 994
Raglan, Robert  336, 782, 829
Raine, Norman Reilly  101, 704, 921
Raine, Patricia  165
Raines, Ella  228, 471, 644, 736
Raines, Steve  724, 787, 872
Rainey, Norman  898
Rains, Claude  443
Raison, Milton  140, 516, 547, 548, 767, 786, 902
Raker, Lorin  91, 145, 960
Ralph, Jessie  494
Ralston, Esther  246, 282
Ralston, Rudy  25, 40, 81, 150, 157, 179, 191, 194, 208, 304, 327, 427, 431, 475, 480, 530, 535, 587, 631, 696, 711, 811, 831, 914
Ralston, Tobyna  1027
Ralston, Vera  2, 18, 46, 219, 230, 235, 304, 357, 364, 402, 475, 535, 581, 593, 766, 800, 836, 912, 928; *see also* Vera Hruba; Vera Hruba Ralston
Ralston, Vera Hruba  155, 413, 419, 510, 779; *see also* Vera Hruba; Vera Ralston
Rama, Rudy  610
Rambeau, Marjorie  377
Rameau, Emil  274, 456, 701
Rameau, Paul H.  383
Ramirez, Dario  84
Ramos, Bobby, Band  345
Ramos, Carla  48
Ramos, Fernando  48
The Ranch Boys  376
Rand, Edwin  637, 884
Rand, Sally  56
Randall, Addison (Jack Randall)  521
Randall, Stuart  25, 49, 316, 671, 676, 903, 989
Randell, Pamela  926
Randell, Ron  782
Randle, Karen  779
Randolph, Charley P.  975
Randolph, Isabel  42, 46, 358, 391, 418, 536, 643, 708, 713, 809, 831
Randolph, Jane  392, 769

Randolph, Lillian  333, 358, 749, 821
Randolph, Marion  538
Ranevsky, Boris  553
Rankin, Gil  2
Rankin, William  788
Ranson, Lois  19, 205, 252, 295, 296, 486, 503, 582, 877
Rapf, Maurice  91
Rapport, Fred  779
Raquello, Edward  906
Rasp, Fritz  454
Rasumny, Mikhail  345, 937
Rathmell, John  276, 647, 763, 957, 961, 1007, 1008, 1010
Ratib, Gamil  558
Rauh, Stanley  429
Ravel, Stelita  505
Rawlinson, A. R.  553
Rawlinson, Herbert  35, 80, 158, 168, 260, 408, 483, 503, 557, 722, 833, 956, 985, 986, 991, 995, 1000, 1003
Ray, Albert  113, 432, 873
Ray, Charles  1033
Ray, Jack  408
Ray, Jimmy  741
Ray, Joey  283, 710
Ray, Michel  184
Ray, Nicholas  399
Ray, Roland  554
Ray, Wade  977
Raybould, Harry  283
Raymond, Dean  148
Raymond, Jack  485, 742, 963
Raymond, Paula  121
Raymond, Robin  710
Raymond, Royal  627
Rayo, Ian  961
Rebaus, Hershel  942
Redman, Lee  595
Redmond, Liam  184
Redwing, Rodd  390, 956
Reed, Alan  273
Reed, Donald  957
Reed, Florence  250
Reed, George  747
Reed, Ione  489
Reed, Marshall  15, 52, 62, 68, 74, 90, 143, 171, 174, 255, 260, 378, 402, 420, 483, 502, 512, 519, 538, 549, 589, 638, 685, 697, 730, 831, 861, 895, 928,

# Name Index

954, 966, 970, 974, 976, 977, 1005, 1011, 1019, 1084
Reed, Maxwell 772
Reed, Myrtle 901
Reed, Philip 637
Reed, Walter 18, 431, 830, 903, 969, 973
Reedy, Beverly 467
Rees, Ed 364, 505
Rees, Lanny 87, 350
Reeves, Bob 39, 70, 168, 214, 310, 377, 394, 524, 528, 539, 624, 691, 723, 795, 889, 948, 950, 951, 959, 960, 964, 970
Reeves, Richard 120, 219, 357, 472, 581, 1006
Reeves, Theodore 187
Regan, Charles 954, 961, 963, 971, 988, 1004
Regan, Phil 240, 311, 341, 429, 477, 568, 715
Regas, George 282
Regas, Pedro 887, 995
Regnier, Charles 454
Reicher, Frank 22, 55, 107, 350, 364, 513, 609, 761, 834, 919, 933, 952
Reicher, Hedwig 360
Reichow, Otto 397, 986
Reid, Carl Benton 766
Reid, Margaret 742
Reid, Wallace, Jr. 985
Reihl, Kay 627
Reinhardt, Elizabeth 345
Relph, Michael 772
Remley, Ralph 568
Renaldo, Duncan 93, 142, 146, 195, 231, 266, 267, 310, 332, 406, 541, 590, 660, 672, 687, 722, 761, 983, 986, 988, 993, 1001, 1005, 1010
Renaldo, Tito 215, 546
Renavent, Georges 109, 708, 717, 779, 995, 1001, 1004, 1005
Renay, Paul 965
Rennie, Guy 665
Rennie, Michael 790
Rentschler, Mickey 244, 904
Republic Pictures 790
The Republic Rhythm Riders 73, 129, 426, 547, 548, 762, 894
Retford, Ella 596
Rettig, Tommy 290, 418

Revere, Anne 714
Rex, Jack 518
Reyes, Chuy 814
Reynolds, Alan 838, 994
Reynolds, Burt 787
Reynolds, Craig 291, 664, 899
Reynolds, Harrington 869
Reynolds, Lee 694
Reynolds, Marjorie 657
Rhein, Al 800
Rhinehart, O'Leta 149, 579
Rhodes, Betty 507
Rhodes, Christopher 428
Rhodes, Grandon 460, 535, 900, 925
Rhodes, Marjorie 596, 808
Riano, Renie 367, 466, 568, 749, 917
Rice, Albert 268
Rice, Darol 762
Rice, Florence 187, 500
Rice, Frank 554
Rice, Jack 29, 503, 588
Rice, Joan 165
Rice, Marie 439
Rich, Dick 162, 377, 408, 460, 710, 998
Rich, Gloria 180, 410, 542, 567, 961
Rich, Irene 15, 86
Richards, Addison 34, 50, 75, 116, 145, 173, 231, 243, 262, 281, 301, 315, 517, 609, 648, 723, 821, 834, 909
Richards, Danny, Jr. 325
Richards, Frank 32, 90, 612, 758
Richards, Keith 65, 201, 269, 323, 533, 754, 768, 866, 950, 976, 977, 978, 981, 1019
Richards, Paul 698
Richards, Robert L. 424
Richardson, Duncan 305, 605
Richardson, Jack 50
Richman, Charles 414
Richmond, Kane 246, 507, 579, 834, 842, 974, 1004, 1076
Richmond, Leo C. 164, 898
Richmond, Warner 190, 322, 435, 523, 601, 738, 847
Ricigliano, Mike 16
Rickert, Shirley 377
Ricks, Archie 23, 303

Rico, Mona 1010
Ridgely, John 816, 826
Ridges, Stanley 220, 500, 586
Riebe, Loren 132, 308, 947, 953, 955, 960, 961, 966, 975, 978, 985, 986, 987, 993, 995, 1000, 1003, 1004, 1010
Riedmann, Gerhard 454
Rienits, Rex 152
Riesner, Charles F. 477
Riesner, Dean 58
Rigby, Edward 596
Rigby, Gordon 272, 347, 560, 733, 927
Riley, Clements 546
Riley, Elaine 437
Riley, Mike, and His Musical Maniacs 814
Rilla, Walter 300, 841
Rimpau, Al 987
Rinehart, Dick 318, 680, 812, 862
Rinehart, Jim 959, 977
Ring, Cyril 235, 351, 368, 397, 612, 743, 937
Riordan, Robert 978
Ripper, Michael 707
Riquelme, Carlos 924
Risdon, Elisabeth 192, 301, 340, 371, 662, 733, 749
Riss, Dan 32
Ritter, Fred 104
The Ritz Brothers 1032
Rivas, Carlos 575
Rivero, Charles 195
Rivero, Julian 48, 144, 195, 266, 310, 432, 460, 546, 650, 681, 711, 761, 828, 888, 914, 940
Rivkin, Allen 45, 211, 654, 836
RKO Pictures 250, 651, 683, 757, 790, 822, 962
Roach, Bert 468, 476, 664
Roadman, Betty 60, 988
Roan, Vinegar 67, 308, 965, 987, 993, 1003, 1008, 1010, 1011
Roark, Garland 219, 898
Robards, Jason, Sr. 397, 599, 615, 748, 1012
"Robbie," the Dog 665
Robbins, Archie 439, 665
Robbins, Gale 191
Robbins, Marty 619
Robel, Bernard 428

Roberson, Chuck 230, 249, 593, 651, 836, 977, 978
Robert, Jacqueline 165
The Robertos 749
Roberts, Allene 830
Roberts, Beatrice 59, 590
Roberts, Ben 501
Roberts, Beverly 94, 366, 457, 810
Roberts, Charles E. 153, 215, 314, 356, 539
Roberts, Don 276
Roberts, J. H. 790
Roberts, Jack 67, 961, 963, 968, 1003
Roberts, Jeanie 639
Roberts, John S. 678
Roberts, Lee 143, 179, 460, 903, 922, 959, 977, 981, 991, 1019
Roberts, Leona 262, 365, 453, 819
Roberts, Lynn 83, 95, 117, 159, 319, 961, 987; see also Mary Hart; Lynne Roberts
Roberts, Lynne 44, 55, 116, 214, 285, 339, 349, 441, 452, 455, 459, 512, 586, 588, 597, 656, 678, 706, 739, 754, 815, 835, 917; see also Mary Hart; Lynn Roberts
Roberts, Paul 379
Roberts, Roy 228, 239, 357, 362, 423, 685, 704
Roberts, Stanley 130, 331, 331, 526, 574, 601, 629, 823
Roberts, Tracey 900
Robertson, Dale 156, 324
Robertson, Willard 246, 263, 421, 457
Robie, Earl 418
Robin, Sue 941
Robinson, Bartlett 283
Robinson, Bob 955, 962, 970, 986, 988
Robinson, Dewey 28, 247, 326, 415, 459, 639, 820, 856
Robinson, Edward G. 506
Robinson, Frances 364
Robinson, Ralph 915
Robinson, Ruth 46, 112, 142, 195, 373, 406, 812
Robson, Flora 596
Roc, Patricia 700
Rocco, Eddie 953, 958

Rochelle, Ben 144
Rochelle, Claire 69, 307, 650
Rockwell, Jack 9, 35, 41, 54, 55, 56, 62, 67, 106, 128, 137, 154, 162, 167, 169, 257, 306, 394, 433, 463, 470, 512, 569, 584, 601, 620, 624, 630, 633, 634, 670, 672, 723, 725, 735, 770, 794, 799, 860, 863, 878, 895, 916, 939, 949, 956, 987
Rockwell, Robert 10, 47, 65, 181, 224, 447, 610, 627, 853, 881, 925, 1025
Rodgers, Gene 814
Rodman, Nancy 160
Rodriguez, Estelita 13, 47, 90, 153, 215, 224, 269, 292, 314, 345, 371, 492, 546, 549, 572, 762, 796, 801, 802, 857, 865
Rodriguez, Ismael 160
Roe, Vingie 581
Roebuck, Tiny 1000
Roeca, Sam 335, 619
Roehn, Franz 838
Roettinger, Heinz 379
Rogell, Albert S. 203, 343, 377, 450, 455, 612, 682, 743, 941
Rogers, Bob 992
Rogers, Bradford 368
Rogers, Charles "Buddy" 1028
Rogers, Jean 268
Rogers, Roy 13, 21, 24, 27, 35, 49, 50, 51, 60, 71, 79, 106, 126, 134, 144, 162, 167, 189, 192, 214, 221, 256, 269, 292, 294, 310, 317, 320, 323, 344, 350, 369, 371, 372, 374, 378, 393, 394, 408, 419, 442, 463, 466, 467, 513, 522, 528, 533, 549, 559, 572, 622, 625, 633, 648, 657, 662, 663, 672, 680, 688, 723, 725, 732, 750, 752, 753, 755, 758, 760, 763, 768, 771, 795, 796, 798, 799, 801, 846, 854, 865, 871, 876, 878, 883, 899, 934, 939, 940, 1031; see also Leonard Slye; Dick Weston
Roy Rogers, Riders 371, 572, 758
Rogers, Ruth 526

Rogers, Will 791
Roginsky, Miguel 403
Roland, Armand 109
Roland, Gilbert 19, 84
Roman, Ric 199, 357, 711, 758, 811, 900
Roman, Ruth 713, 779
Romanoff, Constantine 534, 887
Romer, Jeanne 348
Romer, Lynn 348
Romer, Sax 965
Romero, Cesar 1028, 1032, 1033
Romney, Edana 11
Romoff, Nicco 534
Rooney, Mickey 32, 390, 867, 1030
Roope, Fay 32
Roosevelt, Buddy 20, 405, 543, 958, 960, 962, 968, 972, 982, 984, 986, 988, 1000, 1001, 1003, 1004
Roosevelt, President Franklin D. 603
Root, Wells 67, 325, 473
Roper, Bob 650
Roper, Jack 155, 332, 592, 616, 899, 965
Ropes, Bradford 19, 22, 47, 117, 144, 238, 266, 310, 341, 342, 397, 466, 485, 487, 623, 635, 649, 649, 733, 750, 777
Roquemore, Henry 322, 617, 738
Rorke, Hayden 211
Rory, Rossana 324
Rosalean and Seville 477
Rosanska, Countess 534
Rosas, Raymond 390
Roscoe, Gerald 537
Rose, Billy 765
Rose, Dudley 889
Rose, George 772, 841
Rose, Harry 16
Rose, Polly 765
Rose, Robert 269
Rose, Wally 962, 975
Rosemond, Clinton 162, 322
Rosen, Phil 77, 101, 151, 248, 271, 388, 396, 603, 870, 942
Rosenbloom, Maxie 263, 296, 870
Rosener, George 27, 106, 126, 374, 723

# Name Index

Rosett, Rose 345
Rosing, Bodil 322, 493
Ross, Bob 1034
Ross, Dennis 418
Ross, Earl 110, 647
Ross, George 324
Ross, Jack 376
Ross, Shirley 682, 749, 1034
Ross, Stanley 604
Roth, Gene 422, 724; see also Gene Stutenroth
Roubert, Matty 257, 291, 551, 583, 680, 725, 844, 949, 958, 971
Rousseau, Louise 608, 872
Rouverol, Jean 439, 906
Roux, Tony 267, 800
Rowan, Dan 1007
Rowan, Don 5, 705
Rowan, Frank 459
Rowland, Henry 364, 585, 727, 787, 979, 1009
Rowland, William 749
Rowles, Polly 770
Roy, Billy 509
Roy, John 975, 983, 996
Royal, Charles Francis 127, 263, 307, 440, 445, 542, 650
Royce, Frosty 74, 541, 977
Royce, John 1001
Royce, Lionel 1001
Royle, Selena 505
Royle, William 256, 332, 491, 629, 965, 975
Rub, Christian 247, 347, 388, 438
Rubenstein, Arthur 389
Rubin, Benny 206
Rubini, Jan 36
Ruby, Mike 10
Ruby, Wade 131
Rudd, Norman 65
Ruetting, Barbara 383
Ruggles, Wesley 1033
Ruhl, William 125, 168, 266, 267, 541, 812
Ruick, Mel 520, 603
Ruiz, Albert 344
Rule, Janice 924
Rumann, Sig 67, 103, 636
Rumistrzewicz, Krystyna 184
Rush, Dick 612, 693, 953, 962
Ruskin, Shimen 416
Russell, Elizabeth 702
Russell, Gail 15, 505, 531, 898

Russell, Grace Denbigh 808
Russell, Harriet 148
Russell, Jane 1033
Russell, John 200, 219, 228, 329, 357, 402, 423, 539, 677, 791
Russell, Mary 56, 476, 647, 655
Russell, Rosland 1028
Russell, William 1
Russey, Donia 6
Rutherford, Ann 135, 196, 313, 433, 448, 453, 489, 510, 554, 611, 738, 1034
Rutherford, Jack 554, 667, 883
Rutherford, Margaret 858
Rutherford, Tom 180, 1028
Ruysdael, Basil 713
Ryan, Ben 429
Ryan, Dick 709
Ryan, Don 119, 172, 172, 904
Ryan, Irene 536, 894
Ryan, Peggy 715
Ryan, Sheila 338, 577, 753, 787, 1027
Ryan, Ted 922
Ryan, Tim 153, 343, 367, 462, 612, 804, 937
Ryan, Tommy 141, 205, 296, 494, 503, 514, 557, 601, 726, 788, 810, 1002
Rydon, Ryck 901

Saal, William 250
Sabu 390
Sacha, Jean 558
Sachs, Leonard 829
Sackheim, Jerry 222, 321, 424, 456, 653, 678, 769, 852, 879
Sadovsky, Felix 419
The Sagebrush Serenaders 468
St. Angelo, Robert 966
St. Clair, Leonard 380
St. Clair, Malcolm 486
St. Clair and Vilova 815
St. George, Thomas R. 98
St. John, Adela Rogers 813
St. John, Al 20, 26, 94, 252, 395, 435, 498, 773, 812, 822
St. Leo, Leonard 1004
St. Leon, George 987
St. Luke's Choristers 113, 492, 559

St. Polis, John 660
Sais, Marin 13, 50, 481, 679, 693, 728, 774, 868, 982
Saks, Patty 643
Sale, Charles "Chic" 272
Sale, Richard 86, 98, 197, 381, 534, 637, 767
Sale, Virginia 159
Salew, John 683
Salgari, Emilio 518
Salkow, Sidney 133, 232, 240, 259, 280, 525, 609, 715, 778, 788, 919, 945
"Salty," the Chimp 325
Samuels, Maurice 382
Sande, Walter 29, 412, 484, 614, 810
Sanders, George 562
Sanders, Hugh 362, 423, 882
Sanders, Sandy 959, 964, 969, 1019
Sands, Johnny 6, 217
Baby Sandy 398
Sanford, Erskine 285, 451, 898
Sanford, Ralph 104, 210, 344, 513, 705, 739, 902
Sanger, John 841
Sansom, Robert 700
Santell, Alfred 492, 813
Santley, Fred 91, 397, 743
Santley, Joseph 45, 79, 91, 112, 158, 195, 204, 293, 313, 330, 348, 367, 391, 397, 429, 487, 488, 613, 636, 666, 669, 714, 740, 742, 821, 825, 843, 937
Santos, Jack 282
Sarafian, Richard C. 475, 535
Sarecky, Barney A. 949, 957, 965, 985, 992, 996, 997, 1007, 1012
Sarecky, Louis 405
Sarfati, Maurice 558
Sargent, Charles 434, 907
Sarie and Sallie 376
Saris, Marilyn 431
Sarno, Hector V. 109, 155, 965, 1010
Sarracino, Ernest 947, 949, 965, 986, 992, 1012
Sassoli, Dina 242
"Satan," the Gorilla 995; see also Emil Van Horn
Satterlee, Peggy 48
Sauber, Harry 477, 568
Saunders, Lloyd 1008

Saunders, Stuart 185
Savage, Ann 424, 922
Savage, Archie 994
Savage, Carol 278
Savitsky, Sam 534
Savitt, Jan, and His Top Hatters 815
Sawyer, Joe 71, 162, 195, 278, 438, 488, 520, 605, 677, 742
Saxe, Carl 987
Sayers, Eric 384
Sayles, Francis 612, 615, 618, 710, 773, 947, 961, 968, 987
Saylor, Syd 50, 212, 307, 485, 522, 705, 728, 797, 822, 927, 931
Sayre, Bigelow 963
Sayre, George W. 289, 617
Sayre, Jeffrey 952
Scannell, Frank 10, 16, 44, 344
Scar, Sam 227, 357
Scardon, Paul 416, 469
Schaefer, Armand 6, 16, 27, 42, 78, 94, 96, 139, 193, 212, 225, 232, 240, 252, 263, 265, 274, 278, 279, 280, 285, 286, 295, 315, 330, 333, 349, 358, 375, 376, 391, 393, 462, 490, 507, 509, 513, 536, 537, 543, 545, 586, 592, 653, 667, 669, 681, 701, 705, 718, 738, 739, 757, 778, 788, 803, 804, 809, 815, 848, 850, 864, 866, 893, 897, 936
Schaefer, Fred 955, 962, 963, 968, 988, 992
Schaeffer, Rube 1007
Schallert, William 46, 357, 447, 838, 1019
Schary, Dore 45, 412
Scheerer, Robert 16
Schild, Marlyn 941
Schildkraut, Joseph 113, 236, 260, 414, 534, 546, 593
Schiller, Fanny 924
Schiller, Fred 591, 917
Schiller, Miriam 765
Schiller, Norbert 562
Schilling, Gus 18, 86, 112, 345, 356, 367, 451
Schlesinger, John 184
Schlesinger, Leon 715
Schlom, Herman 29, 117,
133, 200, 366, 493, 494, 403, 515, 525, 557, 606, 609, 664, 677, 717
Schnitzer, Gerald 702
Schofield, Joan 901
Schofield, Johnnie 122
Schomberg, Hermann 118
Schonauer, Marianne 379
Schonbock, Karl 136
Schor, Lou 418
Schrecker, Frederick 184
Schrier, Harold G. Capt. 689
Schrock, Raymond L. 311, 610, 741
Schroeder, Doris 26, 39, 166, 264, 395, 405, 498, 541, 583, 746, 773, 812, 868, 899, 908
Schubert, Bernard 322
Schumann, Erik 454
Schumm, Hans 1004
Schunzel, Reinhold 593
Schuster, Hugo 707
Scott, Bob 65
Scott, DeVallon 325, 484
Scott, Dick 288, 370, 419, 482, 783, 955, 986, 1003
Scott, Dorothy 604
Scott, Hampton J. 816
Scott, Jacques 401
Scott, John 468
Scott, Karen 484
Scott, Lester 1003
Scott, Linda 377
Scott, Lizabeth 901
Scott, Martha 206, 377, 1034
Scott, Randolph 71, 1032
Scott, Robert 213
Scott, Wallace 898
Scott, Zachary 237
Scotti, Vito 215
Scotto, Aubrey 244, 311, 347, 366, 552, 833
Scully, Bill 981
Seabrook, Gay 339
Seal, Peter 534
Seaman, Earl 433
Seamon, Helen 322, 397
Searl, Jackie 870
Sears, Allan 738
Seay, James 43, 351, 463, 541, 648, 744, 787
Sebastian, Dorothy 24, 405, 672
Sebby, Sam 46, 998
Sedan, Rolfe 180, 552, 640
Seddon, Margaret 252, 359
Seese, Dorothy Ann 486
Seff, Manuel 348, 881
Seidel, Tom 243, 747, 805, 908, 961, 972
Seidner, Irene 614
Seiter, William A. 111, 418, 458
Sekely, Steve 216, 419, 512
Selander, Lesley 63, 75, 92, 109, 115, 222, 234, 298, 529, 559, 579, 584, 588, 656, 720, 722, 775, 824, 842, 845, 887, 900
Selano, Guido 242
Selby, Sarah 304
Self, William 481, 689
Selk, George 1006
Sells, Paul 394
Selznick, Joyce 665
Semels, Harry 410, 674, 855, 1001
Semon, Maxine 98, 769
Sennett, Mack 1033
Sentries, Gene Gary 534
Sen Yung, Victor 2, 235, 402, 713, 902, 1006
Sepulveda, Carl 52, 62, 74, 92, 167, 483, 593, 678, 686, 692, 722, 775, 965, 978, 988, 996, 1002, 1011, 1012
Serato, Massimo 242, 259
Serbaroli, Alex 259
Seroff, Muni 534, 779
Serrano, Sam 983
Serret, John 428, 700
Servis, Helen 56
Sessions, Almira 329, 539, 544, 923
Seton, Bruce 233, 336, 782
Severn, Clifford, Jr. 266
Seward, Edmond 200
Seymour, Al 962, 992, 1004, 1007
Seymour, Dan 805
Seymour, James 683
Shackelford, Floyd 448, 887
Shade, Jamesson 258, 555
Shadnoff, George 765
Shahan, Rocky 402, 977, 1002
Shakespeare, William 451
"Shamrock," the Horse 50
Shane, Maxwell 225, 757
Shannon, Frank 5
Shannon, Harry 7, 131, 199, 213, 315, 327, 369, 373,

# NAME INDEX

377, 424, 474, 587, 605, 736, 747, 753, 807, 934
Shannon, Peggy  942
Shannon, Robert T  3, 42, 235, 299, 368, 385, 577, 743, 755, 932
Sharbutt, Del  344
Sharpe, David  51, 146, 190, 526, 674, 725, 801, 823, 912, 930, 947, 948, 949, 951, 954, 955, 961, 962, 963, 964, 965, 966, 969, 971, 973, 976, 977, 980, 982, 983, 984, 985, 986, 988, 992, 995, 999, 1004
Sharpe, Lester  260, 779, 818, 881
Shavelson, Melville  367, 740
Shaw, Betty  149, 155, 309
Shaw, C. Montague  16, 438, 647, 717, 869, 955, 962, 972, 992, 1007, 1012
Shaw, Denis  901
Shaw, Hazel  25
Shaw, Janet  220
Shaw, Richard  233, 336, 829
Shaw, Susan  837
Shay, Mildred  375, 643
Shayne, Konstantin  18
Shayne, Robert  2, 157, 381, 418, 480, 497, 838, 981, 1006
Shayne, Tamara  534
Shea, Jack  495, 998, 1009
Shean, Al  31, 252, 388
Sheehan, Howard  749, 777
Sheehan, John  12, 400, 429, 459, 464, 501, 833
Sheffield, Reed  1003
Sheldon, Dick  1003
Sheldon, Jerry  975
Sheldon, Kathryn  117, 368
Sheldon, Kelsey  641
Sheldon, Norman  9, 207
Sheldon, Sidney  501
Shelley, Jordan  709
Shelton, Gilman  963
Shelton, Marla  48, 710
Shepard, Elaine  738, 957
Shepard, Miles  401
Shepley, Michael  185, 859
Sheridan, Ann  131
Sheridan, Daniel M.  87
Sheridan, Frank  140, 439, 764
Sheridan, Tommy  628

Sherlock, Charles  512, 961, 963
Sherman, Annyse  779
Sherman, Fred  333, 718, 784
Sherman, George  20, 26, 119, 130, 142, 146, 154, 172, 175, 220, 257, 277, 331, 376, 395, 405, 406, 413, 444, 445, 478, 491, 498, 517, 524, 526, 551, 567, 570, 574, 583, 614, 615, 629, 641, 645, 660, 674, 693, 702, 746, 761, 773, 779, 812, 823, 844, 862, 868, 877, 905, 915, 930, 931, 932
Sherman, Jack  912
Sherman, Ransom  239, 803, 933
Sheron, Molio  534
Sherrier, Julian  428
Sherven Brothers' Rodeoliers  352
Sherwood, C. L.  624
Sherwood, George  137, 368, 467, 570, 710, 776, 931, 952, 969, 1004
Shield, Robert  328
Shields, Arthur  616
Shields, Frank  5
Shindall, Cy  975
Shindle, Gus  949
Shiner, Ronald  428
Shingler, Helen  428
Shipman, Barry  103, 123, 159, 257, 304, 327, 427, 436, 445, 559, 585, 602, 621, 660, 784, 844, 882, 955, 960, 961, 963, 968, 975, 987, 988, 993, 1000, 1003, 1010, 1019
Shirley, Anne  464
Shirley, Bill  187, 243, 333, 363, 368, 666, 682, 802, 821
Shirley, Irene  368, 747
Shoemaker, Ann  359, 464
Sholem, Lee  325, 838
Shooting Star  642
Shor, Sol  164, 754, 947, 948, 949, 950, 953, 954, 955, 961, 963, 965, 966, 968, 970, 971, 975, 977, 978, 984, 985, 988, 992, 999, 1002, 1012
Short, Antrim  56
Short, Luke  329, 644
Shotter, Barbara  808

Shoup, Col. D. M.  689
Shrum, Cal, and His Gang  699
Shrum, Walt, and His Colorado Hillbillies  66, 542
Shuken, Phillip  595
Shulman, Irving  111, 811
Shumate, Harold  76, 210, 473
Shumway, Lee  26, 142, 169, 172, 254, 289, 351, 357, 368, 395, 464, 465, 498, 512, 526, 555, 564, 602, 615, 662, 674, 776, 868, 928, 963, 965, 978, 986
Shumway, Walter  586, 967
Shurtz, Sewell  419
Siegel, Sol C.  28, 70, 83, 132, 162, 308, 319, 339, 342, 421, 473, 488, 514, 542, 611, 615, 624, 715, 726, 770, 820, 855, 878, 915, 919, 926, 945, 961, 968, 975, 987, 1000, 1003, 1010
Sigaloff, Eugene  534, 668
Sillman, Leonard  16
Silva, Petra  800
Silvani, Aldo  780
"Silver," the Horse  50
"Silver Chief," the Horse  987, 988
Silverheels, Jay  534, 888, 912
Silvers, Phil  342, 367
Silverstein, David  158, 487, 833
Silvestre, Armando  830
Sima, Oskar  136
Simmons, George  319
Simmons, Georgia  24, 664
Simmons, Richard  241, 363, 830, 922, 985, 986, 989
Simmons, Richard Arlen  418
Simms, Eddie  891
Simon, Robert F.  665
Simon, Scott  2
Simon, Simone  805
Simon, William H., Jr.  98
The Simp-Phonies  139
Simpson, Ivan  385, 941
Simpson, Mickey  230, 437, 800, 898
Simpson, Mimi  698
Simpson, Napoleon  627
Simpson, Russell  55, 88, 119, 217, 313, 423, 464, 791, 793, 820, 936
Sims, Joan  185, 186, 772, 808, 858

Sinclair, Betty  101
Sinclair, Eric  218, 447
Sinclair, Hugh  11, 30, 683
Sinclair, Peter  152, 859
Sinden, Donald  1, 165, 186
Singh, Gurdial  67
The Singing Riders  907
Singleton, Doris  4
Singleton, Penny  568
Singley, Arthur  642
Singuineau, Frank  829
Siodmak, Curt  220, 413, 444, 478, 614
Siodmak, Robert  747
Sistrom, William  683, 790
Siterman, Fred  909
Sitka, Emil  402, 581, 703
Six Hits and a Miss  342
Skarstedt, Vance  474, 531
Skipworth, Alison  347, 410, 412, 870
Sky Eagle, George  956
Slater, Barbara  941
Slater, John  683, 987, 1008
Slaughter, Anna May  1024
Slaven, Buster  601
Slavin, Slick  206
Sledge, John  384
Sleeper, Martha  869
Slifer, Elizabeth  329, 894
Sloane, Michael  166, 670
Sloane, Olive  471
Slocum, Cy  955, 963, 985, 986, 992, 995, 1004
Slye, Leonard  56, 543; *see also* Roy Rogers; Dick Weston
Smile, Ted  402
Smirnova, Dina  534
Smith, Alexis  211
Smith, Alson Jesse  431
Smith, Art  17
Smith, C. Aubrey  637, 701, 709
Smith, Charles  98, 688, 941
Smith, Drake  914
Smith, Ernie  1007
Smith, Evelynne  894
Smith, Gerald Oliver  385
Smith, Gerald Oliver  613, 622, 737
Smith, Harry  956, 974, 980, 995, 1005
Smith, Jack C.  34, 190, 226, 286, 307, 435, 440, 522, 578, 673, 847, 860
Smith, John  150, 431

Smith, Paul  781
Smith, Paul Gerard  339, 459
Smith, Queenie  46, 610
Smith, Robert  346
Smith, Roberta  532
Smith, Tom  24, 106, 115, 162, 234, 372, 466, 488, 489, 541, 602, 615, 839, 844, 863, 897, 936, 939
Smith, Walter  979, 994
The SMU 50  56
Snell, Earle  9, 14, 85, 107, 128, 137, 142, 167, 267, 354, 481, 541, 556, 584, 626, 656, 660, 675, 694, 721, 774, 792, 844, 891, 896
Snowden, Alec C.  700
Snowden, Eric  245
Snyder, Howard  613
Soderberg, Charles  955
Sodering, Walter  64, 251, 288, 566, 933, 941, 982
Soederbaum, Kristina  118
Sokal, Henry  917
Sokolove, Richard  455
Sokolskaya, Myra  534
Sokou, Ekali  185
Soldani, Charles  164, 467, 956
Soldati, Mario  188
Soldi, Steve  866
Solon, Ewen  808
Solow, Eugene  78
Somers, Esther  807
Somlo, Josef  11
"Sonny," the Horse  74, 97, 171, 337, 470, 502, 569, 895
Sons of the Pioneers  13, 21, 50, 51, 56, 91, 144, 189, 214, 228, 269, 310, 317, 323, 344, 350, 353, 370, 408, 442, 463, 466, 467, 513, 528, 543, 549, 622, 633, 648, 651, 662, 663, 688, 732, 750, 752, 753, 755, 760, 771, 795, 798, 799, 871, 876, 883, 934
Soo Hoo, Hayward  55
Sooter, Rudy  60, 465, 641
Sorel, George  534, 717, 1001
Sosso, Pietro  974
Sothern, Hugh  408, 940, 952, 968
Soule, Olan  153, 181
Sowards, George  114, 956
Space, Arthur  350, 460, 516,

527, 675, 884, 889, 951, 973, 994
Spadaro, Umberto  242
Spain, Fay  150
Spalding, Kim  460
Sparks, Jack  292, 323, 727, 792
Speaker, Tris  407
Spellman, Martin  693
Spence, Ralph  593, 740
Spence, Sandra  228
Spencer, Douglas  460
Spencer, Jim I.  975
Spencer, Johnny  979
Spencer, Marian  790
Spencer, Sarah  357, 894
Spencer, Tim  56, 543, 648, 755
Spier, William  417
Spiker, Ray  981
The Sportsmen  330, 613
Spottswood, James  349
Springsteen, R. G.  4, 14, 22, 47, 88, 128, 131, 137, 143, 152, 170, 191, 215, 238, 253, 273, 290, 312, 321, 326, 340, 353, 354, 356, 362, 456, 468, 481, 482, 495, 519, 539, 556, 560, 581, 584, 627, 638, 675, 694, 706, 707, 721, 724, 736, 748, 774, 786, 792, 793, 840, 841, 857, 872, 891, 896, 909, 990
Stack, Robert  84, 1034
Stader, Paul  329, 402, 766, 800, 1009
Staff, Ivan  772
Stafford, Bess  439
Stafford, Bucko  766
Stafford, John  30
The Stafford Sisters  291, 542
Stahl, William  960, 961, 963, 968, 975, 985, 992, 1007
Stallings, Laurence  791
Stamp-Taylor, Enid  11
Stander, Lionel  57, 378, 765, 805
Stanhope, Ted  288, 992
Stanley, Barbara  312
Stanley, Edwin  27, 60, 76, 368, 391, 462, 476, 507, 536, 577, 960, 968, 992
Stanley, Helene  37
Stanley, John  765
Stanley, Louise  202, 302, 432, 827

Stanning, Arthur 709
Stanton, Ernie 175
Stanton, Paul 28, 149, 388, 410, 598, 815, 942
Stanton, Will 5
Stanwyck, Barbara 484
Stapp, Marjorie 698
The Stardusters 856
Starling, Pat 688
Starr, Jimmy 559, 699
Staub, Ralph 5, 140, 400, 459, 476, 485, 520, 601, 741, 906
Stebbins, Bobby 218
Steele, Bob 23, 38, 64, 72, 106, 110, 123, 127, 177, 190, 199, 202, 213, 226, 227, 264, 267, 299, 302, 303, 440, 445, 561, 564, 573, 578, 585, 602, 621, 634, 646, 650, 652, 679, 685, 692, 696, 697, 712, 721, 822, 827, 832, 844, 860, 866, 877, 885, 904, 908
Steele, Freddie 592, 773
Steele, Tom 52, 54, 55, 95, 105, 115, 121, 124, 174, 234, 305, 337, 376, 446, 483, 502, 563, 565, 569, 621, 647, 687, 730, 731, 752, 774, 845, 854, 861, 887, 891, 895, 948, 950, 951, 952, 953, 954, 956, 958, 959, 961, 963, 964, 966, 967, 968, 969, 970, 971, 972, 973, 974, 976, 977, 978, 979, 980, 981, 982, 983, 984, 986, 989, 990, 991, 992, 994, 995, 996, 997, 998, 999, 1001, 1002, 1004, 1005, 1006, 1007, 1009, 1011, 1019
Steele, William 727
Steers, Larry 89, 310, 502, 512, 521, 678, 709, 927, 950, 961, 968
Stefanelli, Count 360
Stein, Paul L. 596, 683
Stein, Sammy 57, 251, 612, 636, 728, 742
Steinbeck, John 628
Stepanek, Herbert 379
Stepanek, Karel 30, 233, 471, 707
Stephens, Frank 13
Stephens, Martin 184
Stephens, Marvin 232

Stephenson, Henry 416, 478, 709
Stephenson, James 918
Stept, Samuel 937
Sterling, Joseph 553
Stevans, Landers 59
Stevens, Bill 446, 967
Stevens, Charles 67, 90, 402, 473, 538, 697, 727, 888, 897, 989
Stevens, Jean 492, 813
Stevens, Kathryn 1034
Stevens, Landers 400, 945
Stevens, Laura 950
Stevens, Louis 71, 126
Stevens, Onslow 77, 246, 310, 369, 799, 911
Stevens, Ruthelma 853
Stevens, Warren 2, 474
Stevenson, Bob 397, 885, 965, 998, 1004
Stevenson, Houseley 155, 505, 539
Stevenson, Martin 56
Stevenson, Tom 444, 478
Stewart, Anna Marie 885
Stewart, Athole 596
Stewart, Calvin 700
Stewart, Eleanor 303, 624, 968
Stewart, Jack 859, 960, 1000
Stewart, Larry 742
Stewart, Nick 237
Stewart, Nicodemus 155, 220, 358, 529, 763
Stewart, Peggy 9, 39, 88, 115, 124, 137, 166, 234, 386, 482, 555, 605, 630, 670, 675, 720, 721, 731, 774, 775, 834, 848, 861, 883, 887, 891, 996, 1002
Stewart, Richard 700
Stewart, Sheila 555
Stiritz, Walter 949
Stirling, Linda 114, 155, 386, 453, 516, 604, 652, 687, 691, 719, 722, 839, 892, 896, 953, 978, 990, 997, 1005, 1011
Stirling, Pamela 184
Stockdale, Carl 439, 537, 987
Stockwell, Harry 12
Stone, Bobby 364, 397, 710, 849
Stone, George E. 7, 512
Stone, Irving 27

Stone, Marianne 165, 553, 808, 829
Stone, Milburn 126, 172, 299, 583, 791, 822, 849, 942
Stooge 76
Storey, June 42, 66, 104, 130, 193, 209, 266, 494, 352, 375, 376, 508, 623, 643, 653, 706, 761, 849
Storm, Gale 394, 463, 633, 679, 921
Storm, Lesley 11
Storm, Rafael 360
Stossel, Ludwig 273, 419, 791
Straight, Clarence 129, 221, 292, 589, 600
Strang, Harry 133, 146, 162, 172, 266, 364, 512, 521, 541, 615, 662, 763, 844, 952, 955, 960, 965, 967, 968, 982, 990, 992, 1000, 1003, 1010
Strange, Glenn 66, 87, 162, 167, 217, 260, 304, 402, 427, 434, 523, 526, 654, 663, 72, 679, 687, 731, 798, 800, 888, 907, 928, 988
Strange, Robert 53, 175, 221, 365, 438, 657, 760, 818, 947, 952, 972, 985, 995, 1009
Stratford, Peggy 439
Stratton-Porter, Gene 313, 493
Strauch, Joe, Jr. 48, 52, 91, 318, 351, 874
Strauss, Alfred 782
Strauss, Robert 32
Strauss, Theodore 505
Stravenger, Frank 306
Strawn, Arthur 6
Street, David 16, 505
Striker, Fran 987, 988
Stritz, Walter 965
Strong, Leonard 328
Strong, Mark 976
Strudwick, Shepperd 628
Strueby, Katherine 30, 122
Stuart, Angela 534
Stuart, Gloria 330
Stuart, Nicholas 184
Stubbs, Harry 282, 365, 737, 764
Stutenroth, Gene 260, 354, 481, 540, 948, 950, 964,

970, 977, 978, 994; see also
  Gene Roth
Sujata 219
Sullivan, Barry 484
Sullivan, Brick 189, 981
Sullivan, Charles 50, 161,
  169, 207, 236, 258, 402,
  408, 410, 464, 483, 512,
  543, 560, 586, 818, 842,
  861, 887, 920, 950, 958,
  961, 963, 971, 976, 982,
  989, 994, 1006
Sullivan, Denny 985
Sullivan, Elliott 263, 271,
  740, 972
Sullivan, Wallace 429, 639
Sully, Frank 507, 743
Summerfield, Eleanor 808
Summers, Bill 407
Summers, Brian 782
Summers, Don 978
Summers, Georgia 526
Summerville, Slim 613
Sumner, Geoffrey 186
Sundberg, Clinton 802
Sundholm, William 397
Suss, Bernard 508, 955, 963
Sutherland, Eddie 1033
Sutherland, Sidney 78, 429,
  439, 741
Sutton, Grady 159, 187, 216,
  301, 455, 593, 824
Sutton, Kay 757
Sutton, Paul 373
Suzanne, George 947, 965,
  991, 995
Swabacker, Leslie 1008
Swan, Bob 150, 431, 484,
  766, 828
Swann, Francis 47
Swickard, Josef 491, 963,
  1010
Switzer, Carl "Alfalfa" 42, 46,
  363, 398, 635, 669, 714, 894
Sydney, Derek 829
Sylvester, Henry 957, 960,
  961, 1000

Tabori, Paul 782
Tafler, Sidney 772
Taggart, Ben 112, 410, 464,
  710, 952, 955, 973
Taggart, James 323, 425
Talbot, Helen 50, 89, 99,
  138, 189, 218, 446, 566, 591,
  688, 752, 804, 845, 967,
  982

Talbot, Lyle 5, 94, 179, 247,
  365, 535, 750, 783, 838,
  1006, 1019
Talbott, Gloria 806
Taliaferro, Hal 35, 71, 80, 90,
  106, 126, 144, 162, 260, 299,
  303, 317, 319, 369, 374,
  378, 394, 466, 473, 590,
  593, 633, 648, 663, 667,
  680, 697, 703, 723, 732,
  753, 755, 812, 855, 874,
  883, 892, 934, 939, 949,
  967, 974, 983, 987, 993,
  996, 1011
Taller, Oril 377
Talley, Marion 244
Tallichet, Margaret 180, 182,
  1028
Talman, William 121, 472
Talton, Alice 626
Tamblyn, Russ 407
Tamez, Al 935
Tang, Frank 438
Tann, Tom 700
Tannen, Julius 459
Tannen, William 208, 382,
  796
Tansey, Emma 261, 302, 634
Tansey, Sherry 23, 67, 69,
  190, 226, 261, 302, 306,
  307, 433, 434, 435, 440,
  523, 578, 634, 827, 860
Tapley, Colin 778, 926
Tashman, Lilyan 250
Tasker, Robert 7, 351, 710
Tate, Reginald 596
Tatum, Burl 987
Tauvera, Harry 972
Taylor-Smith, Jean 186
Taylor, Al 54, 60, 62, 64, 70,
  91, 95, 106, 123, 132, 134,
  135, 142, 154, 162, 169, 171,
  264, 266, 277, 286, 291,
  306, 332, 372, 394, 433,
  463, 465, 470, 483, 491,
  541, 564, 565, 585, 601,
  620, 621, 624, 625, 629,
  652, 657, 692, 723, 773,
  775, 832, 860, 868, 907,
  908, 930, 936, 947, 949,
  954, 955, 956, 959, 960,
  961, 962, 963, 965, 968,
  980, 985, 986, 987, 988,
  992, 1000, 1008, 1010,
  1012
Taylor, Alma 808
Taylor, Bobby 539

Taylor, Brad 31, 348, 734,
  804
Taylor, Carlie 964, 986
Taylor, Dub 551, 787, 921
Taylor, Duke 50, 565, 947,
  948, 951, 953, 955, 959,
  962, 965, 966, 972, 973,
  976, 977, 978, 980, 981,
  983, 985, 986, 987, 988,
  990, 992, 993, 995, 996,
  999, 1002, 1003, 1004, 1010,
  1011
Taylor, Eric 129, 181, 311,
  320, 520, 533, 557, 572,
  664, 758, 927
Taylor, Ferris 139, 162, 209,
  260, 295, 358, 410, 457,
  462, 468, 473, 508, 623,
  649, 693, 757, 927, 945
Taylor, Forrest 14, 39, 52, 73,
  115, 123, 125, 145, 170, 177,
  202, 226, 288, 331, 351,
  370, 373, 387, 405, 408,
  502, 519, 528, 565, 566,
  573, 604, 634, 648, 649,
  674, 675, 676, 694, 732,
  737, 742, 752, 753, 755,
  762, 774, 798, 821, 832,
  844, 868, 877, 883, 884,
  903, 933, 950, 953, 961,
  962, 963, 964, 967, 968,
  974, 983, 986, 988, 990,
  995, 1011
Taylor, George 81
Taylor, Kent 224, 707, 841,
  853
Taylor, Lawrence Edmund
  380
Taylor, Megan 367, 368
Taylor, Norma 863
Taylor, Opal 656
Taylor, Phil 367, 368
Taylor, Ray 822, 960, 993,
  1000, 1008
Taylor, Rex 476, 741, 955,
  961, 963, 965, 975
Teague, Guy 727, 890, 948,
  959, 964, 969, 976, 981,
  989, 998
Teal, Ray 161, 189, 197, 217,
  271, 312, 534, 844, 900,
  906, 949, 1010
Tearle, Godfrey 30
Tedrow, Irene 690
The Teen-Agers 550
Telaak, Bill 48
Tellegen, Mike 196

# Name Index

Temple, George 10
Tempo, Nino 628
Tenbrook, Harry 346, 464, 616, 655, 961, 962, 975
The Tennessee Ramblers 536, 642, 803, 936
Terhune, Max 14, 56, 70, 95, 132, 276, 308, 319, 331, 341, 346, 412, 459, 473, 477, 526, 567, 570, 574, 615, 624, 629, 642, 645, 647, 655, 693, 722, 823, 855, 915
Terrell, Ken 68, 74, 124, 142, 145, 269, 294, 469, 482, 483, 541, 565, 572, 621, 656, 846, 861, 947, 948, 949, 950, 952, 953, 954, 955, 956, 958, 962, 963, 965, 966, 967, 969, 970, 971, 972, 974, 976, 977, 978, 980, 982, 983, 985, 986, 991, 992, 995, 997, 998, 999, 1001, 1002, 1004, 1005, 1006, 1009, 1011, 1012
Terry, Al 465
Terry, Gordon 335
Terry, Phillip 612
Terry, Robert 961, 963
Terry, Robert A. 880
Terry, Ruth 7, 91, 113, 293, 310, 317, 391, 419, 466, 512, 517, 591, 666, 733, 734, 743, 777, 809, 821, 941
Terry, Sheila 289
Terry, Tex 9, 13, 21, 129, 207, 260, 323, 332, 402, 405, 422, 467, 555, 565, 590, 593, 630, 652, 654, 670, 687, 739, 795, 797, 800, 802, 831, 836, 866, 928, 964, 978, 989, 1002
Terry, William 44, 785, 821
Teske, Charles 189, 885
Tetley, Walter 601, 877
The Texas Wanderers 893
Thane, Dirk 570, 868, 968, 995, 1010
Thatcher, Heather 1028
Thayer, Julia 59, 308, 993
Theodoli, Niccolo 188
The Theodores 741
Thiel, Walter 972
Thiele, William 453
Thimig, Helene 785
Thom, Bob 955, 961
Thomas, Bob 680

Thomas, Buckwheat 128
Thomas, Charles 862, 868, 949, 955, 985, 986, 987
Thomas, Dagmar 379
Thomas, Evan 962, 965, 1000
Thomas, Frank M. 27, 509, 515, 680, 728, 798, 799, 931
Thomas, Jerry 8
Thomas, Lyn 143, 499, 631
Thomas, Madoline 772
Thomas, Ralph 1, 165, 185, 186
Thomas, Robert C. 276, 642
Thompson, Bobby 987
Thompson, Carlos 454, 898, 920
Thompson, Janice 738
Thompson, June 738
Thompson, Kay, and Her Ensemble 477
Thompson, Larry 155, 982, 1000
Thompson, Mort 527
Thompson, Nick 374, 583, 974
Thompson, Peggy 410
Thompson, R. P. 965
Thomson, Kenneth 396
Thorgersen, Ed 341
Thornton, Cyril 288
Thornton, Frank 553
Thorpe, Buddy 973
Thorpe, Jim 887
Thorpe, Ted 998
Thorsen, Duane 951
The Three Cheers 343
The Three Chocolateers 504
Thrower, Maxie 979
"Thunder," the Horse 50, 88, 115, 128, 137, 298, 792, 896
Thunder Cloud, Chief 67, 642, 647, 738, 940, 956, 987, 988, 996
Thurston, Helen 952, 980, 992, 995, 999, 1070
Thyssen, Greta 2
Tickell, Jerrard 165
Tiffany Pictures 932
The Tiger-Men 957
Tilbury, Zeffie 640, 723
Timblin, Charles 421
The Tipica Orchestra 751
Tobey, Dan 57, 201, 349, 592
Tobey, Ruth 1034
Tobias, Charles 937
Tobin, Genevieve 200
Todd, Ann 596

Todd, Ann E. 354, 945, 1034
Todd, Mabel 515, 788
Todd, Sally 880
Tolman, Daniel Day 593
Tolson, Pearl 397
Tomack, Sid 355, 357
Tombes, Andrew 46, 180, 189, 195, 363, 375, 419, 485, 503, 507, 539, 664, 688, 740, 833, 893, 918
Tombragel, Maurice 787
Tomei, Louis 1004
Tomlin, Pinky 193, 330
Toney, Jim 448
Tong, Kam 397, 965, 983
Toomey, Regis 83, 156, 515, 788
Toone, Geoffrey 596
Toones, Fred "Snowflake" 20, 26, 34, 51, 172, 200, 234, 257, 266, 291, 308, 337, 433, 448, 491, 498, 537, 551, 624, 629, 643, 645, 674, 735, 812, 862, 868, 915, 934, 936, 955, 975
Topetchy, Bryan 956
Topper, Burt 531, 595
Tor, Michael 259
Tor, Sigurd 1001
Torvay, Jose 924
Tosi, Luigi 518
Totheroh, Dan 665
Totman, Wellyn 158, 196, 212, 232, 263, 282, 311, 438, 818
Tottenham, Merle 596
Totter, Audrey 111, 474, 888, 922
Tourneur, Jacques 187
Tours, Joan 397
Tovar, Lupita 761, 868
Towb, Harry 1
Towne, Aline 312, 671, 889, 964, 976, 998, 1006, 1009, 1019
Towne, Rosella 271, 660
Townley, Jack 12, 50, 116, 139, 141, 150, 153, 215, 218, 263, 293, 296, 314, 330, 339, 348, 352, 356, 367, 391, 397, 503, 513, 514, 539, 550, 557, 592, 613, 664, 666, 669, 699, 726, 740, 850, 882, 883, 934
Townley, Toke 185
Townsend, Leo 782

Toxton, Candy 505
Travers, Bill 772
Travers, Henry 235
Travers, Victor 779
Travis, June 117, 212, 225, 400, 525
Travis, Richard 120, 447, 560
Treacher, Arthur 347
Treadway, Charlotte 717
Treadway, Wayne 418
Treadwell, Laura 397
Trebach, John 18, 235
Tree, Dorothy 515, 521
Treen, Mary 309, 310, 343, 517, 550, 783, 909
Tregaskis, Richard 219, 912
Trenk, William 348
Trent, Philip 299, 564
Trevor, Claire 162, 357
Triana, Antonio 413
"Trigger," the Horse 13, 21, 24, 35, 49, 50, 51, 71, 106, 120, 144, 167, 189, 192, 214, 221, 256, 269, 292, 294, 310, 317, 320, 323, 344, 350, 369, 371, 372, 374, 394, 408, 442, 463, 466, 467, 513, 522, 528, 533, 549, 559, 572, 622, 625, 633, 648, 657, 662, 663, 672, 680, 688, 723, 725, 732, 750, 752, 753, 755, 758, 760, 763, 768, 771, 795, 796, 798, 799, 801, 846, 854, 865, 871, 876, 878, 883, 899, 934, 939, 940
Trivers, Barry 28, 180, 243, 356
Trowbridge, Charles 212, 218, 263, 357, 361, 606, 618, 705, 881, 886, 952, 986, 992
Troy, Helen 893
Troy, Louise 665
Troy, Sid 961, 962, 963, 1004
Truex, Ernest 270, 459, 742
Truman, Michael 184
Trumbo, Dalton 392
Tsiang, H. T. 378
Tubb, Ernest, and His Texas Troubadors 391
Tucker, Forrest 80, 90, 228, 241, 283, 326, 357, 402, 422, 428, 538, 594, 644, 659, 685, 689, 859, 888, 912

Tucker, Harland 344
Tucker, Jerry 225, 961
Tucker, Melville 14, 87, 430, 499, 544, 563, 589, 608, 626, 661, 686, 730, 736, 748, 759, 793, 826, 835, 872, 875, 884, 889
Tucker, Richard 141, 339
"Tuffie," the Dog 955, 975
Tufts, Sonny 131
Tuitama, Kuka 898
Tully, Montgomery 700
Tully, Tom 704
Tumiati, Gualtiero 188
Tunberg, William 814
Turich, Felipe 402
Turich, Rosa 153, 314, 402, 587, 948, 1010
Turnbull, Glenn 363
Turner, Anna 808
Turner, George 891, 955, 1002
Turner, Glenn 971
Turner, Lana 1032
Turner, Martin 110
Turner, Ray 296, 957
Turner, Roscoe 240
Tuttle, Lurene 451
Twelvetrees, Helen 254, 764
20th Century–Fox 84, 173, 339, 363
Twitchell, Archie 35, 45, 494, 843, 939, 962, 992; see also Michael Branden
Tyler, Harry 31, 45, 108, 216, 326, 370, 396, 486, 581, 616, 917, 923, 942
Tyler, Leon 2, 298, 404, 436, 562, 802
Tyler, Tom 64, 123, 267, 526, 564, 585, 621, 646, 692, 712, 822, 832, 846, 885, 895, 904, 908, 947
Tyne, George 628, 689
Tyrrell, Alice 16, 87

UFA 136
Ulman, William+A., Jr. 196
Ulric, Lenore 534
Ung, Tom 1003
United Artists 167
United States Department of Agriculture 1022
United States Marines 817
United States Navy 817
Universal Jack 115
Universal Pictures 69, 889

Urchel, Tony 975
Urecal, Minerva 21, 22, 27, 212, 290, 373, 415, 460, 462, 464, 479, 539, 563, 609, 622, 678, 706, 739, 755, 793, 895, 922
Uris, Michael 593
Usher, Guy 48, 70, 299, 373, 405, 415, 493, 551, 603, 612, 649, 672, 674, 718, 764, 878, 904

Vachon, Jean 418
Vadnay, Laslo 57
Vague, Vera 203, 333, 669, 803, 1028; see also Barbara Jo Allen
Valdes, Tito and Corinne 144
Valdez, Corinne 415
Valentine, Elizabeth 692
Valk, Frederick 454, 707, 790
Valkis, Helen 542
Vallee, Rudy 216
Vallin, Rick 534, 619, 646, 743, 895, 920, 941, 981, 1019
Vallon, Michael 807, 965
Vallon, Nanette 824
Vallone, Raf 188
Valmy, Andre 558
Van, Frankie 201
Van, Gus 31
Van, Jean 678
Van Atta, Lee 960, 1007
Van Cleef, Lee 2, 362, 427, 460, 619, 654, 888
Van Cleve, Patricia 1027
Vandeleur, Iris 841
Vandergrift, Monte 476
Van Dine, S. S. 603
Van Every, Billie 521, 1003
Van Horn, Emil 368, 742, 995; see also "Satan," the Gorilla
Van Hulzen, Joop 259
Van Loewen, Jan 122
Van Pelt, John 647, 735
Van Sickel, Bill 954
Van Sickel, Dale 51, 107, 121, 178, 201, 292, 410, 441, 446, 540, 638, 671, 831, 852, 854, 889, 948, 950, 951, 952, 953, 954, 958, 959, 964, 966, 967, 969, 970, 971, 972, 973, 974, 976, 977, 978, 982, 984, 985,

989, 990, 991, 996, 997, 998, 999, 1002, 1005, 1006, 1009, 1011, 1019, 1070
Van Sloan, Edward 209, 646, 778, 885, 952, 991
Van Zandt, Philip 65, 150, 173, 362, 425, 581
Varconi, Victor 155, 410, 701
Varden, Norma 113, 285
Varela, Gloria 402
Varela, Nina 402, 922
Varga, Billy 10
Varley, Beatrice 596
Varno, Roland 182, 820, 824, 885
The Vass Family 139
Vaughan, Dorothy 60, 493, 656, 813, 848
Vaughn, Robert 327
Vaughn, William (William Von Brincken) 397, 614, 983, 1001
Veeck, Bill 407
Vehr, Nick 1004
Vejar, Harry 898
Velasco and Lopez 297
The Velascos (Fred and Mary) 266
Veloz and Yolanda 79
Venable, Evelyn 311, 349
Veness, Amy 186, 683
Venturini, Giorgio 518
Venuta, Benay 364
Venuti, Joe 47
Verdi, Joe 148
Verdugo, Elena 575
Verebes, Erno 180, 504, 534
Verga, Giavani 716
Ver Halen, C. J., Jr. 335
Vernon, Billy 510
Vernon, Dorothy 352
Vernon, Glenn 46, 321, 912
Vernon, Howard 3
Vernon, Mickey 407
Vernon, Wally 566, 591, 702, 729, 731, 775, 805, 62, 89, 93, 99, 258, 330, 409, 469
Vernon and Draper 688
Versois, Odile 165
Victor, Charles 683
Vigran, Herb 539, 595, 710
Villiers, Mavis 837
Villoldo, Jorge 33
Vincenot, Louis 438
Vincent, Allen 28, 412
Vincent, Billy 4, 687, 691

Vincent, June 120, 129, 708, 894
Vincent, Leslie 709
Vincent, Russ 21, 153, 865, 990
Vincent, Sailor 955, 963, 982
Vincent, Yves 558
Vinson, Helen 78, 413
Vinyals, F. A. 859
Visaroff, Michael 155, 534
Vittes, Louis 580
Vogan, Emmett 10, 13, 44, 99, 112, 121, 128, 138, 174, 192, 209, 218, 236, 251, 260, 268, 323, 354, 361, 377, 408, 410, 512, 517, 536, 572, 582, 599, 605, 631, 641, 752, 759, 776, 786, 819, 838, 850, 856, 883, 887, 923, 934, 937, 953, 997
Vogeding, Fredrik 360
Vohs, Joan 147, 811
The Voice of Experience 341
"Volcano," the Stallion Horse 346
Volding, Louise 999
Volk, George 357, 973, 976
Von Eltz, Theodore 396, 461, 833, 853, 942
von Morhart, Hans 1001, 1004
Von Nauckhoff, Rolf 118
Von Stroheim, Erich 11, 148, 297, 413, 701, 779
Von Stroheim, Erich, Jr. 335
Von Twardowski, Hans 397
Von Ziegler, Peter 963
Vorhaus, Bernard 7, 19, 361, 368, 410, 416, 501, 810, 820, 917
Vosper, John 46, 61, 169
Vye, Murvyn 283

Wade, John P. 331, 645, 961
Wade, Mary Ruth 594
Wadham, Joe 336
Wadsworth, Henry 741
Wagenheim, Charles 779, 786
Wager, Anthony 1
Waggner, George 100, 230, 580
Waggner, Leah 357
Waggner, Shy 230
Wagner, Gorgeous George 10

Wagner, Max 360, 418, 628, 710
Wainer, Lee 16
Wainwright, Godfrey 981
Waite, Eric 368
Waizman, Max 949, 962, 986, 1004
Wakely, Jimmy 318, 680, 812, 862
Wakely, Jimmy, and His Rough Riders 680, 812, 862
Wakely, Jimmy, Trio 318
Walbrook, Anton 790
Walburn, Freddie 91
Walburn, Raymond 6, 113, 162, 593, 613, 637
Walcott, George 476, 906
Walcott, Gregory 828
Wald, John 10, 510, 871
Wald, Malvin 787
Waldis, Otto 708, 925
Waldo, Elizabeth 751
Waldo, Janet 551
Waldor, David 595
Waldridge, Harold 347
Waldron, Charles 210, 819, 820
Waldron, Tom 782
Wales, Ethel 167, 256, 372, 378, 807, 939
Wales, John 108
Walker, Bill 561, 979
Walker, Bob 308, 1003
Walker, Cheryl 370, 712, 749, 821
Walker, Cindy 257, 643
Walker, Francis 307, 434, 448, 526, 847, 965, 1000
Walker, Gertrude 44, 149, 209, 382, 517, 729, 910
Walker, Helen 510
Walker, Nellie 978
Walker, Patricia 278
Walker, Peter 900
Walker, Ray 32, 83, 100, 149, 268, 429, 464, 512, 588, 589, 656, 729, 815, 875
Walker, Robert 787
Walker, Robert G. 948, 954
Walker, Tommy 32
Wall, Geraldine 285, 453
Walla, Marianne 184
Wallace, Beryl 798
Wallace, Edgar 77
Wallace, George 998
Wallace, Helen 481, 505, 560, 739, 766, 786

Wallace, Irving 814
Wallace, John 972, 1012
Wallace, Morgan 60, 552
Waller, Eddy 37, 38, 40, 61, 68, 90, 91, 95, 104, 107, 111, 125, 143, 155, 170, 174, 178, 179, 208, 253, 255, 305, 315, 378, 437, 458, 464, 479, 480, 519, 524, 540, 593, 600, 612, 638, 670, 672, 676, 684, 696, 724, 732, 792, 793, 812, 831, 890, 913, 928, 929
Wallington, Jimmy 349
Walsh, Arthur 238, 305, 418, 786, 998
Walsh, John 350, 742
Walsh, Maurice 616, 859
Walsh, Raoul 162
Walsh, Don 998
Walters, Elizabeth 58
Walters, Luana 491, 862, 965
Walthall, Henry B. 322
Walton, Douglas 395, 778
Walton, Fred 245, 360
Walzman, Max 123, 621
Wanka, Rolf 118
Wanzer, Arthur 272, 322
Warburton, John 316
Ward, Alan 39, 251
Ward, Amelita 804
Ward, Bill 335, 531
Ward, Blackjack 567, 693, 812
Ward, Frank 91
Ward, Jerome 988, 1008, 1012
Ward, John 70, 647, 960, 965, 1000
Ward, Len 1008
Ward, Luci 24, 95, 97, 130, 406, 422, 465, 491, 524, 570, 629, 693, 693, 848
Ward, Lucille 313, 439, 521, 639
Ward, Michael 808, 858
Ward, Ronald 808
Warde, Anthony 101, 133, 210, 271, 410, 649, 950, 954, 962, 982, 983, 991, 997, 999, 1001
Warde, Harlan 898
Ware, Irene 223
Warner, H. B. 28, 77, 101, 197, 218, 326, 783
Warner, Hansel 167, 590
Warner, Jack 772
Warner, Wes 306, 308, 681, 735, 1107, 1008

Warner Bros. 5, 512, 747
Warren, C. E. T. 1
Warren, Charles Marquis 228, 538, 921
Warren, Elmer 936
Warren, Frank 665
Warren, Janet 917
Warren, John 707, 858
Warren, Phil 954, 971
Warren, Ruth 419
Warren, Steve 43, 304
Warrick, Ruth 197, 665
Warwick, John 858
Warwick, Nick 982
Warwick, Robert 28, 67, 83, 133, 173, 376, 377, 464, 639, 855, 1008
Washbourne, Mona 186, 808
Washburn, Bryant 105, 705, 712, 947, 985
Washington, Bill 979
Wastal, M. Lou 521
Waterfield, Bob 147
Waterman, Willard 238
Watkin, Pierre 31, 43, 46, 59, 101, 140, 141, 155, 161, 209, 217, 272, 278, 318, 341, 368, 371, 394, 415, 421, 436, 453, 462, 484, 493, 515, 522, 582, 586, 593, 635, 659, 710, 739, 741, 796, 824, 831, 899, 913, 937, 951
Watling, Jack 859
Watson, Cecil 322
Watson, John 336, 782
Watson, Minor 500, 814
Watson, Wylie 683
Watt, Nate 257, 521, 541
Wattis, Richard 186
Watts, George 500
Watts, Twinkle 89, 99, 138, 309, 419, 469, 566, 722, 731, 775, 839, 845
Wave, Virginia 155
Waxman, Stanley 357, 853, 1009, 1019
Wayne, Antonia 616
Wayne, Billy 239, 412, 810
Wayne, Frank 947, 955, 961, 965, 983, 985, 1003
Wayne, Fredd 472
Wayne, John 15, 84, 155, 162, 230, 231, 236, 243, 373, 377, 411, 415, 416, 423, 433, 434, 448, 462, 523, 524, 526, 554, 570, 574, 616,

629, 651, 689, 693, 820, 823, 898, 907, 916, 930
Wayne, Melinda 616
Wayne, Michael 616
Wayne, Patrick 616, 651, 791
Wayne, Robert 963, 985, 992
Wayne, Steve 781, 912
Wear, Claire's, Embassy Orchestra 11
Weaver, Doodles 818
Weaver, Frank 27, 193, 252, 295, 375, 393, 507, 509, 545, 718, 864
Weaver, June 27, 193, 252, 295, 375, 393, 507, 509, 545, 718, 864
Weaver, Leon 27, 193, 252, 295, 375, 393, 507, 509, 545, 664, 718, 864
Weaver, Loretta 27, 252, 295, 332, 375, 393, 507
Webb, James R. 35, 247, 394, 522, 606, 618, 723, 757, 760
Webb, Richard 402, 689, 976
Webber, Peggy 451
Weber, Dave 574
Weber, Herbert 960, 961, 963, 1000, 1003
Webster, M. Coates 61, 102, 141, 143, 176, 180, 253, 305, 351, 437, 480, 519, 527, 638, 671, 684, 750, 755, 831, 876, 903, 929
Webster, Mary 206
Wedlock, Hugh, Jr. 613
Weeks, Anson and His Orchestra 57
Weeks, Jane 478
Weeks, Ranny 59, 319, 942, 1003
Weil, Richard 44, 57, 297, 370
Weiman, Rita 603
Weiser, Bud 983
Weitzenkorn, Louis 410
Welch, Elisabeth 11
Welch, Niles 738
Welch, William 110
Welden, Ben 200, 225, 231, 330, 335, 366, 424, 500, 525, 604, 609, 710, 810, 918
Weldon, Marion 127, 177, 226
Welles, Christopher 451
Welles, Dorit 184
Welles, Mel 227

# Name Index

Welles, Orson 451, 851, 859
Welles, Rebecca 404
Wells, Alan 989
Wells, Jacqueline 34, 406, 625, 939; *see also* Julie Bishop
Wells, Ted 75, 861, 961, 965, 988
Wellum, Patricia 700
Welsch, Howard 359
Welsh, Bill 32
Welsh, John 184, 471, 808, 841
Wendell, Howard 227
Wendhausen, F. R. 30
Wengraf, John 898
Wengren, Dave 955
Wentworth, Martha 354, 481, 556, 675, 694, 774, 891
Wenzel, Art 761
Wessel, Dick 29, 48, 71, 111, 155, 175, 220, 271, 299, 356, 357, 378, 408, 633, 663, 673, 689, 732, 799, 850, 882, 894, 932, 975
West, Nathanael 76, 244, 388, 603, 640, 833
West, Wally 35, 50, 66, 67, 123, 127, 144, 172, 226, 249, 264, 276, 346, 435, 467, 488, 615, 634, 647, 822, 847, 860, 955, 960, 963, 992, 1008
Westbrook, Jolene 398
Westcott, Helen 384
Westerby, Robert 772
Westermeier, Paul 136
Westley, Helen 416
Weston, Cecil 356
Weston, Dick 542, 915; *see also* Roy Rogers; Leonard Slye
Weston, Doris 76
Weston, Garnett 151, 299
Weston, Leslie 1
Whalen, Michael 515, 805
Whelan, Arleen 619, 677, 685, 791
Whiley, Manning 122
Whipper, Leigh 317, 657
Whitaker, Slim 56, 67, 130, 307, 373, 377, 420, 434, 466, 488, 524, 570, 623, 643, 673, 732, 761, 863, 868, 878, 939, 986, 987, 988
White, Alice 410
White, Bert 961

White, Christine 575
White, Crystal 230
White, Dan 55, 304, 376, 402, 601, 602, 654, 672, 737, 949
White, Dorothy Ann 796
White, Edward J. 13, 21, 47, 49, 50, 51, 55, 62, 73, 74, 89, 99, 105, 116, 129, 168, 169, 171, 192, 214, 221, 257, 258, 269, 292, 293, 294, 320, 323, 350, 371, 387, 426, 469, 472, 502, 512, 528, 533, 547, 548, 549, 565, 566, 572, 575, 591, 622, 662, 688, 746, 750, 758, 762, 768, 794, 796, 801, 804, 846, 854, 861, 865, 871, 876
White, Frank 950
White, Jesse 111, 328
White, Lee "Lasses" 296, 541, 674, 993
White, Leo 747
White, Leonard 808
White, Leslie T. 842, 918
White, Paul 104, 415
White, Sammy 341
White, Will J. 431
Whiteford, Blackie 219, 372, 652, 987
Whitehead, Joe 291, 725, 997
Whitehead, Peter 128
Whiteley, Jon 901
Whiteman, Paul, and His Orchestra 31
Whiteman, Russ 9, 512, 671
Whiteman, Thorpe 460
Whitespear, Greg Star 642, 993
Whitfield, "Smoki" 338, 560
Whitfield, Anne 404
Whitley, Crane 217, 271, 382, 697, 952, 956, 972, 991, 1004, 1005
Whitlock, Lloyd 29, 397, 521, 642, 797, 955, 968, 992, 1000, 1007
Whitman, Ernest 592, 791
Whitman, Gayne 512, 639, 949, 991, 1077, 1078, 1082, 1083
Whitman, Russ 971
Whitman, Stuart 981
Whitney, Art 112
Whitney, Claire 255, 540
Whitney, Eve 65, 999

Whitney, John 689, 853, 861
Whitney, Peter 534
Whitney, William 21
Whittell, Josephine 6, 53, 244, 421
Whitten, Marguerite 743
Whittingham, Jack 184
Whynemah, Princess 173
Wickerhauser, Willy 364
Wickland, J. Laurence 960, 993, 1000, 1008
Widenaar, Clair 328
Widrin, Tanya 1027
The Wiere Brothers 310
Wigton, Anne 297, 783
Wilbur, Robert 968, 1012
Wilcox, Frank 43, 46, 103, 327, 781
Wilcox, Herbert 428, 851, 859
Wilcox, Robert 992
Wilcoxon, Henry 151, 398, 603, 609, 919
Wilde, Lee 98
Wilde, Lois 735, 1007
Wilde, Lyn 98, 724
Wilder, Frank 468
Wilder, W. Lee 288, 297, 604, 783, 933
Wildes, Newlin B. 318
Wilding, Michael 851
Wiley, Jan 962
Wilhelm, Wolfgang 683
Wilke, Robert 50, 52, 55, 65, 75, 89, 92, 107, 109, 115, 124, 134, 138, 144, 161, 178, 207, 234, 298, 337, 376, 380, 446, 467, 483, 559, 670, 687, 691, 719, 720, 722, 775, 793, 795, 839, 842, 845, 865, 866, 892, 929, 934, 949, 950, 952, 953, 954, 955, 958, 962, 966, 968, 970, 971, 974, 977, 982, 991, 996, 997, 1003, 1004, 1005, 1011, 1084
Wilkerson, Billy 656, 659
Wilkerson, Guy 101, 319, 473, 576, 936
Wilkins, Martin 887, 994
Wilkinson, Ronald 186
Wilkus, Bill 949, 953, 955, 962, 963, 965, 969, 985, 986, 992, 1004
Willenz, Max 534
Willey, Leonard 385
Williams, "Sleepy," and His

Three Shades of Rhythm 358
Williams, Ben 683, 772
Williams, Ben Ames 747
Williams, Bill 90, 314, 580
Williams, Bob 2, 38, 52, 68, 75, 88, 92, 169, 170, 174, 178, 199, 255, 337, 442, 446, 479, 482, 540, 544, 569, 589, 607, 626, 648, 678, 724, 730, 748, 835, 875, 889; *see also* Bob Williams and "Red Dust"
Williams, Bob, and "Red Dust" 1030; *see also* Bob Williams
Williams, Bransby 30
Williams, Buddy 673, 960
Williams, Charles 31, 76, 91, 92, 209, 323, 349, 368, 370, 396, 397, 419, 479, 499, 579, 678, 710, 987
Williams, David 80, 593, 928
Williams, Duke 627
Williams, Elmo 325
Williams, Guinn "Big Boy" 28, 80, 139, 144, 159, 193, 310, 335, 788, 822, 897, 1008
Williams, Jack 343
Williams, Ken 791
Williams, Kenneth 851
Williams, Larry 50, 464
Williams, Mack 181, 766
Williams, Maston 95, 319, 331, 611, 961, 987, 993
Williams, Mervin 357
Williams, Rex 220, 614
Williams, Rhys 90, 399, 495, 636, 727
Williams, Robert B. 589
Williams, Roger 59, 95, 128, 132, 226, 307, 331, 432, 508, 526, 629, 641, 647, 988, 1003, 1010
Williams, Rush 1006
Williams, Sumner 399
Williams, Sydney M. 57
Williams, Zack 887
Williamson, Thames 80, 422, 697, 806
Willing, Foy, and the Riders of the Purple Sage 14, 49, 87, 192, 221, 292, 294, 320, 425, 533, 559, 768, 796, 801, 835, 846, 854, 865, 872

Willis, F. McGrew 740
Willis, Lee 923
Willis, Norman 38, 267, 408, 593, 609, 972, 985, 1009
Willis, Ted 858
Willock, Dave 47, 368, 823
Wills, Bob, and His Texas Playboys 488
Wills, Chill 121, 329, 538, 644, 651, 659, 703, 836
Wills, Edwin 739
Wills, Henry 54, 55, 75, 124, 138, 298, 406, 427, 522, 555, 564, 593, 625, 663, 670, 679, 687, 691, 719, 732, 752, 760, 775, 798, 845, 939, 947, 965, 975, 995, 996, 997, 1012
Wills, Walter 146, 526, 693, 961, 988
Wilsey, Jay (Buffalo Bill, Jr.) 66
Wilson, Charles 232, 272, 347, 464, 525, 579, 639, 732, 810
Wilson, Clarence 252, 488, 870
Wilson, Don 333, 391, 893
Wilson, Ernest 583
Wilson, Harry 92, 410, 927, 974
Wilson, Ian 837
Wilson, James 562
Wilson, Jan 336
Wilson, John 632
Wilson, Lois 77, 100, 639, 1027
Wilson, Marie 666, 726
Wilson, Neil 837
Wilson, Wally 987
Wilton, Eric 53, 245, 709
Winans, Robin 356
Windsor, Barbara 808
Windsor, Claire 1027
Windsor, Marie 112, 121, 230, 326, 328, 530, 727
Wing, Toby 246
Winkler, Robert 66, 573, 612, 955
Winn, Derek 233, 336, 782
Winninger, Charles 111, 381, 581, 791
Winston, Helen 838
Winston, Mildred 341
Winston, Steve 555
Winter, Val 787
Winters, David 665

Winton, Barry 245
Wisbar, Frank 452
Wisdom, Norman 858
Wise, Vic 772
Wiseberg, Aubrey 345
Wiseman, Joseph 111
Withers, Grant 6, 17, 46, 49, 50, 59, 63, 102, 111, 155, 161, 201, 208, 219, 230, 231, 260, 274, 284, 293, 326, 327, 345, 355, 357, 377, 378, 387, 402, 422, 427, 437, 495, 528, 539, 546, 576, 594, 651, 653, 659, 697, 703, 729, 754, 768, 791, 852, 854, 857, 883, 884, 887, 898, 921, 928, 934, 1019
Withers, Isabel 769, 879
Withers, Jane 6, 218, 398, 511, 1028, 1032
Witherspoon, Cora 250, 389, 919
Witney, William 49, 51, 73, 120, 129, 192, 194, 214, 221, 227, 269, 292, 294, 316, 320, 323, 332, 350, 371, 387, 404, 426, 528, 533, 547, 548, 549, 561, 565, 572, 575, 690, 711, 758, 762, 768, 771, 781, 784, 796, 801, 846, 854, 855, 865, 871, 894, 912, 947, 949, 953, 955, 961, 962, 963, 965, 968, 972, 975, 980, 983, 985, 986, 987, 988, 992, 993, 995, 1003, 1004, 1010, 1012
Wolf, Pappy 936
Wolfe, Bill 67, 74, 114, 128, 236, 394, 465, 524, 570, 691, 693, 839, 878, 939
Wolfe, Bud 63, 145, 402, 441, 948, 950, 953, 954, 955, 958, 961, 962, 963, 966, 971, 972, 974, 976, 977, 978, 982, 984, 986, 988, 992, 995, 999, 1002, 1004, 1005, 1070
Wolfe, David 239, 610
Wolfe, Ian 17, 67, 439, 552, 557
Wolfe, Sam 341
Wolfit, Donald 471
Wolfson, P. J. 867
Wolheim, Dan 961, 1003
Wong, Anna May 1028

# Name Index

Wong, Beal 438
Wong, Victor 438, 968
Wood, Allan 318
Wood, Britt 774
Wood, Douglas 57, 322, 521, 530
Wood, Harley 72
Wood, Jeane 951
Wood, Marjorie 802
Wood, Mary Laura 185
Wood, Natalie 197
Wood, Robert W. 635, 898
Wood, Wilson 98, 382, 826, 998, 1009
Woodbridge, George 300, 808
Woodbury, Joan 42, 374, 799, 933
Woodell, Barbara 516
Woodruff, Frank 591
Woodruff, Richard 709
Woods, Buck 318
Woods, Craig 15
Woods, Donald 248, 664
Woods, Edward 520
Woods, Harry 54, 66, 74, 92, 134, 162, 167, 217, 260, 326, 329, 372, 377, 423, 433, 486, 582, 624, 625, 663, 723, 731, 833, 928, 991
Woods, Ira Buck 464
Woods, Shorty 987
Woods, Thomas F. 324
Woodward, Bob 34, 35, 71, 154, 162, 234, 267, 352, 373, 374, 394, 405, 522, 540, 621, 687, 693, 755, 763, 771, 797, 798, 890, 965
Wooley, Sheb 399, 840
Wootton, Stephen 784
Worden, Hank 2, 15, 99, 123, 145, 230, 266, 276, 326, 441, 526, 561, 616, 654, 766, 921
Worlock, Frederic 222, 444, 478, 701, 709, 1001
Wormser, Richard 102, 249, 561, 581, 593, 600, 676, 727, 890
Worth, Barbara 617
Worth, Constance 972
Worth, Harry 56, 167, 405, 646, 947, 949
Worth, Nancy 620

Worth, William 397
Wray, John 117, 263, 461, 603, 745, 810
Wren, Chris 298
Wright, Ben 987
Wright, Cobina, Jr. 1034
Wright, Douglas 641
Wright, Florence 937
Wright, Gilbert 770, 883, 915
Wright, Howard 316, 784
Wright, Jean 951
Wright, John Wayne 721
Wright, Mack V. 56, 100, 135, 346, 624, 647, 655, 667, 735, 916, 1000, 1008
Wright, Patricia 698
Wright, Wen 88
Wright, Will 14, 80, 301, 330, 359, 377, 380, 381, 399, 453, 550, 637, 697, 742, 796, 1026
Wright, William 164, 182, 409, 666, 668
Wrixon, Maris 288, 393, 545, 755, 797
Wunder, Thelma 477
Wyatt, Charlene 493
Wyatt, Jane 280, 359, 361
Wyenn, Than 43
Wyldeck, Martin 700
Wyler, Robert 232
Wynn, Gordon 698
Wynn, May 472, 806
Wynne, Norman 336
Wynne, Peggy 174, 178, 604, 950
Wynters, Charlotte 206, 586, 606

Yaconelli, Frank 10, 196, 388, 452, 822
Yarborough, Barton 101
Yard, Lester 713
Yates, George Worthing 182, 464, 515, 961, 987
Yates, Hal 459
Yates, Herbert J. 17, 46, 120, 131, 227, 241, 357, 362, 363, 399, 402, 423, 460, 484, 495, 513, 534, 627, 654, 713, 766, 800, 802, 836, 859, 867, 882, 888, 912, 922
Yawitz, Paul 881

Ybarra, Roque 928
Yetter, William 1001
Yordan, Philip 399, 923
York, Carl 474
York, Duke 87, 345, 612, 822, 833, 961, 968, 1003
York, Jeff 800
Yost, Robert 99, 106, 569, 585, 585, 799, 832, 940
Young, Billy 568
Young, Carleton 123, 132, 159, 286, 311, 331, 400, 461, 498, 520, 542, 551, 673, 760, 868, 947, 949, 960, 968, 983, 988, 1003, 1004, 1012
Young, Clara Kimball 537
Young, Clifton 49, 448, 684, 846, 1009
Young, Faron 160, 335, 619
Young, Gig 121, 898
Young, Harold 665, 677
Young, Ned 268
Young, Shaun Terence 790
Young, Tony 336
Yowlachie, Chief 556, 564, 679
Yrigoyen, Bill 949, 953, 956, 963, 965, 987, 988, 992, 996, 1007, 1011, 1012
Yrigoyen, Joe 73, 465, 488, 656, 678, 861, 916, 922, 948, 949, 951, 952, 953, 955, 956, 958, 963, 965, 966, 968, 970, 979, 982, 986, 987, 988, 991, 993, 996, 1001, 1012
Yu, Chin 553
Yule, Joe 510
Yurka, Blanche 235, 415

"Zane," the Horse 1000
Zaner, Jimmy 512, 967
Zarco, Estelita 940
Zaremba, John 938
ZeBrack, Raymond 298
Zelaya, Don 280
Zepeda, Elsa 17
Zilzer, Wolfgang 397
Zimet, Julian 182, 323, 728
Zobel, Victor 282, 476, 639
Zucco, George 312, 706
Zwolsman, Carl 947
Zynda, Henry 1004